D0598572

Sams **Teach Yourself**

Big Data Analytics with Microsoft HDInsight®

in **24 Hours**

SAMS   800 East 96th Street, Indianapolis, Indiana, 46240 USA

Sams Teach Yourself Big Data Analytics with Microsoft HDInsight® in 24 Hours

ISBN-13: 978-0-672-33727-7
ISBN-10: 0-672-33727-4

Library of Congress Control Number: 2015914167

Printed in the United States of America

First Printing November 2015

Trademarks

All terms mentioned in this book that are known to be trademarks or service marks have been appropriately capitalized. Sams Publishing cannot attest to the accuracy of this information. Use of a term in this book should not be regarded as affecting the validity of any trademark or service mark.

HDInsight is a registered trademark of Microsoft Corporation.

Warning and Disclaimer

Every effort has been made to make this book as complete and as accurate as possible, but no warranty or fitness is implied. The information provided is on an "as is" basis. The authors and the publisher shall have neither liability nor responsibility to any person or entity with respect to any loss or damages arising from the information contained in this book.

Special Sales

For information about buying this title in bulk quantities, or for special sales opportunities (which may include electronic versions; custom cover designs; and content particular to your business, training goals, marketing focus, or branding interests), please contact our corporate sales department at corpsales@pearsoned.com or (800) 382-3419.

For government sales inquiries, please contact governmentsales@pearsoned.com.

For questions about sales outside the U.S., please contact international@pearsoned.com.

Editor-in-Chief
Greg Wiegand

Acquisitions Editor
Joan Murray

Development Editor
Sondra Scott

Managing Editor
Sandra Schroeder

Senior Project Editor
Tonya Simpson

Copy Editor
Krista Hansing Editorial Services, Inc.

Senior Indexer
Cheryl Lenser

Proofreader
Anne Goebel

Technical Editors
Shayne Burgess
Ron Abellera

Publishing Coordinator
Cindy Teeters

Cover Designer
Mark Shirar

Compositor
codeMantra

Contents at a Glance

Introduction 1

Part I: Understanding Big Data, Hadoop 1.0, and 2.0

HOUR 1 Introduction of Big Data, NoSQL, and Business Value Proposition 9

2 Introduction to Hadoop, Its Architecture, Ecosystem, and
Microsoft Offerings 31

3 Hadoop Distributed File System Versions 1.0 and 2.0 65

4 The MapReduce Job Framework and Job Execution Pipeline 113

5 MapReduce—Advanced Concepts and YARN 145

Part II: Getting Started with HDInsight and Understanding Its Different Components

HOUR 6 Getting Started with HDInsight, Provisioning Your HDInsight
Service Cluster, and Automating HDInsight Cluster Provisioning 179

7 Exploring Typical Components of HDFS Cluster 219

8 Storing Data in Microsoft Azure Storage Blob 233

9 Working with Microsoft Azure HDInsight Emulator 245

Part III: Programming MapReduce and HDInsight Script Action

HOUR 10 Programming MapReduce Jobs 255

11 Customizing the HDInsight Cluster with Script Action 277

Part IV: Querying and Processing Big Data in HDInsight

HOUR 12 Getting Started with Apache Hive and Apache Tez in HDInsight 287

13 Programming with Apache Hive, Apache Tez in HDInsight,
and Apache HCatalog 323

14 Consuming HDInsight Data from Microsoft BI Tools over
Hive ODBC Driver: Part 1 371

15 Consuming HDInsight Data from Microsoft BI Tools over
Hive ODBC Driver: Part 2 385

16 Integrating HDInsight with SQL Server Integration Services............ 423

17 Using Pig for Data Processing 433

18 Using Sqoop for Data Movement Between RDBMS and HDInsight ... 445

Part V: Managing Workflow and Performing Statistical Computing

HOUR 19 Using Oozie Workflows and Job Orchestration with HDInsight........ 455

20 Performing Statistical Computing with R 467

Part VI: Performing Interactive Analytics and Machine Learning

HOUR 21 Performing Big Data Analytics with Spark.............................. 479

22 Microsoft Azure Machine Learning.. 491

Part VII: Performing Real-time Analytics

HOUR 23 Performing Stream Analytics with Storm............................... 519

24 Introduction to Apache HBase on HDInsight............................. 535

Index... 553

Table of Contents

Introduction   1

Part I: Understanding Big Data, Hadoop 1.0, and 2.0

HOUR 1: Introduction of Big Data, NoSQL, and Business Value Proposition   9

Types of Analysis 9

Types of Data 11

Big Data 12

Managing Big Data 15

NoSQL Systems 17

Big Data, NoSQL Systems, and the Business Value Proposition 26

Application of Big Data and Big Data Solutions 27

Summary 29

Q&A 29

HOUR 2: Introduction to Hadoop, Its Architecture, Ecosystem, and Microsoft Offerings   31

What Is Apache Hadoop? 31

Architecture of Hadoop and Hadoop Ecosystems 33

What's New in Hadoop 2.0 42

Architecture of Hadoop 2.0 43

Tools and Technologies Needed with Big Data Analytics 46

Major Players and Vendors for Hadoop 50

Deployment Options for Microsoft Big Data Solutions 57

Summary 61

Q&A 61

HOUR 3: Hadoop Distributed File System Versions 1.0 and 2.0   65

Introduction to HDFS 65

HDFS Architecture 67

Rack Awareness 88

WebHDFS 89

Accessing and Managing HDFS Data 90

What's New in HDFS 2.0 95

Summary 107

Q&A 108

HOUR 4: The MapReduce Job Framework and Job Execution Pipeline   **113**

Introduction to MapReduce 113

MapReduce Architecture 116

MapReduce Job Execution Flow 119

Summary 140

Q&A 140

HOUR 5: MapReduce—Advanced Concepts and YARN   **145**

DistributedCache 145

Hadoop Streaming 146

MapReduce Joins 148

Bloom Filter 149

Performance Improvement 150

Handling Failures 154

Counter 158

YARN 160

Uber-Tasking Optimization 170

Failures in YARN 171

Resource Manager High Availability and Automatic Failover in YARN 173

Summary 175

Q&A 175

Part II: Getting Started with HDInsight and Understanding Its Different Components

HOUR 6: Getting Started with HDInsight, Provisioning Your HDInsight Service Cluster, and Automating HDInsight Cluster Provisioning   **179**

Introduction to Microsoft Azure 179

Understanding HDInsight Service 181

Provisioning HDInsight on the Azure Management Portal 186

Automating HDInsight Provisioning with PowerShell 199

Managing and Monitoring HDInsight Cluster and Job Execution 212

Summary 214

Q&A 214

Exercise 215

HOUR 7: Exploring Typical Components of HDFS Cluster   **219**

HDFS Cluster Components 219

HDInsight Cluster Architecture 223

High Availability in HDInsight 228

Summary 231

Q&A 231

HOUR 8: Storing Data in Microsoft Azure Storage Blob   **233**

Understanding Storage in Microsoft Azure 233

Benefits of Azure Storage Blob over HDFS 234

Azure Storage Explorer Tools 235

Summary 243

Q&A 243

HOUR 9: Working with Microsoft Azure HDInsight Emulator   **245**

Getting Started with HDInsight Emulator 245

Setting Up Microsoft Azure Emulator for Storage 251

Summary 253

Q&A 254

Part III: Programming MapReduce and HDInsight Script Action

HOUR 10: Programming MapReduce Jobs   **255**

MapReduce Hello World! 255

Analyzing Flight Delays with MapReduce 258

Serialization Frameworks for Hadoop 262

Hadoop Streaming 270

Summary 276

Q&A 276

HOUR 11: Customizing the HDInsight Cluster with Script Action   **277**

Identifying the Need for Cluster Customization 277

Developing Script Action 278

Consuming Script Action 280

Running a Giraph job on a Customized HDInsight Cluster 282

Testing Script Action with HDInsight Emulator 285

Summary 285

Q&A 285

Part IV: Querying and Processing Big Data in HDInsight

HOUR 12: Getting Started with Apache Hive and Apache Tez in HDInsight   **287**

Introduction to Apache Hive 287

Getting Started with Apache Hive in HDInsight 288

Azure HDInsight Tools for Visual Studio 302

Programmatically Using the HDInsight .NET SDK 311

Introduction to Apache Tez 316

Summary 321

Q&A 321

Exercise 322

HOUR 13: Programming with Apache Hive, Apache Tez in HDInsight,
and Apache HCatalog   **323**

Programming with Hive in HDInsight 323

Using Tables in Hive 331

Serialization and Deserialization 340

Data Load Processes for Hive Tables 343

Querying Data from Hive Tables 346

Indexing in Hive 363

Apache Tez in Action 365

Apache HCatalog 368

Summary 370

Q&A 370

Exercise 370

HOUR 14: Consuming HDInsight Data from Microsoft BI Tools over
Hive ODBC Driver: Part 1   **371**

Introduction to Hive ODBC Driver 371

Introduction to Microsoft Power BI 378

Accessing Hive Data from Microsoft Excel 379

Summary 384

Q&A 384

HOUR 15: Consuming HDInsight Data from Microsoft BI Tools over
Hive ODBC Driver: Part 2   **385**

Accessing Hive Data from PowerPivot 385

Accessing Hive Data from SQL Server 409

Accessing HDInsight Data from Power Query 417

Summary 421

Q&A 421

Exercise 422

HOUR 16: Integrating HDInsight with SQL Server Integration Services   **423**

The Need for Data Movement 423

Introduction to SSIS 424

Analyzing On-time Flight Departure with SSIS 424

Provisioning HDInsight Cluster 427

Summary 431

Q&A 431

HOUR 17: Using Pig for Data Processing   **433**

Introduction to Pig Latin 433

Using Pig to Count Cancelled Flights 434

Using HCatalog in a Pig Latin Script 438

Submitting Pig Jobs with PowerShell 440

Summary 443

Q&A 443

HOUR 18: Using Sqoop for Data Movement Between RDBMS and HDInsight   **445**

What Is Sqoop? 445

Using Sqoop Import and Export Commands 448

Using Sqoop with PowerShell 451

Summary 452

Q&A 452

Part V: Managing Workflow and Performing Statistical Computing

HOUR 19: Using Oozie Workflows and Job Orchestration with HDInsight   **455**

Introduction to Oozie 455

Determining On-time Flight Departure Percentage with Oozie 457

Submitting an Oozie Workflow with HDInsight .NET SDK 463

Coordinating Workflows with Oozie 464

Oozie Compared to SSIS 465

Summary 466

Q&A 466

HOUR 20: Performing Statistical Computing with R   **467**

Introduction to R 467

Integrating R with Hadoop 471

Enabling R on HDInsight 472

Summary 477

Q&A 477

Part VI: Performing Interactive Analytics and Machine Learning

HOUR 21: Performing Big Data Analytics with Spark   **479**

Introduction to Spark 479

Spark Programming Model 481

Blending SQL Querying with Functional Programs 485

Summary 489

Q&A 489

HOUR 22: Microsoft Azure Machine Learning   **491**

History of Traditional Machine Learning 491

Introduction to Azure ML 493

Azure ML Workspace 495

Processes to Build Azure ML Solutions 497

Getting Started with Azure ML 498

Creating Predictive Models with Azure ML 506

Publishing Azure ML Models as Web Services 512

Summary 515

Q&A 515

Exercise 516

Part VII: Performing Real-time Analytics

HOUR 23: Performing Stream Analytics with Storm   519

Introduction to Storm 519

Using SCP.NET to Develop Storm Solutions 522

Analyzing Speed Limit Violation Incidents with Storm 524

Summary 533

Q&A 533

HOUR 24: Introduction to Apache HBase on HDInsight   535

Introduction to Apache HBase 535

HBase Architecture 538

Creating HDInsight Cluster with HBase 545

Summary 552

Q&A 552

Index   553

About the Authors

Arshad Ali has more than 13 years of experience in the computer industry. As a DB/DW/BI consultant in an end-to-end delivery role, he has been working on several enterprise-scale data warehousing and analytics projects for enabling and developing business intelligence and analytic solutions. He specializes in database, data warehousing, and business intelligence/analytics application design, development, and deployment at the enterprise level. He frequently works with SQL Server, Microsoft Analytics Platform System (APS, or formally known as SQL Server Parallel Data Warehouse [PDW]), HDInsight (Hadoop, Hive, Pig, HBase, and so on), SSIS, SSRS, SSAS, Service Broker, MDS, DQS, SharePoint, and PPS. In the past, he has also handled performance optimization for several projects, with significant performance gain.

Arshad is a Microsoft Certified Solutions Expert (MCSE)–SQL Server 2012 Data Platform, and Microsoft Certified IT Professional (MCITP) in Microsoft SQL Server 2008–Database Development, Data Administration, and Business Intelligence. He is also certified on ITIL 2011 foundation.

He has worked in developing applications in VB, ASP, .NET, ASP.NET, and C#. He is a Microsoft Certified Application Developer (MCAD) and Microsoft Certified Solution Developer (MCSD) for the .NET platform in Web, Windows, and Enterprise.

Arshad has presented at several technical events and has written more than 200 articles related to DB, DW, BI, and BA technologies, best practices, processes, and performance optimization techniques on SQL Server, Hadoop, and related technologies. His articles have been published on several prominent sites.

On the educational front, Arshad holds a Master in Computer Applications degree and a Master in Business Administration in IT degree.

Arshad can be reached at arshad.ali@live.in, or visit http://arshadali.blogspot.in/ to connect with him.

Manpreet Singh is a consultant and author with extensive expertise in architecture, design, and implementation of business intelligence and Big Data analytics solutions. He is passionate about enabling businesses to derive valuable insights from their data.

Manpreet has been working on Microsoft technologies for more than 8 years, with a strong focus on Microsoft Business Intelligence Stack, SharePoint BI, and Microsoft's Big

Data Analytics Platforms (Analytics Platform System and HDInsight). He also specializes in Mobile Business Intelligence solution development and has helped businesses deliver a consolidated view of their data to their mobile workforces.

Manpreet has coauthored books and technical articles on Microsoft technologies, focusing on the development of data analytics and visualization solutions with the Microsoft BI Stack and SharePoint. He holds a degree in computer science and engineering from Panjab University, India.

Manpreet can be reached at manpreet.singh3@hotmail.com.

Dedications

Arshad:

To my parents, the late Mrs. and Mr. Md Azal Hussain, who brought me into this beautiful world and made me the person I am today. Although they couldn't be here to see this day, I am sure they must be proud, and all I can say is, "Thanks so much—I love you both."

And to my beautiful wife, Shazia Arshad Ali, who motivated me to take up the challenge of writing this book and who supported me throughout this journey.

And to my nephew, Gulfam Hussain, who has been very excited for me to be an author and has been following up with me on its progress regularly and supporting me, where he could, in completing this book.

Finally, I would like to dedicate this to my school teacher, Sankar Sarkar, who shaped my career with his patience and perseverance and has been truly an inspirational source.

Manpreet:

To my parents, my wife, and my daughter. And to my grandfather, Capt. Jagat Singh, who couldn't be here to see this day.

Acknowledgments

This book would not have been possible without support from some of our special friends. First and foremost, we would like to thank Yaswant Vishwakarma, Vijay Korapadi, Avadhut Kulkarni, Kuldeep Chauhan, Rajeev Gupta, Vivek Adholia, and many others who have been inspirations and supported us in writing this book, directly or indirectly. Thanks a lot, guys—we are truly indebted to you all for all your support and the opportunity you have given us to learn and grow.

We also would like to thank the entire Pearson team, especially Mark Renfrow and Joan Murray, for taking our proposal from dream to reality. Thanks also to Shayne Burgess and Ron Abellera for reading the entire draft of the book and providing very helpful feedback and suggestions.

Thanks once again—you all rock!

Arshad

Manpreet

We Want to Hear from You!

As the reader of this book, *you* are our most important critic and commentator. We value your opinion and want to know what we're doing right, what we could do better, what areas you'd like to see us publish in, and any other words of wisdom you're willing to pass our way.

We welcome your comments. You can email or write to let us know what you did or didn't like about this book—as well as what we can do to make our books better.

Please note that we cannot help you with technical problems related to the topic of this book.

When you write, please be sure to include this book's title and authors as well as your name and email address. We will carefully review your comments and share them with the authors and editors who worked on the book.

Email: consumer@samspublishing.com

Mail: Sams Publishing
         ATTN: Reader Feedback
         800 East 96th Street
         Indianapolis, IN 46240 USA

Reader Services

Visit our website and register this book at informit.com/register for convenient access to any updates, downloads, or errata that might be available for this book.

Introduction

"The information that's stored in our databases and spreadsheets cannot speak for itself. It has important stories to tell and only we can give them a voice." —Stephen Few

Hello, and welcome to the world of Big Data! We are your authors, Arshad Ali and Manpreet Singh. For us, it's a good sign that you're actually reading this introduction (so few readers of tech books do, in our experiences). Perhaps your first question is, "What's in it for me?" We are here to give you those details with minimal fuss.

Never has there been a more exciting time in the world of data. We are seeing the convergence of significant trends that are fundamentally transforming the industry and ushering in a new era of technological innovation in areas such as social, mobility, advanced analytics, and machine learning. We are witnessing an explosion of data, with an entirely new scale and scope to gain insights from. Recent estimates say that the total amount of digital information in the world is increasing 10 times every 5 years. Eighty-five percent of this data is coming from new data sources (connected devices, sensors, RFIDs, web blogs, clickstreams, and so on), and up to 80 percent of this data is unstructured. This presents a huge opportunity for an organization: to tap into this new data to identify new opportunity and areas for innovation.

To store and get insight into this humongous volume of different varieties of data, known as Big Data, an organization needs tools and technologies. Chief among these is Hadoop, for processing and analyzing this ambient data born outside the traditional data processing platform. Hadoop is the open source implementation of the MapReduce parallel computational engine and environment, and it's used quite widely in processing streams of data that go well beyond even the largest enterprise data sets in size. Whether it's sensor, clickstream, social media, telemetry, location based, or other data that is generated and collected in large volumes, Hadoop is often on the scene to process and analyze it.

Analytics has been in use (mostly with organizations' internal data) for several years now, but its use with Big Data is yielding tremendous opportunities. Organizations can now leverage data available externally in different formats, to identify new opportunities and areas of innovation by analyzing patterns, customer responses or behavior, market trends, competitors' take, research data from governments or organizations, and more. This provides an opportunity to not only look back on the past, but also look forward to understand what might happen in the future, using predictive analytics.

In this book, we examine what constitutes Big Data and demonstrate how organizations can tap into Big Data using Hadoop. We look at some important tools and technologies in the Hadoop ecosystem and, more important, check out Microsoft's partnership with Hortonworks/Cloudera. The Hadoop distribution for the Windows platform or on the Microsoft Azure Platform (cloud computing) is an enterprise-ready solution and can be integrated easily with Microsoft SQL Server, Microsoft Active Directory, and System Center. This makes it dramatically simpler, easier, more efficient, and more cost effective for your organization to capitalize on the opportunity Big Data brings to your business. Through deep integration with Microsoft Business Intelligence tools (PowerPivot and Power View) and EDW tools (SQL Server and SQL Server Parallel Data Warehouse), Microsoft's Big Data solution also offers customers deep insights into their structured and unstructured data with the tools they use every day.

This book primarily focuses on the Hadoop (Hadoop 1.* and Hadoop 2.*) distribution for Azure, Microsoft HDInsight. It provides several advantages over running a Hadoop cluster over your local infrastructure. In terms of programming MapReduce jobs or Hive or PIG queries, you will see no differences; the same program will run flawlessly on either of these two Hadoop distributions (or even on other distributions), or with minimal changes, if you are using cloud platform-specific features. Moreover, integrating Hadoop and cloud computing significantly lessens the total cost ownership and delivers quick and easy setup for the Hadoop cluster. (We demonstrate how to set up a Hadoop cluster on Microsoft Azure in Hour 6, "Getting Started with HDInsight, Provisioning Your HDInsight Service Cluster, and Automating HDInsight Cluster Provisioning.")

Consider some forecasts from notable research analysts or research organizations:

"Big Data is a Big Priority for Customers—49% of top CEOs and CIOs are currently using Big Data for customer analytics."—McKinsey &Company, McKinsey Global Survey Results, *Minding Your Digital Business,* 2012

"By 2015, 4.4 million IT jobs globally will be created to support Big Data, generating 1.9 million IT jobs in the United States. Only one third of skill sets will be available by that time."—Peter Sondergaard, Senior Vice President at Gartner and Global Head of Research

"By 2015, businesses (organizations that are able to take advantage of Big Data) that build a modern information management system will outperform their peers financially by 20 percent."—Gartner, Mark Beyer, *Information Management in the 21st Century*

"By 2020, the amount of digital data produced will exceed 40 zettabytes, which is the equivalent of 5,200GB of data for every man, woman, and child on Earth."—Digital Universe study

IDC has published an analysis predicting that the market for Big Data will grow to over $19 billion by 2015. This includes growth in partner services to $6.5 billion in 2015 and growth in software to $4.6 billion in 2015. This represents 39 percent and 34 percent compound annual growth rates, respectively.

We hope you enjoy reading this book and gain an understanding of and expertise on Big Data and Big Data analytics. We especially hope you learn how to leverage Microsoft HDInsight to exploit its enormous opportunities to take your organization way ahead of your competitors.

We would love to hear your feedback or suggestions for improvement. Feel free to share with us (Arshad Ali, arshad.ali@live.in, and Manpreet Singh, manpreet.singh3@hotmail.com) so that we can incorporate it into the next release. Welcome to the world of Big Data and Big Data analytics with Microsoft HDInsight!

Who Should Read This Book

What do you hope to get out of this book? As we wrote this book, we had the following audiences in mind:

- **Developers**—Developers (especially business intelligence developers) worldwide are seeing a growing need for practical, step-by-step instruction in processing Big Data and performing advanced analytics to extract actionable insights. This book was designed to meet that need. It starts at the ground level and builds from there, to make you an expert. Here you'll learn how to build the next generation of apps that include such capabilities.

- **Data scientists**—As a data scientist, you are already familiar with the processes of acquiring, transforming, and integrating data into your work and performing advanced analytics. This book introduces you to modern tools and technologies (ones that are prominent, inexpensive, flexible, and open source friendly) that you can apply while acquiring, transforming, and integrating Big Data and performing advanced analytics.

  By the time you complete this book, you'll be quite comfortable with the latest tools and technologies.

- **Business decision makers**—Business decision makers around the world, from many different organizations, are looking to unlock the value of data to gain actionable insights that enable their businesses to stay ahead of competitors. This book delves into advanced analytics applications and case studies based on Big Data tools and technologies, to accelerate your business goals.

- **Students aspiring to be Big Data analysts**—As you are getting ready to transition from the academic to the corporate world, this books helps you build a foundational skill set to ace your interviews and successfully deliver Big Data projects in a timely manner. Chapters were designed to start at the ground level and gradually take you to an expert level.

Don't worry if you don't fit into any of these classifications. Set your sights on learning as much as you can and having fun in the process, and you'll do fine!

How This Book Is Organized

This book begins with the premise that you can learn what Big Data is, including the real-life applications of Big Data and the prominent tools and technologies to use Big Data solutions to quickly tap into opportunity, by studying the material in 24 1-hour sessions. You might use your lunch break as your training hour, or you might study for an hour before you go to bed at night.

Whatever schedule you adopt, these are the hour-by-hour details on how we structured the content:

▶ Hour 1, "Introduction of Big Data, NoSQL, and Business Value Proposition," introduces you to the world of Big Data and explains how an organization that leverages the power of Big Data analytics can both remain competitive and beat out its competitors. It explains Big Data in detail, along with its characteristics and the types of analysis (descriptive, predictive, and prescriptive) an organization does with Big Data. Finally, it sets out the business value proposition of using Big Data solutions, along with some real-life examples of Big Data solutions.

This hour also summarizes the NoSQL technologies used to manage and process Big Data and explains how NoSQL systems differ from traditional database systems (RDBMS).

▶ In Hour 2, "Introduction to Hadoop, Its Architecture, Ecosystem, and Microsoft Offerings," you look at managing Big Data with Apache Hadoop. This hour is rooted in history: It shows how Hadoop evolved from infancy to Hadoop 1.0 and then Hadoop 2.0, highlighting architectural changes from Hadoop 1.0 to Hadoop 2.0. This hour also focuses on understanding other software and components that make up the Hadoop ecosystem and looks at the components needed in different phases of Big Data analytics. Finally, it introduces you to Hadoop vendors, evaluates their offerings, and analyzes Microsoft's deployment options for Big Data solutions.

▶ In Hour 3, "Hadoop Distributed File System Versions 1.0 and 2.0," you learn about HDFS, its architecture, and how data gets stored. You also look into the processes of reading from HDFS and writing data to HDFS, as well as internal behavior to ensure fault tolerance. At the end of the hour, you take a detailed look at HDFS 2.0, which comes as a part of Hadoop 2.0, to see how it overcomes the limitations of Hadoop 1.0 and provides high-availability and scalability enhancements.

▶ In Hour 4, "The MapReduce Job Framework and Job Execution Pipeline," you explore the MapReduce programming paradigm, its architecture, the components of a MapReduce job, and MapReduce job execution flow.

▶ Hour 5, "MapReduce—Advanced Concepts and YARN," introduces you to advanced concepts related to MapReduce (including MapReduce Streaming, MapReduce joins, distributed caches, failures and how they are handled transparently, and performance optimization for your MapReduce jobs).

In Hadoop 2.0, YARN ushers in a major architectural change and opens a new window for scalability, performance, and multitenancy. In this hour, you learn about the YARN architecture, its components, the YARN job execution pipeline, and how failures are handled transparently.

▶ In Hour 6, "Getting Started with HDInsight, Provisioning Your HDInsight Service Cluster, and Automating HDInsight Cluster Provisioning," you delve into the HDInsight service. You also walk through a step-by-step process for quickly provisioning HDInsight or a Hadoop cluster on Microsoft Azure, either interactively using Azure Management Portal or automatically using PowerShell scripting.

▶ In Hour 7, "Exploring Typical Components of HDFS Cluster," you explore the typical components of an HDFS cluster: the name node, secondary name node, and data nodes. You also learn how HDInsight separates the storage from the cluster and relies on Azure Storage Blob instead of HDFS as the default file system for storing data. This hour provides more details on these concepts in the context of the HDInsight service.

▶ Hour 8, "Storing Data in Microsoft Azure Storage Blob," shows you how HDInsight supports both the Hadoop Distributed File System (HDFS) and Azure Storage Blob for storing user data (although HDInsight relies on Azure storage blob as the default file system instead of HDFS for storing data). This hour explores Azure Storage Blob in the context of HDInsight and concludes by discussing the impact of blob storage on performance and data locality.

▶ Hour 9, "Working with Microsoft Azure HDInsight Emulator," is devoted to Microsoft's HDInsight emulator. HDInsight emulator emulates a single-node cluster and is well suited to development scenarios and experimentation. This hour focuses on setting up the HDInsight emulator and executing a MapReduce job to test its functionality.

▶ Hour 10, "Programming MapReduce Jobs," expands on the content in earlier hours and provides examples and techniques for programming MapReduce programs in Java and C#. It presents a real-life scenario that analyzes flight delays with MapReduce and concludes with a discussion on serialization options for Hadoop.

▶ Hour 11, "Customizing the HDInsight Cluster with Script Action," looks at the HDInsight cluster that comes preinstalled with a number of frequently used components. It also introduces customization options for the HDInsight cluster and walks you through the process for installing additional Hadoop ecosystem projects using a feature called Script Action. In addition, this hour introduces the HDInsight Script Action feature and illustrates the steps in developing and deploying a Script Action.

▶ In Hour 12, "Getting Started with Apache Hive and Apache Tez in HDInsight," you learn about how you can use Apache Hive. You learn different ways of writing and executing

HiveQL queries in HDInsight and see how Apache Tez significantly improves overall performance for HiveQL queries.

▶ In Hour 13, "Programming with Apache Hive, Apache Tez in HDInsight, and Apache HCatalog," you extend your expertise on Apache Hive and see how you can leverage it for ad hoc queries and data analysis. You also learn about some of the important commands you will use in Apache Hive for data loading and querying. At the end this hour, you look at Apache HCatalog, which has merged with Apache Hive, and see how to leverage the Apache Tez execution engine for Hive query execution to improve the performance of your query.

▶ Hour 14, "Consuming HDInsight Data from Microsoft BI Tools over Hive ODBC Driver: Part 1," shows you how to use the Microsoft Hive ODBC driver to connect and pull data from Hive tables from different Microsoft Business Intelligence (MSBI) reporting tools, for further analysis and ad hoc reporting.

▶ In Hour 15, "Consuming HDInsight Data from Microsoft BI Tools over Hive ODBC Driver: Part 2," you learn to use PowerPivot to create a data model (define relationships between them, apply transformations, create calculations, and more) based on Hive tables and then use Power View and Power Map to visualize the data from different perspectives with intuitive and interactive visualization options.

▶ In Hour 16, "Integrating HDInsight with SQL Server Integration Services," you see how you can use SQL Server Integration Services (SSIS) to build data integration packages to transfer data between an HDInsight cluster and a relational database management system (RDBMS) such as SQL Server.

▶ Hour 17, "Using Pig for Data Processing," explores Pig Latin, a workflow-style procedural language that makes it easier to specify transformation operations on data. This hour provides an introduction to Pig for processing Big Data sets and illustrates the steps in submitting Pig jobs to the HDInsight cluster.

▶ Hour 18, "Using Sqoop for Data Movement Between RDBMS and HDInsight," demonstrates how Sqoop facilitates data migration between relational databases and Hadoop. This hour introduces you to the Sqoop connector for Hadoop and illustrates its use in data migration between Hadoop and SQL Server/SQL Azure databases.

▶ Hour 19, "Using Oozie Workflows and Job Orchestration with HDInsight," looks at data processing solutions that require multiple jobs chained together in particular sequence to accomplish a processing task in the form of a conditional workflow. In this hour, you learn to use Oozie, a workflow development component within the Hadoop ecosystem.

▶ Hour 20, "Performing Statistical Computing with R," focuses on the R language, which is popular among data scientists for analytics and statistical computing. R was not designed to work with Big Data because it typically works by pulling data that persists elsewhere into memory. However, recent advancements have made it possible to leverage R for Big Data analytics. This hour introduces R and looks at the approaches for enabling R on Hadoop.

▶ Hour 21, "Performing Big Data Analytics with Spark," introduces Spark, briefly explores the Spark programming model, and takes a look at Spark integration with SQL.

▶ In Hour 22, "Microsoft Azure Machine Learning," you learn about an emerging technology known as Microsoft Azure Machine Learning (Azure ML). Azure ML is extremely simple to use and easy to implement so that analysts with various backgrounds (even nondata scientists) can leverage it for predictive analytics.

▶ In Hour 23, "Performing Stream Analytics with Storm," you learn about Apache Storm and explore its use in performing real-time Stream analytics.

▶ Hour 24, "Introduction to Apache HBase on HDInsight," you learn about Apache HBase, when to use it, and how you can leverage it with HDInsight service.

Conventions Used in This Book

In our experience as authors and trainers, we've found that many readers and students skip over this part of the book. Congratulations for reading it! Doing so will pay big dividends because you'll understand how and why we formatted this book the way we did.

Try It Yourself

Throughout the book, you'll find Try It Yourself exercises, which are opportunities for you to apply what you're learning right then and there. I believe in knowledge stacking, so you can expect that later Try It Yourself exercises assume that you know how to do stuff you did in previous exercises. Therefore, your best bet is to read each chapter in sequence and work through every Try It Yourself exercise.

System Requirements

You don't need a lot, computer wise, to perform all the Try It Yourself exercises in this book. However, if you don't meet the necessary system requirements, you're stuck. Make sure you have the following before you begin your work:

▶ **A Windows-based computer**—Technically, you don't need a computer that runs only Microsoft Windows: Microsoft Azure services can be accessed and consumed using web browsers from any platform. However, if you want to use HDInsight emulator, you need to have a machine (virtual or physical) with the Microsoft Windows operating system.

▶ **An Internet connection**—Microsoft HDInsight service is available on the cloud platform, so while you are working with it, you'll be accessing the web.

▶ **An Azure subscription**—You need an Azure subscription to use the platform or services available in Azure. Microsoft offers trial subscriptions of the Microsoft Azure subscription service used for learning or evaluation purposes.

Okay, that's enough of the preliminaries. It's time to get started on the Big Data journey and learn Big Data analytics with HDInsight. Happy reading!

Introduction of Big Data, NoSQL, and Business Value Proposition

---

What You'll Learn in This Hour:

▶ Types of Analysis

▶ Types of Data

▶ Big Data

▶ Managing Big Data

▶ NoSQL Systems

▶ Big Data, NoSQL Systems, and the Business Value Proposition

▶ Application of Big Data and Big Data Solutions

This hour introduces you to the world of Big Data and shows how an organization can leverage the power of Big Data analytics to triumph over its competitors. You examine Big Data in detail, identify its characteristics, and look at the different types of analysis (descriptive, predictive, and prescriptive) an organization performs.

Later in the hour, you explore NoSQL technologies to manage and process Big Data and see how NoSQL systems differ from traditional database systems (RDBMS). You delve into the different types of NoSQL systems (like key-value store databases, columnar or column-oriented [also known as column-store databases], document-oriented databases, and graph databases) and explore the benefits and limitations of using NoSQL systems. At the end of the hour, you learn about the business value proposition of using Big Data solutions and take a look at some real-life examples of Big Data solutions in use.

Types of Analysis

The world of data is changing rapidly. Analytics has been identified as one of the recent mega-trends (social, mobility, and cloud technology are others) and is at the heart of this data-centric world. Now organizations of all scales are collecting vast amounts of data with their own systems, including data from these areas:

▶ Operations

▶ Production and manufacturing

▶ Sales

▶ Supply chain management

▶ Marketing campaign performance

Companies also use external sources, such as the social networking sites Facebook, Twitter, and LinkedIn, to analyze customer sentiment about their products and services. Data can even be generated from connected mobile devices, government, and research bodies for use in analyzing market trends and opportunities, industry news, and business forecasts.

The capability to collect a vast amount of data from different sources enables an organization to gain a competitive advantage. A company can then better position itself or its products and services in a more favorable market (*where* and *how*) to reach targeted customers (*who*) at their most receptive times (*when*), and then listen to its customers for suggestions (*feedback* and *customer service*). More important, a company can ultimately offer something that makes sense to customers (*what*).

Analytics essentially enables organizations to carry out targeted campaigns, cross-sales recommendations, online advertising, and more. But before you start your journey into the world of Big Data, NoSQL, and business analytics, you need to know the types of analysis an organization generally conducts.

Companies perform three basic types of analysis on collected data (see Figure 1.1):

▶ **Diagnostic or descriptive analysis**—Organizations seek to understand what happened over a certain period of time and determine what caused it to happen. They might try to gain insight into historical data with reporting, Key Performance Indicators (KPIs), and scorecards. For example, this type of analysis can use clustering or classification techniques for customer segmentation to better understand customers and offer them products based on their needs and requirements.

Diagnostic analysis	Predictive analysis	Prescriptive analysis
What happened and why?	What will happen in the future?	What is the next best action?
How was the performance over past period?	Forecasting and propensity to buy.	Channel management or portfolio optimization.
Used for customer segmentation.	Predict with time series, neural networks, regression, etc.	Linear programming, Monte Carlo simulation, or game theory.
Diagnose with clustering or classification techniques.		

FIGURE 1.1
Business intelligence and Big Data analysis types.

▶ **Predictive analysis**—Predictive analysis helps an organization understand what can happen in the future based on identified patterns in the data, using statistical and machine learning techniques. Predictive analysis is also referred to as data mining or machine learning. This type of analysis uses time series, neural networks, and regression algorithms to predict the future. Predictive analysis enables companies to answer these types of questions:

   ▶ Which stocks should we target as part of our portfolio management?

   ▶ Did some stocks show haphazard behavior? Which factors are impacting the stock gains the most?

   ▶ How and why are users of e-commerce platforms, online games, and web applications behaving in a particular way?

   ▶ How do we optimize the routing of our fleet of vehicles based on weather and traffic patterns?

   ▶ How do we better predict future outcomes based on an identified pattern?

▶ **Prescriptive analysis**—Some researchers refer to this analysis as the final phase in business analytics. Organizations can predict the likely outcome of various corrective measures using optimization and simulation techniques. For example, prescriptive analysis can use linear programming, Monte Carlo simulation, or game theory for channel management or portfolio optimization.

Types of Data

Businesses are largely interested in three broad types of data: structured, unstructured, and semi-structured data.

Structured Data

Structured data adheres to the predefined fixed schema and strict data model structure—think of a table in the relational database system. A row in the table always has the same number of columns of the same type of other rows (although some columns might contain blank or NULL values), per the predefined schema of the table. With structured data, changes to the schema are assumed to be rare and, hence, the data model is rigid.

Unstructured Data

Unlike structured data, *unstructured data* has no identifiable internal structure. It does not have a predefined, fixed schema, but instead has a free-form structure. Unstructured data includes proprietary documents, bitmap images and objects, text, and other data types that are not part of a database system. Examples include photos and graphic images, audio and video, streaming instrument data, web pages, emails, blog entries, wikis, portable document format (PDF) documents, Word or Excel documents, and PowerPoint presentations. Unstructured data constitutes most enterprise data today.

In Excel documents, for example, the content might contain data in structured tabular format, but the Excel document itself is considered unstructured data. Likewise, email messages are organized on the email server in a structured format in the database system, but the body of the message has a free-form structure with no structure.

Semi-Structured Data

Semi-structured data is a hybrid between structured and unstructured data. It usually contains data in structured format but a schema that is not predefined and not rigid. Unlike structured data, semi-structured data lacks the strict data model structure. Examples are Extensible Markup Language (XML) or JavaScript Object Notation (JSON) documents, which contain tags (elements or attributes) to identify specific elements within the data, but without a rigid structure to adhere to.

Unlike in a relational table, in which each row has the same number of columns, each entity in semi-structured data (analogous to a row in a relational table) has a different number of attributes or even nested entities.

NOTE

By the Way

For simplicity, we use "structured and unstructured data" to refer to the collection of structured, semi-structured, and unstructured data. Semi-structured data usually is grouped with unstructured data even though it differs slightly from purely unstructured data.

Big Data

The phrase *data explosion* refers to the vast amount of data (structured, semi-structured, and unstructured) organizations generate every day, both internally and externally, at a speed that is practically impossible for their current data processing systems to collect and process. Ironically, organizations cannot afford to ignore the data because it provides insight into how they can gain competitive advantages. In some cases, organizations are *required* to store large amounts of structured and unstructured data (documents, email messages, chat history, audio, video, and other forms of electronic communication) to comply with government regulations. Fortunately, the cost of storage devices has decreased significantly, enabling companies to store Big Data that they previously would have purged regularly.

Big Data is primarily characterized by the three Vs (see Figure 1.2):

- ► Volume

- ► Variety

- ► Velocity

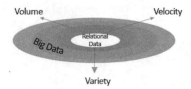

FIGURE 1.2
Big Data characteristics.

Businesses currently cannot capture, manage, and process the three Vs using traditional data processing systems within a tolerable elapsed time.

Volume Characteristics of Big Data

Big data can be stored in volumes of terabytes, petabytes, and even beyond. Now the focus is not only human-generated data (mostly structured, as a small percentage of overall data), but also data generated by machines such as sensors, connected devices, and Radio-Frequency Identification (RFID) devices (mostly unstructured data, as a larger percentage overall). (See Figure 1.3.)

FIGURE 1.3
Volume characteristics of Big Data.

Variety Characteristics of Big Data

Variety refers to the management of structured, semi-structured, and unstructured data (see Figure 1.4). Semi-structured and unstructured data includes but is not limited to text, images, legacy documents, audio, video, PDFs, clickstream data, web log data, and data gathered from social media. Most of this unstructured data is generated from sensors, connected devices, clickstream, and web logs, and can constitute up to 80 percent of overall Big Data.

FIGURE 1.4
Variety characteristic of Big Data.

Velocity Characteristics of Big Data

Velocity refers to the pace at which data arrives and usually refers to a real-time or near-real-time stream of data (see Figure 1.5). Examples include trading and stock exchange data and sensors attached to production line machinery to continuously monitor status.

FIGURE 1.5
Velocity characteristic of Big Data.

For Big Data, velocity also refers to the required speed of data insight.

Recently, some authors and researchers have added another *V* to define the characteristic of Big Data: *variability*. This characteristic refers to the many possible interpretations of the same data. Similarly, *veracity* defines the uncertainty (credibility of the source of data might not be verifiable and hence suitability of the data for target audience might be questionable) in collected data. Nonetheless, the premise of Big Data remains the same as discussed earlier.

Big Data is generally synonymous with Hadoop, but the two are not really the same. *Big Data* refers to a humongous volume of different types of data with the characteristics of volume, variety, and velocity that arrives at a very fast pace. Hadoop, on the other hand, is one of the tools or technologies used to store, manage, and process Big Data.

GO TO ▶ We talk in greater detail about Hadoop and its architecture in **Hour 2, "Introduction to Hadoop, Its Architecture, Ecosystem, and Microsoft Offerings."**

What Big Data Is Not

Big Data does not refer to the tools and technologies that manage and process the Big Data (as discussed earlier) itself. Several tools and technologies can manage Big Data, and Hadoop is one among them. Hadoop is a mature, fault-tolerant platform that can handle the distributed storage and processing of Big Data.

GO TO ▶ We talk about Hadoop in greater detail in **Hour 2**.

So far, we have talked about Big Data and looked at future trends in analytics on Big Data. Now let's dive deeper to understand the different tools and technologies used to store, manage, and process Big Data.

Managing Big Data

An organization cannot afford to delete data (especially Big Data) if it wants to outperform its competitors. Tapping into the opportunities Big Data offers makes good business sense for some key reasons.

More Data, More Accurate Models

A substantial number and variety of data sources generate large quantities of data for businesses. These include connected devices, sensors, RFIDs, web clicks, and web logs (see Figure 1.6). Organizations now realize that data is too valuable to delete, so they need to store, manage, and process that data.

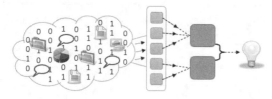

FIGURE 1.6
Getting insight into Big Data.

More—and Cheaper—Computing Power and Storage

The dramatic decline in the cost of computing hardware resources (see Figure 1.7), especially the cost of storage devices, is one factor that enables organizations to store every bit of data or Big Data. It also enables large organizations to cost-effectively retain large amounts of structured and unstructured data longer, to comply with government regulations and guard against future litigation.

FIGURE 1.7
Decreasing hardware prices.

Increased Awareness of the Competition and a Means to Proactively Win Over Competitors

Companies want to leverage all possible means to remain competitive and beat their competitors. Even with the advent of social media, a business needs to analyze data to understand customer sentiment about the organization and its products or services. Companies also want to offer customers what they want through targeted campaigns and seek to understand reasons for customer *churn* (the rate of attrition in the customer base) so that they can take proactive measures to retain customers. Figure 1.8 shows increased awareness and customer demands.

FIGURE 1.8
Increased awareness, realization, and demand.

Availability of New Tools and Technologies to Process and Manage Big Data

Several new tools and technologies can help companies store, manage, and process Big Data. These include Hadoop, MongoDB, CouchDB, DocumentDB, and Cassandra, among others. We cover Hadoop and its architecture in more detail in Hour 2.

NoSQL Systems

If you are a Structured Query Language (SQL) or Relational Database Management System (RDBMS) expert, you first must know that you don't need to worry about NoSQL—these two technologies serve a very different purpose. NoSQL is not a replacement of the familiar SQL or RDBMS technologies, although, of course, learning these new tools and technologies will give you better perspective and help you think of an organizational problem in a holistic manner. So why do we need NoSQL? The sheer volume, velocity, and variety of Big Data are beyond the capabilities of RDBMS technologies to process in a timely manner. NoSQL tools and technologies are essential for processing Big Data.

NoSQL stands for **Not Only SQL** and is complimentary to the existing SQL or RDBMS technologies. For some problems, storage and processing solutions other than RDBMS are more suitable—both technologies can coexist, and each has its own place. RDBMS still dominates the market, but NoSQL technologies are catching up to manage Big Data and real-time web applications.

In many scenarios, both technologies are being used to provide an enterprise-wide business intelligence and business analytics systems. In these integrated systems, NoSQL systems store and manage Big Data (with no schema) and RDBMS stores the processed data in relational format (with schema) for a quicker query response time.

NoSQL Versus RDBMS

RDBMS systems are also called *schema-first* because RDBMS supports creating a relation, or a table structure to store data in rows and columns (a predefined normalized structure) and then join them using a relationship between the primary key and a foreign key. Data gets stored in these relations/tables. When querying, we then retrieve data either from a single relation or from multiple relations by joining them. An RDBMS system provides a faster query response time, but loading data into it takes longer; a significant amount of time is needed especially when you are developing and defining a schema. The rigid schema requirement makes it inflexible—changing the schema later requires a significant amount of effort and time. As you can see in Figure 1.9, once you have a data model in place, you must store the data in stages, apply cleansing and transformation, and then move the final set of data to the data warehouse for analysis. This overall process of loading data into an RDBMS system is not suitable for Big Data. Figure 1.9 shows the stages in analysis of structured data in RDBMS—Relation Data Warehouse.

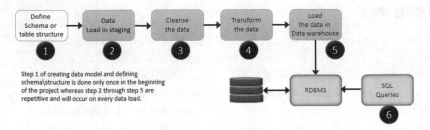

FIGURE 1.9
Stages in the analysis of structured data in RDBMS—Relation Data Warehouse.

In contrast to RDBMS systems, NoSQL systems are called *schema-later* because they don't have the strict requirement of defining the schema or structure of data before the actual data load process begins. For example, you can continue to store data in a Hadoop cluster as it arrives in Hadoop Distributed File System (HDFS; you learn more about it in Hour 3, "Hadoop Distributed File System Versions 1.0 and 2.0") (in files and folders), and then later you can use Hive to define the schema for querying data from the folders. Likewise, other document-oriented NoSQL systems support storing data in documents using the flexible JSON format. This enables the application to store virtually any structure it wants in a data element in a JSON document. A JSON document might have all the data stored in a row that spans several tables of a relational database and might aggregate it into a single document. Consolidating data in documents this way might duplicate information, but the lower cost of storage makes it possible. As you can see in Figure 1.10, NoSQL lets you continue to store data as it arrives, without worrying about the schema or structure of the data, and then later use an application program to query the data. Figure 1.10 shows the stages of analyzing Big Data in NoSQL systems.

FIGURE 1.10
Stages in analysis of Big Data in NoSQL systems.

Apart from efficiency in the data load process for Big Data, RDBMS systems and NoSQL systems have other differences (see Figure 1.11).

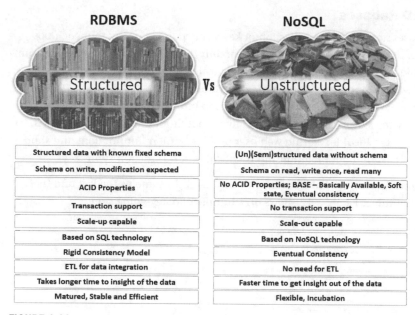

RDBMS	NoSQL
Structured	**Unstructured**
Structured data with known fixed schema	(Un)(Semi)structured data without schema
Schema on write, modification expected	Schema on read, write once, read many
ACID Properties	No ACID Properties; BASE – Basically Available, Soft state, Eventual consistency
Transaction support	No transaction support
Scale-up capable	Scale-out capable
Based on SQL technology	Based on NoSQL technology
Rigid Consistency Model	Eventual Consistency
ETL for data integration	No need for ETL
Takes longer time to insight of the data	Faster time to get insight out of the data
Matured, Stable and Efficient	Flexible, Incubation

FIGURE 1.11
Differences between RDBMS and NoSQL systems.

Major Types of NoSQL Technologies

Several NoSQL systems are used. For clarity, we have divided them into the typical usage scenarios (for example, Online Transaction Processing [OLTP] or Online Analytical Processing [OLAP]) we often deal with.

No current NoSQL system purely supports the need for OLTP; they all lack a couple important supports. This section covers the following four categories of NoSQL systems used with OLTP:

▶ Key-value store databases

▶ Columnar, or column-oriented, or column-store databases

▶ Document-oriented databases

▶ Graph databases

GO TO ▶ For more information on supports for OLTP, refer to the **"Limitations of NoSQL Systems"** section, later in this hour.

Key-Value Store Databases

Key-value store databases store data as a collection of key-value pairs in a way that each possible key appears once, at most, in a collection. This is similar to the hash tables of the programming world, with a unique key and a pointer to a particular item of data. This database stores only pairs of keys and values, and it facilitates retrieving values when a key is known. These mappings are usually accompanied by cache mechanisms, to maximize performance. Key-value stores are probably the simplest type and normally do not fit for all Big Data problems. Key-value store databases are ideal for storing web user profiles, session information, and shopping carts. They are not ideal if a data relationship is critical or a transaction spans keys.

A file system can be considered a key-value store, with the file path/name as the key and the actual file content as the value. Figure 1.12 shows an example of a key-value store.

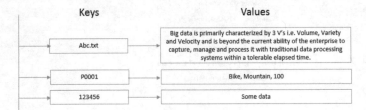

FIGURE 1.12
Key-value store database storage structure.

In another example, with phone-related data, `"Phone Number"` is considered the key, with associated values such as `"(123) 111-12345"`.

Dozens of key-value store databases are in use, including Amazon Dynamo, Microsoft Azure Table storage, Riak, Redis, and MemCached.

Amazon Dynamo

Amazon Dynamo was developed as an internal technology at Amazon for its e-commerce businesses, to address the need for an incrementally scalable, highly available key-value storage system. It is one of the most prominent key-value store NoSQL databases. Amazon S3 uses Dynamo as its storage mechanism. The technology has been designed to enable users to trade off cost, consistency, durability, and performance while maintaining high availability.

Microsoft Azure Table Storage

Microsoft Azure Table storage is another example of a key-value store that allows for rapid development and fast access to large quantities of data. It offers highly available, massively scalable key-value–based storage so that an application can automatically scale to meet user demand. In Microsoft Azure Table, key-value pairs are called *Properties* and are useful in filtering and specifying selection criteria; they belong to Entities, which, in turn, are organized into Tables. Microsoft Azure Table features optimistic concurrency and, as with other NoSQL databases, is schema-less. The properties of each entity in a specific table can differ, meaning that two entities in the same table can contain different collections of properties, and those properties can be of different types.

Columnar or Column-Oriented or Column-Store Databases

Unlike a row-store database system, which stores data from all the columns of a row stored together, a column-oriented database stores the data from a single column together. You might be wondering how a different physical layout representation of the same data (storing the same data in a columnar format instead of the traditional row format) can improve flexibility and performance.

In a column-oriented database, the flexibility comes from the fact that adding a column is both easy and inexpensive, with columns applied on a row-by-row basis. Each row can have a different set of columns, making the table sparse. In addition, because the data from single columns is stored together, the database has high redundancy and achieves a greater degree of compression, improving the overall performance.

Column-oriented or column-store databases are ideal for site searches, blogs, content management systems, and counter analytics. Figure 1.13 shows the difference between a row store and a column store.

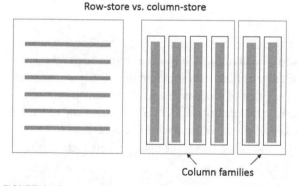

Row-store vs. column-store

Column families

FIGURE 1.13
Row-store versus column-store storage structure.

Some RDBMS systems have begun to support storing data in a column-oriented structure, such as SQL Server 2012 and onward. The following NoSQL databases also support column-oriented storage and, unlike RDBMS systems, in which the schema is fixed, allow a different schema for each row.

Apache Cassandra

Facebook developed Apache Cassandra to handle large amounts of data across many commodity servers, providing high availability with no single point of failure. It is the perfect platform for mission-critical data. Cassandra is a good choice when you need scalability and high availability without compromising on performance. Cassandra's support for replicating across multiple data centers is best-in-class, providing lower latency for users and providing peace of mind that you can survive even regional outages.

Apache HBase

Apache HBase is a distributed, versioned, column-oriented database management system that runs on top of HDFS. An HBase system comprises a set of tables. Each table contains rows and columns, much like in a traditional relational table. Each table must have an element defined as a primary key, and all access attempts to HBase tables must use this primary key. An HBase column represents an attribute of an object. HBase enables many columns to be grouped together into column families, so the elements of a column family are all stored together. This differs from a relational table, which stores together all the columns of a given row. HBase mandates that you predefine the table schema and specify the column families. However, it also enables you to add columns to column families at any time. The schema is thus flexible and can adapt to changing application requirements. Apache HBase is a good choice when you need random, real-time read/write access to your sparse data sets, which are common in many Big Data use cases. HBase supports writing applications in Avro, REST, and Thrift.

Document-Oriented Databases

Document-oriented databases, such as other NoSQL systems, are designed for horizontal scalability or *scale-out* needs. (Scaling out refers to spreading the load over multiple hosts.) As your data grows, you can simply add more commodity hardware to scale out and distribute the load. These systems are designed around a central concept of a document. Each document-oriented database implementation differs in the details of this definition, but they all generally assume that documents encapsulate and encode data in some standard formats or encodings, such as XML, Yet Another Markup Language (YAML), and JSON, as well as binary forms such as Binary JSON (BSON) and PDF.

In the case of a relational table, every record in a table has the same sequence of fields (they contain NULL\empty if they are not being used). This means they have rigid schema. In contrast, a document-oriented database contains collections, analogous to relational tables. Each collection might have fields that are completely different across collections: The fields and their value data types can vary for each collection; furthermore, even the collections can be nested. Figure 1.14 shows the document-oriented database storage structure.

A collection with four fields

```
{
        name: "ABC"
        age:30
        status: "Married"
        department: ["Finance", "Management"]
}
```
....
A collection with nested collections

```
{
        name: "XYZ"
        age:35
        status: "Married"
        department: "IT Support"
        Expertise:
        {
                skill: {"SQL Server", level: "Expert"}
                skill: {"SSIS", level: "Intermediate"}
                skill: {"SSAS", level: "Expert"}
                skill: {"SSRS", level: "Beginner"}
        }
}
```

FIGURE 1.14
Document-oriented database storage structure.

Document-oriented databases are ideal for storing application logs, articles, blogs, and e-commerce applications. They are also suitable when aggregation is needed. These databases are not ideal when transactions or queries span aggregations.

Several implementations of document-oriented databases exist, including MongoDB, CouchDB, Couchbase, and Microsoft DocumentDB.

MongoDB

MongoDB derives its name from word *humongous* and stores data as JSON-like documents with dynamic and binary schemas called *BSON*. MongoDB has databases, collections (like a table in the relational world), documents (like a record in the relational world), and indexes, much like a traditional relational database system. In MongoDB, you don't need to define fields in advance. No schema exists for fields within a document—the fields and their value data-types can vary from one document to another. In practice, you typically store documents of the same structure within collections. In fact, a collection itself is not defined. The database creates a collection on the first `insert` statement.

CouchDB

Similar to MongoDB, CouchDB is a document-oriented database that stores data in JSON document format. CouchDB has a fault-tolerant storage engine that puts the safety of the data first. Each CouchDB database is a collection of independent documents; each document maintains its own data and self-contained schema. You can use JavaScript as the CouchDB query language for MapReduce programming (for more on this, see Hour 4, "The MapReduce Job Framework and Job Execution Pipeline"); you can use HTTP for an API because it completely supports the Web and is particularly suited for interactive web applications.

Graph Databases

Graph databases have a concept of nodes, with relationships and properties. Unlike relational tables of rows and columns, and with the rigid structure of RDBMS, a flexible graph model is used that can scale across many machines. A graph database is designed for data that can be better represented as a graph (elements interconnected with an undetermined number of relationships between them). For example, this could be social relationships, public transport links, road maps, or network topologies. Examples of graph databases include Sones GraphDB and Neo4j. Figure 1.15 shows the structure of graph databases at a high level.

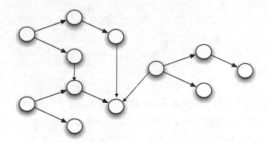

FIGURE 1.15
Graph database structure.

Benefits of Using NoSQL Systems

NoSQL systems offer several advantages over traditional relational systems. Consider some advantages of using NoSQL systems:

▶ You don't need to define the data model, schema, or structure at the beginning of the project. Just keep dumping all the data coming into the NoSQL systems, and process only required data by defining schema for it at the time of the query or when a reporting need arises. This is why NoSQL systems are called schema at read systems.

▶ You don't need to spend time developing complex ETL (extract, transform, and load) packages for data integration. No overhead is incurred in running those ETL packages on schedule.

▶ You don't need to worry about data staging or multiple data hops. Simply keep loading the data into the NoSQL system (for example, Hadoop) and analyze the data where it lands.

▸ No upfront investment in data cleansing and massaging is required. Just keep storing all the data that comes in and extract whatever you need for analysis when you need it.

▸ NoSQL systems are designed to be dynamic, horizontal, or scale-out solutions, scaling from a few hosts to hundreds or even thousands of hosts. They distribute the data across multiple hosts as the load increases and, in parallel, process them locally on each node where data exists (minimizing data movement across nodes) in a distributed manner.

▸ Most of these NoSQL systems run on commodity hardware (for less expense) and have built-in redundancy and automatic recovery, in case of failure at the software level.

Limitations of NoSQL Systems

NoSQL systems have some limitations. Updates appear every few days or weeks, however, and these systems are maturing with every new release.

▸ NoSQL systems are still evolving, whereas RDBMS systems have been in use for several decades and have both stable and mature functionality. Many key features have not yet been implemented in NoSQL systems.

▸ Most NoSQL systems are open-source projects, without strong support teams and high-level support. Almost all major RDBMS systems, on the other hand, come from big companies (such as Microsoft, Oracle, and IBM). Some companies have started to provide their own distribution of NoSQL systems and offer support for them, but reaching the level of support and confidence that RDBMS vendors provide will take time.

▸ NoSQL systems load data more quickly (because this is a schema-less system), but ad-hoc query and analysis does not work as fast as an RDBMS system. You can choose to have a combination of NoSQL and RDBMS, with NoSQL used for data storage and RDBMS used for processing data or querying for needed data.

▸ Installation, configuration, and maintenance for most NoSQL systems is a hassle, at least for now. If you intend to use Hadoop, you can use Microsoft HDInsight, which is already installed and configured on a cloud platform, offered as Platform As A Service (PaaS). We talk in greater detail about Microsoft HDInsight in Hour 6, "Getting Started with HDInsight, Provisioning Your HDInsight Service Cluster, and Automating HDInsight Cluster Provisioning."

▸ NoSQL systems are evolving, so users must learn a completely new technology. (This skill shortage does seem to be changing rapidly, though.) On the flip side, almost everyone who has worked on data has experience working with RDBMS (even the shift from one RDBMS system to another one is easier because all the systems are based on ANSI standards for standard features).

Big Data, NoSQL Systems, and the Business Value Proposition

Previously, big companies and well-funded government agencies were the main organizations capable of creating Big Data solutions because implementing those solutions required huge amounts of hardware, software, training, and time. Now, however, the capability to store and process massive amounts of data is within reach for many organizations because the cost of hardware has gone down dramatically. Consider these business value propositions of managing Big Data and using NoSQL systems:

- ▶ Data is too valuable to delete. Government mandates also require organizations to store every type of data (structured, semi-structured, and unstructured) for future reference.

- ▶ Organizations are doing analytics to understand what has happened in the past, and also doing predictive analytics to understand or forecast the future and prescriptive analytics to identify the best course of action.

- ▶ The flexible design (a schema-less architecture) of NoSQL databases makes them a great tool to leverage the power of Big Data.

- ▶ Horizontal or dynamic scaling (scale-out) of NoSQL systems makes it affordable to start with a small set of commodity hardware (reducing the overall upfront investment in hardware resources) and then add hardware as the load or demand increases.

- ▶ Built-in redundancy and fault-tolerant capabilities are present at the software level, ensuring higher availability.

- ▶ A distributed architecture, parallel processing, and load-balancing capabilities are built in to NoSQL systems, enabling them to complete processing in a timely manner. NoSQL is designed for distributed data stores for very large-scale data needs.

- ▶ NoSQL can handle hierarchical nested data structures easily, as is typical in social networking applications and in the semantic web. Storing and managing such types of complex data in a traditional RDBMS system would require multiple relational tables with all kinds of keys; joining them with massive amounts of data would degrade performance.

- ▶ The recent integration of NoSQL systems with cloud computing makes NoSQL systems significantly cheaper to use (you pay only for usage) and much faster to set up. For example, now you can create a Hadoop cluster with Microsoft HDInsight in just a few minutes. If your requirements change and you need a larger cluster, you can simply delete your existing cluster and create a bigger (or smaller) one in a few minutes without losing any data.

Application of Big Data and Big Data Solutions

This section discusses some application or usage scenarios for Big Data, Big Data solutions, and NoSQL systems.

Customer churn analysis. The cost of retaining an existing customer is far less than the cost of acquiring a new one. Organizations do customer churn (attrition in the customer base) analysis to identify customers who are most likely to discontinue use of the service or product and then take proactive, corrective measures to retain those customers.

Fraud detection and prevention. Fraud is any intentional act or omission to deceive others for unfair or unlawful gain. Big Data helps you identify current fraud and any future possibilities, and they provide a robust mechanism to prevent them. Big Data helps organizations analyze the data from different data sources across a wide range of channels and identify trends, patterns, and anomalies in the transactions. It helps in identifying the outliers and raises red flags on doubtful transactions and situations, to provide a robust mechanism for preventing them.

Credit scoring and analysis. The possibility that a borrower will default on payments is termed *credit risk*. With the help of Big Data, the financial services industry creates credit scores and strategies based on both demographic and customer behavior data, to maintain an optimal ratio of revenue to risk. With this credit scoring, financial services organizations can offer more products to customers who have a lower credit risk and shy away from customers with a higher credit risk. If organizations do offer a product to a customer with a high credit risk, they can use higher interest rates. If a customer is deemed significantly high-risk, the solution can even automatically decline a transaction, to prevent fraud from ever happening.

Targeted campaigning and recommendations for cross-selling. Big Data paves the way for the marketing team to put the right content in front of the right prospect at the right time to significantly increase profitability, productivity, and business success by producing automatic recommendations of useful content. For example, an e-commerce site might suggest products you might be interested in buying; this is one example of the recommendation engine kicking in to provide suggestions based on your interests, likes, or purchase history. The engine also can suggest product alternatives, as well as bundling opportunities, or other products that similar customers purchased.

Social network analysis. Social media has grown up exponentially, and with it comes new opportunities to improve customer experience management. With the help of text discovery and sentiment analysis, social network analysis focuses on identifying and forecasting connections, relationships, and influence among individuals and groups and their sentiments. Organizations can now better understand the impact and influence of their products or services by doing sentimental analysis on data collected from social media, culled from varied populations and geographies. Based on positive and negative sentiments of products and services, organizations can optimize their offerings for a better customer experience.

Weather forecasting. Previously, mostly government agencies used weather forecasting (think of the numerical weather-prediction methods from the National Oceanic and Atmospheric Administration [NOAA] Climate Forecast System and the European Centre for Medium-Range Weather Forecasts [ECMWF]) in rescue operations if a natural calamity was forecast to happen in a particular region. But now even business organizations are leveraging weather forecasting as a way to better target, position, and serve its products and services to its customers.

▶ Businesses take the weather into account when determining how, when, and where to distribute products. For example, an air conditioning business can correlate heat waves to its supply of air conditioners by looking at historical weather patterns, to ensure their stores (in that specific part of the country) have an adequate supply of air conditioners in summer. Businesses also derive related benefits, such as not having to pay for shipping items from one part of the country to another.

▶ A transportation company might use weather forecasting to route or reroute vehicles appropriately to avoid delay and save on cost.

▶ The energy sector is leveraging Big Data analysis to transform how it forecasts the risk of extreme weather events on the horizon. From gas and power futures to grid infrastructure planning, the implications of Big Data analysis for the energy sector are huge. Although companies still use conventional forecasting tools for short- and medium-range forecasts, accurate forecasting with these conventional methods beyond a seven-day window has remained challenging. Companies have started to reap the benefit of doing Big Data analysis to identify trends and probabilities from patterns within massive volumes of data, as powerful new techniques for risk reduction and decision making.

▶ Insurance companies use weather forecasting data to optimize their insurance products. They can charge a higher premium for products offered in regions more prone to natural calamity than other regions.

Life science research. The huge volume of life sciences data is unstructured: It resides in the text of scientific papers and journals, web pages, electronic medical records, emails, and so on. The inability to search text for relevant information in a timely manner has undoubtedly led to missed opportunities for faster and less expensive drug discovery and development. Big Data helps the life sciences community sustain the pace of discovery and deliver next-generation treatments more quickly and affordably. It can leverage models such as regression and neural network to predict the occurrence of disease, as well as mortality rates from diabetes, heart failure, cancer, and many more. Furthermore, advanced analytics can be applied across the entire life sciences spectrum, from drug discovery through marketing.

Predicting disease outbreak. A Big Data solution can quickly mine terabytes or petabytes of data from both internal and external sources (real-time data mining from Twitter, Facebook, or other sources) for clues and then apply sophisticated statistical data exploration and machine-learning techniques to identify patterns. Organizations then can predict disease outbreaks by comparing those patterns to current conditions to make predictions on the probability of disease outbreaks. This enables government agencies or non-government organizations (NGOs) to improve their planning and risk mitigation efforts and save tens of thousands of lives—plus billions of dollars.

Summary

In this hour, you learned about

▶ The importance of data and how advanced data analytics can help an organization remain competitive

▶ The different types of analysis an organization does: diagnostic/descriptive analysis, predictive analysis, and prescriptive analysis

▶ Big Data and its characteristics

▶ NoSQL systems and how they differ from traditional RDBMS

▶ The different types of NoSQL systems used in different (OLTP versus OLAP) usage scenarios

▶ The benefits and limitations of NoSQL systems

▶ The business value proposition of Big Data, Big Data solutions, and NoSQL systems

▶ Real-world applications or use cases for Big Data and Big Data Analytics

Q&A

Q. What types of analysis does an organization generally do?

A. Organizations basically do three types of analysis. *Descriptive analysis* helps organizations to understand what happened in the past and what caused it to happen. *Predictive analysis* helps organizations understand what can happen in the future, based on an identified pattern using statistical and machine-learning techniques. *Prescriptive analysis* helps organizations take a corrective measure or a next-best action, based on descriptive analysis or predictive analysis.

Q. What different types of data does an organization deal with?

A. An organization deals with three broad data types. *Structured data* has a predefined fixed schema and a strict data model structure. *Unstructured data* has no identifiable internal structure and does not have a predefined fixed schema—it basically has a free-form structure. *Semi-structured data* is a hybrid between structured data and unstructured data. It usually contains data in a structured format, but the schema is not predefined or rigid, and it lacks the strict data model structure of structured data.

Q. What is Big Data and what are its different characteristics?

A. Big Data refers to the data that is beyond the current capability of the enterprise to capture, manage, and process with traditional data processing systems within a tolerable elapsed time. Big Data is primarily characterized by three Vs: *Volume* is the huge volume of data (up to terabytes, petabytes, and even beyond). *Variety* refers to the management of structured, semi-structured, and unstructured data. *Velocity* refers the pace at which data arrives and usually refers to real-time or near-real-time stream of data.

Q. What are NoSQL systems and what are the different categories of NoSQL systems?

A. The sheer volume, velocity, and variety of Big Data are beyond the capabilities of RDBMS technologies to process in a timely manner; hence, NoSQL tools and technologies are needed for processing Big Data. NoSQL systems can be broadly grouped into four categories: Key-value store databases; columnar or column-oriented or column-store databases; document-oriented databases; and graph databases.

Q. What are some examples of Big Data usage in the real world?

A. Covering all the use cases of Big Data in the real world in a single paragraph isn't possible, but consider a few prominent ones:

▶ Customer churn analysis

▶ Fraud detection and prevention

▶ Credit scoring and analysis

▶ Targeted campaigning and recommendation for cross-selling

▶ Social network analysis

▶ Weather forecasting

▶ Life science research

▶ Disease outbreak prediction

HOUR 2

Introduction to Hadoop, Its Architecture, Ecosystem, and Microsoft Offerings

What You'll Learn in This Hour:

▶ What Is Apache Hadoop?
▶ Architecture of Hadoop and Hadoop Ecosystems
▶ What's New in Hadoop 2.0
▶ Architecture of Hadoop 2.0
▶ Tools and Technologies Needed with Big Data Analytics
▶ Major Players and Vendors for Hadoop
▶ Deployment Options for Microsoft Big Data Solutions

In this hour, you explore the world of Big Data and look at how to manage Big Data with Apache Hadoop. You learn about its history and how Hadoop evolved from infancy to Hadoop 1.0 and then Hadoop 2.0, and you compare the architecture of Hadoop 1.0 and Hadoop 2.0. You also focus on other software or components that make up the Hadoop ecosystem. Finally, you gain some familiarity with Hadoop vendors and their offerings. At the end of this hour, you evaluate deployment options for Big Data solutions from Microsoft and see what makes a unique business value proposition to leverage Microsoft Big Data solutions.

What Is Apache Hadoop?

Apache Hadoop (http://hadoop.apache.org/) is a top-level open source project of the Apache Software Foundation based on Java. Hadoop provides a scalable and fault-tolerant framework for distributed storage and processing of Big Data across many nodes in the cluster in parallel. Hadoop makes it possible to store and process Big Data with thousands of nodes, involving hundreds or thousands of terabytes of data.

Doug Cutting, Hadoop's original creator, named the framework after his child's yellow stuffed toy elephant. Now it's being built and used by a global community of contributors and users.

Yahoo! has been the largest contributor to the project and uses Hadoop extensively across its businesses.

Hadoop has become the de facto industry framework for Big Data processing because of its inherent benefits. Players including Microsoft, Google, Yahoo!, and IBM largely use it for applications that involve search engines, advertising, and sentimental analysis.

These characteristics of Hadoop make it an ideal platform for Big Data storage and processing:

▶ **Flexibility**—Hadoop can quickly analyze massive collections of records without needing data to first be modeled, cleansed, and loaded, as you generally need to do with relational systems. This means business or IT professionals can skip the data modelling and instead focus on getting insight into the data. Hadoop also enables you to generate value from data that was once considered too expensive to be stored and processed in traditional database platforms. With Hadoop, you can store and process all types of data and extract more meaningful business insights as needed.

▶ **Scalability**—The Hadoop framework is distributed in nature and based on a scale-out model. As the load increases, you can keep increasing nodes for additional storage and processing power. Hadoop also provides an easy-to-use batch mode parallel programming paradigm for writing and executing analysis programs that scale to thousands of nodes and petabytes of data.

▶ **Lower cost**—Hadoop has lower up-front software and hardware costs because it runs on commodity hardware. Unlike RDBMS systems, which rely heavily on expensive proprietary hardware to store and process data and need a scale-up capability for more power, Hadoop enables distributed parallel processing of Big Data across inexpensive commodity servers. Those servers store and process the data and can scale out virtually without limits, in terms of the number of nodes in the Hadoop cluster.

▶ **Fault tolerance**—The Hadoop framework has a built-in redundancy mechanism and load balancing at the software level that makes it highly fault tolerant. In fact, Hadoop assumes that both hardware and software failures are common, and its built-in mechanism handles these failures gracefully, without developers and administrators having to worry about it. In other words, instead of relying on hardware to deliver high availability, the framework itself is designed to detect and handle failures at the application layer. Hence, it delivers a highly available service on top of a cluster of computers, in which each computer (disk, node, or rack) might be prone to failure.

Architecture of Hadoop and Hadoop Ecosystems

Apache Hadoop consists of two core components, Hadoop Distributed File System (HDFS) and MapReduce. The other software or components that you see in Figure 2.1 (many others exist, but they are omitted here for the sake of simplicity) are different components that sit on and around Hadoop and make up the Hadoop ecosystem.

TIP

In Figure 2.1, components with a dark gray background are part of Hadoop and components with a light gray background are other components from Microsoft that are part of the Hadoop ecosystem. Components with a white background are other open-source components in the Hadoop ecosystem.

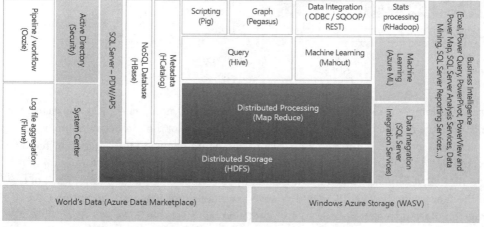

FIGURE 2.1
Hadoop architecture and ecosystems.

Hadoop Distributed File System

The inspiration for the Hadoop Distributed File System (HDFS) was the Google File System (GFS). HDFS is a distributed, scalable, load-balanced, and fault-tolerant (with built-in redundancy) storage component of Hadoop.

HDFS has a master-slave architecture (see Figure 2.2). The master is called a *name node* and the slaves are called *data nodes*. A client application talks to the name node to get metadata information about the file system and connects data nodes to transfer data between the client and the data nodes. (The client communicates with the name node to get only metadata. Actual data transfer happens between the client and the data nodes; the name node is not involved in the actual data transfer.)

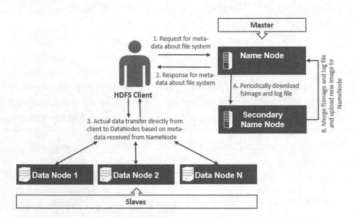

FIGURE 2.2
Data transfer process from client to HDFS.

Contrary to its name, the secondary name node is not a standby name node; it is not meant for failover in case the name node fails. To understand the purpose of the secondary name node, it is important to first look at how the name node stores metadata related to the addition or removal of blocks of files in the file system. The name node stores the HDFS metadata information in a metadata file called fsimage. This image file is not updated on every addition or removal of a block in the file system. Instead, these add/remove operations are logged and maintained in a separate log file. Appending updates to a separate log helps achieve faster I/O. The primary purpose of the secondary name node is to periodically download the name node fsimage and log files, to create a new image by merging the fsimage and log files and uploading the new image back to the name node. With the secondary name node performing this task periodically, the name node can restart relatively more quickly (otherwise, the name node would need to do this merge operation upon restarting). The secondary name node is also responsible for backing up the name node fsimage.

HDFS is optimized for high throughput and for reading and writing large files (generally, in gigabytes or larger). HDFS breaks the files into 64MB blocks (configurable and changeable, as needed) and distributes them across data nodes. Furthermore, HDFS transparently maintains three copies of each block (configurable and changeable, as needed) for redundancy and to make HDFS fault tolerant.

GO TO ▶ We talk in detail about the Hadoop Distributed File System (HDFS) in **Hour 3, "Hadoop Distributed File System Versions 1.0 and 2.0."**

MapReduce

As with HDFS, Google MapReduce served as the inspiration for Hadoop's MapReduce. The Hadoop MapReduce framework is a batch-oriented, distributed computing framework for processing vast amount of data in parallel on large clusters (with hundreds or thousands of nodes) made up of commodity hardware in a reliable, fault-tolerant manner.

Similar to HDFS, the MapReduce framework is also based on an architecture of master and slaves (see Figure 2.3). The master is called the *JobTracker*, and the slaves are called *TaskTrackers*. The JobTracker is responsible for scheduling the jobs' component tasks (a job is made of up one or more tasks) on the TaskTrackers, monitoring them, and re-executing failed tasks. TaskTrackers execute the tasks that the JobTracker gives them.

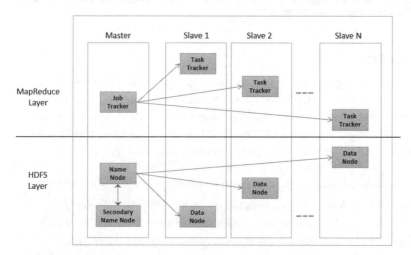

FIGURE 2.3
Hadoop architecture with N number of slaves.

In the Figure 2.3 architecture diagram, you can see one master and *N* number of slaves. The master consists of a JobTracker (MapReduce part) and a name node (HDFS part); each slave consists of a TaskTracker (MapReduce part) and a data node (HDFS part).

NOTE

Single-Node Cluster

In some architecture, such as a single-node cluster, you can have both a master (with a JobTracker and a name node) and a slave (with a TaskTracker and a data node) running on a single machine. This type of cluster is generally suited for learning or development and is not recommended for production.

MapReduce has two primary functions for each job. The first is the Mapper function, which processes data, splits it into chunks in a completely parallel manner, and performs filtering and sorting for input to the second function. That function, called Reducer, performs a summary operation on the processed data. Typically, both the input and the output of the job are stored in a file system (such as HDFS). The MapReduce framework takes care of scheduling tasks, monitoring them, and re-executing failed tasks.

GO TO ▶ A more detailed discussion of MapReduce is included in **Hours 4, "The MapReduce Job Framework and Job Execution Pipeline," and 5, "MapReduce–Advanced Concepts and YARN."**

Hadoop Ecosystems

More than a dozen components or systems make up the Hadoop ecosystem, and new ones are added regularly. Covering them all in a single book is not feasible; therefore, we cover only Hadoop and some components that make using Hadoop easier: Apache Hive, Apache Pig, and Sqoop. We also detail NoSQL databases, such as HBase, in this book. This section briefly talks about some of the other components and provides references for further study.

Apache Hive

You can think of Hive as a SQL abstraction over MapReduce with a SQL-like query engine. Hive lets you write query in a SQL-like declarative language called HiveQL, which is similar to relational database systems. When you execute the HiveQL query, Hive translates the query into a series of equivalent MapReduce jobs, saving you the time and effort of writing actual MapReduce jobs on your own. Hive comes in handy for analysts with strong SQL skills, providing a quicker and easier migration into the world of Hadoop.

Hive is a distributed data warehouse software that facilitates easy data summarization, ad hoc queries, and analysis of large data sets stored in HDFS. It comes closer in concept to RDBMS and thus is appropriate for use with more structured data. Hive is designed for a data warehouse type of workload and is best suited for batch jobs over large sets of append-only data (such as web logs); it does not work well with OLTP-type workloads that require real-time queries or row-level updates.

GO TO ▶ We investigate Hive and demonstrate its use in **Hours 12, "Getting Started with Apache Hive and Apache Tez in HDInsight"; 13, "Programming with Apache Hive, Apache Tez in HDInsight, and Apache HCatalog"; 14, "Consuming HDInsight Data from Microsoft BI Tools over Hive ODBC Driver: Part 1"; and 15, "Consuming HDInsight Data from Microsoft BI Tools over Hive ODBC Driver: Part 2."**

Apache HCatalog

Apache HCatalog is a metadata layer for interoperability, a data storage abstraction layer built on top of the Hive metastore. It incorporates components from the Hive DDL and provides an abstraction of Hadoop data with a relational view of the data stored in HDFS—users don't need to worry about where their data is stored in HDFS or what format it takes. HCatalog thus delivers complete data storage independence: A change in storage format has no ripple effect on other applications dependent on it.

HCatalog is a table and storage management layer for Hadoop, providing table and storage abstraction that enables you to think about data in the HDFS as if it were a set of tables. Users with different data processing tools, such as MapReduce, Hive, and Pig, can more easily read and write data on the HDFS. HCatalog presents a common table layer or shared schema and data types to each data processing tool and gives each user the same data model, for interoperability across these tools. Figure 2.4 shows how HCatalog interfaces between HDFS and data processing tools.

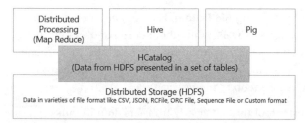

FIGURE 2.4
How HCatalog interfaces between HDFS and data processing tools.

No matter who creates a table in HCatalog, the table will be available to other data processing tools, providing a greater degree of interoperability. Also, it's worth noting that many HCatalog tables can be created over a single data set, allowing many views over the same data.

GO TO ▶ HCatalog has been merged with Hive. We talk more about HCatalog and Hive in **Hours 12** and **13**.

Apache Pig

Apache Pig is a high-level platform and data flow language for processing Big Data on Hadoop clusters. The Pig Latin data flow scripting language that Pig uses supports writing queries on large datasets. Pig also provides an execution environment for running programs from a console.

A program written in Pig Latin consists of a dataset transformation series converted under the covers to equivalent MapReduce jobs, much like in Apache HiveQL. Its abstractions provide a richer data structure than MapReduce and is fully extensible using user-defined functions (UDFs). These UDFs can be written in Java, Python, C# (on Windows platform), or JavaScript and can be used in the processing path of Pig Latin to customize each processing path stage while transforming the data.

NOTE

Pig Versus Hive

Pig Latin is a data flow language, whereas HiveQL is a declarative query language. HiveQL works for asking a question of your data; Pig Latin is useful for writing a data flow that describes how your data will be transformed from one form to another (extract, transform, load [ETL] or extract, load, transform [ELT]).

GO TO ▶ We talk more about Apache Pig and demonstrate its use in **Hours 17, "Using Pig for Data Processing," and 18, "Using Sqoop for Data Movement Between RDBMS and HDInsight."**

Apache Sqoop

So far, we have talked about managing and processing Big Data in Hadoop, but a good amount of data exists in relational data processing systems as well. What about doing analysis on these data or combining that data with Big Data and then doing analysis on top of that? What about moving processed data to relational data processing systems so that it can then be quickly accessed in different reports? Here comes Apache Sqoop to the rescue.

Apache Sqoop is a command-line data transfer tool that efficiently transfers data in bulk between Hadoop and relational data processing systems (such as SQL server) or other relational database management systems.

▶ **Import**—You can use Sqoop to import external structured data from relational data processing systems into the HDFS or related systems such as HBase.

▶ **Export**—You can also use Sqoop to extract data from Hadoop and export the extracted data to the external relational data processing systems.

Sqoop is leveraged by Microsoft in SQL Server Connector for transferring data between SQL Server and Hadoop. Likewise, CouchBase, Inc. provides the CouchBase Hadoop Connector to move data between the NoSQL product and Hadoop.

GO TO ▶ We talk more about Apache Sqoop and demonstrate its use in **Hour 18, "Using Sqoop for Data Movement Between RDBMS and HDInsight."**

Apache HBase

As you learned in Hour 1, "Introduction of Big Data, NoSQL, and Business Value Proposition," Apache HBase is a distributed, versioned, column-oriented database management system that runs on top of HDFS (you learn more about HDFS in Hour 3). An HBase system consists of a set of tables. Each table contains rows and columns, much like in a traditional relational table. Each table must have an element defined as a primary key, and all access attempts to HBase tables must use this primary key. An HBase column represents an attribute of an object. HBase allows many columns to be grouped together into column families; the elements of a column family are all stored together, unlike in a relational table, where all the columns of a given row are stored together.

HBase mandates that you predefine the table schema and specify the column families. However, it also provides flexibility in adding columns to column families at any time, making the schema adaptable to changing application requirements. It is well suited to times when you need random, real-time read/write access to your sparse data sets, which are common in many Big Data use cases. HBase supports writing applications in Avro, REST, and Thrift.

GO TO ▶ We talk more about Apache HBase and demonstrate its use in **Hour 24, "Introduction to Apache HBase on HDInsight."**

Apache Mahout

Apache Mahout is a distributed and scalable open source machine learning library that is implemented on top of Apache Hadoop. It uses the MapReduce paradigm and facilitates building scalable machine learning solutions. It focuses on clustering, classification, batch-based collaborative filtering (recommendations), and frequent item-set mining categories of algorithms.

No single algorithm is right for every situation. Mahout offers an implementation of various machine learning algorithms (although several other algorithms are still missing), and the list is growing. Some of these algorithms can be used in local mode, and some in distributed mode (for use with Hadoop). Each algorithm in the Mahout library is invoked using the Mahout command line.

NOTE

Mahout?

Mahout is a Hindi word that refers to a person who drives an elephant—a mahout is often found sitting near the animal's neck while riding it.

Apache Flume

Apache Flume is a distributed, highly reliable, scalable, and available service for efficiently collecting, aggregating, and moving large log data (streaming data) from multiple sources to HDFS. Flume does this by collecting a high volume of web logs in real time. The Flume architecture is based on a streaming data flow and an extensible data model. It is robust and fault tolerant, with tunable and reliable mechanisms, along with many failover and recovery mechanisms.

As you can see in Figure 2.5, an external source such as a web server sends an event (a unit of data flow) to an agent, and the agent puts it into an external repository such as HDFS.

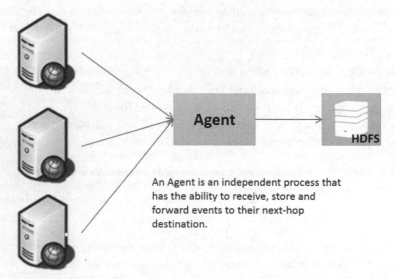

FIGURE 2.5
High-level view of log data collection process in Flume.

Flume supports multi-hop data flows in which events travel through multiple agents before they reach the final destination. Then an agent forwards the event to the next Agent (next hop) in the flow.

Apache Oozie

Apache Oozie is a server-based pipeline or workflow scheduler system used to manage and execute Hadoop jobs sequentially in the defined workflow.

To build complex data transformations, you can create a workflow in Oozie, which is a logical collection of multiple jobs (called *actions* in Oozie) of MapReduce, Pig, Hive, and Sqoop arranged in a control dependency directed acyclic graph (DAG). You do this by specifying a sequence of actions to execute.

The Oozie workflow provides greater control over complex data transformation jobs and makes it easier to repeat those jobs at predetermined intervals. We talk more about Apache Oozie and demonstrate its use in Hour 19.

Pegasus

Pegasus (Peta GraAph mining System) is an open source, peta-scale graph mining system that runs in parallel with and, in a distributed manner, on top of Hadoop. It is fully written in Java. Before Pegasus, the graph mining systems were capable of mining millions of objects. With the help of Pegasus, you can develop an algorithm that runs in parallel on top of a Hadoop cluster and mines graphs (network or interconnected objects) that contain billions of objects for finding patterns, communities, and outliers.

Pegasus supports typical graph mining tasks such as computing the radius of each node in the graph, computing the diameter of the graph, and finding the connected components through a generalization of matrix-vector multiplication.

NOTE

Graph Mining

Graph mining is a data mining mechanism for finding the patterns, rules, and anomalies that characterize graphs. In this context, a graph is a set of interconnected object sets with links between any two objects in the set. This structure type defines an interconnection or relationship among objects and characterizes networks everywhere, including pages linked on the Web, computer and social networks (Facebook, Twitter, LinkedIn), and many biological and physical systems.

RHadoop

Before we discuss RHadoop, we need to first explain R. R is a programming language used for data analysis, statistical computing (linear and nonlinear modeling, classical statistical tests, time-series analysis, classification, clustering, and so on), and data visualization that uses strong graphical capabilities. The R programming language is highly extensible and has object-oriented features. It compiles and runs on UNIX, Linux, Windows, and MacOS using a command-line interpreter, although some IDEs are available (including RStudio and JGR) for ease in development.

R and Hadoop complement each other well: Hadoop provides an environment for storing and managing Big Data, and R provides data analysis, statistical computing, and data visualization capabilities on Big Data stored in a Hadoop cluster.

This combination is called RHadoop. Developed by RevolutionAnalytics, RHadoop is a collection of four R packages that enable users to manage and analyze data within Hadoop:

- **rmr**—Provides Hadoop MapReduce functionality in R.

- **rhdfs**—Provides HDFS file management in R.

- **rhbase**—Provides HBase distributed database management from within R.

- **plyrmr**—Offers higher-level, plyr-like (with a split-apply-combine strategy) data processing for structured data, powered by rmr.

Integration with Microsoft Business Intelligence Tools and Technologies

Microsoft Business Intelligence (MSBI) is a leader in the business intelligence technology domain. MSBI includes the SQL Server Database Engine for structured data storage and management; SQL Server Integration Services for integrating data from heterogeneous data sources; SQL Server Analysis Services for analytical processing and data mining solutions for predictive analysis; and SQL Server Reporting Services for alerting, reporting, or dashboards. MSBI extends its capabilities with familiar tools such as Excel, PowerPivot, Power BI, and SharePoint, for hosting reports or dashboards and supporting collaboration.

You can leverage these tried-and-tested MSBI tools and technologies with HDInsight or Hadoop on your Windows platform by using the ODBC driver or the Hive ODBC driver and the Hive Add-in for Excel.

This brings up an interesting use case: You can keep storing all your Big Data in a Hadoop cluster, and then you can process the needed data and transfer it to SQL Server or SQL Server Analysis services, to bring down your query response time to seconds (from several minutes or hours), as if it had been in a Hadoop cluster.

What's New in Hadoop 2.0

Hadoop 1.0 was designed and developed more than 7 years ago. The concern then was the need to process a massive amount of data in parallel, distributed over hundreds of thousands of nodes in a batch-oriented way. Now hardware is even cheaper, making companies demand more horizontal scaling while also ensuring high availability. Companies want to process data interactively along with batch data processing. Hadoop 2.0 overcomes these limitations with its new architecture and components. The next sections discuss some of the limitations of Hadoop 1.0 and show how Hadoop 2.0 can come to the rescue.

Single Point of Failure

Although you can use a secondary name node in Hadoop 1.0, it's not a standby node and, hence, does not provide failover capabilities. The same holds true for the JobTracker: It is also a single point of failure. JobTracker rarely fails, but when it does, the job clients must resubmit all the running and queued jobs.

Limited to Running MapReduce Jobs on HDFS

The MapReduce component of Hadoop 1.0 was designed for batch mode processing, with no true support for interactive and streaming query support. Iterative applications implemented using MapReduce were several times slower and were not suitable for graph processing. In Hadoop 1.0, only MapReduce can access data in HDFS. This is fairly restrictive and does not allow for multitenancy, forcing some other application (which does not work on batch mode processing) to store data in other storage than the HDFS (as a result of that, HDFS used to be underutilized).

Low Computing Resource Utilization

Computing resources on each node are divided as Map slots and Reduce slots (we talk about MapReduce, the Mapper, the Reducer, and different slot types in Hours 4 and 5) in a hard partition manner. Suppose that, at a given a time, many Mappers and only a few Reducers are running. All the Map slots thus are in use, but only a few Reduce slots are being used. No sharing of resource takes place to better use the computing resources. In other words, Mappers can use only Map slots; if Map slots are not available, Mappers must wait, even though some Reduce slots might be available at the same time. The same is true for Reducers and Reducer slots.

Horizontal Scaling Performance Issue

As the number of nodes grows beyond a certain number (or more than 40,000 concurrent tasks), performance of the name node and JobTracker degrades, setting a kind of upper limit to the number of nodes in a cluster.

Overly Crowded JobTracker

The JobTracker is solely responsible for managing resources and the application life cycle. The more jobs are run currently, the greater the chance for failure, causing users to resubmit all the jobs because all the running and queued jobs were killed upon restart.

NOTE

HDFS 1.0 Versus HDFS 2.0

HDFS has proven its metal and is now considered a fault-tolerant and highly reliable file system. A study by Yahoo! in 2009 (https://www.youtube.com/watch?v=zbycDpVWhp0) indicated loss of a mere 650 blocks out of 329 million total blocks on 10 different Hadoop clusters across 20,000 nodes. Even most of these 650 blocks were lost because of a few bugs that were fixed long ago. Despite this success rate, two prime hindrances have limited the widespread use of HDFS. First, in Hadoop 1.0, the name node of HDFS is a single point of failure (which might be acceptable to the batch processes but is not feasible for an interactive query). Second, HDFS data can be accessed only using batch-oriented MapReduce jobs (basically, limiting its use and applicability).

The question is, if HDFS is such a reliable file system, why not make it highly available (by taking care of the single point of failure issue) and allow other applications (other than batch-oriented MapReduce jobs) to access it? And the answer to this question is, Hadoop 2.0. That version comes with a host of new features and solves these issues related to HDFS or Hadoop 1.0.

Architecture of Hadoop 2.0

As you learned earlier in the section "Architecture of Hadoop and Hadoop Ecosystems," Hadoop 1.0 has two main components: HDFS, a highly reliable and highly available primary distributed storage for Hadoop, and MapReduce, a batch-oriented, distributed, parallel processing engine for Hadoop. In Hadoop 2.0, the work of MapReduce is split, and another new component, called Yet Another Resource Negotiator (YARN), was added (see Figure 2.6). YARN takes care of resource management, job scheduling, and monitoring, making MapReduce a pure batch mode computational layer on top of YARN.

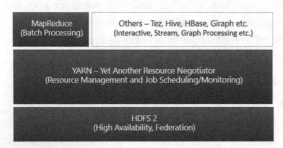

FIGURE 2.6
Hadoop 2.0 architecture and components.

In Hadoop 2.0, HDFS was overhauled. The following important features were added to overcome the limitations of Hadoop 1.0. It's called HDFS 2.

HDFS High Availability

In the Hadoop 1.0 cluster, the name node was a single point of failure. Name node failure gravely impacted the complete cluster availability. Taking down the name node for maintenance or upgrades meant that the entire cluster was unavailable during that time. The HDFS high availability feature introduced with Hadoop 2.0 addresses this problem. It is now possible to have two name nodes in a cluster, in an active-passive configuration—one node is active at a time, and the other node is in standby mode. The active and standby nodes remain synchronized. If the active name node fails, the standby node takes over and promotes itself to active state.

HDFS Federation

Horizontal scaling is rare and needed in only very large implementations, such as for Yahoo! or Facebook, but it was a challenge with a single name node in Hadoop 1.0. This single name node had to take care of an entire namespace (a namespace consists of information related to directories, files, and blocks) and storage of blocks on all data nodes, which doesn't require coordination. In Hadoop 1.0, the number of files that can be managed in HDFS was limited to the amount of RAM on the machine. At the same time, read/write operation throughput is limited by that machine.

In Hadoop 2.0, HDFS Federation is a way of partitioning the file system namespace over multiple separated name nodes. Each name node manages only an independent slice of the overall file system namespace. These name nodes are part of a single cluster, but they don't talk to each other; they are actually federated and do not require any coordination with each other. HDFS Federation is useful for small clusters, for file system namespace isolation (for multitenants), as well as large clusters, for horizontal scalability.

HDFS Snapshot

Hadoop 2.0 has added a new capability to take a snapshot (read-only and copy-on-write) of the file system (data blocks) stored on the data nodes.

GO TO ▶ We talk about HDFS and its new features in Hadoop 2.0 in **Hour 3**.

In Hadoop 2.0, even MapReduce has gone through a complete overhaul, and a new layer on top of HDFS has been created. This new layer, called YARN, takes care of two major functions: resource management and application life-cycle management (the JobTracker alone previously handled these functions). Now MapReduce is just a batch mode computational layer that sits on top of YARN. YARN acts like an operating system for the Hadoop cluster, making Hadoop a general-purpose data-processing platform that is not constrained to MapReduce only. This brings some important benefits:

- **Segregation of duties**—Now MapReduce can focus on what it is good at: batch mode data processing. YARN focuses on resource management and application life-cycle management.

- **Multitenancy**—Applications other than MapReduce can connect to YARN and gain access to the data stored in HDFS, enabling a broader array of interaction patterns for the data stored in HDFS beyond MapReduce. This broadens the horizon. Now you have interactive, streaming, and graphics processing support (and much more) for accessing data from HDFS by leveraging YARN and by all sharing a common resource management framework. YARN now can handle much more than batch-oriented MapReduce jobs and can assign cluster capacity accordingly to the different applications, to meet the service level demands of a particular workload and address constraints such as queue capacities and user limits.

- **Scalability**—Unlike the JobTracker, which previously handled resource management and application life-cycle management together, YARN has a new global resource manager and per-machine node managers. They manage the resources of the cluster and form the computation fabric of the cluster. At the same time, YARN has an application-specific application master that negotiates resources from the resource manager and manages the application life cycle. This segregation brings a new level of scalability to Hadoop 2.0.

NOTE

MapReduce 1.0 Versus MapReduce 2.0

In Hadoop 2.0, MapReduce is referred to as MapReduce 2.0 or MRv2, NextGen MapReduce, or YARN (Yet Another Resource Negotiator). Different artifacts use different nomenclature. But just to summarize, the resource management and application life-cycle management capabilities were removed from MapReduce and assigned to YARN. This way, MapReduce can focus on what it does best: batch-mode data processing. YARN then can work as the operating system for the Hadoop cluster, serving requests from multiple applications instead of being limited to MapReduce.

In other words, MapReduce 2 and YARN are two different things. Referring to them as if they are interchangeable is misleading. YARN is a generic framework or data operating system that provides Hadoop cluster resource management and job scheduling and monitoring capabilities. YARN sits on top of HDFS and provides these services to any application targeting it, to leverage the services in Figure 5.3. MapReduce 2 is just one application among many applications that leverage services that YARN provides.

Note that YARN is not tied to MapReduce only. It can be leveraged by any application targeting to use it. You can find out the latest details on other applications that leverage the power of YARN at http://wiki.apache.org/hadoop/PoweredByYarn.

GO TO ▶ We talk about YARN and its features in Hadoop 2.0 in **Hour 5**.

Tools and Technologies Needed with Big Data Analytics

Big Data Analytics is a big topic, with a broad horizon and different phases. To help you understand the tools or technologies you might need during each phase, this section highlights a useful categorization and explains some tools suited to each individual phase. Note, however, that this is not an exhaustive list—we provide it here merely as a guide.

Data Acquisition

In this section, you explore options for acquiring data from different data sources:

▶ **SQL Server StreamInsight**—Service that provides high-throughput, low-latency complex event processing (CEP) for near-real-time stream analysis (Hot Stream) and storage (Cold Stream).

▶ **Flume**—Distributed log file aggregation service for moving data into HDFS from several web servers.

▶ **Sqoop**—Bidirectional distributed bulk transfer of data between Hadoop and a relational database management system. Data can be imported directly into HDFS or into Hive/HBase, or can be exported to relational tables.

▶ **SQL Server Integration Services (SSIS)**—Scalable enterprise data integration platform with ETL or ELT options, as well as integration capabilities.

Data Storage

Here you explore different options of data storage:

▶ **HDFS and MapReduce (Hadoop)**—Apache Hadoop is an open-source software framework that supports data-intensive distributed applications to work with thousands of computational commodity computers and petabytes of data.

▶ **HBase**—HBase is a distributed, versioned, column-oriented database management system that runs on top of HDFS. An HBase system consists of a set of tables. Each table contains rows and columns, much like a traditional relational table.

▶ **SQL Server RDBMS**—Relational database management system for storing structured data, often used to store processed data (for example, from Hadoop) for quicker response time.

▶ **SQL Server Parallel Data Warehouse**—Massively Parallel Processing (MPP) distributed architecture for a relational database management system, for storing a huge volume of structured data. Often used to store processed or needed data (for example, from Hadoop) for quicker response time.

▶ **Azure Storage (SQL Database, Tables, and Blobs)**—SQL Database is a cloud-based RDBMS. Azure Table storage is an example of a key-value store NoSQL database. The schema-less design of Azure Tables allows for rapid development and fast access to large quantities of data. It offers highly available, massively scalable key-value-based storage so that your application can automatically scale to meet user demand. Azure Blobs are used to store unstructured data such as binary and text data.

Data Analysis

Next, you can take a look at ways to perform analysis on the collected and stored data:

▶ **Apache Hive**—Hive is a distributed data warehouse software that facilitates easy data summarization, ad hoc queries, and analysis of large data sets stored in an HDFS. It lets you write your query in HiveQL, a declarative language for querying. Hive is designed for a data warehouse type of workload and is best suited for batch jobs over large sets of append-only data (such as web logs).

▶ **Apache Pig**—Pig is a high-level platform and data flow language for processing and transforming Big Data stored in the Hadoop cluster. The Pig Latin data flow scripting language, which comes with Apache Pig, supports writing queries on large datasets, and provides an execution environment running programs from a console.

▶ **SQL Server Analysis Services (SSAS)**—SQL Server Analysis Services (SSAS) delivers online analytical processing (OLAP) and data mining functionality for business intelligence applications. Analysis Services supports OLAP by letting you design, create, and manage multidimensional structures that contain data aggregated from different data sources, including Hadoop. This results in much faster query response time. As an example, Yahoo! has a 24TB cube on 2 petabytes (PB) of aggregated data from Hadoop.

▶ **SQL Server StreamInsight**—With this option, you get high-throughput, low-latency, complex event processing (CEP) for near-real-time stream analysis (Hot Stream) and storage (Cold Stream).

▶ **Azure ML**—Azure ML is a new cloud-based machine learning platform offered as a fully managed cloud service to enable data scientists and developers to efficiently embed predictive analytics into their applications. This helps organizations use massive amounts of data as a source for predicting, forecasting, and changing future outcomes. At the same time, it brings all the benefits of the cloud platform to the machine learning process.

▶ **RHadoop**—RHadoop is a collection of R packages for data analysis, statistical computing, and data visualization that uses strong graphical capabilities on Big Data from the Hadoop cluster.

▶ **Pegasus**—Pegasus is an open source, peta-scale graph mining system. With the help of Pegasus, you can develop an algorithm that runs in parallel on top of a Hadoop cluster and mines graphs (network or interconnected objects) that containing billions of objects for finding patterns, communities, and outliers.

▶ **Apache Mahout**—Mahout is a distributed and scalable open source machine-learning library implemented on top of Apache Hadoop. It facilitates building scalable machine learning solutions. Mahout focuses on clustering, classification, batch-based collaborative filtering (recommendations), and frequent item-set mining categories of algorithms.

Data Visualization

The following are the different visualization tools for exploring and analyzing data:

▶ **Excel, PowerPivot, and Power BI**—This Microsoft Office analytical tool with PowerPivot is a powerful data mashup and data exploration tool.

▶ **SharePoint (Excel Services, Power View, and so on)**—This is a collaboration and hosting platform that provides (among other things) HTML-based rendering of Excel spreadsheets, along with the analytical information that supplies them. You can use Power View for ad hoc reporting.

▶ **SQL Server Reporting Services**—SQL Server Reporting Services works for data alerting, reporting, and creating dashboards.

▶ **RHadoop**—RHadoop is a collection of R packages for data analysis, statistical computing, and data visualization. It uses strong graphical capabilities on Big Data from the Hadoop cluster.

Data Management

These tools come in handy during data management:

▶ **Apache Oozie**—Oozie is a server-based pipeline or workflow scheduler system that manages and executes Hadoop jobs sequentially in the define workflow.

▶ **Apache HCatalog**—HCatalog is a table and storage management layer for Hadoop that provides table and storage abstraction. You can thus think about data in the HDFS as if it were a set of tables. Users with different data processing tools, such as MapReduce, Hive, and Pig, can more easily read and write data on the HDFS.

▶ **Active Directory**—Active Directory manages corporate identities, validates credentials, protects information, and handles system and application settings for authorization and authentication.

Development and Monitoring Tools

These tools come in handy during data development and monitoring:

▶ **System Center Operations Manager**—A comprehensive IT infrastructure, virtualization, and cloud management platform for monitoring and managing your IT infrastructure.

▶ **Team Foundation Server**—The collaboration platform at the core of Microsoft's Application Lifecycle Management (ALM) solution. It also includes source control for maintaining versions of changes to the code.

▶ **Visual Studio**—A powerful integrated development environment (IDE) that eases the development process and ensures quality code throughout the entire application life cycle, from design to deployment.

▶ **Azure VNet**—A virtual private network (VPN) within the Azure cloud Infrastructure As a Service (IaaS) environment that is connected via a private IPSec VPN tunnel or ExpressRoute with on-premises networks. You can have a Hadoop cluster running in the virtual machines in Azure (IaaS) and connect the Hadoop cluster from your corporate network using Azure VNet.

Major Players and Vendors for Hadoop

Apache Hadoop is an open-source software framework from the Apache Software Foundation. Any organization can use it freely under the Apache License 2.0.

Many enterprises avoid using Hadoop because of its lack of enterprise support. Lately, however, some companies have started to support Hadoop. They have a strong support team that provides high-level training and support to smaller companies as well as larger enterprises. Let's take a look at some of the prominent players.

Cloudera

Cloudera is one of the earliest companies that started providing Apache Hadoop-based software, support and services, and training to business customers. Cloudera Distribution Including Apache Hadoop (CDH) targets enterprise-class deployments of Hadoop and adds two crucial elements to its distribution of Apache Hadoop Software:

▶ **Cloudera Manager**—Cloudera Manager offers automated deployment, configuration, and cluster management. Cloudera Manager is a wizard-based installation with configuration menus for deploying Hadoop. It provides a single, central console to enact configuration changes across your cluster. It incorporates a full range of reporting and diagnostic tools to help you optimize performance and utilization.

▶ **Cloudera Support**—Cloudera Support features predictive and proactive support capabilities, focused on securing more uptime, rapid issue resolution and prevention, better performance for your mission-critical applications, and faster delivery of the all features you care about. Support services include configuration checks, escalation and issue resolution, integration with third-party systems, and knowledge bases, articles, and other technical resources.

Hortonworks

Twenty-four engineers from the original Yahoo! Hadoop development and operations team founded Hortonworks in 2011. These professionals had worked on Hadoop during development, designing and testing the core of the Hadoop platform. This is another one of the earliest companies to provide Hadoop-based software, support and services, training, and consulting to business customers. Hortonworks claims to have years of experience in Hadoop operations and support for an enterprise's mission-critical Hadoop project.

Hortonworks provides the Hortonworks Data Platform (HDP), a 100 percent open source distribution of Apache Hadoop. Hence, all solutions in HDP are developed as projects through the Apache Software Foundation (ASF), and no proprietary extensions or add-ons are required. HDP works in-cloud, on-premises, or from an appliance across both the Linux and Windows platforms.

Similar to Cloudera Manager, Hortonworks includes Apache Ambari, a wizard-driven, completely open-source operational framework for cluster provisioning and managing and monitoring Apache Hadoop clusters. The intuitive web interface enables you to easily provision a Hadoop cluster and configure and test all the Hadoop services and core components from a single user interface. It further enables you to start, stop, and test Hadoop services; change configurations when needed; and manage ongoing growth of your cluster. It enables you to preconfigure alerts for watching Hadoop services and visualize cluster operational data in the same intuitive web interface. The interface also includes job diagnostic tools to visualize job interdependencies and view task timelines as a way to troubleshoot historic job performance execution.

To enable seamless integration with existing tools such as Microsoft System Center and Teradata Viewpoint, Ambari provides a RESTful API.

MapR

MapR Technologies is another company that provides Apache Hadoop distribution and contributes to Apache Hadoop projects. Its distribution overcomes the limitation of Hadoop 1.0 being a single point of failure (discussed in detail in Hours 4 and 6) and provides full data protection.

With this distribution, Hadoop can be accessed as easily as Network Attached Storage (NAS) via Network File System (NFS). Instead of using Direct Attached Storage (DAS) in the data nodes, this distribution uses a POSIX-compliant random read-write file system to mount the cluster as a volume via NFS.

As of this writing, the MapR Hadoop distribution is available in three editions:

▶ **M3**—Standard Edition, available for free download and unlimited production use.

▶ **M5**—Enterprise Edition, including everything from M3, plus high availability, self-healing, and data protection with snapshot and mirroring.

▶ **M7**—Enterprise Database Edition for Hadoop. Includes everything from M5, plus consistent low latency with no compactions, instant recovery, snapshots, and mirroring for tables.

Amazon uses the MapR Hadoop distribution for the Amazon Elastic MapReduce (EMR) service, discussed next.

Amazon

Amazon Web Services introduced Amazon Elastic MapReduce (EMR), a rapidly scalable web service that runs on the Amazon Elastic Compute Cloud (Amazon EC2) and Amazon Simple Storage Service (Amazon S3). EMR uses Hadoop to distribute processing across different nodes of a cluster running in the Amazon cloud. CloudWatch monitors cluster performance and raises alarms. You can thus instantly provision as much capacity as you need for data-intensive tasks such as log analysis, web indexing, data warehousing, machine learning, financial analysis, scientific simulation, and bioinformatics research.

Beyond data processing, you can use another services-based version of Karmasphere Analyst, a visual desktop workspace for analyzing data on EMR. Karmasphere provides visual tools to use SQL and other languages to do ad hoc queries and analyses on structured and unstructured data located on EMR. You can quickly and cost-effectively build powerful Apache Hadoop-based applications to generate insights from your data.

Microsoft

Microsoft Windows is the most widely used platform globally. To make Hadoop compatible on a Windows platform, Microsoft partners with Hortonworks. Together, they produce the Hadoop distribution that runs on Windows (the Hortonworks Data Platform, or HDP, on Windows) and contributes back to the community.

Microsoft delivers that distribution as a service in Azure as well, with HDInsight. HDInsight is a Platform As a Service (PaaS) service in Microsoft Azure, although customers can run HDP, CDH, and others in an IaaS environment in Azure.

Microsoft provides an end-to-end approach for Big Data analytics on the Windows platform. The breadth of offering from a single vendor makes it a unique and worthwhile business value proposition (see Figure 2.7).

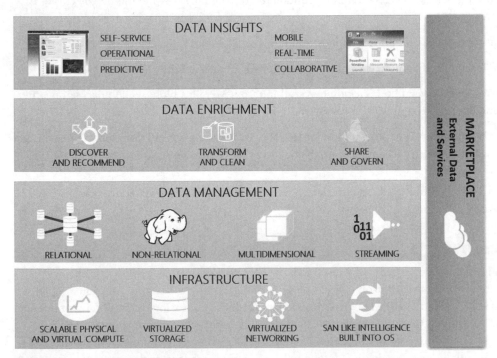

FIGURE 2.7
Microsoft Big Data platform—end-to-end approach.

▶ **Infrastructure**—Included is an option to set up a Hadoop cluster on-premises on the Windows platform or in the cloud as a service in Microsoft Azure. You can scale out with confidence, based on your increasing needs.

▶ **Data management**—This category integrates well with SQL Server, StreamInsight. It supports storing structured, unstructured, and streaming data together on a single Windows platform, while being able to seamlessly move data from one type to another and both monitor and manage all your data, regardless of the type of data or its data structure. With on-premises deployment, you can integrate with Active Directory, System Center, and more to achieve integrated and unified monitoring, management, and security and governance. The application doesn't have to worry at all about scale, performance, security, and availability.

▶ **Data enrichment**—You can use tools such as SQL Server Integration Services (SSIS) and Data Quality Services (DQS) to integrate, cleanse, and transform your data. You can even leverage external data or services (from reliable providers such as the U.S. Census Bureau, the United Nations, and Dunn and Bradstreet, to name a few) from the Microsoft Azure Marketplace to cleanse your data. For example, imagine that you have customer address data with a correct zip code but not the correct city or state information. You can use data available on Microsoft Azure Marketplace to fill in the missing information.

▶ **Data insights**—Existing Microsoft BI tools integrate seamlessly with Hadoop offerings from Microsoft. For example, you can use SQL Server Analysis Services for in-memory, online analytical processing to produce a blazing fast query response; SQL Server Data Mining for predictive analytics; Power BI for self-service BI; SQL Server Reporting Services (SSRS) for operational reporting; Microsoft Excel and PowerPivot, Power View for data mashup or ad hoc reporting; and SharePoint as a collaboration platform for hosting these reports and dashboards.

Why Microsoft Big Data Solutions?

Using Hadoop on the Windows platform offers these advantages:

▶ **Integration with Microsoft's data platform**—The Microsoft Big Data offering integrates seamlessly with Microsoft's data platform (SQL Server and Microsoft Analytics Platform System [APS, formerly known as Parallel Data Warehouse, or PDW]). This integration has new Hadoop connectors, one for SQL Server and one for the Microsoft APS. Customers can easily integrate Hadoop with Microsoft Enterprise Data Warehouses (EDW) or PDW and BI solutions to gain deeper business insights from both structured and unstructured data. Microsoft offers three ways to integrate with its data warehouse and BI tools: a Hive ODBC Driver, a Hive add-in for Excel, and two Hadoop connectors for SQL Server and APS. As a result, SQL Server customers can enrich their analyses by including insights from Hadoop environments in the enterprise data.

▶ **Integration with Microsoft BI tools**—The Microsoft Big Data offering integrates seamlessly with Microsoft Business Intelligence (BI) tools. For example, with powerful Microsoft BI tools such as Power Query, PowerPivot, Power View, and Power Map in Excel, your employees can easily analyze all data types, including unstructured data from on-premises Hadoop clusters or HDInsight service from Microsoft Azure.

▶ **Power Query**—You can use Power Query to find the data you need internally or externally, including unstructured data from Hadoop clusters and the HDInsight service from Microsoft Azure.

▶ **PowerPivot**—With PowerPivot, you can do data modelling (define relationship for your tables; create measures, KPIs, and hierarchies; and so on) on the data extracted from the same or completely different data sources.

▶ **Power View**—Power View allows intuitive, interactive, ad hoc data exploration, visualization, and presentation. It empowers end users to do ad hoc analysis and create reports quickly, with different visualization options. In other words, it lets end users spend less time formatting reports and more time visualizing the data so that they can gain insights and dig deeper into business questions or problems. Power View enables end users to explore data in new ways, to uncover hidden insights. It brings data to life with interactive visualization.

▶ **Power Map**—Power Map extends the capability of Power View by enabling end users to visualize data in 3D visualization format. It plots geographical and temporal data visually so that you can analyze it in 3D visualization format and create an interactive, guided, cinematic tour to discover new insights by seeing your data in geographic space. You can even see time-stamped data change over time (which you might not have seen in traditional 2D tables and charts), and you can share your insights with others. Figure 2.8 shows a sample 3D Power Map report.

▶ **SQL Server Integration Services (SSIS)**—This is an enterprise-scale data integration platform with both ETL and ELT capabilities. It has dozens of out-of-the-box transformation components for you to easily use.

▶ **SQL Server Analysis Services (SSAS)**—SSAS delivers online analytical processing (OLAP) and data mining functionality for business intelligence applications with its in-memory capabilities. Analysis Services supports OLAP by letting you design, create, and manage multidimensional structures that contain data aggregated from different data sources, including Hadoop. It provides an extremely fast query response.

▶ **SQL Server Reporting Services**—SQL Server Reporting Services are useful for data alerts, reporting (standard, preformatted, and drill-down reports), and dashboard creation.

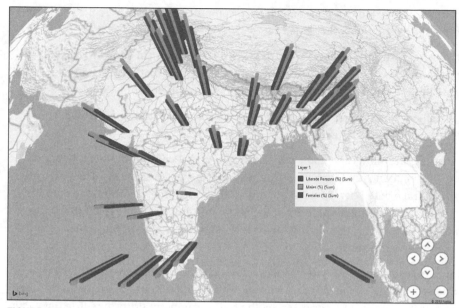

FIGURE 2.8
Sample 3D Power Map report.

▶ **Simplicity and manageability of Windows**—Hadoop integrates well with other Microsoft products as well, including Active Directory. IT thus can secure the Hadoop cluster using enterprise-based security policies. Integration with Microsoft System Center allows IT to easily manage Hadoop clusters just like any other IT asset and provides the governance capabilities needed to scale with confidence.

▶ **Simplified programming**—Microsoft simplifies programming on Hadoop through integration with .NET, new JavaScript libraries, and the HDInsight SDK. Developers can use the new JavaScript libraries to easily write MapReduce programs in JavaScript and then run MapReduce jobs from a web browser. Microsoft is committed to proposing changes to Hadoop for broad use by the Hadoop community. For instance, Microsoft will offer the new JavaScript libraries it is developing for Hadoop to the Hadoop community.

▶ **Cloud advantage**—Even if you're not a big enterprise or don't want to have a dedicated infrastructure to support a Hadoop cluster on-premises, you can use this Microsoft Azure–based HDInsight Hadoop service: an enterprise-ready Hadoop service in the cloud. You can create a Hadoop cluster with Microsoft HDInsight in a few minutes. If your requirements change and you need a larger cluster, or if you no longer need your running cluster, you can simply delete it. You can later create a new cluster of the same size or a different size (for example, you might want a bigger one if you want more power) in a few minutes without losing any data. The best part is that an organization pays for only as long as the cluster is running. You can delete the cluster whenever you don't need it and create it again when you do. Storage is decoupled from compute, so data on WASB can still be accessible if the cluster is de-provisioned.

▶ **Predictive Analytics with Microsoft Azure Machine Learning (in short, Azure ML)—** Predictive analytics with machine learning is not a new concept; it has been in use for a while now. But the traditional approach of machine learning has some problems:

  ▶ It is usually deployed in an on-premises infrastructure and self-managed by a sophisticated engineering team.

  ▶ It has a steep learning curve for a rather complex process: It uses mathematics and statistical computing, and it requires trained and expert data scientists. The financial cost of having a data scientist onboard and, at the same time, cleansing the data for correct and accurate inferences is often too costly for companies to exploit their data, even though they know that data analysis is an effective way to improve their services and optimize their strategies.

  ▶ Building machine learning systems takes a long time. Data scientists must build the training sets and guide the machine learning system through its first step in a complex and expensive process. In some cases, by the time a company starts to realize the value of the model, the model might not be relevant with the current circumstances.

Microsoft Azure ML is a new cloud-based machine learning platform offered as fully managed cloud service. It enables data scientists and developers to efficiently embed predictive analytics into their applications, helping organizations use massive amounts of data as a source for predicting, forecasting, and changing future outcomes. At the same time, it brings all the benefits of the cloud platform to the machine learning process.

NOTE

Machine Learning Made Easy with Azure ML

"You take data from your enterprises and make several hypotheses and experiment with them. When you find a hypothesis that you can believe in, that seems to work and [that] it seems to validate, you want to put that into production so you can keep monitoring that particular hypothesis with new data all the time and track your predictions of what is going to happen versus what's actually happening and adjust your position. And that process is now so much easier now with Azure ML."

—Joseph Sirosh, Corporate Vice President, Machine Learning, Microsoft (see http://www.citeworld.com/article/2366161/big-data-analytics/microsoft-azure-ml-overview.html)

Azure ML offers a data science experience to make inferences from your massive amount of data that is directly accessible to domain experts or business analysts (now not limited to data scientists only). It does this by reducing complexity and broadening participation through better, more user-friendly tooling. For example, its predefined templates, workflows, and intuitive user interface (UI) have been built to help analysts or data scientists dig deeper and forecast future outcomes with predictive analytics much more quickly than with traditional methods. Although you still must understand and formulate your queries appropriately, the web- and workflow-based visual tool helps you build questions easily. You can publish APIs on top of the Azure ML platform so that others can further easily hook them up from any enterprise application, or even from any mobile application for building intelligence, by taking in new data and delivering recommendations.

Azure ML has been made extremely simple to use and easier to implement. Analysts with various backgrounds (even nondata scientists) can leverage it. As a user, you just need to know your data and know how to set up and frame your problem. Then you leverage Azure ML to build the predictive model. Unlike with traditional methods, in which an IT team with sophisticated programming experience handled deployment, Azure ML helps you do it yourself.

The best part of Azure ML is that it is tried, tested, and based on more than 20 years of machine learning. Its powerful algorithms are being used in several Microsoft products, including Xbox, Kinect, Microsoft Malware Protection Center, Cortana, Skype Translator, and Bing. Microsoft released a data mining component for predictive analytics with SQL Server 2005, and it is available in later versions as well.

Early adopters of Azure ML include a large retail customer that was helped by MAX451, a Microsoft partner, to predict the products a customer is most likely to purchase next, based on both e-commerce and brick-and-mortar store data. The retailer used this information to stock its stores even before the demand rose. Another Microsoft partner, OSISoft, is working with Carnegie Mellon University (http://www.microsoft.com/casestudies/Power-BI-for-Office-365/Carnegie-Mellon-University/University-Improves-Operational-Efficiency-Cuts-Energy-Consumption-by-30-Percent-with-BI-Solution/710000003921) on real-time fault detection and the diagnosis of energy output variations across university campus buildings. The university can predict and then plan for mitigation activities, to reduce or optimize overall energy usage and cost in a real-time-like scenario.

GO TO ▶ We look at Azure ML in greater detail in **Hour 22, "Microsoft Azure Machine Learning."**

Deployment Options for Microsoft Big Data Solutions

Now we evaluate the different options of deploying and running Big Data solutions on Microsoft Big Data Platform.

On-Premises

Several organizations have been maintaining infrastructure locally and are not yet ready to move to the cloud because of technical or legal reasons. For those organizations, Microsoft has offerings to run Hadoop on the local infrastructure.

HDInsight on Windows Platform

If your organization needs to have a dedicated local or on-premises Hadoop cluster, you can use HDInsight (based on the Hortonworks Data Platform) to set up a Hadoop cluster on your local hardware infrastructure. If you have HDInsight running on your local infrastructure, you can integrate it with other Microsoft software, such as Active Directory, to enable enterprise-based security policies, and System Center, to easily manage Hadoop clusters just like any other IT asset. This option provides governance capabilities needed to scale with confidence.

Microsoft Analytics Platform System

The Microsoft APS has evolved from Microsoft SQL Server PDW. This single appliance can host both PDW and HDInsight workloads together while running on the local infrastructure.

NOTE
_____
Microsoft SQL Server Parallel Data Warehouse (PDW) is a Massively Parallel Processing (MPP) relational database to store and process vast amount of structured data in distributed manner.
_____

The Analytics Platform System brings Microsoft's MPP data warehouse technology—the SQL Server PDW—together with HDInsight (100 percent Apache Hadoop distribution) in a single integrated appliance. The Analytics Platform System platform was designed for data warehousing and Big Data analytics, offering deep data integration, high-speed query processing, highly scalable storage, and simple maintenance for end-to-end business intelligence solutions.

The Analytics Platform System includes PolyBase, a new and enhanced query engine to query data from Hadoop and the PDW relational data warehouse. It enables you to join data from Hadoop and the PDW relational data warehouse on the fly. PolyBase supports the parallel import of data from HDFS to PDW tables for persistent storage, and the parallel export of PDW data into HDFS (including "round-tripping" of data). PolyBase has a single T-SQL query model for PDW and Hadoop that offers the rich features of T-SQL, including joins without a special ETL operation. SQL Server developers and database administrations can become instantly productive by using T-SQL, tying together siloes of Hadoop solutions with the PDW relational data warehouse. Figure 2.9 shows the PolyBase Query Engine and its interactions with other systems or components.

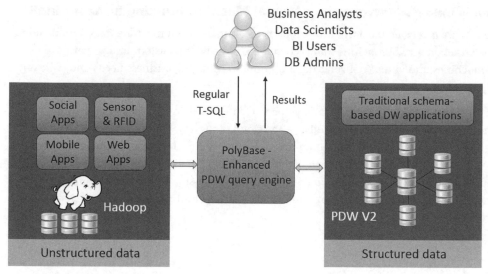

FIGURE 2.9
PolyBase Query Engine and its interaction.

Cloud

Many organizations are now moving to the cloud because of the inherent benefits it provides. In this section, you check out the different offerings for Hadoop running in the cloud (Microsoft Azure).

Microsoft Azure HDInsight Service

Big companies and well-funded government agencies previously were the only entities capable of creating Big Data solutions because doing so required a huge up-front investment in infrastructure and a significant amount of time to implement it. But now the capability to store and process a massive amount of data is within reach for many companies. HDInsight service in Microsoft Azure is a Hadoop-based, enterprise-ready service from Microsoft that brings a 100 percent Apache Hadoop solution to the cloud. HDInsight is a modern, cloud-based data platform that manages data of any type (structured or unstructured) and any size. HDInsight makes it possible for you to gain the full value of your Big Data.

GO TO ▶ Refer to **Hour 6, "Getting Started with HDInsight, Provisioning Your HDInsight Service Cluster, and Automating HDInsight Cluster Provisioning,"** for more information on the Microsoft Azure HDInsight service.

HDP on Windows Platform on a Virtual Machine Running in Azure IaaS

Microsoft Azure is a cloud platform that supports creating a virtual machine (IAAS) on demand. It can be based on virtual machine images available already or a custom image you have. Virtual machines and virtual networks quickly adapt to changing business needs and scale out quickly on demand.

As with HDP on your local infrastructure, you can create an HDInsight cluster on virtual machines from Microsoft Azure (basically, in the cloud platform) without worrying about upfront capital investment and managing the machines locally. This also delivers flexibility in scaling out to more virtual machines when demand increases. With the virtual network service of Microsoft Azure, you can configure a point-to-site or site-to-site VPN to make your virtual machines from the cloud platform look like or work like a virtual machine from the local infrastructure.

NOTE

Keep in mind that Microsoft Azure–provided virtual machines are not limited to only Windows operating systems; you can set up a Hadoop cluster on Linux-based machines (and others) as well. When you create a virtual machine on Microsoft Azure, you get an option to choose from the images available in the virtual machine image gallery (see Figure 2.10). If none of these predefined images suits your need, you can design your own custom image and use it to create virtual machines on the Microsoft Azure platform.

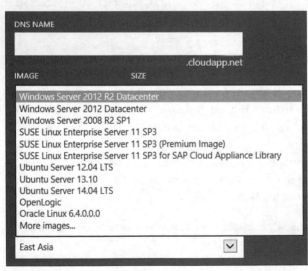

FIGURE 2.10
Creating a virtual machine on Azure with available VM images.

Summary

You learned a lot in this long hour. You dove into the world of Big Data and saw how to manage Big Data with Apache Hadoop. You investigated its history and how Hadoop evolved from infancy to Hadoop 1.0 and then Hadoop 2.0, how the architecture looks in Hadoop 1.0 and the architectural changes in Hadoop 2.0, and how the need arose for Hadoop 2.0. You checked out the software and components that make up the Hadoop ecosystem, and you looked at when and how you can leverage them during the different phases of Big Data analytics. Finally, you got some familiarity with the different Hadoop vendors and their offerings. You also explored deployment options for Big Data solutions from Microsoft and investigated the unique business value proposition of leveraging Microsoft Big Data solutions.

Q&A

Q. What is Hadoop? Who created it? Why the name Hadoop?

A. Apache Hadoop is a top-level open-source project of the Apache Software Foundation that is based on Java. Hadoop provides a scalable and fault-tolerant framework for distributed storage and processing of Big Data across many nodes in the cluster, in parallel. Doug Cutting, the creator of Hadoop, named the framework after his child's yellow stuffed toy elephant. Now Hadoop is being built and used by a global community of contributors and users. Yahoo! has been the largest contributor to the project, and the company uses Hadoop extensively across its businesses.

Q. What are the core components of Hadoop 1.0, and what are some of its limitations?

A. Hadoop 1.0 has two core components. The first is HDFS, a distributed, scalable, load-balanced, and fault-tolerant (with built-in redundancy) storage component of Hadoop. The second is MapReduce, a batch-oriented, distributed computing framework for processing a vast amount of data in parallel on large clusters (with hundreds or thousands of nodes) made up of commodity hardware in a reliable, fault-tolerant manner. These are some of the limitations of HDFS in Hadoop 1.0:

▶ The name node is a single point of failure. HDFS can have only one name node. (The same applies for JobTracker.)

▶ No support exists for horizontally scaling the name node.

These are some of the limitations of MapReduce in Hadoop 1.0:

▶ Only MapReduce can access data in HDFS. This is restrictive and does not allow multitenancy; the other application (which does not work on batch-mode processing) is forced to store data somewhere other than the HDFS.

▶ The JobTracker is overburdened and is solely responsible for managing both resources and the application life cycle.

▶ Computing resources are underutilized. Mappers can use only Map slots; if Map slots are not available, they must wait, even though some Reduce slots might be available. The same applies to Reducers, which must use Reduce slots.

Q. **What changed in Hadoop 2.0? What are the different components in Hadoop 2.0?**

A. The Hadoop architecture introduced some changes to overcome the limitations of Hadoop 1.0. First and foremost, you can take advantage of the high availability of a name node by having a standby name node in passive mode and failing over to it if the active name node fails. For horizontal scaling, you can leverage HDFS Federation, which supports having multiple independent name nodes or namespaces. HDFS with these new features is called HDFS 2 in Hadoop 2.0.

With respect to MapReduce, a new component called YARN (Yet Another Resource Negotiator) was added to take care of resource management and application life-cycle management (originally handled by the JobTracker). This leaves MapReduce to focus on what it does best: batch-mode data processing. YARN then works as the operating system for the Hadoop cluster, serving requests from multiple applications, not just those limited to MapReduce.

Q. **Name a few of the components that make up the Hadoop ecosystem.**

A. These are some of the software or components from Apache that make up the Hadoop ecosystem:

▶ **Apache Hive**—Hive is a distributed data warehouse software that facilitates easy data summarization, ad hoc queries, and the analysis of large datasets stored in HDFS. Hive is best suited for batch jobs over large sets of append-only data (such as web logs). It does not work well with OLTP types of workloads that require real-time queries or row-level updates.

▶ **Apache Pig**—Pig is a high-level platform. It is a data flow and transformation language for processing Big Data on Hadoop clusters. Programs written in Pig Latin consist of dataset transformation series converted under the covers to equivalent MapReduce jobs, very much like in Apache HiveQL.

▶ **Apache Sqoop**—Sqoop is a command-line bulk data transfer tool that efficiently transfers data in bulk between Hadoop and relational data processing systems such as SQL server, or other relational database management systems.

▶ **Apache Oozie**—Oozie is a server-based pipeline or workflow scheduler system for managing and executing Hadoop jobs sequentially. The Oozie workflow delivers greater control over complex data transformation jobs and also makes it easier to repeat those jobs at predetermined intervals, if needed.

▶ **Apache HCatalog**—HCatalog is the table and storage management layer for Hadoop. It provides table and storage abstraction that enables you to think about data in the HDFS as if it were a set of tables. Users with different data processing tools, such as MapReduce, Hive, and Pig, can more easily read and write data on the HDFS. HCatalog presents a common table layer or shared schema and data types to the data processing tools and gives each user the same data model, to enable interoperability across these tools.

▶ **Apache Flume**—Flume is a distributed, highly reliable, scalable, and available service for efficiently collecting, aggregating, and moving large web log data (streaming data) from multiple sources to HDFS, by collecting a high volume of web logs in real time.

Q. Name a few of the vendors for Hadoop.

A. The most prominent vendors are Hortonworks, Microsoft, Cloudera, MapR, Amazon, IBM, Oracle, and Teradata.

Q. What are the deployment options for Big Data solutions from Microsoft?

A. Based on your need, you can have an HDInsight cluster set up either on your local infrastructure or in the cloud.

▶ If your organization needs a dedicated local or on-premises Hadoop cluster, you can use HDInsight (based on the Hortonworks Data Platform) to set up a Hadoop cluster on your local hardware infrastructure.

▶ With Microsoft Azure HDInsight service, you can create a Hadoop cluster in a few minutes without requiring a huge upfront investment in hardware. If your requirement changes in the future or you need a larger cluster, you can simply delete your existing cluster and create a new, bigger one in minutes without losing any data. The best part is that you pay for only as long as you use the cluster. You can delete the cluster anytime you don't need it and create it again when you do need it.

Hadoop Distributed File System Versions 1.0 and 2.0

What You'll Learn in This Hour:

▶ Introduction to HDFS

▶ HDFS Architecture

▶ Rack Awareness

▶ WebHDFS

▶ Accessing and Managing HDFS Data

▶ What's New in HDFS 2.0

In this hour, you take a detailed look at the Hadoop Distributed File System (HDFS), one of the core components of Hadoop for storing data in a distributed manner in the Hadoop cluster. You look at its architecture and how data gets stored. You check out its processes of reading from HDFS and writing data to HDFS, as well as its internal behavior to ensure fault tolerance. In addition, you delve into HDFS 2.0, which comes as a part of Hadoop 2.0, to see how it overcomes the limitations of Hadoop 1.0 and provides high availability and scalability enhancements.

Introduction to HDFS

The Hadoop Distributed File System (HDFS) is based on the Google File System (GFS) and written entirely in Java. Google provided only a white paper, without any implementation; however, around 90 percent of the GFS architecture has been applied in its implementation in the form of HDFS.

HDFS is a highly scalable, distributed, load-balanced, portable, and fault-tolerant (with built-in redundancy at the software level) storage component of Hadoop. In other words, HDFS is the underpinnings of the Hadoop cluster. It provides a distributed, fault-tolerant storage layer for storing Big Data in a traditional, hierarchical file organization of directories and files. HDFS has been designed to run on commodity hardware.

HDFS was originally built as a storage infrastructure for the Apache Nutch web search engine project. It was initially called the *Nutch Distributed File System (NDFS)*.

These were the assumptions and design goals when HDFS was implemented originally:

▶ **Horizontal scalability**—HDFS is based on a scale-out model and can scale up to thousands of nodes, for terabytes or petabytes of data. As the load increases, you can keep increasing nodes (or data nodes) for additional storage and more processing power.

▶ **Fault tolerance**—HDFS assumes that failures (hardware and software) are common and transparently ensures data redundancy (by default, creating three copies of data: two copies on the same rack and one copy on a different rack so that it can survive even rack failure) to provide fault-tolerant storage. If one copy becomes inaccessible or gets corrupted, the developers and administrators don't need to worry about it—the framework itself takes care of it transparently.

In other words, instead of relying on hardware to deliver high availability, the framework itself was designed to detect and handle failures at the application layer. Hence, it delivers a highly reliable and available storage service with automatic recovery from failure on top of a cluster of machines, even if the machines (disk, node, or rack) are prone to failure.

▶ **Capability to run on commodity hardware**—HDFS has lower upfront hardware costs because it runs on commodity hardware. This differs from RDBMS systems, which rely heavily on expensive proprietary hardware with scale-up capability for more storage and processing.

▶ **Write once, read many times**—HDFS is based on a concept of write once, read multiple times, with an assumption that once data is written, it will not be modified. Hence, HDFS focuses on retrieving the data in the fastest possible way. HDFS was originally designed for batch processing, but with Hadoop 2.0, it can be used even for interactive queries.

▶ **Capacity to handle large data sets**—HDFS works for small numbers of very large files to store large data sets needed by applications targeting HDFS. Hence, HDFS has been tuned to support files of a few gigabytes to those several terabytes in size.

▶ **Data locality**—Every slave node in the Hadoop cluster has a data node (storage component) and a TaskTracker (processing component). When you run a query or MapReduce job, the TaskTracker normally processes data at the node where the data exists, minimizing the need for data transfer across nodes and significantly improving job performance because of data locality. This comes from the fact that moving computation near data (especially when the size of the data set is huge) is much cheaper than actually moving data near computation—it minimizes the risk of network congestion and increases the overall throughput of the system.

▶ **HDFS file system namespace**—HDFS uses traditional hierarchical file organization, in which any user or application can create directories and recursively store files inside these directories. This enables you to create a file, delete a file, rename a file, and move a file from one directory to another one.

For example, from the following information, you can conclude that a top-level directory named `user` contains two subdirectories named `abc` and `xyz`. You also know that each of these subdirectories contains one file named `sampleone.txt` in the `abc` subdirectory and one file named `sampletwo.txt` in the `xyz` subdirectory. This is just an example—in practice, a directory might contain several directories, and each of these directories might contain several files.

```
/user/abc/sampleone.txt
/user/xyz/sampletwo.txt
```

▶ **Streaming access**—HDFS is based on the principle of "write once, read many times." This supports streaming access to the data, and its whole focus is on reading the data in the fastest possible way (instead of focusing on the speed of the data write). HDFS has also been designed for batch processing more than interactive querying (although this has changed in Hadoop 2.0.

In other words, in HDFS, reading the complete data set in the fastest possible way is more important than taking the time to fetch a single record from the data set.

▶ **High throughput**—HDFS was designed for parallel data storage and retrieval. When you run a job, it gets broken down into smaller units called *tasks*. These tasks are executed on multiple nodes (or data nodes) in parallel, and final results are merged to produce the final output. Reading data from multiple nodes in parallel significantly reduces the actual time to read data.

In the next section, you explore the HDFS architecture in Hadoop 1.0 and the improvements in Hadoop 2.0.

HDFS Architecture

HDFS has a master and slaves architecture in which the master is called the *name node* and slaves are called *data nodes* (see Figure 3.1). An HDFS cluster consists of a single name node that manages the file system namespace (or metadata) and controls access to the files by the client applications, and multiple data nodes (in hundreds or thousands) where each data node manages file storage and storage device attached to it.

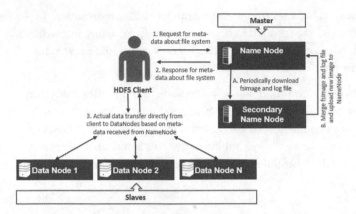

FIGURE 3.1
How a client reads and writes to and from HDFS.

While storing a file, HDFS internally splits it into one or more blocks (chunks of 64MB, by default, which is configurable and can be changed at cluster level or when each file is created). These blocks are stored in a set of slaves, called *data nodes*, to ensure that parallel writes or reads can be done even on a single file. Multiple copies of each block are stored per replication factor (which is configurable and can be changed at the cluster level, or at file creation, or even at a later stage for a stored file) for making the platform fault tolerant.

The name node is also responsible for managing file system namespace operations, including opening, closing, and renaming files and directories. The name node records any changes to the file system namespace or its properties. The name node contains information related to the replication factor of a file, along with the map of the blocks of each individual file to data nodes where those blocks exist. Data nodes are responsible for serving read and write requests from the HDFS clients and perform operations such as block creation, deletion, and replication when the name node tells them to. Data nodes store and retrieve blocks when they are told to (by the client applications or by the name node), and they report back to the name node periodically with lists of blocks that they are storing, to keep the name node up to date on the current status.

A client application talks to the name node to get metadata information about the file system. It connects data nodes directly so that they can transfer data back and forth between the client and the data nodes.

NOTE

The client communicates with the name node to get only metadata; the actual data transfer happens between the client and the data nodes. The name node is not involved in the actual data transfer.

The name node and data node are pieces of software called daemons in the Hadoop world. A typical deployment has a dedicated high-end machine that runs only the name node daemon; the other machines in the cluster run one instance of the data node daemon apiece on commodity hardware. Next are some reasons you should run a name node on a high-end machine:

▶ The name node is a single point of failure. Make sure it has enough processing power and storage capabilities to handle loads. You need a scaled-up machine for a name node.

NOTE

The word *daemon* comes from the UNIX world and refers to a process or service that runs in the background. On a Windows platform, it is generally referred to as a service.

▶ The name node keeps metadata related to the file system namespace in memory, for quicker response time. Hence, more memory is needed.

▶ The name node coordinates with hundreds or thousands of data nodes and serves the requests coming from client applications.

As discussed earlier, HDFS is based on a traditional hierarchical file organization. A user or application can create directories or subdirectories and store files inside. This means that you can create a file, delete a file, rename a file, or move a file from one directory to another.

All this information, along with information related to data nodes and blocks stored in each of the data nodes, is recorded in the file system namespace, called fsimage and stored as a file on the local host OS file system at the name node daemon. This fsimage file is not updated with every addition or removal of a block in the file system. Instead, the name node logs and maintains these add/remove operations in a separate edit log file, which exists as another file on the local host OS file system. Appending updates to a separate edit log achieves faster I/O.

A secondary name node is another daemon. Contrary to its name, the secondary name node is not a standby name node, so it is not meant as a backup in case of name node failure. The primary purpose of the secondary name node is to periodically download the name node fsimage and edit the log file from the name node, create a new fsimage by merging the older fsimage and edit the log file, and upload the new fsimage back to the name node. By periodically merging the namespace fsimage with the edit log, the secondary name node prevents the edit log from becoming too large.

NOTE

Name Node: fsimage and Edit Log File

The fsimage and the edit log file are central data structures that contain HDFS file system metadata and namespaces. Any corruption of these files can cause the HDFS cluster instance to become nonfunctional. For this reason, the name node can be configured to support maintaining multiple copies of the fsimage and edit log to another machine. This is where the secondary name node comes into play.

The name node machine is a single point of failure, so manual intervention is needed if it fails. Hadoop 1.0 does not support the automatic restart and failover of the name node, but Hadoop 2.0 does. Refer to the section "What's New in HDFS 2.0" later in this hour, for more details on changes.

The process of generating a new fsimage from a merge operation is called the *Checkpoint process* (see Figure 3.2). Usually the secondary name node runs on a separate physical machine than the name node; it also requires plenty of CPU and as much as memory as the name node to perform the Checkpoint operation.

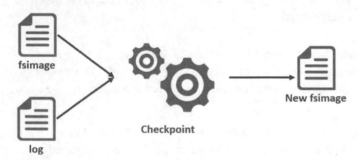

FIGURE 3.2
Checkpoint process.

As you can see in Table 3.1, the `core-site.xml` configuration file for Hadoop 1.0 contains some configuration settings related to the Checkpoint process. You can change these configuration settings to change the Hadoop behavior. See Table 3.1 for a Checkpoint-related configuration example in Hadoop 1.0.

TABLE 3.1 Checkpoint-Related Configuration in Hadoop 1.0

Setting	Location	Description
`fs.checkpoint.dir`	c:\hadoop\HDFS\2nn	Determines where on the local file system the DFS secondary name node should store the temporary images to merge. If this is a comma-delimited list of directories, the image is replicated in all the directories for redundancy.
`fs.checkpoint.edits.dir`	c:\hadoop\HDFS\2nn	Determines where on the local file system the DFS secondary name node should store the temporary edits to merge. If this is a comma-delimited list of directories, the edits are replicated in all the directories for redundancy. The default value is the same as `fs.checkpoint.dir`.
`fs.checkpoint.period`	86400	The number of seconds between two periodic Checkpoints.
`fs.checkpoint.size`	2048000000	The size of the current edit log (in bytes) that triggers a periodic Checkpoint even if the `fs.checkpoint.period` hasn't expired.

Table 3.2 shows some configuration settings related to the Checkpoint process that are available in the `core-site.xml` configuration file for Hadoop 2.0.

TABLE 3.2 Checkpoint-Related Configuration In Hadoop 2.0

Setting	Description
`dfs.namenode.checkpoint.dir`	Determines where on the local file system the DFS secondary name node should store the temporary images to merge. If this is a comma-delimited list of directories, the image is replicated in all the directories for redundancy.
`dfs.namenode.checkpoint.edits.dir`	Determines where on the local file system the DFS secondary name node should store the temporary edits to merge. If this is a comma-delimited list of directories, the edits are replicated in all the directories for redundancy. The default value is the same as `dfs.namenode.checkpoint.dir`.
`dfs.namenode.checkpoint.period`	The number of seconds between two periodic checkpoints.

Setting	Description
`dfs.namenode.checkpoint.txns`	The secondary name node or checkpoint node will create a checkpoint of the namespace every `dfs.namenode.checkpoint.txns` transactions, regardless of whether `dfs.namenode.checkpoint.period` has expired.
`dfs.namenode.checkpoint.check.period`	The secondary name node and checkpoint node will poll the name node every `dfs.namenode.checkpoint.check.period` seconds to query the number of uncheckpointed transactions.
`dfs.namenode.checkpoint.max-retries`	The secondary name node retries failed checkpointing. If the failure occurs while loading fsimage or replaying edits, the number of retries is limited by this variable.
`dfs.namenode.num.checkpoints.retained`	The number of image checkpoint files that will be retained by the name node and secondary name node in their storage directories. All edit logs necessary to recover an up-to-date namespace from the oldest retained checkpoint will also be retained.

With the secondary name node performing this task periodically, the name node can restart relatively faster. Otherwise, the name node would need to do this merge operation when it restarted.

NOTE

Name Node Also Does Checkpoint

The secondary name node periodically performs a Checkpoint operation by merging the namespace fsimage with the edit log and uploading it back to the name node. But the name node also goes through a Checkpoint operation when it starts up. It applies all the transactions from the edit log to the in-memory representation of the fsimage (the name node keeps the fsimage in memory, for quicker response). The name node then writes back this new version of fsimage to the disk. At this time, it can safely truncate the edit log file because it has already been merged.

The secondary name node is also responsible for backing up the name node fsimage (a copy of the merged fsimage), which is used if the primary name node fails. However, the state of the secondary name node lags that of the primary, so if the primary name node fails, data loss might occur.

TIP

If your configuration keeps the name node's metadata files (fsimage and edit log) on the Network File System (NFS), you can take a copy of these files (or point back to them from the secondary name node) to the secondary name node and then run that secondary name node as the primary name node.

File Split in HDFS

As discussed earlier, HDFS works best with small numbers of very large files for storing large data sets that the applications need. As you can see in Figure 3.3, while storing files, HDFS internally splits a file content into one or more data blocks (chunks of 64MB, by default, which is configurable and can be changed when needed at the cluster instance level for all the file writes or when each specific file is created). These data blocks are stored on a set of slaves called *data nodes*, to ensure a parallel data read or write.

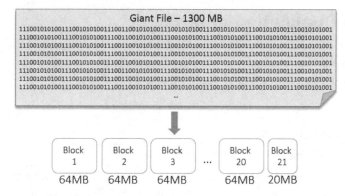

FIGURE 3.3
File split process when writing to HDFS.

All blocks of a file are the same size except the last block, which can be either the same size or smaller. HDFS stores each file as a sequence of blocks, with each block stored as a separate file in the local file system (such as NTFS).

Cluster-wide block size is controlled by the dfs.blocksize configuration property in the hdfs-site.xml file. The dfs.blocksize configuration property applies for files that are created without a block size specification. This configuration has a default value of 64MB and usually varies from 64MB to 128MB, although many installations now use 128MB. In Hadoop 2.0, the default block is 128MB (see Table 3.3). The block size can continue to grow as transfer speeds grow with new generations of disk drives.

TABLE 3.3 Block Size Configuration

Name	Value	Description
dfs. blocksize	134217728	The default block size for new files, in bytes. You can use the following suffix (case insensitive): k (kilo), m (mega), g (giga), t (tera), p (peta), e (exa) to specify the size (such as 128k, 512m, 1g, and so on). Or, provide the complete size in bytes, such as 134217728 for 128MB.

NOTE

Impact of Changing the `dfs.blocksize`

When you change the `dfs.blocksize` configuration setting in the `hdfs-site.xml` configuration file for an existing cluster, it does not affect the already-written files (or blocks). This new setting is effective for new files only. If you want to make it applicable to already written files (or existing files or blocks from HDFS), you must write a logic to rewrite those files to HDFS again (this automatically picks up the new configuration and splits the blocks in size, as defined in the new configuration).

Block Placement and Replication in HDFS

You have already seen that each file is broken in multiple data blocks. Now you can explore how these data blocks get stored. By default, each block of a file is stored three times on three different data nodes: The replication factor configuration property has a default value of 3 (see Table 3.4).

TABLE 3.4   Block Replication Configuration

Name	Value	Description
`dfs.replication`	3	Default block replication. The actual number of replications can be specified when the file is created. The default is used if replication is not specified in create time.
`dfs.replication.max`	512	Maximum block replication.
`dfs.namenode.replication.min`	1	Minimal block replication.

When a file is created, an application can specify the number of replicas of each block of the file that HDFS must maintain. Multiple copies or replicas of each block makes it fault tolerant: If one copy is not accessible or gets corrupted, the data can be read from the other copy. The number of copies of each block is called the *replication factor* for a file, and it applies to all blocks of a file.

While writing a file, or even for an already stored file, an application can override the default replication factor configuration and specify another replication factor for that file. For example, the replication factor can be specified at file creation time and can be even changed later, when needed.

NOTE

Replication Factor for a File

An application or job can also specify the number of replicas of a file that HDFS should maintain. The number of copies or replicas of each block of a file is called the *replication factor* of that file.

The name node has the responsibility of ensuring that the number of copies or replicas of each block is maintained according to the applicable replication factor for each file. If necessary, it instructs the appropriate data nodes to maintain the defined replication factor for each block of a file.

Each data node in the cluster periodically sends a heartbeat signal and a block-report to the name node. When the name node receives the heartbeat signal, it implies that the data node is active and functioning properly. A block-report from a data node contains a list of all blocks on that specific data node.

A typical Hadoop installation spans hundreds or thousands of nodes. A collection of data nodes is placed in rack together for a physical organization, so you effectively have a few dozen racks. For example, imagine that you have 100 nodes in a cluster, and each rack can hold 5 nodes. You then have 20 racks to accommodate all the 100 nodes, each containing 5 nodes.

The simplest block placement solution is to place each copy or replica of a block in a separate rack. Although this ensures that data is not lost even in case of multiple rack failures and delivers an enhanced read operation by utilizing bandwidth from all the racks, it incurs a huge performance penalty when writing data to HDFS because a write operation must transfer blocks to multiple racks. Remember also that communication between data nodes across racks is much more expensive than communication across nodes in a single rack.

The other solution is to put together all the replicas in the different data nodes of a single rack. This scenario improves the write performance, but rack failure would result in total data loss.

To take care of this situation, HDFS has a balanced default block placement policy. Its objective is to have a properly load-balanced, fast-access, fault-tolerance file system:

▶ The first replica is written to the data node creating the file, to improve the write performance because of the write affinity.

▶ The second replica is written to another data node within the same rack, to minimize the cross-rack network traffic.

▶ The third replica is written to a data node in a different rack, ensuring that even if a switch or rack fails, the data is not lost. (This applies only if you have configured your cluster for rack awareness as discussed in the section "Rack Awareness" later in this hour.

You can see in Figure 3.4 that this default block placement policy cuts the cross-rack write traffic. It generally improves write performance without compromising on data reliability or availability, while still maintaining read performance.

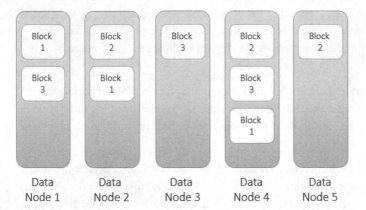

FIGURE 3.4
Data block placement on data nodes.

The replication factor is an important configuration to consider. The default replication factor of 3 provides an optimum solution of both write and read performance while also ensuring reliability and availability. However, sometimes you need to change the replication factor configuration property or replication factor setting for a file. For example, you need to change the replication factor configuration to 1 if you have a single-node cluster.

For other cases, consider an example. Suppose you have some large files whose loss would be acceptable (for example, a file contains data older than 5 years, and you often do analysis over the last 5 years of data). Also suppose that you can re-create these files in case of data loss). You can set its replication factor to 1 to minimize the need for storage requirement and, of course, to minimize the time taken to write it.

You can even set the replication factor to 2, which requires double the storage space but ensures availability in case a data node fails (although it might not be helpful in case of a rack failure). You can change the replication factor to 4 or higher, which will eventually improve the performance of the read operation at the cost of a more expensive write operation, and with more storage space requirement to store another copies.

NOTE

When a Name Node Starts Re-replication

A heartbeat signal from a data node guarantees that the data node is available for serving requests. When a name node realizes that a data node has died, it stops sending any new I/O request to it and concludes that the replication factor of blocks stored on that specific data node has fallen below the specified value, based on its calculation. This swings the name node into action. The name node initiates replication for these blocks to ensure that the replication factor is maintained. Re-replication might be needed for several reasons. For example, a data node itself might have stopped working, or a replica on a data node might have been corrupted. Alternatively, a storage device might have failed on the data node, the network connecting to the data node might have gone bad, or the replication factor of a file might have increased.

When you decrease the replication factor for a file already stored in HDFS, the name node determines, on the next heartbeat signal to it, the excess replica of the blocks of that file to be removed. It transfers this information back to the appropriate data nodes, to remove corresponding blocks and free up occupied storage space.

Writing to HDFS

As discussed earlier, when a client or application wants to write a file to HDFS, it reaches out to the name node with details of the file. The name node responds with details based on the actual size of the file, block, and replication configuration. These details from the name node contain the number of blocks of the file, the replication factor, and data nodes where each block will be stored (see Figure 3.5).

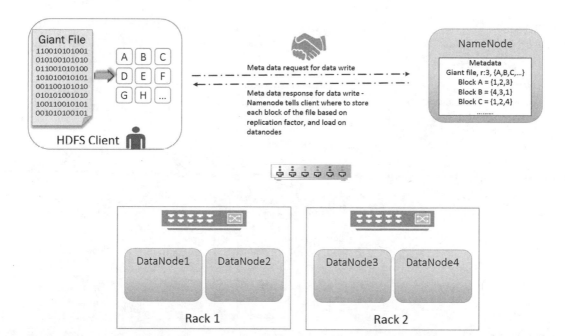

FIGURE 3.5
The client talks to the name node for metadata to specify where to place the data blocks.

Based on information received from the name node, the client or application splits the files into multiple blocks and starts sending them to the first data node. Normally, the first replica is written to the data node creating the file, to improve the write performance because of the write affinity.

TIP

The client or application directly transfers the data to the first data node; the name node is not involved in the actual data transfer (data blocks don't pass through the name node). Along with the block of data, the HDFS client, application, or API sends information related to the other data nodes where each block needs to be stored, based on the replication factor.

As you see in Figure 3.6, Block A is transferred to data node 1 along with details of the two other data nodes where this block needs to be stored. When it receives Block A from the client (assuming a replication factor of 3), data node 1 copies the same block to the second data node (in this case, data node 2 of the same rack). This involves a block transfer via the rack switch because both of these data nodes are in the same rack. When it receives Block A from data node 1, data node 2 copies the same block to the third data node (in this case, data node 3 of the another rack). This involves a block transfer via an out-of-rack switch along with a rack switch because both of these data nodes are in separate racks.

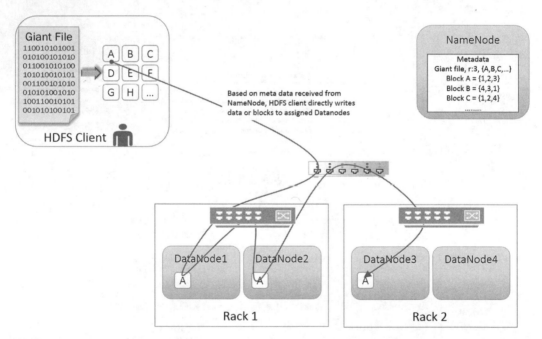

FIGURE 3.6
The client sends data blocks to identified data nodes.

NOTE

Data Flow Pipeline

For better performance, data nodes maintain a pipeline for data transfer. Data node 1 does not need to wait for a complete block to arrive before it can start transferring to data node 2 in the flow. In fact, the data transfer from the client to data node 1 for a given block happens in smaller chunks of 4KB. When data node 1 receives the first 4KB chunk from the client, it stores this chunk in its local repository and immediately starts transferring it to data node 2 in the flow. Likewise, when data node 2 receives first 4KB chunk from data node 1, it stores this chunk in its local repository and immediately starts transferring it to data node 3. This way, all the data nodes in the flow except the last one receive data from the previous one and transfer it to the next data node in the flow, to improve on the write performance by avoiding a wait time at each stage.

When all the instructed data nodes receive a block, each one sends a write confirmation to the name node (see Figure 3.7).

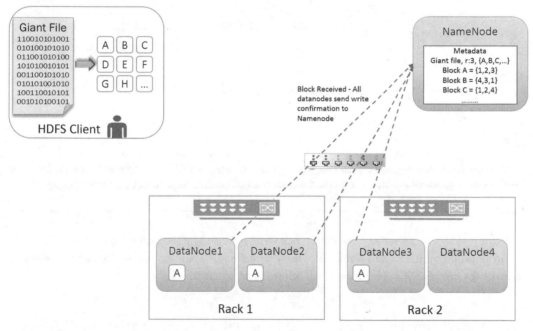

FIGURE 3.7
Data nodes update the name node about receipt of the data blocks.

Finally, the first data node in the flow sends the confirmation of the Block A write to the client (after all the data nodes send confirmation to the name node) (see Figure 3.8).

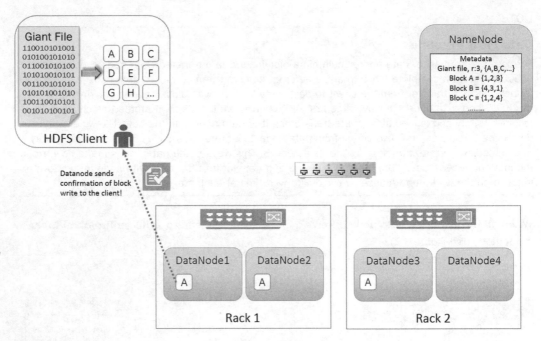

FIGURE 3.8
The first data node sends an acknowledgment back to the client.

NOTE

For simplicity, we demonstrated how one block from the client is written to different data nodes. But the whole process is actually repeated for each block of the file, and data transfer happens in parallel for faster write of blocks.

For example, Figure 3.9 shows how data block write state should look after transferring Blocks A, B, and C, based on file system namespace metadata from the name node to the different data nodes of the cluster. This continues for all other blocks of the file.

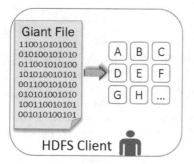
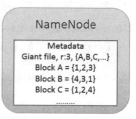

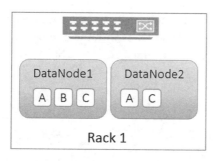
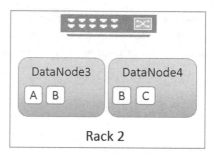

FIGURE 3.9
All data blocks are placed in a similar way.

HDFS uses several optimization techniques. One is to use client-side caching, by the HDFS client, to improve the performance of the block write operation and to minimize network congestion. The HDFS client transparently caches the file into a temporary local file. When it accumulates data as big as a defined block size, the client reaches out to the name node.

At this time, the name node responds by inserting the filename into the file system hierarchy and allocating data nodes for its storage. The client flushes the block of data from the local temporary file to the closest data node and that data node creates copies of the block to other data nodes to maintain replication factor (as instructed by the name node based on the replication factor of the file).

When all the blocks of a file are transferred to the respective data nodes, the client tells the name node that the file is closed. The name node then commits the file creation operation to a persistent store.

CAUTION

Remember that if the name node dies before the file is closed, the file is lost and must be resent.

NOTE

Communication Protocols

All communication from clients to the name node, clients to data nodes, data nodes to the name node, and name node to the data nodes happens over Transmission Control Protocol/Internet Protocol (TCP/IP). The data nodes communicate with the name node using the data node protocol with its own TCP port number (configurable). The client communicates with the name node using the client protocol with its own TCP port number (configurable). By design, the name node does not initiate a remote procedure call (RPC); it only responds to the RPC requests coming from either data nodes or clients.

Reading from HDFS

To read a file from the HDFS, the client or application reaches out to the name node with the name of the file and its location. The name node responds with the number of blocks of the file, data nodes where each block has been stored (see Figure 3.10).

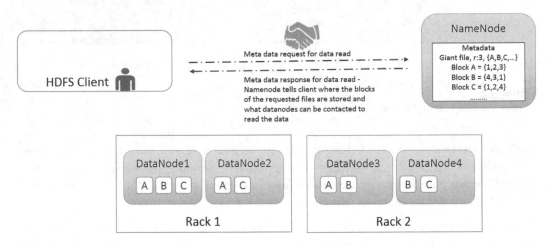

FIGURE 3.10
The client talks to the name node to get metadata about the file it wants to read.

Now the client or application reaches out to the data nodes directly (without involving the name node for actual data transfer—data blocks don't pass through the name node) to read the blocks of the files in parallel, based on information received from the name node. When the client or application receives all the blocks of the file, it combines these blocks into the form of the original file (see Figure 3.11).

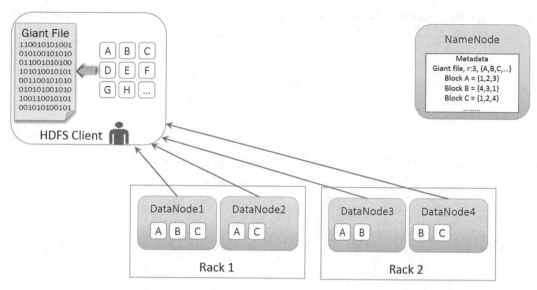

FIGURE 3.11
The client starts reading data blocks of the file from the identified data nodes.

To improve the read performance, HDFS tries to reduce bandwidth consumption by satisfying a read request from a replica that is closest to the reader. It looks for a block in the same node, then another node in the same rack, and then finally another data node in another rack. If the HDFS cluster spans multiple data centers, a replica that resides in the local data center (the closest one) is preferred over any remote replica from remote data center.

NOTE

Checksum for Data Blocks

When writing blocks of a file, the HDFS client computes the checksum of each block of the file and stores these checksums in a separate, hidden file in the same HDFS file system namespace. Later, while reading the blocks, the client references these checksums to verify that these blocks have not been corrupted. (Corruption can happen because of faults in a storage device, network transmission faults, or bugs in the program.) When the client realizes that a block is corrupt, it reaches out to another data node that has the replica of the corrupt block, to get another copy of the block.

Handling Failures

On cluster startup, the name node enters into a special state called safe mode. During this time, the name node receives a heartbeat signal (implying that the data node is active and functioning properly) and a block-report from each data node (containing a list of all blocks on that specific data node) in the cluster. Figure 3.12 shows how all the data nodes of the cluster send a periodic heartbeat signal and block-report to the name node.

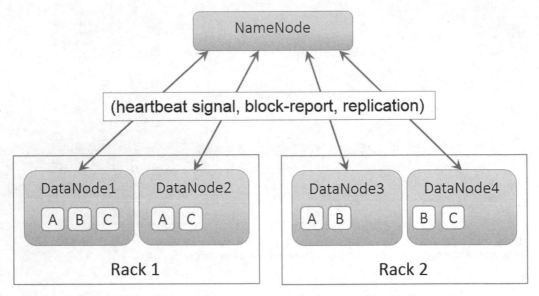

FIGURE 3.12
All data nodes periodically send heartbeat signals to the name node.

Based on the replication factor setting, each block has a specified minimum number of replicas to be maintained. A block is considered safely replicated when the number of replicas (based on replication factor) of that block has checked in with the name node. If the name node identifies blocks with less than the minimal number of replicas to be maintained, it prepares a list.

After this process, plus an additional few seconds, the name node exits safe mode state. Now the name node replicates these blocks (which have fewer than the specified number of replicas) to other data nodes.

Now let's examine how the name node handles a data node failure. In Figure 3.13, you can see four data nodes (two data nodes in each rack) in the cluster. These data nodes periodically send heartbeat signals (implying that a particular data node is active and functioning properly) and a block-report (containing a list of all blocks on that specific data node) to the name node.

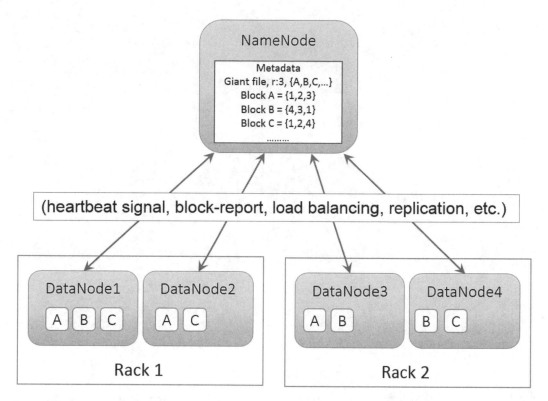

FIGURE 3.13
The name node updates its metadata based on information it receives from the data nodes.

The name node thus is aware of all the active or functioning data nodes of the cluster and what block each one of them contains. You can see that the file system namespace contains the information about all the blocks from each data node (see Figure 3.13).

Now imagine that data node 4 has stopped working. In this case, data node 4 stops sending heartbeat signals to the name node. The name node concludes that data node 4 has died. After a certain period of time, the name nodes concludes that data node 4 is not in the cluster anymore and that whatever data node 4 contained should be replicated or load-balanced to the available data nodes.

As you can see in Figure 3.14, the dead data node 4 contained blocks B and C, so name node instructs other data nodes, in the cluster that contain blocks B and C, to replicate it in manner; it is load-balanced and the replication factor is maintained for that specific block. The name node then updates its file system namespace with the latest information regarding blocks and where they exist now.

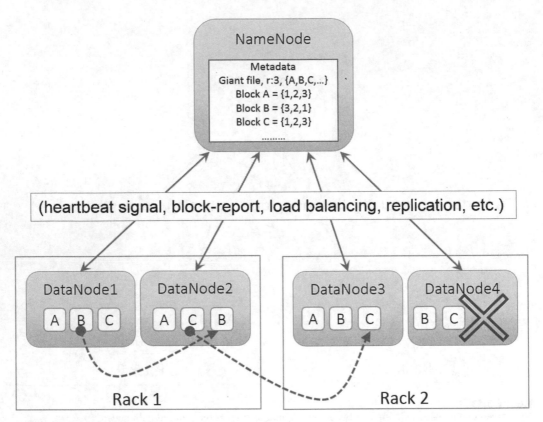

FIGURE 3.14
Handling a data node failure transparently.

Delete Files from HDFS to Decrease the Replication Factor

By default, when you delete a file or a set of files from HDFS, the file(s) get deleted permanently and there is no way to recover it. But don't worry: HDFS has a feature called Trash that you can enable to recover your accidently deleted file(s). As you can see in Table 3.5, this feature is controlled by two configuration properties: fs.trash.interval and fs.trash.checkpoint.interval in the core-site.xml configuration file.

TABLE 3.5 Trash-Related Configuration

Name	Description
fs.trash.interval	The number of minutes after which the checkpoint gets deleted. If zero, the trash feature is disabled. This option can be configured on both the server and the client. If trash is disabled on the server side, the client-side configuration is checked. If trash is enabled on the server side, the value configured on the server is used and the client configuration value is ignored.
fs.trash.checkpoint. interval	The number of minutes between trash checkpoints. Should be smaller than or equal to fs.trash.interval. If zero, the value is set to the value of fs.trash.interval. Each time the checkpoint process runs, it creates a new checkpoint out of the current and removes checkpoints created more than fs.trash.interval minutes ago.

By default, the value for fs.trash.interval is 0, which signifies that trashing is disabled. To enable it, you can set it to any numeric value greater than 0, represented in minutes. This instructs HDFS to move your deleted files to the Trash folder for that many minutes before it can permanently delete them from the system. In other words, it indicates the time interval a deleted file will be made available to the Trash folder so that the system can recover it from there, either until it crosses the fs.trash.interval or until the next trash checkpoint occurs.

By default, the value for fs.trash.checkpoint.interval is also 0. You can set it to any numeric value, but it must be smaller than or equal to the value specified for fs.trash.interval. It indicates how often the trash checkpoint operation should run. During trash checkpoint operation, it checks for all the files older than the specified fs.trash.interval and deletes them. For example, if you have set fs.trash.interval to 120 and fs.trash.checkpoint.interval to 60, the trash checkpoint operation kicks in every 60 minutes to see if any files are older than 120 minutes. If so, it deletes that files permanently from the Trash folder.

When you decrease the replication factor for a file already stored in HDFS, the name node determines, on the next heartbeat signal to it, the excess replica of the blocks of that file to be removed. It transfers this information back to the appropriate data nodes, to remove corresponding blocks and free up occupied storage space.

TIP

In both cases just mentioned, a time delay occurs between when you delete a file or decrease the replication factor for a file and when storage space is actually reclaimed.

Rack Awareness

HDFS, MapReduce, and YARN (Hadoop 2.0) are rack-aware components. This means they can learn about all the nodes of the cluster rack they belong to and act accordingly. The third block from default block placement policy (see the section "Block Placement and Replication in HDFS") applies only if you have configured rack awareness.

If you have not configured rack awareness (in this case, all nodes of the cluster are considered to be on the same rack), or if you have a small cluster with just one rack, one replica of the block goes to the local data node and two replicas go to another two data nodes, selected randomly from the cluster.

CAUTION
_____

This should not be an issue if you have just one rack. However, a larger cluster with multiple racks faces the possibility that all replicas of a block end up in different data nodes in the same rack. This can cause data loss if that specific rack fails.

_____

To avoid this problem, Hadoop (HDFS, MapReduce, and YARN) supports configuring rack awareness. This ensures that the third replica is written to a data node from another rack for better reliability and availability. Even if one rack is getting down, another rack then is available to serve the requests. This also increases the utilization of network bandwidth when reading data because data comes from multiple racks with multiple network switches.

Making Clusters Rack Aware

You can make a Hadoop cluster rack aware by using a script that enables the master node to map the network topology of the cluster. It does so using the properties `topology.script.file.name` or `net.topology.script.file.name`, available in the `core-site.xml` configuration file.

First, you need to change this property to specify the name of the script file. Then you write the script and place it in a file at the specified location. The script should accept a list of IP addresses and return the corresponding list of rack identifiers. For example, the script takes `host.foo.bar` as an argument and returns `/rack1` as the output.

In other words, the script should be able to accept IP addresses or DNS names and return the rack identifier; it is a one-to-one mapping between what the script takes and what it returns. For retrieving the rack identifier, the script might deduce it from the IP address or query some service (similar to the way DNS works). The simplest way is to read from a file that has the mapping from IP address or DNS name to rack identifier.

For example, imagine that you have a mapping file with the following information, where the first column represents the IP address or DNS name of the node and the second column represents the rack it belongs to:

```
hadoopdn001      /hadoop/rack1
hadoopdn002      /hadoop/rack1
hadoopdn006      /hadoop/rack2
hadoopdn007      /hadoop/rack2
```

Given this information, you can write a script that compares the IP address or DNS name of the node with the first column; when they match, the script returns the value from the second column of the corresponding row.

For example, based on the previous information, if you pass hadoopdn001, it should return /hadoop/rack1; if you pass hadoopdn006, it should return /hadoop/rack2. Likewise, if you pass hadoopdn101, it should return /default/rack because there is no entry for hadoopdn101 in the file.

NOTE

Default Rack

If the value for net.topology.script.file.name is not configured, the default value of /default-rack is returned for any IP addresses; thus, all nodes are considered to be on the same rack.

WebHDFS

As long as an application needs to access data stored in HDFS from inside a cluster or another machine on the network, it can use a high-performance native protocol or native Java API and be fine. But what if an external application wants to access or manage files in the HDFS over the Internet or HTTP or the Web?

For these kinds of requirements, an additional protocol was developed. This protocol, called WebHDFS, is based on an industry-standard RESTful mechanism that does not require Java binding. It works with operations such as reading files, writing to files, making directories, changing permissions, and renaming. It defines a public HTTP REST API, which permits clients to access HDFS over the Web. Clients can use common tools such as curl/wget to access the HDFS.

WebHDFS provides web services access to data stored in HDFS. At the same time, it retains the security the native Hadoop protocol offers and uses parallelism, for better throughput.

To enable WebHDFS (REST API) in the name node and data nodes, you must set the value of `dfs.webhdfs.enabled` configuration property to `true` in `hdfs-site.xml` configuration file as shown in the Figure 3.15.

```
<property>
   <name>dfs.webhdfs.enabled</name>
   <value>true</value>
</property>
```

FIGURE 3.15
WebHDFS-related configuration.

Accessing and Managing HDFS Data

You can access the files or data stored in HDFS in many different ways. For example, you can use HDFS FS shell commands, leverage the Java API available in the classes of the `org.apache.hadoop.fs` package (http://hadoop.apache.org/docs/current/api/org/apache/hadoop/fs/package-frame.html), write a MapReduce job, or write Hive or Pig queries. You can even use a web browser to browse the files from an HDFS cluster.

HDFS Command-Line Interface

The HDFS command-line interface (CLI), called FS Shell, enables you to write shell commands to manage your files in the HDFS cluster. It is useful when you need a scripting language to interact with the stored files and data. Figure 3.16 shows the `hadoop fs` command and the different parameter options you can use with it.

FIGURE 3.16
Hadoop CLI for managing the file system.

Some commonly used parameters with the `hadoop fs` command follow:

► `mkdir`—Creates a directory based on the passed URI.

NOTE

The *URI*, or *uniform resource identifier*, refers to the string of characters (compact representation) that identify the name of a resource available to your application on the intranet or Internet.

► `put`—Copies one or more files from the local file system (also reads input from stdin) to the destination file system.

► `copyFromLocal`—Copies one or more files from the local file system to the destination file system. The `-f` option overwrites the destination if it already exists.

► `get`—Copies one or more files to the local file system.

► `copyToLocal`—Copies one or more files to the local file system.

▶ ls—Return statistics on the file or content of a directory.

▶ lsr—Same as ls but recursive in nature.

▶ rm—Deletes a file or directory. The directory must be empty to drop it.

▶ rmr—Same as rm but recursive in nature.

▼ TRY IT YOURSELF

Getting Started with HDFS Commands

In Listing 3.1, line 2 creates a subdirectory named sampledata under the example directory. Line 4 copies a local directory named Gutenberg and its content to the sampledata directory on HDFS. Likewise, line 9 copies one specific file from the local file system to the HDFS folder. Figure 3.17 shows folders from the local file system used with FS Shell commands to move files and folders to the HDFS cluster.

FIGURE 3.17
Source folders and files to copy to HDFS.

LISTING 3.1 **Example of HDFS Command-Line Interface**

```
 1:  @rem --- creating a directory
 2:  hadoop fs -mkdir /example/sampledata
 3:  @rem --- copying a directory
 4:  hadoop fs -copyFromLocal c:\apps\dist\examples\data\gutenberg /example/
     sampledata
 5:  @rem --- listing content of the directory
 6:  hadoop fs -ls /example/sampledata
 7:  hadoop fs -ls /example/sampledata/gutenberg
 8:  @rem --- copying a file
 9:  hadoop fs -copyFromLocal c:\apps\dist\examples\data\sample\sample.log
     /example/sampledata
10:  @rem --- listing content of the directory
```

```
11:   hadoop fs -ls /example/sampledata
12:   @rem --- copying a file to local drive
13:   hadoop fs -copyToLocal /example/sampledata/gutenberg c:\gutenberg
```

Figure 3.18 shows files copied from HDFS to the local file system using the code from line 13 of Listing 3.1.

FIGURE 3.18
Folder and files copied back from HDFS to the local file system.

Figure 3.19 shows the execution result of the code from Listing 3.1.

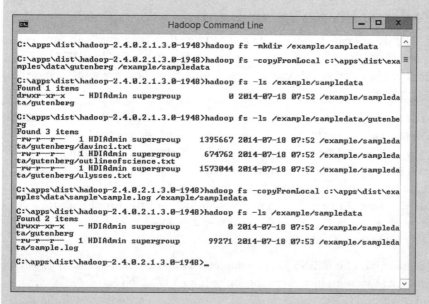

FIGURE 3.19
HDFS command execution from Listing 3.1.

NOTE
_____

In Hadoop 2.0, instead of using `hadoop fs` with the FS Shell, you use `hdfs dfs`. For example, if you used `hadoop fs -ls /example/sampledata` to list the content from the `sampledata` directory in earlier versions of Hadoop, you need to use `hdfs dfs -ls /example/sampledata` instead.

You can learn more about shell commands of Hadoop 2.0 at http://hadoop.apache.org/docs/current/hadoop-project-dist/hadoop-common/FileSystemShell.html.

NOTE
_____

HDFS Administration

DFSAdmin is another CLI for administering an HDFS cluster. Only HDFS administrators use DFSAdmin. For example, `hadoop dfsadmin -safemode enter` puts the cluster in safe mode, `hadoop dfsadmin -safemode leave` brings the cluster back from safe mode, and `hadoop dfsadmin -report` reports basic file system information and statistics, such as how much disk is available and how many data nodes are running.

On Hadoop 2.0, you must use `hdfs dfsadmin -report`. If you don't, you will see the message "DEPRECATED: Use of this script to execute hdfs command is deprecated".

Using MapReduce, Hive, Pig, or Sqoop

FS Shell commands are good as long as you want to move files or data back and forth between the local file system and HDFS. But what if you want to process the data stored in HDFS? For example, imagine that you have stored sale transactions data in HDFS and you want to know the top five states that generated most of the revenue.

This is where you need to use either MapReduce, Hive, or Pig. MapReduce requires programming skills and expertise in Java (see Hour 4, "The MapReduce Job Framework and Job Execution Pipeline"; Hour 5, "MapReduce—Advanced Concepts and YARN"; Hour 10, "Programming MapReduce Jobs"; and Hour 11, "Customizing HDInsight Cluster with Script Action"). People with a SQL background can use Hive (see Hour 12, "Getting Started with Apache Hive and Apache Tez in HDInsight," and Hour 13, "Programming with Apache Hive, Apache Tez in HDInsight, and Apache HCatalog"). Pig helps with data flow and data transformation for data analysis (see Hour 17, "Using Pig for Data Processing").

You can use Sqoop to move data from HDFS to any relational database store (for example, SQL Server), and vice versa. You can learn more about Sqoop in Hour 18, "Using Sqoop for Data Movement Between RDBMS and HDInsight."

GO TO ▶ Refer to **Hour 18, "Using Sqoop for Data Movement Between RDBMS and HDInsight,"** for more details on Sqoop and how you can use it for data movement.

What's New in HDFS 2.0

As you learned in Hour 2,"Introduction to Hadoop, Its Architecture, Ecosystem, and Microsoft Offerings," HDFS in Hadoop 1.0 had some limitations and lacked support for providing a highly available distributed storage system. Consider the following limitations of Hadoop 1.0, related to HDFS; Hadoop 2.0 and HDFS 2.0 have resolved them.

▶ **Single point of failure**—Although you can have a secondary name node in Hadoop 1.0, it's not a standby node, so it does not provide failover capabilities. The name node still is a single point of failure.

▶ **Horizontal scaling performance issue**—As the number of data nodes grows beyond 4,000 the performance of the name node degrades. This sets a kind of upper limit to the number of nodes in a cluster.

In Hadoop 2.0, HDFS has undergone an overhaul. Three important features, as discussed next, have overcome the limitations of Hadoop 1.0. The new version is referred to as HDFS 2.0 in Hadoop 2.0.

HDFS High Availability

In the Hadoop 1.0 cluster, the name node was a single point of failure. Name node failure gravely impacted the complete cluster availability. Taking down the name node for maintenance or upgrades meant that the entire cluster was unavailable during that time. The HDFS High Availability (HA) feature introduced with Hadoop 2.0 addresses this problem.

Now you can have two name nodes in a cluster in an active-passive configuration: One node is active at a time, and the other node is in standby mode. The active and standby name nodes remain synchronized. If the active name node fails, the standby name node takes over and promotes itself to the active state.

In other words, the active name node is responsible for serving all client requests, whereas the standby name node simply acts as a passive name node—it maintains enough state to provide a fast failover to act as the active name node if the current active name node fails.

This allows a fast failover to the standby name node if an active name node crashes, or a graceful failing over to the standby name node by the Hadoop administrator for any planned maintenance.

HDFS 2.0 uses these different methods to implement high availability for name nodes. The next sections discuss them.

Shared Storage Using NFS

In this implementation method, the file system namespace and edit log are maintained on a shared storage device (for example, a Network File System [NFS] mount from a NAS [Network Attached Storage]). Both the active name node and the passive or standby name node have access to this shared storage, but only the active name node can write to it; the standby name node can only read from it, to synchronize its own copy of file system namespace (see Figure 3.20).

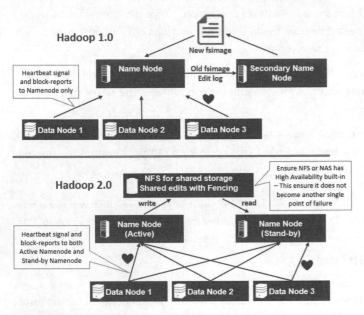

FIGURE 3.20
HDFS high availability with shared storage.

When the active name node performs any changes to the file system namespace, it persists the changes to the edit log available on the shared storage device; the standby name node constantly applies changes logged by the active name node in the edit log from the shared storage device to its own copy of the file system namespace. When a failover happens, the standby name node ensures that it has fully synchronized its file system namespace from the changes logged in the edit log before it can promote itself to the role of active name node.

The possibility of a "split-brain" scenario exists, in which both the name nodes take control of writing to the edit log on the same shared storage device at the same time. This results in data loss or corruption, or some other unexpected result. To avoid this scenario, while configuring high availability with shared storage, you can configure a fencing method for a shared storage device. Only one name node is then able to write to the edit log on the shared storage device at one time. During failover, the shared storage devices gives write access to the new active name node (earlier, the standby name node) and revokes the write access from the old active name node (now the standby name node), allowing it to only read the edit log to synchronize its copy of the file system namespace.

NOTE

Heartbeat Signal from Data Nodes

Whatever method you choose for implementing high availability for name nodes (based on shared storage or quorum-based storage using the Quorum Journal Manager), you must configure all the data nodes in the cluster to send heartbeat signals and block-reports to both the active name node and the standby name node. This ensures that the standby name node also has up-to-date information on the location of blocks in the cluster. This helps with faster failover.

Quorum-based Storage Using the Quorum Journal Manager

This is one of the preferred methods. In this high-availability implementation, which leverages the Quorum Journal Manager (QJM), the active name node writes edit log modifications to a group of separate daemons. These daemons, called *Journal Machines* or *nodes*, are accessible to both the active name node (for writes) and the standby name node (for reads). In this high-availability implementation, Journal nodes act as shared edit log storage.

NOTE

Journal Nodes and Their Count

Journal nodes can be co-located on machines with name nodes, the JobTracker, or the YARN ResourceManager because these are relatively lightweight daemons. However, at least three Journal node daemons must be running to ensure that file system namespace changes (edit log) are written to a majority of these daemons. You can even run these daemons on more than three machines (usually an odd number, such as 3, 5, or 7) to handle an increased number of failures.

Given the previous configuration, in which N is the number of these daemons running, it can survive at max $(N - 1) / 2$ failures of these daemons to work normally. An odd number is chosen to ensure that a majority can be ascertained. For example, if you have five Journal nodes, then $(5 - 1)/2 = 2$ nodes can be taken out because of failure, whereas the majority of the rest of 3 available nodes can be used for decisions.

When the active name node performs any changes to the file system namespace, it persists the change log to the majority of the Journal nodes. The active name node commits a transaction only if it has successfully written it to a quorum of the Journal nodes. The standby or passive name node keeps its state in synch with the active name node by consuming the changes logged by the active name node and applying those changes to its own copy of the file system namespace.

When a failover happens, the standby name node ensures that it has fully synchronized its file system namespace with the changes from all the Journal nodes before it can promote itself to the role of active name node.

Much like the earlier implementation method (shared storage using NFS), the "split-brain" scenario is possible here, too: Both the name nodes could become active, causing data loss or corruption or an unexpected result.

To avoid this scenario, Journal nodes allow only one name node to be a writer, to ensure that only one name node can write to the edit log at one time. During failover, the Journal node gives write access to the new active name node (earlier, the standby name node) and revokes the write access from the old active name node (now the standby name node). This new standby name node now can only read the edit log to synchronize its copy of file system namespace. Figure 3.21 shows HDFS high availability with Quorum-based storage works.

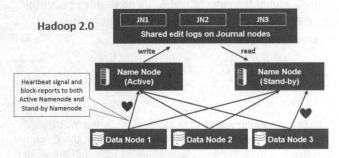

FIGURE 3.21
HDFS high availability with Quorum-based storage.

Do You Need a Secondary Name Node When You Set Up High Availability?

When you enable high availability for your Hadoop 2.0 cluster, the standby name node also takes charge of performing the checkpoint operation of the file system namespace. The secondary name node's task of performing checkpoint and backup becomes redundant with the presence of a standby name node in this new configuration, so having a separate secondary name node is not required in the high availability–enabled cluster. This means you can reuse the same hardware for the secondary name node from the earlier configuration for the standby name node in the new high availability configuration. However, make sure the standby name node has hardware equivalent to that of the active name node (the same amount of physical memory because it holds the same information or file system namespace, and same number of processors because it serves the same number of client requests upon failover).

Failover Detection and Automatic Failover

Automatic failover is controlled by the `dfs.ha.automatic-failover.enabled` configuration property in the `hdfs-site.xml` configuration file. Its default value is `false`, but you can set it to `true` to enable automatic failover. When setting up automatic failover to the standby name node if the active name node fails, you must add these two components to your cluster:

▶ **ZooKeeper quorum**—Set up ZooKeeper quorum using the `ha.zookeeper.quorum` configuration property in the `core-site.xml` configuration file and, accordingly, three or five ZooKeeper services. ZooKeeper has light resource requirements, so it can be co-located on the active and standby name node. The recommended course is to configure the ZooKeeper nodes to store their data on separate disk drives from the HDFS metadata (file system namespace and edit log), for isolation and better performance.

▶ **ZooKeeper Failover Controller (ZKFC)**—ZKFC is a ZooKeeper client that monitors and manages the state of the name nodes for both the active and standby name node machines. ZKFC uses the ZooKeeper Service for coordination in determining a failure (unavailability of the active name node) and the need to fail over to the standby name node (see Figure 3.22). Because ZKFC runs on both the active and standby name nodes, a split-brain scenario can arise in which both nodes try to achieve active state at the same time. To prevent this, ZKFC tries to obtain an exclusive lock on the ZooKeeper service. The service that successfully obtains a lock is responsible for failing over to its respective name node and promoting it to active state.

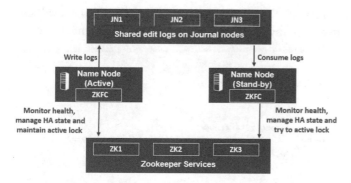

FIGURE 3.22
HDFS high availability and automatic failover.

While implementing automatic failover, you leverage ZooKeeper for fault detection and to elect a new active name node in case of earlier name node failure. Each name node in the cluster maintains a persistent session in ZooKeeper and holds the special "lock" called Znode (an active name node holds Znode). If the active name node crashes, the ZooKeeper session then expires and the lock is deleted, notifying the other standby name node that a failover should be triggered.

ZKFC periodically pings its local name node to see if the local name node is healthy. Then it checks whether any other node currently holds the special "lock" called Znode. If not, ZKFC tries to acquire the lock. When it succeeds, it has "won the election" and is responsible for running a failover to make its local name node active.

NOTE

Automatic failover detection and redirection can be configured for both types of high availability setup (shared storage using NFS or Quorum-based storage using Quorum Journal Manager) in a similar way, even though here we show how to set it up only for Quorum-based storage using the Quorum Journal Manager.

GO TO ▶ Refer to **Hour 6, "Getting Started with HDInsight, Provisioning Your HDInsight Service Cluster, and Automating HDInsight Cluster Provisioning,"** and **Hour 7, "Exploring Typical Components of HDFS Cluster,"** for more details about high availability in HDInsight.

Client Redirection on Failover

As you can see in Figure 3.23, you must specify the Java class name that the HDFS client will use to determine which name node is active currently, to serve requests and connect to the active name node.

```
                              ┌──────────────────┐
                              │ Specify your cluster
                              │ nameservice ID here
                              └──────────────────┘
<property>
  <name>dfs.client.failover.proxy.provider.myhadoop2cluster</name>
  <value>org.apache.hadoop.hdfs.server.namenode.ha.ConfiguredFailoverProxyProvider</value>
</property>
```

FIGURE 3.23
Client redirection on failover.

NOTE

As of this writing, `ConfiguredFailoverProxyProvider` is the only implementation available in Hadoop 2.0, so use it unless you have a custom one.

The session timeout, or the amount of time required to detect a failure and trigger a failover, is controlled by the `ha.zookeeper.session-timeout.ms` configuration property. Its default value is `5000` milliseconds (5 seconds). A smaller value for this property ensures quick detection of the unavailability of the active name node, but with a potential risk of triggering failover too often in case of a transient error or network blip.

HDFS Federation

Horizontal scaling of HDFS is rare but needed in very large implementations such as Yahoo! or Facebook. This was a challenge with single name nodes in Hadoop 1.0. The single name node had to take care of entire namespace and block storage on all the data nodes of the cluster, which doesn't require coordination. In Hadoop 1.0, the number of files that can be managed in HDFS was limited to the amount of RAM on a machine. The throughput of read/write operations is also limited by the power of that specific machine.

HDFS has two layers (see Figure 3.24—for Hadoop 1.0, look at the top section):

▶ **Namespace (managed by a name node)**—The file system namespace consists of a hierarchy of files, directories, and blocks. It supports namespace-related operations such as creating, deleting, modifying, listing, opening, closing, and renaming files and directories.

▶ **Block storage**—Block storage has two parts. The first is Block Management, managed by a name node. The second is called Storage and is managed by data nodes of the cluster.

▶ **Block Management (managed by a name node)**—As the data nodes send periodic block-reports, the Block Management part manages the data node cluster membership by handling registrations, processing these block-reports received from data nodes, maintaining the locations of the blocks, and ensuring that blocks are properly replicated (deleting overly replicated blocks or creating more replicas for under-replicated blocks). This part also serves the requests for block-related operations such as create, delete, modify, and get block location.

▶ **Storage (managed by data nodes)**—Blocks can be stored on the local file system (each block as separate file), with read/write access to each.

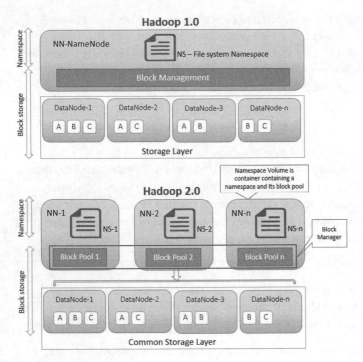

FIGURE 3.24
HDFS Federation and how it works.

In terms of layers, both Hadoop 1.0 and Hadoop 2.0 remain the same, with two layers: Namespace and Block Storage. However, the works these layers encompass have changed dramatically.

In Figure 3.24, you can see that, in Hadoop 2.0 (bottom part), HDFS Federation is a way of partitioning the file system namespace over multiple separated name nodes. Each name node manages only an independent slice of the overall file system namespace. Although these name nodes are part of a single cluster, they don't talk to each other; they are federated and do not require any coordination with each other. A small cluster can use HDFS Federation for file system namespace isolation (for multitenants) or for use in large cluster, for horizontal scalability.

HDFS Federation horizontally scales the name node or name service using multiple federated name nodes (or namespaces). Each data node from the cluster registers itself with all the name nodes in the cluster, sends periodic heartbeat signals and block-reports, stores blocks managed by any of these name nodes, and handles commands from these name nodes. The collection of all the data nodes is used as common storage for blocks by all the name nodes. HDFS Federation also adds client-side namespaces to provide a unified view of the file system.

NOTE

A Data Node Registers with Multiple Name Nodes

A data node can register itself with multiple name nodes (name spaces) in the cluster and can store the blocks for these multiple name nodes.

In Hadoop 2.0, the block management layer is divided into multiple block pools (see Figure 3.24). Each one belongs to a single namespace. The combination of each block pool with its associated namespace is called the *namespace volume* and is a self-contained unit of management. Whenever any name node or namespace is deleted, its related block pool is deleted, too.

NOTE

Balancer in Hadoop 2.0

In Hadoop 2.0, the block balancer has been updated to work with multiple name nodes for balancing block storage at data nodes or balancing storage at the block pool level (this includes balancing block storage at data nodes).

Using HDFS Federation offers these advantages:

- ▶ Horizontal scaling for name nodes or namespaces.

- ▶ Performance improvement by breaking the limitation of a single name node. More name nodes mean improved throughput, with more read/write operations.

- ▶ Isolation of namespaces for a multitenant environment.

- ▶ Separation of services (namespace and Block Management), for flexibility in design.

- ▶ Block pool as a generic storage service (namespace is one application to use this service.)

Horizontal scalability and isolation is fine from the cluster level implementation perspective, but what about client accessing these many namespaces? Wouldn't it be difficult for the client to access these many namespaces at first?

HDFS Federation also adds a client-side mount table to provide an application-centric unified view of the multiple file system namespaces transparent to the client. Clients may use View File System (ViewFs), analogous to client-side mount tables in some Unix/Linux systems, to create personalized namespace views or per cluster common or global namespace views.

HDFS Snapshot

Hadoop 2.0 added a new capability to take a snapshot (read-only copy, and copy-on-write) of the file system (data blocks) stored on the data nodes. The best part of this new feature is that it has been efficiently implemented as a name node-only feature with low memory overhead, instantaneous snapshot creation, and no adverse impact on regular HDFS operations. It does not require additional storage space because no extra copies of data are required (or created) when creating a snapshot; the snapshot just records the block list and the file size without doing any data copying upon creation.

Additional memory is needed only when changes are done for the files (that belong to a snapshot), relative to a snapshot, to capture the changes in the reverse chronological order so that the current data can be accessed directly.

For example, imagine that you have two directories, d1 (it has files f1 and f2) and d2 (it has files f3 and f4), in the root folder at time T1. At time T2, a snapshot (S1) is created for the d2 directory, which includes f3 and f4 files (see Figure 3.25).

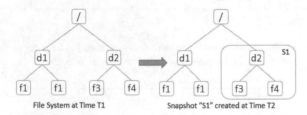

FIGURE 3.25
How HDFS Snapshot works.

In Figure 3.26, at time T3, file f3 was deleted and file f5 was added. At this time, space is needed to store the previous version or deleted file. At time T4, you have to look at the files under the d2 directory; you will find only f4 and f5 (current data). On the other hand, if you look at the snapshot S1, you will still find files f3 and f4 under the d2 directory; it implies that a snapshot is calculated by subtracting all the changes made after snapshot creation from the current data (for example, Snapshot data = Current Data – any modifications done after snapshot creation).

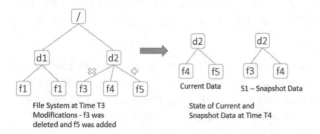

FIGURE 3.26
How changes are applied in HDFS Snapshot.

Consider these important characteristics of the HDFS snapshot feature:

▶ You can take a snapshot of the complete HDFS file system or of any directory or subdirectory in any subtree of the HDFS file system. To take a snapshot, you first must check that you can take a snapshot for a directory or make a directory snapshottable. Note that if any snapshot is available for the directory, the directory can be neither deleted nor renamed before all the snapshots are deleted.

▶ Snapshot creation is instantaneous and doesn't require interference with other regular HDFS operations. Any changes to the file are recorded in reverse chronological order so that the current data can be accessed directly. The snapshot data is computed by subtracting the changes (which occurred since the snapshot) from the current data from the file system.

▶ Although there is no limit to the number of snapshottable directories you can have in the HDFS file system, for a given directory, you can keep up to 65,536 simultaneous snapshots.

▶ Subsequent snapshots for a directory consume storage space for only delta data (changes between data already in snapshot and the current state of the file system) after the first snapshot you take.

▶ As of this writing, you cannot enable snapshot (snapshottable) on nested directories. As an example, if any ancestors or descendants of a specific directory have already enabled for snapshot, you cannot enable snapshot on that specific directory.

▶ The .snapshot directory contains all the snapshots for a given directory (if enabled for snapshot) and is actually a hidden directory itself. Hence, you need to explicitly refer to it when referring to snapshots for that specific directory. Also, .snapshot is now a reserved word, and you cannot have a directory or a file with this name.

Consider an example in which you have configured to take a daily snapshot of your data. Suppose that a user accidently deletes a file named sample.txt on Wednesday. This file will no longer be available in the current data (see Figure 3.27). Because this file is important (maybe it got deleted accidentally), you must recover it. To do that, you can refer to the last snapshot TueSS, taken on Tuesday (assuming that the file sample.txt was already available in the file system when this snapshot was taken) to recover this file.

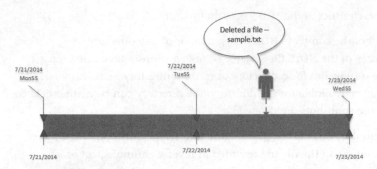

FIGURE 3.27
An example scenario for HDFS Snapshot.

HDFS Snapshot Commands

You can use either of these commands to enable snapshot for a path (the path of the directory you want to make snapshottable):

```
hdfs dfsadmin -allowSnapshot <path>
hadoop dfsadmin -allowSnapshot <path>
```

To disable to take a snapshot for a directory, you can use either of these commands:

```
hdfs dfsadmin -disallowSnapshot <path>
hadoop dfsadmin -disallowSnapshot <path>
```

When a directory has been enabled to take a snapshot, you can run either of these commands to do so. You must specify the directory path and name of the snapshot (an optional argument—if it is not specified, a default name is generated using a time stamp with the format 's'yyyyMMdd-HHmmss.SSS) you are creating. You must have owner privilege on the snapshottable directory to execute the command successfully.

```
hdfs dfs -createSnapshot <path> <snapshotName>
hadoop dfs -createSnapshot <path> <snapshotName>
```

If there is a snapshot on the directory and you want to delete it, you can use either of these commands. Again, you must have owner privilege on the snapshottable directory to execute the command successfully.

```
hdfs dfs -deleteSnapshot <path> <snapshotName>
hadoop dfs -deleteSnapshot <path> <snapshotName>
```

You can even rename the already created snapshot to another name, if needed, with the command discussed next. You need owner privilege on the snapshottable directory to execute the command successfully.

```
hdfs dfs -renameSnapshot <path> <oldSnapshotName> <newSnapshotName>
hadoop dfs -renameSnapshot <path> <oldSnapshotName> <newSnapshotName>
```

If you need to compare two snapshots and identify the differences between them, you can use either of these commands. This requires you to have read access for all files and directories in both snapshots.

```
hdfs snapshotDiff <path> <startingSnapshot> <endingSnapshot>
hadoop snapshotDiff <path> <startingSnapshot> <endingSnapshot>
```

You can use either of these commands to get a list of all the snapshottable directories where you have permission to take snapshots:

```
hdfs lsSnapshottableDir
hadoop lsSnapshottableDir
```

You can use this command to list all the snapshots for the directory specified—for example, for a directory enabled for snapshot, the path component .snapshot is used for accessing its snapshots:

```
hdfs dfs -ls /<path>/.snapshot
```

You can use this command to list all the files in the snapshot s5 for the testdir directory:

```
hdfs dfs -ls /testdir/.snapshot/s5
```

You can use all the regular commands (or native Java APIs) against snapshot. For example, you can use this command to list all the files available in the bar subdirectory under the foo directory from the s5 snapshot of the testdir directory:

```
hdfs dfs -ls /testdir/.snapshot/s5/foo/bar
```

Likewise, you can use this command to copy the file sample.txt, which is available in the bar subdirectory under the foo directory from the s5 snapshot of the testdir directory to the tmp directory:

```
hdfs dfs -cp /testdir/.snapshot/s5/foo/bar/sample.txt /tmp
```

Summary

The Hadoop Distributed File System (HDFS) is a core component and underpinning of the Hadoop cluster. HDFS is a highly scalable, distributed, load-balanced, portable, and fault-tolerant storage compound (with built-in redundancy at the software level). In this hour, we went into greater detail to understand the internal architecture of HDFS.

We looked at how data gets stored in the HDFS, how a file gets divided among one or more data blocks, how blocks are stored across multiple nodes for better performance and fault tolerance, and how replication factor is maintained. We also looked at the process of writing a file to HDFS and reading a file from HDFS, and we saw what happens behind the scenes. Then we used some commands to play around with HDFS for the storage and retrieval of files.

Finally, we looked at different limitations of HDFS in Hadoop 1.0 and how Hadoop 2.0 overcomes them. We then discussed in detail HDFS-related major features in Hadoop 2.0 in this hour.

Q&A

Q. **What is HDFS, and what are the design goals?**

A. HDFS is a highly scalable, distributed, load-balanced, portable, and fault-tolerant storage component of Hadoop (with built-in redundancy at the software level).

When HDFS was implemented originally, certain assumptions and design goals were discussed:

▶ **Horizontal scalability**—Based on the scale-out model. HDFS can run on thousands of nodes.

▶ **Fault tolerance**—Keeps multiple copies of data to recover from failure.

▶ **Capability to run on commodity hardware**—Designed to run on commodity hardware.

▶ **Write once and read many times**—Based on a concept of write once, read multiple times, with an assumption that once data is written, it will not be modified. Its focus is thus retrieving the data in the fastest possible way.

▶ **Capability to handle large data sets and streaming data access**—Targeted to small numbers of very large files for the storage of large data sets.

▶ **Data locality**—Every slave node in the Hadoop cluster has a data node (storage component) and a JobTracker (processing component). Processing is done where data exists, to avoid data movement across nodes of the cluster.

▶ **High throughput**—Designed for parallel data storage and retrieval.

▶ **HDFS file system namespace**—Uses a traditional hierarchical file organization in which any user or application can create directories and recursively store files inside them.

Q. **In terms of storage, what does a name node contain and what do data nodes contain?**

A. HDFS stores and maintains file system metadata and application data separately. The name node (master of HDFS) contains the metadata related to the file system (information about each file, as well as the history of changes to the file metadata). Data nodes (slaves of HDFS) contain application data in a partitioned manner for parallel writes and reads.

The name node contains an entire metadata called namespace (a hierarchy of files and directories) in physical memory, for quicker response to client requests. This is called the fsimage. Any changes into a transactional file is called an edit log. For persistence, both of these files are written to host OS drives. The name node simultaneously responds to the multiple client requests (in a multithreaded system) and provides information to the client to connect to data nodes to write or read the data. While writing, a file is broken down into multiple chunks of 64MB (by default, called blocks). Each block is stored as a separate file on data nodes. Based on the replication factor of a file, multiple copies or replicas of each block are stored for fault tolerance.

Q. What is the default data block placement policy?

A. By default, three copies, or replicas, of each block are placed, per the default block placement policy mentioned next. The objective is a properly load-balanced, fast-access, fault-tolerant file system:

▶ The first replica is written to the data node creating the file.

▶ The second replica is written to another data node within the same rack.

▶ The third replica is written to a data node in a different rack.

Q. What is the replication pipeline? What is its significance?

A. Data nodes maintain a pipeline for data transfer. Having said that, data node 1 does not need to wait for a complete block to arrive before it can start transferring it to data node 2 in the flow. In fact, the data transfer from the client to data node 1 for a given block happens in smaller chunks of 4KB. When data node 1 receives the first 4KB chunk from the client, it stores this chunk in its local repository and immediately starts transferring it to data node 2 in the flow. Likewise, when data node 2 receives the first 4KB chunk from data node 1, it stores this chunk in its local repository and immediately starts transferring it to data node 3, and so on. This way, all the data nodes in the flow (except the last one) receive data from the previous data node and, at the same time, transfer it to the next data node in the flow, to improve the write performance by avoiding a wait at each stage.

Q. What is client-side caching, and what is its significance when writing data to HDFS?

A. HDFS uses several optimization techniques. One is to use client-side caching, by the HDFS client, to improve the performance of the block write operation and to minimize network congestion. The HDFS client transparently caches the file into a temporary local file; when it accumulates enough data for a block size, the client reaches out to the name node. At this time, the name node responds by inserting the filename into the file system hierarchy and allocating data nodes for its storage. The client then flushes the block of data from the local, temporary file to the closest data node, and that data node transfers the block to other data nodes (as instructed by the name node, based on the replication factor of the file). This client-side caching avoids continuous use of the network and minimizes the risk of network congestion.

Q. How can you enable rack awareness in Hadoop?

A. You can make the Hadoop cluster rack aware by using a script that enables the master node to map the network topology of the cluster using the properties `topology.script.file.name` or `net.topology.script.file.name`, available in the `core-site.xml` configuration file. First, you must change this property to specify the name of the script file. Then you must write the script and place it in the file at the specified location. The script should accept a list of IP addresses and return the corresponding list of rack identifiers. For example, the script would take `host.foo.bar` as an argument and return `/rack1` as the output.

Quiz

1. What is the data block replication factor?

2. What is block size, and how is it controlled?

3. What is a checkpoint, and who performs this operation?

4. How does a name node ensure that all the data nodes are functioning properly?

5. How does a client ensures that the data it receives while reading is not corrupted?

6. Is there a way to recover an accidently deleted file from HDFS?

7. How can you access and manage files in HDFS?

8. What two issues does HDFS encounter in Hadoop 1.0?

9. What is a daemon?

Answers

1. An application or a job can specify the number of replicas of a file that HDFS should maintain. The number of copies or replicas of each block of a file is called the replication factor of that file. The replication factor is configurable and can be changed at the cluster level or for each file when it is created, or even later for a stored file.

2. When a client writes a file to a data node, it splits the file into multiple chunks, called blocks. This data partitioning helps in parallel data writes and reads. Block size is controlled by the `dfs.blocksize` configuration property in the `hdfs-site.xml` file and applies for files that are created without a block size specification. When creating a file, the client can also specify a block size specification to override the cluster-wide configuration.

3. The process of generating a new fsimage by merging transactional records from the edit log to the current fsimage is called checkpoint. The secondary name node periodically performs a checkpoint by downloading fsimage and the edit log file from the name node and then uploading the new fsimage back to the name node. The name node performs a checkpoint upon restart (not periodically, though—only on name node start-up).

4. Each data node in the cluster periodically sends heartbeat signals and a block-report to the name node. Receipt of a heartbeat signal implies that the data node is active and functioning properly. A block-report from a data node contains a list of all blocks on that specific data node.

5. When writing blocks of a file, an HDFS client computes the checksum of each block of the file and stores these checksums in a separate hidden file in the same HDFS file system namespace. Later, while reading the blocks, the client references these checksums to verify that these blocks were not corrupted (corruption might happen because of faults in a storage device, network transmission faults, or bugs in the program). When the client realizes that a block is corrupted, it reaches out to another data node that has the replica of the corrupted block, to get another copy of the block.

6. By default, no—but you can change this default behavior. You can enable the Trash feature of HDFS using two configuration properties: `fs.trash.interval` and `fs.trash.checkpoint.interval` in the `core-site.xml` configuration file. After enabling it, if you delete a file, it gets moved to the Trash folder and stays there, per the settings. If you happen to recover the file from there before it gets deleted, you are good; otherwise, you will lose the file.

7. You can access the files and data stored in HDFS in many different ways. For example, you can use HDFS FS Shell commands, leverage the Java API available in the classes of the `org.apache.hadoop.fs` package, write a MapReduce job, or write Hive or Pig queries. In addition, you can even use a web browser to browse the files from an HDFS cluster.

8. First, the name node in Hadoop 1.0 is a single point of failure. You can configure a secondary name node, but it's not an active-passing configuration. The secondary name node thus cannot be used for failure, in case the name node fails. Second, as the number of data nodes grows beyond 4,000, the performance of the name node degrades, setting a kind of upper limit to the number of nodes in a cluster.

9. The word *daemon* comes from the UNIX world. It refers to a process or service that runs in the background. On a Windows platform, we generally refer to it is as a service. For example, in HDFS, we have daemons such as name node, data node, and secondary name node.

The MapReduce Job Framework and Job Execution Pipeline

What You'll Learn in This Hour:

▶ Introduction to MapReduce

▶ MapReduce Architecture

▶ MapReduce Job Execution Flow

This hour primarily introduces you to the MapReduce programming paradigm, its architecture, the components of a MapReduce job, and the MapReduce job execution flow. The examples here serve as a good starting point for writing MapReduce programs. For a more detailed discussion of writing MapReduce programs in Java or any other language (such as C#), turn to Hour 10, "Programming MapReduce Jobs," and Hour 11, "Customizing HDInsight Cluster with Script Action."

In Hour 5, "MapReduce—Advanced Concepts and YARN," you learn about advanced concepts related to MapReduce (including MapReduce streaming, MapReduce joins, distributed caches, different types of failures, and performance optimization for MapReduce jobs) and YARN for Hadoop 2.0 (including architecture, different components, job execution pipeline in YARN, and different types of failures).

Introduction to MapReduce

MapReduce is a fault-tolerant, batch-oriented, parallel programming framework. It enables developers to write a program that processes massive amounts of data (mostly unstructured data) in a distributed manner across hundreds or thousands of nodes in the cluster so that it finishes data processing in a reasonable amount of time on this large volume of data.

As its name implies, the program for the MapReduce framework is divided into two major functions:

▶ **Map**—A Map or Mapper function processes input data to generate intermediate key-value pairs. Basically, input data is split into smaller chunks or key-value pairs. The Map function is applied separately on each chunk or key-value pair, running in parallel with other Map functions on other sets of key-value pairs. The Mapper function creates a new output list (intermediate key-value pair) by applying a function to individual elements of input data (see Figure 4.1).

▶ **Reduce**—A Reduce or Reducer function merges all the values that share the same key to produce the final single output or key-value pair. (The results the Map function generates are shuffled and sorted by the framework to make them available to the Reducer for further processing. Thus, the Reducer can start only after the Mapper completes.) In other words, normally the Reduce function iterates over the input values to produce an aggregate value as output for each specific key. Usually, an output value of 0 or 1 is generated per Reduce function invocation (see Figure 4.1).

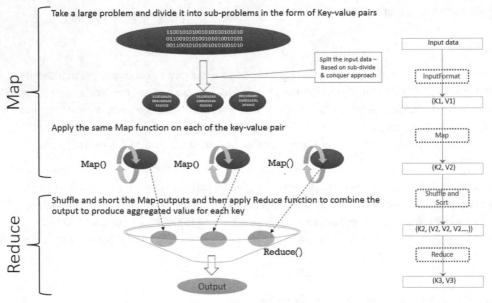

FIGURE 4.1
Typical Map and Reduce functions.

NOTE

Optionally, users can specify a Combiner to perform local aggregation of the intermediate key-value pairs or map outputs. A Combiner typically performs work similar to a Reducer, but locally on each Mapper node. This helps cut down the amount of data that gets transferred from the Mapper to the Reducer.

The MapReduce programming framework provides several benefits that make it ideal for processing a large volume of data in a reasonable amount of time, as discussed next:

▶ **Simplicity in parallelism**—Programs targeted for the MapReduce framework get automatically parallelized and are executed on a large cluster of nodes by the MapReduce framework. This enables even programmers with no experience in parallel and distributed systems to easily write programs targeting the MapReduce framework and to utilize the resources and power of a large cluster made up of commodity hardware.

▶ **Fault tolerance**—The MapReduce framework is based on an architecture of master and slaves. The master is the *JobTracker* and the slaves are *TaskTrackers*. The TaskTrackers keep sending a heartbeat signal to the JobTracker on a certain frequency. When a JobTracker does not hear anything from a TaskTracker in a certain amount of time (configurable), it assumes that the specific TaskTracker is in a failed state or that communication with that specific TaskTracker cannot be established. It then takes corrective measures to ensure that the tasks assigned to that specific TaskTracker are reassigned to another available TaskTracker; no new tasks are assigned to this TaskTracker. The MapReduce framework takes care of this process transparently, without making users worry about rescheduling tasks upon failure.

Because of a bug in the user code, sometimes the MapReduce program fails deterministically. The usual course of action is to fix the bug, but that might not be possible if you are using a third-party library or you don't have access to the source code. In that case, you can configure the MapReduce framework to handle this scenario by skipping those bad records or marking them as something to avoid so that it can make forward progress. Generally, skipping a few bad records is acceptable when doing statistical analysis on a large data set.

GO TO ▶ We talk more about skipping bad records in **Hour 5**.

▶ **Scalability**—The MapReduce framework is distributed in nature and is based on a scale-out model. As the load increases, you can keep increasing additional nodes for more storage and processing power. This means you can use a batch-mode parallel programming paradigm to write and execute analysis programs that scale to thousands of nodes and petabytes of data.

▶ **Data locality**—Network bandwidth is relatively scarce and is the slowest resource in the computing environment, so moving data to the computation is often more expensive than moving computation to the data. Hadoop embraces this fact. As you learned in Hour 3, "Hadoop Distributed File System Versions 1.0 and 2.0," the HDFS part of Hadoop splits a large file into multiple chunks, called data blocks, and then store these data blocks across nodes of the cluster. HDFS also maintains multiple replicas of each data block for fault tolerance and high availability. When you write a MapReduce program to process this data, MapReduce tries to process each block of data needed, in a parallel and distributed manner, where it exists, taking advantage of horizontal partitioned data stored in HDFS. If it does not find available computing resources to process the data on the same node where the data exists, it looks for another node (with the same network switch, to avoid transferring data over the network) in the same rack to process the data.

NOTE

Representing a Problem in Two Functions

It might sound like a different way of programming than what you have traditionally been doing, but many real-world problems can be expressed in these two functions: Map and Reduce. For them, you can leverage the MapReduce framework.

MapReduce Architecture

The MapReduce framework is based on a master and slaves architecture. The master is the JobTracker and the slaves are TaskTrackers. A JobTracker is a daemon running on the master node for submitting, scheduling, monitoring, and tracking the execution of MapReduce jobs across TaskTrackers. If any tasks fail, the JobTracker re-executes them, up to a predefined limit of retries. A TaskTracker is a daemon running on slave nodes that accepts tasks (Map, Reduce, and Shuffle operations) from the JobTracker.

Each TaskTracker in the cluster has a set of computational slots (both Map slots and Reduce slots) available that indicate the number of tasks that specific TaskTracker can accept for processing simultaneously. When a TaskTracker is assigned a task to execute, it spawns a separate Java Virtual Machine (JVM) process to execute the task in it. This isolation ensures that if the task fails, it does not bring down the TaskTracker itself. The TaskTracker monitors these spawned processes and captures their output and exit codes. When these spawned processes execute (either success or failure), the TaskTracker notifies the JobTracker. As discussed next, the TaskTracker also sends out a heartbeat signal to the JobTracker, usually every few minutes (configurable), to let the JobTracker know of its health and the number of available computational slots it holds to take up more work.

NOTE

Number of Map and Reduce Slots

By default, both the `mapred.tasktracker.map.tasks.maximum` and `mapred.tasktracker.reduce.tasks.maximum` configurations have a default value of 2. This means that two Mappers (two slots for maps) and two Reducers (two slots for Reducers) on a TaskTracker can run simultaneously in parallel. For example, if you have 10 nodes (TaskTrackers) in a cluster, you can run up to 20 (2 × 10) Mappers and 20 (2 × 10) Reducers in the cluster.

When assigning a task to a TaskTracker for processing, the JobTracker first tries to locate a TaskTracker with a free slot on the same server that has the data node containing the data (to ensure data locality). If it doesn't find this TaskTracker, it looks for a TaskTracker on another node in the same rack before it goes across the racks to locate a TaskTracker.

JobTracker: A Single Point of Failure Too

As with the name node, JobTracker is a single point of failure in Hadoop 1.0. Hadoop 2.0 has overcome this limitation, as you find in the section "YARN" in the next hour.

MapReduce Job Request and Response Flow

Figures 4.2 and 4.3 illustrate the general flow of job submission, execution, and response back to the job client.

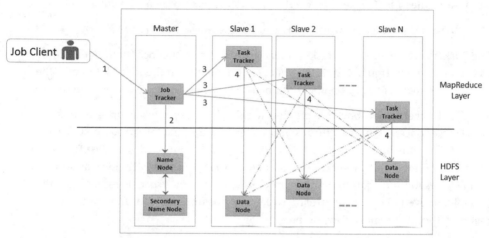

FIGURE 4.2
MapReduce job submission and execution.

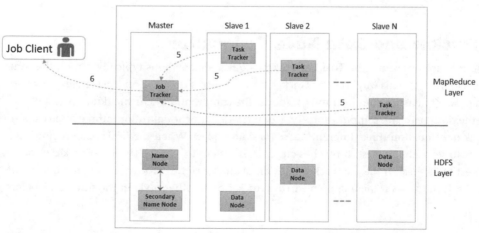

FIGURE 4.3
MapReduce job response back to the client.

Here's what happens:

1. The Job client submits a job (implementation of Map and Reduce functions) to the JobTracker along with the input and output file paths and configurations. The job is queued for execution. From there, the job scheduler picks it up and initializes it for execution. (We discuss the Job Scheduler and its methods in the next hour.)

2. The JobTracker coordinates with the name node to learn about the input data and where it exists to serve the job request. The JobTracker creates an execution plan based on the information it receives from the name node about the data and overall workload. The JobTracker ensures that computation executes as close as possible to the data—in other words, it locates TaskTracker nodes with available slots at or near the data itself.

3. The JobTracker submits the work or tasks to the identified TaskTrackers.

4. The TaskTrackers execute the tasks and use the data from the local data node (shown as the solid line in Figure 4.2). If the data is not available on the local data node, the TaskTracker reaches out to another data node (shown as the dashed line in Figure 4.3).

5. The TaskTrackers report back the progress to the JobTracker using heartbeat signals. If a TaskTracker doesn't send heartbeat signals often enough, the JobTracker assumes that it is in a failed state and reschedules the work assigned to that particular TaskTracker. If the execution of a task fails, the TaskTracker notifies the JobTracker. The JobTracker might decide to resubmit the job to another TaskTracker, mark that specific record as something to avoid, or even blacklist the specific TaskTracker as unreliable for future task assignments so that it can make forward progress.

6. The JobTracker tracks the execution of tasks and manages the phases of its execution. The JobTracker updates its status to the job client during execution and when the job finishes executing.

TaskTracker and Data Node Co-location

Although it is not necessary, the TaskTracker and data node daemons typically run on the same node (see Figure 4.4). This way, the JobTracker tries to process the data on the same node where the data exists (to ensure data locality)—it moves the computation near the data instead of moving the data near the computation. Typically (by default configuration), three replicas of a data block are stored on three different nodes (or data nodes). When the JobTracker requires this data block to serve the request, it reaches out to those nodes to execute the TaskTracker in order from closest to farthest. If the JobTracker finds an available slot to process the request on any of these nodes, it processes it there or spins a TaskTracker on another node in the same rack before it goes across the racks to locate an available slot for TaskTracker execution. In the latter case, data movement might occur across nodes. Although spinning TaskTracker on another rack is not that frequent, it might be required when a local slot is not available where data exists, so that submitted request is not blocked.

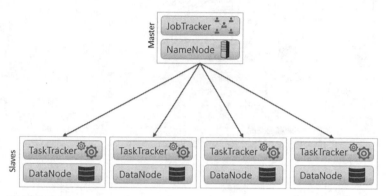

FIGURE 4.4
TaskTracker and data node co-location.

NOTE

A Single Node with All the Daemons Running on It

You can see that Figure 4.4 shows one master and *N* slaves. The master consists of a JobTracker (MapReduce part) and a name node (HDFS part); each slave consists of a TaskTracker (MapReduce part) and a data node (HDFS part).

Some architectures, such as a single-node cluster, can be used for learning or development—for example, you can have both a master (with JobTracker and name node) and a slave (with TaskTracker and data node) running on a single machine. Note, however, that one node cluster is not recommended for production use.

MapReduce Job Execution Flow

A MapReduce job has different components. When you execute a MapReduce job, it goes through several distinct phases. Figure 4.5 shows these components and illustrates the MapReduce job execution flow pipeline at a high level.

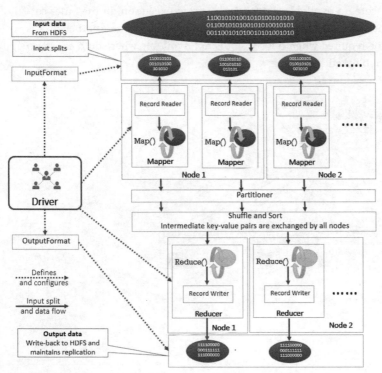

FIGURE 4.5
MapReduce job—high-level execution flow.

In this section, we talk about the following components or classes and identify the role each plays during the MapReduce job execution flow:

- ▶ InputFormat
- ▶ OutputFormat
- ▶ Multiple Input and Output Format
- ▶ Mapper
- ▶ Partitioner
- ▶ Combiner
- ▶ Driver
- ▶ Tool Interface
- ▶ Context Object

We also use the following two examples to explain the execution pipeline of MapReduce jobs:

▶ **MapReduce job for counting the word in an input file**—This job, which comes as a
  sample with Hadoop, counts the number of times each word appears in the input file. The
  output comes in an output text file that consists of lines, each containing a word and the
  total count (a key-value pair) of how often that specific word occurred in the input file.

▶ **MapReduce job for getting the total sales amount for each city**—The input file for this
  job contains a daily sales amount for each city. The MapReduce program computes the
  total sales for each city by grouping on the city. The output comes in an output text file
  that consists of lines, each containing a city and the total sales amount (a key-value tab-
  separated pair) by grouping on city in the input file.

NOTE

The MapReduce framework is suitable not only for structured data processing, but also for
unstructured data. The Mapper part of the MapReduce framework can be leveraged to bring
structure to the unstructured data for further processing.

Note that, in Figure 4.5, Partitioning and Shuffling are shown separately for clarity, although
they both actually happen together. Based on the partitioning process being used, map-outputs
are shuffled across appropriate Reducers.

In addition, in Figure 4.5, the `InputFormat` and `OutputFormat` are defined by the Driver component of the MapReduce job. You can think of the Driver component as a main program that
initializes a MapReduce job and defines the job-specific configuration.

GO TO ▶ You can find more about the Driver component in the **"Driver"** section of this hour.

InputFormat

The MapReduce framework uses the `InputFormat` class to define how to read data from a file
and make it available to the Map functions. It splits the input and spawns one map task for
each `InputSplit` generated by it. This `InputFormat` class basically validates input specification and uses these two interfaces from the `org.apache.hadoop.mapreduce` package to perform two main operations:

▶ **InputSplit interface**—Divides the input data of the files into logical fragments, called
  `InputSplit`, that make up the inputs to individual Mappers (each `InputSplit` is
  assigned to an individual Mapper). An `InputSplit` doesn't copy the data—it just contains
  a reference to the actual data.

▶ **RecordReader interface**—The RecordReader class is responsible for reading records from InputSplits and submitting them (as key-value pairs) to the map functions. It converts the byte-oriented view of the input (provided by the InputSplit) to a record-oriented view, to make it available to the Mapper for processing. It is responsible for processing record boundaries and presenting the tasks with keys and values. It also ensures that they do not miss records that span multiple InputSplit boundaries.

NOTE

InputSplits Versus Data Blocks

InputSplits are a logical division of records, whereas HDFS data blocks are a physical division of the input data of the files. In practice, they might not be perfectly aligned, even though both are the same size. For example, records can cross data block boundaries, but even then, the MapReduce framework ensures the processing of all records. A Mapper ensures fetching a remaining part of the record (when a record has been stored in two data blocks) from the other data block when processing the record from the main block.

Several implementations for InputFormat classes are already available for standard data reading, including the TextInputFormat class to read lines of text files, the SequenceFileInputFormat class to read from a particular binary file, and the DBInputFormat class to read data from a relational database. If you want to process application-specific or custom data, you can also define your own custom InputFormat implementation. For example, the built-in TextInputFormat class reads lines of text files and produces a key (byte offset of the line read) and value (the contents of the line) for each line up to the terminating "\n".

Now suppose that you have a text file in which each record is not available as a new line, but rather is in a single line separated by some special characters. In this case, you can write your own custom implementation of the InputFormat class that parses lines from the file into records by splitting on that specific special character.

NOTE

InputSplit Versus the Map Function

An InputSplit, provided by InputFormat, is a chunk of the input data that is processed by a single map function. Based on the implementation, each InputSplit can be further divided into records, and the map function can process each record (a key-value pair) separately. For example, this might be a range of rows from a table, in the case of the DBInputFormat class.

FileInputFormat is the base class for all implementations of InputFormat that are based on files. With this, you can define which files are included as the input to a MapReduce job execution and specify an implementation for generating splits—the getSplits (JobConf, int) method—for the input files. The subclasses implement the job of dividing an `InputSplit` into records.

GO TO ▶ You can see an example of `FileInputFormat` in the **"Driver"** section later in this hour.

NOTE

Large Number of Small Files Versus Small Number of Large Files

Hadoop is designed to store and process a smaller number of large files and might not yield better performance for a large number of small files. Having a smaller number of larger files is ideal, but you might not always have an ideal situation. If you have a large number of small files, resources will be wasted: More map functions will need to be initiated and the JobTracker will have more overhead in keeping track of it. In this case, you might consider implementing the `CombineFileInputFormat` abstract base class, which combines many files into each split so that fewer map functions are initiated and each map function has more to process. Also, the `CombineFileInputFormat` class has node and rack locality awareness. Take that into consideration when combining files, to ensure minimal data movement and faster processing of the MapReduce job.

OutputFormat

Hadoop has output data formats that validate the output specification of the job. For example, it checks whether the output directory already exists (to avoid overwrite) and provides the `RecordWriter` implementation to write the output `<key, value>` pairs to an output file. Output files of the job are stored in a file system.

These output data formats correspond to the input formats. For example, the `TextInputFormat` input format has the corresponding `TextOutputFormat` output format for writing the reduce function output to plain-text files. Likewise, the `SequenceFileInputFormat` input format has the corresponding `SequenceFileOutputFormat` output format to write the reduce function output to flat files consisting of binary key-value pairs. The `DBInputFormat` input format has the corresponding `DBOutputFormat` output format to write the reduce function output to a SQL table, and so on.

NOTE

Avoiding Input File Splits

If you don't want to split your input files into `InputSplits` and you want each file to be processed as a whole by a single map function, you can override the `isSplitable (FileSystem, Path)` method of the `FileInputFormat` class and set `false` as its return value. This comes in handy if you have XML files as your input and you want to process the whole file (or the entire XML document) as one input so that it gets processed by one map function.

Multiple Input and Output Format

By default, all the input files provided to a MapReduce job are interpreted and parsed by a single InputFormat class. If your input files have a different structure and you want them to be parsed using multiple InputFormat classes or a combination of them, you can use the MultipleInputs class, which enables you to specify the InputFormat and Mapper on each path basis.

```
//Define path1 with a TextInputFormat input to the list of inputs for Mapper1
MultipleInputs.addInputPath(conf, path1, TextInputFormat.class, Mapper1.class);
//Define path1 with a SequenceFileInputFormat input to the list of inputs
for Mapper2
MultipleInputs.addInputPath(conf, path2, SequenceFileInputFormat.class, Mapper2.class);
```

Likewise, you can use the MultipleOutputs class for writing to additional outputs of types other than the job default output. This requires you to pass the OutputCollector to the map() and reduce() methods of the Mapper and Reducer implementations. Each additional output can be configured with its own OutputFormat, its own key class, and its own value class: Output filenames can be derived from the output keys and values.

```
//Defines additional single text based output "text" for the job
MultipleOutputs.addNamedOutput(conf, "text", TextOutputFormat.class,
LongWritable.class, Text.class);
//Defines additional multi sequencefile based output 'sequence' for the job
MultipleOutputs.addMultiNamedOutput(conf, "seq", SequenceFileOutputFormat.class,
LongWritable.class, Text.class);
```

Mapper

The user-defined Mapper class extends the Mapper<KeyIn, ValueIn, KeyOut, ValueOut> base class from the org.apache.hadoop.mapreduce package and performs user-defined work during the first phase of the MapReduce job execution. From the implementation point of view, a Mapper implementation takes input data in the form of a series of input key-value pairs (k1, v1) and produces a set of intermediate output key-value pairs (k2, v2) that eventually are used as inputs for shuffle and sort operations.

For each InputSplit generated by the InputFormat for the MapReduce job, a separate instance of Mapper is instantiated in a separate instance of the Java Virtual Machine (JVM). These multiple instances of Mapper running in parallel cannot communicate, so the local machine governs each Mapper instance.

In our word count MapReduce job example, we use the TextInputFormat (a default InputFormat as well) class. InputSplits generated by TextInputFormat consider each input line as a record that has a byte offset within the file as its key and consider the content of the line as its value (see Figure 4.6).

FIGURE 4.6
InputSplit to Map task.

Four methods extend from the base class:

▶ `setup (Context)`—Called first and executed only once at the beginning of the task to initialize the Mapper. For example, you can leverage this method to read from shared resources. The default implementation is a no-op method.

▶ `map (Object, Object, Context)`—Executed for each key-value pair of the given InputSplit. In this method, you write the business functionality or application-specific logic of the Mapper to process each record or key-value pair.

▶ `cleanup (Context)`—Called only once at the end of the execution of the task (after all the input records are processed) to clean up the Mapper's resources. The default implementation is a no-op method.

▶ `run (Context)`—Can be overridden for more complete control over the execution of the Mapper function. By default, the `run ()` method simply takes each key-value pair supplied by the context and calls the `map ()` method, as discussed earlier. If you want to change this default behavior (such as with multithreaded Mappers), you can override this method.

For optimum performance, the map function does not start writing data to the disk when it starts producing output; it takes advantage of the memory buffer by writing it to the circular buffers assigned to it and presorting for efficiency. By default, each map task has 100MB of circular memory buffer and can be changed using the `io.sort.mb` property.

A background thread starts spilling buffer contents to the disk at a certain threshold, controlled by the `io.sort.spill.percent` property (this defaults to 80 percent). This spillover process can happen even when the map function is writing to the buffer. If the MapReduce job has 0 (zero) Reducer instance, the output of the Mapper is directly written to the `OutputFormat` (FileSystem) without sorting by keys.

The MapReduce framework also enables you to specify whether and how the intermediate outputs are to be compressed (by default, output is not compressed) and which CompressionCodecs are to be used via the job configuration (for faster write to disk, to save disk space, and to minimize load on the network while transferring data to the Reducer).

Mapper Example

For our MapReduce job example, you can see in Figure 4.7 that the text is stored in different blocks on the data node. TextInputFormat reads these blocks and splits the data into multiple InputSplits—this example has two InputSplits, so two instance of Mapper are instantiated. Each Mapper takes each line from the InputSplit as an input and breaks it into words. It emits a key-value pair on each occurrence of the word, followed by a 1.

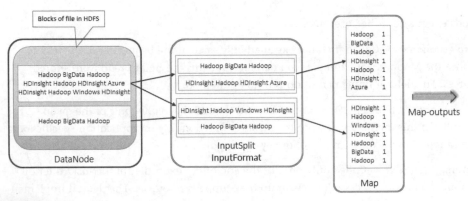

FIGURE 4.7
Map function flow for the word count example.

Listing 4.1 contains the implementation of Mapper for the word count example, which processes one line at a time, as provided by the TextInputFormat. It then splits the line into tokens (words) separated by whitespace, via the StringTokenizer class, and emits a key-value pair of < <word>, 1> as you saw in Figure 4.7.

LISTING 4.1   Mapper Implementation for the Word Count Example

```
 1: public static class WordCountMapper
 2:     extends Mapper<Object, Text, Text, IntWritable>{
 3:
 4: private final static IntWritable one = new IntWritable(1);
 5: private Text word = new Text();
 6:
 7: public void map(Object key, Text value, Context context
 8:                  ) throws IOException, InterruptedException {
 9:    StringTokenizer itr = new StringTokenizer(value.toString());
10:    while (itr.hasMoreTokens()) {
11:        word.set(itr.nextToken());
12:      context.write(word, one);
13:      }
14:    }
15:  }
```

The MapReduce job is executed across many nodes in the Hadoop cluster. To pass data from one node to another, it must be serializable and deserializable. This is where `<data-type>Writable` classes were used as `IntWritable` in Listing 4.1. `<data-type>Writable` classes implement the `Writable` interface, which provides a simple, efficient, serialization protocol based on `DataInput` and `DataOutput`.

NOTE

Serialization is the process of converting structured objects into a byte stream so that it can be persisted over to the disk or transmitted over a network. *Deserialization* is the reverse process of serialization and actually converts the byte stream back into a series of structured objects.

Typically, the data type classes that implement the `Writable` interface can be passed as values. To pass keys, your data type classes must implement the `WritableComparable<T>` interface because keys are sorted before the reduce function can be called; comparability (comparing to each other) thus is needed. The `WritableComparable<T>` interface is a combination of the `Writable` and `java.lang.Comparable<T>` interfaces, so you can use them not only for keys but also for values.

The MapReduce framework comes with basic data type wrapper classes that already have implemented the `WritableComparable` interface (for example, `BooleanWritable`, `ByteWritable`, `DoubleWritable`, `FloatWritable`, `IntWritable`, `LongWritable`, `Text`, `VlongWritable`, and `NullWritable`, a placeholder when the key or value is not needed). If needed, you can create your own custom data type classes by implementing either the `Writable` or `WritableComparable<T>` interfaces.

NOTE

MapReduce API Versions

Hadoop provides two versions of MapReduce APIs. You can find the latest in the `org.apache.hadoop.mapreduce` package. For older ones, look in the `org.apache.hadoop.mapred` package. We recommend using the latest APIs from the `org.apache.hadoop.mapreduce` package and thus refer to it in our examples.

Number of Mappers

The number of Mappers initiated for a MapReduce job depends on the number of `InputSplits` being generated by `FileInputFormat`. Similarly, the number of `InputSplits` generated by `FileInputFormat` depends on a couple other factors. First among them is the `isSplitable` function, which determines whether a file is splittable. If this function returns `false`, the file will not be split and, instead, will be processed as a whole by a single Mapper.

Ideally, the split size is the same as the block size, which is controlled by `dfs.blocksize` (the default value is 64MB or 128MB) and is appropriate for most situations. However, if you want to change the split size, you can use the combination of these three configuration properties to determine the actual split size:

▶ `mapred.min.split.size`—The default value is 1. This configuration comes into the picture only when you set its value to larger than `dfs.blocksize` to set the minimum split size. Changing this property is not recommended in most cases because of the risk of the number of blocks (coming from different data nodes against the data locality policy) that are not local to a given map task. For example, if you set its value to 128MB on a cluster where the block size is 64MB, the input split will be a minimum of 128MB, containing two blocks, each block of 64MB. These two blocks, part of a single input split, might come from two different data nodes.

▶ `mapred.max.split.size`—The default value is the maximum value for the `Long` data type (`Long.MAX_VALUE`), or 9223372036854775807 bytes. This configuration comes into play only when you sets its value to smaller than `dfs.block.size`, forcing the split to be smaller than the block size. Again, setting this value to a lower number causes too many Mappers to be created, which increases overhead in maintaining and monitoring job execution.

▶ `dfs.block.size`—The default value is either `67108864` (64MB) or `134217728` (128MB).

For the actual split size, `max (mapred.min.split.size, dfs.block.size)` sets the lower bound and `min (dfs.block.size, mapred.max.split.size)` sets the upper bound. You calculate the actual split size in the `computeSplitSize()` method of `FileInputFormat`:

`max (mapred.min.split.size, min (mapred.max.split.size, dfs.block.size))`

By default, compressed input files (such as gzip files) are not splittable, although some patches are available for this or you can write your custom code to make it splittable.

NOTE

Recommended Size for InputSplit

Keep each split size small enough for parallelization but large enough to avoid too much overhead in starting and managing too many map tasks. Also, in most cases, using the same size for input split and block size works efficiently.

Partitioner

Partitioning is the process of dividing up the intermediate key-value pairs and determining which Reducer instance will receive which intermediate key-value pairs. A Partitioner class controls the partitioning of the keys of the intermediate map-outputs from Mappers. In other words, the Partitioner class determines which Reducer a given key-value pair (map-output) from Mappers should receive further processing. The default partitioner class, called `HashPartitioner`, partitions the keys typically by a hash function or code that is most suited to the scenario.

You can write your own custom partitioner if you want to change or override the default behavior. In your custom partitioner, you must implement two functions: `configure()` and `getPartition()`. The first uses the MapReduce job configuration to configure the custom partitioner; the second returns an integer between 0 and the number of reduce tasks indexing to which Reducer the (key-value) pair will be sent.

For example, as you can see in Figure 4.8, map-outputs from four Mappers are partitioned (shuffled and moved) to two Reducers (the first contains A and B, and the second contains C and D), based on the partitioning key space mapping. In other words, a single Reducer receives input from several Mappers based on the partitioning key space mapping.

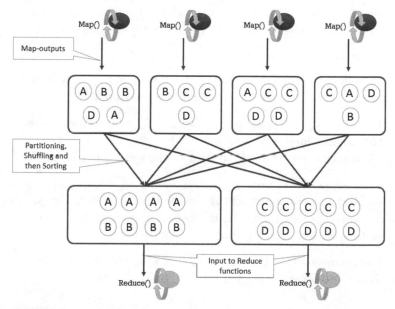

FIGURE 4.8
Partitioning, shuffling, and then sorting map-outputs.

As you see in Figure 4.8, these partitions or subsets of keys (the first subset contains A and B, and the second subset contains C and D) are then input to the Reducers. The total number of partitions or subsets of keys is the same as the number of Reducers for the given MapReduce job.

Each Mapper may emit key-value pairs to any available partition, and all the values for the same key are always sent to the same partition, regardless of the Mappers. Because all Mappers use the same partitioning logic, the destination partition is always the same for a given key, regardless of which Mapper instance generated it.

Reducer

The user-defined Reducer class extends the `Reducer<KeyIn, ValueIn, KeyOut, ValueOut>` base class from the `org.apache.hadoop.mapreduce` package and performs user-defined work during the second phase of the MapReduce job execution. During this phase, the reduce function is invoked for each key in the sorted output, along with an iterator over all the values associated with that key.

From the implementation point of view, a Reducer implementation takes input data in the form of key-value pairs (`k2, list (v2, v2, v2 ...)`) and produces a final key-value output pair, as with (`k3, v3`). In this function, you can write your own logic for each unique key. For example, you can write logic to sum all the values for a given key, or take a maximum value from all the values for that specific key, or take an average of all the values for a specific key.

You can extend from a base class using four methods:

- ▶ `setup (Context)`—Called first and is executed only once in the beginning of the reduce task to initialize the Reducer. The default implementation is a no-op method.

- ▶ `reduce (Object, Iterable<Object>, Context)`—Executed for each unique key and list of its values. A typical implementation of the reduce method iterates over a set of values for each unique key, applies business logic as needed, and writes the result to the output.

- ▶ `cleanup (Context)`—Called only once at the end of the execution of the reduce task (after all the unique keys are processed) to clean up the Reducer's resources. The default implementation is a no-op method.

- ▶ `run (Context)`—Can be overridden for more control (such as with multithreaded Reducers) over the execution of the reduce function.

The Reducer execution has three subphases:

- ▶ **Shuffle**—During shuffling, map-output is copied from each Mapper using HTTP to its intended Reducer (based on key space partitioning).

- ▶ **Sort**—The MapReduce framework merge-sorts map-outputs because different Mappers might produce the same key. The merge-sorted output contains the key-value pairs for a given key contiguously. The shuffle and sort phases occur simultaneously and produce output in the form of keys-values (`k2, (v2, v2, v2...)`) to the reduce function.

▶ **Reduce**—In this phase the `reduce` method is called for each unique key (`<key,` `(collection of values)>`) assigned to the Reducer, and the output is typically written to HDFS with the `RecordWriter` class. The Reducers write their output only to their own output file, which resides in a common directory and typically is named similar to `part-nnnnn`, where nnnnn is the partition ID of the Reducer. As you saw in Figure 4.5, the `RecordWriter` class formats the output from the Reducers when writing to the output files. Note that the output from the reduce method is not sorted again.

As you can see in Figure 4.9, the map-outputs are first shuffled and sorted before making them available to the reduce method. Then the reduce method sums all the ones for each unique key or word and emits a single key-value pair that contains the word followed by the sum of its occurrences.

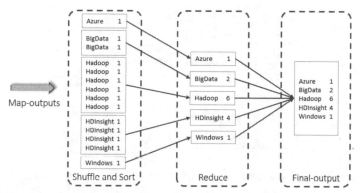

FIGURE 4.9
Reduce function flow for the word count example.

Listing 4.2 shows the implementation of Reducer for the word count example. The reduce method is called for each unique key (or a word, in this case) and then sums the individual count for each word. Finally, it emits a single key-value pair that contains the word followed by the sum of its occurrences.

LISTING 4.2 Reducer Implementation for Word Count Example

```
1:  public static class WordCountReducer
2:      extends Reducer<Text,IntWritable,Text,IntWritable> {
3:  private IntWritable result = new IntWritable();
4:
5:  public void reduce(Text key, Iterable<IntWritable> values,
6:                     Context context
7:                     ) throws IOException, InterruptedException {
8:    int sum = 0;
```

```
 9:    for (IntWritable val : values) {
10:      sum += val.get();
11:    }
12:    result.set(sum);
13:    context.write(key, result);
14:    }
15:  }
```

Figure 4.10 puts together both Mapper and Reducer for the word count example. The map-outputs from both the Mappers (there are two `InputSplits` in this case, so two instances of Mapper have been created) are shuffled and sorted to make them available to the reduce method.

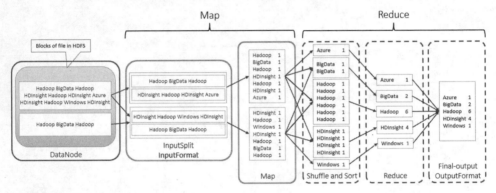

FIGURE 4.10
Map and Reduce functions flow for the word count example.

NOTE

Data Locality Applies to Mappers Only

The concept of data locality applies to the Mapper only as it deals with input files and is not applicable to the Reducer. The MapReduce framework kicks off a Reducer wherever it finds a Reducer slot available; then the map-outputs (based on partition) from all the Mappers are shuffled and sorted, to be executed by the Reduce function on that node.

Combiner

If you notice the amount of data that moves from Mappers to Reducers, you might conclude that you can optimize it with some local aggregation before a data transfer on the network to reach out to the Reducers.

This is where Combiner comes into the picture. You can think of a Combiner as a local or mini Reducer. It operates on data generated by only one Mapper. Optionally, it is useful when there is a possibility to combine at the Mapper level. For example, a Mapper might be emitting more than one record per key, so you can aggregate them locally to pass a single key-value to the Reducer. This lessens the workload (across network shuffle, short, and reduce) that is passed on further to the Reducers, making the Reducers run faster.

This is an optional implementation. When used, it runs after the Mapper and before the Reducers. It receives all data emitted by the Mapper instances as input (still in a circular buffer, as discussed earlier) and tries to combine values with the same key, to compact the map-output (although this does not affect the final output) and minimize the data that needs to be written to local disk or needs to travel to Reducers.

TIP

Although it's not necessary, the Reducer class implementation typically is used for both the Combiner and local aggregation. If you are writing your own class for the Combiner (other than the Reducer implementation), it must extend the `org.apache.hadoop.mapreduce.Reducer` base class and override/implement the `reduce()` method.

Figure 4.11 shows the use of Combiner. Notice the initial 14 key-value pairs as map-outputs; Combiner then does local aggregation, which results in 10 key-value pairs made available to the Reducer. Actually, a Combiner starts gathering the map-output, which comes in the form of (`word`, `1`) in in-memory lists, with one list per key or per word. When a certain number of map-output pairs is gathered, the Combiner is called once per unique key or word, with the in-memory list available as an iterator. Finally, it emits (`key or word`, `count of occurrences`).

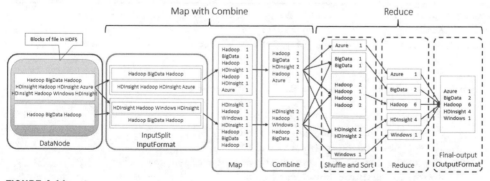

FIGURE 4.11
Map (with combine) and Reduce functions flow for the word count example.

This example seems to have very little compaction, but think of a scenario with a huge data volume in which repetition would be much higher and the Combiner would aggregate to a greater extent.

NOTE

Use the Combiner Wherever Possible

Wherever possible, use the Combiner to optimize and minimize the number of key-value pairs shuffled across the network between Mappers and Reducers, to save on network bandwidth and improve job performance.

The sole objective of the Combiner is to reduce the load on the network or on the Reducer and improve performance. The output of the Reducer must be the same whether or not you are using the Combiner.

Driver

A Driver is a main class that you need to write and use for initializing your MapReduce job. As you saw in Figure 4.5, within the Driver, you specify the job-specific configuration and all the MapReduce components, such as input and output formats, Mapper and Reducer, use of a Combiner (if any), use of a custom partitioner, and so on. The Driver instructs the MapReduce framework to execute your code on a set of specified input files and also controls where the output files will be placed. In addition, the Driver can get the status of the MapReduce job execution. Listing 4.3 shows an implementation of a Driver for the word count example.

LISTING 4.3 Driver Implementation for the Word Count Example

```
1:   public static void main(String[] args) throws Exception {
2:   Configuration conf = new Configuration();
3:   String[] otherArgs = new GenericOptionsParser(conf, args).getRemainingArgs();
4:
5:   if (otherArgs.length != 2) {
6:     System.err.println("Usage: wordcount <in> <out>");
7:     System.exit(2);
8:       }
9:         Job = Job.getInstance(new Configuration());
               job.setJobName("word count");
10:        //Set the Jar by finding where a given class came from.
11:        job.setJarByClass(WordCount.class);
12:
13:        //Set the Mapper for the job.
14:        job.setMapperClass(WordCountMapper.class);
15:        //Set the combiner class for the job.
16:        job.setCombinerClass(WordCountReducer.class);
17:        //Set the Reducer for the job.
```

```
18:             job.setReducerClass(WordCountReducer.class);
19:
20:             //Set only 1 reduce task for this job
21:             job.setNumReduceTasks(1);
22:
23:             job.setOutputKeyClass(Text.class);
24:             job.setOutputValueClass(IntWritable.class);
25:
26:         /**
           * TextInputFormat and TextOutputFormat are defaults and
           * you can skip below two lines. Provided here for clarity sake.
          */
27:             job.setInputFormat(TextInputFormat.class);
28:             job.setOutputFormat(TextOutputFormat.class);
29:             //Path for input file
30:             FileInputFormat.addInputPath(job, new Path(otherArgs[0]));
31:             //Path for output file
32:             FileOutputFormat.setOutputPath(job, new Path(otherArgs[1]));
33:             // Submit the job, then poll for progress until the job is complete
34:             System.exit(job.waitForCompletion(true) ? 0 : 1);
35:         }
36: }
```

As you can see in Listing 4.3, the setMapperClass() and setReducerClass() methods identify the mapping and reducing functions. Likewise, the setCombinerClass, setOutputKeyClass(), and setOutputValueClass() functions identify the Combiner function. They also specify the output data types for the Reducer and setMapOutputKeyClass() and setMapOutputValueClass() functions, to specify the output data types for the Mapper. If these function calls are absent, the Reducer output data types are assumed to be the output types of the Mapper as well. You can use the submit method to submit the job to the cluster and return immediately, or you can use the waitForCompletion method to submit the job to the cluster and wait for it to finish.

Listing 4.4 contains the complete program for the word count example. As you can see, it has the implementations of Mapper, Reducer, and Driver. Driver is the main program you need to invoke to kick off MapReduce job execution.

LISTING 4.4   Complete Program for Word Count Example

```
package org.apache.hadoop.examples;
import java.io.IOException;
import java.util.StringTokenizer;
import org.apache.hadoop.conf.Configuration;
import org.apache.hadoop.fs.Path;
import org.apache.hadoop.io.IntWritable;
import org.apache.hadoop.io.Text;
```

```java
import org.apache.hadoop.mapreduce.Job;
import org.apache.hadoop.mapreduce.Mapper;
import org.apache.hadoop.mapreduce.Reducer;
import org.apache.hadoop.mapreduce.lib.input.FileInputFormat;
import org.apache.hadoop.mapreduce.lib.output.FileOutputFormat;
import org.apache.hadoop.util.GenericOptionsParser;

/**
 * This is a word count example - MapReduce job that
 * reads the text input files, breaks each line into words
 * and counts them. The output is a locally sorted list of words and the
 * count of how often they occurred.
 */
public class WordCount {

/**
* Counts the words in each line of the InputSplit.
* For each line, it breaks the line into words and emits them as
* (word, 1).
*/
public static class WordCountMapper
    extends Mapper<Object, Text, Text, IntWritable>{

private final static IntWritable one = new IntWritable(1);
private Text word = new Text();

public void map(Object key, Text value, Context context
                ) throws IOException, InterruptedException {
  StringTokenizer itr = new StringTokenizer(value.toString());
  while (itr.hasMoreTokens()) {
    word.set(itr.nextToken());
    context.write(word, one);
    }
  }
}

/**
 * A reducer class that just emits the sum of the input values
 * for each unique key or word
 */
public static class WordCountReducer
    extends Reducer<Text,IntWritable,Text,IntWritable> {
private IntWritable result = new IntWritable();

public void reduce(Text key, Iterable<IntWritable> values,
                   Context context
                   ) throws IOException, InterruptedException {
  int sum = 0;
```

```java
    for (IntWritable val : values) {
      sum += val.get();
    }
    result.set(sum);
    context.write(key, result);
    }
}


/**
 * A Driver is a main program that you need to write and use
 * it for initializing your MapReduce job.
 * User needs to invoke this method to submit the map/reduce job.
 */
public static void main(String[] args) throws Exception {
Configuration conf = new Configuration();
String[] otherArgs = new GenericOptionsParser(conf, args).getRemainingArgs();

if (otherArgs.length != 2) {
  System.err.println("Usage: wordcount <in> <out>");
  System.exit(2);
    }


    Job job = Job.getInstance(new Configuration());
     job.setJobName("word count");
    //Set the Jar by finding where a given class came from.
    job.setJarByClass(WordCount.class);

    //Set the Mapper for the job.
    job.setMapperClass(WordCountMapper.class);
    //Set the combiner class for the job.
    job.setCombinerClass(WordCountReducer.class);
    //Set the Reducer for the job.
    job.setReducerClass(WordCountReducer.class);

    //Set only 1 reduce task for this job
    job.setNumReduceTasks(1);

    job.setOutputKeyClass(Text.class);
    job.setOutputValueClass(IntWritable.class);
    /**
     * TextInputFormat and TextOutputFormat are defaults and
     * you can skip below two lines. Provided here for clarity sake.
     */
    //job.setInputFormatClass(TextInputFormat.class);
    //job.setOutputFormatClass(TextOutputFormat.class);
    //Path for input file
    FileInputFormat.addInputPath(job, new Path(otherArgs[0]));
    //Path for output file
```

```
        FileOutputFormat.setOutputPath(job, new Path(otherArgs[1]));
        // Submit the job, then poll for progress until the job is complete
        System.exit(job.waitForCompletion(true) ? 0 : 1);
    }
}
```

Another MapReduce Job Example

The word count MapReduce job is the simplest example, but you can express many real-world problems in terms of Map and Reduce—hence, you can leverage the MapReduce framework to solve and process them.

For example, consider that you have city-wide sales data stored daily basis in an HDFS block (see the leftmost box in Figure 4.12). You want to write a MapReduce job to compute the total sales for each city, by grouping on the city. Your MapReduce job implementation will be similar to the earlier example for word count, but instead of emitting 1 as a value from the Mapper, you will get an actual sales amount, such as (NYC, 75) or (LAX, 60).

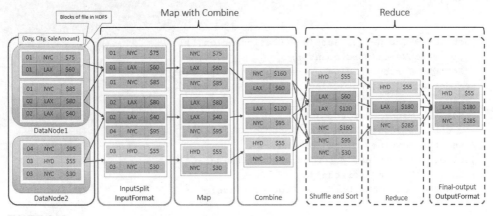

FIGURE 4.12
Map (with combine) and Reduce functions flow for total sales by city.

Figure 4.12 shows the MapReduce job execution flow for this requirement. As you can see, the InputFormat splits the input data from HDFS into InputSplits, which eventually becomes input for the Mapper (remember, for each input split, one instance of the Mapper is created). The Combiner then combines the map-outputs (local aggregation), and on the Reducer side, it gets shuffled and sorted to make it available to the reduce method. Finally, the reduce method sums all the values for each city and produces the final output, as shown in the rightmost box in Figure 4.12.

Tool Interface

If you look at the code for Driver, you will see that all the configuration information is hard-coded. For any change in configuration, you must apply it in the source code, compile and rebuild another JAR file, and deploy the JAR again to Hadoop. This is not only complicated and time consuming, but also prone to error because you must change the code every time the configuration changes.

To help you in this scenario, the Hadoop framework has a Tool interface that supports the handling of generic command-line options. You can pass your configuration information from the command-line interface (CLI) or when you are actually executing your MapReduce job. For example, the driver code has the configuration `job.setNumReduceTasks(1)`, which sets one reduce task for the job. However, if you want to pass another value (for example, `10`) when executing your code, you can pass it from the CLI as shown here:

```
hadoop jar "/example/jars/hadoop-mapreduce.jar" wordcount -D mapred.reduce.tasks=10
"/example/data/HDInsight.txt" "/example/data/"
```

You can supply some additional useful generic options from the command line while executing the job:

- ▶ `-conf <configuration file>`—Specify an application configuration file
- ▶ `-D <property=value>`—Use a value for a given property
- ▶ `-fs <local|namenode:port>`—Specify a local or remote name node
- ▶ `-jt <local|jobtracker:port>`—Specify a local or remote JobTracker
- ▶ `-files <comma separated list of files>`—Specify comma-separated files to be copied to the MapReduce cluster
- ▶ `-libjars <comma separated list of jars>`—Specify comma-separated JAR files to include in the classpath
- ▶ `-archives <comma separated list of archives>`—Specify comma-separated archives to be unarchived on the compute

When you decide to use the Tool interface, you need to use the ToolRunner utility to help run classes that implement the Tool interface. It works with the `GenericOptionsParser` class to parse the generic Hadoop command-line arguments; it modifies the configuration of the Tool interface.

Context Object

The Context object enables the Mapper, Reducer, and Driver to interact with the rest of the Hadoop system even though they are executed in different processes. It includes configuration data for the job, as well as interfaces that enable it to collect and emit output (`context.write (Key, Value)`) and to exchange required system- and job-wide information. You can use the Context object for one of these actions:

▶ Report progress

▶ Set application-level status messages

▶ Update counters

▶ Indicate they are alive

GO TO ▶ Refer to **Hour 5** for detailed information on counters.

NOTE
_____

MapReduce for Hadoop 1.0 and Hadoop 2.0

MapReduce went through a complete overhaul in Hadoop 2.0 and is now called MapReduce 2. However, the MapReduce programming model has not changed; you can still use the MapReduce APIs as discussed throughout the book. YARN provides a new resource management and job scheduling model, and its implementation executes MapReduce jobs. In most cases, your existing MapReduce jobs will run without any changes. In some cases, minor changes and recompilation might be needed.
_____

Summary

MapReduce is a fault-tolerant, batch-oriented, parallel programming framework. It enables developers to write a program that processes a massive amount of data in a distributed manner across hundreds or thousands of nodes in the cluster so that it finishes data processing in a reasonable amount of time on the large volume of data.

In this hour, you looked in detail at the MapReduce programming paradigm, its architecture, the different components of a MapReduce job, and the MapReduce job execution flow. In the next hour, you explore advanced concepts related to MapReduce (such as MapReduce streaming, MapReduce joins, distributed caches, different types of failures, and performance optimization for MapReduce jobs) and YARN of Hadoop 2.0 (architecture, different components, job execution pipeline in YARN, different types of failures, and so on).

Q&A

Q. What are the benefits of using the MapReduce framework?

A. The MapReduce framework offers several benefits over the traditional way of programming. For example, the MapReduce framework uses the concept of data locality, which means that it moves the computation near the data instead of moving the data to the computation. In doing so, it significantly improves performance. The framework breaks a bigger problem into smaller problems and executes these smaller problems on several nodes in parallel, to ensure that the problem can be solved in a reasonable amount of time. It scales up to hundreds of thousands of nodes, for extremely parallel execution. The framework has built-in fault tolerance capabilities, so if any task fails, the framework itself recovers and re-executes it transparently.

Q. What is the difference between a JobTracker and a TaskTracker?

A. The MapReduce framework is based on a master and slaves architecture in which the master is called the JobTracker and the slaves are called TaskTrackers. A JobTracker is a daemon that runs on the master node for submitting, scheduling, monitoring, and tracking the execution of the MapReduce jobs across TaskTrackers; it also re-executes failed tasks, up to a predefined limit of retries. A TaskTracker is a daemon that runs on slave nodes and accepts tasks (Map, Reduce, and Shuffle operations) from the JobTracker for execution.

Q. What does a Mapper do?

A. A Mapper function processes input data to generate intermediate key-value pairs as output. Basically, input data is split into smaller chunks or key-value pairs, and the Map function is applied on each chunk or key-value pair separately; they run in parallel with other Map functions on other sets of key-value pairs. The Mapper function creates a new output list (intermediate key-value pair) by applying a function to individual elements of an input data.

Q. What does a Reducer do?

A. A Reducer merges all the values that share the same key to produce the final single output or key-value pair. Results generated from the Map function are shuffled and sorted by framework to make them available to the Reducer for further processing; this means that the Reducer can start only after the Mapper completes. In other words, the Reduce function iterates over the input values to produce an aggregate value as output for each specific key. Usually 0 (zero) or 1 (one) output value is generated per Reduce function invocation.

Q. What does a Partitioner do?

A. A Partitioner determines to which Reducer a given intermediate key-value pair from the Mappers should go. Based on the partitioning process being used, map-outputs from all the Mappers are shuffled across appropriate Reducers.

Q. What does a Driver do?

A. A Driver is a program for initializing and configuring MapReduce jobs. Within the Driver, you specify the job-specific configuration and also specify all the MapReduce components (input and output formats, Mapper and Reducer, use of a Combiner, use of a custom partitioner, and so on). The Driver instructs the MapReduce framework to execute your code on a set of specified input files and also controls where the output files will be placed. The driver can also get the status of the MapReduce job execution.

Q. What is the use of the Context object?

A. The Context object allows the Mapper, Reducer, and Driver to interact with the rest of the Hadoop system, even though they are executed in different processes across different nodes of the cluster. You can use the Context object to report progress, set application-level status messages, update Counters, indicate whether the Mapper and Reducer are alive, and more.

Quiz

1. What is the difference between the Combiner and the Reducer?

2. How are resources from a TaskTracker considered for use?

3. How does the JobTracker identify a TaskTracker for task execution?

4. Explain the concept of data node and TaskTracker co-location.

5. How can you ensure that you can pass different configuration values when you are executing your MapReduce jobs without actually compiling every time?

Answers

1. Both the Combiner and the Reducer normally perform the same operation—the difference lies in the dataset they work on and where they run. The Combiner runs right after the Mapper function and works on the dataset generated by that specific Mapper function. This is not absolutely necessary, but it is added to the flow to optimize performance by reducing the amount of data that needs to move across nodes in the cluster. The Reducer, on the other hand, runs on the dataset (after the shuffle and sort) that comes from all the Mapper functions and produces the final output.

2. Each TaskTracker in the cluster has a set of computational slots (Map slots as well as Reduce slots). The available slots indicate the number of tasks that the specific TaskTracker can accept for processing simultaneously.

By default, the configurations `mapred.tasktracker.map.tasks.maximum` and `mapred.tasktracker.reduce.tasks.maximum` both have a default value of 2. This means that two Mappers (two slots for maps) and two Reducers (two slots for Reducers) at a given instance on a TaskTracker can run simultaneously in parallel.

3. When assigning a task to a TaskTracker for processing, the JobTracker first tries to locate a TaskTracker with an available free slot on the same server that has the data node containing the data (to ensure data locality). If it doesn't find this TaskTracker, it looks for a TaskTracker on another node in the same rack before it goes across the racks to locate a TaskTracker.

4. Typically, both the TaskTracker and data node daemons run on the same node. This way, the JobTracker tries to process the data on the same node where the data exists (to ensure data locality). Typically (by default configuration), three replicas of a data block are stored on three different nodes (or data nodes). When the JobTracker requires this data block to serve the request, it reaches out to the nodes for executing the TaskTracker in order from closest to farthest. If the JobTracker finds an available slot to process the request on any of these nodes, it processes the request there; otherwise, it spins a TaskTracker on another node in the same rack before it goes across racks to locate an available slot for TaskTracker execution (which is very rare). In the latter case, data movement might occur across nodes. Although spinning a TaskTracker on another rack is not that frequent it might be required when a local slot is not available where data exists, so that submitted request is not blocked.

5. The tool interface supports the handling of generic command-line options: You can pass your configuration information from CLI or when you are actually executing your MapReduce job. The hard-coded configuration in the driver program is overwritten by these passed-on configuration values while executing the program.

MapReduce—Advanced Concepts and YARN

What You'll Learn in This Hour:

▶ DistributedCache

▶ Hadoop Streaming

▶ MapReduce Joins

▶ Bloom Filter

▶ Performance Improvement

▶ Handling Failures

▶ Counter

▶ YARN

▶ Uber-Tasking Optimization

▶ Failures in YARN

▶ Resource Manager High Availability and Automatic Failover in YARN

In Hour 4, "The MapReduce Job Framework and Job Execution Pipeline," you learned about the MapReduce programming paradigm, its architecture, the different components of a MapReduce job, and MapReduce job execution flow. This hour primarily focuses on advanced concepts related to MapReduce (including MapReduce streaming, MapReduce joins, distributed caches, different types of failures, and performance optimization for MapReduce jobs).

In this hour, you also explore YARN, which brings a major architectural change to the Hadoop platform and opens a new window for scalability, performance, and multitenancy. You dive deep into the YARN architecture, its different components, and its job execution pipeline, and you look at how YARN transparently handles different types of failures.

DistributedCache

The MapReduce framework DistributedCache feature enables you to share static data globally among all nodes in the cluster. Unlike reading from HDFS, in which data from a single file typically is read from a single Mapper, the distributed cache comes in handy when you want to share some data (for example, global lookup JAR files [or archives] that contain executable code) with all the Mappers of the job, or for initialization or libraries of code that all nodes in the cluster might need to access.

Distributed cache files can be either private or public. Private distributed cache files are cached in a local directory private to the user whose jobs need these files (shared by all tasks and jobs of the specific user only). Public distributed cache files are cached in a global directory; file access is set up so that they are publicly visible to all users and are shared by tasks and jobs of all users on all the machines of the cluster.

To use distributed cache functionality, the data location should be set before the MapReduce job starts. To do this, you must create an instance of the `DistributedCache` class while setting up your job; then use the `DistributedCache.addCacheFile()` method to add files that should be sent to all nodes in the cluster (or to the machines where the actual execution is to start) and make them available for local use.

Likewise, to access these distributed cache files on a machine where Mapper is running, call the `DistributedCache.getLocalCacheFiles()` method to get the list of paths local to the current node for the copies of the cached files. Then you can use regular Java file I/O mechanisms, such as `java.io.FileInputStream`, to access and read the file of the returned path.

Hadoop Streaming

Hadoop was written entirely in Java; therefore, Java is a native language for writing MapReduce jobs. However, if you don't come from a Java background, you don't need to worry: Hadoop provides the Hadoop Streaming utility (implemented in the form of a JAR file) that enables you to create Map and Reduce executables in other languages than Java (C#, Python, and so on) and execute them in the Hadoop cluster.

When you execute your executables (Map and Reduce) that were written in languages other than Java, the Hadoop Streaming utility creates a MapReduce job, submits the job to the intended Hadoop cluster, monitors the progress of the job until it completes, and reports back. During execution, the Mapper and Reducer executables read the input data line by line from the standard input stream (STDIN) and emit the output data to the standard output stream (STDOUT).

By default, the Hadoop Streaming utility processes a line-oriented or text data stream in which each line is considered to be a record. It works on key-value pairs just like the standard Java

MapReduce programs; it uses the first tab character to separate the key from the value of each record. The first part is considered to be the key and the rest is considered to be the value. When a record has no tab, the entire record is considered the key, leaving the value an empty string. You can change this default behavior. For example, suppose your data itself contains a tab character—you can then use another character to separate the key from the value.

When executing an executable for the Mapper or the Reducer task, the Mapper or Reducer task launches a separate process after initialization and runs a specified executable in it (see Figure 5.1). In the case of the Mapper, the Mapper task converts the input data into lines and feeds them to the STDIN of the process (launched for the Mapper executable). The Mapper collects line-oriented outputs from the STDOUT of the process and converts each line into key-value pairs. Likewise, in the case of the Reducer, the Reducer task converts input key-value pairs into lines and feeds them to the STDIN of the process (launched for the Reducer executable).

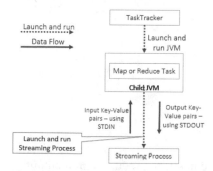

FIGURE 5.1
Hadoop Streaming process flow.

The Hadoop Streaming utility sorts and groups these key-value pairs according to the key before calling the reduce method. The Reducer task collects the line-oriented outputs from the STDOUT of the process and converts each line into a key-value pair. In both cases, during task execution, the Mapper or Reducer Java process passes input key-value pairs to the external process (the executable you have specified). The external process runs it through the user-defined map or reduce function and passes the output key-value pairs back to the Mapper or Reducer Java process.

The TaskTracker assumes that the child Java process running in the child JVM runs the map or reduce function.

In both cases, during task execution, the Mapper or Reducer Java JVM process passes input key-value pairs to the external process (the executable you specified). The external process runs it through the user-defined map or reduce function (in those external processes) and passes the output key-value pairs back to the Mapper or Reducer Java JVM process. During this whole process, the TaskTracker assumes that the child Java JVM process runs the map or reduce function and is not aware of the external processes.

As Hadoop Streaming goes through an additional layer, it might be slightly slower than when running native Java-based MR jobs.

GO TO ▶ We talk in detail about using Hadoop Streaming and demonstrate how to use the C# language to write MapReduce job in **Hour 10, "Programming MapReduce Jobs,"** and **Hour 11, "Customizing HDInsight Cluster with Script Action."**

MapReduce Joins

The MapReduce job example, in Hour 4, is based on a single dataset. It's not uncommon, how-ever, to have multiple datasets in a single problem and to join them to produce the final output. For example, as you can see in Figure 5.2, you might have one dataset that contains sale infor-mation and another one that contains product information. You might need to join these two datasets to produce your desired result.

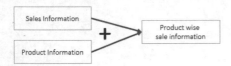

FIGURE 5.2
Joining sales information with product information.

The MapReduce framework enables you to join two or more datasets to produce a final output. Writing these types of MapReduce jobs requires much effort and expertise, so it's often easier to use a high-level framework such as Hive or Pig to write queries that involve joining several datasets. You can easily use Hive to write a query in the HiveQL query language (similar to SQL) in just a few lines of code, which would translate into hundreds of lines of code in a MapReduce job. We explore joining multiple datasets using Hive and Pig in subsequent hours; this section gives you the basics on joining datasets in MapReduce.

Based on implementation, if the Mapper of the MapReduce job performs the join, it is called a *map-side join*; if the Reducer performs the join, it is called a *reduce-side join*. If one dataset is small enough (which is the case in most Big Data scenarios), you can consider using the DistributedCache (to cache the smaller table and use it as lookup reference during the join oper-ation by each Mapper) to do joining during the map phase only. If both datasets are large, first see whether the map-side join is possible before you opt for the reduce-side join.

Map-Side Join

The map-side join is most efficient in terms of performance, but it requires input data to each map task, to be partitioned and sorted by the same key (joining key). All the records for a par-ticular key (joining key) must reside in the same partition. If you have two datasets partitioned into the same number of partitions, and all the partitions are sorted on the key (joining key), the Mapper can locate the right data and perform a join on it during the map phase itself. For example, in Figure 5.2, if both pieces of output data are partitioned and sorted on ProductID, the map-side join can be applied to perform the join.

If not, then to provide the partitioned and sorted input data to the Mappers (which are supposed to do the join), you can use another MapReduce job before it, to get your output data in the way your Mapper needs (partitioned and sorted) to join the data. Note that sometimes running an extra MapReduce job to structure the data your Mapper needs for the join defeats the efficiency gain.

Reduce-Side Join

Reduce-side joins are common, flexible, and much simpler to implement, but they can be inefficient. For a reduce-side join, you don't need to have overhead to provide a structured dataset (as in the case of a map-side join, discussed earlier). However, because of the overhead in the huge volume of data transferred from Mappers to Reducers during the shuffle and sort phase (the shuffle and sort of the large datasets across the network can be resource intensive), this type of join is less efficient. Remember, the join does not happen until the reduce phase.

In most cases, most of the data is dropped from the result set during join operations; therefore, it is better to eliminate unnecessary data in the Mapper only (so that unnecessary data does not move across network)—and even better to perform the join during the map phase only.

The basic idea with the reduce-side join is that the Mapper produces a record with a partitioned group key (a joining key—this is ProductID in Figure 5.2) and is tagged with additional data as the value in its key-value pair. The MapReduce framework ensures that the same keys end up in the same partitioner or Reducer, so by default, data is already organized to be joined. Now the Reducer needs to cache a key and compare it against incoming keys. As long as the keys match, it can join the values (tagged data) from the corresponding keys.

Bloom Filter

We talked about joining two datasets earlier. If both datasets are large enough, you might have to use an inefficient reduce-side join. The problem with reduce-side joins is that a huge volume of data is shuffled and sorted across the network before the Reducer can begin. Later, during the join, the Reducer might drop most of these records. If one of the datasets is small, you can use a map-side join with the DistributedCache, which is quite efficient. But the problem is, it works only if one dataset is small. Otherwise, you might start getting memory out of exception, leaving you no choice than to use a reduce-side join.

To help you in this case, Hadoop enables you to use the *Bloom Filter*, a data structure that tests the containment of a given element in a set. One dataset can be augmented into a Bloom Filter (encodes the dataset into a bit vector), which is a smaller representation of the actual data and can be replicated easily to each node.

At the Mapper, each record fetched can be used to check whether an individual record is present in the Bloom Filter (a smaller table representation of one of the input datasets) and only if it exists then to emit that particular record for passing on to the Reducer. Because a Bloom Filter is guaranteed not to provide false negatives, the result is always accurate. In other words, with the help of the Bloom Filter, the Mapper can filter out all the records not matched in the join and pass only a subset of the dataset matched in the join to the Reducer to work on this.

The Bloom Filter object supports these two main methods:

▶ **add method**—Adds an object, an element, or, more specifically, a key to the set.

▶ `contains` or `membershipTest` **method**—Returns either `true` or `false`, based on whether an object or an element or a key is in the set. Per the Bloom Filter property, it can return a false positive but never a false negative (for assurance that the set doesn't have the object, element, or key queried).

Performance Improvement

This section explores techniques for improving performance.

Use of Compression

We talked about using the Combiner to combine the map output before sending it to the Reducer, to reduce the overall overhead on network I/O during the shuffle and sort operation across the network. Using the Combiner wherever applicable makes sense to improve performance, but you can also easily use compression on intermediate data, produced by Mappers, to reduce the amount of disk space needed for storage and network I/O during the shuffle and sort operation.

Hadoop has built-in support to compress and decompress the intermediate data (the Mapper's output) using these two properties and works transparently to the developer. As a developer, you just need to set these properties; the framework compresses the output from Mappers and decompresses it back when input to the Reducers. As a developer, you don't need to write any code for this, other than setting appropriate properties—it also works transparently.

▶ `mapred.compress.map.output`—This is set to either `true` or `false` to indicate whether the Mapper output should be compressed.

▶ `mapred.map.output.compression.codec`—This is considered only if the previous property has a `true` value. It indicates which `CompressionCodec` should be used for compressing the Mapper's output. Some built-in codec classes available to use include `DefaultCodec`, `GzipCodec`, and `BZip2Codec`.

NOTE

A *codec* is an implementation of a compression-decompression algorithm.

```
conf.setBoolean("mapred.output.compress", true);
conf.setClass("mapred.output.compression.codec", BZip2Codec.class,
CompressionCodec.class);
```

When deciding whether to use compression, you need to make sure the file format that you intend to use is splittable. For example, the sequence file format supports compression and offers splitta-bility; hence, it is recommended in most cases. Synchronization markers denote splittable boundar-ies. You can set the output format to `SequenceFileOutputFormat` to use sequence file format.

The Hadoop framework allows compression and decompression at two levels. In the default, record-level compression, each record is compressed separately. In block-level compression, a block of records is compressed together, achieving a higher compression ratio as it applies a more aggressive compression and the possibilities of higher redundancy in the data. In block compression, data is not compressed until it reaches a threshold (block size); then all key-value pairs are compressed together as a block.

NOTE

Even if you have data stored in uncompressed format in HDFS, using compression and decompres-sion for intermediate data makes sense because it minimizes the amount of data Mappers produce that is written to disk and transferred across the network to reach the Reducers.

Reusing Java Virtual Machine

As discussed earlier, by default, a TaskTracker kicks off a Mapper or Reducer task in a separate Java Virtual Machine (JVM) as a child process. Separation and isolation sound like good ideas so that the failure of map task does not break the TaskTracker itself, but an initialization cost is incurred each time a separate JVM spins off for the task execution. This additional initialization cost increases further if the task needs to read a large data structure in memory (DistributedCache or data needed for joining).

If the execution of the task take several minutes, this additional initialization cost is not significant compared to the overall time the task takes. But with small, fast-running tasks, this additional initialization cost might be significant.

To solve this problem, the MapReduce framework has the property `mapred.job.reuse.jvm.num.tasks`, which enables you to reuse a JVM across multiple tasks of the same job. The additional initialization cost can be compensated or shared across many tasks of the same job.

`mapred.job.reuse.jvm.num.tasks` has a default value of 1. This means JVMs are not used across tasks (of the same job), though you can set it to any positive value greater than 1 to indicate that each specific JVM can be reused (for execution of the tasks from the same job) up to that many times. For example, if you set it to 5, the MapReduce framework will try to reuse a JVM-created instance up to five times after it is created. If you are not sure, you can set it to -1 to indicate no limit on the number of tasks (of the same job) a JVM can run and let the MapReduce framework decide on maximum reuse of JVM.

NOTE

Reuse of JVM in YARN

As of this writing, YARN does not support reusing JVM for task execution.

MapReduce Job Scheduling

Earlier, the MapReduce framework used the first in, first out (FIFO) method to process the job requests or with job scheduling. When a client submitted a job, it was queued at one end, and the JobTracker picked it up from the other end (the oldest one) for execution. This approach had no concept of the priority or size of the job. Sharing a large, shared MapReduce cluster between users or applications was difficult because a large running job starves subsequent jobs in its queue.

This approach might seem reasonable for a traditional batch processing workload in which clients submitted jobs and JobTracker executed them in that order. When you have varieties of workloads (from small jobs to large ones) and you want to support different types of job processing needs by users or applications, you need greater control over the scheduling mechanism. You must provide guaranteed capacity to each job in a fair way.

Initially, this FIFO approach for processing jobs was intermixed with JobTracker logic, making it inflexible and giving administrators no control over this. But later, Hadoop made it extensible and started support for a *pluggable job scheduling component*. Now you can use the FIFO method, the Capacity Scheduler, the Fair Scheduler (one of the most widely used), or any other available or custom scheduling component to plug in to your Hadoop cluster to resolve job contention.

Fair Scheduler

Facebook developed the Fair Scheduler (Hadoop-3746 Jira). It organizes jobs into pools; each user is assigned to a pool, and each job submitted belongs to a specific pool (based on the pool the user has been assigned to). The idea behind fair scheduling is to provide a fair share (an equal share of resource over time, on average) of resources to every jobs.

If a single job is running at a given point in time in the cluster, it can request entire cluster resources, but as additional jobs are submitted, resources (Map slots or Reduce slots) that are free or are being freed up are assigned fairly to the new jobs in a way to ensure that each job gets roughly the same amount of resources, on average. Smaller jobs that require less time can access the resources and finish, while bigger jobs that require more resources run simultaneously.

This approach also allows some interactivity among jobs, allowing greater responsiveness of the Hadoop cluster to the variety of job types submitted. In a pool, you can set priority on jobs to give more capacity to a job higher in priority.

Apart from that, the Fair Scheduler also allows a guaranteed minimum share of resources to each pool, to ensure that certain users or applications always get sufficient resources. When a pool contains jobs for execution, it is guaranteed to get a minimum share, but when the pool does not need its full guaranteed minimum share, the excess is split among other pools.

To keep a single user from flooding the clusters with hundreds of jobs, the Fair Scheduler can limit the number of jobs per application or pool. If it exceeds this number, the additional jobs need to wait until the previously submitted jobs complete.

The Fair Scheduler also introduces the notion of preemption. If a pool has not received its guaranteed minimum share for a certain period of time, the Fair Scheduler kills tasks in pools that are running over capacity (tasks in the other pools), to give the resources to the pool running under capacity. When the Fair Scheduler kills tasks, it picks the most recently launched tasks from the pools running over capacity, to minimize the waste of computation time.

TIP

Even though the Fair Scheduler kills tasks from pools running over capacity, it does not cause the job to fail. In fact, Hadoop ensures that jobs are resubmitted transparently, without users knowing.

Capacity Scheduler

Yahoo! developed the Capacity Scheduler (Hadoop-3445 Jira). It shares some of the scheduling principles of the Fair Scheduler but takes a slightly different approach to multi-tenants or multi-applications (for example, short interactive jobs, large batch jobs, and guaranteed-capacity production jobs) scheduling. It offers an assurance to meet service-level agreements (SLA) under peak or near-peak conditions.

The Capacity Scheduler can be used in a larger cluster that has multiple independent target users and target applications that require a guarantee of minimum capacity so that they can meet their SLA. As in the Fair Scheduler's pool, the Capacity Scheduler has the similar concept of a queue. Hadoop cluster resources are allocated to those queues of the Capacity Scheduler, to guarantee minimum resources; administrators can configure soft limits and optional hard limits on the resource capacity allocated to each queue.

The queues of the Capacity Scheduler can be even more hierarchical—for example, a queue can be the child of another queue. A Hadoop cluster resource is made up of a number of queues, each with an allocated guaranteed minimum capacity (configurable number of map and Reduce slots). The sum of all the queue's guaranteed minimum capacity should not be more than the overall capacity of the Hadoop cluster.

Inside each queue of the Capacity Scheduler, jobs are scheduled using the FIFO method. This helps organizations simulate FIFO scheduling, with priorities, in each queue targeted for the specific application or tenant. Also, as these queues are monitored, the Capacity Scheduler ensures that if a queue is not consuming its allocated resource capacity, the unused or excess resource capacity can be loaned to other starved queues; the queue can always reclaim it when needed. This provides a greater level of elasticity in a most cost-effective manner.

One difference with respect to the Fair Scheduler is the presence of strict access control lists (ACLs) on queues. ACLs control which users can submit a job to a specific queue (basically, a person or an organization is tied to a specific queue). A user cannot submit a job to a queue, or that user will not be able to view or modify the jobs from a queue on which he or she does not have access.

NOTE

Job Scheduler in YARN

The job scheduling mechanism has been described in the context of JobTracker (Hadoop 1.0), but it applies to YARN (Hadoop 2.0) as well and works in a similar way.

Handling Failures

Failures are inevitable—no matter what you do, it's going to happen sometime. Fortunately, the MapReduce framework has been designed to handle most of these types of failures on its own, to complete job execution even without user intervention.

JobTracker Failure

The JobTracker is a single point of failure (in Hadoop 1.0), and its failure is a serious issue. All jobs that were running when it failed must be resubmitted when the JobTracker restarts. The possibility of JobTracker failure is very low, but when it happens, all jobs need to be resubmitted. The good news is that, with Hadoop 2.0 YARN, things have changed and it's no longer a problem.

GO TO ▶ We talk about high availability and automatic failover in the section **"Resource Manager High Availability and Automatic Failover in YARN"** at the end of this hour.

TaskTracker Failure

Using heartbeat signals, each TaskTracker reports to the JobTracker with its progress and the number of Map and Reduce slots available. If a TaskTracker doesn't send heartbeat signals often enough, the JobTracker assumes it to be in a failed state; the JobTracker then reschedules the work that particular TaskTracker was doing (or supposed to be doing) and reassigns it to a different TaskTracker.

When the JobTracker stops receiving heartbeat signals from a TaskTracker, it waits for 10 minutes before it assumes that the TaskTracker is lost and removes it from its list of TaskTrackers. (In the Hadoop version, the JobTracker can be configured with either the `mapred.tasktracker.expiry.interval` property or the `mapreduce.jobtracker.expire.trackers.interval` property. It is specified in milliseconds; the default value is `600000`, or 10 minutes.) Any in-progress tasks or completed map tasks of incompleted job are rescheduled to run on another available TaskTracker. Completed map tasks are rescheduled again because intermediate output from the previous execution (on the failed TaskTracker) might not be available to the JobTracker.

The JobTracker declares a TaskTracker blacklisted if the tasks from the same job the TaskTracker executed failed four times (controlled with the properties `mapred.max.tracker.failures` and `mapred.max.tracker.blacklists`), even if the TaskTracker itself did not fail. TaskTrackers are blacklisted in two ways:

▶ **Per-MapReduce job blacklisting**—Prevents the scheduling of new tasks from that specific MapReduce job, although the TaskTracker can still accept tasks from other MapReduce jobs, as long as it is not blacklisted cluster-wide. This happens when a TaskTracker has task failure from a single MapReduce job greater than the value for the `mapred.max.tracker.failures` property.

▶ **Cluster-wide blacklisting**—Prevents the scheduling of new tasks from all MapReduce jobs. A TaskTracker is blacklisted cluster-wide if the number of blacklists from successful jobs (the fault count) exceeds the value for the `mapred.max.tracker.blacklists` property or has been manually blacklisted using the `hadoop job -blacklist-tracker <host>` command.

TIP

Blacklisted TaskTrackers continue to send heartbeat signals to the JobTracker and continue to run tasks assigned to them so that they finish them. These blacklisted TaskTrackers return to normalcy after one day, after you restart them, or after they rejoin the cluster.

Task Failure

A TaskTracker creates a child JVM instance, reduces the count of available map or Reduce slots based on the task it intends to execute, and starts executing the map or reduce task in it. During execution, if a task running in the child JVM fails because of a bug in the function or because of any other runtime exception, the task reports the failure to the parent TaskTracker before it exits. The error then is logged into the user logs. At this time, the TaskTracker marks that specific task execution attempt as failed and releases the resource (Map slot or Reduce slot, based on the task running) allocated to it so that another task can use it.

Next, the TaskTracker notifies the JobTracker (using the heartbeat message) about the task failure. The JobTracker reschedules this task to be executed again, probably on another TaskTracker.

By default, four failures of a task are absorbed; the JobTracker keeps rescheduling before it finally gives up and declares the job as failed. The number of failures the JobTracker absorbs is controlled by the `mapred.map.max.attempts` property for map tasks and the `mapred.reduce.max.attempts` property for reduce tasks.

When you are doing analysis on a large volume of data, hundreds of thousands of tasks sometimes are kicked off to process your request. In such a case, if a few failures occur, you want to ignore them and continue processing so that the job completes. MapReduce enables you to define the percentage of task failures that can be ignored and avoid marking the job as a failure if the task failures are within that defined percentage. Based on the Hadoop version, you use either the `mapred.max.map.failures.percent` property or the `mapreduce.map.failures.maxpercent` property to set the maximum percentage of acceptable failures for a map task. You use the `mapred.max.reduce.failures.percent` property or the `mapreduce.reduce.failures.maxpercent` property for a reduce task to specify the percentage of failures the MapReduce framework should ignore.

In certain cases, such as when the MapReduce framework might kill a task, if one task from the speculative execution (more on this in the next section) completes successfully, the MapReduce framework automatically kills the other one. Likewise, if the TaskTracker itself fails, the MapReduce framework kills all the tasks that specific TaskTracker kicked off. These killed tasks are not counted as failed attempts (with respect to the `mapred.map.max.attempts` or `mapred.reduce.max.attempts` properties) because they were not killed as the fault of the task itself.

If a TaskTracker does not hear a progress update (to indicate that the task is alive) from the child JVM, it could be because it is hanged or a task is taking a significant amount of time during execution. The TaskTracker then assumes that the task has failed and kills the child JVM instance. The amount of time a TaskTracker has to wait to take this decision is controlled by the `mapred.task.timeout` property (you can set this at the cluster or job level; it is specified in milliseconds, with a default value of `600000`, or 10 minutes). You might need to set this property to a higher value (or to `0`, to indicate that no timeout should happen) if your task is doing some complex processing and is expected to take a long time.

Speculative Execution

As discussed earlier, the MapReduce framework breaks a bigger problem into smaller subproblems or tasks and then executes each one in parallel across many nodes of the cluster. If any of the tasks fail during execution, the built-in fault tolerant feature of the MapReduce framework identifies this and re-executes the same task either on the same node or on another node of the cluster so that the job can complete successfully.

Now consider that one of the tasks takes longer than expected to execute (which is not actually a failure and, hence, does not cause re-execution by the MapReduce framework), causing an overall delay in the execution of the job. Remember, Reducers will not be started until all the Mappers of the job have completed; likewise, a job is not considered completed until

▶ All the Mappers have completed, if the job has no Reducer(s)

▶ All the Reducers have completed, if the job has Reducer(s)

To take care of this problem, the MapReduce framework uses the concept of speculative execution: It launches a backup or speculative task for an identified slow-running task to do the same work the original task was doing, in parallel. In other words, it identifies a task that is running slower than expected and kicks off a backup or speculative task (maybe on the same or on another node that contains the replica of the same data) that does the same work the slow-running task was doing.

The important point to note here is that a speculative or backup task is executed only when the MapReduce framework identifies a task that is running slower than expected (identification is done based on the overall progress it has made with respect to other tasks of the same job). The MapReduce framework never kicks off two copies of the same task at the beginning of job execution itself, to avoid a race between them to get the best execution time. Speculative execution is intended only to prevent slow tasks from dragging down the job's overall execution time.

The MapReduce framework keeps monitoring both the tasks (the original and the speculative or backup). Whichever task completes first (either the original or the speculative task) is taken into consideration. The MapReduce framework kills the other task (which was supposed to do the same work) because the other completed task finished the same work.

Speculative execution might be helpful when an issue with hardware or network configuration causes the task to hang or slow down. But if the issue is a bug in the program, that might be likely to cause trouble every time it gets executed. In that case, it's better to fix the bug in the program and then run the job again.

By default, speculative execution is ON, but you can turn it OFF or ON for map tasks or reduce tasks separately using the `mapred.map.tasks.speculative.execution` or `mapred.reduce.tasks.speculative.execution` properties either at cluster level or at the job level. Keeping speculative execution ON is recommended, but sometimes you want to turn it OFF to increase cluster efficiency (speculative execution has an overhead, and on a busy cluster, this reduces overall throughput) or to avoid conflict from both tasks (original one and speculative). For example, if a task is expected to write to an external shared file, these two tasks (the original and the speculative) might collide with each other in an attempt to create or write to the same external shared files.

Handling Bad Records

The MapReduce framework tries to execute a task four times before it marks the job as failed. It attributes the task failure to hardware, the network, or some other reason beyond the task's control and assumes that, on subsequent execution, the task should run successfully. This approach works as long as no data is causing the task to fail. Then the task will fail every time you run at the same place with the same reason.

Depending on the analysis you are doing (for example, if you are doing analysis on a large volume of data), skipping or ignoring a few records might be acceptable. In that case, you might write your Mapper or Reducer to gracefully handle those bad records while processing without actually causing the runtime exception to happen or the task to fail. But in some cases, such as if you are using a third-party library or you don't have access to the source code, that might not be possible. Then you can instruct the MapReduce framework to automatically skip bad records on subsequent task retries.

By default, skipping mode is disabled because of the extra overhead or bookkeeping it requires. You can enable it by using the `SkipBadRecords` class either in Mapper or Reducer or in both. When enabled, two task failures are considered to be a normal failure. On the third failure, the MapReduce framework captures the data that caused the failure. The fourth time, the MapReduce framework skips the identified data to avoid failure again.

All the bad records that are detected and skipped are written to HDFS in the sequence file format in the job's output directory under the `_logs/skip` subdirectory, for later analysis as needed.

Counter

The MapReduce framework provides built-in counters to gather application-level statistics or metrics that can be used for maintaining quality control, diagnosing a problem, monitoring and tracking the progress of jobs, and more. Some of these built-in counters report various metrics for your job: for example, `FILE_BYTES_READ`, `FILE_BYTES_WRITTEN`, `NUM_KILLED_MAPS`, `NUM_KILLED_REDUCES`, `NUM_FAILED_MAPS`, and `NUM_FAILED_REDUCES`. The MapReduce framework increments their values automatically in response to the respective events.

Beside built-in counters, the MapReduce framework enables developers to create and define user-defined or custom counters, in case the existing built-in counters do not suit your need. You can increment (with a positive value as the parameter) or decrement (with a negative value as the parameter) the value of the counter inside the Mapper, Reducer, or Driver—they are globally available to the job. The increment method is synchronized, to avoid a race condition in incrementing and decrementing a counter value with parallel executing code.

NOTE

Counter for Communication

Think of counters as lightweight objects that provide a simple mechanism for communication between a Driver, a Mapper, and a Reducer during execution. You can use counters to gather job-related statistics and metrics, and you can access them from anywhere (Mapper, Reducer, or Driver) in your application.

You can create and define the custom counter using a Java enum that contains the names of all the custom counters for your job and acts as a group of user-defined counters:

```
public enum MyCounters {
MapperCounter,
ReducerCounter
}
```

You can use the increment method of the context object to increment or decrement the value of a counter (in either the Mapper or the Reducer). The MapReduce framework then globally aggregates the value of the counter:

```
//Incrementing counter value by 1
context.getCounter(MyCounters.MapperCounter).increment(1);
//Decrementing counter value by 1
context.getCounter(MyCounters.MapperCounter).increment(-1);
```

Alongside the built-in counters, the values for your custom counters are displayed on a summary web page for your job. Alternatively, you can access them programmatically using the following statements:

```
long mapperCounterValue = job.getCounters().findCounter(MyCounters.MapperCounter);
long reducerCounterValue = job.getCounters().findCounter(MyCounters.MapperCounter);
```

During execution, each task periodically sends the counters and their values to the TaskTracker. In return, the task is sent to the JobTracker, where it is consolidated to provide a holistic view for the complete job.

Because overhead is incurred when having and maintaining too many counters (remember, storing each counter requires additional memory used by the JobTracker), the maximum number of counters is limited to 120, by default, to ensure that no single job accidentally uses all the available JobTracker memory. You can change this, however, using the `mapreduce.job.counters.limit` property in the `mapred-site.xml` configuration file for a cluster-wide change; alternatively, you can change it in your job, which makes it applicable to your job only.

```
<property>
  <name>mapreduce.job.counters.limit</name>
  <value>1200</value>
</property>
```

NOTE

Counters Come with an Overhead

Counters are a good means for tracking some important global data on an application level. But counters are fairly expensive in terms of the memory needed to store them (counters from each map or reduce task) at the JobTracker level during the entire application execution cycle. Thus, they are not recommended for use to aggregate very fine-grained statistics of applications.

YARN

Hadoop 1.0 was designed and developed more than seven years ago. The need then was to process a massive amount of data in parallel, distributed over hundreds of thousands of nodes in a batch-oriented manner. Now times have changed, and the hardware has gotten even cheaper. Companies today demand more horizontal scaling while, at the same time, ensuring high availability; companies want to process data interactively as well as with batch mode data processing. Hadoop 2.0 overcomes these limitations with its new architecture and components. Consider some of the limitations of Hadoop 1.0, with respect to the MapReduce processing framework and the advances of Hadoop 2.0:

▶ **Single point of failure**—JobTracker, like name node, is a single point of failure.

▶ **Limited to running MapReduce jobs on HDFS, a lack of support for interactive queries, or an underutilized HDFS**—The MapReduce component of Hadoop 1.0 was designed for batch mode processing, and it had no true support for interactive and streaming query support. Iterative applications implemented using MapReduce were several times slower and thus were not suitable for usage-like graph processing. In Hadoop 1.0, only MapReduce can access data in HDFS. This is restrictive and does not allow multitenancy, forcing other applications (which do not work on batch mode processing) to store data somewhere other than the HDFS or to use HDFS via MapReduce only.

▶ **Low computing resource utilization**—Computing resources on each node are divided as Map slots and Reduce slots in a hard partition manner. Suppose that, at a given time, many Mappers are running and only a few Reducers are running. All the Map slots would be used, but only a few Reduce slots are being used. No resources are being shared for better utilization. In other words, Mappers can use only Map slots—if they are not available, the Mappers must wait, even though some Reduce slots might be available.

▶ **Overly crowded JobTracker**—The JobTracker alone is responsible for managing both resources and the application life cycle. As more jobs are run concurrently, the chance of failure is higher. All the jobs then need to be resubmitted by the users because all the running and queued jobs are killed upon restart. The JobTracker suffers from an increased memory requirement (for a larger cluster or complex MapReduce jobs), causing problems related to scalability and reliability. The JobTracker also has a rigid threading model.

In Hadoop 2.0, MapReduce has undergone a complete overhaul, with a new layer on top of HDFS. In Figure 5.3, the shaded box indicates core Hadoop components and the white box indicates different technologies in the Hadoop ecosystem. This new layer is called YARN (Yet Another Resource Negotiator). YARN takes care of two major functions, called resource management and application life-cycle management. the JobTracker took care of these previously.

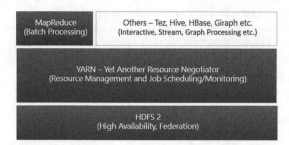

FIGURE 5.3
Hadoop 2.0 high-level architecture and components.

Now MapReduce is just a batch-mode computational layer sitting on top on YARN. YARN, however, acts like an operating system for the Hadoop cluster, providing resource management and application life-cycle management functionalities and making Hadoop a general-purpose data-processing platform that is not constrained only to MapReduce. This change brings some important benefits:

▶ **Segregation of duties**—Now MapReduce can focus on what it is good at doing: batch mode data processing. YARN focuses on resource management and application life-cycle management.

▶ **Multitenancy**—Other applications than MapReduce can connect to YARN and gain access to the data stored in HDFS. This brings a broader array of interaction patterns for the data stored in HDFS beyond just MapReduce. It broadens the horizon. Now you have interactive, streaming graphics processing support for accessing data from HDFS by leveraging YARN, all sharing common resource management. Now YARN can handle much more than batch-oriented MapReduce jobs and can assign cluster capacity to the different applications so that it meets the service level demands of a particular workload and stays in line with constraints such as queue capacities and user limits.

▶ **Scalability and performance**—Unlike the JobTracker, which previously handled resource management and application cycle management together, YARN has a new global Resource Manager and per-machine Node Manager to manage the resources of the cluster and form the computation fabric of the cluster. At the same time, it has an application-specific Application Master that negotiates resources from the Resource Manager and manages the application life cycle. This segregation brings the new scalability and performance of Hadoop 2.0.

NOTE

MapReduce 2.0 Versus YARN

In Hadoop 2.0, MapReduce is referred to as MapReduce 2.0, MRv2, NextGen MapReduce, or YARN. You will find this different nomenclature used in different artifacts. But just to summarize, the resource management and application life-cycle management capabilities have been moved from the classic MapReduce into the YARN layer. MapReduce can now focus on what it does best (batch-mode data processing), and YARN can work as an operating system for the Hadoop cluster serving requests from multiple applications, not just limited to MapReduce.

In other words, MapReduce 2 and YARN are different; referring to them as the same thing is misleading or deceiving. YARN is a generic framework or data operating system that provides Hadoop with cluster resource management and job scheduling/monitoring capabilities. YARN sits on top of HDFS and provides these services to any application targeting it, to leverage the services in Figure 5.3, whereas MapReduce 2 is just one application among many applications leveraging services provided by YARN.

Note that YARN is in no way tied to MapReduce only and can be leveraged by any application wanting to use it. You can find the latest details on other applications that leverage the power of YARN here: http://wiki.apache.org/hadoop/PoweredByYarn.

As you saw in Figure 5.3, YARN now takes care of resource management, job scheduling, and monitoring, making MapReduce a pure computational layer on top of YARN for batch processing. It's now possible for the other components to be written natively over YARN, but that doesn't just happen. Even in a Hadoop 2.0 cluster, many things still translate down into MR: The community is working on YARN versions of most components, and these are in various states of completion.

Different Components of YARN

Aligning with the original master-slave architecture principle, even YARN has a global or master Resource Manager for managing cluster resources. YARN also has a per–node/slave Node Manager that takes direction from the Resource Manager and manages resources on that specific node. This forms the computation fabric for YARN. Apart from that, a per-application Application Master is nothing but an application-specific library tasked with negotiating resources from the global Resource Manager and coordinating with the Node Manager(s) to execute and monitor the execution of the tasks. Other components are containers, a group of computing resources such as memory, CPU, disk, and network. This section covers these components in detail.

Resource Manager

For a YARN-based Hadoop cluster, a global Resource Manager manages the global assignment of compute resources to the applications targeting the Hadoop cluster. The Resource Manager has two main components (see Figure 5.4).

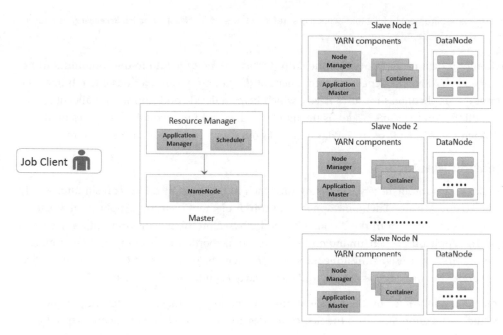

FIGURE 5.4
YARN components.

Resource Manager—Application Manager

The job client initiates a talk with the Application Manager, a component of the Resource Manager that handles job submission and negotiates for the first container (from the Scheduler, as discussed next) so that the application-specific Application Master can be executed. The Application Manager also provides services to restart the application-specific Application Master container in case it detects any failure of an Application Master instance.

Resource Manager—Scheduler

The Scheduler component of the Resource Manager plays a role in scheduling and allocating cluster resources that are subject to various constraints, such as capacities, queues, and SLA. This is based on the resource requirements of the applications. The cluster resources are described in terms of the number of containers (memory, CPU, disk, network, and so on) and the application-specific tasks in those containers, based on the chosen pluggable scheduling policy (FIFO, Fair Scheduler, Capacity Scheduler, and so on). The `yarn.resourcemanager.scheduler.class` property is in the `yarn-default.xml` configuration file. The Scheduler component is a pure scheduler, which means it performs the scheduling functions to allocate computing resources to run the applications' tasks, based on the resource requirements of the applications. The Scheduler does not itself monitor or track the status of the execution of the applications' tasks or restart any failed tasks.

GO TO ▶ To learn more about pluggable schedulers, refer to the section **"MapReduce Job Scheduling,"** earlier in this hour.

The notion of moving computation to the data (instead of moving data to the computation) has not changed in YARN. The Scheduler component of the Resource Manager has enough information about the application's resource needs, which helps it decide on locating and allocating containers available on the same nodes as the data. If it does not find available resources on those nodes (which contain replicas of the data), it looks out for another node in the same rack.

Application Master

Hadoop 2.0 added multitenancy capabilities in which multiple applications can simultaneously utilize the Hadoop cluster. Each new application can implement a custom Application Master, which requests resources from the Resource Manager based on the specific application need and manages the application's scheduling and task execution coordination. Many of these applications use the Hadoop cluster simultaneously with the help of Application Masters; these applications run under the notion of isolation, and each one gets guaranteed capacity.

Based on the job submitted by the job client, the Application Manager executes that application-specific Application Master in the first container assigned. Next, the application-specific Application Master has the responsibility to negotiate the appropriate resources from the Scheduler component of the Resource Manager, based on that specific application's need. Other responsibilities include maintaining the task queue, managing the application or job life-cycle by coordinating with the Node Manager(s) to launch the tasks, monitoring the tasks' execution progress, tracking their status, and handling task failure.

In terms of responsibilities, an Application Master is similar to the JobTracker. However, unlike the JobTracker, which runs on the master node, the Application Master runs on the slave node. The Application Master relieves the Resource Manager (master node) from being overcrowded, manages the life cycle of that specific application, and provides the scaled-out model for the Application Master so that many applications can work together.

Multiple Application Masters from different versions of the same application also can run side by side, allowing users to implement a rolling upgrade of the user application or the cluster according to their own schedule. For example, you can run multiple versions (each version might be served by the same Application Master or a different one) of the MapReduce jobs on the same cluster.

NOTE

Common Application Master

Typically, you will find a separate Application Master for each application, but that is not a rule. You could have a single common Application Master for more than one application.

When the task finishes executing, the Application Master releases the container assigned to it and returns it to the Resource Manager so that other queued requests can use it. When all the tasks of the job are completed and all the containers are released, the Application Master deregisters itself with the Resource Manager and then terminates itself—but before that, the Application Master passes the management and metrics information it has accumulated and aggregated from all the tasks of the job to the Job History Server so that it can be accessed later as needed.

NOTE

Job History Server

The application-specific Application Master is instantiated when a request comes in for that specific application and is terminated when the job completes. The Application Master also accumulates and aggregates task metrics and logs—but what happens to those collected metrics and logs when Application Master terminates?

To preserve this useful data, the MapReduce application framework has another daemon, the Job History Server. It is a kind of centralized location for storing all the job or task execution-related metrics and logs so that the information is available even after the Application Master is terminated. By default, job history files are stored in the directory `/mr-history/done` on HDFS. The directories are organized by date when the MapReduce jobs were executed. To access this history log later, the Job History server provides REST APIs to get the status on finished applications.

NOTE

Timeline Server

Currently, the Job History server supports only MapReduce and provides information on finished MapReduce jobs only. This information is very specific to MapReduce because it contains the MapReduce counter, Mappers, and Reducers. This is fine if you have only MapReduce, but YARN is intended to be used beyond MapReduce. YARN thus introduces a new Timeline Server to collect job execution logs beyond MapReduce, which will eventually take over the Job History server.

The Timeline Server provides generic information about completed applications and per-framework information for running, along with completed applications through two different interfaces.

Application-generic information provides an execution log related to YARN resource management or application-level data, such as queue name, username, application attempts, containers used by each application, and metrics related to those containers. Application-specific information is specific to an application, as with MapReduce, counters, Mappers, and Reducers.

Based on the failure of the Application Master, the Resource Manager (or, more specifically, the Application Manager component of Resource Manager) can relaunch the Application Master in another container.

NOTE

Multitenancy

You can think of Apache MapReduce, Apache Giraph, Apache Tez, Distributed Shell, and Open MPI as applications. Each has an Application Master specific to it. Here, *multitenancy* means running these many types of applications side by side, targeting the same YARN-based cluster.

Node Manager

You can think of Node Manager the same as TaskTracker of earlier MapReduce (classic MapReduce or MapReduce 1.0) in terms of functionalities it provides, though it's more efficient and flexible than TaskTracker. The Node Manager daemon runs on each slave node in the cluster, as you saw in Figure 5.4, and accepts instructions from the Application Master to launch the task in the allocated container, monitor their resource usage (CPU, memory, disk and network), ensures it does not use more resources than it has been allocated, and sends the resource usage report to the Scheduler component of Resource Manager.

Container

You can think of a container as a basic processing unit and an encapsulation of cluster resources (CPU, memory, disk, network and so on), allocated always on a single node (a container does not share cluster resources across nodes—refer to Figure 5.4). It is flexible and contains a specific amount of resources allocated, based on its request. On a single node, more than one container and multiple tasks can be executed in these multiple containers in parallel.

Unlike the notion of fixed-type Map and Reduce slots in Hadoop 1.0—which had a significant negative impact on Hadoop cluster utilization because at different times either Map or Reduce slots were not fully utilized—Hadoop 2.0 introduces the concept of containers to overcome this issue in Hadoop 1.0.

Typically, an Application Master (itself also a container or one run in a container) receives the additional containers from the Resource Manager during resource negotiation and then talks to the Node Manager to start or stop containers and tasks of the job requested. And unlike classic MapReduce, in which resources are split into hard-coded Map and Reduce slots, the container can be of variable size, based on each application's (or, more specifically, task) specific requirement.

NOTE

Containers Allocated to the Application Master

You can think of a container granted to an application as a right provided to the application-specific Application Master to use a specific amount of node resources (CPU cores, memory, and so on) on a specific host. The Application Master reaches out to the Node Manager on which the container has been granted, to launch the tasks by utilizing the allocated resource.

Note that the application-specific Application Master was written by application developers, so the Node Manager should not trust it fully. The Node Manager verifies the container allocation information presented to it by the Application Master with Resource Manager in secure mode (remember, the Resource Manager and Node Managers form the computation framework in YARN) so that it can be sure it does not respond to the fake container allocation information received from the Application Master.

NOTE

As of this writing, only CPU cores and memory (refer to this article for configuring YARN and MapReduce memory: http://docs.hortonworks.com/HDPDocuments/HDP2/HDP-2.0.6.0/bk_installing_manually_book/content/rpm-chap1-11.html) are supported as part of the container. Changes are frequent in the Hadoop world, though, so you might see more support for other resources (disk, network, and so on) by the time this book reaches you.

Job Execution Flow in YARN

Figures 5.5 and 5.6 illustrated the job execution or request/response pipeline and flow. The following description matches the numbering in Figures 5.5 and 5.6, for better understanding.

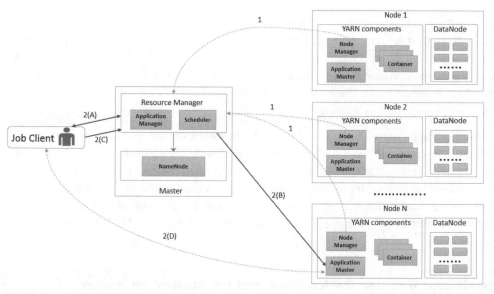

FIGURE 5.5
Job execution on flow in YARN—part 1.

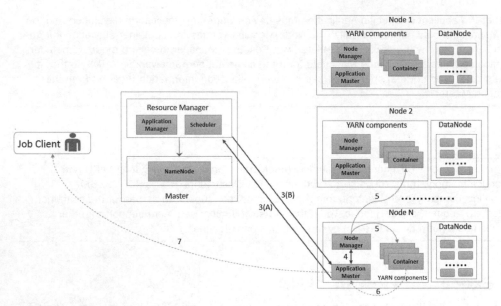

FIGURE 5.6
Job execution on flow in YARN—part 2.

1. All the Node Managers of the cluster register with the Resource Manager (by individual Node ID so that Resource Manager can identify them) upon restart or when they join the cluster. Through heartbeat signals, they send the Resource Manager information about the counters (cluster resources) they hold (either in use or free). Based on this information, the Resource Manager builds the inventory of cluster resources.

2. To submit a job in YARN, the job client reaches out to the Application Manager component of the Resource Manager (2A) with the necessary specifications. The Resource Manager requests that the Scheduler component allocate the first container so that it can initiate an instance of the application-specific Application Master (2B). At this time, the Application Manager informs the job client of his status (2C). The Application Master is initiated; going forward, the job client can directly talk to the Application Master for job status (2D). For MapReduce applications, the Application Master is MRAppMaster.

NOTE

Communication Between the Job Client and the Application Master

The instantiated Application Master registers itself with the Resource Manager so that the Resource Manager can identify it and provide information about it to the job client. Then on the job client, once the information is received from the Resource Manager, the job client can directly communicate with its own Application Master.

3. The Application Master requests cluster resources, defined in terms of containers, from the Scheduler component of the Resource Manager (3A). The Scheduler responds with allocated resources needed for job execution (3B). This does not necessarily have to happen at the beginning of job execution: During execution, the Application Master can request additional containers if there is a need or can release a container when its use is complete.

   While allocating computing resources or containers, the Scheduler takes into account data locality information (hosts and racks) that was computed by InputFormat and stored inside InputSplits on HDFS. It tries to allocate a container on the same data node (on which the data exists); if it does not find any, the Scheduler looks for another data node in the same rack.

4. The Application Master reaches out to the Node Manager(s) to execute the tasks in the allocated containers. For a MapReduce job, the MRAppMaster application master retrieves InputSplits (created by job client and copied to HDFS) and then creates map tasks based on the number of input splits and reduce tasks based on the mapreduce.job.reduces property. Based on mapreduce.job.ubertask.enable property and the size of the MapReduce job, the Application Master (MRAppMaster) either executes the MapReduce job in the same JVM or container (as of the Application Master) or reaches out to the Node Manager(s) for job execution.

5. The Node Manager executes the containers. This involves a Java process with YarnChild as the main class. It is executed in a separate dedicated JVM; it copies required resources (such as configuration or JAR files) locally and executes the map or reduce tasks.

   The Node Manager kicks off the tasks and reports the resource utilization back to the Resource Managers (step 1 in Figure 5.5). When a task completes, the allocated container is released and the Resource Manager is informed so that the container can be reused for some other purpose.

6. The Application Master tracks the execution of the tasks and containers, monitors progress, and reruns the tasks if any failures occur. Tasks executed in the containers report their status to the parent Application Master, where the Application Master accumulates and aggregates status information and execution metrics.

7. The Application Master keeps updating the job client (directly, not via a Resource Manager) about the overall progress of the job execution. The job client polls every second for the status update from an Application Master and poll interval can be configured with the mapreduce.client.progressmonitor.pollinterval property. Unlike classic MapReduce, where TaskTracker just keeps on passing status information to JobTracker and JobTracker has responsibilities to accumulate and aggregate the information to assemble the current status of the job, in case of YARN the Application Master accumulates and aggregates the information to assemble current status of the job and client query it from the Application Master (without going through the Resource Manager).

NOTE

Communication Between the Job Client and Application Master after Application Master Failure

When the Resource Manager instantiates an Application Master during job initialization, it passes the Application Master's address to the job client. The job client then caches the address and reaches out directly to the Application Master for a job progress update. This way, after job initialization, the client bypasses the Resource Manager (reducing the overall overload on the Resource Manager) and gets a job status update directly from the Application Master. But what happens when the Application Master fails? How does a job client know about the new Application Master instance and its new address?

The job client keeps communicating to the Application Master on the cached address (which it got from the Resource Manager). Upon Application Master failure, the job client encounters the time-out exception while trying to reach out to the Application Master. Then it reaches out again to the Resource Manager to find out the address for the new instance of the Application Master. At this point, it discards the previous cached address and caches the new address for the new instance of the Application Master; from then on, it directly communicates to this new instance of the Application Master.

Uber-Tasking Optimization

The concept of uber-tasking optimization in YARN applies to the smaller jobs: Smaller jobs are executed in the same container or in the same JVM in which the Application Master is running. The basic idea behind uber-tasking optimization is that the distributed task allocation and management overhead exceeds the benefits of executing tasks in parallel for smaller jobs; executing smaller jobs in the same JVM or container of Application Master is better.

In other words, the Application Master will not negotiate an additional counter for the smaller jobs. Instead, those smaller jobs will be executed in the same single, first container allocated to the Application Master. The `maxmaps`, `maxreduces`, and `maxbytes` properties control the definition of smaller jobs. By default, this feature is disabled, but you can change this feature and its behavior with these properties:

▶ `mapreduce.job.ubertask.enable`—The default value is `false`; you can change it to `true` to enable it. As of this writing, this feature is in technical preview, so check the YARN documentation for its general availability and recommendations for using it in production systems.

▶ `mapreduce.job.ubertask.maxmaps`—The default value is `9`. You can change it to any downward value. This property indicates a threshold for maximum maps tasks, beyond which a job is considered too large for uber-tasking optimization.

▶ `mapreduce.job.ubertask.maxreduces`—The default value is `1`. You can changed it to any downward value only for now (currently, no more than one Reducer is supported). This property indicates a threshold for reduce tasks, beyond which a job is considered too large for uber-tasking optimization.

▶ `mapreduce.job.ubertask.maxbytes`—The default value is the HDFS block size and is controlled by the property `dfs.block.size`. You can change this to any downward value if the underlying file system is not HDFS. This property indicates a threshold for the number of input bytes, beyond which a job is considered too big for the uber-tasking optimization.

Failures in YARN

This section talks about failures that can happen in YARN, in the context of a MapReduce job running on YARN or the MRAppMaster Application Master.

Task Failure

A task (or container) is executed in a child JVM by the Node Manager. It's more likely to fail than any other components because of a bug in the function or because of another runtime exception. When a task fails, it reports the failure to the Application Master. The Application Master then marks that specific task execution attempt (not the task itself) as failed.

If it doesn't receive a ping from a task (or container) in the defined time (controlled with the `mapreduce.task.timeout` property), the Application Master assumes that the task is in a failed state and cannot be contacted. In this case, too, it marks the specific task execution attempt (not the task itself) as failed.

The Application Master reschedules it for an execution attempt, probably on another Node Manager. By default, rescheduling takes place four times, as controlled by the `mapreduce.map.maxattempts` property for Mappers and the `mapreduce.reduce.maxattempts` property for Reducers. When all the attempts are exhausted, the task itself is now marked as failed.

As with classic MapReduce, MapReduce 2.0 enables you to define the percentage of task failures to ignore and avoid marking the job as a failure if the task failures are within a defined percentage. You define the percentage with `mapreduce.map.failures.maxpercent` to set the maximum percentage of acceptable failures for a map task, and you use `mapreduce.reduce.failures.maxpercent` for a reduce task.

TIP
Sometimes when you are doing analysis on a large volume of data, hundreds of thousands of tasks are kicked off to process your request. When this occurs, if there are few failures and you would like to ignore those failures, then continue processing until the job is complete.

Application Master Failure

An Application Master is similar to the JobTracker in terms of the responsibilities it performs. Unlike classic MapReduce, however, YARN can gracefully handle the failure of the Application

Master. The Application Master sends heartbeat signals to the Resource Manager. If the Application Master fails, or if no heartbeat signal is received from the Application Master, the Resource Manager allocates a new container and initiates a new instance of Application Master to run in it for a specified number of times, as well as to recover the completed tasks.

You can configure the `yarn.resourcemanager.am.max-attempts` property in the `yarn-site.xml` configuration file to specify the maximum number of Application Master restart attempts. By default, its value is 2, so at least one restart of the Application Master will be done in case of failure. This setting is a global value that applies to all Application Masters, although each Application Master can specify, via API (or via the `mapreduce.am.max-attempts` property in the `mapred-site.xml` configuration file for the MapReduce Application Master), its individual maximum value (which must be less than or equal to the global value).

The new instance of Application Master can recover the state of tasks executed by the previous failed instance of the Application Master, to avoid duplicate runs of these tasks. You can control this behavior for MapReduce with the help of the `yarn.app.mapreduce.am.job.recovery.enable` property in the `mapred-site.xml` configuration file.

Node Manager Failure

Node Managers are similar to TaskTrackers in classic MapReduce in terms of the responsibilities they perform. Each Node Manager sends status updates (including information about in-use and free containers or resources) to the Resource Manager using heartbeat signals. If a Node Manager doesn't send heartbeat signals often enough, the Resource Manager assumes it to be in failed state and removes it from the pool of available Node Managers after 10 minutes (you can control this with the `yarn.nm.liveness-monitor.expiry-interval-ms` property in the `yarn-default.xml` configuration file; the default value is `600000` milliseconds, or 10 minutes). Then the Resource Manager will not schedule or allocate a container from the failed Node Manager.

The Application Master or the task that was executing on that Node Manager restarted, as discussed earlier.

Resource Manager Failure

As discussed earlier, JobTracker in Hadoop 1.0 is a crucial central component. Unfortunately, it has not been designed to recover from failures, so it is a single point of failure. When a JobTracker fails, the administrator must bring it up manually and the job clients must submit all the queued and running jobs again. When Hadoop 1.0 was designed, its main intent was to do batch processing (running in parallel across several nodes). Now, however, Hadoop is not just limited to batch processing—it's intended to be used for interactive querying, stream processing, graph processing, and more. With so many use cases and uses by different applications, having a component with a single point of failure that must be recovered manually is not acceptable.

To overcome this challenge, YARN in Hadoop 2.0 has come up with the Resource Manager high availability feature. This new feature lets the Resource Manager save its state to the persistent shared storage device. When the stand-by Resource Manager changes its role to become active when the earlier active Resource Manager fails, it reads out the saved application state information from the shared persistent storage device and assumes the responsibilities of the active Resource Manager (see Figure 5.7).

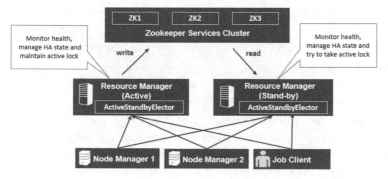

FIGURE 5.7
Resource Manager—automatic failover with ZooKeeper.

By default, this feature is not enabled, but you can turn it ON using the `yarn.resourcemanager.recovery.enabled` and `yarn.resourcemanager.store.class` properties in the `yarn-default.xml` configuration file. See the next section to learn more about how Resource Manager high availability works.

NOTE
_____

JobTracker Versus Resource Manager Failure

Resource Manager does not perform the same duties as JobTracker, but it's a crucial central component in the YARN architecture. Its failure can bring down the Hadoop cluster if the high availability feature is not enabled.

_____

Resource Manager High Availability and Automatic Failover in YARN

The Resource Manager high availability and automatic failover feature requires you to add another redundant Resource Manager (refer to Figure 5.7), which works as a standby Resource Manager and takes over the active role when the active Resource Manager crashes. The failover trigger happens either manually using the admin (through CLI) or through the integrated failover-controller when automatic failover is enabled.

Resource Manager high availability is controlled by two main properties, `yarn.resourcemanager.recovery.enabled` and `yarn.resourcemanager.store.class`. You can use either of these two state storage types as persistent state storage:

- ▶ **`FileSystemRMStateStore`**—A file-based state-store built on top of any simple file systems. You use this property to specify the URI for the file system location: `yarn.resourcemanager.fs.state-store.uri`.

- ▶ **`ZKRMStateStore`**—A ZooKeeper-based state-store implementation. The best part of this store implementation is that the store is implicitly fenced; only one Resource Manager can write to the store at any point in time and hence is recommended as a store for Resource Manager high availability setup.

By default, automatic detection and failover happens through the Zookeeper-based `ActiveStandbyElector` (a failure detector and a leader elector component). The `ActiveStandbyElector` elects the active Resource Manager when the earlier active Resource Manager crashes. At this point, the standby Resource Manager transitions to active state, loads the internal state from the designated state store, starts all the internal services, and resubmits the applications (all those running applications when the earlier active Resource Manager was active). The Resource Manager won't resubmit the applications if they were already completed before the earlier active Resource Manager died.

`ActiveStandbyElector` or the failover controller is embedded in the Resource Manager itself. Unlike HDFS, no additional ZooKeeper Failover Controller (ZKFC) daemon needs to be running on the Resource Manager.

When the active Resource Manager fails, in-progress Application Masters and Node Managers keep running, wait for the Resource Manager to come back and keep buffering their updates. When the Resource Manager comes back online (or the standby Resource Manager turns to active), Application Masters synchronize with it, whereas all the Node Managers start sending status reports to it.

How to Reach an Active Resource Manager

When you set up Resource Manager high availability, you must specify the addresses for all the Resource Managers in the `yarn-site.xml` configuration files used by clients, Application Masters, and Node Managers to communicate with the Resource Managers. Clients, Application Masters, and Node Managers try to connect to the Resource Managers in a round-robin manner until they reach the active Resource Manager and then cache this address—until it starts getting a communication exception (when the active Resource Manager dies) and have to go again through the round-robin to identify the new active Resource Manager.

NOTE

MapReduce for Hadoop 1.0 and Hadoop 2.0

MapReduce has undergone a complete overhaul in Hadoop 2.0 and is now called MapReduce 2. However, the MapReduce programming model has not changed—you can still use the MapReduce APIs as discussed in this book. YARN provides a new resource-management and job scheduling model, and its implementation executes MapReduce jobs. In most cases, your existing MapReduce jobs will run without any changes. In some cases, you might need to make minor changes and deal with recompilation.

Summary

In this hour, you learned advanced concepts related to MapReduce, including the MapReduce Streaming utility, MapReduce joins, Distributed Caches, different types of failures, and performance optimization for MapReduce jobs.

You also took a look at YARN, which brings a major architectural change in the Hadoop framework and opens a new window for scalability, performance, and multitenancy. You explored the YARN architecture, its components, its job execution pipeline, and how YARN transparently handles different types of failures.

Q&A

Q. What is DistributedCache and why it is used?

A. The DistributedCache feature shares static data globally among all nodes in the cluster. Unlike reading from HDFS, in which data from a single file typically is read from a single Mapper, DistributedCache comes in handy when you want to share some data (for example, global lookup, or JAR files or archives that contain executable code) among all the Mappers of the job or for initialization, or when libraries of code need to be accessed on all nodes in the cluster.

Q. What benefits does reuse of JVM provide?

A. By default, a TaskTracker kicks off a Mapper or Reducer task in a separate JVM as a child process. Although separation or isolation sounds like a good idea, to keep a failed map task from breaking the TaskTracker itself, an initialization cost is incurred each time a separate JVM spins off for the task execution. This additional initialization cost increases even further if the task needs to read a large data structure in memory (for example, DistributedCache or data needed for joining).

To solve this problem, the MapReduce framework has the property `mapred.job.reuse.jvm.num.tasks`, which supports reuse of a JVM across multiple tasks of the same job. Hence, the additional initialization cost can be compensated or shared across many tasks.

Q. How does job scheduling happen in Hadoop?

A. The earlier MapReduce framework used a first in, first out (FIFO) method to process the job requests. When a client submitted a job, it was queued at one end and JobTracker picked it up from the other end (the oldest one) for execution. This FIFO approach for processing jobs was intermixed with JobTracker logic, making it inflexible and giving administrators no control over this. Later, however, Hadoop made it extensible and started support for a pluggable job scheduling component. Now you can use either the FIFO approach, the Capacity Scheduler or Fair Scheduler, or any other available scheduling component that plugs in to your Hadoop cluster to resolve job contention and schedule a job.

Q. What is a speculative task and when it is executed?

A. The MapReduce framework has a concept of speculative execution, in which it launches a backup or speculative task for an identified slow-running task to do the same work, in parallel, as the original task. The MapReduce framework keeps monitoring both tasks (the original one and the speculative or backup); whichever task completes first is taken into consideration. The MapReduce framework kills the other task (which was doing the same work). Speculative execution is intended to prevent the slow tasks from dragging down the job's overall execution time.

The important point to note here is that a speculative or backup task is executed only when the MapReduce framework identifies a task running slower than expected (based on the overall progress it has made with respect to other tasks of the same job). The MapReduce framework never kicks off two copies of the same task at the beginning of job execution, to avoid a race for the best execution time.

Q. What are counters and why are they used?

A. Counters provide a means of gathering application-level statistics for assessing quality control, diagnosing a problem, monitoring and tracking the progress of job, and so on. Some built-in counters report various metrics for your job, including FILE_BYTES_READ, FILE_BYTES_WRITTEN, NUM_KILLED_MAPS, NUM_KILLED_REDUCES, NUM_FAILED_MAPS, and NUM_FAILED_REDUCES.

You can create and define other user-defined or custom counters as well.

Q. What is YARN and what does it do?

A. In Hadoop 2.0, MapReduce has undergone a complete overhaul, with a new layer created on top of HDFS. This new layer, called YARN (Yet Another Resource Negotiator), takes care of two major functions: resource management and application life-cycle management. The JobTracker previously handled those functions. Now MapReduce is just a batch-mode computational layer sitting on top of YARN, whereas YARN acts like an operating system for the Hadoop cluster by providing resource management and application life-cycle management functionalities. This makes Hadoop a general-purpose data processing platform that is not constrained only to MapReduce.

Q. **What is uber-tasking optimization?**

A. The concept of uber-tasking in YARN applies to smaller jobs. Those jobs are executed in the same container or in the same JVM in which that application-specific Application Master is running. The basic idea behind uber-tasking optimization is that the distributed task allocation and management overhead exceeds the benefits of executing tasks in parallel for smaller jobs, hence its optimum to execute smaller job in the same JVM or container of the Application Master.

Quiz

1. Hadoop is written in Java, so Hadoop natively supports writing MapReduce jobs in Java. Imagine that you are not a Java expert, though. Do you have any other option for writing MapReduce jobs in any other language?

2. What's the difference between a map-side join and reduce-side join? Which offers better performance?

3. Why is JobTracker a single point of failure?

4. How can you handle bad records when you are doing analysis on the large set of data?

5. What are the different components of YARN?

Answers

1. Hadoop provides the Hadoop Streaming utility (implemented in the form of a JAR file) for creating Map and Reduce executables in other languages (including C# and Python) for execution on a Hadoop cluster. When you execute your executables (Map and Reduce), the Hadoop Streaming utility creates a MapReduce job, submits the job to the intended Hadoop cluster, monitors the progress of the job until it completes, and reports back. During execution, the Mapper and Reducer executables read the input data line by line from STDIN and emit the output data to STDOUT.

2. Based on implementation, if the join is performed by the Mapper of the MapReduce job, it is called a map-side join. If the Reducer performs the join, it is called a reduce-side join.

   Map-side joins are better in terms of performance and thus are recommended. If one of the datasets is small enough (which is the case in most Big Data scenarios), you can consider using the Distributed Cache (to cache the smaller table and use it as lookup during the join by each Mapper) to do joining during the map phase only. If both datasets are large, though first see whether a map-side join is possible before you opt for a reduce-side join.

3. If the JobTracker fails, all the job clients must resubmit all the running and queued jobs because there is no built-in mechanism to recover from the failure. The possibility of JobTracker failure is low, but its failure is a serious issue.

   The good news is that JobTracker failure is no longer a problem in Hadoop 2.0 YARN.

4. When you are doing analysis in a large dataset, it's generally acceptable to ignore a small percentage of bad records so that job execution completes successfully. You might write your Mapper or Reducer to gracefully handle these bad records while processing without actually causing the runtime exception to happen or the task to fail. But in some cases, such as if you are using a third-party library or you don't have access to the source code, you won't have that option. In those cases, you can use the MapReduce framework to skip bad records automatically on subsequent task retries.

   When you enable this feature, two task failures are considered to be normal failure. On the third failure, the MapReduce framework captures the data that caused the failure. On the fourth failure, it skips those identified data to avoid the failure again. All the bad records detected and skipped are written to HDFS in the sequence file format in the job's output directory under the `_logs/skip` subdirectory, for later analysis.

5. Aligning to the original master-slave architecture principle, even YARN has a global or master Resource Manager for managing cluster resources and a per-node and -slave Node Manager that takes direction from the Resource Manager and manages resources on the node. These two form the computation fabric for YARN. Apart from that is a per-application Application Master, which is merely an application-specific library tasked with negotiating resources from the global Resource Manager and coordinating with the Node Manager(s) to execute the tasks and monitor their execution. Containers also are present—these are a group of computing resources, such as memory, CPU, disk, and network.

Getting Started with HDInsight, Provisioning Your HDInsight Service Cluster, and Automating HDInsight Cluster Provisioning

What You'll Learn in This Hour:

▶ Introduction to Microsoft Azure

▶ Understanding HDInsight Service

▶ Provisioning HDInsight on the Azure Management Portal

▶ Automating HDInsight Provisioned with PowerShell

▶ Managing and Monitoring an HDInsight Cluster and Job Execution

In the last few hours, you extensively studied the need for Big Data and how you can leverage Hadoop to store and process Big Data. You also took a detailed look at the new features and enhancements in Hadoop 2.0. With so much theory in place, you can now up your sleeves and get started with some practical application.

In this hour, you delve into HDInsight to see how you can quickly provision HDInsight or a Hadoop cluster on Microsoft Azure either manually, using the Azure Management Portal, or automatically, using PowerShell scripting.

Introduction to Microsoft Azure

Before we go into the details of HDInsight, one of the services Microsoft Azure provides, we should briefly look at Microsoft Azure itself.

Microsoft Azure is an open and flexible cloud computing (Platform As a Service, PaaS) and infrastructure platform (Infrastructure As a Service, IaaS) that enables customers to rapidly build, deploy, and manage secure applications to scale on premises, in the cloud, or both. Gartner has ranked Microsoft Azure an industry leader for both PaaS and IaaS. It is one of the most popular and widely used cloud computing platforms because of its breadth of offering—and, of course, seamless integration between the offerings or with other Microsoft technologies.

The world of cloud computing is constantly changing, and so is Microsoft Azure. Microsoft Azure has a growing collection of integrated services—compute, storage, data, networking, and application—that help you move faster, do more, and save money. Microsoft Azure has a broad range of services; Figure 6.1 shows some of the most widely used services.

NOTE

Practically, it's not possible to talk about the broad range of Microsoft Azure services in a single hour or even a single book. Instead, this hour focuses specifically on the Microsoft Azure HDInsight service and its other related services (such as storage).

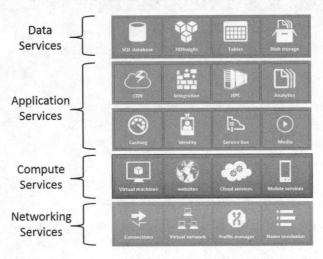

FIGURE 6.1
Some widely used services in Microsoft Azure.

Microsoft Azure is subscription based, so before you can start using it, you must procure a Microsoft Azure subscription. Microsoft Azure uses different pricing models. For example, you can choose the "pay as you go" (PAYG) model for short-term computing, with no upfront cost or capital investment and no penalty for termination. Large organizations can choose the Enterprise Agreement (EA) model for long-term computing and a discount over the regular cost.

NOTE

Refer to the latest Microsoft Azure pricing plan (http://azure.microsoft.com/en-us/pricing/) for services you want to use; the pricing changes with new releases or based on market dynamics.

If you already have a subscription, you can either use it or choose to use a trial subscription for learning purposes. Microsoft offers a one-month free subscription with $200 of credit to spend on Azure services if you sign up. See http://azure.microsoft.com/en-us/pricing/free-trial/.

GO TO ▶ For local development or evaluation, you can also use HDInsight Emulator, which we cover in **Hour 9, "Working with Microsoft Azure HDInsight Emulator."**

Azure Storage Service

The Microsoft Azure Storage service is a robust, general-purpose, Hadoop-compatible Azure storage solution that integrates seamlessly with HDInsight. It provides anywhere and anytime access of your data via a secure cloud storage system. It is highly durable, available, and massively scalable, so you can store and process hundreds of terabytes of data to support any Big Data scenarios you require with your scientific, financial analysis, and media applications.

Although the Microsoft Azure Storage service enables you to store different types of data (blob storage, table storage, queue storage, and file storage), our focus in this hour is to use blob storage (mainly for binary data storage) because this is what HDInsight uses for data storage by default. The Azure Storage Blob stores file data such as text, binary data, and other Big Data (such as logs and large datasets).

A storage account can contain any number of containers, and a container can contain any number of blobs, up to the 500TB capacity limit of the storage account. You can configure more than one storage account on a cluster, or you can configure a single storage account with multiple containers to go beyond the 500TB limit.

A container is a way of organizing each blob and provides a useful way to assign security policies to groups of objects as a unit.

Microsoft Azure also has the Azure Import/Export Service, which enables you to ship a hard drive to Microsoft to import or export data directly from the data center. This is relevant if you have large datasets and uploading over the wire isn't realistic.

NOTE

When using the Microsoft Azure Storage service, you pay only for what you use and only when you use it.

Understanding HDInsight Service

Microsoft Azure offers HDInsight in partnership with Hortonworks. HDInsight brings a 100 percent Apache Hadoop–based solution to the cloud platform. It provides the capability to gain the full value of Big Data with a modern, cloud-based data platform that manages data of any type, whether structured or unstructured, and of any size.

Earlier, only big companies and well-funded government agencies were able to create Big Data solutions because doing so required a huge upfront investment for the infrastructure and a lot of time to implement it. But now the capability to store and process a massive amount of data is within reach for many companies. HDInsight makes it possible for you to gain the full value of your Big Data in a quicker and cost-effective way.

With HDInsight, now any organization (small or big) can create a Hadoop cluster in a few minutes (instead of having to create a Hadoop cluster on the local infrastructure in days or months), without a huge upfront investment for hardware.

If your requirement changes and you need a larger cluster, you can simply delete your cluster and create a new, bigger one in minutes without losing any data. The best part is, you pay for only as long as you use the cluster. You can delete the cluster when you don't need it and create it again when the need arises.

Even better, you can script this into a workflow so that your workload is to "create cluster, run workload, delete cluster." This way, you don't have to think about managing the cluster.

HDInsight Cluster Deployment

An HDInsight cluster deployment consists of multiple nodes: two head nodes to provide high availability for master daemons, two secure gateway nodes to provide access to the HDInsight cluster, and one or more worker or data nodes that you select for computation.

As you can see in Figure 6.2 (and discussed in Hour 3, "Hadoop Distributed File System Versions 1.0 and 2.0," and Hour 5, "MapReduce—Advanced Concepts and YARN"), to maintain high availability of head nodes, the cluster leverages ZooKeeper services for fault detection and to elect a new active head node in case the currently active head node fails.

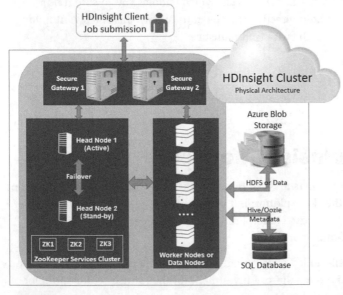

FIGURE 6.2
Physical architecture of the HDInsight cluster.

▶ **Head nodes**—Head nodes run master daemons such as NameNode and Secondary NameNode for data storage and run the Resource Manager (or JobTracker) for processing, along with other data services daemons such as HiveServer, HiveServer2, Pig, and Sqoop. Head nodes also run operational services such as Oozie and Ambari.

▶ **Secure gateway nodes**—Secure gateway nodes are proxies that serve as a gateway to your Azure HDInsight cluster. They perform authentication and authorization and expose endpoints for WebHcat, Ambari, HiveServer, HiveServer2, and Oozie on port 443. To authenticate to the HDInsight cluster, you use the username and password you specified at the time of HDInsight cluster provisioning. Secure gateway nodes are also responsible for connecting you to the current active head node (in case of head node failover).

▶ **Data or worker nodes**—Data or worker nodes run all the slave daemons, including data node, TaskTracker, NodeManager, Pig, and Hive Client. In a typical scenario, you have multiple data or worker nodes for the distributed processing of your Big Data.

▶ **ZooKeeper nodes**—The ZooKeeper services cluster monitors and manages the state of the head nodes. The HDInsight cluster leverages it for fault detection of the currently active head node and to elect a new active head node in case the currently active head node fails, to ensure high availability (it overcomes the limitation of the master node being a single point of failure in earlier Hadoop releases).

▶ **SQL database**—When you want to use Hive or Oozie, you can use the Azure SQL database to store metadata related to Hive or Oozie.

▶ **Azure Storage Blob**—By default, HDInsight uses Azure Storage Blob (also called *WASB*, short for Windows Azure Storage Blob) for data storage. It has been implemented so that it appears as a full-featured Hadoop Distributed File System (HDFS) to end users. The best part of WASB is that Hadoop users still use the HDFS commands as usual to interact with it; at the same time, it can be accessed using Azure Storage Blob REST APIs or some other applications, or through one of the many popular Azure Storage Explorer tools.

Although you can change the configuration to make local drives of the HDInsight cluster (or, more specifically, the data or worker nodes) for data storage as an HDFS layer, we recommend that you use the default Azure Storage Blob because it is optimized for the storage of Big Data and computations on that data.

NOTE

WASB Versus Local Disk Storage for HDFS

Microsoft has implemented a mesh grid network called Azure Flat Network Storage (also known as Quantum 10 or Q10 network) to offer a high-bandwidth, high-speed connectivity between WASB and worker or data nodes of your HDInsight cluster.

To minimize network data transfer, the implementation uses WASB during the initial and final streaming phases. Most of the other tasks are performed intra-node (the map, reduce, and sort tasks typically are performed on the local disk residing with the worker or data nodes themselves).

GO TO ▶ Hour 8, "Storing Data in Microsoft Azure Storage Blob," looks at why HDInsight chooses WASB as the default storage option and how it makes sense both technically and from a business perspective.

NOTE

HDInsight Service and the Azure Storage Service

Azure Storage Blob is a high-capacity, highly scalable, highly available storage option that costs significantly less and can be shared by other applications that run outside your HDInsight cluster. Storing data in an Azure Storage Blob enables the HDInsight clusters used for computation to be safely released without losing data: The data is stored in Azure Storage Blob and not on the local drives in the HDInsight cluster.

In other words, you pay for the HDInsight cluster just for the time you are using it for computation. Data is stored in the Azure Storage Blob, which is already a low-cost storage option and is decoupled from the HDInsight cluster. You also don't need an operational HDInsight cluster for uploading or downloading data from the Azure Storage Blob—you can do it anytime, anywhere with Azure Storage Blob REST APIs, using PowerShell, or through one of the many popular Azure Storage Explorer tools (see http://azure.microsoft.com/en-us/documentation/articles/hdinsight-upload-data/).

When you need to do computation again, you can simply provision another HDInsight cluster based on your new requirement (either smaller than, bigger than, or the same size as the earlier cluster), point it back to the same Azure Storage Blob, and use the data again for further computation.

The two head nodes and multiple data or worker nodes (or as many as you have requested) are billed on an hourly basis, prorated to the nearest minute a cluster exists. The secure nodes, along with ZooKeeper nodes, are free as of this writing. Charges start when cluster creation completes and stops when you request that the cluster be deleted.

Unlike the virtual machine in Microsoft Azure, which can be shut down or deallocated when not in use to save on cost, there is no concept of deallocating or putting the HDInsight cluster on hold. As mentioned earlier, you can delete your cluster safely at any time(by default, your data gets stored in Azure Storage Blob—uploading data to Azure Storage Blob and downloading it from there does not require operational HDInsight cluster, so you can use different methods for uploading or downloading). Then you can create another instance of the HDInsight cluster with the same specification or a different one, based on your new need. Afterward, you can start processing again without losing your data. By doing this, you save on cost by paying for only when you are using the HDInsight cluster.

See Figure 6.3 for Hadoop costs and Figure 6.4 for Hadoop + HBase costs as of this writing. You have many other options for VM size than mentioned in Figures 6.3 and 6.4, and you can choose from this list based on your requirements, such as a memory-intensive option, a compute-intensive option, or faster VMs with Solid State Drive (SSD). As advised earlier, always refer to the Microsoft Azure pricing site for the latest VM size options and pricing models.

Hadoop Pricing

NODE TYPE	PRICE
Two Head Nodes (on an Extra Large (A4) instance):	$1.28 per hour (~$952 per month)
Two Head Nodes (on a Large (A3) instance):	$0.64 per hour (~$476 per month)
Each Data Node (on a Large (A3) instance):	$0.32 per hour (~$238 per month)
Two Secure Gateway Nodes (on a Medium (A2) instance):	Free
Three ZooKeeper Nodes (on a Small (A1) instance):	Free

* Monthly price estimates are based on 744 hours of usage per month.

FIGURE 6.3
HDInsight costs for Hadoop only.

Hadoop + HBase Pricing

NODE TYPE	PRICE
Two Head Nodes (on an Extra Large (A4) instance):	$1.28 per hour (~$952 per month)
Two Head Nodes (on a Large (A3) instance):	$0.64 per hour (~$476 per month)
Each Data Node (on a Large (A3) instance):	$0.32 per hour (~$238 per month)
Two Secure Gateway Nodes (on a Medium (A2) instance):	Free
Additional cost for HBase: Three ZooKeeper Nodes (on a Medium (A2) instance)	$0.48 per hour (~$357 per month)

* Monthly price estimates are based on 744 hours of usage per month.

FIGURE 6.4
HDInsight costs for Hadoop + HBase.

NOTE

Other Microsoft Azure services associated with HDInsight, such as Storage and Data Transfers, are
billed separately using the standard rates for Storage and Data Transfers. Standard data transfer
charges also are applied when transferring data from one region to another.

Provisioning HDInsight on the Azure Management Portal

When you have an active Microsoft Azure subscription attached to your live account, you can
log in to the Azure Management Portal. You will notice a nice-looking home page (see
Figure 6.5). On the left side of the home page is a list of services Microsoft Azure offers. Because
we have logged on for the first time here, we don't have anything right now.

FIGURE 6.5
Azure Management Portal home page.

Click the icon at the bottom left to call up a nice-looking user interface where you can select the
service you want to provision. For example, in this case, we want to provision the HDInsight
service (Hadoop cluster) in Figure 6.6; hence, we selected Data Services, HDInsight, Custom
Create. You can quickly provision a service by using other options, but using Custom Create
gives you more control in specifying different parameters.

FIGURE 6.6
Provisioning a new HDInsight service.

On the first page of the New HDInsight Cluster Provision Wizard, you specify the name for your cluster, which should be unique on the `azurehdinsight.net` domain. Next, you specify the cluster type (only Hadoop, Hadoop + HBase, or Storm—pricing differs based on the cluster type you choose, so refer to the Azure pricing page for the latest information). See Figure 6.7.

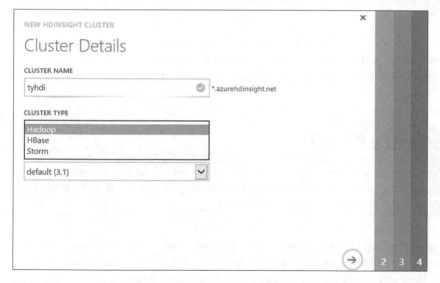

FIGURE 6.7
HDInsight Cluster Provision Wizard, page 1.

On the first page of the New HDInsight Cluster Provision Wizard (see Figure 6.8), you must also specify the HDInsight version. As of this writing, the default version is 3.1, which is based on Hortonworks Data Platform (HDP) 2.1 and includes the Hadoop 2.4 distribution from Hortonworks. You can see some older versions to choose from as well.

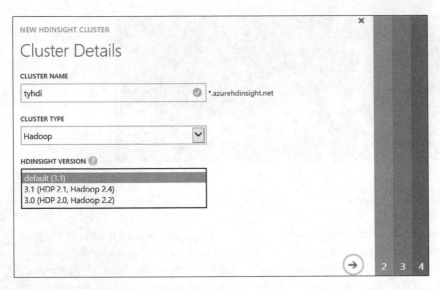

FIGURE 6.8
HDInsight Cluster Provision Wizard, page 1—HDInsight versions.

You can get details on the latest HDInsight releases based on different Hadoop versions and the components each of these HDInsight releases contain at http://azure.microsoft.com/en-us/documentation/articles/hdinsight-component-versioning/.

NOTE

Hadoop Distributions for HDInsight

As of now, HDInsight is based on the Hortonworks Data Platform (HDP). Recently, however, Microsoft entered into a partnership with Cloudera, so you can expect to see a future option to create an HDInsight service based on Cloudera Enterprise. This will give customers more options to deploy their Hadoop distribution of choice on Microsoft Azure.

On the second page of the New HDInsight Cluster Provision Wizard (see Figure 6.9), you specify the number of data or worker nodes that you want to be part of the provisioned cluster. In addition, you need to specify the Azure data center location or virtual network.

NOTE

Virtual Network (sometimes referred to as VNET) enables Virtual Private Networks (VPN) to be created within Microsoft Azure and securely connect with on-premises IT infrastructure or share resources on the Microsoft Azure.

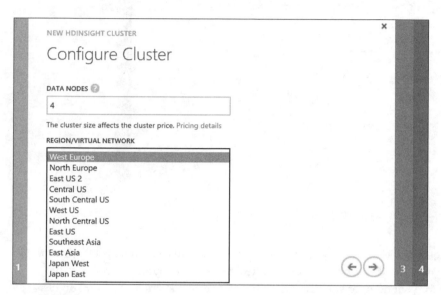

FIGURE 6.9
HDInsight Cluster Provision Wizard, page 2.

Microsoft Azure has a long list of data centers geographically dispersed across the globe. You can choose one nearest to your location. (As of this writing, HDInsight is not supported on all the data centers Microsoft Azure has, but the Microsoft team is working hard to bring it onto the newly added data centers as early as possible; refer to the HDInsight documentation for its availability in different data centers.)

On the third page of the New HDInsight Cluster Provision Wizard (see Figure 6.10), you specify the administrator for the cluster. If you already have an Azure SQL Database available, you can also choose to specify it for the storage of metadata related to Hive and Oozie. This is useful if you have Hive or Oozie metadata that you want to be used across many cluster creations.

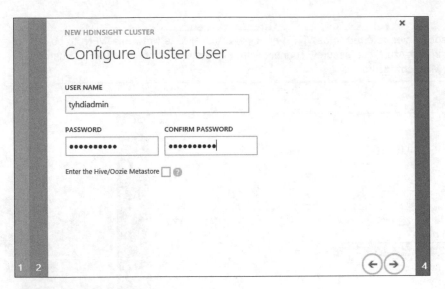

FIGURE 6.10
HDInsight Cluster Provision Wizard, page 3.

On the fourth page of the New HDInsight Cluster Provision Wizard (see Figure 6.11), you specify the Azure storage account. If you have already created a storage account, you can use the existing one here for your data, or you can choose to create a new storage account. You also must specify a default container (a way of organizing blob contents as a group) that will be created inside the storage account to store blob data.

NOTE

Normally, you create the storage account first, upload all the data that needs to be processed, and only then create the HDInsight cluster to actually process the data. When the data processing is complete, you can save the result to the storage account for later analysis and then can safely delete your cluster. This way, you are paying only for storage (a nominal cost) and data transfer and are paying for HDInsight (or for computation) only for the duration you are using it. This represents a huge savings on overall cost. When you need the HDInsight cluster again, you can provision the cluster, do the processing, and delete it again after saving the result back to storage.

TIP

Make sure you have a storage account and HDInsight cluster in the same data center for cluster creation. This also ensures data and compute node co-locality, for better performance.

FIGURE 6.11
HDInsight Cluster Provision Wizard, page 4.

Customizing Your HDInsight or Hadoop Cluster

The New HDInsight Cluster Provision Wizard includes a new page to specify custom scripts for your provisioned HDInsight cluster (or to change the default configuration of applications on the cluster) with your requirement-specific custom scripts (see Figure 6.12). These can be executed on both head nodes and worker nodes.

For example, as part of cluster provisioning, you can specify scripts to install Apache Spark or the R Programming Language on the HDInsight cluster, or you can change the Hadoop configuration files (such as `core-site.xml` and `hive-site.xml`), or add shared libraries (such as Hive and Oozie) into common locations in the HDInsight cluster.

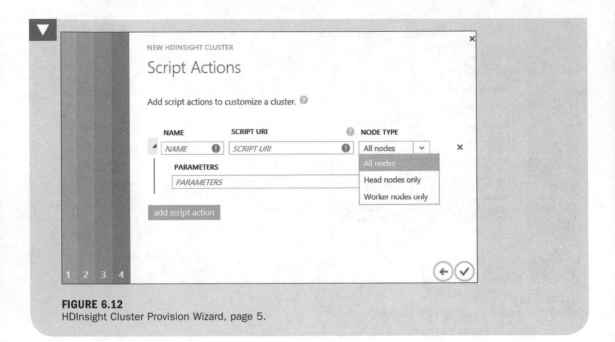

FIGURE 6.12
HDInsight Cluster Provision Wizard, page 5.

NOTE

HDInsight also provides sample scripts to install Apache Spark and the R Programming Language on an HDInsight cluster: See http://azure.microsoft.com/en-us/documentation/articles/hdinsight-hadoop-customize-cluster/.

You are now finished specifying all the parameters for cluster provisioning, so click the icon on the last page of the New HDInsight Cluster Provision Wizard to start provisioning the HDInsight service (Hadoop cluster).

Based on the size of the cluster you are creating, this might take a few minutes. You can monitor the progress while it's provisioning. When the HDInsight cluster is provisioned successfully, you will see a message about its running status on the Azure Management Port (see Figure 6.13).

FIGURE 6.13
HDInsight service provisioning—progress check.

Enabling a Remote Desktop Connection via the Remote Desktop Protocol

For security reasons, by default, remote desktop connectivity to the head node of the HDInsight cluster is not enabled. If you want to do remote logging to the head node, you need to first enable remote logging to the HDInsight cluster.

To enable remote desktop connectivity, go to the Azure Management Portal, click the HDInsight cluster for which you want to enable it, and go to the Configuration tab in Figure 6.14. At the bottom of the page, click the Enable Remote icon to enable remote desktop connectivity for this HDInsight cluster.

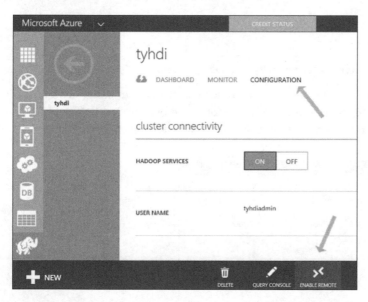

FIGURE 6.14
Enabling remote desktop connectivity for an HDInsight cluster.

On the Configure HDInsight Cluster page of the Configure Remote Desktop Wizard, you specify the username and password you will be using for the remote desktop connection (see Figure 6.15). By default, remote desktop connectivity can be enabled for a maximum of one week.

FIGURE 6.15
Specifying credentials for remote desktop connectivity.

Click the icon to enable remote desktop connectivity; it takes few seconds to get it enabled.

When remote desktop connectivity is enabled, look for an icon on the bottom of the Azure Management Portal (see Figure 6.16) to connect to the remote head node of the HDInsight cluster. The Disable Remote icon offers an option to disable remote desktop connectivity.

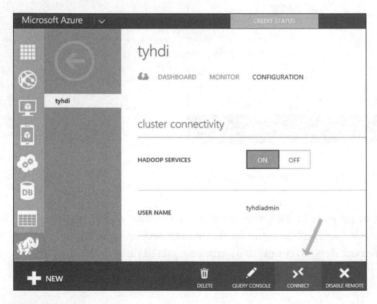

FIGURE 6.16
Connecting to the head node of the HDInsight cluster.

While connecting to the remote head node of the HDInsight cluster, you must specify the username and password that you provided when enabling the remote desktop connectivity (see Figure 6.17).

FIGURE 6.17
Specifying credentials for remote connectivity.

When you are connected to the head node of the HDInsight cluster, you will see these Hadoop-related shortcut icons on the desktop of the head node machine (see Figure 6.18).

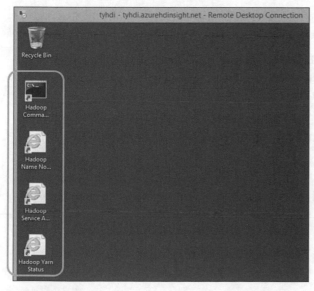

FIGURE 6.18
Desktop head node when connected via remote desktop connectivity.

Verifying HDInsight Setup

You verify the installation and configuration of the provisioned HDInsight cluster in different ways. Let's first start by executing the sample word count example to see how it works. Although you can do this in different ways, this section uses the Hadoop command prompt.

Click the Hadoop command prompt icon on the desktop of the head node of the HDInsight cluster (refer to Figure 6.18).

Next, execute the commands in Listing 6.1 to verify the existence of a JAR file and data files; then execute the JAR file to kick off the word count example with the appropriate arguments and produce the result of the word count for the provided input file.

LISTING 6.1   Verifying the Existence of Necessary Files for the Word Count MapReduce Job Execution

```
1: hadoop fs -ls /
2: hadoop fs -ls /example
3: hadoop fs -ls /example/jars
4: hadoop fs -ls /example/data
5: hadoop fs -ls /example/data/gutenberg
6: hadoop fs -cat /example/data/gutenberg/davinci.txt
```

Line 1 of Listing 6.1 shows all the files and folders at the root level. By default, the HDInsight cluster uses Azure Storage Blob, so these contents are coming from the default container of the associated Azure Storage Blob.

Line 2 shows the files and folders from the `example` directory, and line 3 shows the files and folders from the `jars` subdirectory of the `example` directory.

Line 4 shows the files and folders from the `data` subdirectory of the `example` directory. Likewise, line 5 shows the files and folders of the `gutenberg` subdirectory of the `data` subdirectory of the `example` directory, which is available at root level.

Line 6 shows the content of the `davinci.txt` file on the console (or on the standard output), available in the `gutenberg` subdirectory of the `data` subdirectory of the `example` directory.

Figure 6.19 shows the execution result of the scripts from Listing 6.1. (As you can see, folder names are appended with the version of the applications, and this might be different for you based on the HDInsight version you are using.)

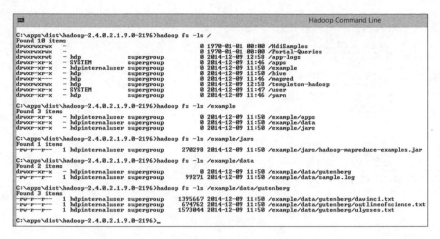

FIGURE 6.19
Verifying the HDInsight installation and configuration by running HDFS commands.

Listing 6.2 shows the Hadoop command for executing the word count MapReduce job. The first parameter is the name of the class from the JAR file to be executed, the second parameter is an input file, and the third parameter is a directory where output is produced as a result of the execution. Line 1 executes the JAR file from the Azure Storage Blob; line 2 executes the JAR file from the local drive (you can choose to execute either of these).

LISTING 6.2   Executing a MapReduce Job from a JAR File

```
1: hadoop jar /example/jars/hadoop-mapreduce-examples.jar wordcount /example/data/
   gutenberg/davinci.txt /example/data/wordcountexample
2: hadoop jar C:\apps\dist\hadoop-2.4.0.2.1.9.0-2196\hadoop-mapreduce-examples.jar
   wordcount /example/data/gutenberg/davinci.txt /example/data/wordcountexample
```

Figure 6.20 shows the execution result of the word count MapReduce job. You can also see other runtime information captured during Hadoop MapReduce job execution.

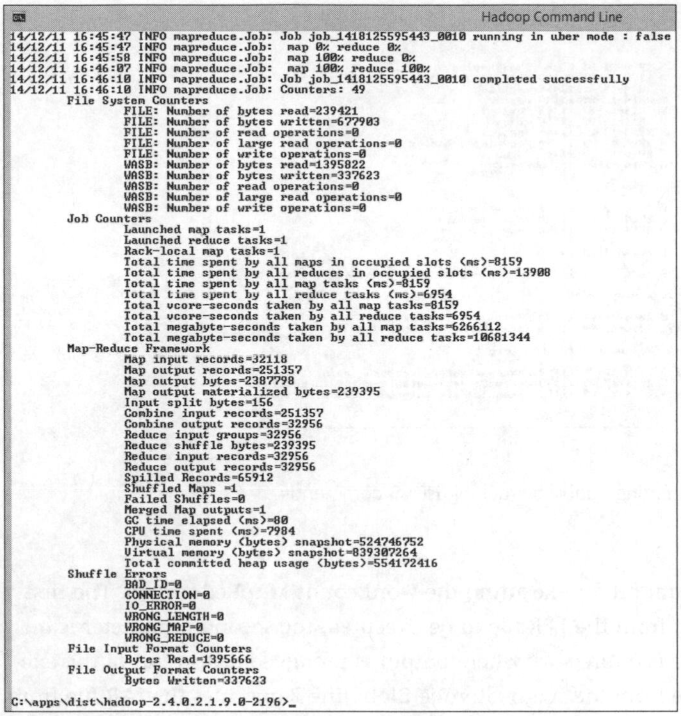

FIGURE 6.20
Execution result of a MapReduce job for the word count example.

Listing 6.3 shows a script to analyze the output produced by the word count MapReduce job executed earlier. The MapReduce framework creates output files with a specific naming pattern: part-x-yyyyy, where x is either m (representing output from a map-only job) or r (representing output from a Reducer), and yyyyy is the Mapper or Reducer task number starting with a zero index.

LISTING 6.3   Verifying the MapReduce Job Output

```
1: hadoop fs -cat /example/data/wordcountexample/part-r-00000
2: hadoop fs -tail /example/data/wordcountexample/part-r-00000
```

Figure 6.21 shows the output of the word count MapReduce job execution. As you can see, for each word is a count of the occurrence of that specific word.

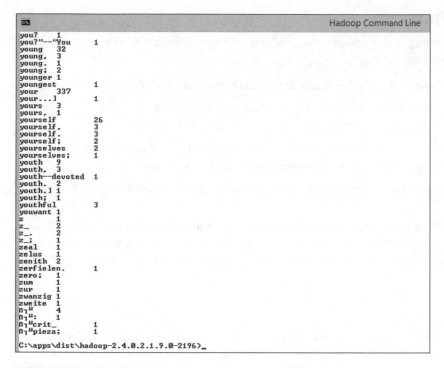

FIGURE 6.21
Verifying the output produced by the word count MapReduce job.

Automating HDInsight Provisioning with PowerShell

We talked in detail about how you can use the Azure Management Portal to create an HDInsight cluster by using a wizard-based interface interactively. But it's not uncommon to automate this process of creating an HDInsight cluster so that you can execute it quickly whenever you need to, either manually or with a scheduler or a workflow process. Microsoft Azure provides PowerShell cmdlets to automate the process of provisioning an HDInsight cluster.

Prerequisites

Before you start writing or executing PowerShell for automatic HDInsight provisioning, you need to check in to these prerequisites:

▶ An active Microsoft Azure subscription under which you want to create an HDInsight cluster

▶ Windows PowerShell Version 2.0 (see Install Windows PowerShell 2.0: http://msdn.microsoft.com/en-us/library/ff637750(v=azure.10).aspx) or later

▶ Microsoft Azure PowerShell with Microsoft Azure SDK (see Install Microsoft Azure PowerShell: http://azure.microsoft.com/en-us/downloads/?fb=en-us)

▶ Azure subscription certificates and the `publishsettings` file downloaded and imported

To execute PowerShell cmdlets for managing services in the Azure subscription, you need to first download the required certificates or `publishsettings` file on the local machine to set up a secure relationship between your local PowerShell scripting environment and the Microsoft Azure subscription.

CAUTION

You can allow connectivity between your local machine and your Microsoft Azure subscription in two ways. You can do so either manually, by configuring the management certificate and subscription details with the `Set-AzureSubscription` and `Select-AzureSubscription` cmdlets, or automatically, by downloading and importing the `PublishSettings` file from Microsoft Azure. The relationship establishment settings for Microsoft Azure and Windows PowerShell are stored as a JSON file in the folder `<user>\AppData\Roaming\Windows Azure PowerShell`.

The `PublishSettings` file contains an encoded management certificate that serves as a credential to connect and administer all aspects of your Azure subscription. Be sure to store this file in a secure location and delete it when you are done with it.

You can write and execute PowerShell scripts in different ways. This example uses the Windows PowerShell interactive scripting environment (ISE) for writing and executing all the PowerShell scripts. You can see in Figure 6.22 that the top-left section of the Windows PowerShell ISE is for writing and executing your scripts, the right section shows module-wise PowerShell cmdlets, with a brief description of each cmdlet and with a search capability. The bottom section shows the progress and result of the script execution; you can also verify the runtime values for variables or objects in this section while debugging.

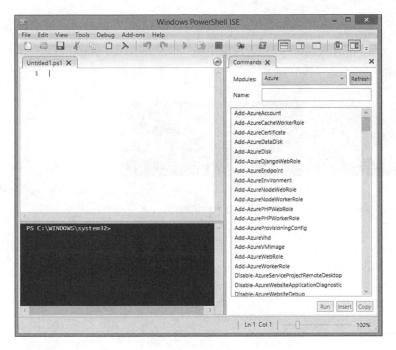

FIGURE 6.22
Windows PowerShell ISE.

Listing 6.4 shows scripts for downloading certificates or the publishsettings file from the
Azure subscription and then import them back into the local PowerShell scripting environment.

LISTING 6.4 Downloading and Importing an Azure Subscription Certificate
and Establishing a Secure Relationship Between the Local PowerShell Scripting
Environment and the Azure Subscription

```
 1: # Check if Windows Azure PowerShell is available
 2: if ((Get-Module -ListAvailable Azure) -eq $null)
 3: {
 4:    throw "Microsoft Azure PowerShell is not installed! Please check pre-requisites"
 5: }
 6:
 7: Get-AzureAccount
 8:
 9: Get-AzureSubscription
10:
11: Get-AzurePublishSettingsFile
12:
13: Import-AzurePublishSettingsFile "C:\azure-credentials.publishsettings"
14:
15: Get-AzureSubscription
```

Lines 2–4 check whether the Microsoft Azure PowerShell has been installed on the current machine. Lines 7 and 9 check whether a relationship already has been established between the local PowerShell scripting environment and the Azure subscription. At this point in time, we have not defined any relationship (see Figure 6.23).

```
PS C:\WINDOWS\system32> Get-AzureAccount
PS C:\WINDOWS\system32> Get-AzureSubscription
PS C:\WINDOWS\system32> Get-AzurePublishSettingsFile
PS C:\WINDOWS\system32> Import-AzurePublishSettingsFile "C:\azure-credentials.publishsettings"
PS C:\WINDOWS\system32> |
```

FIGURE 6.23
Verifying the relationship between the local PowerShell and the Azure subscription.

Line 11 of Listing 6.4 downloads the certificate from the Azure subscription. When you execute this command, it opens the Azure subscription certificate download page in the browser (you must log in with your account to connect to the Azure subscription and download its certificate). See Figure 6.24.

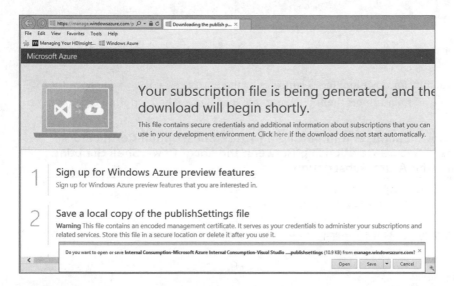

FIGURE 6.24
Downloading the certificate for the Azure subscription.

After you have downloaded the certificate onto your local machine, you can execute line 13 of Listing 6.4 to import the certificate in the local PowerShell scripting environment. Next, you execute line 15 to verify the imported certificate PowerShell scripting environment (see Figure 6.25).

FIGURE 6.25
Verifying the imported certificate in the PowerShell scripting environment.

Provisioning HDInsight Cluster

When you have the prerequisites in place, you start creating the HDInsight cluster with the script in Listing 6.5.

LISTING 6.5   Provisioning an HDInsight Cluster with PowerShell

```
 1: # Declare all the variables and specify their values
 2: $location = "Central US"
 3:
 4: $defaultStorageAccount = "tyhdistorageauto"
 5: $defaultStorageContainer = "adventureworksauto"
 6:
 7: $clusterAdminUserName = "tyhdiadminauto"
 8: $clusterAdminPassword = "Passw@rd01"
 9:
10: $clusterName = "tyhdiclusterauto"
11: $clusterSizeInNodes = 4
12:
13:
14: # Check if storage account already exists then use it
15: # or else create a new storage account with the specified name
16: $storageAccount = Get-AzureStorageAccount -StorageAccountName
    $defaultStorageAccount `
17:    -ErrorAction SilentlyContinue
```

```
18: if ($storageAccount -eq $null)
19: {
20:    Write-Host "Creating new storage account $defaultStorageAccount."
21:    $storageAccount = New-AzureStorageAccount -StorageAccountName
    $defaultStorageAccount `
22:        -Location $location
23: }
24: else
25: {
26:    Write-Host "Using existing storage account $defaultStorageAccount."
27: }
28:
29: # Check if specified storage container already exists then use it
30: # or else create a new storage container with the specified
31: # name in the specified storage account
32: $storageContext = New-AzureStorageContext -StorageAccountName
    $defaultStorageAccount `
33:    -StorageAccountKey (Get-AzureStorageKey $defaultStorageAccount).Primary
34: $storageContainer = Get-AzureStorageContainer -Name $defaultStorageContainer `
35:    -Context $storageContext -ErrorAction SilentlyContinue
36: if ($storageContainer -eq $null)
37: {
38:    Write-Host "Creating new storage container $defaultStorageContainer."
39:    $storageContainer = New-AzureStorageContainer -Name $defaultStorageContainer `
40:        -Context $storageContext
41: }
42: else
43: {
44:    Write-Host "Using existing storage container $defaultStorageContainer."
45: }
46:
47: # if cluster admin user name and password are specified use it
48: # or else prompt for entering user name and password for cluster administrator
49: if ($clusterAdminUserName -eq "" -or $clusterAdminPassword -eq "")
50: {
51:    Write-Host "Enter administrator credential to use when provisioning the
    cluster."
52:    $credential = Get-Credential
53:    Write-Host "Administrator credential captured successfully, please use these '
54:        credentials to login to the cluster when the script is complete."
55: }
56: else
57: {
```

```
58:     $clusterAdminPasswordSecureString = ConvertTo-SecureString
        $clusterAdminPassword `
59:         -AsPlainText -Force
60:     $credential = new-object -typename System.Management.Automation.PSCredential
        -argumentlist `
61:         $clusterAdminUserName, $clusterAdminPasswordSecureString
62: }
63:
64:
65: Write-Host "Creating HDInsight cluster : $clusterName in $location location."
66:
67: New-AzureHDInsightCluster -Name $clusterName -Location $location `
68:     -DefaultStorageAccountName ($defaultStorageAccount + ".blob.core.windows.
        net") `
69:     -DefaultStorageAccountKey (Get-AzureStorageKey $defaultStorageAccount).
        Primary `
70:     -DefaultStorageContainerName $defaultStorageContainer `
71:     -Credential $credential `
72:     -ClusterSizeInNodes $clusterSizeInNodes
73:
74: Write-Host "HDInsight cluster : $clusterName in $location location created
        successfully."
```

In lines 2–11, you specify parameters required for creating the HDInsight cluster (including the name of the HDInsight cluster, the number of worker or data nodes in the cluster, and the data center location). Lines 14–27 check whether the specified storage account already exists; the code either uses the existing storage account or creates a new storage account with the specified name (to be used as storage account for the HDInsight cluster). Similarly, lines 29–45 check whether the storage account container already exists; the code either uses the existing storage account container or creates a new storage account container with the specified name (to be used as the default storage account container for the HDInsight cluster).

Lines 47–62 are a bit tricky. The code first checks whether you have specified any values for cluster administrator (username and password). If so, the script uses this information or prompts you to enter it during script execution. Be careful when you use variables to pass on values for cluster administrator: The username and password are stored as plain text in the script file, and you need to keep your script file secure.

Lines 67–72 create a new HDInsight cluster based on the configuration parameters specified. Figure 6.26 shows the result of the complete script (see Listing 6.5).

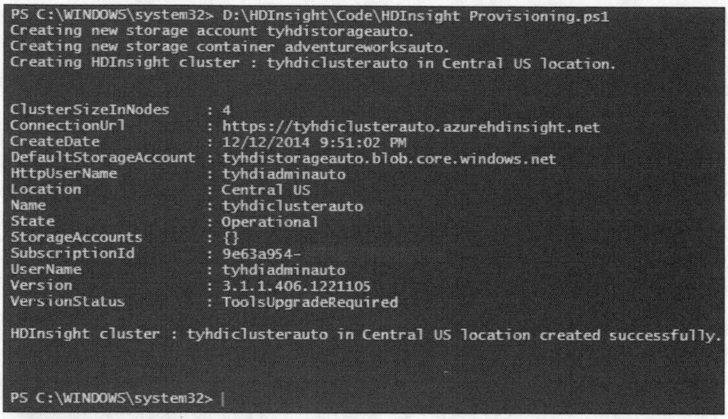

```
PS C:\WINDOWS\system32> D:\HDInsight\Code\HDInsight Provisioning.ps1
Creating new storage account tyhdistorageauto.
Creating new storage container adventureworksauto.
Creating HDInsight cluster : tyhdiclusterauto in Central US location.


ClusterSizeInNodes      : 4
ConnectionUrl           : https://tyhdiclusterauto.azurehdinsight.net
CreateDate              : 12/12/2014 9:51:02 PM
DefaultStorageAccount   : tyhdistorageauto.blob.core.windows.net
HttpUserName            : tyhdiadminauto
Location                : Central US
Name                    : tyhdiclusterauto
State                   : Operational
StorageAccounts         : {}
SubscriptionId          : 9e63a954-
UserName                : tyhdiadminauto
Version                 : 3.1.1.406.1221105
VersionStatus           : ToolsUpgradeRequired

HDInsight cluster : tyhdiclusterauto in Central US location created successfully.


PS C:\WINDOWS\system32> |
```

FIGURE 6.26
Execution result of HDInsight cluster creation with PowerShell.

With the help of PowerShell scripting, you can quickly create an HDInsight cluster when you need it for computation and drop it when not in use, as in Listing 6.6. If you need another computation, you can re-create the cluster automatically with PowerShell scripting in just few minutes and simply pay for the duration you actually use it (by deleting it when not in use).

LISTING 6.6   Managing an HDInsight Cluster with PowerShell

```
1: # To get all HDInsight clusters in the current subscription
2: Get-AzureHDInsightCluster
3:
4: # To show details of the specific HDInsight cluster
5: # in the current subscription
6: Get-AzureHDInsightCluster -Name <ClusterName>
7:
8: # To delete an existing HDInsight cluster when not in use
9: Remove-AzureHDInsightCluster -Name <ClusterName>
```

NOTE

For demonstration and simplicity purposes, we have used only a few of the important parameters while creating an HDInsight cluster; you can use many more, based on your specific need. For example, you might want to use multiple storage accounts or you might want to use Hive or Oozie, and thus need to store metadata in the Azure SQL database.

Verifying HDInsight Setup with PowerShell

To verify installation and configuration of the provisioned HDInsight cluster, you do the same verification you did in the earlier section: You run the word count MapReduce job. This time, however, we do it slightly differently:

▶ First, we use only PowerShell scripting (running the MapReduce job from the local machine with PowerShell scripting).

▶ Second, we upload input files from the local machine to the Azure Storage Blob (even before creating the HDInsight cluster, to demonstrate that uploading files to Azure Storage does not require an operational HDInsight cluster). After processing, we download the resultant files from the Azure Storage Blob for further analysis. This demonstrates how these two Azure services (Azure Storage and HDInsight) run separately but still integrate seamlessly. Microsoft Azure uses high-speed Azure Flat Network Storage technology for high-speed data transfer so that it does not compromise on performance.

You can still store (upload or download) data in the Azure Storage Blob without needing to have an operational HDInsight cluster. Whenever you need Hadoop computation capability, you can simply create an HDInsight cluster, point it to the Azure Storage Blob, process the data stored there, and store the result, if any, back to the Azure Storage Blob. And of course, when computation is done, you can delete the HDInsight cluster without losing the data (it is stored separately in the Azure Storage Blob, by default).

In Listing 6.7, for lines 2–8, you must specify parameters required for transferring local files from the local machine to the Azure Storage Blob (these include the data center location, storage account, container name, and local and remote folder names).

LISTING 6.7   Uploading Files from the Local Machine to the Azure Storage Blob

```
1: # Declare all the variables and specify their values
2: $location = "Central US"
3:
4: $defaultStorageAccount = "tyhdistorageauto"
5: $defaultStorageContainer = "adventureworksauto"
6:
7: $localFolder = "D:\HDInsight\Data"
8: $azureStorageFolder = "davinci"
9:
10: # Check if storage account already exists then use it
11: # or else create a new storage account with the specified name
12: $storageAccount = Get-AzureStorageAccount -StorageAccountName
    $defaultStorageAccount `
13:    -ErrorAction SilentlyContinue
```

```
14: if ($storageAccount -eq $null)
15: {
16:    Write-Host "Creating new storage account $defaultStorageAccount."
17:    $storageAccount = New-AzureStorageAccount -StorageAccountName
    $defaultStorageAccount `
18:        -Location $location
19: }
20: else
21: {
22:    Write-Host "Using existing storage account $defaultStorageAccount."
23: }
24:
25: # Check if specified storage container already exists then use it
26: # or else create a new storage container with the specified
27: # name in the specified storage account
28: $storageContext = New-AzureStorageContext -StorageAccountName
    $defaultStorageAccount `
29:    -StorageAccountKey (Get-AzureStorageKey $defaultStorageAccount).Primary
30: $storageContainer = Get-AzureStorageContainer -Name $defaultStorageContainer `
31:    -Context $storageContext -ErrorAction SilentlyContinue
32: if ($storageContainer -eq $null)
33: {
34:    Write-Host "Creating new storage container $defaultStorageContainer."
35:    $storageContainer = New-AzureStorageContainer -Name $defaultStorageContainer `
36:        -Context $storageContext
37: }
38: else
39: {
40:    Write-Host "Using existing storage container $defaultStorageContainer."
41: }
42:
43: $filesToUpload = Get-ChildItem $localFolder
44: foreach ($file in $filesToUpload)
45: {
46:    $localFileName = "$localFolder\$file"
47:    $fileToUpload = "$azureStorageFolder/$file"
48:    Write-Host "Copying $localFileName to Azure storage as $fileToUpload"
49:    # Copy the file from local workstation to the Blob container
50:    Set-AzureStorageBlobContent -File $localFileName `
51:        -Container $defaultStorageContainer `
52:        -Blob $fileToUpload `
53:        -context $storageContext
54: }
55: Write-Host "All files from $localFolder workstation folder copied to
    $azureStorageFolder folder on Azure storage"
```

Lines 10–23 check whether the specified storage account already exists, and then either use it or create a new storage account with the specified name. Similarly, lines 25–41 check whether the storage account container already exists, and then either use it or create a new storage account container with the specified name.

Lines 43–54 iterate through the local specified folder and copy or upload each file from the local folder to the destination folder (in the Azure Storage Blob's container). Figure 6.27 shows the execution result of PowerShell scripts from Listing 6.7. You can see that five files in the local folder (five copies of the same `davinci.txt` file available as part of sample data) were successfully uploaded to the Azure Storage Blob.

```
PS C:\WINDOWS\system32> D:\HDInsight\Code\HDInsight Provisioning_5.ps1
Using existing storage account tyhdistorageauto.
Using existing storage container adventureworksauto.
Copying D:\HDInsight\Data\davinci_01.txt to Azure storage as davinci/davinci_01.txt


    Container Uri: https://tyhdistorageauto.blob.core.windows.net/adventureworksauto


Name                                         BlobType    Length
----                                         --------    ------
davinci/davinci_01.txt                       BlockBlob   1427785
Copying D:\HDInsight\Data\davinci_02.txt to Azure storage as davinci/davinci_02.txt
davinci/davinci_02.txt                       BlockBlob   1427785
Copying D:\HDInsight\Data\davinci_03.txt to Azure storage as davinci/davinci_03.txt
davinci/davinci_03.txt                       BlockBlob   1427785
Copying D:\HDInsight\Data\davinci_04.txt to Azure storage as davinci/davinci_04.txt
davinci/davinci_04.txt                       BlockBlob   1427785
Copying D:\HDInsight\Data\davinci_05.txt to Azure storage as davinci/davinci_05.txt
davinci/davinci_05.txt                       BlockBlob   1427785
All files from D:\HDInsight\Data workstation folder copied to davinci folder on Azure storage


PS C:\WINDOWS\system32>
```

FIGURE 6.27
Execution result of copying files from the local folder to the Azure Storage Blob.

The PowerShell scripts from Listing 6.8 define a MapReduce job for word count for the files we uploaded and submit it for execution to the HDInsight cluster. The code then waits for the MapReduce job to complete and shows execution-related metrics (see Figure 6.28).

LISTING 6.8   Executing a MapReduce Job from a Local Machine Using PowerShell Scripting

```
 1: # Declare all the variables and specify their values
 2: $subscriptionName = "Visual Studio Ultimate with MSDN"
 3: $clusterName = "tyhdiclusterauto"
 4:
 5: # Define the word count MapReduce job to be executed
 6: $jobDefinition = New-AzureHDInsightMapReduceJobDefinition `
 7:    -JarFile "wasb:///example/jars/hadoop-mapreduce-examples.jar" `
 8:    -ClassName "wordcount" `
 9:    -Arguments "wasb:///davinci/", "wasb:///davinciwordcountresult"
10:
```

```
11: # Submit the MapReduce job
12: Select-AzureSubscription $subscriptionName
13: $wordCountMapReduceJob = Start-AzureHDInsightJob -Cluster $clusterName
    -JobDefinition $jobDefinition
14:
15: Write-Host "WordCount MapReduce Job submitted..."
16: # Wait for the MapReduce job to complete
17: Wait-AzureHDInsightJob -Job $wordCountMapReduceJob -WaitTimeoutInSeconds 3600
18: # Get the MapReduce job standard error output
19: Get-AzureHDInsightJobOutput -Cluster $clusterName -JobId $wordCountMapReduceJob.
    JobId -StandardError
20: Write-Host "WordCount MapReduce Job completed..."
```

```
PS C:\WINDOWS\system32> D:\HDInsight\Code\HDInsight Provisioning_6.ps1
WordCount MapReduce Job submitted...


Cluster         : tyhdiclusterauto
ExitCode        : 0
Name            : wordcount
PercentComplete : map 100% reduce 100%
Query           :
State           : Completed
StatusDirectory : f50c4321-baa5-4c08-92b6-d5c528427eb8
SubmissionTime  : 12/13/2014 6:22:27 PM
JobId           : job_1418490106721_0007

14/12/13 18:22:42 INFO impl.TimelineClientImpl: Timeline service address: http://headnode
14/12/13 18:22:42 INFO client.RMProxy: Connecting to ResourceManager at headnodehost/100.
14/12/13 18:22:42 INFO client.AHSProxy: Connecting to Application History server at headn
14/12/13 18:22:43 INFO input.FileInputFormat: Total input paths to process : 5
14/12/13 18:22:44 INFO mapreduce.JobSubmitter: number of splits:5
14/12/13 18:22:44 INFO mapreduce.JobSubmitter: Submitting tokens for job: job_14184901067
14/12/13 18:22:44 INFO mapreduce.JobSubmitter: Kind: mapreduce.job, Service: job_14184901
14/12/13 18:22:44 INFO mapreduce.JobSubmitter: Kind: RM_DELEGATION_TOKEN, Service: 100.78
14/12/13 18:22:45 INFO impl.YarnClientImpl: Submitted application application_14184901067
14/12/13 18:22:45 INFO mapreduce.Job: The url to track the job: http://headnodehost:9014/
14/12/13 18:22:45 INFO mapreduce.Job: Running job: job_1418490106721_0008
14/12/13 18:22:55 INFO mapreduce.Job: Job job_1418490106721_0008 running in uber mode : f
14/12/13 18:22:55 INFO mapreduce.Job:  map 0% reduce 0%
14/12/13 18:23:13 INFO mapreduce.Job:  map 20% reduce 0%
14/12/13 18:23:14 INFO mapreduce.Job:  map 60% reduce 0%
14/12/13 18:23:15 INFO mapreduce.Job:  map 80% reduce 0%
14/12/13 18:23:17 INFO mapreduce.Job:  map 100% reduce 0%
14/12/13 18:23:23 INFO mapreduce.Job:  map 100% reduce 100%
14/12/13 18:23:25 INFO mapreduce.Job: Job job_1418490106721_0008 completed successfully
14/12/13 18:23:26 INFO mapreduce.Job: Counters: 50
    File System Counters
```

FIGURE 6.28
Execution result of the word count MapReduce job submitted using PowerShell.

Lines 2 and 3 of Listing 6.8 declare variables and their values to be used during execution.
Lines 5–9 define the MapReduce job, including the JAR filename, the class name from the JAR
file, input files or folder name, and output location. Line 13 submits the defined job for execution to the HDInsight cluster. Lines 17 and 18 wait for the submitted job to complete and show
the execution result of the completed job on the console.

PowerShell scripts from Listing 6.9 download the execution output file (generated from the word
count MapReduce job) from the Azure Storage Blob. Lines 2–6 show the variables and their
values to be used during script execution. Lines 8 and 9 create a context to connect the storage
account. Lines 13–15 download the execution output file from the Azure Storage Blob to local
disk. Line 18 displays the content of the execution output file; Figure 6.29 shows the last few lines.

LISTING 6.9   Downloading Files (Output Files from a MapReduce Job) from Azure Storage Blob Using PowerShell

```
1: # Declare all the variables and specify their values
2: $defaultStorageAccount = "tyhdistorageauto"
3: $defaultStorageContainer = "adventureworksauto"
4:
5: $localFolder = "D:\HDInsight\Data"
6: $executionResultBlob = "davinciwordcountresult/part-r-00000"
7:
8: $storageContext = New-AzureStorageContext -StorageAccountName
   $defaultStorageAccount `
9:    -StorageAccountKey (Get-AzureStorageKey $defaultStorageAccount).Primary
10:
11: # Downloads a storage blob from the specified storage account
12: Get-AzureStorageBlobContent -Context $storageContext `
13:    -Container $defaultStorageContainer `
14:    -Blob $executionResultBlob `
15:    -Destination $localFolder
16:
17: # Display content of the resultant file
18: Cat $localFolder\davinciwordcountresult\part-r-00000
```

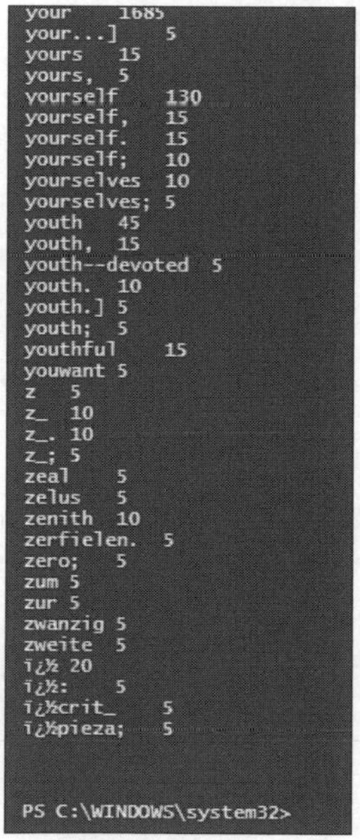

```
your    1685
your...]   5
yours   15
yours,  5
yourself    130
yourself,   15
yourself.   15
yourself;   10
yourselves  10
yourselves; 5
youth   45
youth,  15
youth--devoted  5
youth.  10
youth.] 5
youth;  5
youthful    15
youwant 5
z    5
z_  10
z_. 10
z_; 5
zeal    5
zelus   5
zenith  10
zerfielen.  5
zero;   5
zum 5
zur 5
zwanzig 5
zweite  5
ï¿½ 20
ï¿½:    5
ï¿½crit_    5
ï¿½pieza;   5


PS C:\WINDOWS\system32>
```

FIGURE 6.29
Content of the downloaded execution result file (word count MapReduce job) from local disk.

You can provision and manage an HDInsight cluster in a couple other ways:

▶ Using the Cross-Platform Command-Line Interface (implemented in `Node.js`) to provision and manage Hadoop clusters in HDInsight. See http://azure.microsoft.com/en-us/documentation/articles/hdinsight-administer-use-command-line/.

▶ Using the HDInsight .NET Software Development Kit (SDK) to programmatically provision and manage the HDInsight cluster. The HDInsight .NET SDK also provides classes related the creation, configuration, submission, and monitoring of Hadoop jobs managed by an Azure HDInsight Service. See http://msdn.microsoft.com/en-us/library/azure/dn469975.aspx.

Managing and Monitoring HDInsight Cluster and Job Execution

You can manage and monitor an HDInsight cluster in different ways. For example, you can use the Azure Management Portal to manage your HDInsight cluster. If you are connected to the head node using remote desktop connectivity, you can click the Hadoop Name Node Status icon to see information about overall cluster (see Figure 6.30).

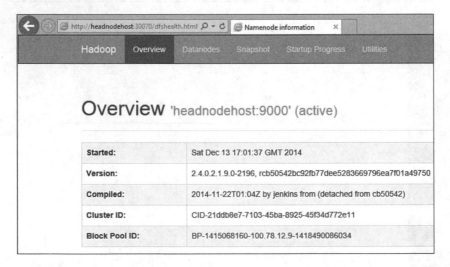

FIGURE 6.30
Hadoop Name Node Status page, part 1.

Figure 6.31 shows a summary of the overall cluster information, such as resources in use, on the Hadoop Name Node Status page.

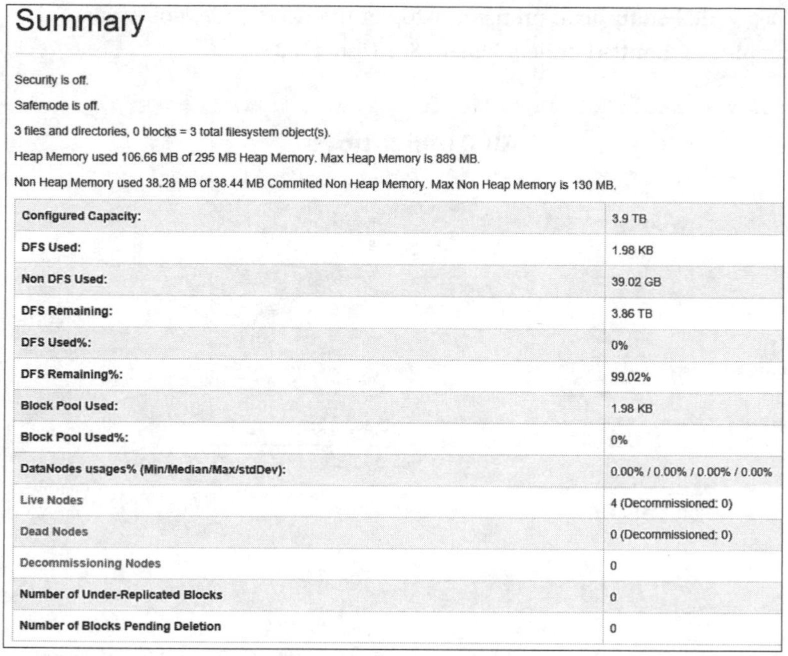

Summary

Security is off.

Safemode is off.

3 files and directories, 0 blocks = 3 total filesystem object(s).

Heap Memory used 106.66 MB of 295 MB Heap Memory. Max Heap Memory is 889 MB.

Non Heap Memory used 38.28 MB of 38.44 MB Commited Non Heap Memory. Max Non Heap Memory is 130 MB.

Configured Capacity:	3.9 TB
DFS Used:	1.98 KB
Non DFS Used:	39.02 GB
DFS Remaining:	3.86 TB
DFS Used%:	0%
DFS Remaining%:	99.02%
Block Pool Used:	1.98 KB
Block Pool Used%:	0%
DataNodes usages% (Min/Median/Max/stdDev):	0.00% / 0.00% / 0.00% / 0.00%
Live Nodes	4 (Decommissioned: 0)
Dead Nodes	0 (Decommissioned: 0)
Decommissioning Nodes	0
Number of Under-Replicated Blocks	0
Number of Blocks Pending Deletion	0

FIGURE 6.31
Hadoop Name Node Status page, part 2.

Figure 6.32 shows the Datanodes tab of the Hadoop Name Node Status page, where you can see all the data nodes in the cluster and their configured capacity and state.

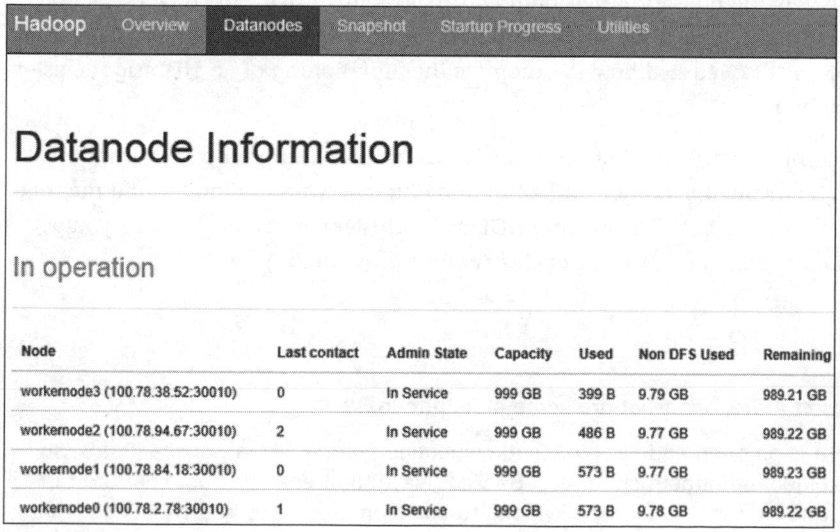

Datanode Information

In operation

Node	Last contact	Admin State	Capacity	Used	Non DFS Used	Remaining
workernode3 (100.78.38.52:30010)	0	In Service	999 GB	399 B	9.79 GB	989.21 GB
workernode2 (100.78.94.67:30010)	2	In Service	999 GB	486 B	9.77 GB	989.22 GB
workernode1 (100.78.84.18:30010)	0	In Service	999 GB	573 B	9.77 GB	989.23 GB
workernode0 (100.78.2.78:30010)	1	In Service	999 GB	573 B	9.78 GB	989.22 GB

FIGURE 6.32
Hadoop Name Node Status page, part 3.

When you click the Hadoop YARN Status icon on the desktop of the head node, you can see all the jobs in their states (running, submitted, failed, killed). See Figure 6.33.

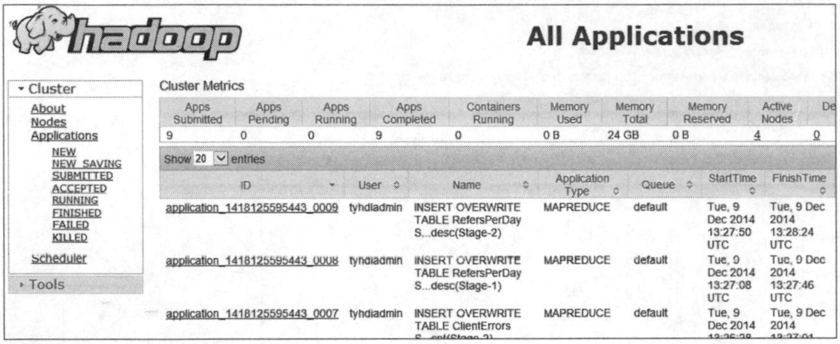

FIGURE 6.33
Hadoop YARN Status page to show job status.

Summary

The past few hours mostly discussed Big Data and how to leverage Hadoop for storing and processing Big Data. This hour focused mainly on getting started on the HDInsight service.

You first looked at Microsoft Azure (a promising cloud computing platform from Microsoft) and the different services it offers. You explored the HDInsight service, in particular, and the related services needed when working with HDInsight.

You investigated different methods for provisioning an HDInsight cluster (basically, a Hadoop cluster). You saw how you can provision an HDInsight cluster interactively using the Azure Management Portal and also learned how to automate the provisioning of an HDInsight cluster with PowerShell scripting.

You also explored running MapReduce job from the Hadoop command prompt and from the local machine using PowerShell. Finally, you looked into different ways to monitor and manage an HDInsight cluster. In Hour 11, "Customizing HDInsight Cluster with Script Action," you go into more detail on customizing an HDInsight cluster while provisioning.

Q&A

Q. What is Microsoft Azure, and what are some of its offerings?

A. Microsoft Azure is an open and flexible cloud computing Platform As a Service (PaaS) and infrastructure platform (Infrastructure As a Service [IaaS]) that enables customers to rapidly build, deploy, and manage secure applications to scale on premises, in the cloud, or both.

Microsoft Azure has a growing collection of integrated services (compute, storage, data, net-working, and application) that help you move faster, do more, and save money. Microsoft Azure offers a broad range of services. Figure 6.1 shows some of the widely used services.

Q. What is HDInsight? What are different ways of creating HDInsight cluster?

A. HDInsight is one service that Microsoft Azure offers. HDInsight brings a 100 percent Apache Hadoop–based solution to the cloud platform, in partnership with Hortonworks. It provides the capability to gain the full value of Big Data with a modern, cloud-based data platform that manages data of any type, whether structured or unstructured, and any size.

With the Microsoft Azure HDInsight service, now any organization (small or big) can create a Hadoop cluster in just few minutes (compared to creating a Hadoop cluster on the local infrastructure in days or months) and without requiring a huge upfront hardware investment. If in the future you need a larger cluster, you can simply delete your current cluster and create a new, bigger one in minutes without losing any data. The best part is that an organization pays for only the time it uses the cluster.

You can provision the HDInsight service (Hadoop cluster) either using the Azure Management Portal interactively or using PowerShell scripting for automatic provisioning.

Exercise

On the Azure Management Portal, select your HDInsight cluster and click the Query Console icon (see Figure 6.34) to log in to the HDInsight cluster dashboard. You are prompted to enter the cluster administrator username and password; use the ones you specified when creating your HDInsight cluster.

NOTE

HDInsight Cluster Dashboard

When you provision an HDInsight cluster, a cluster dashboard in the form of a web application is deployed to your HDInsight cluster. You can use it to run Hive queries, check job logs, and browse the Azure Storage Blob. The URL to access this web application is `<ClusterName>.azurehdinsight.net`.

FIGURE 6.34
The Azure Management Portal—HDInsight details.

After successfully logging in, you are taken to the HDInsight Query Console or the cluster dash-board (see Figure 6.35). Follow the onscreen instructions to execute some built-in solutions with sample data (such as Sensor Data Analysis and Website Log Analysis), and see yourself how it's working and executing.

FIGURE 6.35
HDInsight Query Console—sample solutions.

Now go to the Job History tab on the HDInsight Query Console and analyze the details of jobs that have executed and those in progress. This looks similar to Figure 6.36. You can click the View Details link to see the details of each job submitted to the HDInsight cluster.

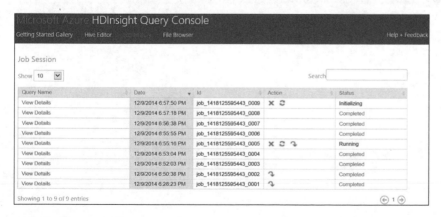

FIGURE 6.36
Exploring job execution history on the HDInsight Query Console.

Each HDInsight cluster has two head nodes configured for higher availability. To determine which head node is currently active and to check on the status of the services running on that head node, connect to the HDInsight cluster using remote desktop connectivity; click the Hadoop Service Availability icon on the desktop and identify the active head node (see Figure 6.37).

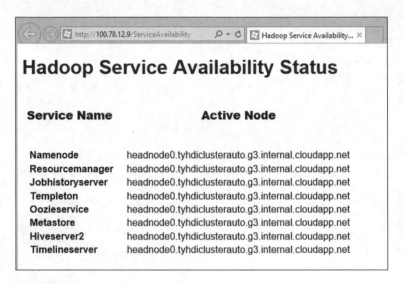

FIGURE 6.37
Hadoop Services Availability icon on the active head node.

HDInsight also includes Ambari, which facilitates the management and monitoring of cluster resources. Ambari includes a collection of operator tools and a set of RESTfull APIs that mask the complexity of Hadoop, simplifying the operation of the cluster.

Exploring Typical Components of HDFS Cluster

What You'll Learn in This Hour:

▶ HDFS Cluster Components

▶ HDInsight Cluster Architecture

▶ High Availability in HDInsight

This hour explores the typical components of an HDFS cluster: the name node, secondary name node, and data nodes. The name node acts as the cluster master and manages and controls the data nodes, or the slaves. Data nodes are responsible for user data storage on HDFS.

HDInsight separates the storage from the cluster and relies on Azure blob storage (not HDFS) as the default file system for storing data. Until Hadoop 1.0, the name node was a single point of failure for the cluster, but as of Hadoop 2.0, high availability (HA) is now standard.

This hour provides more details on these concepts in the context of HDInsight service.

HDFS Cluster Components

Hadoop relies on HDFS, or the Hadoop Distributed File System, for efficient storage of data in the cluster. Hour 3, "Hadoop Distributed File System Versions 1.0 and 2.0," introduced HDFS and explained how Hadoop leverages it to store user data.

An HDFS cluster has these typical components:

▶ Name node

▶ Secondary name node

▶ Standby name node

▶ Data nodes

An HDFS cluster is based on the classic master/slave architecture. The name node, or the cluster master, acts as the brain of the cluster and manages the data nodes, or the slaves.

Understanding Name Node Functionality

The *name node* is responsible for maintaining file system metadata, apart from managing coordination among the data nodes. The name node keeps track of the hierarchies of files and directories (called the *namespace*) stored in the file system and maps file blocks to the data nodes in the cluster.

For example, imagine that a text file (File A) has been split into two blocks (Block 1 and Block 2) and stored on Data Nodes 1, 2, and 3 on the cluster (assuming a replication factor of 3). The name node must keep track of the location of files and file blocks on the file system (see Figure 7.1).

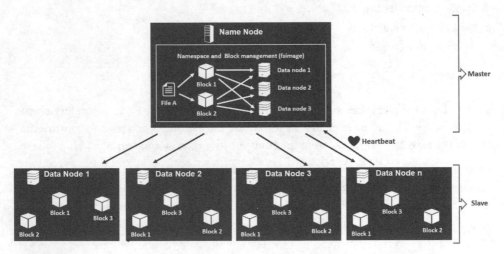

FIGURE 7.1
Components of an HDFS cluster.

The name node also keeps track of alive and available nodes in a cluster by means of a heartbeat it receives from individual data nodes at periodic intervals.

The name node also responds to client requests. When client applications reach out to the name node with data read/write requests, the name node responds by providing clients with the necessary metadata and a list of data nodes that store the required data. Clients subsequently talk directly to relevant data nodes (see Figure 7.2). The name node itself does not store the actual data; it is only a metadata provider for client data requests.

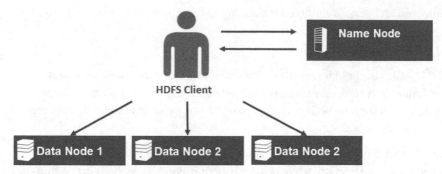

FIGURE 7.2
The client gets a list of data nodes from the name node and interacts directly with data nodes.

Why the Secondary Name Node Is Not a Standby Node

Contrary to its name, the *secondary name node* is not a standby name node. To understand the purpose of a secondary name node, you must understand how a name node stores metadata related to the addition or removal of blocks in the file system.

The name node stores the HDFS metadata information in a metadata file titled `fsimage`. This image file is not updated on every addition or removal of a block in the file system. Instead, these add/remove operations are logged and maintained in a separate log file. Appending updates to a separate log achieves faster I/O.

The primary purposes of the secondary name node are to periodically download the name node image and log files, create a new image by merging the image and log files, and upload the new image back to the name node. The process of generating a new `fsimage` from a merge operation is called the *checkpoint* (see Figure 7.3). Without a secondary name node, the name node itself would have to perform this time-consuming work every time it restarted. Because the secondary name node performs this task periodically, the name node can restart faster.

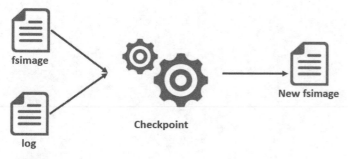

FIGURE 7.3
A secondary name node generating a new `fsimage`.

The secondary name node is also responsible for backing up the name node image.

Standby Name Node

Before Hadoop 2.0.0, a cluster could have only one name node. Thus, the name node was the single point of failure in a Hadoop cluster. Name node failure gravely impacted cluster availability. Likewise, when a name node had to be taken down for maintenance or upgrades, the entire cluster was unavailable.

The HDFS high availability feature introduced in Hadoop 2.0 addressed this problem. Now a cluster can have two name nodes in an active-passive configuration (one node is active and the other node is in standby mode). The active node and the standby node remain in synch. If the active node fails, the standby node takes over and promotes itself to the active state.

The data nodes are configured with the location of both name nodes. Data nodes send periodic heartbeats to both name nodes as a confirmation that the data node is operational and that the blocks hosted by it are available. This is important in ensuring faster failover.

Figure 7.4 illustrates this major difference between the secondary name node and the standby name node. As you can see, data nodes are not aware of the secondary name node.

TIP

A cluster configured for high availability does not require a secondary name node. The task of performing checkpoint and backup becomes redundant with the presence of a standby name node, so the cluster is not required to have a separate secondary name node. In fact, you can reuse the hardware used for the secondary name node to host the standby node.

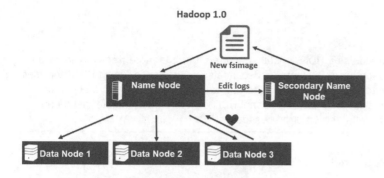

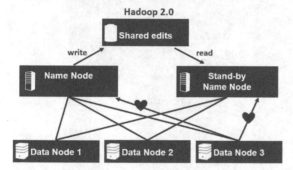

FIGURE 7.4
The differences between the secondary name node and the standby name node.

HDInsight Cluster Architecture

HDInsight deviates from the conventional Hadoop architecture by separating the storage from the cluster. HDInsight relies on Azure blob storage (wasb) as the default file system for storing data instead of using HDFS. Use of blob storage provides the following additional benefits:

▶ Blob storage allows safe decommissioning of HDInsight cluster without the loss of user data.

▶ Because data storage is not dependent on the cluster, you can easily decommission the cluster whenever it is not in use, thus providing additional cost benefits.

▶ Multiple clusters and other apps can access the same blob storage.

GO TO ▶ **Hour 8, "Storing Data in Microsoft Azure Storage Blob,"** explores Azure Storage Blob and looks at how locality of data to compute nodes is maintained, in spite of the separation of data from the cluster.

NOTE

HDFS Is Still Supported

The traditional approach of storage using HDFS is still supported, but it is more transitory in nature, and any data stored in HDFS is lost when a cluster is decommissioned. Hence, using HDFS for user data storage is not recommended. A better solution is to use traditional HDFS to store any temporary job data. Furthermore, HDInsight also uses traditional HDFS to store intermediate results and temporary data from MapReduce jobs and other processes.

Figure 7.5 provides a visual representation of the typical HDInsight cluster architecture.

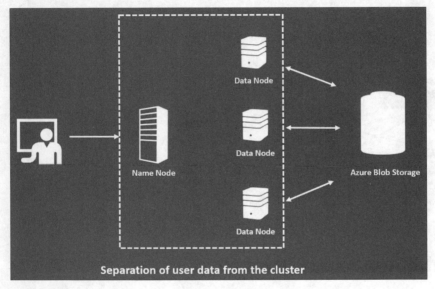

FIGURE 7.5
HDInsight cluster architecture.

The HDInsight head node is conceptually equivalent to the traditional Apache Hadoop name node, discussed in the previous sections. The head node runs the following core Hadoop services:

► Name node

► Secondary name node

► Resource Manager and MapReduce JobHistoryServer (previously part of the Job Tracker service)

NOTE

Where Are the Job Tracker and Task Tracker?

In Hadoop 2.0 (with the YARN framework), Job Tracker capabilities are divided into components: the Resource Manager (responsible for resource management) and the MapReduce Application Master (manages the application's life cycle and terminates when an application/MapReduce job is complete). The Job History Server has the task of providing information about completed jobs. Similarly, the Node Manager has replaced the Task Tracker on the compute nodes.

TRY IT YOURSELF

Exploring the Services on HDInsight Name Node

From the Services console on the name node and compute nodes, you can view the HDInsight services corresponding to the Hadoop daemons listed earlier:

1. Log in to the Azure management portal.

2. Click HDInsight on the left pane to bring up the list of HDInsight clusters.

3. Click the HDInsight cluster of interest.

4. From the top of the page, click Configuration.

5. If a remote desktop connection is not enabled, from the bottom of the page, click Enable Remote to configure a user for remote login (see Figure 7.6); otherwise, click Connect to connect to the name node.

6. This brings up the desktop of the cluster's name node (see Figure 7.7).

7. Launch the Services console by typing `services.msc` in the Run window or selecting View Local Services from Administrative tools in the Control Panel.

8. Examine the Apache Hadoop services in the Services windows; look for the `namenode`, `secondarynamenode`, `resourcemanager`, and `MapReduce JobHistoryServer` services (see Figure 7.8).

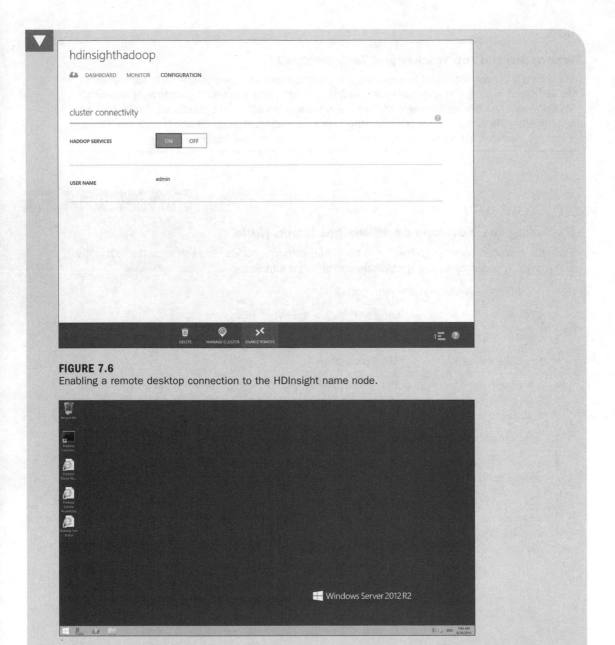

FIGURE 7.6
Enabling a remote desktop connection to the HDInsight name node.

FIGURE 7.7
HDInsight name node desktop.

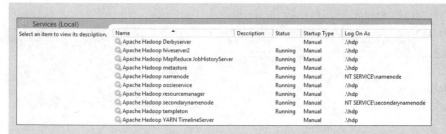

FIGURE 7.8
HDInsight name node services.

9. To view the services running on data nodes, open the Hadoop Name Node Status link on the desktop.

10. Click the Datanodes table to view the data node information (see Figure 7.9).

FIGURE 7.9
HDInsight data node information.

11. Use a remote desktop connection to remotely log in to one of the data nodes from within the name node.

12. Launch the Services console again on the data node and look for the `datanode` and `nodemanager` Apache Hadoop services (see Figure 7.10).

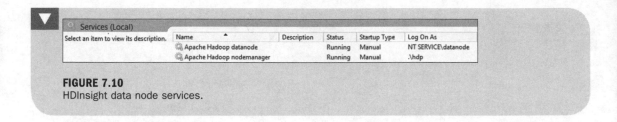

FIGURE 7.10
HDInsight data node services.

High Availability in HDInsight

HDInsight clusters (from HDI Version 2.1 onward) also support a second standby/passive head node, to support the name node high availability feature discussed in the earlier part of this hour. HA relies on quorum-based storage and failover detection using ZooKeeper, as the following sections explain.

HA Based on Quorum-Based Storage

HDInsight 3.1 is based on HDP 2.1, which utilizes the Quorum Journal Manager to achieve high availability. In this configuration, the active node writes edit log modifications to the journal machines.

To be considered successful, a journal log modification should be written to the majority of the journal nodes. The standby, or passive, name node keeps its state in synch with the active node by consuming the file system journal logged by the active name node.

If a failover occurs, the standby name promotes itself to active state only after ensuring that it has read all the edits from the journal nodes.

Failover Detection Using ZooKeeper

The ZooKeeper Failover Controller (ZKFC) service running on the name nodes is responsible for detecting a failure and recognizing a need to fail over to the standby node (see Figure 7.11). ZKFC uses the ZooKeeper service for coordination and to detect a need for failover.

Because ZKFC runs on both active and standby name nodes, it risks a split-brain scenario in which both nodes try to achieve active state at the same time. To prevent this, ZKFC tries to obtain an exclusive lock on the ZooKeeper service. The service that successfully obtains a lock is responsible for failing over to its respective name node and promoting it to active state.

An examination of the entries in the hosts file reveals names and IP addresses of the machines in the cluster (see Figure 7.12).

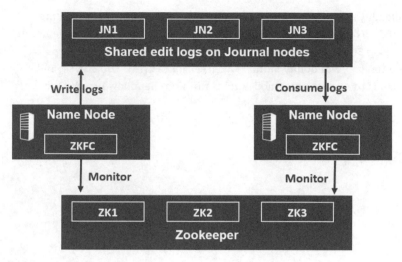

FIGURE 7.11
High availability in HDInsight using Quorum-based storage and ZooKeeper.

FIGURE 7.12
Examining the host entries in the name node.

If you log in to zookepernode0 and examine the services running in the Services console, you can see that zkServer (the ZooKeeper Service) is indeed running on the machine (see Figure 7.13).

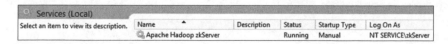

FIGURE 7.13
Windows Service for ZooKeeper server.

The Hadoop Service Availability Status page helps determine the active name node and the status of services on the node. To examine the status of services and determine the active name node, double-click the Hadoop Service Availability Status icon on the name node desktop. This launches the Hadoop Service Availability Status page (see Figure 7.14). You can see in Figure 7.14 that `headnode0` is the active name node and is running the following services:

- ▶ Namenode
- ▶ Resourcemanager
- ▶ Jobhistory
- ▶ Templeton
- ▶ Oozieservice
- ▶ Metastore
- ▶ Hiveserver2

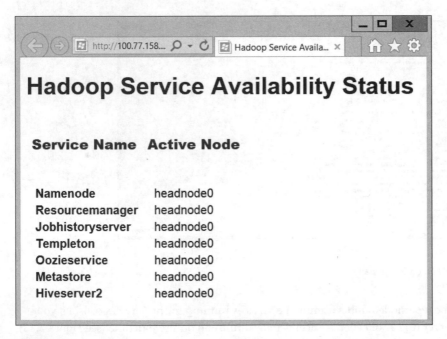

FIGURE 7.14
Checking the Hadoop service availability status.

Summary

In this hour, you explored the typical components of a Hadoop cluster and understood their importance in the context of HDInsight. You also saw why the secondary name node is not actually a standby name node. In addition, you learned why blob storage is recommended over HDFS for user data storage in HDInsight Cluster. Traditional HDFS is transitory in nature and is better suited for storing intermediate processing results. The hour concluded with an overview of the name node HA feature supported by HDInsight service.

Q&A

Q. Are any other mechanisms available for attaining high availability?

A. Yes, a similar approach is based on shared storage instead of the journal nodes. In a shared storage mechanism, instead of logging to journal nodes, the active node logs a record to a file in shared storage that the standby node then reads.

Q. Does switching to a high-availability configuration incur extra cost because it involves provisioning a separate standby name node?

A. Switching to a high-availability configuration does not incur extra costs if the default large-size (A3) head node is used for provisioning. Choosing a higher configuration for the head node (extra-large and above) does involve additional costs with high-availability configuration. Refer to http://azure.microsoft.com/en-us/pricing/details/hdinsight/ for more details on pricing.

Q. How can data be transferred to and from traditional HDFS?

A. You can access traditional HDFS using `hdfs://<namenodehost>/<path>`. The HDFS commands for data transfer and retrieval work as expected. For example, you can use the following command to copy files to HDFS:

```
hadoop fs -copyFromLocal C:\data\*.txt hdfs://<namenodehost>/<path>
```

Without the URI specified, this command copies the files to the default file system (blob storage, in an HDInsight cluster).

Quiz

1. What is the purpose of the secondary name node, and how does it differ from the standby name node?

2. What major change does HDInsight bring about in storing user data on the cluster?

3. What are the main functions of a name node in an HDFS cluster?

Answers

1. The primary purpose of the secondary name node is to perform checkpoints and back up the name node image. The secondary name node is not actually a standby name node; it does not contribute to attaining name node high availability.

2. HDInsight relies on Azure blob storage as the default file system and separates user data from the cluster.

3. The name node is responsible for handling namespace and block management, keeping track of active data nodes, and responding to client requests.

Storing Data in Microsoft Azure Storage Blob

What You'll Learn in This Hour:

▶ Understanding Storage in Microsoft Azure
▶ Benefits of Azure Storage Blob over HDFS
▶ Azure Storage Explorer Tools

HDInsight supports both the Hadoop Distributed Files System (HDFS) and Azure Storage Blob for storing user data. HDInsight relies on Azure Storage Blob as the default file system for storing data, which is a major deviation in HDInsight (compared to other Hadoop distributions) from the conventional Hadoop architecture. Separating storage from the cluster challenges the principle of data locality.

This hour explores Azure storage in the context of HDInsight and concludes by looking at the impact of blob storage on both performance and data locality.

Understanding Storage in Microsoft Azure

Microsoft Azure storage is a scalable, durable, and highly available storage service. Access to Microsoft Azure Storage services is routed through a unique namespace known as the Azure storage account. Each storage account can contain up to 500TB of combined blob, queue, table, and file data.

Microsoft Azure offers the following storage services:

▶ **Blob storage**—An effective means of storing large amounts of unstructured data on the cloud. Blob storage works for text or binary data files (documents, images, Big Data sets such as log files, and more). Blobs are organized into containers. Blob storage offers two types of blobs, block blobs (optimized for streaming and storing cloud objects) and page blobs (optimized for random writes). The maximum size for a block blob is 200GB, and the maximum size for a page blob is 1TB.

▶ **Table storage**—The key/attribute store for Microsoft NoSQL.

▶ **Queue storage**—A messaging solution for communication between applications.

▶ **File storage**—Shared storage for legacy applications.

See Figure 8.1 for a visual representation of these concepts.

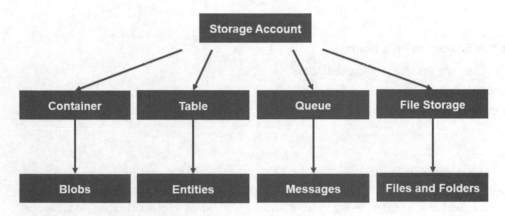

FIGURE 8.1
Visual representation of storage concepts in Microsoft Azure.

NOTE

Because HDInsight currently supports only block blobs, this hour focuses only on blob storage. This book does not discuss the other Azure storage services.

Benefits of Azure Storage Blob over HDFS

Hadoop clusters have been relying on traditional HDFS for storage from the early days. However, HDInsight relies on blob storage to store user data and uses HDFS only as a temporary storage for storing intermediate processing results and temporary job data. These primary motivating factors strengthen the case for the use of blob storage:

▶ Blob storage facilitates the safe decommissioning of HDInsight cluster without the loss of user data.

▶ Because the data storage is not dependent on the cluster, it is possible to easily decommission the cluster whenever it is not in use, thus delivering additional cost benefits.

Blob storage also provides some secondary benefits:

▶ Because the data resides in the Blob store instead of HDFS on a compute cluster, multiple HDInsight clusters and other applications can easily share this data.

▶ Blob storage has built-in scaling capabilities. With HDFS storage, on the other hand, scaling out storage would involve adding data nodes in the cluster. This further implies that storage can be scaled out without scaling out the compute, and vice versa. This is much harder to achieve with traditional HDFS, in which storage and compute are tied together.

▶ Blob storage can be georeplicated and provides the additional benefits of geographic recovery and data redundancy.

Azure Storage Explorer Tools

Several tools are available for accessing Azure Storage. This section explores some of them.

Azure Storage Explorer

Azure Storage Explorer is a Windows Explorer–like free tool available for download on CodePlex at http://azurestorageexplorer.codeplex.com/.

To use Azure Storage Explorer, you must have an Azure storage account name and an account key. To obtain the account name and access key, navigate to the Azure Management Portal and, from the Storage tab, select Manage Access Keys item from the bottom of the page. This brings up details related to the account name and access keys (see Figure 8.2).

Click the Add Account button in Azure Storage Explorer and populate the storage account name and storage account key you obtained earlier (see Figure 8.3).

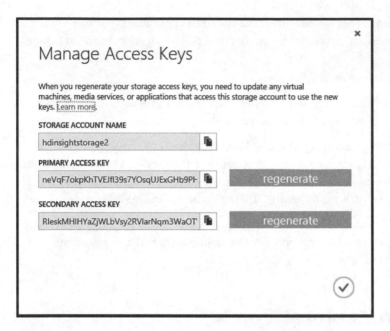

FIGURE 8.2
Retrieving the Azure storage account name and access keys.

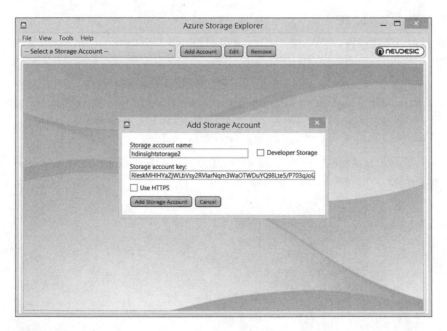

FIGURE 8.3
Populating storage account name and key in Azure Storage Explorer.

Azure Storage Explorer is now ready for use. With its Windows Explorer–like interface, Azure Storage Explorer allows for the convenient addition and removal of containers and files.

AZCopy

AZCopy is a command-line utility that you can incorporate into custom applications to transfer data into and out of Azure storage. AZCopy is similar in use to other Microsoft file copy utilities, such as robocopy, and also supports nested directories and files.

For example, the following command copies all subdirectories and files in the `C:\Data` directory on the local disk as block blobs to the container named `MyStorageContainer` in the storage account `MyStorageAccount`. Use of the `/S` switch (recursive mode) ensures that files in any subdirectories are also copied.

```
AzCopy C:\Data https://MyStorageAccount.blob.core.windows.net/MyStorageContainer/
/destkey:AccessKey /S
```

Azure PowerShell

Azure PowerShell provides cmdlets to manage Azure through Windows PowerShell. Azure PowerShell is installed from the Microsoft Web Platform Installer (see Figure 8.4).

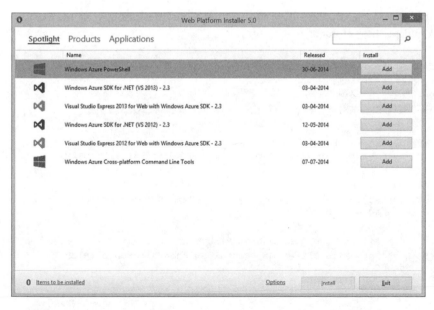

FIGURE 8.4
Installing Windows Azure PowerShell.

The cmdlets need subscription details to connect and manage the services. You provide subscription information in two ways:

▶ Using a management certificate

▶ Signing directly into Azure with user credentials (the Azure AD method)

The Azure AD method is the easier method, but the credentials are available to Azure PowerShell for only 12 hours before they expire. Before you can use Azure PowerShell to upload data to Blob Storage, you need the name of the destination storage account and the container. The easiest way to obtain an existing storage account and container name or create a new one is to navigate to the Storage tab on the Azure Management Portal. Clicking the New button creates a new storage account; selecting an existing account and clicking the Containers tab lists existing containers for a storage account.

To copy a file from local disk to Azure Storage Blob, follow these steps:

1. Launch the Azure PowerShell console and type **Add-AzureAccount**. This opens a pop-up window.

2. Provide the email address and password associated with the Azure subscription in the pop-up window.

3. After Azure authentication, use the following script to upload the Sample.txt file from the C:\Data folder to blob storage:

```
$storageAccountName = "Storage Account Name"
$containerName = "Container Name"
$fileName ="C:\Data\Sample.txt"
$blobName = "example/data/sample.txt"

# Obtain the storage account's primary key
$storageaccountkey = get-azurestoragekey $storageAccountName | %{$_.Primary}

# Create a storage context object
$destContext = New-AzureStorageContext -StorageAccountName $storageAccountName
-StorageAccountKey $storageaccountkey

# Finally, copy a local file to the destination Blob container
Set-AzureStorageBlobContent -File $fileName -Container $containerName -Blob
$blobName -context $destContext
```

NOTE

Blob Storage Is a Key/Value Pair Store

Using the / character in the filename in the previous example (instead of using the key name) does not imply the existence of example or data directories on Blob storage. Because Blob storage is a key/value pair store, no underlying hierarchical directory structure is present.

Hadoop Command Line

You can use Hadoop commands to manipulate files and folders on the Azure Storage Blob. The following exercise explores the process of uploading data to default file system (Azure Storage Blob for HDInsight) using Hadoop commands.

NOTE

Behavior of Native HDFS-Specific Commands

Only commands that are specific to the native HDFS implementation (referred to as DFS), such as fschk and dfsadmin, will show different behavior on Azure storage blob. Other HDFS commands show similar behavior in Azure storage blob as in conventional HDFS storage.

TRY IT YOURSELF

Uploading Data to the Default File System Using the Hadoop Command Line

Follow these steps to upload a sample file to HDFS using the copyFromLocal command:

1. Use a remote desktop connection to remotely log in to the name node of the HDInsight cluster.

GO TO ▶ Refer to **Hour 7, "Exploring Typical Components of HDFS Cluster,"** for more details on enabling a remote desktop connection to the HDInsight name node.

2. Create a text file with some content in the C:\temp directory (call it sample.txt) on the name node.

3. Open the Hadoop command line from the desktop shortcut and run the following command:

   hadoop fs -copyFromLocal C:\temp\sample.txt /example/data/sample.txt command

4. Because the HDInsight default file system is Azure Storage Blob, the file example/sample.txt is actually uploaded on Azure Storage Blob, not HDFS.

5. Optionally, to verify whether the file has been uploaded to Azure Storage Blob, browse the blob storage with Azure Storage Explorer and look for the file example/data/sample.txt.

HDInsight Storage Architecture Details

HDInsight supports both the Hadoop Distributed File System (HDFS) and Azure Storage Blob for storing data. Azure Storage Blob is the default file system.

TIP
***
Using traditional HDFS for user data storage is not recommended. Traditional HDFS is more transitory in nature, and HDInsight uses it to store intermediate results generated by MapReduce jobs and packages.
***

Microsoft's implementation of HDFS based on Azure Storage Blob is called *Windows Azure Storage—Blob (WASB)*. Figure 8.5, adopted from azure.microsoft.com, shows the architecture of an HDInsight cluster. The figure illustrates the existence of Azure Storage Blob and HDFS side by side.

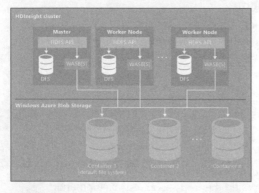

FIGURE 8.5
HDInsight Blob storage architecture.

As you can see in Figure 8.5, the conventional HDFS storage (DFS) is still available to the head node (master) and compute nodes (workers), along with the full-featured HDFS implementation on WASB.

Conventional HDFS storage is accessed using the following URI:

```
hdfs://<namenodehost>:<port>/<path>
```

You can access blob storage using the following fully qualified URI scheme:

```
wasb[s]://<containername>@<accountname>.blob.core.windows.net/<path>
```

The URI with the `wasb` prefix provides unencrypted access. The `wasbs` prefix provides SSL encrypted access.

NOTE

ASV Versus WASB

The term *ASV* (Azure Storage Vault), used in earlier versions of HDInsight to refer to Azure Storage Blob, has been deprecated in favor of WASB. Therefore, the syntax `asv://` is no longer supported from HDInsight version 3.0 onward; it has been replaced with `wasb://` syntax.

The fully qualified URI scheme containing the container name and storage account name is not required while accessing the files on blob storage, configured as the default file system, from the Hadoop command line. In fact, you cannot use the relative path and the absolute path interchangeably.

For example, the `sample.txt` file uploaded earlier can be referred to using any one of the following URI three schemes from the Hadoop command line:

```
wasb://mycontainer@myaccount.blob.core.windows.net/example/data/sample.txt
```

```
wasb:///example/data/sample.txt
```

```
/example/data/sample.txt
```

NOTE

Fully Qualified Domain Name with WASB

When using `wasb`, the fully qualified domain name is required and cannot be skipped.

To query the traditional HDFS, determine the HDFS URI by examining the `dfs.namenode.rpc-address` property in the file `%hadoop_home%\etc\hadoop\hdfs-site.xml`. For example, if the HDFS URI is `hdfs://headnodehost:9000`, you can query the HDFS contents using the following command:

```
hadoop fs -ls hdfs://headnodehost:9000/
```

Configuring the Default File System

Blob storage is the default storage for an HDInsight cluster; however, it is possible (though not recommended) to change the default file system to local HDFS. Because local HDFS is transitory in nature, data stored on HDFS is lost when the cluster is decommissioned.

To modify this setting, connect remotely to the HDInsight name node. (For detailed instructions on remote login, refer to the Try It Yourself "Exploring the Services on HDInsight Name Node" in Hour 7.) You can change the default file system setting by modifying the `fs.defaultFS` property in the file `%hadoop_home%\etc\ hadoop\core-site.xml` (see Figure 8.6).

Determine the HDFS URI by examining the file `dfs.namenode.rpc-address property in %hadoop_home%\etc\hadoop\hdfs-site.xml`. Open the file `core-site.xml` in Notepad and modify the `fs.defaultFS` property value to use HDFS as the default storage. Save and close the file.

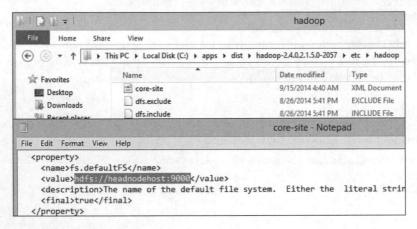

FIGURE 8.6
Modifying the default file system.

Use the command `hadoop fs -ls /` to query the default file system and verify that it has changed to HDFS.

Understanding the Impact of Blob Storage on Performance and Data Locality

A core principle of Hadoop is *data locality*—the data to be processed resides close to the compute nodes on local disks. This proximity minimizes data movement because each compute node is supposed to work on the data set available locally.

In complete contrast, in HDInsight, data is stored on Azure Storage Blob, separated out from the cluster. This seems to conflict with the idea of data locality and involves moving data to compute instead of moving compute to data. Not really!

Azure Flat Network Storage provides performance comparable to reads from disk. In addition, not all queries operate on complete data in the cluster. Most queries ask for a subset of data, which further reduces the amount of data to be read and transferred from blob storage.

NOTE

When it comes to writes, Azure Storage Blob is a clear winner. The write operation to HDFS (assuming a replication factor of 3) is not complete until all three copies are written. With Azure Storage Blob, on the other hand, the write operation is complete after the first copy is written. Azure subsequently takes care of replication, for better write performance.

Overall, Azure Storage Blob seems to be a reasonably good choice for storage.

Summary

This hour introduced Microsoft Azure Storage services and discussed the benefits associated with use of Azure Storage Blob as the default file system in HDInsight. Traditional Hadoop distributions have been using HDFS as the default file system, but Azure Storage Blob provides several additional benefits that favor its use as the default file system in HDInsight. This hour also introduced popular Azure Storage Explorer tools and examined the impact of blob storage on performance and data locality.

Q&A

Q. Are other Microsoft Azure Storage Explorer tools available besides the ones discussed in this hour?

A. Yes, many other tools are available. For an elaborate list of tools and a feature comparison, refer to a blog post from the Microsoft Azure Storage team, at http://blogs.msdn.com/b/windowsazurestorage/archive/2014/03/11/windows-azure-storage-explorers-2014.aspx.

Q. Are Windows Azure and Microsoft Azure the same technologies?

A. Yes. Windows Azure was renamed Microsoft Azure on April 3, 2014. Refer to the following announcement related to this name change from Microsoft: http://azure.microsoft.com/blog/2014/03/25/upcoming-name-change-for-windows-azure/.

Quiz

1. What is the default file system in HDInsight cluster?

2. Is the traditional HDFS still available and accessible in HDInsight cluster?

3. Which command-line tool can be used conveniently in custom applications to transfer data to and from Microsoft Azure storage?

Answers

1. Microsoft Azure Storage Blob is the default file system in HDInsight clusters.

2. Traditional HDFS is still available; however, it is more transitory and its use is generally discouraged.

3. AZCopy is a command-line utility that can be incorporated into custom applications to transfer data into and out of Azure storage. AZCopy is similar to other Microsoft file copy utilities, such as robocopy, and also supports nested directories and files.

Working with Microsoft Azure HDInsight Emulator

What You'll Learn in This Hour:

▶ Getting Started with HDInsight Emulator
▶ Setting Up Microsoft Azure Emulator for Storage

Using HDInsight cluster for development, exploration, and experimentation is not always feasible because of the costs involved in having a multinode cluster constantly up and running. Although you can drop and spin up an HDInsight cluster on demand to test map reduce job functionality, to save cost, you have a better alternative.

Microsoft provides HDInsight emulator for such scenarios. The emulator is a single node cluster that is well suited for development scenarios and experimentation.

This hour focuses on the steps involved in setting up HDInsight emulator and firing a MapReduce job to test the emulator functionality.

Getting Started with HDInsight Emulator

As the name suggests, HDInsight emulator provides an emulation for the Azure HDInsight cluster. With the costs involved in keeping a multinode cluster up and running for development and testing, developing and testing in the Azure HDInsight environment is not always feasible.

HDInsight emulator comes to the rescue by providing a single-node local development environment (a pseudo cluster) for Azure HDInsight.

Keep the following important points in mind when developing on HDInsight emulator:

▶ HDInsight emulator is a pseudo cluster, a single-node deployment with all services (name node, data node, and so on) running on the same node.

▶ HDFS is the default file system for the single-node cluster.

▶ The emulator is meant for development scenarios only.

Although the default file system for the emulator is HDFS, it is possible to switch over to Microsoft Azure blob storage. In fact, HDInsight emulator can pair up with the Microsoft Azure emulator to emulate the Azure storage development experience locally, as you explore in subsequent sections.

Setting Up Microsoft HDInsight Emulator

You can set up Microsoft HDInsight emulator on a workstation that meets certain prerequisites.

Only the 64-bit version of the following operating systems are supported:

▶ Windows 7 Service Pack 1

▶ Windows Server 2008 R2 Service Pack1

▶ Windows 8

▶ Windows Server 2012

In addition, Microsoft Azure PowerShell must be installed and configured.

▼ TRY IT YOURSELF

Installing the Microsoft HDInsight Emulator

To install the Microsoft HDInsight emulator, follow these steps:

1. Navigate to the Microsoft HDInsight Emulator installation page (http://www.microsoft.com/web/gallery/install.aspx?appid=HDINSIGHT) and click the Install Now button.

2. Run the `HDINSIGHT.exe` file that you downloaded in the previous step. This launches the Web Platform Installer in Figure 9.1.

3. Click the Install button. This brings up a list of products that you need to download and install, along with licensing terms (see Figure 9.2).

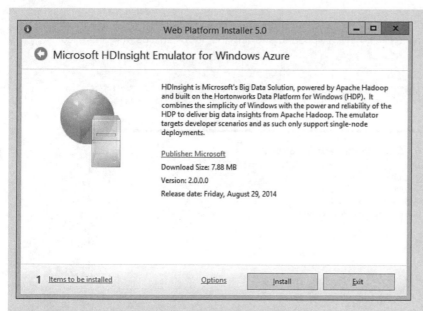

FIGURE 9.1
Setting up the Microsoft HDInsight emulator using the Web Platform Installer.

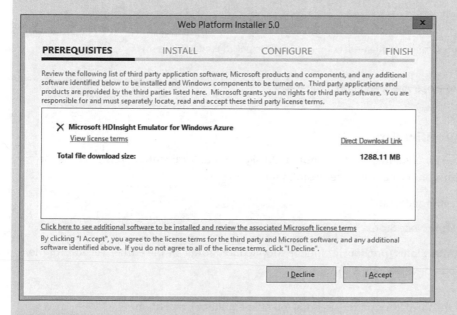

FIGURE 9.2
Web Platform Installer—licensing terms for HDInsight Emulator installation.

4. Click the I Accept button to accept the licensing terms and begin the installation. When installation completes, Figure 9.3 appears, showing the list of successfully installed products.

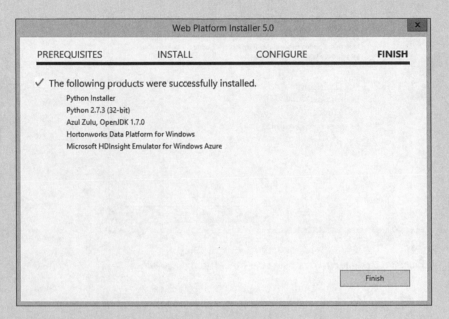

FIGURE 9.3
HDInsight emulator installation—list of successfully installed products.

5. Click Exit to close the Web Platform Installer.

Installation Verification

One of the simplest preliminary ways to verify HDInsight emulator installation is to check for three shortcut icons on the desktop after installation:

▶ Hadoop Command Line

▶ Hadoop Name Node Status

▶ Hadoop YARN Status (previously Hadoop MapReduce Status, in the earlier versions of the emulator based on Hadoop 1.0)

Figure 9.4 shows the three icons on the user desktop after emulator installation. You can also examine the installation log at `C:\HadoopFeaturePackSetup\` `HadoopFeaturePackSetupTools\gettingStarted.winpkg.install.log`.

FIGURE 9.4
Verifying shortcut icons placed on the desktop after HDInsight emulator installation.

Launch the Yarn Status page and click the About tab to verify whether the Resource Manager is in STARTED state. Apart from the shortcut icons, several services are provisioned as a part of the installation. Launch the Services Management Consoles (services.msc) to examine all the services prefixed with Apache Hadoop that were provisioned during the installation. Figure 9.5 shows the services provisioned as a part of HDInsight Emulator installation.

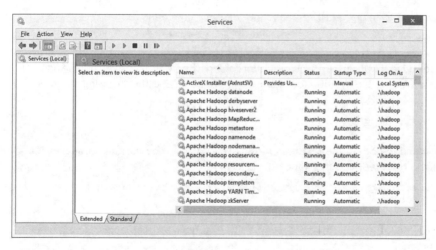

FIGURE 9.5
Services provisioned during HDInsight emulator installation.

Ensure that these services are running before you proceed further.

Running a MapReduce Job

As a final verification, run a MapReduce job to test the installation. HDInsight comes with some samples packaged into the hadoop-mapreduce-examples-2.4.0.2.1.3.0-1981.jar file, located in C:\hdp\hadoop-2.4.0.2.1.3.0-1981\share\hadoop\mapreduce.

To test the installation, run the classic Word Count sample, which counts the number of words in a text file.

GO TO ▶ We look at other ways of executing and monitoring a map reduce job in **Hour 10, "Programming MapReduce Jobs."**

The simplest way to execute a MapReduce job is via the Hadoop command line using the `hadoop jar` command. You simply provide the name of the JAR file, the classname containing the `main` function, and other required arguments:

```
hadoop jar <jar file name> [mainClass] arguments
```

▼ TRY IT YOURSELF

Running a Word Count Job

To run the Word Count example, follow these steps:

1. Launch the Hadoop command line from the desktop shortcut.

2. Create a `/WordCount` folder on HDFS using the following command:

   ```
   hadoop fs -mkdir /WordCount
   ```

3. Create a folder titled Input inside the WordCount folder. The `/WordCount/Input` folder will store input text files for the WordCount MapReduce program. Use the following command to create the Input folder:

   ```
   hadoop fs -mkdir /WordCount/Input
   ```

4. Use this command to copy some text files for analysis to the `/WordCount/Input` folder (to copy multiple text files, use the wildcard `*.txt`):

   ```
   hadoop fs -copyFromLocal C:\Hadoop\MapReduce\Data\WordCountData.txt
   /WordCount/Input/
   ```

5. Query the `/WordCount/Input` folder to ensure that the file has been copied using the following command:

   ```
   hadoop fs -ls /WordCount/Input/
   ```

6. Navigate to `C:\hdp\hadoop-2.4.0.2.1.3.0-1981\share\hadoop\mapreduce`.

7. Run this command to run the WordCount sample MapReduce job:

   ```
   hadoop jar hadoop-mapreduce-examples-2.4.0.2.1.3.0-1981.jar wordcount
   /WordCount/Input /WordCount/Output
   ```

8. When the job successfully completes (when both the map and reduce steps report 100 percent completion), you can use the following command to view the final output:

   ```
   hadoop fs -cat /WordCount/Output/part-r-00000
   ```

Setting Up Microsoft Azure Emulator for Storage

HDInsight emulator uses HDFS as the default file system in contrast to the HDInsight cloud service, which relies on Microsoft Azure blob storage for this purpose. However, this limitation can be overcome by pairing up HDInsight emulator with Microsoft Azure storage emulator to emulate Azure blob storage. This enables developers to develop and test code locally on HDInsight emulator, in an environment similar to HDInsight cloud service.

Setting Up Microsoft Storage Emulator

Follow these steps to set up the Microsoft storage emulator and configure HDInsight emulator to use it as default storage:

1. Navigate to `http://azure.microsoft.com/en-us/downloads/` and install the .NET version of the Microsoft Azure SDK for either Visual Studio 2012 or 2013.

NOTE

Standalone installer for Microsoft Azure Storage

Microsoft Azure Storage Emulator is available as a standalone package as well. However, installing Microsoft Azure SDK is better because you will need it every now and then.

2. After installation, launch the Windows Azure storage emulator from the Start menu.

3. To start or stop the emulator, right-click the blue Azure icon in the Windows System Tray, as shown in Figure 9.6, and then click Show Storage Emulator UI.

FIGURE 9.6
Starting Microsoft Azure emulator.

NOTE

Microsoft Azure Emulator Port Conflict Issue

Hadoop Hiveserver2 service uses port 10000, so you might get an error stating that the Windows Azure storage emulator launch failed due to port conflict. To resolve the issue, stop the Apache Hadoop Hiveserver2 services from the Services Management Console and restart the Microsoft Azure simulator. Then restart the Hadoop Hiveserver2 later.

4. Launch Visual Studio (2012/2013) and open the Server Explorer pane.

5. Expand the Blobs section in the Development section under the Azure Storage node, as in Figure 9.7.

6. Create a new container (name it container1), as in Figure 9.7.

FIGURE 9.7
Creating a new storage container.

7. After you create the container, the emulated blob storage is ready for use. From the Hadoop command line, use the following command to see the contents of the emulated blob storage (which is empty at this point):

```
hadoop fs -ls wasb://container1@storageemulator/
```

Next, follow these steps to configure the emulated blob storage container as the default file system:

1. Open C:\hdp\hadoop-2.4.0.2.1.3.0-1981\etc\hadoop in Notepad.

2. Locate the fs.defaultFS property (see Figure 9.8).

```
<property>
  <name>fs.defaultFS</name>
  <value>hdfs://YOURMACHINENAME:8020</value>
  <description>The name of the default file system.
  <final>true</final>
</property>
```

FIGURE 9.8
Examining the fs.defaultFS default file system configuration property.

3. Replace the value of `fs.defaultFS` with the following XML snippet:

```
<property>
<name>fs.defaultFS</name>
<value>wasb://container1@storageemulator</value>
<description>The name of the default file system.  Either the literal string
"local" or a host:port for HDFS.</description>
<final>true</final>
</property>
<property>
<name>dfs.namenode.rpc-address</name>
<value>hdfs://YOURMACHINEHOSTNAME:8020</value>
<description>A base for other temporary directories.</description>
</property>
```

4. Save and close the file.

5. Invoke the following command to ensure that the default file system has been changed to the emulated blob storage:

```
hadoop fs -ls / command
```

NOTE

Browsing the Traditional HDFS

You can browse the traditional HDFS using this command from the Hadoop command line: `hadoop fs ls hdfs://YOURHOSTNAME:8020/`.

Summary

This hour introduced you to Microsoft HDInsight emulator and detailed the steps for setting it up. HDInsight emulator proves useful in development scenarios and can be paired with Microsoft Azure Emulator for blob storage emulation. The hour also introduced you to the steps involved in validating an HDInsight emulator deployment.

Q&A

Q. Can the blob storage emulator be used for Big Data sets?

A. No. The blob storage emulator is meant for development scenarios only and cannot support Big Data sets. It is best suited for working with smaller datasets that contain a subset of actual production data.

Q. Can HDInsight Emulator be connected to Microsoft Azure blob storage on the cloud instead of using the Azure storage emulator?

A. Yes. However, network speed comes into play in such a scenario. When HDInsight emulator runs on the premises (in a developer workstation), the network speed between the developer machine and Azure storage determines performance of the pseudo cluster and MapReduce jobs.

Quiz

1. What is the default file system in HDInsight emulator?

2. How many nodes are in HDInsight emulator?

Answers

1. Traditional HDFS, not blob storage, is used as the default file system in HDInsight clusters.

2. HDInsight emulator is a pseudo cluster, with all the Apache Hadoop services running on a single node.

Programming MapReduce Jobs

What You'll Learn in This Hour:

▶ MapReduce Hello World!

▶ Analyzing Flight Delays with MapReduce

▶ Serialization Frameworks for Hadoop

▶ Hadoop Streaming

Hours 4, "The MapReduce Job Framework and Job Execution Pipeline," and 5, "MapReduce—Advanced Concepts and YARN," introduced the MapReduce Framework and methodologies for programming MapReduce jobs. This hour builds on the content in earlier hours and provides examples and techniques for programming MapReduce programs in Java and C#. A real-life scenario that analyzes flight delays with MapReduce is also presented. The hour concludes with a discussion on serialization options for Hadoop.

MapReduce Hello World!

The word count scenario in Hour 4 is the Hello World problem in the MapReduce space. Recall that the word count MapReduce program in Hour 4 counted the occurrence of all the words in the set of input text files. Hour 4 also explored the process of developing the word count MapReduce program in Java.

The following section explores the steps involved in running a Java MapReduce program on the HDInsight emulator using the Java code in Hour 4. You can use the same steps to submit a job to the HDInsight cluster on Azure.

Running a Java MapReduce Program on HDInsight Emulator

A MapReduce program written in Java must be compiled with the Java compiler before it can be executed on the HDInsight emulator or cluster. HDInsight comes with the javac compiler, which you can use for that purpose.

▼ TRY IT YOURSELF

Submitting a MapReduce Job Programmed in Java for Execution

This section explores the steps involved in compiling a Java MapReduce program and submitting it for execution.

1. To compile the word count MapReduce program on an HDInsight emulator, first save the program listing from Hour 4 in a text file and name it `WordCount.java`.

2. Create a new folder at, say, `C:\Hadoop\MapReduce\WordCountJava`, and copy the `WordCount.java` file to the folder.

3. Launch the Hadoop command line from the desktop shortcut and browse to the `C:\Hadoop\MapReduce\WordCountJava` folder.

4. The Java compiler requires references to the following JAR files for compiling `WordCount.java` (version numbers might vary for your environment):

   ▶ `hadoop-common-2.4.0.2.1.3.0-1981.jar`

   ▶ `hadoop-mapreduce-client-core-2.4.0.2.1.3.0-1981.jar`

   ▶ `commons-cli-1.2.jar`

   ▶ `hadoop-annotations-2.4.0.2.1.3.0-1981.jar`

5. Issue the following javac command on the command prompt, passing in the dependency JAR filenames using the `classpath` parameter, the name of the file containing the MapReduce Java source code (`WordCount.java`, in this case), and the name of an existing subdirectory where compiled classes will be placed:

   ```
   %JAVA_HOME%\bin\javac -classpath %hadoop_home%\share\hadoop\common\hadoop-
   common-2.4.0.2.1.3.0-1981.jar;%hadoop_home%\share\hadoop\mapreduce\hadoop-
   mapreduce-client-core-2.4.0.2.1.3.0-1981.jar;%hadoop_home%\share\hadoop\
   common\lib\commons-cli-1.2.jar;%hadoop_home%\share\hadoop\common\lib\hadoop-
   annotations-2.4.0.2.1.3.0-1981.jar -d wordcount_classes WordCount.java
   ```

6. Package the compiled classless from the `wordcount_classes` folder into the `WordCount.jar` file using the following JAR command:

   ```
   %JAVA_HOME%\bin\jar -cvf WordCount.jar -C wordcount_classes .
   ```

7. At this point, the WordCount MapReduce job is ready for submission. Create a text file (for example, `WordCountData.txt`) containing some English language sentences at `C:\Hadoop\MapReduce\Data`. Then create a folder called `/WordCount/Input` on HDFS and copy the text file from `local` to the folder using the following commands:

   ```
   hadoop fs -mkdir /WordCount
   hadoop fs -mkdir /WordCount/Input
   hadoop fs -copyFromLocal C:\Hadoop\MapReduce\Data\WordCountData.txt
   /WordCount/Input
   ```

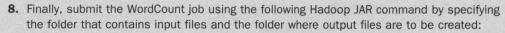

8. Finally, submit the WordCount job using the following Hadoop JAR command by specifying the folder that contains input files and the folder where output files are to be created:

```
hadoop jar WordCount.jar org.apache.hadoop.examples.WordCount /WordCount/Input
/WordCount/Output
```

CAUTION

Do Not Create the Output Folder

Do not create the /WordCount/Output folder—if you do, the MapReduce job fails because the output directory already exists. To delete the output directory (if already created), use the following command: `hadoop fs -rm -r /WordCount/Output`.

9. When map and reduce are 100% complete (see Figure 10.1), examine the contents of the /WordCount/Output folder to see the processing results. Use the following command to display the content of an output file:

```
hadoop fs -cat /WordCount/Output/part-r-00000
```

FIGURE 10.1
Submitting a Java MapReduce job.

Figure 10.2 shows the results of the MapReduce job execution.

```
Administrator: Hadoop Command Line                     _  □  X

C:\hadoop\MapReduce\WordCountJava>hadoop fs -cat /WordCount/Output/part-r-00000
Azure   1
BigData 2
HDInsight       4
Hadoop  6
Windows 1

C:\hadoop\MapReduce\WordCountJava>_
```

FIGURE 10.2
WordCount Java MapReduce job output.

GO TO ▶ The sample data file for this illustration comes from the Word Count illustration in **Hour 4**. Therefore, the MapReduce job produces the same output as in Hour 4.

Analyzing Flight Delays with MapReduce

This section presents a practical MapReduce example for analyzing flight delays.

The example uses the on-time performance of airline flight data from the Research and Innovative Technology Administration, Bureau of Transportation Statistics (RITA).

NOTE

The data is available for download and analysis at http://www.transtats.bts.gov/DL_SelectFields.asp?Table_ID=236&DB_Short_Name=On-Time.

The data set contains the overall flight delay time subdivided into five delay reasons: carrier delay, weather delay, national air system delay, security delay, and late aircraft delay.

Analyzing Flight Delay Reasons with MapReduce

This section explores the steps involved in creating a practical MapReduce job to analyze flight delay reasons. The MapReduce scenario seeks to identify the total number of flight delays caused by a delay reason. The factor with the maximum delay time value is considered the primary delay factor for the flight. Flights with zero delay time value for all delay factors are rolled into the category of no delay. To create a MapReduce program and submit it for execution, follow these steps:

1. Download the on-time performance of airline flight data for January 2014 (all geographies) from http://www.transtats.bts.gov/DL_SelectFields.asp?Table_ID=236&DB_Short_Name=On-Time. Be sure to include following columns in the CSV file: YEAR,MONTH,FL_DATE, CARRIER, TAIL_NUM, ORIGIN, ORIGIN_STATE_ABR, ORIGIN_STATE_NM, DEST,DEST_STATE_ABR, DEST_STATE_NM, CARRIER_DELAY, WEATHER_DELAY, NAS_DELAY, SECURITY_DELAY, and LATE_AIRCRAFT_DELAY. A downloaded sample file (`475719775_T_ONTIME.zip`) is also included in the accompanying code samples for this chapter.

2. The downloaded file is a comma-separated value (CSV) file. Delete the first row of the file that contains the column headers. The row has already been deleted from `475719775_T_ONTIME.zip`.

3. Upload the CSV file to the `/FlightDelayAnalyzer/Input` folder using the command `hadoop fs -copyFromLocal`.

4. Create a new text file named `FlightDelayAnalyzer.java`.

5. Use Listing 10.1 for the `Mapper` function. The listing splits the line input to the `Mapper` function by comma (splitting by comma is not the best way to parse a CSV file, but it works fine for this demonstration) and obtains the delay times for various delay factors. The factor with the maximum delay time value is considered the primary delaying cause for the flight and is written to the context.

LISTING 10.1 Flight Delay Mapper Function

```
public static class FlightDelayMapper
        extends Mapper<Object, Text, Text, IntWritable>{

    private final static IntWritable one = new IntWritable(1);
    private Text delayReason;

    public void map(Object key, Text value, Context context
                    ) throws IOException, InterruptedException {

    String line = value.toString();
    String[] cols = line.split(",",-1);
```

```
    if(cols.length<16){
        return;
    }

    float[] carrierDelay= new float[6];

    if(cols[11] != null && !cols[11].isEmpty())
        carrierDelay[1]=Float.parseFloat(cols[11]);

    if(cols[12] != null && !cols[12].isEmpty())
        carrierDelay[2]=Float.parseFloat(cols[12]);

    if(cols[13] != null && !cols[13].isEmpty())
        carrierDelay[3]=Float.parseFloat(cols[13]);

    if(cols[14] != null && !cols[14].isEmpty())
        carrierDelay[4]=Float.parseFloat(cols[14]);

    if(cols[15] != null && !cols[15].isEmpty())
        carrierDelay[5]=Float.parseFloat(cols[15]);

    int maxIndex = 0;

    for (int i = 1; i < carrierDelay.length; i++){
        if ((carrierDelay[i] > carrierDelay[maxIndex])){
        maxIndex = i;
        }
    }

    switch (maxIndex) {
        case 1:  delayReason = new Text("Carrier");
                break;
        case 2:  delayReason = new Text("Weather");
                break;
        case 3:  delayReason = new Text("NAS");
                break;
        case 4:  delayReason = new Text("Security");
                break;
        case 5:  delayReason = new Text("LateAircraft");
                break;
        default: delayReason = new Text("NoDelay");
                break;
    }

    context.write(delayReason,one);
    }
}
```

6. The Reducer logic is similar to the word count scenario. The reducer sums up the flight count for a delay reason. Refer to the `FlightDelayAnalyzer.java` file in the accompanying source code for this hour for the reducer function source code.

7. Compile the Java code using the following command:

```
%JAVA_HOME%\bin\javac -classpath %hadoop_home%\share\hadoop\common\hadoop-
common-2.4.0.2.1.3.0-1981.jar;%hadoop_home%\share\hadoop\mapreduce\hadoop-
mapreduce-client-core-2.4.0.2.1.3.0-1981.jar;%hadoop_home%\share\hadoop\
common\lib\commons-cli-1.2.jar;%hadoop_home%\share\hadoop\common\lib\
hadoop-annotations-2.4.0.2.1.3.0-1981.jar -d FlightDelayAnalyzer_classes
FlightDelayAnalyzer.java
```

8. Package the class files into the Jar file using the following command:

```
%JAVA_HOME%\bin\jar -cvf FlightDelayAnalyzer.jar -C FlightDelayAnalyzer_
Classes
```

9. Submit the MapReduce job for execution using the `hadoop jar` command:

```
hadoop jar FlightDelayAnalyzer.jar org.myorg.FlightDelayAnalyzer
/FlightDelayAnalyzer/Input /FlightDelayAnalyzer/Output
```

10. When the job completes, examine the generated output using the `hadoop fs -cat` command. Figure 10.3 illustrates the MapReduce job output, with a list of flight delay reasons and number of flights delayed due to each reason.

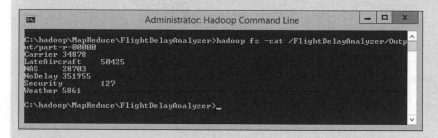

FIGURE 10.3
Flight Delay Analyzer MapReduce job output.

11. Optionally, rerun the job by downloading data for more months.

Serialization Frameworks for Hadoop

For semi-structured scalar or tabular data—when each record is on a new line—serialization might not be a big concern. However, this is rarely the case in real-world situations. Sometimes you need to deal with complicated scenarios that involve composite or hierarchical data that doesn't fit easily into a format of one record per line. For example, you would find it tough to fit the following employee record containing multiple addresses and phone numbers into a format of one record per line:

```
EmployeeID:888,
Name:Chris Smith,
DOB:1-Jan-1980,
Address:{Street:50th,City:NYC,Zipcode:10019,Primary:true},{Street:20th,city:NYC,Zip
code:10008}
PhoneNumbers:16462389999, 16462389991
EmployeeType:Permanent
```

In addition, sometimes you might have to store text fields with binary data, as with the employee photograph in the previous example, and apply compression to data. This results in text fields with binary data and requires specialized serialization techniques. However, serialization and compression don't play well with the MapReduce framework because both tend to remove the record boundaries. Recall that when the MapReduce framework cannot determine a logical division of records, it presents the entire data file to a single mapper. Parallelism then fails to work.

A tedious and impractical way to solve the problem is to manually split the input file into smaller parts. That way, even if HDInsight presents a single file to a map job, the presence of multiple files ensures that multiple mappers are spawned. Hence, parallelism works.

Better ways are available to handle the previous scenarios. Serialization frameworks provide the answer.

NOTE

Java and Hadoop Built-in Serialization

Java also provides serialization mechanisms. However, Java serialization is not very lean and compact, and it doesn't provide precise control over serialization. Extensibility (schema modification and addition or removal of fields) is also not easy to achieve, and Java serialization is not portable to other programming languages. Furthermore, although Hadoop built-in serialization formats (such as Hadoop Sequence Files) are compact and fast, they don't have much support outside the Java language.

Hadoop has a pluggable serialization framework. The package `org.package.hadoop.io` has a Serialization interface. Implement this interface and set the `io.serializations` property to wire up custom serialization. `WritableSerialization` has an implementation of this interface out of box that provides writable types.

Serialization frameworks, such as Avro, Protocol Buffers (developed by Google), and Thrift (developed by Facebook) provide the solution. Avro requires the schema to be always present with the data, unlike in Thrift or Protocol Buffers. This means that data can be just a sequence of bytes (eliminating the need for field identifiers) and resulting in more compact encoding of data.

This section focuses on Avro because it was designed with MapReduce in mind and is best supported in HDInsight.

Avro

Avro is a serialization framework developed by Doug Cutting. It supports programming language portability (including support for C# because of the C# Avro Serialization library that Microsoft provides) and is both compact and extensible. For example, in the employee record described earlier, it's possible to introduce a new email address attribute without causing any breaking changes in existing applications that rely on the older schema.

The Avro file format consists of a header followed by a sequence of data blocks (see Figure 10.4). The header contains the schema information and sync marker (the character used as a marker to separate data blocks). Data blocks consist of a record count (the number of records in the block), the block size, and the actual serialized data. Optionally, the data blocks can be compressed.

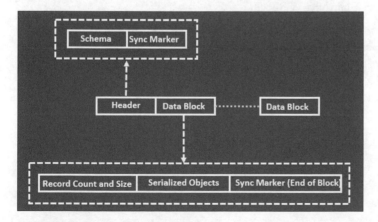

FIGURE 10.4
Flight delay analyzer MapReduce job output.

The presence of record boundaries makes Avro data files splitable and, hence, suitable for efficient MapReduce.

▼ TRY IT YOURSELF

Writing an Avro Data File Using C#

This section covers the process of writing an Avro data file using C#. The example uses a JSON schema in Listing 10.2 to specify a generic record. Because the schema is included in the serialized data, the data reader does not need to know the schema beforehand. The data from the on-time performance of airline flights data CSV file is converted to `AvroRecord` objects and then stored in an object container file represented by the `AvroContainer` class.

LISTING 10.2   JSON Schema for the On-time Performance of Airline Flights Record

```
{
    "type":"record",
    "name":"AirlineDelayRecord",
    "fields":
        [
            { "name":"flightdate", "type":"int" },
            { "name":"carrierdelay", "type":"double" },
            { "name":"weatherdelay", "type":"double" },
            { "name":"nasdelay", "type":"double" },
            { "name":"securitydelay", "type":"double" },
            { "name":"lateaircraftdelay", "type":"double"
}
```

Follow these steps to create an Avro data file using C# (Microsoft.NET library for Avro) which will later be read from java to illustrate language portability:

1. Create a new Visual C# Console Application project named SerializationWithAvro in Visual Studio. Ensure that you select .NET Framework version 4.0 or later.

2. Right-click the project and select Manage NuGet Packages (see Figure 10.5).

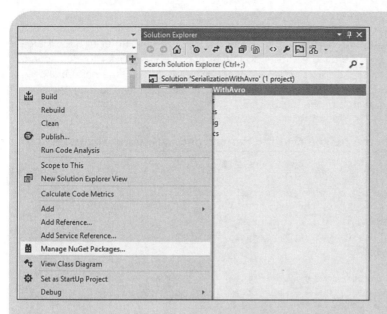

FIGURE 10.5
Managing NuGet packages in Visual Studio.

3. Search for `Microsoft.Hadoop.Avro` in the Online Search box, and click the Install button next to Microsoft.NET Library for Avro (see Figure 10.6). This also installs the `Newtonsoft.Json` NuGet package because it's a dependency.

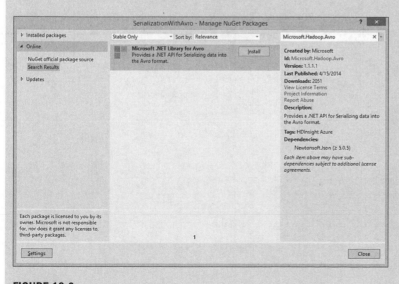

FIGURE 10.6
Installing Microsoft .NET Library for Avro.

4. Paste the `SerializationWithGenericRecord` function code from Listing 10.3 into the console application and invoke the function from the `Main()` function. Refer to the C# project SerializationWithAvro in the code samples accompanying this chapter for the full source code. The function `SerializationWithGenericRecord` reads the on-time performance CSV file line by line and converts each record from the CSV file to an Avro record. The Avro record collection is then written to the file system.

LISTING 10.3   JSON Schema for the On-time Performance of Airline Flights Record

```
public static void SerializationWithGenericRecord()
{
    Console.WriteLine("Reading on-time performance of airline flights CSV file");

    // Source csv file path
    string sourceFilePath = @"C:\Hadoop\MapReduce\AvroFlightDelayAnalyzer\
      475719775_T_ONTIME.csv";

    // Path for target Avro Object Container File
    string targetFilePath = @"C:\Hadoop\MapReduce\AvroFlightDelayAnalyzer\
      475719775_T_ONTIME.avro";

    // JSON schema definition
    const string Schema =
                    @"{
                        ""type"":""record"",
                        ""name"":""AirlineDelayRecord"",
                        ""fields"":
                            [
                                { ""name"":""flightdate"", ""type"":""int"" },
                                { ""name"":""carrierdelay"", ""type"":""double"" },
                                { ""name"":""weatherdelay"", ""type"":""double"" },
                                { ""name"":""nasdelay"", ""type"":""double"" },
                                { ""name"":""securitydelay"", ""type"":""double"" },
                                { ""name"":""lateaircraftdelay"",
                                  ""type"":""double"" }
                            ]
                    }";

    // Generic serializer object based on the JSON schema
    var serializer = AvroSerializer.CreateGeneric(Schema);
    var rootSchema = serializer.WriterSchema as RecordSchema;

    // Create a generic record to represent the data
    var genericRecord = new List<AvroRecord>();
```

```
// Read source csv file line by line and write to destination avro record
Console.WriteLine("Reading source csv file line by line and creating avro
  records");
var reader = new StreamReader(File.OpenRead(sourceFilePath));
while (!reader.EndOfStream)
{
    var line = reader.ReadLine();
    var sourceRecord = line.Split(',');

    // Create a new destination record
    dynamic destinationRecord = new AvroRecord(rootSchema);
    int flightDate = Convert.ToInt32(DateTime.Parse(sourceRecord[2]).
      ToString("yyyyMMdd"));

    double carrierDelay;
    double.TryParse(sourceRecord[11], out carrierDelay);
    double weatherDelay;
    double.TryParse(sourceRecord[12], out weatherDelay);
    double nasDelay;
    double.TryParse(sourceRecord[13], out nasDelay);
    double securityDelay;
    double.TryParse(sourceRecord[14], out securityDelay);
    double lateaircraftDelay;
    double.TryParse(sourceRecord[15], out lateaircraftDelay);

    destinationRecord.flightdate = flightDate;
    destinationRecord.carrierdelay = carrierDelay;
    destinationRecord.weatherdelay = weatherDelay;
    destinationRecord.nasdelay = nasDelay;
    destinationRecord.securitydelay = securityDelay;
    destinationRecord.lateaircraftdelay = lateaircraftDelay;
    genericRecord.Add(destinationRecord);
}

// Serialize and save data to file
using (var buffer = new MemoryStream())
{
    Console.WriteLine("Serializing data to file");

    // Serialize sequence of On-time flight performance generic records to
      stream
    // Null compression codec is used i.e. no compression applied
    using (var writer = AvroContainer.CreateGenericWriter(Schema, buffer,
      Codec.Null))
    {
        using (var streamWriter = new SequentialWriter<object>(writer, 24))
```

```
            {
                // Serialize the data to stream using the sequential writer
                genericRecord.ForEach(streamWriter.Write);
            }
        }

        if (File.Exists(targetFilePath))
        {
            File.Delete(targetFilePath);
        }

        // Save buffer to file
        using (FileStream fs = File.Create(targetFilePath))
        {
            buffer.Seek(0, SeekOrigin.Begin);
            buffer.CopyTo(fs);
        }
    }
}
```

The next section explores the steps involved in reading an Avro data file.

▼ TRY IT YOURSELF

Reading an Avro Data File Using Java

To demonstrate language interoperability with Avro, this section explores the process of reading the on-time performance of airline flights Avro file created with C# using Java. Because the schema is contained in an Avro file, you don't need to specify a schema to the reader Java application. The following steps illustrate this:

1. Create the file `AvroDeSerialization.java` with the Java code in Listing 10.4. The code listing reads the Avro file and loops through AvroRecords using a `DataFileReader` object.

LISTING 10.4   Reading the On-time Performance of Airline Flights Avro File with Java

```
import java.io.File;
import java.io.IOException;
import org.apache.avro.file.DataFileReader;
import org.apache.avro.generic.GenericDatumReader;
import org.apache.avro.generic.GenericRecord;
import org.apache.avro.io.DatumReader;
```

```
public class AvroDeSerialization {

    public static void DeSerializationWithGenericRecord () throws IOException {

        // create a record using schema
        File AvroFile = new File("475719775_T_ONTIME.avro");
        DatumReader<GenericRecord> datumReader = new GenericDatumReader<Generic
          Record>();
        DataFileReader<GenericRecord> dataFileReader = new DataFileReader<Generic
          Record>(AvroFile, datumReader);
        GenericRecord avroRecord = null;
        System.out.println("Deserialized data is :");
        while (dataFileReader.hasNext()) {
            avroRecord = dataFileReader.next(avroRecord);
            // print the complete record
            System.out.println(avroRecord);

            // To access specific fields
            // System.out.println(avroRecord.get( "flightdate" ));
        }
    }

    public static void main(String[] args) throws IOException {
        AvroDeSerialization.DeSerializationWithGenericRecord();
    }
}
```

2. JAR files `avro-1.7.4.jar`, `jackson-core-asl-1.8.8.jar`, and `jackson-mapper-asl-1.8.8.jar` need to compile and run the Java program. The files are available in the folder `%HADOOP_HOME%\share\hadoop\tools\lib`. Copy the JAR files to the same location where the file `AvroDeSerialization.java` is present.

3. Compile the code using the following command from the Hadoop command line:

```
%JAVA_HOME%\bin\javac -cp avro-1.7.4.jar;jackson-core-asl-1.8.8.jar;jackson-mapper-asl-1.8.8.jar; AvroDeSerialization.java
```

4. Package the `AvroDeSerialization.class` file into the JAR file using the following command:

```
%JAVA_HOME%\bin\jar -cvf AvroDeSerialization.jar AvroDeSerialization.class
```

5. Finally, run the program using this command:

```
%JAVA_HOME%\bin\java -cp avro-1.7.4.jar;jackson-core-asl-1.8.8.jar;jackson-mapper-asl-1.8.8.jar; AvroDeSerialization
```

The Java application loops through all the records in the Avro file and prints them in the console windows (see Figure 10.7).

```
securitydelay": 0.0, "lateaircraftdelay": 0.0}
("flightdate": 20140118, "carrierdelay": 0.0, "weatherdelay": 0.0, "nasdelay": 0
.0, "securitydelay": 0.0, "lateaircraftdelay": 0.0}
("flightdate": 20140119, "carrierdelay": 0.0, "weatherdelay": 0.0, "nasdelay": 0
.0, "securitydelay": 0.0, "lateaircraftdelay": 0.0}
("flightdate": 20140120, "carrierdelay": 0.0, "weatherdelay": 0.0, "nasdelay": 0
.0, "securitydelay": 0.0, "lateaircraftdelay": 0.0}
("flightdate": 20140121, "carrierdelay": 0.0, "weatherdelay": 0.0, "nasdelay": 0
.0, "securitydelay": 0.0, "lateaircraftdelay": 0.0}
("flightdate": 20140122, "carrierdelay": 0.0, "weatherdelay": 0.0, "nasdelay": 0
.0, "securitydelay": 0.0, "lateaircraftdelay": 0.0}
("flightdate": 20140123, "carrierdelay": 0.0, "weatherdelay": 0.0, "nasdelay": 0
.0, "securitydelay": 0.0, "lateaircraftdelay": 0.0}
("flightdate": 20140124, "carrierdelay": 0.0, "weatherdelay": 0.0, "nasdelay": 0
.0, "securitydelay": 0.0, "lateaircraftdelay": 0.0}
("flightdate": 20140125, "carrierdelay": 0.0, "weatherdelay": 0.0, "nasdelay": 0
.0, "securitydelay": 0.0, "lateaircraftdelay": 0.0}
("flightdate": 20140126, "carrierdelay": 0.0, "weatherdelay": 0.0, "nasdelay": 0
.0, "securitydelay": 0.0, "lateaircraftdelay": 0.0}
("flightdate": 20140127, "carrierdelay": 0.0, "weatherdelay": 0.0, "nasdelay": 0
.0, "securitydelay": 0.0, "lateaircraftdelay": 0.0}
("flightdate": 20140128, "carrierdelay": 0.0, "weatherdelay": 0.0, "nasdelay": 0
.0, "securitydelay": 0.0, "lateaircraftdelay": 0.0}
("flightdate": 20140129, "carrierdelay": 0.0, "weatherdelay": 0.0, "nasdelay": 1
3.0, "securitydelay": 0.0, "lateaircraftdelay": 0.0}
```
Administrator: Hadoop Command Line

FIGURE 10.7
Reading an Avro data file using Java.

Hadoop Streaming

The Hadoop streaming API enables you to write MapReduce programs in languages other than Java. Any executable or script can serve as a Mapper or a Reducer. Standard input and output streams work for communication between MapReduce Framework and Mapper and Reducer functions.

Using Hadoop streaming, you can program MapReduce jobs in C#. However, certain performance trade-offs arise when using Hadoop streaming. MapReduce programs developed with streaming APIs do not perform as well as native MapReduce programs written in Java. This is attributed to the use of standard input and output streams for communication (feeding data to the Mapper and obtaining output from the Reducer). Furthermore, interprocess communication (as with Hadoop streaming) is always less efficient than in-process communication (as with native Java MapReduce); therefore, a C# streaming MapReduce program is much slower than an equivalent native program written in Java.

Developing a MapReduce program in C# involves the following activities:

▶ Creating a console application for the Mapper in Visual Studio

▶ Creating a console application for the Reducer in Visual Studio

▶ Uploading Mapper and Reducer executables to the default file system

▶ Submitting the MapReduce job for execution

Programming MapReduce in C#

This section demonstrates the steps involved in programming a MapReduce program in C# using an Avro MapReduce example. You will upload the on-time performance analysis of airline flights Avro file that you created in the previous section to HDFS. The Avro Mapper executable written in C# will associate a delay reason to a flight, followed by a C# Reducer performing summarization to generate the final output containing a list of flight delay reasons and the number of flights delayed because of the particular reason.

1. Create a new console application in C# named AvroFlightDelayAnalyzerMapper and add a reference to the `System.Runtime.Serialization` framework assembly.

2. Paste the code from Listing 10.5 into the `Program.cs` file. The Mapper function receives an Avro record from standard input, uses JSON deserialization to get the delay record object, and determines the flight delay reason and writes it to standard output.

LISTING 10.5 Hadoop Streaming Avro Mapper

```
using System;
using System.IO;
using System.Runtime.Serialization;
using System.Runtime.Serialization.Json;
using System.Text;

namespace AvroFlightDelayAnalyzerMapper
{
    class Program
    {
        [DataContract]
        class DelayRecord
        {
            [DataMember]
            public int flightdate { get; set; }
            [DataMember]
            public double carrierdelay { get; set; }
            [DataMember]
            public double weatherdelay { get; set; }
            [DataMember]
            public double nasdelay { get; set; }
            [DataMember]
            public double securitydelay { get; set; }
            [DataMember]
            public double lateaircraftdelay { get; set; }
        }
```

```csharp
static void Main(string[] args)
{
    if (args.Length > 0)
    {
        Console.SetIn(new StreamReader(args[0]));
    }

    string line;

    try
    {
        while ((line = Console.ReadLine()) != null)
        {
            // Get json record object
            DataContractJsonSerializer ser = new DataContractJsonSerializer
              (typeof(DelayRecord));
            MemoryStream stream = new MemoryStream(Encoding.UTF8.
              GetBytes(line));
            DelayRecord jsonRecord = (DelayRecord)ser.ReadObject(stream);

            double[] flightDelay = new double[6];
            flightDelay[1] = jsonRecord.carrierdelay;
            flightDelay[2] = jsonRecord.weatherdelay;
            flightDelay[3] = jsonRecord.nasdelay;
            flightDelay[4] = jsonRecord.securitydelay;
            flightDelay[5] = jsonRecord.lateaircraftdelay;

            int maxIndex = 0;

            for (int i = 1; i < flightDelay.Length; i++)
            {
                if ((flightDelay[i] > flightDelay[maxIndex]))
                {
                    maxIndex = i;
                }
            }

            string delayReason = string.Empty;
            switch (maxIndex)
            {
                case 1: delayReason = "Carrier";
                    break;
                case 2: delayReason = "Weather";
                    break;
                case 3: delayReason = "NAS";
                    break;
```

```
                    case 4: delayReason = "Security";
                        break;
                    case 5: delayReason = "LateAircraft";
                        break;
                    default: delayReason = "NoDelay";
                        break;
                }

                Console.WriteLine(delayReason);
            }
        }
        catch (Exception ex)
        {
            Console.WriteLine(ex.Message);

        }
    }
}
}
```

3. Create another C# console application project named AvroFlightDelayAnalyzerReducer.

4. Paste the code from Listing 10.6 into the `Program.cs` file. The reducer function loops through the standard input lines and maintains a counter for the number of times a word occurs in the input. When it encounters the end of input, it writes the word and number of occurrences to standard output.

LISTING 10.6 Hadoop Streaming Avro Reducer

```
using System;
using System.IO;

namespace AvroFlightDelayAnalyzerReducer
{
    class Program
    {
        static void Main(string[] args)
        {
            string word, lastWord = null;
            int count = 0;

            if (args.Length > 0)
            {
                Console.SetIn(new StreamReader(args[0]));
            }
```

```
        while ((word = Console.ReadLine()) != null)
        {
            if (word != lastWord)
            {
                if (lastWord != null)
                    Console.WriteLine("{0}[{1}]", lastWord, count);

                count = 1;
                lastWord = word;
            }
            else
            {
                count += 1;
            }
        }
        Console.WriteLine("{0}[{1}]", lastWord, count);
    }
  }
}
```

5. Build the mapper and the reducer project, and copy the files `AvroFlightDelayAnalyzerMapper.exe` and `AvroFlightDelayAnalyzerReducer.exe` from the debug folder to the `C:\AvroMapReduce` reducer folder.

6. Download the files `avro-mapred-1.7.4-hadoop2.jar`, `avro-1.7.4.jar`, and `avro-tools-1.7.4.jar` from https://archive.apache.org/dist/avro/avro-1.7.4/java/ to the folder `C:\AvroMapReduce`.

7. Copy the file `475719775_T_ONTIME.avro` you generated in the previous section into the folder `C:\AvroMapReduce`.

8. Create the folder `AvroFlightDelayAnalyzer` with the subfolders `Apps` and `Input` on HDFS using the following commands:

```
hadoop fs -mkdir /AvroFlightDelayAnalyzer
hadoop fs -mkdir /AvroFlightDelayAnalyzer/Apps
hadoop fs -mkdir /AvroFlightDelayAnalyzer/Input
```

9. Use these commands to upload files from `C:\AvroMapReduce` to HDFS in the folders created previously:

```
hadoop fs -copyFromLocal C:\AvroMapReduce\AvroFlightDelayAnalyzerMapper.exe
/AvroFlightDelayAnalyzer/Apps/AvroFlightDelayAnalyzerMapper.exe
hadoop fs -copyFromLocal C:\AvroMapReduce\AvroFlightDelayAnalyzerReducer.exe
/AvroFlightDelayAnalyzer/Apps/AvroFlightDelayAnalyzerReducer.exe
hadoop fs -copyFromLocal C:\AvroMapReduce\475719775_T_ONTIME.avro
/AvroFlightDelayAnalyzer/Input/475719775_T_ONTIME.avro
```

10. Create the folder `Avro` on HDFS using this command:

```
hadoop fs -mkdir /Avro
```

11. Copy the dependency JAR files `avro-mapred-1.7.4-hadoop2.jar`, `avro-1.7.4.jar`, and `avro-tools-1.7.4.jar` that you downloaded in step 6 to this folder using these commands:

```
hadoop fs -copyFromLocal C:\AvroMapReduce\avro-1.7.4.jar /Avro/avro-1.7.4.jar
hadoop fs -copyFromLocal C:\AvroMapReduce\avro-tools-1.7.4.jar /Avro/avro-
tools-1.7.4.jar
hadoop fs -copyFromLocal C:\AvroMapReduce\avro-mapred-1.7.4-hadoop2.jar /Avro/
avro-mapred-1.7.4-hadoop2.jar
```

12. Set the `LIBJARS` variable with the location of the dependency JAR files `avro-mapred-1.7.4-hadoop2.jar`, `avro-1.7.4.jar`, and `avro-tools-1.7.4.jar`. The JAR files are placed into distributed cache and made available to all task trackers. Use the following command to set the `LIBJARS` variable:

```
SET LIBJARS="/Avro/avro-mapred-1.7.4-hadoop2.jar,/Avro/avro-1.7.4.jar,/Avro/
avro-tools-1.7.4.jar"
```

13. Submit the streaming MapReduce job using this command:

```
hadoop jar %HADOOP_HOME%\share\hadoop\tools\lib\hadoop-
streaming-2.4.0.2.1.3.0-1981.jar -files
"hdfs://localhost:8020//AvroFlightDelayAnalyzer/Apps/
AvroFlightDelayAnalyzerMapper.exe,hdfs:// localhost:8020/
AvroFlightDelayAnalyzer/Apps/AvroFlightDelayAnalyzerReducer.exe" -libjars
%LIBJARS% -input "/AvroFlightDelayAnalyzer/Input/" -output "/
AvroFlightDelayAnalyzer/Output" -mapper "AvroFlightDelayAnalyzerMapper.exe"
-reducer "AvroFlightDelayAnalyzerReducer.exe" -
inputformat org.apache.avro.mapred.AvroAsTextInputFormat
```

14. When the job finishes executing, examine the contents of the output folder to view the final output. As you can see in Figure 10.8, the final output shows the list of delay reasons and number of flights delayed due to a particular reason.

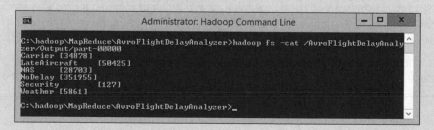

FIGURE 10.8
Hadoop streaming MapReduce job output.

Summary

This hour explored the steps involved in programming and submitting a MapReduce job for execution. The hour also introduced serialization frameworks for Hadoop, focusing on Avro. The hour concluded with an example of writing a MapReduce program in C#.

Q&A

Q. How do I add dependencies (such as third-party libraries) and other files to my MapReduce job for use during runtime?

A. You can accomplish this by using a distributed cache. A distributed cache helps distribute files that MapReduce jobs need to the cluster. You specify a comma-separated list of files using the `-libjars` parameter of the `hadoop jar` command while submitting the MapReduce job for execution. The MapReduce framework copies the necessary files from the HDFS path specified using the `libjars` parameter to the nodes before job execution.

Q. Is it possible to stop a MapReduce job in the middle of execution?

A. Yes, you can use the command `hadoop job -kill <<jobid>>` for this purpose.

Quiz

1. Why are serialization frameworks needed when Java provides built-in serialization support?

2. Is it possible to program MapReduce programs in languages other than Java?

Answers

1. Java serialization is not very lean and compact, and it doesn't provide precise control over serialization. Extensibility (schema modification addition and removal of fields) also is not easy to achieve, and Java serialization is not very portable to other programming languages. In addition, the input data might not be in a format native to Hadoop (for example, it might be in a custom log file format being generated by a legacy system). Recall that when the MapReduce framework cannot determine the logical division of records, it presents the entire data file to a single mapper; parallelism fails to work. A serialization library would come handy in such a scenario for parsing the data and determining record boundaries.

2. Yes, Hadoop streaming APIs provide for this feature. Theoretically, you can write MapReduce programs in any programming language that supports reading from standard input and writing to standard output.

HOUR 11
Customizing the HDInsight Cluster with Script Action

What You'll Learn in This Hour:

▶ Identifying the Need for Cluster Customization
▶ Developing Script Action
▶ Consuming Script Action
▶ Running a Giraph Job on a Customized HDInsight Cluster
▶ Testing Script Action with HDInsight Emulator

The HDInsight cluster comes preinstalled with some frequently used components. You can also customize the HDInsight cluster and install additional Hadoop ecosystem projects using a feature called Script Action. This hour introduces the HDInsight Script Action feature and illustrates the steps in developing and deploying a Script Action.

Identifying the Need for Cluster Customization

When HDInsight cluster is provisioned, various Hadoop ecosystem projects (such as Pig, Hive, Oozie, and HCatalog) are preinstalled, depending on the version of HDInsight (and Hortonworks Data Platform distribution) chosen. Although the preinstalled components will likely meet most users' needs, you can also leverage the capabilities of other Hadoop ecosystem projects.

For example, HDInsight version 3.1 currently does not come installed with the components Giraph, Solr, Spark, and R. Users interested in leveraging the graph processing capabilities of Giraph or the search capabilities of Solr on Big Data might want to install the respective projects on their HDInsight cluster. This is achieved via the Script Action feature. Using the Script Action cluster customization feature, you can install additional Hadoop projects on the HDInsight cluster during cluster deployment.

NOTE

Script Action Feature Is Supported from HDInsight Version 3.1 Onward

Only HDInsight version 3.1 (Hadoop 2.4) and above support the Script Action feature; therefore, you should always validate the Hadoop version in the action script before proceeding further with script execution. You can use the `Get-HDIHadoopVersion` helper method, covered later in this hour, to check the Hadoop version.

Developing Script Action

Script Action scripts are developed in PowerShell. To better understand the process of script development, consider the following steps for installing Giraph on HDInsight cluster:

1. Obtain Giraph source code and build Giraph for a specific version of HDInsight.

2. Download and import the `HDInsightUtilities` module file, which contains the Helper methods for performing common tasks (The PowerShell script developed later in Listing 11.1 includes the download URI.)

3. Download the zipped Giraph binary files from a private or public file share accessible from the cluster to a temporary location.

4. Unzip the downloaded file to the installation directory under `C:\apps` (`C:\hdp` for an HDInsight emulator).

5. Optionally, copy the samples to `/example/jars/` on the default file system.

6. Configure the environment variable `GIRAPH_HOME` to point to the installation directory.

NOTE

Building Giraph from Source Is Optional

Building Giraph from source is optional because Microsoft has already provided Script Actions and binaries for installing several popular Hadoop projects, including Giraph. For example, you can obtain zipped Giraph binaries targeting HDInsight 3.1 from https://hdiconfigactions.blob.core.windows.net/giraphconfigactionv01/giraph-1.2.0.zip.

Using the `HDInsightUtilities` Module

To ease the process of Script Action development, Script Action provides helper methods to perform common installation tasks. The `HDInsightUtilities` module file defines these methods. Table 11.1 lists some commonly used methods and their purposes.

TABLE 11.1   Common Helper Methods in Script Action

Method	Purpose
Get-HDIHadoopVersion	Gets Hadoop version information
Save-HDIFile	Downloads a file from the specified URI and saves to the local file system
Expand-HDIZippedFile	Extracts the ZIP file to a specified location
Write-HDILog	Uses the PowerShell Write-Output cmdlet to write output from script
Get-[HDI]Services	Lists all services or HDInsight-specific services in any state
Get-[HDI]Service	Gets the details of any service or HDInsight-specific service by specifying the service name as the parameter
Get-[HDI]ServicesRunning	Lists all services or HDInsight services in running state
Get-[HDI]ServiceRunning	Verifies whether a service (or HDInsight service) is in running state by specifying the name as the parameter
Test-IsHDIHeadNode, Test-IsActiveHDIHeadNode, Test-IsHDIDataNode	Determines whether the computer running the scripts is a headnote or active headnote or a data node

Listing 11.1 provides the script to install Giraph, leveraging helper methods in Table 11.1.

LISTING 11.1   Script to Install Giraph

```
#Source and destination paths
$HDInsightUtilitiesDownloadLoc="https://hdiconfigactions.blob.core.windows.net/
configactionmodulev01/HDInsightUtilities-v01.psm1"
$giraphSrcLoc="https://hdiconfigactions.blob.core.windows.net/giraphconfigactionv01/
giraph-1.2.0.zip"
$installationFolder=(Get-Item "$env:HADOOP_HOME").parent.FullName;
$HDInsightUtilitiesLoc=$installationFolder+"\HDInsightUtilities.psm1"

#Stop execution, if giraph installation directory already exists
#This ensures that script can be executed again safely when a VM is reimaged
if (Test-Path ($installationFolder + '\' + 'giraph-1.2.0'))
{
    Write-HDILog "Installation directory already exists!";
    exit;
}
```

```
#Download HDInsightUtilities module
$utilWebClient = New-Object System.Net.WebClient;
$utilWebClient.DownloadFile($HDInsightUtilitiesDownloadLoc,$HDInsightUtilitiesLoc);

#Import HDInsightUtilities module
Import-Module $HDInsightUtilitiesLoc;

# Download Giraph binary file to temporary location
$temporaryZipFile = $env:temp + '\' + [guid]::NewGuid() + '.zip';
Save-HDIFile -SrcUri $giraphSrcLoc -DestFile $temporaryZipFile;

# Unzip the downloaded file to installation directory
Expand-HDIZippedFile -ZippedFile $temporaryZipFile -UnzipFolder $installationFolder;

# Delete temporary files
Remove-Item $temporaryZipFile;
[Environment]::SetEnvironmentVariable('GIRAPH_HOME', $installationFolder+ '\' +
'giraph-1.2.0', 'Machine');
```

Remember the following considerations when developing Script Action:

▶ The location containing script files should be accessible to cluster nodes. Using blob storage is best.

▶ Safely executing the same script more than once on a node should be possible. This is helpful when a VM in the cluster gets reimaged and requires re-execution of the Script Action.

▶ Use either C:\Apps or D:\ as the installation path. Other locations on the C: drive are reserved locations and should not be used.

▶ If a script modifies the Hadoop configuration or an operating system setting, restart HDInsight services, if needed.

Consuming Script Action

Script action can be configured for execution from the Windows Azure Management Portal, PowerShell, or HDInsight .NET SDK when you provision a new cluster.

Using Script Action with the Azure Management Portal

When provisioning the HDInsight cluster with a custom create option, you can add Script Action for cluster customization by specifying the Script Action name and script and then selecting the nodes on which the script is to be executed (see Figure 11.1). You can add multiple Script Actions by clicking the Add Script Action button.

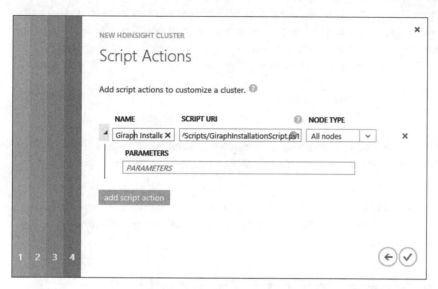

FIGURE 11.1
Adding Script Actions to customize the HDInsight cluster.

Using Script Action with PowerShell

You can also invoke Script Actions using the `Add-AzureHDInsightScriptAction` PowerShell cmdlet while provisioning the HDInsight cluster with PowerShell.

The following code snippet illustrates how to use `Add-AzureHDInsightScriptAction` to add Script Action to a cluster configuration object:

```
$clusterConfig = Add-AzureHDInsightScriptAction -Config $clusterConfig -Name
"Giraph Installer" -ClusterRoleCollection HeadNode -Uri <<replace with script uri>>
```

The `Add-AzureHDInsightScriptAction` cmdlet accepts as arguments the cluster configuration object, the Script Action name, the nodes on which the customization script is to be run (`HeadNode`, `DataNode`, or both), the script URI, and, optionally, any input parameters that script requires.

The cluster configuration object created is supplied as an argument to the `New-AzureHDInsightCluster` cmdlet. The rest of the cluster-provisioning process is similar to the process described in Hour 6, "Getting Started with HDInsight, Provisioning Your HDInsight Service Cluster, and Automating HDInsight Cluster Provisioning."

Using Script Action with HDInsight .NET SDK

In addition, you can invoke Script Actions when provisioning the cluster with the HDInsight .NET SDK. Recall from Hour 6 that you can use the `ClusterCreateParameters` class to specify cluster configuration properties during cluster provisioning. You can add Script Actions to the `ConfigActions` property of the `ClusterCreateParameters` class using the `ScriptAction` class object, as the following code snippet illustrates:

```
clusterConfig.ConfigActions.Add(new ScriptAction("Giraph Installer", new
ClusterNodeType[] { ClusterNodeType.HeadNode },
new Uri("<<replace with script uri>>"),null));
```

Here the `ScriptAction` constructor accepts as arguments the Script Action name, the nodes on which the customization script is to be run, the script URI, and, optionally, any input parameters the script requires.

The cluster configuration object created is supplied as an argument to the `CreateCluster` function (defined in `HDInsightClient` class), and the rest of the cluster provisioning process is similar to the process described in Hour 6.

Running a Giraph Job on a Customized HDInsight Cluster

A customized cluster with Giraph installed can run Giraph jobs. To understand the steps involved in running a Giraph job, consider the `SimpleShortestPathsComputation` example from Apache Giraph documentation, at http://giraph.apache.org/quick_start.html. The example calculates the length of the shortest path from a given source node to all the nodes in a graph using the following directed graph data (see Figure 11.2):

```
[0,0,[[1,1],[3,3]]]
[1,0,[[0,1],[2,2],[3,1]]]
[2,0,[[1,2],[4,4]]]
[3,0,[[0,3],[1,1],[4,4]]]
[4,0,[[3,4],[2,4]]]
```

This data is in the format [*source_node*,*source_node_value*,[[*dest_node*, *edge_value*],...]]. For example, the first line states that source node 0 has a value of 0 and is connected to destination node 1 via edge, with a weight of 2, and destination node 3 via edge, with a weight of 3. The simple shortest path example treats node 1 as the source node and calculates the shortest path from it to all other nodes.

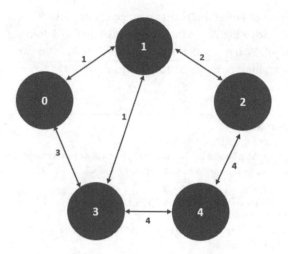

FIGURE 11.2
Visual representation of graph data used in the `SimpleShortestPathComputation` example.

Listing 11.2 provides the PowerShell script to submit a Giraph job. The simple shortest path computation algorithm has been implemented as one of the examples in `giraph-examples.jar`. Table 11.2 lists the arguments the Giraph job requires. The `GiraphRunner` helper class runs Giraph jobs by consuming the arguments provided.

TABLE 11.2   Parameters the Giraph Job Requires

Method	Purpose
-ca	Specifies custom arguments.
-vif	Specifies the vertex input format class name. The class interprets the input text file (which is in JSON format in this example).
-vip	Specifies the vertex input path, the location of the file containing the graph's representation.
-vof	Specifies the output format. In this example, the output is in the format vertex ID and value of the shortest path.
-op	Specifies the output path.
-w	Specifies the number of workers.

Before submitting the Giraph job, copy the `giraph-examples.jar` from `%GIRAPH_HOME%\giraph-examples.jar` to `/example/jars/giraph-examples.jar` in blob storage. Also, save the graph vertex data to a text file and copy it to `/example/data/tiny_graph.txt` in blob storage. You can use a cloud storage explorer tool or PowerShell for this purpose (see Hour 8, "Storing Data in Microsoft Azure Storage Blob"). Save the PowerShell script in Listing 11.2 to a file and execute the script using Azure PowerShell. When job execution comples, the results are stored in /giraphoutput/shortestpath in two files: part-m-00001 and part-m-00002.

LISTING 11.2   Submitting a Giraph Job

```
$hdInsightClusterName = "HDInsight Cluster Name"
$giraphExamplesJarFile = "/example/jars/giraph-examples.jar"
$giraphJobParameters = "org.apache.giraph.examples.SimpleShortestPathsComputation",
            "-ca", "mapred.job.tracker=headnodehost:9010",
            "-vif",
"org.apache.giraph.io.formats.JsonLongDoubleFloatDoubleVertexInputFormat",
            "-vip", "/example/data/tiny_graph.txt",
            "-vof", "org.apache.giraph.io.formats.IdWithValueTextOutputFormat",
            "-op",  "/giraphoutput/shortestpath",
            "-w", "2"
# Create the definition
$giraphJobDefinition = New-AzureHDInsightMapReduceJobDefinition -JarFile
$giraphExamplesJarFile -ClassName "org.apache.giraph.GiraphRunner" -Arguments
$giraphJobParameters

# Get HDInsight crendentials
$creds = Get-Credential

# Submit job for execution
$giraphJob = Start-AzureHDInsightJob -Cluster $hdInsightClusterName -JobDefinition
$giraphJobDefinition -Credential $creds

# Print job ID
Write-Host "JobID:" $giraphJob.JobId -ForegroundColor Green
```

The following is the combined output from the two output files:

```
0 1.0
4 5.0
2 2.0
1 0.0
3 1.0
```

You can infer that the shortest path from node 1 to node 0 has a value (travel cost or weight) of 1. Similarly, the shortest path from node 1 to node 4 has a value of 5 (the sum of the shortest distance from node 1 to node 3 and from node 3 to node 4).

Testing Script Action with HDInsight Emulator

You can test most Script Actions on an HDInsight emulator by manually invoking the PowerShell script. In HDInsight emulator, Hadoop components are installed in the `C:\hdp` folder instead of the `C:\apps` folder used with an HDInsight cluster. You can accommodate this in the script by extracting the correct installation path from Hadoop home by using the expression `(Get-Item "$env:HADOOP_HOME").parent.FullName`.

CAUTION

You might not be able to test scripts that have a dependency on specific HDInsight cluster services that are not available in an HDInsight emulator. Such scripts can be tested only on an HDInsight cluster.

Summary

This hour explored the process of Script Action development to install custom Hadoop projects on an HDInsight cluster. Giraph is a Hadoop project that is well suited to graph computations. The hour demonstrated the steps involved in developing a Script Action to install Giraph on an HDInsight cluster and use it to process a graph problem.

Q&A

Q. When is a Script Action invoked?

A. Script actions are invoked during the cluster provisioning process, after the cluster creation is complete but before the cluster becomes operational. Script actions are also invoked when a VM in the cluster is reimaged.

Q. What are the advantages of using Giraph for graph processing, compared to directly writing MapReduce programs?

A. Graph problems often involve multiple iterations and state transitions. Hopping and transmission of messages between vertices are other common computation operations. Modelling such problems in conventional MapReduce is not a trivial task. Having a MapReduce job for each iteration requires creating multiple jobs, which leads to multiple key/value pair–based read/write operations for saving and retrieving state among multiple graph iterations. Giraph attempts to solve these problems by providing a MapReduce–based graph-processing solution to conveniently model graph problems. Modelling a graph problem as a set of vertices and edges instead of mappers and reducers allows for a simpler and more elegant implementation of graph problems. Vertices can both send messages to other vertices and receive messages sent from previous iterations in the computation, also called Supersteps. Initial Giraph implementations kept graph state in memory for the entire time during a computation, to accomplish this with minimum disk read/write operations. However, the implementation changed later. With out-of-core capability implemented, beyond a certain limit, Giraph partitions and messages now get written to disk. Partitions are swapped between disk and memory, based on usage. Hence, Giraph delivers when it comes to performing graph computations.

Quiz

1. What physical locations can you use to install custom components?

2. Which helper method can you use to check whether an HDInsight service is in running state?

Answers

1. Use either `C:\Apps` or `D:\` as the installation path. Other locations on the `C:` drive are reserved and should not be used.

2. You can use the `Get-HDIServiceRunning` helper method to verify whether an HDInsight service is in running state, specifying the name as the parameter.

Getting Started with Apache Hive and Apache Tez in HDInsight

What You'll Learn in This Hour:

▶ Introduction to Apache Hive
▶ Getting Started with Apache Hive in HDInsight
▶ Azure HDInsight Tools for Visual Studio
▶ Programmatically Using the HDInsight .NET SDK
▶ Introduction to Apache Tez

In the last few hours, you learned in detail about Hadoop (HDFS for data storage and MapReduce as a programming framework). You also looked into the writing programs (Mapper, Reducer, and Driver) that target the MapReduce framework. But you might have noticed that writing a MapReduce program, whether in Java or any other programming language of your choice using Hadoop Streaming, is not easy. It requires a great deal of expertise, a different approach in programming, and a significant amount of time for the development. The task becomes even more difficult if you have two or more datasets to join to get a result.

This is where Apache Hive comes in handy. Apache Hive runs on top of the Hadoop framework and enables you to write your data processing logic (with joins, groups, sorts, and so on) in a Structured Query Language (SQL)-like declarative language (which you probably have been familiar with for several years). With the help of Apache Hive, you can write your queries in just a few lines, saving you time and effort. For example, a simple query of less than 10 lines translates to a MapReduce program with more than 100 lines of code.

In this hour, you delve into how to use Apache Hive, the different ways of writing and executing HiveQL queries in HDInsight, and how Apache Tez improves the overall performance severalfold for HiveQL queries.

Introduction to Apache Hive

You can think of Hive as a SQL abstraction layer over Hadoop MapReduce with a SQL-like query engine. Hive enables you to write data processing logic or queries in a SQL-like declarative language, called HiveQL, that is similar to SQL, as in the case of relational database systems.

As you can see in Figure 12.1, when you execute the HiveQL query, Hive translates the query into a series of equivalent MapReduce, saving you the time and effort of writing actual MapReduce jobs on your own. Then Hive executes the query.

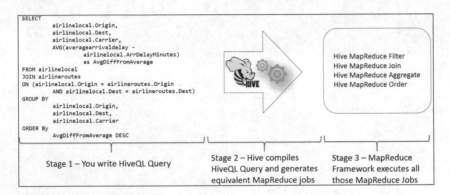

```
SELECT
        airlinelocal.Origin,
        airlinelocal.Dest,
        airlinelocal.Carrier,
        AVG(averagearrivaldelay -
                airlinelocal.ArrDelayMinutes)
                as AvgDiffFromAverage
FROM airlinelocal
JOIN airlineroutes
ON (airlinelocal.Origin = airlineroutes.Origin
        AND airlinelocal.Dest = airlineroutes.Dest)
GROUP BY
        airlinelocal.Origin,
        airlinelocal.Dest,
        airlinelocal.Carrier
ORDER By
        AvgDiffFromAverage DESC
```

Hive MapReduce Filter
Hive MapReduce Join
Hive MapReduce Aggregate
Hive MapReduce Order

Stage 1 – You write HiveQL Query

Stage 2 – Hive compiles HiveQL Query and generates equivalent MapReduce jobs

Stage 3 – MapReduce Framework executes all those MapReduce Jobs

FIGURE 12.1
High-level Hive query execution flow.

Hive comes in handy for data analysts with strong SQL skills, providing an easier and quicker migration into the world of Hadoop. You can think of Hive as distributed data warehouse software that facilitates easy data summarization, ad hoc queries, and the analysis of large data set stored in HDFS. Hive comes closer in concept to Relational Database Management System (RDBMS). Hive is designed for a data warehouse type of workload and is best suited for batch jobs over large sets of append-only data (such as web logs). It does not work well with an OLTP type of workload that requires real-time queries or row-level updates.

NOTE

Hive Development

Hive, a data warehousing layer over Hadoop, was initially developed at Facebook. It continues to be in active development at Facebook and in the open source community.

This new abstraction layer allows for data to be exposed as structured tables that supports both simple and sophisticated ad hoc queries using a query language called HiveQL for data summarization, ad hoc queries, and analysis.

Hive follows a "schema on read" approach, unlike RDMBS, which enforces "schema on write." In other words, Hive has no control over the underlying storage until you read the data.

Getting Started with Apache Hive in HDInsight

Microsoft Azure HDInsight enables you to write and execute HiveQL queries in different ways. You can choose either method based on your role or your comfort level. For example, normally, an administrator uses the Hive command-line interface or PowerShell scripting, a business user prefers to use the Cluster Dashboard, and a developer or development team likes to interact with Hive using Azure HDInsight Tools for Visual Studio or programmatically using HDInsight .NET SDK (Software Development Kit).

NOTE

Hive Metastore

When you create Hive objects (databases, tables, columns, views, and so on), the information about these objects is, by default, stored in an attached database as part of the HDInsight cluster itself. This means that when you delete your HDInsight cluster, this database also gets deleted and you lose metadata information.

To preserve metadata information (even after HDInsight cluster deletion), you can specify that an Azure SQL database be used as a metastore for Hive and Oozie (see Figure 12.2), while provisioning your HDInsight cluster using Azure Management Portal or by using the `Add-AzureHDInsightMetastore` cmdlet with PowerShell scripting (when provisioning the HDInsight cluster with PowerShell scripting), as Hour 6, "Getting Started with HDInsight, Provisioning Your HDInsight Service Cluster, and Automating HDInsight Cluster Provisioning," details.

You can safely delete your HDInsight cluster without losing this information because it is stored externally in an Azure SQL database. Next time, when needed, you can provision another HDInsight cluster and point it to the same Azure SQL database (which contains metadata information from the previous cluster instance) and you will find all those objects again.

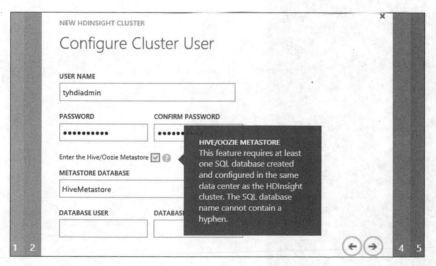

FIGURE 12.2
Specifying a metastore for Hive/Oozie while cluster provisioning.

In this section, you look at some common methods of interacting with Hive and writing HiveQL queries from the remote head node machine or from your local workstation.

GO TO ▶ In this section, we restrict discussion to demonstrating different ways of executing HiveQL queries only. Refer to **Hour 13, "Programming with Apache Hive, Apache Tez in HDInsight, and Apache HCatalog,"** for a detailed discussion of some important Hive commands (along with its different clauses) in HiveQL and real examples of how to use it.

NOTE

Running HiveQL Queries from Cross-Platforms

Although this hour does not cover the task, you can also write and execute your HiveQL queries from non-Windows-based machines. For example, you can leverage a REST API named WebHCat for cross-platform access.

Using the Hive Command-Line Interface

When you connect to the remote head node machine of your HDInsight or Hadoop cluster, you see a shortcut icon for the Hadoop command prompt (command-line interface [CLI]) on the desktop (see Figure 12.3). Double-click that icon to open the Hadoop command prompt.

FIGURE 12.3
Shortcut icons on the desktop of the head node in HDInsight or a Hadoop cluster.

To switch from the Hadoop command prompt to the Hive CLI, execute the command `cd %hive_home%\bin` at the Hadoop command prompt, type **hive**, and press Enter. After a few seconds, you switch to the Hive CLI.

Alternatively, you can move one folder back at the Hadoop command prompt, where you will find a folder for Hive (see Figure 12.4). (As you can see, folder names are appended with the version of the applications, and this might be different for you based on the HDInsight version you are using.) Move inside the Hive folder and then to the `bin` folder; type **hive** and press Enter.

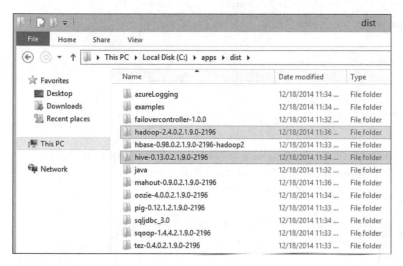

FIGURE 12.4
The Hadoop components folder structure.

As you can see in Figure 12.5, from the Hive CLI, you can start executing HiveQL commands (a HiveQL command terminates with a semicolon, ;). For example, you can see that the executed `show tables` command returns the name of the sample table from the default database, which comes by default. When you execute a HiveQL command, you also see the total time to execute your command and the number of rows retrieved.

```
                                              Hadoop Command Line - hive
C:\apps\dist\hadoop-2.4.0.2.1.9.0-2196>cd..

C:\apps\dist>cd hive-0.13.0.2.1.9.0-2196

C:\apps\dist\hive-0.13.0.2.1.9.0-2196>cd bin

C:\apps\dist\hive-0.13.0.2.1.9.0-2196\bin>hive

Logging initialized using configuration in file:/C:/ap
SLF4J: Class path contains multiple SLF4J bindings.
SLF4J: Found binding in [jar:file:/C:/apps/dist/hadoop
SLF4J: Found binding in [jar:file:/C:/apps/dist/hbase-
SLF4J: See http://www.slf4j.org/codes.html#multiple_bi
SLF4J: Actual binding is of type [org.slf4j.impl.Log4j
hive> show tables;
OK
hivesampletable
Time taken: 1.109 seconds, Fetched: 1 row(s)
hive> _
```

FIGURE 12.5
Hive console and command execution.

Now you can create another table in the default database (see Figure 12.6), with the script available in Listing 12.1. As you see in Figure 12.6, the result of the show tables command now shows two tables (one that came by default and one we created).

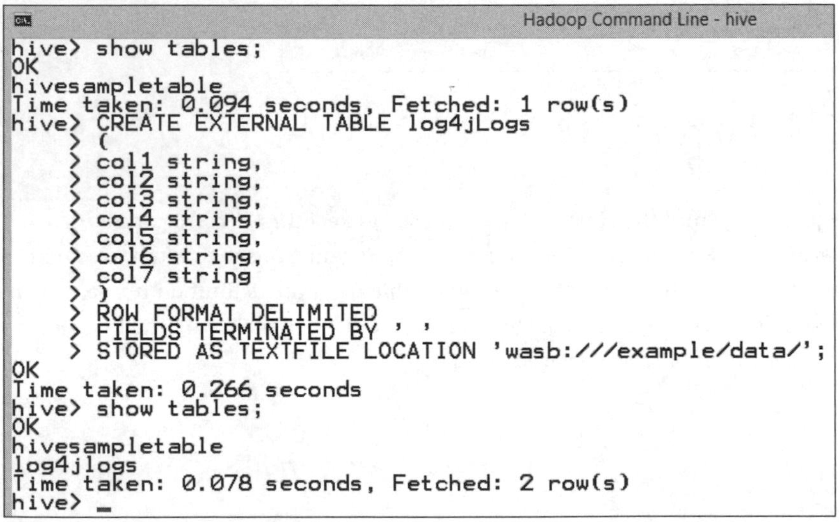

```
                                              Hadoop Command Line - hive
hive> show tables;
OK
hivesampletable
Time taken: 0.094 seconds, Fetched: 1 row(s)
hive> CREATE EXTERNAL TABLE log4jLogs
    > (
    >   col1 string,
    >   col2 string,
    >   col3 string,
    >   col4 string,
    >   col5 string,
    >   col6 string,
    >   col7 string
    > )
    > ROW FORMAT DELIMITED
    > FIELDS TERMINATED BY ' '
    > STORED AS TEXTFILE LOCATION 'wasb:///example/data/';
OK
Time taken: 0.266 seconds
hive> show tables;
OK
hivesampletable
log4jlogs
Time taken: 0.078 seconds, Fetched: 2 row(s)
hive> _
```

FIGURE 12.6
Creating a table using the Hive console.

LISTING 12.1 Creating a Hive Table

```
DROP TABLE IF EXISTS log4jLogs;
CREATE EXTERNAL TABLE log4jLogs
(
col1 string,
col2 string,
col3 string,
col4 string,
col5 string,
col6 string,
col7 string
)
ROW FORMAT DELIMITED
FIELDS TERMINATED BY ' '
STORED AS TEXTFILE LOCATION 'wasb:///example/data/';
```

Next, you execute a HiveQL query to retrieve data from the table you created with the script available in Listing 12.2. As discussed earlier, Hive generates an equivalent MapReduce job internally; you can see in Figure 12.7 that it shows the progress of the MapReduce job (which the Hive framework creates and kicks off internally) when you execute your HiveQL query. At the end of execution, it shows the data returned from the query (see Figure 12.7).

LISTING 12.2 Executing a HiveQL Query

```
SELECT col4 AS Severity, count(*) AS CountOfOccurence
FROM log4jLogs
GROUP BY col4
ORDER BY col4 DESC limit 5;
```

Generally, the Hive framework generates an equivalent MapReduce job internally, executes it, and returns the final set of processed data back to you (if applicable), as Figure 12.7 shows. The Hive framework is smart enough to decide when the MapReduce job is needed to serve the query request and when it's not. For example, if you execute the query SELECT * FROM log4jLogs, Hive goes directly to HDFS and returns all the data to you; it does not generate a MapReduce job in this case because this query requires no data processing or computation.

```
Hadoop Command Line - hive
hive> SELECT col4 AS Severity, count(*) AS CountOfOccurence
   > FROM log4jLogs
   > GROUP BY col4
   > ORDER BY col4  DESC limit 5;
Query ID = tyhdiremoteadmin_20141218161818_718c1c2c-518a-4c9e-bb5f-9efcc90a44c
Total jobs = 2
Launching Job 1 out of 2
Number of reduce tasks not specified. Estimated from input data size: 1
In order to change the average load for a reducer (in bytes):
  set hive.exec.reducers.bytes.per.reducer=<number>
In order to limit the maximum number of reducers:
  set hive.exec.reducers.max=<number>
In order to set a constant number of reducers:
  set mapreduce.job.reduces=<number>
Starting Job = job_1418902687855_0030, Tracking URL = http://headnodehost:9014.
Kill Command = C:\apps\dist\hadoop-2.4.0.2.1.9.0-2196\bin\hadoop.cmd job  -kil
Hadoop job information for Stage-1: number of mappers: 1; number of reducers:
2014-12-18 16:18:30,999 Stage-1 map = 0%,  reduce = 0%
2014-12-18 16:18:41,948 Stage-1 map = 100%,  reduce = 0%, Cumulative CPU 2.077
2014-12-18 16:18:51,651 Stage-1 map = 100%,  reduce = 100%, Cumulative CPU 5.1
MapReduce Total cumulative CPU time: 5 seconds 139 msec
Ended Job = job_1418902687855_0030
Launching Job 2 out of 2
Number of reduce tasks determined at compile time: 1
In order to change the average load for a reducer (in bytes):
  set hive.exec.reducers.bytes.per.reducer=<number>
In order to limit the maximum number of reducers:
  set hive.exec.reducers.max=<number>
In order to set a constant number of reducers:
  set mapreduce.job.reduces=<number>
Starting Job = job_1418902687855_0031, Tracking URL = http://headnodehost:9014.
Kill Command = C:\apps\dist\hadoop-2.4.0.2.1.9.0-2196\bin\hadoop.cmd job  -kil
Hadoop job information for Stage-2: number of mappers: 1; number of reducers:
2014-12-18 16:19:06,552 Stage-2 map = 0%,  reduce = 0%
2014-12-18 16:19:17,040 Stage-2 map = 100%,  reduce = 0%, Cumulative CPU 2.828
2014-12-18 16:19:27,791 Stage-2 map = 100%,  reduce = 100%, Cumulative CPU 5.8
MapReduce Total cumulative CPU time: 5 seconds 890 msec
Ended Job = job_1418902687855_0031
MapReduce Jobs Launched:
Job 0: Map: 1  Reduce: 1   Cumulative CPU: 5.139 sec   HDFS Read: 0 HDFS Write
Job 1: Map: 1  Reduce: 1   Cumulative CPU: 5.89 sec    HDFS Read: 554 HDFS Writ
Total MapReduce CPU Time Spent: 11 seconds 29 msec
OK
[WARN]  4
[TRACE] 816
[INFO]  96
[FATAL] 1
[ERROR] 3
Time taken: 76.467 seconds, Fetched: 5 row(s)
hive> _
```

FIGURE 12.7
Executing a HiveQL query on the Hive console.

▼ TRY IT YOURSELF

Hive on an HDInsight Emulator

The scripts in Listings 12.1 and 12.2 were tested on an Azure HDInsight cluster and should run as is there.

We recommend that you use an Azure HDInsight cluster service whenever possible so that you have access to all the features of HDInsight. A free trial version is available for one month or for up to $200 worth of credit, whichever is earlier. Refer to Hour 6 for details on provisioning an HDInsight cluster easily and quickly. Remember to delete the cluster whenever you are not using it, to save on the cost; you can provision it again, when needed. (Let your data be stored on the default Azure Storage Blob, and use the SQL database as the Hive metastore so that you don't lose anything after cluster deletion.)

If you still want to use scripts on the Azure HDInsight Emulator from Listings 12.1 and 12.2, you must run these additional steps:

1. Copy the `example` folder from this hour's content folder to the `c:` drive of the machine where you have the HDInsight Emulator running.

2. Execute these commands at the Hadoop command prompt on the HDInsight Emulator to create the necessary folders and load data into HDFS:

```
hadoop fs -mkdir /example
hadoop fs -mkdir /example/data
hadoop fs -copyFromLocal c:\example\data\sample.log /example/data
```

3. Replace the `Location` clause, as highlighted here for Listing 12.1. (Listing 12.2 makes no change.)

```
DROP TABLE IF EXISTS log4jLogs;
CREATE EXTERNAL TABLE log4jLogs
(
col1 string,
col2 string,
col3 string,
col4 string,
col5 string,
col6 string,
col7 string
)
ROW FORMAT DELIMITED
FIELDS TERMINATED BY ' '
STORED AS TEXTFILE LOCATION '/example/data/';
```

Using PowerShell Scripting

Hour 6 demonstrated how to use PowerShell scripting to provision an HDInsight cluster and execute a MapReduce job. With PowerShell scripting, you can also execute Hive and Pig jobs.

In this section, you explore two ways to execute Hive jobs with PowerShell scripting: asynchronously and synchronously.

NOTE

Azure PowerShell Installation and Configuration

If you are using PowerShell scripting for the first time, you must install and configure Azure PowerShell. Refer to Hour 6 for more details on how to get started with PowerShell scripting (installation and configuration) to manage HDInsight cluster or jobs (MapReduce, Hive, Pig, and so on).

Listing 12.3 shows a PowerShell script to submit a Hive job to create an external table in Hive. It waits for job completion and displays the standard output when it completes.

LISTING 12.3 Creating a Hive Table with PowerShell Scripting

```
# Declare all the variables and specify their values
$subscriptionName = "Visual Studio Ultimate with MSDN"
$clusterName = "tyhdicluster"

# Create an external table based on sample data
$queryString = "CREATE EXTERNAL TABLE log4jLogs ( col1 string, col2 string, col3
string, col4 string, col5 string, col6 string, col7 string ) ROW FORMAT DELIMITED
FIELDS TERMINATED BY ' ' STORED AS TEXTFILE LOCATION 'wasb:///example/data/';"

# Create a Hive job definition for
# external table creation
$myHiveJobDefinition = New-AzureHDInsightHiveJobDefinition -Query $queryString

# Submit the job to the cluster
# for external table creation asynchronously
Select-AzureSubscription $subscriptionName
Write-Host "Submit the Hive job to the cluster : $clusterName !"
$myHiveJob = Start-AzureHDInsightJob -Cluster $clusterName `
    -JobDefinition $myHiveJobDefinition

# Wait for the Hive job to complete
Wait-AzureHDInsightJob -Job $myHiveJob -WaitTimeoutInSeconds 3600

# Print the standard error and the standard output of the Hive job.
Get-AzureHDInsightJobOutput -Cluster $clusterName `
    -JobId $myHiveJob.JobId -StandardOutput

Write-Host "Hive job in the cluster : $clusterName completed."
```

Figure 12.8 shows the execution result of the PowerShell scripts from Listing 12.3.

```
PS C:\Windows\System32\WindowsPowerShell\v1.0> D:\Running Hive Query with PowerShell.ps1
Submit the Hive job to the cluster : tyhdicluster !
WARNING: When submitting a query use the -RunAsFile switch to prevent errors with query


Cluster          : tyhdicluster
ExitCode         : 0
Name             : Hive: CREATE EXTERNAL TABL
PercentComplete  :
Query            : CREATE EXTERNAL TABLE log4jLogs ( col1 string, col2 string, col3 strin
State            : Completed
StatusDirectory  : 142515e9-fb7a-4ed5-aed9-d94cf2a1a27d
SubmissionTime   : 12/19/2014 6:42:56 AM
JobId            : job_1418969231336_0008

Hive job in the cluster : tyhdicluster completed.


PS C:\Windows\System32\WindowsPowerShell\v1.0>
```

FIGURE 12.8
Creating a table in Hive using PowerShell scripting.

Notice in Listing 12.3 that we have used a generic job runner, `Start-AzureHDInsightJob`, to asynchronously start the Hive job on an HDInsight cluster. Thus, it returns immediately even before the job has completed.

Next, to retrieve the information after job completion, you use the `Wait-AzureHDInsightJob` cmdlet to wait until the job is executing and then use the `Get-AzureHDInsightJobOutput` cmdlet to retrieve information written to STDOUT or STDERR by the job after completion (see Listings 12.3 and 12.4).

TIP

You can use the `Stop-AzureHDInsightJob` cmdlet to stop an already running job.

In contrast to Listing 12.3, which executes a Data Definition Language (DDL) command to create an external table in Hive, Listing 12.4 queries data from the created table by first grouping it on the Severity column and then sorting by highest number of occurrences.

LISTING 12.4   Executing a HiveQL Query with PowerShell Scripting Asynchronously

```
# Declare all the variables and specify their values
$subscriptionName = "Visual Studio Ultimate with MSDN"
$clusterName = "tyhdicluster"

# Query the created external table to find out count
# by grouping on col4
$queryString = "SELECT col4 AS Severity, count(*) AS CountOfOccurence FROM
log4jLogs GROUP BY col4 ORDER BY CountOfOccurence  DESC limit 5;"

# Create a Hive job definition for the query
$myHiveJobDefinition = New-AzureHDInsightHiveJobDefinition -Query $queryString

# Submit the job to the cluster for execution asynchronously
Select-AzureSubscription $subscriptionName
Write-Host "Submit the Hive job to the cluster : $clusterName !"
$myHiveJob = Start-AzureHDInsightJob -Cluster $clusterName -JobDefinition
$myHiveJobDefinition

# Wait for the Hive job to complete
Wait-AzureHDInsightJob -Job $myHiveJob -WaitTimeoutInSeconds 3600

# Print the standard error and the standard output of the Hive job.
Get-AzureHDInsightJobOutput -Cluster $clusterName -JobId $myHiveJob.JobId
-StandardOutput

Write-Host "Hive job in the cluster : $clusterName completed."
```

Figure 12.9 shows the execution result of the PowerShell scripts from Listing 12.4.

```
PS C:\Windows\System32\WindowsPowerShell\v1.0> D:\Running Hive Query with PowerShell_2.ps1
Submit the Hive job to the cluster : tyhdicluster !
WARNING: When submitting a query use the -RunAsFile switch to prevent errors with query ler

Cluster          : tyhdicluster
ExitCode         : 0
Name             : Hive: SELECT col4 AS Sever
PercentComplete  : map 100% reduce 100%
Query            : SELECT col4 AS Severity, count(*) AS CountOfOccurence FROM log4jLogs GROL
State            : Completed
StatusDirectory  : d8b0a1e9-4700-4df7-857f-9b57bcd62cfc
SubmissionTime   : 12/19/2014 9:53:33 AM
JobId            : job_1418969231336_0044

[TRACE] 816
[DEBUG] 434
[INFO]  96
NULL    22
[WARN]  4

Hive job in the cluster : tyhdicluster completed.


PS C:\Windows\System32\WindowsPowerShell\v1.0>
```

FIGURE 12.9
Querying data from a Hive table using PowerShell scripting.

Unlike `Start-AzureHDInsightJob`, which is a generic runner and can be used for executing
MapReduce, Hive, and Pig jobs asynchronously, the `Invoke-Hive` cmdlet runs a Hive query
synchronously, waits for it to complete, and retrieves the output of the query as one action
(see Listing 12.5).

LISTING 12.5 Executing a HiveQL Query with PowerShell Scripting Synchronously

```
# Declare all the variables and specify their values
$subscriptionName = "Visual Studio Ultimate with MSDN"
$clusterName = "tyhdicluster"

# Query the created external table to find out count
# by grouping on col4
$queryString = "SELECT col4 AS Severity, count(*) AS CountOfOccurence FROM
log4jLogs GROUP BY col4 ORDER BY col4  DESC limit 5;"

# Connect to the cluster
# When using Invoke-Hive cmdlet you must first set the cluster to use
Select-AzureSubscription $subscriptionName
Use-AzureHDInsightCluster $clusterName

Write-Host "Submit the Hive job to the cluster : $clusterName !"
# Submit the job to the cluster for execution synchronously
$myHiveJobResponse = Invoke-Hive -Query $queryString
Write-Host $myHiveJobResponse
Write-Host "Hive job in the cluster : $clusterName completed."
```

Figure 12.10 shows the execution result of the PowerShell scripts from Listing 12.5.

```
PS C:\Windows\System32\WindowsPowerShell\v1.0> D:\Running Hive Query with PowerShell_3.ps1
Successfully connected to cluster tyhdicluster
Submit the Hive job to the cluster : tyhdicluster !
Submitting Hive query.. Started Hive query with jobDetails Id : job_1418969231336_0041 Hive
 [TRACE]    816
[DEBUG] 434
[INFO]  96
NULL    22
[WARN]   4

Hive job in the cluster : tyhdicluster completed.

PS C:\Windows\System32\WindowsPowerShell\v1.0> |
```

FIGURE 12.10
Querying data from a Hive table using the `Invoke-Hive` cmdlet.

Writing your actual Hive query in-line with PowerShell scripting sounds like an easy way out, but we recommend that you write your query in a file (save it with the extension `.hql`), upload it to Azure Storage Blob, and then execute the query from the file using the `-File` parameter. This gives you several benefits, especially if you have a large query. For example, while keeping a query in a file, you can

▶ Avoid query truncation because of query length

▶ Avoid the potential of special characters getting inside your query

▶ Share or execute your Hive query from anywhere (using PowerShell, the Hive console, HDInsight .NET SDK and so on)

Using the Cluster Dashboard

When you provision an HDInsight cluster, a cluster dashboard in the form of a web application is deployed to your HDInsight cluster. You can use it to run Hive queries, check job logs, and browse the Azure Storage Blob. The URL to access this web application is *<ClusterName>*.`azurehdinsight.net`.

From the Azure Management Portal, select your HDInsight cluster and click the Query Console icon (see Figure 12.11) to log in to the HDInsight Cluster Dashboard. You are prompted to enter the cluster administrator username and password; use the ones you specified while creating your HDInsight cluster.

After successfully logging in, you come to the HDInsight Query Console, or Cluster Dashboard. The Cluster Dashboard contains several tabs. Click the Hive Editor tab. You now can execute your HiveQL query in a nice interface (see Figure 12.12). In the first text box, in the Hive Editor, name your query for easy identification. In the second multiline text box, write your query. When you are finished, click the Submit button at the bottom to send your query to the Hive framework for execution. As you can see in Figure 12.12, we executed a query to create a table based on the script in Listing 12.1.

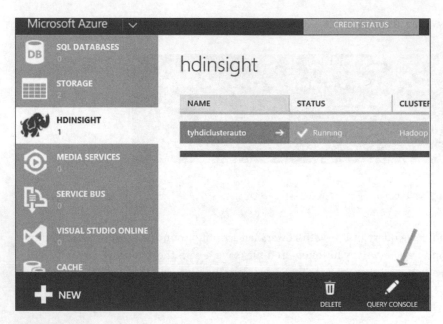

FIGURE 12.11
Azure Management Portal—HDInsight details.

FIGURE 12.12
Hive Editor in the Cluster Dashboard.

With the help of the Hive Editor in the Cluster Dashboard, you can execute as many queries as you want. For example, you can see in Figure 12.13 that we executed the query in Listing 12.2 to return the data from the table by grouping first on one of the columns of the table.

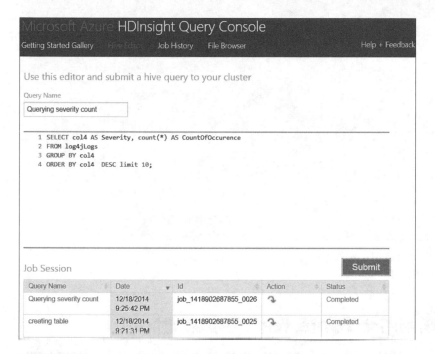

FIGURE 12.13
Executing a query in the Hive Editor on the Cluster Dashboard.

Based on the query you are executing, it might take some time to execute; you can click the hyperlink in the table in the bottom section to see the details of the job (for in-progress, completed, and failed jobs). On the job detail page, you can see the query submitted, the job or query output, and job logs (see Figure 12.14); you can also download this information as local files.

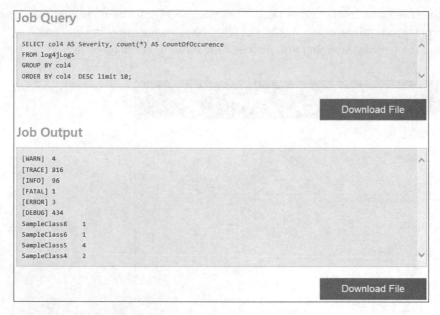

FIGURE 12.14
Viewing the details of Hive job execution.

Azure HDInsight Tools for Visual Studio

If you have experience working with SQL Server Management Studio (SSMS) or SQL Server Data Tools (SSDT) in SQL Server, you will find the experience of using HDInsight Tools for Visual Studio similar and intuitive. HDInsight Tools for Visual Studio connects to your HDInsight cluster from within Visual Studio, shows databases and its objects, and lets you manage them with an intuitive graphical user interface.

HDInsight Tools for Visual Studio is available with Microsoft Azure SDK 2.5 and later. With the help of HDInsight tools in Visual Studio, some of the activities that can be performed are as follows:

▶ Browse the Hive metastore (databases, tables, views) in an intuitive graphical user interface

▶ Create and manage databases and schemas

▶ Create a table using an intuitive graphical user interface

▶ Preview an existing table and its data

▶ Author, run, and manage a Hive query and view the query results

▶ Create a Hive project for team collaboration

NOTE

To use the Azure HDInsight Tools for Visual Studio, you first must install Microsoft Azure SDK 2.5 for .NET (or later, if any) with Web Platform Installer (see Figure 12.15) by going to http://go.microsoft.com/fwlink/?linkid=255386&clcid=0x409.

Based on the Visual Studio version you are using, you might have to select it. At minimum, you need to have Visual Studio 2012 with Update 4, or Visual Studio 2013 with Update 3.

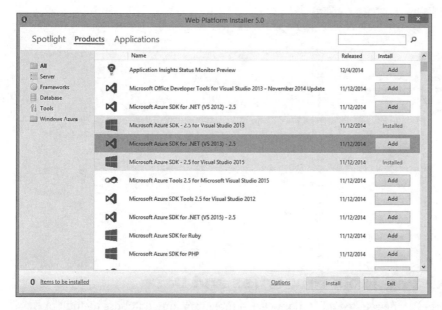

FIGURE 12.15
Installing Microsoft Azure SDK 2.5.

Connecting to HDInsight Cluster from Visual Studio

After you have installed Microsoft Azure SDK 2.5 for .NET, launch Visual Studio, click the View menu, and then click Server Explorer (you can use the shortcut key combination Ctrl+Alt+S, to open Server Explorer) (see Figure 12.16).

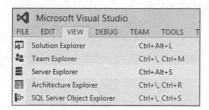

FIGURE 12.16
Server Explorer in Visual Studio.

In Server Explorer, click the Azure icon (see Figure 12.17) and sign in to your Azure subscription. When you are signed in, you can see nodes for Azure services. Expand the HDInsight node. When you see your HDInsight clusters (if you have already created them), expand them further and analyze the Hive databases and attached storage accounts (defaults and also linked storage accounts, if any).

FIGURE 12.17
Signing in to your Azure subscription.

Viewing Existing Table Properties and Data

To view the properties of the selected table, right-click a table from any database (default or user-created database), and then click Properties (see Figure 12.18).

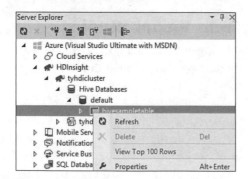

FIGURE 12.18
Viewing the properties of a Hive table.

The properties page shows different properties of the selected table, such as all the columns of the table with their data types, the location of data files, the number of files, and partitioning information, if any (see Figure 12.19).

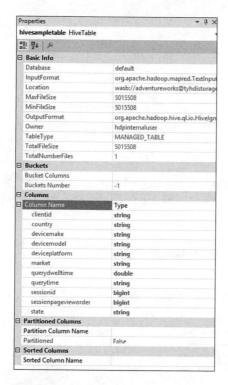

FIGURE 12.19
A Hive table Properties page.

You can even view the top few hundred records from the selected Hive table. To do so, right-click a table from any database (a default or user-created database), and then click View Top 100 Rows (see Figure 12.20).

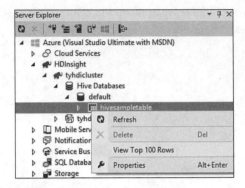

FIGURE 12.20
Viewing the top 100 rows from the selected Hive table.

Figure 12.21 shows the first 100 records retrieved for the selected Hive table. You can change the number of rows to retrieve and click the Refresh icon to bring a new set of data from the Hive table.

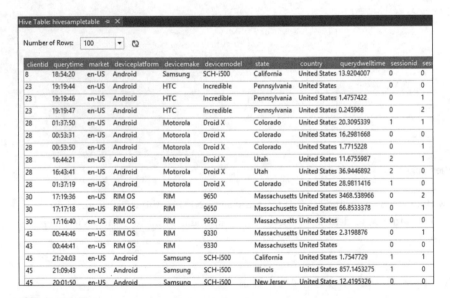

FIGURE 12.21
Data retrieved from a Hive table.

Viewing Hive Jobs on HDInsight Cluster

You can view in Visual Studio all the Hive jobs submitted on a cluster (for their status, such as running, failed, or completed). To do so, right-click the cluster and then click View Hive Jobs (see Figure 12.22).

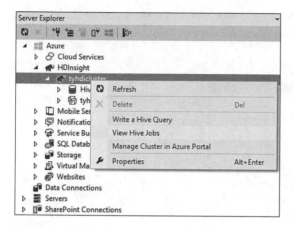

FIGURE 12.22
Viewing Hive jobs submitted on the cluster.

Figure 12.23 shows the Hive Job Browser window. You can browse all jobs here, whether they are running, cancelled, completed, or failed.

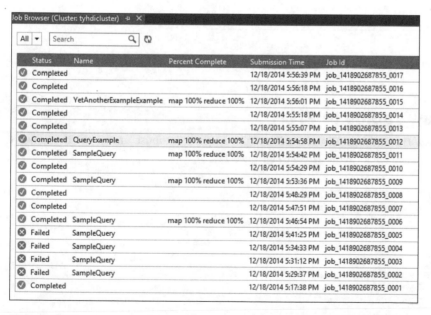

FIGURE 12.23
Hive Job Browser window.

You can select any job in the Job Browser and view its properties, including who executed it, start time, end time, job ID, parent job ID (if any), the query for the job, its output, job logs, and more (see Figure 12.24).

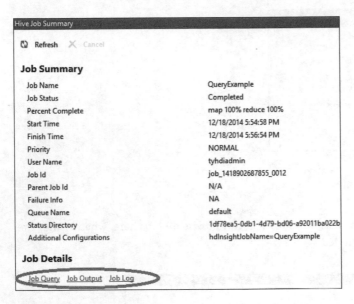

FIGURE 12.24
Viewing Hive job properties.

Creating New Tables in Hive

You can create a new Hive table in Visual Studio. Right-click the database under which you want to create a table and then click Create Table (see Figure 12.25).

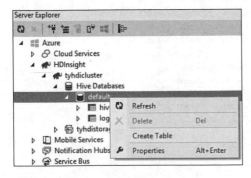

FIGURE 12.25
Creating a Hive table in Visual Studio.

Visual Studio has an intuitive graphical user interface for creating a table (see Figure 12.26). You can specify parameters, such as columns and their data types, partitioning information (if any), and delimiter. Click Create Table to submit a request to the Hive engine to create the table.

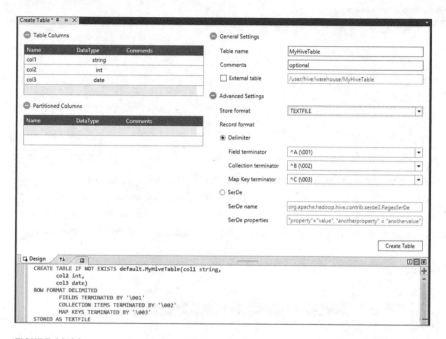

FIGURE 12.26
Specifying different parameters when creating a Hive table in Visual Studio.

Based on your selection and parameter definition, you get a complete Hive query, as in Figure 12.26, if you want to preserve it in the source repository or execute it later.

Writing Hive Queries

HDInsight Tool for Visual Studio also enables you to create a Hive query and submit it directly from Visual Studio to the HDInsight cluster. To do so, right-click the cluster and then click Write a Hive Query (see Figure 12.27).

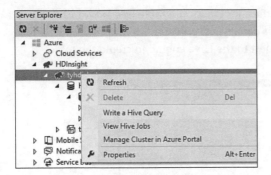

FIGURE 12.27
Writing a Hive query in Visual Studio.

This gives you a nice query editor for writing your HiveQL query and submitting it to the HDInsight cluster (see Figure 12.28). You have two options for submitting your query to the HDInsight cluster: Click either Submit or Submit (Advanced). With the advanced option, you can configure the Hive job name, arguments, additional configurations, status directory, and so on.

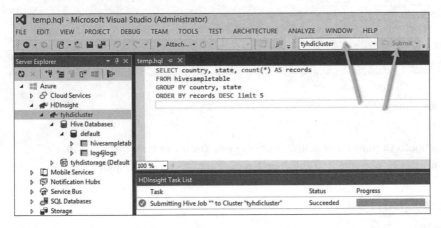

FIGURE 12.28
Executing a Hive query in Visual Studio.

Creating a Hive Application

From better team collaboration and to maintain source code repository, the HDInsight tool for Visual Studio enables you to create a Hive application. Go to the File menu in Visual Studio, click New, and then click Project. Select HDInsight from the left pane, select Hive Application in the middle pane, specify the name and location for your Hive application, and then click OK (see Figure 12.29).

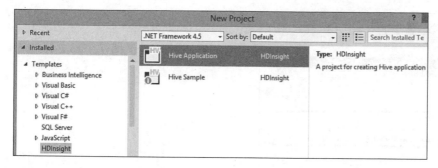

FIGURE 12.29
Creating a Hive application.

As you can see in Figure 12.29, you can also create a Hive sample application that includes Sensor Data Analysis and Web Data Analysis as samples so that you get started on Hive quickly and easily.

After you create a Hive application, you will notice that, by default, a blank Hive script file (Script.hql) is already added to the solution. You can open this file to start putting your scripts in it. You can also create additional script files to let multiple developers work on the same solution at the same time.

Programmatically Using the HDInsight .NET SDK

Sometimes as a developer (or while creating an application), you need to manage all the aspects of HDInsight cluster, including executing queries and jobs (MapReduce, Hive, or Pig) programmatically. To help you in that scenario, Microsoft has released .NET client libraries (a Hadoop client tool) to use in the .NET application, written in any supported programming language.

To use .NET client libraries in your .NET application, you need to first install Microsoft Azure SDK 2.5 for .NET (or later, if any), as Figure 12.15 illustrated with the Web Platform Installer (http://go.microsoft.com/fwlink/?linkid=255386&clcid=0x409).

Next, you must add references to these DLLs in your project (you might need to add DDLs for some other functionalities), as shown in Figure 12.30, to start executing your Hive queries programmatically from your .NET project.

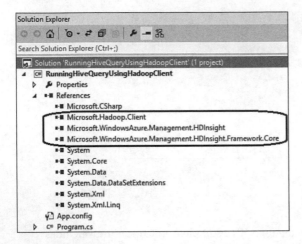

FIGURE 12.30
Referencing Hadoop client DLLs in your application.

Figure 12.31 shows the code for submitting Hive queries to the HDInsight cluster. The top few lines reference important namespaces, and the `main` method calls two methods.

```csharp
using System;
using System.Collections.Generic;
using System.Linq;
using System.Text;
using System.Threading.Tasks;
using Microsoft.Hadoop.Client;
using System.IO;
using System.Threading;
using System.Security.Cryptography.X509Certificates;
using Microsoft.WindowsAzure.Management.HDInsight;

namespace ConsoleApplication1
{
    0 references
    class Program
    {
        0 references
        static void Main(string[] args)
        {
            ExecuteHiveQueryWithBasicCredential();
            ExecuteHiveQueryWithCertificate();
        }

        1 reference
        private static void ExecuteHiveQueryWithBasicCredential()...
        1 reference
        private static void ExecuteHiveQueryWithCertificate()...
        2 references
        private static void WaitForHadoopJobCompletion(JobCreationResults jobInforma
    }
}
```

FIGURE 12.31
Application code to execute Hive queries.

Listing 12.6 uses basic authentication to connect to the HDInsight cluster and executes a Hive query to create a table. Then it waits for the job to complete before it returns to the main method.

LISTING 12.6   Executing a Hive Query with Basic Credentials

```
private static void ExecuteHiveQueryWithBasicCredential()
{
    var jobCredential = new BasicAuthCredential();
    jobCredential.UserName = "<Cluster Administration - User Name>";
    jobCredential.Password = "<Cluster Administration - Password>";
    jobCredential.Server = new Uri("https://<Cluster Name>.azurehdinsight.net//");


    // Connect to the HDInsight cluster
    var jobClient = JobSubmissionClientFactory.Connect(jobCredential);

    // define the Hive job
    var myHiveJobDefinition = new HiveJobCreateParameters()
    {
        JobName = "creating a Hive table",
        Query = "CREATE EXTERNAL TABLE log4jLogs ( col1 string, col2 string, col3
string, col4 string, col5 string, col6 string, col7 string ) ROW FORMAT DELIMITED
FIELDS TERMINATED BY ' ' STORED AS TEXTFILE LOCATION 'wasb:///example/data/';",
        StatusFolder = "/samplequeryoutput"
    };
    var jobResults = jobClient.CreateHiveJob(myHiveJobDefinition);

    // Wait for the job to complete
    WaitForHadoopJobCompletion(jobResults, jobClient);
}
```

Listing 12.7 uses a certificate to connect to the HDInsight cluster and executes a Hive query to query data from a Hive table. Then it waits for the job to complete and shows the retrieved data on the console.

LISTING 12.7   Executing a Hive Query with a Certificate

```
private static void ExecuteHiveQueryWithCertificate()
{
    // Set the variables
    string subscriptionID = "<Unique Subscription ID>";
    string clusterName = "<Cluster Name>";
    string certFriendlyName = "<Certificate Friendly Name>";
```

```
    // Get the certificate object from certificate store using the friendly name to
        identify it
    X509Store store = new X509Store();
    store.Open(OpenFlags.ReadOnly);
    X509Certificate2 certAzure = store.Certificates.Cast<X509Certificate2>().
First(item => item.FriendlyName == certFriendlyName);

    if (certAzure == null)
        Console.WriteLine("No Certificate found with specified friendly name...");


    JobSubmissionCertificateCredential jobCredential = new JobSubmissionCertificate
Credential(new Guid(subscriptionID), certAzure, clusterName);

    // define the Hive job
    HiveJobCreateParameters myHiveJobDefinition = new HiveJobCreateParameters()
    {
        JobName = "querying from sample table",
        StatusFolder = "/samplequeryoutput",
        Query = "SELECT country, state, count(*) AS records FROM hivesampletable
GROUP BY country, state ORDER BY records DESC limit 10;"
    };

    // Submit the Hive job
    var jobClient = JobSubmissionClientFactory.Connect(jobCredential);
    JobCreationResults jobResults = jobClient.CreateHiveJob(myHiveJobDefinition);

    // Wait for the job to complete
    WaitForHadoopJobCompletion(jobResults, jobClient);

    // Print the Hive job output
    using (var responseStream = jobClient.GetJobOutput(jobResults.JobId))
    {
        StreamReader reader = new StreamReader(responseStream);
        Console.WriteLine(reader.ReadToEnd());

        Console.WriteLine("Press ENTER to continue.");
        Console.ReadLine();
    }

}
```

Figure 12.32 shows the data returned by running the Hive query of Listing 12.7 programmatically from the .NET application.

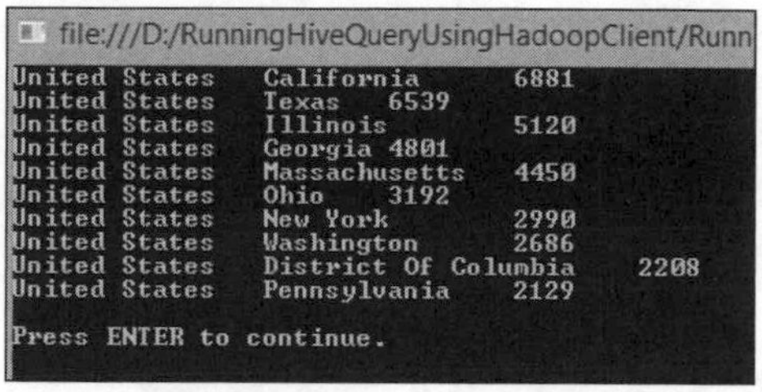

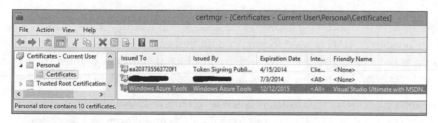

FIGURE 12.32
Data retrieved using .NET client libraries—Hadoop client tool.

Listing 12.8 implements a method to wait until the specified job either completes or fails.

LISTING 12.8 Waiting for a Job to Complete (Either Success or Failure)

```
private static void WaitForHadoopJobCompletion(JobCreationResults jobInformation,
IJobSubmissionClient clientReference)
{
    var runningJob = clientReference.GetJob(jobInformation.JobId);
    //Keep on waiting until either the job completes or fails
    while (runningJob.StatusCode != JobStatusCode.Completed && runningJob.
StatusCode != JobStatusCode.Failed)
    {
        runningJob = clientReference.GetJob(runningJob.JobId);
        Thread.Sleep(TimeSpan.FromSeconds(10));
    }
}
```

As you learned in Hour 6, you can configure the certificate on your local workstation by running the `Get-AzurePublishSettingsFile` and `Import-AzurePublishSettingsFile` PowerShell cmdlets. When done, you can open `certmgr.msc` (run it on the RUN window) from your local workstation and find the certificate by expanding Personal/Certificates (see Figure 12.33). The Azure subscription certificates created by the PowerShell cmdlets have Windows Azure Tools for both the Issued To and Issued By fields (see Figure 12.33).

FIGURE 12.33
Azure subscription certificate.

We have demonstrated how you can leverage .NET client libraries (Hadoop client tool) to execute Hive jobs on your HDInsight cluster, but this is not limited to Hive jobs: You can also execute MapReduce, Pig, Sqoop, and streaming jobs using .NET client libraries (see Figure 12.34).

```
namespace Microsoft.Hadoop.Client
{
    public interface IJobSubmissionSyncClient : IJobSubmissionClientBase, IDisposable, ILog
    {
        JobCreationResults CreateHiveJob(HiveJobCreateParameters hiveJobCreateParameters);
        JobCreationResults CreateMapReduceJob(MapReduceJobCreateParameters mapReduceJobCrea
        JobCreationResults CreatePigJob(PigJobCreateParameters pigJobCreateParameters);
        JobCreationResults CreateSqoopJob(SqoopJobCreateParameters sqoopJobCreateParameters
        JobCreationResults CreateStreamingJob(StreamingMapReduceJobCreateParameters streami
        void DownloadJobTaskLogs(string jobId, string targetDirectory);
        JobDetails GetJob(string jobId);
        Stream GetJobErrorLogs(string jobId);
        Stream GetJobOutput(string jobId);
        Stream GetJobTaskLogSummary(string jobId);
        JobList ListJobs();
        JobDetails StopJob(string jobId);
    }
}
```

FIGURE 12.34
Type of jobs supported for execution on an HDInsight cluster.

Introduction to Apache Tez

The MapReduce framework has been designed as a batch-mode processing platform running over a large amount of data, but this does not fit well in some important current uses cases (such as Machine Learning and interactive query response) that expect near-real-time query processing and response. This is why Apache Tez, a new, distributed execution framework, came into the picture. Apache Tez expresses computations as a data flow graph and allows for dynamic performance optimizations based on real information about the data (statistics) and the resources required to process it. It meet demands for fast response time and extreme throughput at a petabyte scale.

Originally developed by Hortonworks, Apache Tez is an engine built on top of Apache Hadoop YARN to provide the capability to build an application framework that allows for a complex directed acyclic graph (DAG) of tasks for high-performance data processing in either batch or interactive mode.

Projects such as Apache Hive or Apache Pig (or even MapReduce) can leverage the Apache Tez engine to execute a complex DAG of tasks to process data that earlier required multiple MapReduce jobs (in a Map-Reduce -> Map-Reduce pattern; in which the Mapper of the next step takes input from the Reducer of the previous step via intermediate storage of data in HDFS).

Now you can use a single Apache Tez job (which is based on a Map-Reduce-Reduce pattern; in which a single Mapper has multiple Reducers, allowing data streaming from one processor to another, without writing intermediate data to HDFS and hence achieving much better performance) as shown in Figure 12.35, which has been adapted from the Apache Tez documentation.

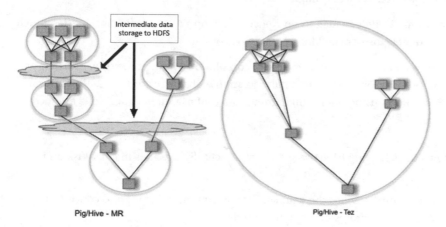

FIGURE 12.35
The MapReduce framework versus the Tez framework for processing.

Apache Tez provides a highly extensible, customizable, pluggable framework and developer API to write native YARN applications. These applications bridge the spectrum of interactive and batch workloads (without forcing people to go out of their way to make things work) and handle petabyte-scale datasets.

Tez provides a distributed parallel-execution framework that negotiates resources from the Resource Manager (a component of YARN) and ensures the recovery of failed steps (or, more specifically, a vertex, discussed next) inside a job. It is capable of horizontal scaling, provides resource elasticity, and comes with a shared library of ready-to-use components (DAP API and Runtime API).

If you are writing your application targeting Tez as a distributed execution engine, you must understand two main components of Tez:

▶ A master for the data processing application, with which you can put together arbitrary data-processing tasks into a task represented as DAG to process data as desired using the DAG API.

▶ **DAG**—Defines the overall job. The user creates a DAG object for each data processing job because a data processing job typically looks like a DAG only.

▶ **Vertex**—Defines the user data transformation logic and the resources and environment needed to execute it. The user creates a Vertex object for each step in the job and adds it to the DAG.

▶ **Edge**—Defines the connection between producer and consumer vertices (the data movement from producers to consumers). The user creates an Edge object and connects the producer and consumer vertices using it.

The generic master is implemented as an Apache Hadoop YARN Application Master, much like the one available for Apache MapReduce, Hive, or Pig.

▶ The data processing pipeline engine where you can plug in input, processing, and output implementations to perform arbitrary data processing with the runtime API. The runtime API provides interfaces using the runtime framework and user application code interact with each other.

Every task in Tez has the following triplet to specify what actually executes in each task on the cluster nodes:

▶ **Input (key/value pairs)**—Reads the data correctly from native format and converts it into the data format that the processor can understand

▶ **Processor**—Applies your business logic on the data received as input by applying filters, transformations, and so on

▶ **Output**—Collects the processed key/value pairs and writes the output correctly so that end users or the next consumer/input can consume it

---

NOTE

If you are writing your application targeting Tez as an execution engine, you can refer to this series of articles from Hortonworks: http://hortonworks.com/blog/apache-tez-a-new-chapter-in-hadoop-data-processing.

Consider the benefits of using the Tez execution framework:

▶ **Eliminated storage of intermediate output to HDFS**—(Remember, by default, 3x replication for intermediate data in HDFS causes overhead.) With Tez, either the next consumer or the next input directly consumes the output (see Figure 12.35), without writing an intermediate result to the HDFS.

▶ **Minimized queue length**—Job launch overhead of workflow jobs is eliminated, as is queue and resource contention suffered by workflow jobs (or to launch an application master) that are started after a predecessor job completes.

▶ **Efficient use of resources**—Tez reuses resource containers to maximize its utilization and minimizes the overhead of initializing it every time. In various cases, it can prelaunch and prewarm the container, for better performance.

▶ **Higher developer productivity**—Application developers can focus on application business logic instead of Hadoop internals. (Tez takes care of Hadoop internals anyway.)

▶ **Reduced network usage**—Tez uses new data shuffle and movement patterns for better data locality and minimal data transfer.

▶ **Simple deployment**—Tez is a completely client-side application that leverages YARN local resources and distributed cache. You can simply upload Tez libraries to HDFS and then use your Tez client to submit requests with those libraries. Tez allows side-by-side execution, in which you can have two or more versions of the libraries on your cluster. This helps you evaluate a new release on the same cluster side by side where the older version is used in production workloads.

Traditionally, Hive and Pig use MapReduce as their execution engine. Any query produces a graph of MapReduce jobs potentially interspersed with some local/client-side work. This leads to many inefficiencies in the planning and execution of queries. However, the latest releases of Apache Hive (0.13 release and onward) and Apache Pig (expected to start with the 0.14 release) have been updated to leverage the Tez distributed execution framework as well; hence, when you can run your Hive or Pig jobs leveraging Tez, you will notice significant improvements in response times (see Figure 12.36, taken from Apache Tez documentation from HorntonWorks).

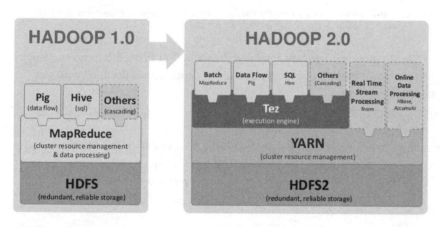

FIGURE 12.36
Hadoop 1.0 to Hadoop 2.0.

Apart from the benefits just discussed, some additional characteristics make Hive on Tez perform better:

▶ **Cost-based optimization plans**—A cost-based optimization (CBO) engine uses statistics (table and column levels) within Hive tables to produce more efficient and optimal query plans. This eventually leads to better cluster utilization.

▶ **Performance improvements of vectorized queries**—When you enable the vectorization feature, it fetches data in batches of 1000 rows at a time instead of 1 row at time for processing, enabling improved cluster utilization and faster processing. For now, the vectorization feature works only on Hive tables with the Optimized Row Columnar (ORC) file format.

Using the Apace Tez Engine with Hive on HDInsight

The good news is, HDInsight supports executing your Hive queries on the Apache Tez distributed execution engine; it comes with Apache Tez preinstalled and preconfigured. By default, however, this is not enabled. The execution engine for Hive is MapReduce, so if you want to run your Hive queries on the Tez execution engine, you need to either run `set hive.execution.engine=tez;` on the Hive client machine for each Hive session or change this value permanently in `hive-site.xml`. You can revert or disable usage of the Tez execution engine by running `set hive.execution.engine=mr;` on the Hive client machine.

Because Tez performs much faster than MapReduce, we recommend using it as the default engine. If you have a particular query that Tez can't handle, or for backward compatibility, you can change to MapReduce for just that query.

GO TO ▶ Refer to **Hour 13** to learn how to leverage Apache Tez for Hive queries. You can also see a small performance comparison on using Apache Tez over the default MapReduce engine.

Vectorization allows Hive to process a batch of rows together as a unit instead of processing one row at a time for the files stored in ORC format. By default, vectorization is disabled; you can enable it by running this command:

```
set hive.vectorized.execution.enabled=true;
```

With vectorization enabled, Hive examines the query and the data to determine whether vectorization can be applied. If it cannot, Hive executes the query without vectorization. The Hive client logs, at the info level, whether a query's execution leveraged vectorization.

NOTE

Tez Engine for MapReduce

As discussed earlier, even the MapReduce framework can leverage the Tez execution engine for better performance. To enable it, set `mapreduce.framework.name` to `yarn-tez` in the `mapred-site.xml` configuration file.

Summary

In this hour, you learned about Apache Hive, a data warehousing layer that runs on top of the Hadoop framework. It enables you to write data processing logic or queries in a SQL-like declarative language, called HiveQL, which is similar to relational database systems. With the help of Apache Hive, you can write your queries in just a few lines, saving you time and effort. For example, a simple query of fewer than 10 lines translates to a MapReduce program with more than 100 lines of code.

You explored the different methods of writing and executing HiveQL in HDInsight. You also looked into Apache Tez, which improves the performance of Hive queries several fold and can be used in HDInsight.

In the next hour, you extend your knowledge of Apache Hive and see how you can leverage it for ad hoc queries and data analysis. That hour goes into detail about some important commands you will generally use in Apache Hive for data loading and querying.

Q&A

Q. **What methods commonly are used to write and execute Hive queries in HDInsight?**

A. Microsoft Azure HDInsight enables you to write and execute HiveQL queries in different ways. You can choose among these methods based on your role or your comfort level:

- ▶ Using the Hive command-line interface (CLI)
- ▶ Using PowerShell scripting
- ▶ Using the Cluster Dashboard
- ▶ Using Azure HDInsight Tools for Visual Studio
- ▶ Programmatically using HDInsight .NET
- ▶ Using a REST API called WebHCat for cross-platform access

Q. **Where is metadata information for Hive objects stored, and how can you preserve it so that it is not lost after cluster deletion?**

A. When you create Hive objects (databases, tables, columns, views, and so on), the information about these objects is, by default, stored in an embedded database as part of the HDInsight cluster itself. When you delete your HDInsight cluster, this embedded database also gets deleted and you lose metadata information.

To preserve metadata information (even after HDInsight cluster deletion), you can specify a SQL database to be used as metastore for Hive and Oozie when provisioning your HDInsight cluster. You can then safely delete your HDInsight cluster without losing this information because it is stored externally in a SQL database. The next time you need it, you can provision another HDInsight cluster and point it to the same SQL database (which contains metadata information from the previous cluster instance) to find all those objects again.

Q. **What is Apache Tez? How can Hive leverage it for interactive query response?**

A. Apache Tez is a new, distributed execution framework. It provides generalization in expressing computations as a data flow graph and allows for dynamic performance optimizations based on real information about the data (statistics) and the resources required to process it. It meets demands for fast response times and extreme throughput at a petabyte scale.

HDInsight supports executing your Hive queries on the Apache Tez distributed execution engine. By default, however, this is not enabled: The default execution engine for Hive is MapReduce. If you want to run your Hive queries on the Tez execution engine, you need to either run `set hive.execution.engine=tez;` on the Hive client machine each time for each Hive session or change this value permanently in `hive-site.xml` (manually or through Ambari). You can revert it or disable usage of Tez execution engine by running this `set hive.execution.engine=mr;` on the Hive client machine.

Exercise

Exercise 1: Provision an HDInsight cluster and use the SQL database as a metastore for Hive. When the HDInsight cluster is provisioned, create some Hive tables (you can use the script from Listing 12.1) by following any of the methods discussed earlier.

Exercise 2: Execute this query on the Azure SQL database to find out about the Hive tables, along with the columns and data types created on the HDInsight cluster, when connected to this SQL database.

```
SELECT TBL_NAME, TBL_TYPE, COLUMN_NAME, TYPE_NAME
FROM [dbo].[TBLS] T
INNER JOIN [dbo].[COLUMNS_V2] C ON T.TBL_ID = C.CD_ID;
```

Programming with Apache Hive, Apache Tez in HDInsight, and Apache HCatalog

---

What You'll Learn in This Hour:

▶ Programming with Hive in HDInsight
▶ Using Tables in Hive
▶ Serialization and Deserialization
▶ Data Load Processes for Hive Tables
▶ Querying Data from Hive Tables
▶ Indexing in Hive
▶ Apache Tez in Action
▶ Apache HCatalog

In the last hour, you took a detailed look at Apache Hive and Apache Tez, and you saw how you can leverage Apache Tez in HDInsight to significantly improve the performance of Hive queries. You also explored different ways of writing and executing HiveQL queries in HDInsight.

In this hour, you extend your knowledge of Apache Hive, to see how you can leverage it for ad hoc queries and data analysis. You learn some of the important commands you will use in Apache Hive for data loading and querying.

You also explore Apache HCatalog, which has now merged with Apache Hive, and you see how leveraging the Apache Tez execution engine, for Hive query execution, significantly improves the performance of your query.

Programming with Hive in HDInsight

First, let's prepare some datasets for ad hoc queries and data analysis using Apache Hive.

The examples will use some of the publically available on-time performance of airline flights data from the Research and Innovative Technology Administration (RITA), Bureau of

Transportation Statistics (BTS). The data is available for download and analysis at http://www.transtats.bts.gov/DL_SelectFields.asp?Table_ID=236&DB_Short_Name=On-Time.

Download the prezipped (which includes a CSV file with all the columns and `readme.html` documentation about those columns) on-time performance file for a couple months so that you can see the different features of Hive. For example, you can create a monthly partition to see partition elimination in action. After downloading the files, unzip them and then either use PowerShell scripting (see Hour 6, "Getting Started with HDInsight, Provisioning Your HDInsight Service Cluster, and Automating HDInsight Cluster Provisioning") to upload them to the Azure Storage Blob folder or use any of the available Azure Storage Explorer tools (http://blogs.msdn.com/b/windowsazurestorage/archive/2014/03/11/windows-azure-storage-explorers-2014.aspx).

NOTE

For demonstration purposes, we used the CloudXplorer tool here to upload these files in the folder `/OnTimePerformance/Data/` (see Figure 13.1).

CloudXplorer has a simple and intuitive Windows File Explorer–like interface to assist you in exploring your Windows Azure storage (it supports copy and paste, drag and drop, and so on). You can download evaluation edition of this tool here: http://clumsyleaf.com/products/cloudxplorer.

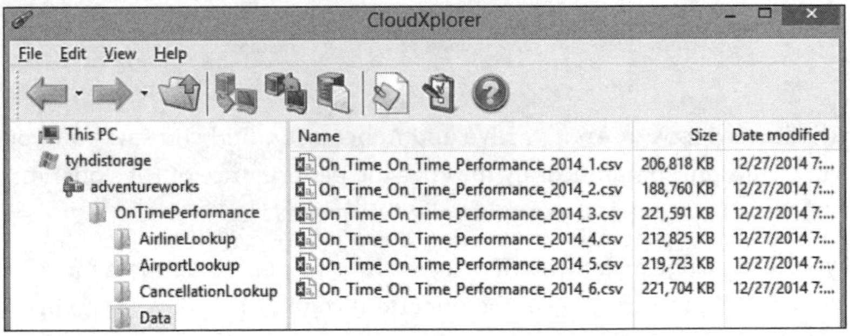

FIGURE 13.1
Uploading on-time performance flight data to Azure Storage Blob.

Download lookup data related to airline codes and descriptions from http://www.transtats.bts.gov/Download_Lookup.asp?Lookup=L_AIRLINE_ID. Then upload it to the folder `/OnTimePerformance/AirlineLookup/` in the Azure Storage Blob (see Figure 13.2).

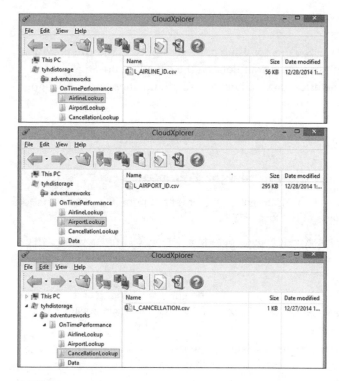

FIGURE 13.2
Uploading lookup data to Azure Storage Blob.

Download lookup data related to airport codes and descriptions from http://
www.transtats.bts.gov/Download_Lookup.asp?Lookup=L_AIRPORT_ID. Then upload it to the
folder /OnTimePerformance/AirportLookup/ in the Azure Storage Blob (see Figure 13.2).

Download lookup data related to flight cancellation codes and descriptions from http://
www.transtats.bts.gov/Download_Lookup.asp?Lookup=L_CANCELLATION. Then upload it to the
folder /OnTimePerformance/CancellationLookup/ in the Azure Storage Blob (see Figure 13.2).

The HDInsight cluster in Azure leverages Azure Storage Blob as the default file system for data
storage, whereas HDInsight emulator uses HDFS on the local disk as the default file system.

Running Examples on HDInsight Emulator

All examples in this hour have been tested on an Azure HDInsight cluster and should run as is
on an Azure HDInsight cluster.

We recommend that you use the Azure HDInsight cluster service whenever possible so you have
access to all the features of HDInsight.

GO TO ▶ Refer to **Hour 6** to review how to provision HDInsight cluster easily and quickly.

Remember to delete the cluster whenever you are not using it, to save on cost. You can provision it again when you need it. In the meantime, store your data on the default Azure Storage Blob and use the SQL database as a Hive metastore so you don't lose anything after cluster deletion.

▼ TRY IT YOURSELF

Running Flight Performance Data on HDInsight Emulator

If you are running examples from this hour on HDInsight Emulator, perform the following steps to create the required folders and copy files to the local HDFS:

1. Download and copy the on-time flight performance data files (using the link provided earlier in this section) to the `C:\OnTimePerformance\Data` folder on the machine where you have HDInsight emulator running.

2. Download and copy the file `L_AIRLINE_ID.csv` (using the link provided earlier in this section) to the `C:\OnTimePerformance\AirlineLookup` folder on the machine where you have HDInsight emulator running.

3. Download and copy the file `L_AIRPORT_ID.csv` (using the link provided earlier in this section) to the `C:\OnTimePerformance\AirportLookup` folder on the machine where you have HDInsight emulator running.

4. Download and copy the file `L_CANCELLATION.csv` (using the link provided earlier in this section) to the `C:\OnTimePerformance\CancellationLookup` folder on the machine where you have HDInsight emulator running.

5. Download the CSV SerDe file from http://ogrodnek.github.io/csv-serde/ and copy it to the `C:\OnTimePerformance` folder on the machine where you have HDInsight emulator running.

6. Now execute these commands at the Hadoop command prompt to upload these files appropriately to HDFS:

```
hadoop fs -mkdir /OnTimePerformance

hadoop fs -copyFromLocal C:\OnTimePerformance\AirlineLookup
/OnTimePerformance/
hadoop fs -copyFromLocal C:\OnTimePerformance\AirportLookup
/OnTimePerformance/
hadoop fs -copyFromLocal C:\OnTimePerformance\CancellationLookup
/OnTimePerformance/
hadoop fs -copyFromLocal C:\OnTimePerformance\Data /OnTimePerformance/

hadoop fs -copyFromLocal C:\OnTimePerformance\csv-serde-1.1.2.jar
/OnTimePerformance/
```

7. Replace `ADD JAR wasb:///OnTimePerformance/csv-serde-1.1.2.jar;` with `ADD JAR /OnTimePerformance/csv-serde-1.1.2.jar;` wherever referenced in the scripts provided in the hour.

8. Copy the `example` folder from this hour's content folder to the C: drive of the machine where you have HDInsight emulator running.

9. Create these folders in HDFS if they are already not available:

```
hadoop fs -mkdir /example/data/internaldemo01
hadoop fs -mkdir /example/data/internaldemo02
hadoop fs -mkdir /example/data/externaldemo01
```

10. Copy these files for internal and external table examples:

```
hadoop fs -copyFromLocal c:\example\data\sample.log /example/data/
internaldemo01/sample01.log
hadoop fs -copyFromLocal c:\example\data\sample.log /example/data/
internaldemo01/sample02.log

hadoop fs -copyFromLocal c:\example\data\sample.log /example/data/
internaldemo02/sample01.log
hadoop fs -copyFromLocal c:\example\data\sample.log /example/data/
internaldemo02/sample02.log
hadoop fs -copyFromLocal c:\example\data\sample.log /example/data/
internaldemo02/sample03.log

hadoop fs -copyFromLocal c:\example\data\sample.log /example/data/
externaldemo01/sample01.log
hadoop fs -copyFromLocal c:\example\data\sample.log /example/data/
externaldemo01/sample02.log
hadoop fs -copyFromLocal c:\example\data\sample.log /example/data/
externaldemo01/sample03.log
hadoop fs -copyFromLocal c:\example\data\sample.log /example/data/
externaldemo01/sample04.log
```

Comparison with RDBMS Databases

Apache Hive includes HiveQL, a declarative query language much like the Structured Query Language (SQL) of RDBMS. It has some differences from RDBMS, however:

▶ When you create a Hive table, the data lives in unstructured files (unlike structured table storage, in the case of RDBMS).

▶ CREATE TABLE in Hive provides a way to give structure to the unstructured data stored in these data files on the WASB or local HDFS.

▶ An external table in Hive provides a relational view on existing files in either WASB or the local HDFS. Basically, it references the files and does not create another copy of the data or control it (more on this later in this hour).

▶ Data for a table in Hive can be stored either as text files or as sequence files. While storing data in a file, you can choose to separate values with delimiters or based on a custom serializer/deserializer (more on this later in this hour).

▶ Like a relational table, a Hive table can be partitioned, clustered, and sorted

▶ Hive enables you to define indexes and maintains limited statistics (only file size). Hence, it supports limited optimizations only (such as partition elimination).

▶ Hive has Inserts only, no Updates, and no transaction support (however, as of this writing, upcoming Apache Hive releases are expected to offer these features).

▶ Hive is designed for batch execution. (With Apache Tez, interactive execution of the queries is allowed, although it's still not comparable to the interactive response time RDBMS systems provide.)

▶ HiveQL is limited to what can be executed using MapReduce jobs (limited joins).

Database or Schema

Apache Hive includes a default database where you can create objects, for better segregation, to avoid table name collisions, or for better manageability. This is especially relevant if you are working on multiple applications and you need to create an application-specific database or schema. Apache Hive includes commands to create, alter, and drop databases whenever needed. For example, with the help of the CREATE DATABASE command, you can create a database named airlinesdb:

```
CREATE DATABASE IF NOT EXISTS airlinesdb
COMMENT 'This database or namespace or schema contains all the tables related to
on-time-performance flight information';
```

Note the use of the optional IF NOT EXISTS keyword. When specified, it creates the database only if a database with the same name does not exist already. Also, by default, the root directory for the database is set as /hive/warehouse/<database name>.db. If you want to change it to some other folder location, you can use the LOCATION clause when creating a database to specify a different location.

The SHOW DATABASES command shows all the databases available in Hive:

```
SHOW DATABASES;
```

If you want to filter databases based on some pattern, you can use the LIKE clause to filter all the databases that start with air:

```
SHOW DATABASES LIKE 'air*';
```

Although the ALTER DATABASE command exists in Hive, its role is limited to modifying database properties and the database owner. You cannot modify other properties, such as the database name and location.

```
ALTER DATABASE airlinesdb SET DBPROPERTIES ('CreatedBy' = 'Arshad', 'ModifiedBy' =
'Manpreet');
```

The DESCRIBE DATABASE command shows metadata information about the database, such as its name, comment (if specified while creating it), root directory location on the WASB or HDFS where data for tables will be stored, and database creator.

```
DESCRIBE DATABASE airlinesdb;
```

You can use the DROP DATABASE command to delete a database. The IF EXISTS clause is optional; it drops the database only if it exists. If you don't specify the IF EXISTS clause and you try to delete a database that doesn't exist, you get the error FAILED: SemanticException [Error 10072]: Database does not exist: <your specified database name>:

```
DROP DATABASE IF EXISTS airlinesdb;
```

By default, the DROP DATABASE command uses the RESTRICT clause, which means, it will drop the database only if it has no tables. If you want to drop a database by first deleting its table and then deleting the database, you need to use the CASCADE clause:

```
DROP DATABASE IF EXISTS airlinesdb CASCADE;
```

Figure 13.3 shows the execution result of these commands on the Hive command-line interface (CLI).

GO TO ▶ The scripts in Figure 13.3 can be executed using any method of Hive query execution, as discussed in **Hour 12, "Getting Started with Apache Hive and Apache Tez in HDInsight."**

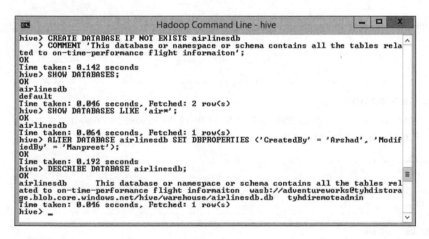

FIGURE 13.3
Execution result for database management scripts.

We discussed how you can create databases in your cluster. If you have multiple databases, you must switch the database context so that you work on the right set of tables in the right database. The USE command changes the database context:

```
USE airlinesdb;
SET hive.cli.print.current.db=true;
SHOW TABLES;
USE default;
SHOW TABLES;
SET hive.cli.print.current.db=false;
```

When you are working on the Hive command-line interface, you might find it confusing to work with multiple databases. In this case, you can use the SET hive.cli.print.current.db=true; command to include your current database name as part of Hive prompt (see Figure 13.4). You can use the SET hive.cli.print.current.db=false; command to revert this setting.

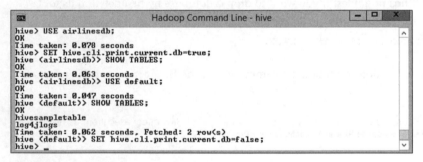

FIGURE 13.4
Execution result of scripts for database usage.

NOTE

Two-Part Naming Convention

Instead of using USE *<database>* to change the context or working database, you can use a two-part naming convention such as *<database name>*.*<table name>*. This convention works perfectly fine in Hive.

NOTE

Database Versus Schema

Unlike RDBMS, in which a schema is an object inside a database, SCHEMA and DATABASE are interchangeable in Hive—they both refer to the same thing. This means that the commands

CREATE DATABASE adventureworks and CREATE SCHEMA adventureworks are the same. If a database with the adventureworks name already exists and you try executing CREATE SCHEMA adventureworks, the command will throw an error.

Using Tables in Hive

Apache Hive enables you to create two types of tables, *internal,* or *managed,* tables (because they are actually managed by Hive) and *external* tables. The type of table you create depends on where the data should reside and how it should be managed and controlled when the table is deleted.

The next sections discuss internal and external tables.

Internal Table

When you create an internal or managed table, Hive manages the data. This means that Hive copies data from the source files to a subdirectory (each table has a subdirectory with the same name as the table) of the root directory of the database (by default, location /hive/warehouse/) at the time data is loaded.

TIP

Specifying a different location than the default location does not copy data—it only points to that location.

When you drop an internal or managed table, Hive deletes the associated data and the metadata information about the table.

Note that the TRUNCATE TABLE command is applicable for internal or managed tables only, to delete all the rows of the table or specific partitions of the table.

Before you see how an internal table works, let's create two folders (internaldemo01 and internaldemo02) in the /example/data/ location and then copy the sample.log file (/example/data/sample.log) to these folders (see Figure 13.5).

TIP

You can copy multiple copies of this file, for better clarity. For example, we have created multiple copies of sample.log, with names such as sample01.log and sample02.log and so on.

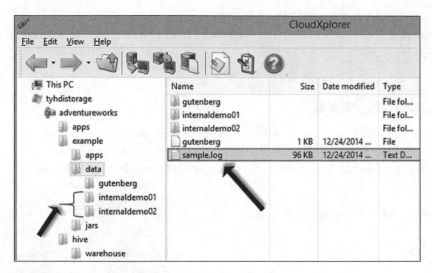

FIGURE 13.5
Datasets for an internal table demo.

Next, create an internal table (the absence of the `EXTERNAL` clause in the `CREATE TABLE` command indicates an internal table) in the `airlinesdb` database without specifying the `LOCATION` clause. This means that this table will be created by default in the `/hive/warehouse/` `airlinesdb.db` folder:

```
USE airlinesdb;
DROP TABLE IF EXISTS log4jLogsInternal01;
CREATE TABLE log4jLogsInternal01
(
col1 string,
col2 string,
col3 string,
col4 string,
col5 string,
col6 string,
col7 string
)
ROW FORMAT DELIMITED FIELDS TERMINATED BY ' '
STORED AS TEXTFILE;
```

TIP

If you don't have this database already, create it with the script shown earlier in the section, "Database or Schema."

Using the following command, you can load data from the `internaldemo01` folder into this table. Note that this moves the data from the `internaldemo01` folder to the `log4jlogsinternal01` subfolder (same name as the table) inside the `/hive/warehouse/airlinesdb.db` folder (see Figure 13.6).

```
LOAD DATA INPATH '/example/data/internaldemo01' INTO table log4jLogsInternal01;
```

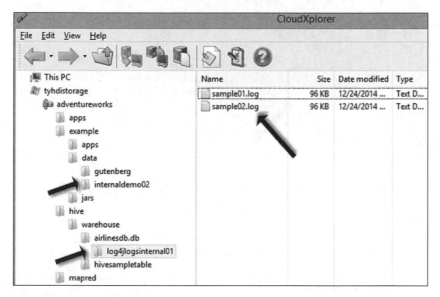

FIGURE 13.6
Internal table stored in the default location.

Now let's create another internal table by specifying the `LOCATION` clause, as in this script:

```
USE airlinesdb;
DROP TABLE IF EXISTS log4jLogsInternal02;
CREATE TABLE log4jLogsInternal02
(
col1 string,
col2 string,
col3 string,
col4 string,
col5 string,
col6 string,
col7 string
)
ROW FORMAT DELIMITED FIELDS TERMINATED BY ' '
STORED AS TEXTFILE
LOCATION '/example/data/internaldemo02/';
```

The script creates an internal table, but it points to the original location of /example/data/ internaldemo02/ instead of pointing to the default /hive/warehouse/ location (see Figure 13.7). Unlike the previous internal table you created, in this case, no new folder gets created in the default folder /hive/warehouse/ with the name of the table.

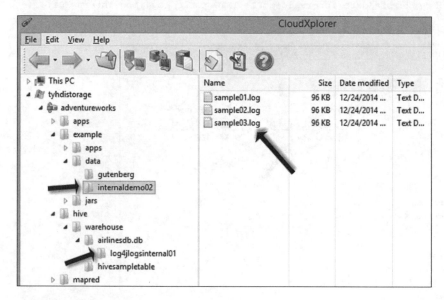

FIGURE 13.7
Internal table stored outside the default location.

You can execute this script to verify the internal tables and their properties:

```
SHOW TABLES;
DESCRIBE EXTENDED log4jLogsInternal01;
DESCRIBE EXTENDED log4jLogsInternal02;
```

Now let's drop these two tables and analyze the impact on the data. To drop these tables, you can run this script:

```
DROP TABLE IF EXISTS log4jLogsInternal01;
DROP TABLE IF EXISTS log4jLogsInternal02;
```

As you see in Figure 13.8, even the associated data got deleted when you dropped the internal tables.

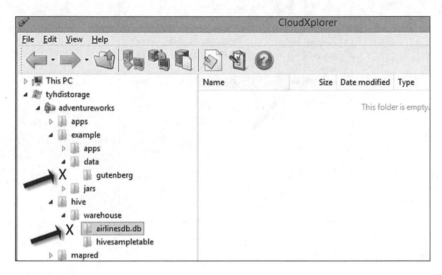

FIGURE 13.8
Data gets deleted when you drop internal tables.

External Table

When you create an external table, Hive does not copy data from the source files to a subdirectory of the root directory of the database (by default, location `/hive/warehouse/`). Instead, Hive just creates a table, its metadata, and a reference to the data in its original location. Of course, unlike with an internal table, when you drop an external table, only the table's metadata gets deleted, not the actual data (because the table does not own data).

Let's now see how an external table works. First, however, create a folder (`externaldemo01`) in the `/example/data/` location and then copy the `sample.log` file (`/example/data/sample.log`) to this folder. (You can copy multiple copies of this file, for better clarity; we have created multiple copies of `sample.log`, with names such as `sample01.log` and `sample02.log`) (See Figure 13.9.)

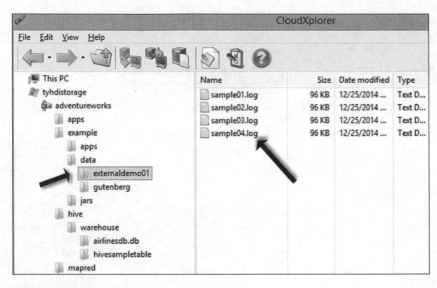

FIGURE 13.9
Creating a folder and data for an external table demo.

Next, create an external table (the EXTERNAL clause is mandatory when creating an external table) in the `airlinesdb` database with the LOCATION clause (if you don't have this database already, create it with script available in the earlier section). The external table is created in Hive (only metadata about the table gets created in Hive) and references the location specified with the LOCATION clause for the data.

```
USE airlinesdb;
DROP TABLE IF EXISTS log4jLogsExternal01;
CREATE EXTERNAL TABLE log4jLogsExternal01
(
col1 string,
col2 string,
col3 string,
col4 string,
col5 string,
col6 string,
col7 string
)
ROW FORMAT DELIMITED FIELDS TERMINATED BY ' '
STORED AS TEXTFILE
LOCATION '/example/data/externaldemo01/';
```

Now let's drop the external table with the following command and study its impact:

```
USE airlinesdb;
DROP TABLE IF EXISTS log4jLogsExternal01;
```

As you see in Figure 13.10, when you drop an external table, Hive drops only the metadata related to the table. The data this external table referenced remains intact.

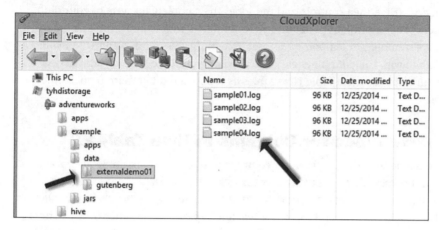

FIGURE 13.10
Impact of deleting an external table.

NOTE

IF EXISTS and IF NOT EXISTS Clauses

You can use the IF NOT EXISTS clause with the CREATE TABLE command to create a table only if it does not already exist or if it gracefully exits if the table already exists. If you don't specify IF NOT EXISTS and you run the CREATE TABLE command with a table name that already exists, it will throw an exception.

Likewise, you can use the IF EXISTS clause with the DROP TABLE command to drop a table only if the table exists or the command gracefully exits if the table is not available. If you don't specify IF EXISTS and you run the DROP TABLE command with a table name that is not available, it will throw an exception.

NOTE

ALTER TABLE Command

You can use the ALTER TABLE command to change the structure of the table, such as to rename the table, modify table properties, modify SerDe, add or drop columns, add or drop partitions in a partitioned table, or move the data in a partition from a table to another table that has the same schema but does not already have that partition.

Internal and External Tables

You might prefer to create an internal table if you want Hive to completely manage data along with the table structure. (Hive then controls and manages the complete lifecycle of your data, including its deletion.) You also might prefer an internal table if data is not shared across applications or if you have a smaller or temporary dataset. External tables work better when you want to decouple tables with the data they reference or when your data is being shared across other applications (this applies to multiple Hive tables as well when all of them point to the same single dataset).

Supported Data Types for Columns in Hive Tables

Hive enables you to define several data types for columns in a table. For example, it supports common primitive data types such as TINYINT, SMALLINT, INT, BIGINT, BOOLEAN, FLOAT, DOUBLE, STRING, BINARY, TIMESTAMP, DECIMAL, DECIMAL (precision, scale), VARCHAR, and CHAR. Hive also enables you to combine primitive data types (or even other complex data types), to form complex data types such as an array type, a structure type, a union type, and a map type. Note that the list of supported data types is increasing with almost every new release of Hive. Check the latest documentation for all current supported data types.

Other Clauses Used When Creating a Table in Hive

With the CREATE TABLE command, you might have noticed that you specified several other clauses beyond just the table name and its columns details. This section goes into detail about these clauses with CREATE TABLE command:

▶ ROW FORMAT DELIMITED FIELDS TERMINATED BY—Indicates how fields are separated in a row. You can use a space, a comma, or a tab (\t) for a field separator.

▶ STORED AS—Indicates how data gets stored:

  ▶ TEXTFILE—The default storage format for data in a plain-text file with comma-separated values (CSVs) or tab-separated values (TSVs). Note that rows are always separated by a newline character (\n) when TEXTFILE is used.

  The default TEXTFILE storage format makes sharing data with other tools easy, but because these are conveniently viewable or editable files, they are not space-efficient, compared to binary storage formats. You can use compression, but again, you will get more efficient use of disk space and better disk I/O performance when using binary file formats.

  ▶ SEQUENCEFILE—Creates flat files that consist of binary key-value pairs. When Hive converts queries to MapReduce jobs during execution, it decides on the appropriate key-value pairs to use for each given record. SEQUENCEFILE is a basic file format that Hadoop provides, and it is supported by other tools in the Hadoop ecosystem, including Hive.

Similar to TEXTFILE, SEQUENCEFILE can also be compressed, although it gets compressed at the block and record levels and fits well in the map-reduce output format. The compression ratio is better and is useful in optimizing disk space utilization and minimizing I/O, while still supporting the capability to split files on block boundaries for parallel processing.

SEQUENCEFILE performs better than TEXTFILE and is an optimal solution for Hive because it saves a complete row as a single binary value. This means that Hive must read a full row and decompress it, even if only a few columns are being requested. Now think of a scenario in which you have hundreds of columns and only few are being queried. In such a case, SEQUENCEFILE does not work as a better solution.

▶ RCFILE—Record Columnar File is another binary storage format that has been optimized for a table with a larger number of columns. The RCFILE storage format splits data horizontally into row groups first, which are stored in an HDFS file. Furthermore, inside each row group, it vertically saves the row group data in columnar format. The benefit of this storage is that parallelism still applies: The row groups in different files are distributed redundantly across the Hadoop cluster and are processed at the same time. Subsequently, while processing, each processing node reads only the columns relevant to a query from the file (row group) and skips irrelevant ones. This also results in a better compression ratio because of the higher redundancy (only a few distinct entries) in the data of the columns.

▶ ORC—Optimized Row Columnar (ORC) is one of the most efficient storage formats. It significantly reduces the data storage space; improves performance when Hive is reading, writing, and processing data; and overcomes several challenges that other formats faced. ORC can result in a small performance loss when writing data, but it makes up for it with a huge performance gain while reading.

▶ AVRO—Apache Avro is a popular binary data interchange and data serialization format in the Hadoop technology stack. It relies on language-agnostic schemas stored in JSON format to store and load data. Thus, many different tools can read and interpret Avro files. Avro stores all the data in a binary format, making the files more compact, and even adds markers in the data to help MapReduce jobs find where to break large files, for more efficient processing.

GO TO ▶ You can learn more about Avro in **Hour 10, "Programming MapReduce Jobs."**

▶ LOCATION—Specifies the location of the data for the table. If this optional clause is not specified, the default location is either a subdirectory in the /hive/warehouse/ directory for a table in the default database or a subdirectory in the `/hive/warehouse/<database name>.db/` directory for a table in a user-created database. The name of the subdirectory is the same as the name of the table.

▶ COMMENT—Provides a description or comment for the table or for each column of the table after the data type.

▶ PARTITIONED BY—Allows a Hive table to be partitioned by one or more columns. You must specify it when you create a table with the CREATE TABLE command or when you modify it with the ALTER TABLE command, to improve performance. For a partitioned table, data is stored in one directory per partition. Hive uses a partition elimination technique to query only partitions that have the requested data; it ignores the other partitions of the table if they don't hold qualifying rows requested by the query. You will see examples of creating a partitioned table later in this hour.

NOTE

Partitioning is a process of horizontal slicing of data which allow large datasets to be segmented into more manageable smaller chunks.

Serialization and Deserialization

A Serializer and Deserializer (SerDe) enables Hive to read data from a table with a custom format after deserializing a row of data from the bytes in the file to objects that Hive uses internally to operate on that row of data. SerDe then writes the data back out to the HDFS in any custom format after serializing Hive's internal representation of a row of data into the bytes written to the output file. For example, imagine that you have data in an XML file—you can write SerDe to pick up the data encapsulated in an XML file.

A SerDe encapsulates the logic for converting the unstructured bytes in a record (gives the instructions on how to process a record), which is stored as part of a file, into a record that Hive can use. You can write your own custom SerDe for any specific custom data formats, although Hive comes with several built-in SerDe (for example, SerDe are available for Avro, ORC, CSV, and RegEx), and many other third-party SerDe are also available.

A Hive table can be configured to process data using a SerDe by specifying the SerDe when creating the table with the CREATE TABLE command or modifying it using the ALTER TABLE command.

GO TO ▶ In the section **"Writing Data Analysis Queries,"** later in this hour, you see how to use CSVSerDe to process the CSV files to appropriately handle embedded commas in the data. This CSVSerDe also ignores the first row if the column header information is the part of the file.

CREATE TABLE AS SELECT **Command**

The CREATE TABLE AS SELECT (CTAS) command creates a new table with the schema and data derived from the results of the following SELECT command. If the SELECT command does not specify column aliases, the column names automatically are assigned to _col0, _col1, _col2, and so on.

In addition, the new table is created using a specific storage format and a SerDe independent of the source tables specified in the SELECT command.

```
CREATE TABLE AggregatedLogs
ROW FORMAT DELIMITED
FIELDS TERMINATED BY ' '
STORED AS TEXTFILE
AS
SELECT col4 AS Severity, count(*) AS CountOfOccurence
FROM log4jLogsExternal01
GROUP BY col4
ORDER BY col4 DESC limit 5;
```

As you can see in the script, the SELECT command aggregates the data. When it gets executed, it generates a MapReduce job to perform this operation.

Next, the resultant data of the SELECT command is loaded into the new table. When you select all the rows of this table using the script that follows, it shows you data (already aggregated when the table got created and loaded) as is from the HDFS without generating a MapReduce job (see Figure 13.11).

```
SELECT * FROM AggregatedLogs;
```

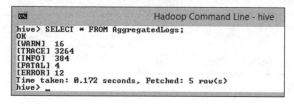

```
Hadoop Command Line - hive
hive> SELECT * FROM AggregatedLogs;
OK
[WARN]  16
[TRACE] 3264
[INFO]  384
[FATAL] 4
[ERROR] 12
Time taken: 0.172 seconds, Fetched: 5 row(s)
hive> _
```

FIGURE 13.11
Querying data from a table generated using the CTAS command.

With CTAS, you can create only internal, nonpartitioned, and nonbucketed tables.

CREATE TABLE LIKE **Command**

The CREATE TABLE LIKE command lets you create an internal or external table, based on the schema of an existing table. This command creates a table with the schema of the existing table (copy of an existing table) but does not copy the data of the existing table:

```
CREATE EXTERNAL TABLE log4jLogsExternal02
LIKE log4jLogsExternal01;
SELECT * FROM log4jLogsExternal02;
```

By default, the location for the table is a subdirectory in the /hive/warehouse/ folder for a table in default database, or a subdirectory in the /hive/warehouse/<database name>.db/ folder in a user-created database. Optionally, you can use the LOCATION clause to specify a different location than the default.

Temporary Table

Hive enables you to create a user session–specific temporary table (available in Hive 0.14.0 and later) for temporary storage of data during processing. When you create a temporary table (the partition and index are not supported on a temporary table), it is visible to you only in your current session; data for this table is stored in the user's scratch directory. Hive automatically drops temporary tables at the end of the session.

Creating Table Views

Hive enables you to create one or more views on one or more tables with the CREATE VIEW command. This simplifies your queries by encapsulating your joins or filters in an underlying SELECT query of the view.

Unlike the CTAS command that executes the underlying SELECT command at the time of CTAS command execution, when you create a view, it just creates the metadata. Actual query execution of the underlying SELECT query happens only when you query from the view. This proves that a view is a purely logical object with no associated data storage.

NOTE

As of this writing, you cannot create materialized views in Hive.

```
USE airlinesdb;
DROP VIEW IF EXISTS WarningMessageOnly;
CREATE VIEW WarningMessageOnly
AS
SELECT col1, col2, col3, col4, col5
FROM log4jLogsExternal01
WHERE col4 = '[WARN]';

SELECT * FROM WarningMessageOnly;
```

By default, Hive automatically derives column names from the underlying SELECT command, although you can specify different names for the columns of the view:

```
USE airlinesdb;
DROP VIEW IF EXISTS ErrorMessageOnly;
CREATE VIEW ErrorMessageOnly
(new_col1, new_col2, new_col3, new_col4, new_col5)
AS
SELECT col1, col2, col3, col4, col5
FROM log4jLogsExternal01
WHERE col4 = '[ERROR]';

SELECT * FROM ErrorMessageOnly;
```

Names of views or tables should be unique inside a database. Your view creation script will fail if you specify a view name with the same name of an existing table. You can use the same SHOW TABLES command to list both tables and views inside a database. You can use the DESCRIBE command to analyze the details of views in the same way you do for a table:

```
SHOW TABLES;
DESCRIBE FORMATTED WarningMessageOnly;
DESCRIBE FORMATTED ErrorMessageOnly;
```

Views are read-only and cannot be used as the target of loading data with LOAD or INSERT commands. You can include ORDER BY and LIMIT clauses as part of the underlying SELECT command of the view. While querying from view, you again can use the query-level ORDER BY and LIMIT clauses, although query-level clauses are evaluated after the view clauses.

Data Load Processes for Hive Tables

Hive is smart enough to identify and consider new files available in the referenced location (either the default location of /hive/warehouse/ or any exact location specified) of the table (supported for both internal and external tables). This gives flexibility in just dumping files into the appropriate location by the external data dumping process, and when you query from the Hive table, you get data from this newly dumped files as well.

If you don't have a data load process already in place, you can leverage the LOAD DATA command in Hive to move data files from either the local file system or from WASB or HDFS into the location that the Hive table references. Hive performs the copy operation if the specified source location is on the local machine; otherwise, it moves the data files from its original location to the location that the table references. This command helps especially if you have partitioned table.

```
LOAD DATA [LOCAL] INPATH <source location of data files> [OVERWRITE] INTO TABLE
  <table_name> [PARTITION (partition_column1=value, partition_column2=value...)];
```

The LOCAL clause is specified if the source file system is on the local machine. It can be omitted if it is a WASB or HDFS location. With INPATH, you specify either a specific file to copy\move or you specify a specific folder to copy\move all the files from that folder.

Unlike the `LOAD DATA` command, which enables you to load data from data files, Hive includes an `INSERT` command to load data from one Hive table to another.

```
INSERT [OVERWRITE] <target_table_name> [PARTITION (partition_column1=value,
partition_column2=value...)]
SELECT col1, col2,.... FROM <source_table_name>;
```

`OVERWRITE` is an optional clause (in both the `LOAD DATA` and `INSERT` commands). If it is specified, the contents of the specified target table (or partition) are deleted and replaced by new incoming data. If this clause is absent, Hive appends data to the specified target table (or partition), keeping the existing data intact.

We go into detail on these methods of data loading in the next section.

Data Manipulation Language

Starting with Hive 0.14, you can use `INSERT`, `UPDATE`, and `DELETE` commands for data manipulation.

The `INSERT` statement enables you to insert row-wise data into a Hive table or a partition of a Hive table with syntax that supports atomicity, consistency, isolation, and durability (ACID). (If a table is to be used in ACID writes [`INSERT`, `UPDATE` and `DELETE`], the table property `transactional` must be set on that table.) As you can see, no column specification is given for the target table; hence, values or nulls for all the columns must be specified for each column of the target table:

```
INSERT INTO TABLE <target_table_name> [PARTITION (partition_column1=value,
partition_column2=value...)]
VALUES ( values_row [, values_row ...] );
```

The `UPDATE` statement updates column values for rows of a table that match the `WHERE` clause with the following syntax. The `UPDATE` statement works only for tables that support ACID.

```
UPDATE <target_table_name> SET column1 = value [, column2 = value ...] [WHERE
expression];
```

The `DELETE` statement deletes rows of a table that match the `WHERE` clause with the following syntax. The `DELETE` statement works only for tables that support ACID.

```
DELETE FROM <target_table_name> [WHERE expression];
```

Built-in Functions in Hive

Hive includes several built-in functions to handle almost all aspects of data manipulation (aggregation, string handling, date-related functions, mathematical functions, type conversion functions, collection functions, conditional functions, and more). You can find out about the latest available list of built-in functions with this command (see Figure 13.12):

```
SHOW FUNCTIONS;
DESCRIBE FUNCTION substring;
DESCRIBE FUNCTION EXTENDED substring;
```

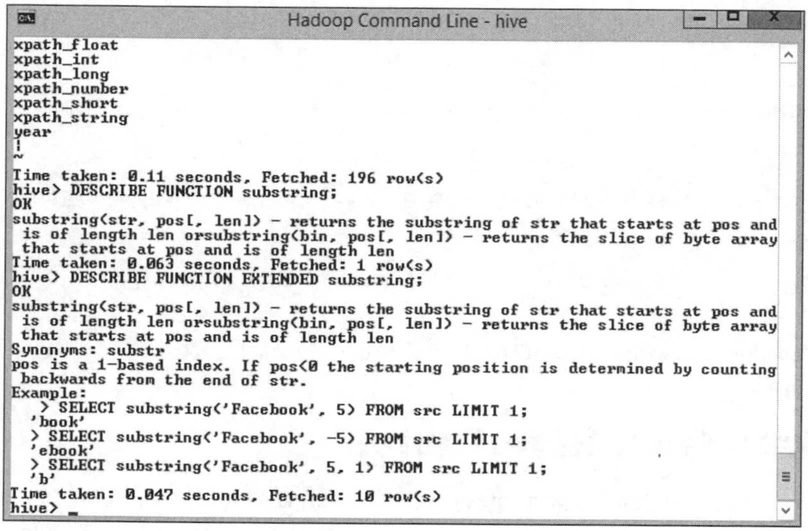

FIGURE 13.12
Viewing available functions and their descriptions.

Hive primarily has three types of functions:

▶ **User-defined functions (UDFs)**—Operate row-wise (take one or more columns from a row and return a single value), generally during map execution. These are the simplest functions to write, but they are constrained in their functionality.

▶ **User-defined table-generating functions (UDTFs)**—Also execute row-wise (take zero or more inputs), but they produce multiple rows of output (generating a table instead of a single value). An example is the built-in `explode` function.

▶ **User-defined aggregating functions (UDAFs)**—Take one or more columns from zero to many rows and return a single result. They are typically used with the GROUP BY clause. Examples are the `count` and `sum` built-in functions.

You also can write your own custom UDF to extend existing functionalities or for some specific custom processing. To create a UDF, you first extend the UDF class and implement the `evaluate()` function. You can overload the `evaluate` method with different parameters; Hive picks the method that matches with passed-in parameters.

During HiveQL query processing, an instance of your user-defined function class is instantiated for each use of the function in a HiveQL query. The `evaluate()` method is called for each input row.

```
public class <your UDF class name> extends UDF {
    public <your UDF class name>(){

    }
    public <return type> evaluate(<data type> parameter1){

    }
    public <return type> evaluate(<data type> parameter1, <data type> parameter2){

    }
}
```

You can also extend functionalities with custom UDTF or UDAF.

Querying Data from Hive Tables

Hive has a mature query language that supports querying data from Hive tables with the SELECT command. (You can also use SET `hive.cli.print.header=true`; to instruct Hive to show the column names above the returned result set.) It enables you to specify the following:

▶ Columns to be selected, column expressions, and use of aggregate functions, with an option to select all the column values or only distinct values

▶ Filters with the WHERE clause

▶ Grouping on a result set with the GROUP BY clause

▶ Ordering by using the SORT BY clause to sort data per Reducer, or by using the ORDER BY clause to sort a complete data set

▶ Limit on the number of rows to be returned

The syntax for the SELECT command follows:

```
SELECT [ALL | DISTINCT] column1, column2, ...
FROM table_reference
[WHERE where_condition]
[GROUP BY col_list]
[HAVING BY col_list]
[CLUSTER BY col_list
  | [DISTRIBUTE BY col_list]
  [SORT BY col_list]]
[ORDER BY col_list]
[LIMIT number]
```

As in an RDBMS system that enables you to create a temporary result set by deriving it from a query specified with Common Table Expression (CTE), Hive also supports creating a common table expression derived from a simple query specified in a WITH clause.

```
WITH CTEExample
AS
(
SELECT col4 AS Severity, count(*) AS CountOfOccurence
FROM log4jLogsExternal01
GROUP BY col4
ORDER BY col4 DESC limit 5;
)
SELECT * FROM CTEExample;
```

Hive enables you to join two or more tables with an inner join, a left outer join, a right outer join, a full join, a cross join, and so on.

```
join_table:
    table_reference JOIN table_factor [join_condition]
  | table_reference {LEFT|RIGHT|FULL} [OUTER] JOIN table_reference join_condition
  | table_reference LEFT SEMI JOIN table_reference join_condition
  | table_reference CROSS JOIN table_reference [join_condition]
```

NOTE

Hive Supports Equi-joins Only

As of this writing, Hive supports only equi-joins (a specific type of comparator-based join that uses equality comparisons in the join-predicate). Also, for better performance, put the largest table on the rightmost side of the join.

Hive allows two datasets (the number and names of columns returned by each SELECT statement must be the same) to be combined with the UNION ALL statement. Hive supports only UNION ALL, which does not remove duplicates in the final combined result set.

```
SELECT *
FROM (
  select_statement
  UNION ALL
  select_statement
) unionResult;
```

Hive supports subqueries in the FROM and WHERE clauses. When used with the FROM clause, the subquery must be given a name; columns in the subquery must have unique names. With the WHERE clause, you can also reference columns from the parent query to make it a correlated query.

```
SELECT * FROM (SELECT col1, col2, ... FROM t1) t2;

SELECT * FROM A
WHERE A.key IN (SELECT B.key FROM B);
SELECT * FROM A
WHERE A.key NOT IN (SELECT B.key FROM B);

SELECT * FROM A
WHERE A.key EXISTS (SELECT B.key FROM B);
SELECT * FROM A
WHERE A.key NOT EXISTS (SELECT B.key FROM B);
```

Writing Data Analysis Queries

You have seen in detail how internal and external tables are created and maintained. This section demonstrates how you can partition these tables, how to load data into partitioned tables, and how you can leverage SerDe in loading data from CSV files.

At the beginning of this hour, you downloaded prezipped airline flights data from RITA BTS. Now you will load this data into an external partitioned table.

Also, because this data is in CSV files, you will use the `com.bizo.hive.serde.csv.CSVSerde` SerDe to interpret these CSV files. This SerDe is defined in `csv-serde-1.1.2.jar`, which you can download from http://ogrodnek.github.io/csv-serde/. We downloaded the JAR file and uploaded it to `/OnTimePerformance/` on the Azure Storage Blob.

In the next script, you first add the reference of this JAR file with the `ADD JAR` command so that you can use SerDe in the current Hive session. Then you create a table with partitions by year and month (the columns are named PartitionYear and PartitionMonth because the Year and Month columns are already part of the data).

The CSV files contain the first row as a column header, so to skip the first row, we have used `TBLPROPERTIES`. We specified a location for this table that does not contain any data files for now; hence, `SELECT COUNT (*)` will return zero rows.

You can partition (partitioning is a process of horizontal slicing of data that enables large datasets to be segmented into more manageable smaller chunks) a table on one or more columns; when you specify more than one column, it becomes hierarchical. In this case, you will have a top-level partition for the year, followed by child-level partitions for each month in the year:

```
ADD JAR wasb:///OnTimePerformance/csv-serde-1.1.2.jar;
DROP TABLE IF EXISTS OnTimePerformancePartition01;
CREATE EXTERNAL TABLE OnTimePerformancePartition01 (
Year INT, Quarter INT, Month INT, DayofMonth INT, DayOfWeek INT, FlightDate STRING,
UniqueCarrier STRING, AirlineID INT, Carrier STRING,
```

```
TailNum STRING, FlightNum INT, OriginAirportID INT, OriginAirportSeqID int,
OriginCityMarketID int, Origin STRING, OriginCityName STRING,
OriginState STRING, OriginStateFips INT, OriginStateName STRING, OriginWac INT,
DestAirportID INT, DestAirportSeqID INT, DestCityMarketID INT,
Dest STRING, DestCityName STRING, DestState STRING, DestStateFips INT, DestStateName
STRING, DestWac INT, CRSDepTime INT, DepTime INT,
DepDelay FLOAT, DepDelayMinutes FLOAT, DepDel15 FLOAT, DepartureDelayGroups INT,
DepTimeBlk STRING, TaxiOut FLOAT, WheelsOff INT, WheelsOn INT,
TaxiIn FLOAT, CRSArrTime INT, ArrTime INT, ArrDelay FLOAT, ArrDelayMinutes FLOAT,
ArrDel15 FLOAT, ArrivalDelayGroups INT, ArrTimeBlk STRING,
Cancelled INT, CancellationCode STRING, Diverted INT, CRSElapsedTime FLOAT,
ActualElapsedTime FLOAT, AirTime FLOAT, Flights FLOAT, Distance FLOAT,
DistanceGroup INT, CarrierDelay FLOAT, WeatherDelay FLOAT, NASDelay FLOAT,
SecurityDelay FLOAT, LateAircraftDelay FLOAT, FirstDepTime INT, TotalAddGTime
FLOAT,
LongestAddGTime FLOAT, DivAirportLandings INT, DivReachedDest FLOAT,
DivActualElapsedTime FLOAT, DivArrDelay FLOAT, DivDistance FLOAT, Div1Airport
STRING,
Div1AirportID INT, Div1AirportSeqID INT, Div1WheelsOn INT, Div1TotalGTime FLOAT,
Div1LongestGTime FLOAT, Div1WheelsOff INT, Div1TailNum STRING,
Div2Airport STRING, Div2AirportID INT, Div2AirportSeqID INT, Div2WheelsOn INT,
Div2TotalGTime FLOAT, Div2LongestGTime FLOAT, Div2WheelsOff INT,
Div2TailNum STRING, Div3Airport STRING, Div3AirportID STRING, Div3AirportSeqID
STRING, Div3WheelsOn STRING, Div3TotalGTime STRING, Div3LongestGTime STRING,
Div3WheelsOff STRING, Div3TailNum STRING, Div4Airport STRING, Div4AirportID STRING,
Div4AirportSeqID STRING, Div4WheelsOn STRING, Div4TotalGTime STRING,
Div4LongestGTime STRING, Div4WheelsOff STRING, Div4TailNum STRING, Div5Airport
STRING, Div5AirportID STRING, Div5AirportSeqID STRING, Div5WheelsOn STRING,
Div5TotalGTime STRING, Div5LongestGTime STRING, Div5WheelsOff STRING, Div5TailNum
STRING
)
PARTITIONED BY (PartitionYear INT, PartitionMonth INT)
ROW FORMAT SERDE 'com.bizo.hive.serde.csv.CSVSerde'
STORED AS TEXTFILE
LOCATION '/OnTimePerformance/OnTimePerformancePartition01/'
TBLPROPERTIES ("skip.header.line.count"="1");

--This will return no data as the specified folder does not have any files
SELECT COUNT(*) FROM OnTimePerformancePartition01;
```

NOTE

Partitioning Columns and Folders Structure

Whatever partitioning columns you specify for a partitioned table, they eventually become columns in the table itself and are called *virtual columns* or *pseudo-columns*. This means that any column in the table with the same of partition column will not work; it must be unique. That's why we used the names PartitionYear and PartitionMonth for partition columns—the Year and Month columns are already part of the data itself.

When you encounter the exception "FAILED: Error in semantic analysis: Column repeated in partitioning columns," it means you are trying to include the partitioned column in the data of the table itself.

If you worked on SQL Server, you know that you need to create the first partition function and partitioning scheme, and the partitioning column must be part of the partitioned table explicitly. As an administrator or developer, you need to have overhead in maintaining partitions of the partitioned table for this sliding window scenario. Fortunately, Hive takes care of most of this overhead and you just need to appropriately load the data. Hive automatically writes the data of each partition into different folders. In this case, there will be a top-level partition or folder for YEAR and then child-level partitions or folders for each month in that specific year. While reading, Hive automatically locates the right partitions or folders based on the folder structure (eliminating the other partitions or folders) and returns the partitioning columns (also called *virtual columns*) as columns in the result set.

Notice that the PartitionYear and PartitionMonth values are encoded in directory names; there's no reason to have this data in the data files themselves, too.

Take a look at the Azure Storage Blob. You can see that a file has been created with the same name of the table (see Figure 13.13).

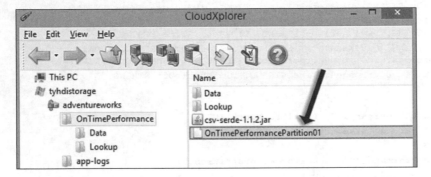

FIGURE 13.13
External partitioned table with no data.

Now you can load the data you downloaded earlier. Each file contains one month of data, so you can correctly load it in the correct partition with the PARTITION clause:

```
--Data Load for Jan 2014
LOAD DATA INPATH '/OnTimePerformance/Data/On_Time_On_Time_Performance_2014_1.csv'
INTO TABLE OnTimePerformancePartition01 PARTITION (PartitionYear=2014,
PartitionMonth=1);
--Data Load for Feb 2014
LOAD DATA INPATH '/OnTimePerformance/Data/On_Time_On_Time_Performance_2014_2.csv'
```

```
INTO TABLE OnTimePerformancePartition01 PARTITION (PartitionYear=2014,
PartitionMonth=2);
--Data Load for Mar 2014
LOAD DATA INPATH '/OnTimePerformance/Data/On_Time_On_Time_Performance_2014_3.csv'
INTO TABLE OnTimePerformancePartition01 PARTITION (PartitionYear=2014,
PartitionMonth=3);
--Data Load for Apr 2014
LOAD DATA INPATH '/OnTimePerformance/Data/On_Time_On_Time_Performance_2014_4.csv'
INTO TABLE OnTimePerformancePartition01 PARTITION (PartitionYear=2014,
PartitionMonth=4);
--Data Load for May 2014
LOAD DATA INPATH '/OnTimePerformance/Data/On_Time_On_Time_Performance_2014_5.csv'
INTO TABLE OnTimePerformancePartition01 PARTITION (PartitionYear=2014,
PartitionMonth=5);
--Data Load for Jun 2014
LOAD DATA INPATH '/OnTimePerformance/Data/On_Time_On_Time_Performance_2014_6.csv'
INTO TABLE OnTimePerformancePartition01 PARTITION (PartitionYear=2014,
PartitionMonth=6);
```

If you go back again to the Azure Storage Blob, you will see that a top-level folder has been created for PartitionYear, followed by the PartitionMonth subfolders inside it, for as much data as you loaded into these partitions. You can also see that data has been correctly loaded in each partitions. For example, the partition for March contains a March data file (see Figure 13.14).

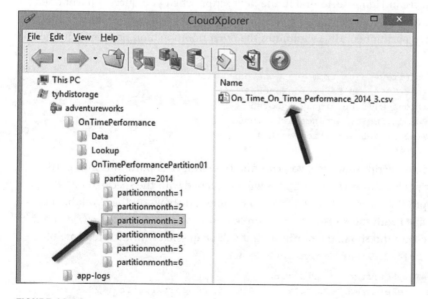

FIGURE 13.14
Data loaded into a partitioned table.

As you can see in Figure 13.15 and in the script that follows, when you query a partitioned table either without specifying the WHERE predicate or when the WHERE predicate does not refer to partitioning a column, you retrieve data from all the available partitions at that time.

```
--This query will retrieve data from all the partitions as there
--is no WHERE predicate defined for partition elimination
SELECT COUNT(*) FROM OnTimePerformancePartition01;
```

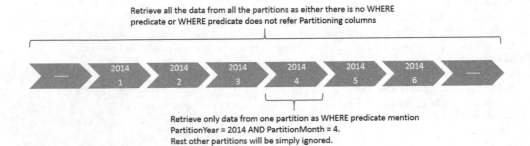

FIGURE 13.15
Partition elimination in action.

Similarly, as you can see in Figure 13.15 and in the next script, when you query a partitioned table with a WHERE predicate that references a partitioning column, you retrieve data for only that specific referenced partition(s). Hive eliminates the other nonmatching partitions during processing.

```
--This query will retrieve data from just one partition
--WHERE PartitionYear=2014 AND PartitionMonth=4
--rest other partitions will be simply ignored
SELECT COUNT(*) FROM OnTimePerformancePartition01
WHERE PartitionYear=2014 AND PartitionMonth=4
```

Figure 13.16 and the next script show how you can find the number of partitions in a partitioned table. The script also shows what partitions will be queried with the specified WHERE predicate. For example, the second SHOW PARTITIONS command shows all the available partitions that will be queried with the WHERE PartitionYear = 2014 predicate. Likewise, the third SHOW PARTITIONS command shows the partition that will be queried with the predicate WHERE PartitionYear = 2014 AND PartitionMonth = 4.

```
SHOW PARTITIONS OnTimePerformancePartition01;
SHOW PARTITIONS OnTimePerformancePartition01 PARTITION (PartitionYear=2014);
SHOW PARTITIONS OnTimePerformancePartition01 PARTITION (PartitionYear=2014,
PartitionMonth=4);
```

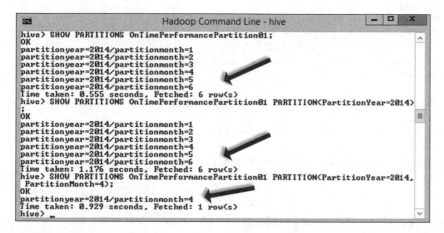

FIGURE 13.16
Partition information for a table.

NOTE

Partitioning Considerations

Partitioning improves the performance of your query by eliminating unneeded partitions from query processing. However, having too many smaller partitions results in overhead for Hive because it must scan directories recursively (with too much metadata to be maintained in the memory of name node). You need to strike a balance in the number of partitions and the expected query performance.

You also must ensure that the partitions of a table are roughly similar in size, to avoid data skewness and prevent a single long, running thread from holding things up.

We talked about creating partitions on one or more columns of a table with the PARTITION BY clause to improve performance. Furthermore, partitions of a table can be clustered, bucketed, or segmented into buckets (Hive uses the hash function to distribute partition data across buckets) using the CLUSTERED BY clause. Data can be sorted within that bucket using the SORT BY clause. This can improve performance with certain kinds of queries, especially when you are sampling data. If you have not done bucketing, random sampling on the table still works, but it is not efficient because the query must scan all the data.

The following script shows how you can create buckets for a partitioned table. Using the CLUSTERED BY clause, you specify the column to be hashed and bucketed and the number of buckets to be created (in this example, you are creating five buckets). Each bucket then contains multiple AirlineIDs, while restricting each AirlineID to a single bucket.

```
ADD JAR wasb:///OnTimePerformance/csv-serde-1.1.2.jar;
DROP TABLE IF EXISTS OnTimePerformancePartition03;
CREATE EXTERNAL TABLE OnTimePerformancePartition03 (
<Put all the columns as mentioned above for OnTimePerformancePartition01 table in
section "Writing Data Analysis Queries">
)
PARTITIONED BY (PartitionYear INT, PartitionMonth INT)
CLUSTERED BY (AirlineID) INTO 5 BUCKETS
ROW FORMAT SERDE 'com.bizo.hive.serde.csv.CSVSerde'
STORED AS TEXTFILE
LOCATION '/OnTimePerformance/OnTimePerformancePartition03/'
TBLPROPERTIES ("skip.header.line.count"="1");
```

Partition Switching or Swapping

You learned how to use the LOAD DATA command to load data appropriately in the right partitions of a partitioned table. But what if you already have data placed appropriately in folders, and you want it to be part of a partitioned table without the data movement that the LOAD DATA command causes?

You can use the ALTER TABLE command to add a new partition (switch-in) or drop an existing partition (switch-out) from a partitioned table. The next script adds a new seventh partition in the existing partitioned table; this new partition references the location for the data files for the seventh partition.

Using the ALTER TABLE command, you can drop an existing partition, too (based on whether the table is internal or external). Data then is dropped or remains as is. Figure 13.17 shows the execution result of the following script to add a new partition or remove an existing partition from the partitioned table.

```
ALTER TABLE OnTimePerformancePartition01
ADD PARTITION (PartitionYear=2014, PartitionMonth=7)
LOCATION '/OnTimePerformance/OnTimePerformancePartition01/partitionyear=2014/
partitionmonth=7/';
SHOW PARTITIONS OnTimePerformancePartition01;

ALTER TABLE OnTimePerformancePartition01
DROP IF EXISTS PARTITION (PartitionYear=2014, PartitionMonth=7);
SHOW PARTITIONS OnTimePerformancePartition01;
```

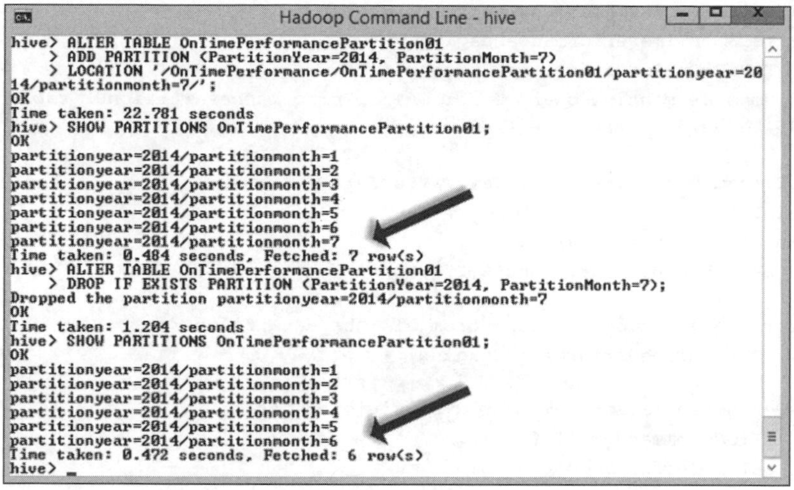

FIGURE 13.17
Modifying a partitioned table to add a partition or remove a partition.

Dynamic Partition Insert

You have learned about two different methods for creating or loading data into specific partitions of a partitioned table. Although these methods work in most cases, you might encounter a problem if you have a data file that contains data pertaining to more than one partition of the partitioned table. For example, suppose that you have a data file that contains data for the years 2012, 2013, and 2014, and you want to load it into a partitioned table that is partitioned yearly.

In this case, how and where will you place the data file? How will you distribute data correctly across partitions for 2012, 2013, and 2014 from a single file? To help you in this scenario, Hive includes dynamic partition insert functionality to dynamically determine which partitions should be created and populated while scanning the input dataset. During the data insert process, the input column values are evaluated to determine which partition this specific row should be inserted into. If the target partition is already available, the row gets inserted into it; otherwise, a new partition is created automatically and then the row gets inserted into it.

The dynamic partition insert feature is disabled by default. To leverage this feature, follow these steps:

▶ **Load data into a nonpartitioned staging table first.** The following code creates a staging table that points to the /OnTimePerformance/Data/ folder, which contains all the available files. (We used the LOAD DATA command earlier to load files into this specific folder. If you have deleted them from there for any reason, you must execute the LOAD DATA command again to bring those files back to complete this example.)

```
ADD JAR wasb:///OnTimePerformance/csv-serde-1.1.2.jar;
DROP TABLE IF EXISTS OnTimePerformanceStaging;
CREATE EXTERNAL TABLE OnTimePerformanceStaging (
<Put all the columns as mentioned above for OnTimePerformancePartition01 table
in section "Writing Data Analysis Queries">
)
ROW FORMAT SERDE 'com.bizo.hive.serde.csv.CSVSerde'
STORED AS TEXTFILE
LOCATION '/OnTimePerformance/Data/'
TBLPROPERTIES ("skip.header.line.count"="1");

--This will return total number of rows from all the data files
SELECT COUNT(*) FROM OnTimePerformanceStaging;

--As the OnTimePerformanceStaging is not a partitioned table
--this SHOW PARTITION command will fail
SHOW PARTITIONS OnTimePerformanceStaging;
```

▶ **Create a partitioned table, if one is not already available.** With this command, you
create another partitioned table. The referenced folder with the LOCATION clause does not
contain any data file, so this table will have no records as of now.

```
DROP TABLE IF EXISTS OnTimePerformancePartition02;
CREATE EXTERNAL TABLE OnTimePerformancePartition02 (

<Put all the columns as mentioned above for OnTimePerformancePartition01 table
in section "Writing Data Analysis Queries">

)
PARTITIONED BY (PartitionYear INT, PartitionMonth INT)
ROW FORMAT DELIMITED
FIELDS TERMINATED BY '\001'
STORED AS TEXTFILE
LOCATION '/OnTimePerformance/OnTimePerformancePartition02/';
--This will no return as the specified folder does not have any files
SELECT COUNT(*) FROM OnTimePerformancePartition02;
SHOW PARTITIONS OnTimePerformancePartition02;
```

▶ **Enable dynamic partitioning in Hive.** With the next script, you can enable the dynamic
partition insert functionality in the current Hive session:

```
--Enable dynamic partitions insert
SET hive.exec.dynamic.partition = true;
SET hive.exec.dynamic.partition.mode = nonstrict;
```

▶ **Use the INSERT INTO command to load data.** You must include partition columns as the
last columns (in the same order in which they appear in the PARTITION BY clause of the
partitioned table) in the SELECT query from the staging table, as in the following script.
Figure 13.18 shows the execution result of the INSERT INTO command. You can see that
data gets loaded from the staging table appropriately to the right partitions of the target
partitioned table, based on values for partition columns.

```
ADD JAR wasb:///OnTimePerformance/csv-serde-1.1.2.jar;
INSERT OVERWRITE TABLE OnTimePerformancePartition02 PARTITION (PartitionYear,
PartitionMonth)
SELECT *, Year AS PartitionYear, Month AS PartitionMonth FROM
OnTimePerformanceStaging;
```

```
┌────────────────────── Hadoop Command Line - hive ──────── ─ □ X ──┐
│2014-12-27 14:10:35,265 Stage-1 map = 100%,  reduce = 72%, Cumulative CPU 420.08 ▲│
│3 sec                                                                             │
│2014-12-27 14:10:56,471 Stage-1 map = 100%,  reduce = 73%, Cumulative CPU 467.48 │
│9 sec                                                                             │
│2014-12-27 14:10:57,547 Stage-1 map = 100%,  reduce = 86%, Cumulative CPU 467.92 │
│6 sec                                                                             │
│2014-12-27 14:10:59,658 Stage-1 map = 100%,  reduce = 100%, Cumulative CPU 472.2 │
│07 sec                                                                            │
│MapReduce Total cumulative CPU time: 7 minutes 52 seconds 207 msec               │
│Ended Job = job_1419686544792_0003                                               │
│Loading data to table airlinesdb.ontimeperformancepartition02 partition (partiti │
│onyear=null, partitionmonth=null)                                                │
│        Loading partition (partitionyear=2014, partitionmonth=6)                 │
│        Loading partition (partitionyear=2014, partitionmonth=1)                 │
│        Loading partition (partitionyear=2014, partitionmonth=5)                 │
│        Loading partition (partitionyear=2014, partitionmonth=4)                 │
│        Loading partition (partitionyear=2014, partitionmonth=3)                 │
│        Loading partition (partitionyear=2014, partitionmonth=2)                 │
│MapReduce Jobs Launched:                                                         │
│Job 0: Map: 4  Reduce: 2   Cumulative CPU: 472.207 sec   HDFS Read: 0 HDFS Write │
│: 0 SUCCESS                                                                       │
│Total MapReduce CPU Time Spent: 7 minutes 52 seconds 207 msec                    │
│OK                                                                         ≡     │
│Time taken: 252.426 seconds                                                      │
│hive> _                                                                     ▼    │
└─────────────────────────────────────────────────────────────────────────────────┘
```

FIGURE 13.18
Inserting data into a partitioned table with dynamic partition tables.

As you can see in Figure 13.19, with the next script, you can find the number of partitions in a partitioned table that were created after the data load with the INSERT INTO command. The script also shows what partitions are queried with the WHERE predicate.

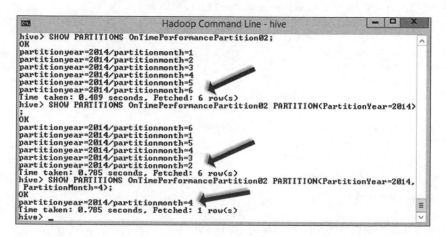

FIGURE 13.19
Partition information for a table that got data from the dynamic partition insert process.

For example, the second `SHOW PARTITIONS` command shows all the available partitions that will be queried with the `WHERE PartitionYear = 2014` predicate. Likewise, the third `SHOW PARTITIONS` command shows the partition that will be queried with the `WHERE PartitionYear = 2014 AND PartitionMonth = 4` predicate.

```
SHOW PARTITIONS OnTimePerformancePartition02;
SHOW PARTITIONS OnTimePerformancePartition02 PARTITION (PartitionYear=2014);
SHOW PARTITIONS OnTimePerformancePartition02 PARTITION (PartitionYear=2014,
PartitionMonth=4);
```

Creating Datasets for Analysis

Let's create some more datasets for use in the data analysis examples in subsequent sections and also in Hour 14, "Consuming HDInsight Data from Microsoft BI Tools over Hive ODBC Driver: Part 1." With the next script, you first create a lookup table (AirlineLookup) based on the data from the `L_AIRLINE_ID.csv` file you downloaded and then uploaded to the Azure Storage Blob at the start of this hour.

This table contains airline information from across the globe, but you have on-time flight information for airlines operating in the USA only; therefore, you will do the join and create another table (DimAirline) that operates in the USA only.

```
ADD JAR wasb:///OnTimePerformance/csv-serde-1.1.2.jar;
DROP TABLE IF EXISTS AirlineLookup;
CREATE EXTERNAL TABLE AirlineLookup (
AirlineID INT, Airline STRING)
ROW FORMAT SERDE 'com.bizo.hive.serde.csv.CSVSerde'
STORED AS TEXTFILE LOCATION '/OnTimePerformance/AirlineLookup/'
TBLPROPERTIES ("skip.header.line.count"="1");
--1580 records
SELECT COUNT(*) FROM AirlineLookup;
DROP TABLE IF EXISTS DimAirline;
CREATE TABLE DimAirline
ROW FORMAT DELIMITED FIELDS TERMINATED BY '\001'
AS
SELECT DISTINCT AirlineLookup.AirlineID, AirlineLookup.Airline
FROM OnTimePerformancePartition02
INNER JOIN AirlineLookup ON OnTimePerformancePartition02.AirlineID = AirlineLookup.
AirlineID;
--14 records
SELECT COUNT(*) FROM DimAirline;
```

In the next script, you first create a lookup table (AirportLookup) based on the data from the `L_AIRPORT_ID.csv` file you downloaded and then uploaded to the Azure Storage Blob at the beginning of this hour. This table contains airport information from across the globe, but you have on-time flight information for airports in the USA only; hence, you will do the join and create another table (DimAirport) that will contain only airports from the USA.

```
ADD JAR wasb:///OnTimePerformance/csv-serde-1.1.2.jar;
DROP TABLE IF EXISTS AirportLookup;
CREATE EXTERNAL TABLE AirportLookup (
AirportID INT, Airport STRING)
ROW FORMAT SERDE 'com.bizo.hive.serde.csv.CSVSerde'
STORED AS TEXTFILE LOCATION '/OnTimePerformance/AirportLookup/'
TBLPROPERTIES ("skip.header.line.count"="1");
--6311 records
SELECT COUNT(*) FROM AirportLookup;
DROP TABLE IF EXISTS DimAirport;
CREATE TABLE DimAirport
ROW FORMAT DELIMITED FIELDS TERMINATED BY '\001'
AS
SELECT DISTINCT AirportLookup.AirportID, AirportLookup.Airport
FROM OnTimePerformancePartition02
INNER JOIN AirportLookup ON OnTimePerformancePartition02.OriginAirportID =
AirportLookup.AirportID;
--319 records
SELECT COUNT(*) FROM DimAirport;
```

In the following script, you are first creating a table (DimCancellation) based on the data from the L_CANCELLATION.csv file you downloaded and then uploaded to the Azure Storage Blob at the beginning of this hour.

Next, you create another table (DimDate) based on unique date-related data information available for on-time flight performance data. Finally, you create a table (DimGeography) based on unique geography-related data information available for on-time flight performance data.

```
ADD JAR wasb:///OnTimePerformance/csv-serde-1.1.2.jar;
DROP TABLE IF EXISTS CancellationLookup;
CREATE EXTERNAL TABLE CancellationLookup (
CancellationID INT, Cancellation STRING)
ROW FORMAT SERDE 'com.bizo.hive.serde.csv.CSVSerde'
STORED AS TEXTFILE LOCATION '/OnTimePerformance/CancellationLookup/'
TBLPROPERTIES ("skip.header.line.count"="1");

DROP TABLE IF EXISTS DimCancellation;
CREATE TABLE DimCancellation
ROW FORMAT DELIMITED FIELDS TERMINATED BY '\001'
AS
SELECT DISTINCT CancellationID, Cancellation
FROM CancellationLookup;
--4 records
SELECT COUNT(*) FROM DimCancellation;
DROP TABLE IF EXISTS DimDate;
CREATE TABLE DimDate
ROW FORMAT DELIMITED FIELDS TERMINATED BY '\001'
AS
```

```
SELECT DISTINCT Year, Quarter, Month, DayofMonth, FlightDate
FROM OnTimePerformancePartition02;
--181 records
SELECT COUNT(*) FROM DimDate;
DROP TABLE IF EXISTS DimGeography;
CREATE TABLE DimGeography
ROW FORMAT DELIMITED FIELDS TERMINATED BY '\001'
AS
SELECT DISTINCT 'USA' AS Country, 'United States of America' AS CountryName,
OriginState, OriginStateName, OriginCityName
FROM OnTimePerformancePartition02;
--315 records
SELECT COUNT(*) FROM DimGeography;
```

Data Analysis of Timely Departure Percentage, Based on Airline

In this section, you conduct analysis to determine which airlines have the best percentage of timely flight departure history, based on the data collected. In this section, you use an approach to create intermediate internal tables for storing data; in the next section, you learn about writing direct queries to do analysis without creating intermediate tables.

NOTE

Hive Internal Temporary Files

Hive always inserts the results of the SELECT command into a table, internally written to some temporary file and displayed to the Hive client side.

In the following script, you first create a table (TotalFlights) that contains the total number of flights that departed, based on on-time flight performance data for 6 months. Then you create another table (OnTimeDepartureFlights) that contains the total number of flights that departed earlier than or at the scheduled time (flights with delays are excluded), based on on-time flight performance data for 6 months.

```
DROP TABLE IF EXISTS TotalFlights;
CREATE TABLE TotalFlights
ROW FORMAT DELIMITED FIELDS TERMINATED BY ','
AS
SELECT AirlineID, COUNT(*) AS Flights
FROM OnTimePerformancePartition02
GROUP BY AirlineID;
DROP TABLE IF EXISTS OnTimeDepartureFlights;
```

```
CREATE TABLE OnTimeDepartureFlights
ROW FORMAT DELIMITED FIELDS TERMINATED BY ','
AS
SELECT AirlineID, COUNT(*) AS Flights
FROM OnTimePerformancePartition02
WHERE CAST(DepDelay AS INT) <= 0
GROUP BY AirlineID;
```

Next, you create a table (OnTimeDeparturePercent) that contains the percentage of timely flight departures.

```
DROP TABLE IF EXISTS OnTimeDeparturePercent;
CREATE TABLE OnTimeDeparturePercent
ROW FORMAT DELIMITED FIELDS TERMINATED BY ','
AS
SELECT DimAirline.Airline,
100.0*OnTimeDepartureFlights.Flights/TotalFlights.Flights AS
OnTimeDeparturePercentage
FROM TotalFlights
INNER JOIN DimAirline ON DimAirline.AirlineID = TotalFlights.AirlineID
LEFT JOIN OnTimeDepartureFlights ON TotalFlights.AirlineID = OnTimeDepartureFlights.
AirlineID;
```

Then you query the data. As you can see in Figure 13.20, Hawaiian Airlines has the highest, with a timely departure history of close to 82 percent. Southwest Airlines has the lowest ranking, with a timely departure history of 39 percent for the 6 months of data collected.

```
SELECT Airline, OnTimeDeparturePercentage FROM OnTimeDeparturePercent
ORDER BY OnTimeDeparturePercentage DESC;
```

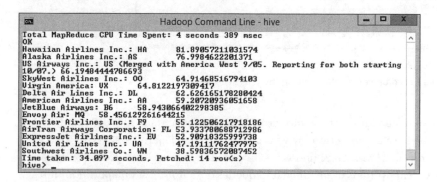

FIGURE 13.20
Partition information for a table that got data from the dynamic partition insert process.

Data Analysis of Cancelled Flights, Based on Cancellation Reason

The next script queries on-time flight performance data for 6 months and identifies the count of cancellation, based on cancellation reason, by year and month (see Figure 13.21). As you can see, you have not used any partitioning column in the WHERE predicate, so data is queried from all the available partitions of the table (with no partition elimination).

```
SELECT P.Year, P.Month, C.Cancellation, COUNT(*) AS TotalCancellation
FROM OnTimePerformancePartition02 AS P
INNER JOIN DimCancellation AS C ON P.CancellationCode = C.CancellationID
WHERE P.Cancelled = 1
GROUP BY P.Year, P.Month, C.Cancellation
ORDER BY P.Year, P.Month, C.Cancellation;
```

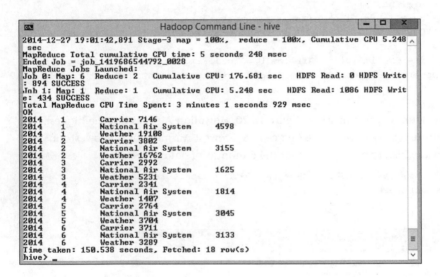

FIGURE 13.21
Flight cancellation count based on cancellation reason, by year and month.

Next, you query the on-time flight performance data for 6 months and identify the count of cancellation based on cancellation reason, by year and month (see Figure 13.22). This time, however, you are using PartitionYear and PartitionMonth in the WHERE predicate. Hive thus eliminates the other partitions of the table and queries data from just one partition that matches the criteria.

```
SELECT P.Year, P.Month, C.Cancellation, COUNT(*) AS TotalCancellation
FROM OnTimePerformancePartition02 AS P
INNER JOIN DimCancellation AS C ON P.CancellationCode = C.CancellationID
WHERE PartitionYear = 2014 AND PartitionMonth = 4 AND P.Cancelled = 1
```

```
GROUP BY P.Year, P.Month, C.Cancellation
ORDER BY P.Year, P.Month, C.Cancellation;
```

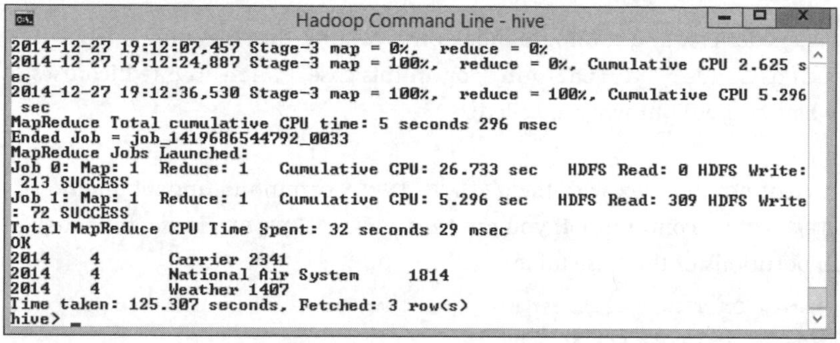

FIGURE 13.22
Partition information for a table that got data from the dynamic partition insert process.

The following script is same as the earlier one, although this time it uses `FlightDate` in the selection and grouping. It also uses `PartitionYear` and `PartitionMonth` in the `WHERE` predicate, so Hive will eliminate the other partitions of the table and query data from just one partition that matches the criteria.

```
SELECT P.Year, P.Month, P.FlightDate, C.Cancellation,
COUNT(*) AS TotalCancellation
FROM OnTimePerformancePartition02 AS P
INNER JOIN DimCancellation AS C ON P.CancellationCode = C.CancellationID
WHERE PartitionYear = 2014 AND PartitionMonth = 4 AND P.Cancelled = 1
GROUP BY P.Year, P.Month, P.FlightDate, C.Cancellation
ORDER BY P.Year, P.Month, P.FlightDate, C.Cancellation;
```

Indexing in Hive

You have learned about partitioned tables and seen how Hive uses partition elimination to consider during query processing only partitions that contain the data requested; Hive ignores the other partitions, to improve performance. This works in most cases, but sometimes you want better performance while reading data from a single partition.

Hive supports creating indexes on a table or on partitions (all or some of the partitions) of a table to further improve performance. Hive enables you to create two types of indexes, Compact and Bitmap:

▶ **Compact index**— With a Compact index, instead of storing the HDFS location of each occurrence of a particular value, Hive stores only the addresses of the HDFS blocks that contain that value. This keeps the index small because there are fewer blocks than the actual rows with those values. This has been optimized for point-lookups, in case a value occurs more than once in nearby rows, but filtering out the other rows from the indexed blocks during query processing requires extra work.

▶ **Bitmap index—** Consider creating a Bitmap index on a column that has only a few distinct values, such as Gender, Marital status, or, in this case, Cancelled (which uses 1 or 0 to indicate whether the flight was cancelled).

Consider the syntax for creating an index with the CREATE INDEX command and rebuilding and index with the ALTER INDEX command. If you omit the PARTITION BY clause, the index spans or rebuilds for all partitions of the base table:

```
CREATE INDEX <index name> ON TABLE <table name> (<column name to be indexed>)
AS ['BITMAP' or 'COMPACT'] WITH DEFERRED REBUILD
[PARTITION (column1, column2,...)];

ALTER INDEX <index name> ON <table name> [PARTITION (column1, column2,...)]
REBUILD;
```

The following script shows how you can create a Compact index on a column of a table using the CREATE INDEX command and then rebuild it using the ALTER INDEX command:

```
CREATE INDEX IDX_OnTimePerformancePartition02_OriginAirportID_C
ON TABLE OnTimePerformancePartition02 (OriginAirportID) AS 'COMPACT'
WITH DEFERRED REBUILD;

ALTER INDEX IDX_OnTimePerformancePartition02_OriginAirportID_C
ON OnTimePerformancePartition02 REBUILD;
```

The next script shows how you can create a Bitmap index on a column of a table using the CREATE INDEX command and then rebuild it using the ALTER INDEX command:

```
CREATE INDEX IDX_OnTimePerformancePartition02_Cancelled_B
ON TABLE OnTimePerformancePartition02 (Cancelled) AS 'BITMAP'
WITH DEFERRED REBUILD;

ALTER INDEX IDX_OnTimePerformancePartition02_Cancelled_B
ON OnTimePerformancePartition02 REBUILD;
```

The clause WITH DEFERRED REBUILD states not to rebuild the index structure right after the CREATE INDEX command execution, even if the table contains data. It just creates the metadata and waits for you to run ALTER INDEX ... REBUILD to build the actual index structure for a table or the partitions of a partitioned table. With the ALTER INDEX ... REBUILD command, you can also specify whether you want an index to be built for all the partitions of the table or some specific partitions only. For example, the next script rebuilds an index for just one partition of the table, where PartitionYear = 2014 and PartitionMonth = 4:

```
ALTER INDEX IDX_OnTimePerformancePartition02_Cancelled_B
ON OnTimePerformancePartition02
PARTITION (PartitionYear = 2014, PartitionMonth = 4) REBUILD;
```

As with indexes in an RDBMS system that need to be rebuilt after a data change (especially if the change is huge), indexes in Hive need to be rebuilt using the ALTER INDEX ... REBUILD command, to bring index data up to date.

NOTE

Index: Overhead Versus Performance Gain

Based on the amount of data you have, an index rebuild can take significant time. Consider rebuilding an index for a partition that went through a change instead of rebuilding indexes for all the partitions of a table.

Note that although an index might improve performance in certain cases, it has overhead both in additional processing time needed whenever data of the base table changes and in disk space to store index data. In our testing, we saw only a small improvement in query performance with an index, whereas an index rebuild took a long time. Be sure to evaluate your need for an index for your query and its possible benefit to you.

This line shows how you can create a Compact index on a column of the table:

```
SHOW FORMATTED INDEX ON OnTimePerformancePartition02;
```

If not needed, you can drop an existing index with this script:

```
DROP INDEX IF EXISTS IDX_OnTimePerformancePartition02_Cancelled_B
ON OnTimePerformancePartition02;
```

Apache Tez in Action

In Hour 12, you looked at Apache Tez in detail. In this section, you learn how to run some queries and analyze performance difference when using default the MapReduce execution engine and the Tez execution engine. The next script queries data from a partitioned table (from all the partitions of a table because there is no partition column in the WHERE predicate) after grouping. Note that we ran this test on an HDInsight cluster with two compute nodes only; with bigger datasets in a bigger cluster, you might expect to get even better performance gain.

```
SELECT P.Year, P.Month, C.Cancellation, COUNT(*) AS TotalCancellation
FROM OnTimePerformancePartition02 AS P
INNER JOIN DimCancellation AS C ON P.CancellationCode = C.CancellationID
WHERE P.Cancelled = 1
GROUP BY P.Year, P.Month, C.Cancellation
ORDER BY P.Year, P.Month, C.Cancellation;
```

Figure 13.23 shows the execution result of this script with the default MapReduce execution engine. This query took 173 seconds.

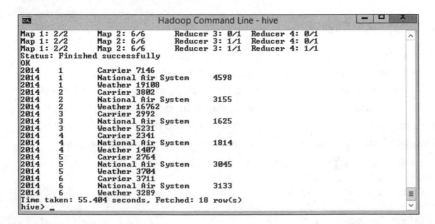

```
Hadoop Command Line - hive

: 894 SUCCESS
Job 1: Map: 1    Reduce: 1    Cumulative CPU: 5.578 sec    HDFS Read: 1086 HDFS Writ
e: 434 SUCCESS
Total MapReduce CPU Time Spent: 3 minutes 13 seconds 292 msec
OK
2014    1        Carrier 7146
2014    1        National Air System    4598
2014    1        Weather 19108
2014    2        Carrier 3802
2014    2        National Air System    3155
2014    2        Weather 16762
2014    3        Carrier 2992
2014    3        National Air System    1625
2014    3        Weather 5231
2014    4        Carrier 2341
2014    4        National Air System    1814
2014    4        Weather 1407
2014    5        Carrier 2764
2014    5        National Air System    3045
2014    5        Weather 3704
2014    6        Carrier 3711
2014    6        National Air System    3133
2014    6        Weather 3289
Time taken: 172.728 seconds, Fetched: 18 row(s)
hive>
```

FIGURE 13.23
Execution result of a query with the default MapReduce execution engine for all the partitions of the table.

Now let's switch the default MapReduce execution engine and use the Tez execution engine in the current Hive session:

```
set hive.execution.engine=tez;
```

Figure 13.24 shows the execution result of this script with the Tez execution engine. Notice that, this time, the same query, with the same set of data, took just 55 seconds. This is an improvement of about three times when using the Tez execution engine.

```
Hadoop Command Line - hive

Map 1: 2/2      Map 2: 6/6      Reducer 3: 0/1    Reducer 4: 0/1
Map 1: 2/2      Map 2: 6/6      Reducer 3: 1/1    Reducer 4: 0/1
Map 1: 2/2      Map 2: 6/6      Reducer 3: 1/1    Reducer 4: 1/1
Status: Finished successfully
OK
2014    1        Carrier 7146
2014    1        National Air System    4598
2014    1        Weather 19108
2014    2        Carrier 3802
2014    2        National Air System    3155
2014    2        Weather 16762
2014    3        Carrier 2992
2014    3        National Air System    1625
2014    3        Weather 5231
2014    4        Carrier 2341
2014    4        National Air System    1814
2014    4        Weather 1407
2014    5        Carrier 2764
2014    5        National Air System    3045
2014    5        Weather 3704
2014    6        Carrier 3711
2014    6        National Air System    3133
2014    6        Weather 3289
Time taken: 55.404 seconds, Fetched: 18 row(s)
hive>
```

FIGURE 13.24
Execution result of query with the Tez execution engine for all the partitions of the table.

Now let's run the following query, which queries data from only a single partition of the main table:

```
SELECT P.Year, P.Month, C.Cancellation, COUNT(*) AS TotalCancellation
FROM OnTimePerformancePartition02 AS P
INNER JOIN DimCancellation AS C ON P.CancellationCode = C.CancellationID
WHERE PartitionYear = 2014 AND PartitionMonth = 4 AND P.Cancelled = 1
GROUP BY P.Year, P.Month, C.Cancellation
ORDER BY P.Year, P.Month, C.Cancellation;
```

Figure 13.25 shows the execution result of this script with the default MapReduce execution engine. Notice that this query took 119 seconds when querying from the selected partition of the table.

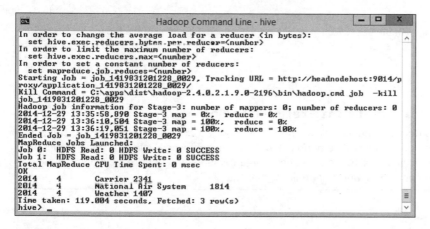

FIGURE 13.25
Execution result of query with the default MapReduce engine for a selected partition of the table.

Figure 13.26 shows the execution result of the previous script (for the selected partition) with the Tez execution engine. This time, the same query, with the same set of data, took just 37 seconds, an improvement of about three times when using the Tez execution engine.

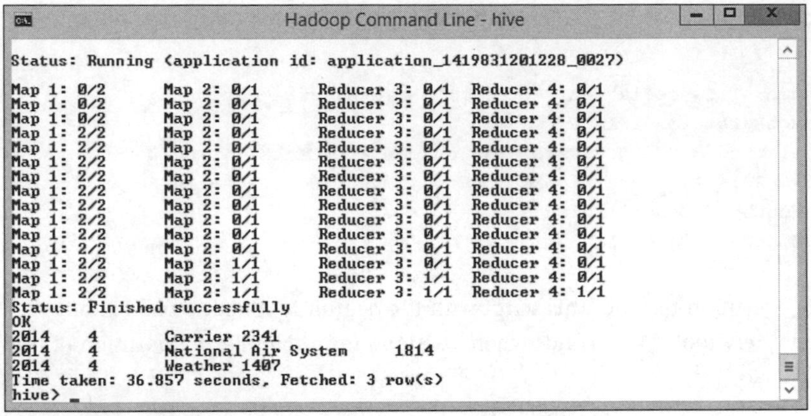

FIGURE 13.26
Execution result of query with the Tez execution engine for the selected partition of the table.

NOTE

Query Performance with the Tez Execution Engine

The previous queries were executed on smaller datasets on an HDInsight cluster with two compute nodes. We could see about a three-time performance improvement when using the Tez execution engine. Think of situations in which where you have large datasets and query execution on a large HDInsight cluster. The difference would be really significant.

Apache HCatalog

Apache HCatalog has merged with Apache Hive in the latest release of HDInsight and has become a key component of Hive. HCatalog supports all the Hive DDL commands except ones that kick off MapReduce jobs in the background (such as CTAS and ALTER INDEX...REBUILD).

Apache HCatalog provides a metadata layer for interoperability or a data storage abstraction layer built on top of the Hive metastore, and it incorporates components from the Hive DDL. It provides an abstraction of Hadoop data, with a relational view of the data stored in HDFS; users don't need to worry about where or in what format their data is stored in HDFS. The end result is complete data storage independence because a change in storage format will not have a ripple effect on the other applications dependent on it.

You can think of Apache HCatalog as a table and storage management layer for Hadoop, providing table and storage abstraction. You can think about data in the HDFS as if it were a set of tables. Users thus can use different data-processing tools, such as MapReduce, Hive, and Pig, to more easily read and write data on the HDFS. It presents a common table layer or a shared schema and data types to each of these data processing tools and gives each user the same data model, to enable interoperability across the tools.

NOTE

As of this writing, HCatalog supports creating tabular view of the data from text file, CSV, JSON, sequence file, RCFile, ORC, and any other file format for which a Hive SerDe is available or can be written. HCatalog has a REST-based API for letting the external system access it.

In Figure 13.27, no matter who creates a table in HCatalog, the table will be available to other data-processing tools. This gives you a greater degree of interoperability.

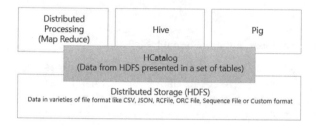

FIGURE 13.27
How HCatalog interfaces between HDFS and data-processing tools.

In summary, take a look at what HCatalog is and the benefits it provides:

▶ Abstracted view of the HDFS data in a relational or tabular format. Tables can be partitioned, too.

▶ No need for users to worry about where or in what format their data is stored in HDFS.

▶ A single, uniform interface for reading and writing data in HDFS with data-processing tools such as Hive, Pig, and MapReduce.

▶ A REST API for external systems to access it.

▶ In recent release, HCatalog merged with Hive to support all the data types that Hive supports.

▶ Support for a subset of the Hive DDL commands. Commands that trigger MapReduce jobs are not supported.

▶ Notification of a new partition or set of new partitions so that workflow tools, such as Oozie, can be notified when new data becomes available. This helps you set up a process to maintain a sliding window scenario for your partitioned table.

Summary

In this hour, you explored programming with Hive. You looked at the different types of tables Hive supports, how table partitioning improves the performance of your queries, and how to efficiently maintain partitions. You investigated loading data into Hive tables based on different scenarios, and you explored writing queries for ad hoc queries, summarization, and data analysis. You also looked into leveraging the Tez execution engine and saw how it significantly improves the performance of the query.

In the next hour, you see how you can consume HDInsight data from Microsoft BI tools by using the Hive ODBC driver.

Q&A

Q. What is the difference between an internal table and an external table?

A. An internal table is also called a managed table because, for this table, Hive manages and controls the data. During internal table creation, Hive copies data from the source files to a subdirectory (for each table, there is a subdirectory with the same name as the table) of the root directory of the database (by default, the location is `/hive/warehouse/`) at the time the data loads. If you specify a different location than the default, it does not copy data but only points to that location. When you drop an internal table, Hive deletes the associated data as well, along with metadata information about the table.

When you create an external table, Hive does not copy data from the source files to a subdirectory of the root directory of the database (by default, the location is `/hive/warehouse/`). Instead, Hive just creates a table, its metadata, and a reference to the data in its original location. Of course, unlike with an internal table, when you drop an external table, only the table's metadata gets deleted, not the actual data (because the table does not own data).

Q. What is partitioning of a table, and how does it help in improving query performance?

A. Partitioning is a process of horizontally slicing data so that large datasets can be segmented into more manageable smaller chunks. A Hive table can be partitioned by one or more columns by specifying it when you create a table using the `CREATE TABLE` command or when you modify it using the `ALTER TABLE` command. For a partitioned table, data is stored in one directory per partition. Hive uses partition elimination to query only the partitions that have the requested data; Hive ignores the other partitions of the table if they don't hold qualifying rows that the query has requested.

Exercise

Execute the queries we explored in this hour with the default MapReduce execution engine (`set hive.execution.engine=mr;`) and the Tez execution engine (`set hive.execution.engine=tez;`). Analyze the difference in the performance.

Consuming HDInsight Data from Microsoft BI Tools over Hive ODBC Driver: Part 1

What You'll Learn in This Hour:

▶ Introduction to Hive ODBC Driver
▶ Introduction to Microsoft Power BI
▶ Accessing Hive Data from Microsoft Excel

The last hour detailed programming in Apache Hive. You learned about the different types of objects you can create and explored how to write HiveQL queries to retrieve data for analysis.

You also created several objects in the last hour that you will use in this hour for further analysis and ad hoc reporting with different Microsoft Business Intelligence (MSBI) reporting tools.

Introduction to Hive ODBC Driver

Microsoft, in collaboration with Simba Technologies, has developed Microsoft Hive ODBC Driver to connect to HDInsight cluster or HDInsight emulator and retrieve Hive-based data directly using either HiveQL or standard SQL commands. This enables business intelligence (BI), analytics, and reporting tools to directly access Hive-based data from Hadoop, virtually in no time. This saves you from writing a separate data movement layer, to first bring in data locally from HDInsight cluster and then do reporting on the local stored data.

While querying, you have a choice of using either standard SQL or HiveQL commands. If you are passing a standard SQL command, the Hive ODBC Driver internally and efficiently transforms it into an equivalent HiveQL query for execution on an HDInsight cluster.

Microsoft Hive ODBC Driver complies with the ODBC 3.52 data standard and is available for installation on either 32-bit or 64-bit Windows machines. If you have 64-bit machine, you should use the 64-bit version for better performance.

If you have a large dataset, you should use 64-bit installation to avoid this exception:

"Memory error: Allocation failure: Not enough storage is available to process this command. If using a 32-bit version of the product, consider upgrading to the 64-bit version or increasing the amount of memory available on the machine.

The current operation was cancelled because another operation in the transaction failed."

32-Bit Versus 64-Bit Hive ODBC Driver

You need to understand these two variants of Hive ODBC Driver to properly configure Hive ODBC Driver or Data Source Names (DSN). Otherwise, it might not work because it's loading the wrong kind of driver.

You can install and configure both variants of Hive ODBC Driver (32-bit and 64-bit) side by side on a 64-bit Windows machine. You should know, however, that 64-bit applications can use only the 64-bit driver or DSN, and 32-bit applications can use only the 32-bit driver or DSN. For example, if you have a 64-bit Windows machine with 32-bit Excel and 64-bit SQL Server, to use the driver correctly from Excel, you must install and configure the 32-bit Hive ODBC Driver. Similarly, to use the driver from SQL Server, you must install and configure the 64-bit Hive ODBC Driver.

Setting Up the Hive ODBC Driver

Microsoft Hive ODBC Driver is a free download that you can find at this link, based on your 32-bit or 64-bit Windows platform and the applications that will be using it (see Figure 14.1): http://www.microsoft.com/en-us/download/details.aspx?id=40886.

Version:	Date Published:
1.1.0.0	11/13/2014
File Name:	**File Size:**
HiveODBC32.msi	9.0 MB
HiveODBC64.msi	10.3 MB

FIGURE 14.1
Hive ODBC Driver deployment options.

After installing the Hive ODBC Driver, you can type **Data Source** in the Search box on Windows 8 to see options to configure both the 32-bit and 64-bit ODBC sources (see Figure 14.2).

FIGURE 14.2
Setting up ODBC data sources—32-bit versus 64-bit.

You can choose either of these, based on your specific need or the bit-ness of the applications that will be accessing Hive-based data.

If you are using other versions of the Windows operating system, you can go to the Control Panel and then open either ODBC Data Sources (32-Bit) or ODBC Data Sources (32-Bit) under Administrative Tools.

By default, on a 64-bit Windows machine, you can access 64-bit ODBC Data Source Administrator from the Control Panel. If you want to use the 32-bit version of ODBC Data Source Administrator on a 64-bit Windows machine, you can execute this command in Run: `C:\WINDOWS\SysWOW64\odbcad32.exe`.

TRY IT YOURSELF ▼

Configuring the 64-Bit Driver

In the ODBC Data Source Administrator (64-Bit) dialog box, go to the System DSN tab and click the Add button (see Figure 14.3).

TIP

A system DSN is available to all users who log in to the machine. A user DSN is available only to the user who creates the DSN.

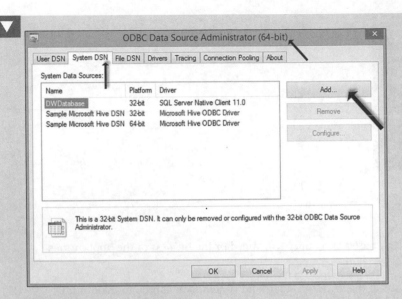

FIGURE 14.3
ODBC Data Source Administrator (64-Bit) dialog box.

In the Create New Data Source Wizard, select Microsoft Hive ODBC Driver (see Figure 14.4) and click Finish. If you don't find Microsoft Hive ODBC Driver listed there, then the 64-bit Hive ODBC Driver is not yet installed.

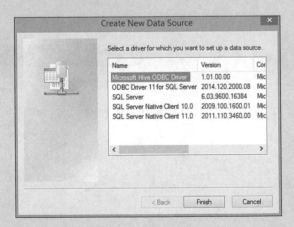

FIGURE 14.4
Create New Data Source Wizard (64-bit).

Clicking Finish brings up the Microsoft Hive ODBC Driver DSN Setup page for 64-bit DSN setup (see Figure 14.5). You must specify the following settings for the DSN:

▶ **Data Source Name**—This is the name for your DSN.

Microsoft Hive ODBC Driver DSN Setup	✕
Data Source Name:	HiveODBC64 to tyhdicluster
Description:	64-bit Hive ODBC DSN to tyhdicluster
Host:	tyhdicluster.azurehdinsight.net
Port:	443
Database:	default
Hive Server Type:	Hive Server 2 ⌄
Authentication	
Mechanism:	Windows Azure HDInsight Service ⌄
Realm:	
Host FQDN:	
Service Name:	
HTTP Path:	
User Name:	tyhdiadmin
Password:	●●●●●●●●●●|
Delegation UID:	
	Advanced Options...
v1.1.0.0 (64 bit)	Test OK Cancel

FIGURE 14.5
Microsoft Hive ODBC Drive DSN setup (64-bit).

▶ **Description**—This is an optional description for your DSN.

▶ **Host**—Specify the cluster name, IP address, or hostname of the Hive server. For the HDInsight service, it should be in the form of `<cluster name>.azurehdinsight.net`.

▶ **Port**—Specify the port number on which the service is listening. The default is 443.

▶ **Database**—Specify the name of the database to refer to when a query does not explicitly specify it. You can still execute queries involving other databases by explicitly specifying the database name in the query with a two-part naming convention (`<database name>.<table name>`).

▶ **Hive Server Type**—You can keep the default of Hive Server 2.

NOTE

Hive Server 2 is the latest implementation that addresses the concurrency limitation imposed by Hive Server 1. Moreover, authentication is available only for Hive Server 2.

▶ **Authentication**—Depending on whether you are connecting to HDInsight Service or HDInsight emulator, select either Windows Azure HDInsight Service or Windows Azure HDInsight Emulator. You can specify a username and password to connect to the HDInsight cluster.

Click the Test button to verify connectivity with the HDInsight cluster, based on the details provided.

Click Advanced Options to specify advanced settings for the Hive ODBC DSN (see Figure 14.6).

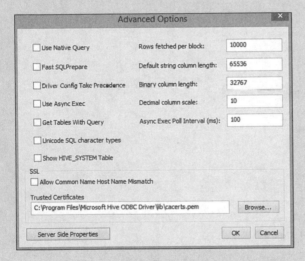

FIGURE 14.6
Advanced options of Hive ODBC DSN.

▶ **Use Native Query**—By default, Hive ODBC Driver uses SQL Connector to translate standard SQL-92 queries into equivalent HiveQL queries. You can check this option to turn off this feature if you are directly passing HiveQL queries.

▶ **Fast SQLPrepare**—Check this option to defer HiveQL query execution to retrieve the result set metadata for SQLPrepare. If the result set metadata is not required after calling SQLPrepare, enabling this option will improve performance.

▶ **Driver Config Take Precedence**—Check this option to allow ODBC Driver–wide configurations to take precedence over connection string and DSN settings.

- ▶ **Use Async Exec**—Check this option to use the asynchronous version of the API call against the Hive Server when executing a query.

- ▶ **Get Tables with Query**—This is applicable only when you are using Hive Server 2. Turn on this option to retrieve the names of tables in a particular database using the SHOW TABLES query.

- ▶ **Unicode SQL Character Types**—Check this option to enable the ODBC Driver to return Unicode characters (of type SQL_WVARCHAR or SQL_WCHAR) instead of non-Unicode characters (of type SQL_VARCHAR or SQL_CHAR).

- ▶ **Show HIVE_SYSTEM Table**—Check this option to enable the ODBC driver to return the HIVE_SYSTEM pseudo table for catalog function calls such as SQLTables and SQLColumns. The pseudo table is under the pseudo schema HIVE_SYSTEM. The table has two String type columns, ENVKEY and ENVVALUE. We demonstrate this in the section "Accessing Hive Data from SQL Server," in Hour 15.

- ▶ **Rows Fetched Per Block**—You can specify any 32-bit positive integer to indicate the number of rows to bundle into a single block. The default value of 10,000 rows per block works best in most scenarios.

- ▶ **Default String Column Length**—Specify the maximum data length for columns, with the string data type, to be considered during query execution.

GO TO ▶ We look more at the string column length setting in the section **"Accessing Hive Data from SQL Server,"** in Hour 15.

- ▶ **Binary Column Length**—Specify the maximum data length for columns, with binary data type, to be considered during query execution.

- ▶ **Decimal Column Scale**—Specify the maximum number of digits to the right of the decimal point for numeric data types.

- ▶ **Async Exec Poll Interval (ms)**—Specify the time (in milliseconds) between each poll of the query execution status (asynchronous RPC call used to execute a query against Hive).

Optionally, you can click the Server Side Properties button (see Figure 14.6) to add, modify, or delete server-side properties. To do so, you specify appropriate keys and values to configure the Hive ODBC Driver to apply each server-side property you set by executing a query when opening a session to Hive Server 2.

Configuring the 32-Bit Driver

In the ODBC Data Source Administrator (32-Bit) dialog box, go to the System DSN tab and click the Add button (see Figure 14.7).

FIGURE 14.7
Microsoft Hive ODBC Driver DSN setup (32-bit).

In the Create New Data Source wizard, select Microsoft Hive ODBC Driver (refer to Figure 14.4) and click the Finish button. If you don't find Microsoft Hive ODBC Driver listed there, it indicates that the 32-bit Hive ODBC Driver is not yet installed.

Clicking Finish brings up the Microsoft Hive ODBC Driver DSN Setup page for 32-bit DSN setup (see Figure 14.7). Specify the values as mentioned in the previous section "Setting Up the Hive ODBC Driver."

As discussed in the previous section, you can click the Test button to verify connectivity with HDInsight cluster. Click the Advanced Options button to specify other advanced settings.

Introduction to Microsoft Power BI

Microsoft Power BI is a cloud-based self-service BI solution for the enterprise. It enables users to get insight into virtually any type of data (including data from HDInsight cluster) in the familiar Microsoft Excel, which users have been using for several decades.

Power BI empowers end users and provides tools to take care of end-to-end business intelligence scenario for Self-Service BI solution—for example:

▶ Leveraging Power Query for data discovery and combining data from different sources including HDInsight cluster

▶ Using PowerPivot to model the data from different sources, such as defining the relationship, creating hierarchies, using KPIs and measures, and so on)

▶ When the model is ready, visualizing the data from different perspectives with different intuitive and interactive visualization options in Power View and Power Map

NOTE

For our purpose, *end users* are people with all levels of skills, including data analysts, power users, business users, data stewards, and folks from the IT department.

Power BI is a broad umbrella that contains four major Excel add-ins (Power Query, PowerPivot, Power View, and Power Map). Power BI also integrates with Office 365, which, in turn, is built on a scalable, manageable, and trusted cloud platform. This integration provides better self-service analytics in the cloud, better collaboration capabilities: Users can now share reports they have created with other folks in the organization with the help of Office 365 online services, access these reports from anywhere in a browser or on mobile devices, ask questions of data in a natural language, and more.

NOTE

You can learn more about Power BI at http://www.microsoft.com/en-us/server-cloud/solutions/business-intelligence/self-service.aspx.

Accessing Hive Data from Microsoft Excel

Microsoft Excel is one of the most widely used applications globally. People from all departments use Microsoft Excel in their daily lives. To empower all those users, Microsoft supports accessing Hive-based data in familiar Excel from HDInsight cluster—so it's not just limited to IT people.

The following Try It Yourself exercise demonstrates how you can use Microsoft Excel 2013 to access Hive-based data from HDInsight cluster.

▼ TRY IT YOURSELF

Accessing Hive-Based Data from an HDInsight Cluster

To begin, open a new Excel file, click the Data tab, click From Other Sources, and then click From Microsoft Query (see Figure 14.8).

TIP

You can also choose From Data Connection Wizard, which has a similar interface, to use Hive ODBC Driver to retrieve Hive-based data.

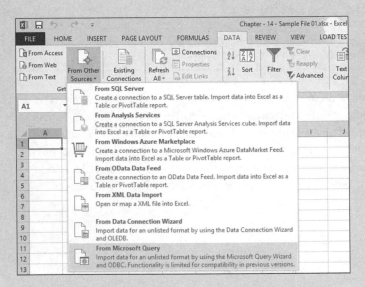

FIGURE 14.8
Accessing Hive-based data using Microsoft Query.

On the Choose Data Source screen, you can select the DSN you created earlier in the section "Setting Up the Hive ODBC Driver" (see Figure 14.9). (Because we have 32-bit Excel, we can see only 32-bit DSNs here.) Click OK to continue; you are prompted to specify the username and password to connect to the HDInsight cluster.

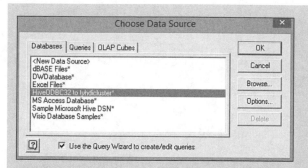

FIGURE 14.9
Choose Data Source screen.

On the Query Wizard—Choose Columns screen, you can see all the Hive tables available on the connected HDInsight cluster. You can choose a table from the left and add columns of the table, to be retrieved, in the right text box (see Figure 14.10).

TIP

In this exercise, we have selected only one table; however, you can select multiple tables and define the relationship between them to get the combined result set.

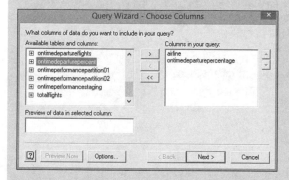

FIGURE 14.10
Choosing tables and columns.

On the Query Wizard—Filter Data screen, you can specify any filter if you want to restrict the row to be returned (see Figure 14.11).

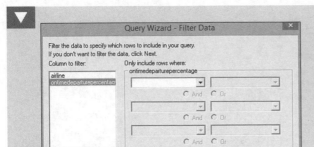

FIGURE 14.11
Specify a filter, if any.

On the Query Wizard—Sort Order screen, you can specify column(s) and their sort order, if any. In our case, we want the result set to be sorted on the OnTimeDeparturePercentage column in descending order.

On the Query Wizard—Finish screen, you can specify where you want the retrieved data to be placed. Click the Save Query button to save the query if you want to use it later. Clicking the Finish button starts retrieving data from the HDInsight cluster; depending on your query and the amount of data, it might take some time.

After the HDInsight cluster retrieves the data, it should look like Figure 14.12. Bringing in data from HDInsight cluster is easy in your familiar Excel tool. Depending on your need, you can apply any of the formatting options or features available in Excel.

For example, based on the data retrieved, we wanted to create a pie chart. We first formatted `OnTimeDeparturePercentage` to have single a digit after the decimal. Then we inserted a pie chart (see Figure 14.13).

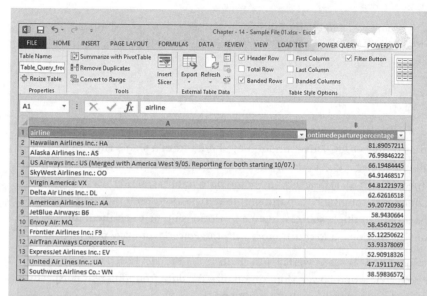

FIGURE 14.12
Retrieved data in Excel from the Hive table.

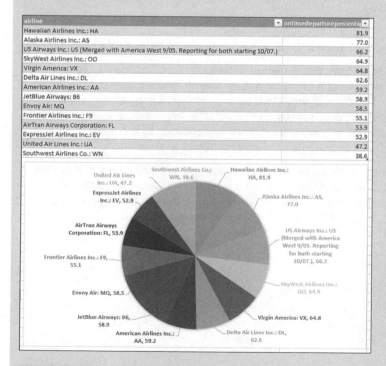

FIGURE 14.13
You can format and visualize the data you want when it is in Excel.

This is the power of the seamless integration of HDInsight cluster with Excel. With just a few clicks and in just a few minutes, you create an appealing report to get insight.

Summary

In this hour, you created a Hive ODBC Driver and retrieved data from a single Hive table. You also created one small report that retrieves data, but it's not limited to that only. Microsoft Excel empowers end users (people with all skill levels, including data analysts, power users, business users, data stewards, and folks from the IT department) to retrieve data from multiple tables (from either a single source or multiple sources), define a relationship between them, apply transformations, create calculations, and much more with the PowerPivot Excel add-in.

In the next hour, you learn how to use PowerPivot to create a data model based on different tables. Then you use Power View and Power Map to visualize the data from different perspectives with different intuitive and interactive visualization options.

Q&A

Q. What is the Hive ODBC Driver? What's the difference between 32-bit and 64-bit drivers?

A. Microsoft Hive ODBC Driver allows SQL Server or other MSBI reporting tools to connect to an HDInsight cluster or HDInsight Emulator and retrieve Hive-based data directly using either HiveQL or standard SQL commands. This enables business intelligence (BI), analytics, and reporting tools to directly access Hive-based data from Hadoop in virtually no time. This saves you from writing a separate data movement layer to first bring in data locally from HDInsight cluster and then do reporting on the local stored data.

Microsoft Hive ODBC Driver is available for installation on either 32-bit or 64-bit Windows machines. You can install and configure both variants of Hive ODBC Driver (32-bit and 64-bit versions on a 64-bit Windows machine) side by side. However, 64-bit applications can use only the 64-bit driver or DSN, and 32-bit applications can use only the 32-bit driver or DSN.

Consuming HDInsight Data from Microsoft BI Tools over Hive ODBC Driver: Part 2

What You'll Learn in This Hour:

▶ Accessing Hive Data from PowerPivot

▶ Accessing Hive Data from SQL Server

▶ Accessing HDInsight Data from Power Query

In the last hour, you checked out the Hive ODBC driver and saw how to retrieve data from a single Hive table in Microsoft Excel. You also created one small report on that retrieved data, but it's not limited to only that.

In this hour, you learn how to use PowerPivot to create a data model (define relationships, apply transformations, create calculations, and more) based on different tables. Then you use Power View and Power Map to visualize the data from different perspectives, with intuitive and interactive visualization options.

NOTE

With the complexity of the topics discussed, some figures in this hour are very detailed. They are intended only to provide a high-level view of the concepts. These figures are representational and are not intended to be read in detail.

Accessing Hive Data from PowerPivot

PowerPivot is an Excel add-in that is supported in both Excel 2010 and Excel 2013. It enables you to do the following:

▶ Create a data model on a massive amount of data from virtually any source, not limited just to the HDInsight cluster

▶ Define relationships among multiple tables, from either a single source or multiple sources

▶ Create measures or calculations, key performance indicators (KPIs), and hierarchies

PowerPivot uses the xVelocity in-memory, column-store engine for lightning-fast analytic performance. It empowers Excel users with powerful, self-service data analysis. With PowerPivot, you can do data mashups on the models you create and explore the data with different visualization options. Your created model can be exposed to Excel, Power View, and Power Map as a report-ready element for analysis and insights.

NOTE

The PowerPivot Excel add-in comes preinstalled with Excel 2013. However, for Excel 2010 you simply need to download the PowerPivot Excel add-in and install it: http://msdn.microsoft.com/en-us/library/gg413462(v=sql.110).aspx.

NOTE

PowerPivot xVelocity Engine

PowerPivot leverages the xVelocity columnar data store engine for storing data in a highly compressed format in memory at runtime, and it gets you past the 1 million row limit in Excel. This technology makes analysis significantly faster in Excel with PowerPivot. Furthermore, PowerPivot can be deployed to SharePoint for collaboration, to share with a wider audience and convert individual or personal business intelligence (BI) solutions to team or organization BI.

▼ TRY IT YOURSELF

Enabling PowerPivot

After you install PowerPivot, you must enable it. Launch an Excel application; click File, Options; select the COM Add-ins for Manage combo box; and then click the Go button (see Figure 15.1).

NOTE

Keep in mind that PowerPivot comes preinstalled with Excel 2013, so you don't need to install it separately.

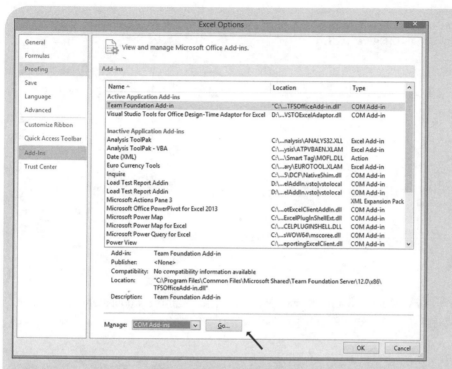

FIGURE 15.1
Excel options to add "add-ins."

As you can see in Figure 15.2, you select PowerPivot, Power View, Power Map, and Power Query, or whichever is available; then click the OK button to return to the Excel document.

GO TO ▶ We talk about other tools for consuming HDInsight data later in this hour.

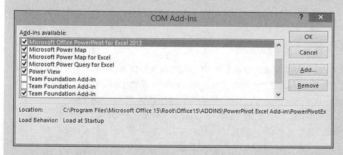

FIGURE 15.2
Submitting Power BI tools for use.

When these tools are enabled, click the PowerPivot tab and then click the Manage icon on the left side of the ribbon (see Figure 15.3).

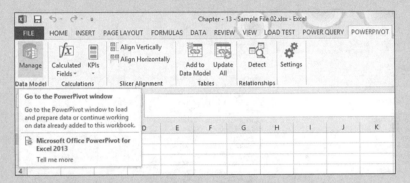

FIGURE 15.3
Launching PowerPivot.

In a PowerPivot document (which automatically gets embedded in an Excel document), click the From Other Source icon to launch the Import Wizard (see Figure 15.4).

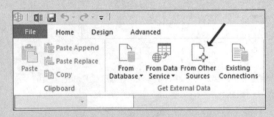

FIGURE 15.4
Launching the Import Wizard.

In the Table Import Wizard, select Others (OLEDB/ODBC) and click the Next button (see Figure 15.5).

On the next screen of the Table Import Wizard, specify a friendly name for the connection (we have named it airlinesdb) and then click the Build button. This launches another dialog box; select the DSN you created in the section "Setting Up the Hive ODBC Driver" in Hour 14, "Consuming HDInsight Data from Microsoft BI Tools over Hive ODBC Driver: Part 1." Specify the username and password to connect to the HDInsight cluster, and click the Test Connection button to verify connectivity to the HDInsight cluster (see Figure 15.6).

FIGURE 15.5
Importing data from ODBC.

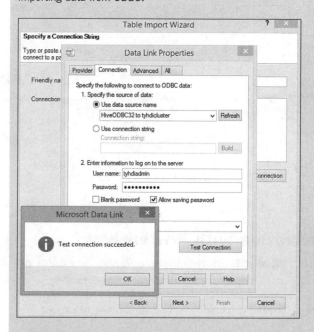

FIGURE 15.6
Creating a connection to an HDInsight cluster and verifying connectivity.

After you verify connection to the HDInsight cluster, click the Next button. On the next screen of the Table Import Wizard, you have two options (you can directly pull data from tables or views, or you can write a query to retrieve data, based on a user-specified query). We demonstrate both of these options later—for now, select the first option to pull data directly from tables or views, and click Next.

The next screen of the Table Import Wizard shows a list of tables or views available on the connected HDInsight cluster. You can select the tables or views to import and specify a friendly name for each one (see Figure 15.7). For each table or view selected, you can preview the data and specify a filter, if needed, to restrict the rows while importing data from the source.

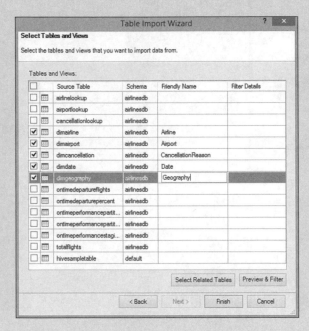

FIGURE 15.7
Selecting tables or views from which to import data.

Reporting and Data Visualization with PowerPivot

In Hour 13, "Programming with Apache Hive, Apache Tez in HDInsight, and Apache HCatalog," you created dimension tables. You use them here to import them into a PowerPivot model.

GO TO ▶ If you don't have these tables already created, refer to the section **"Querying Data from Hive Tables"** in Hour 13 for a guide to creating them.

You also created a fact or transaction table called OnTimePerformancePartition02 that you will import from this table later in this section, by specifying the query and filter with a HiveQL query.

- ▶ DimAirline

- ▶ DimAirport

- ▶ DimCancellation

- ▶ DimDate

- ▶ DimGeography

NOTE

Dimensional Modeling

Dimensional modeling (DM) is a set of techniques and concepts used in data warehouse design and given by Ralph Kimball, one of the original architects of data warehousing. DM always uses the concepts of facts (also called *measures*) and dimensions (also called *context*). Facts are typically (but not always) numeric values that can be aggregated, and dimensions are groups of hierarchies and descriptors or attributes that define the facts (see http://en.wikipedia.org/wiki/Dimensional_modeling).

Dimensions organize data with a relationship to an area of interest—for example, in our case, `Airline`, `Airport`, `Geography`, `CancellationReason`, and `Date` are dimensions. Facts, on the other hand, represent areas of interest—for example, this could include total number of flights, total number of cancelled flights, and average departure delay.

TRY IT YOURSELF

Loading Data into PowerPivot and Visualization

When you click the Finish button (refer to Figure 15.7), data starts importing from the HDInsight cluster. This might take time, depending on the amount of data. You can monitor the progress of the data being loaded into PowerPivot during import and see final information about the load (see Figure 15.8).

TIP

If any error occurs during the data import process, it includes the error message and reason for failure as well.

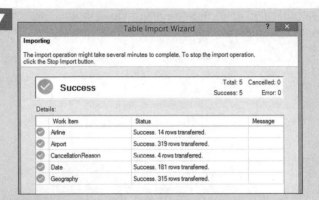

FIGURE 15.8
Data import in progress in the Table Import Wizard.

So far, you have imported all the dimension data by directly importing from Hive tables. Now you will import the data from the OnTimePerformancePartition02 fact table using a query that specifies the data to import with selected columns and filters. Click the Existing Connections icon in the ribbon of the PowerPivot document (see Figure 15.9).

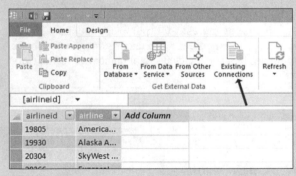

FIGURE 15.9
Importing data from a Hive table from an HDInsight cluster.

In the Table Import Wizard, under PowerPivot Data Connections, select the connection you created earlier in this section (for example, we named it airlinesdb). Then click on Open button available on the bottom; you are prompted to enter a username and password to connect to the HDInsight cluster (see Figure 15.10). Specify these details and click OK to connect and proceed.

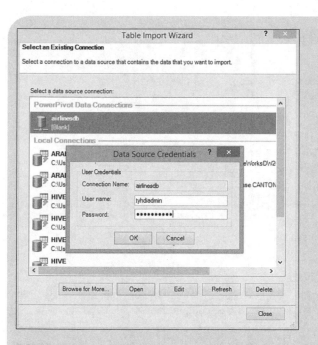

FIGURE 15.10
Connecting to an existing connection.

NOTE

Multiple Data Sources for the PowerPivot Model

In this section, you bring data in from a single data source (HDInsight cluster), for simplicity and brevity. However, PowerPivot enables you to bring data from multiple sources into a single PowerPivot document. You can do data mashups or create appropriate relationships to create your own data model and then publish reports on that model.

On the next screen of the Table Import Wizard, this time select the second option to write your own query (instead of selecting tables or views to import the data) and click Next.

As you can see in Figure 15.11, you must specify a friendly name for your query, and then specify the actual query. This time, to demonstrate, select only a few of the columns from the source table to retrieve data, and specify a filter to bring in data only for May and June.

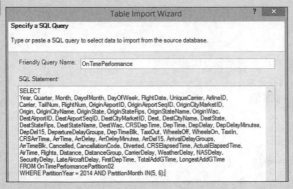

FIGURE 15.11
Specifying a query to retrieve the data from the source.

TIP

As discussed in Hour 13, as the table is partitioned, Hive does not scan the complete table. Instead, it uses partition elimination to retrieve only from partitions that contain data for May and June.

Click Finish to start the data import with the specified query.

Figure 15.12 shows the progress of the data import while executing and shows the final message (whether success or failure—in case of failure, it also gives you failure reason) related to the data import.

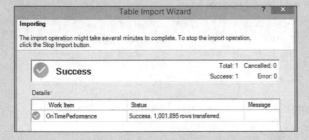

FIGURE 15.12
Status of query execution and data import.

NOTE

Data Refresh in the PowerPivot Model

When we created the PowerPivot data model, we retrieved data from the source (Hive tables in an HDInsight cluster) once. PowerPivot provides a mechanism to refresh the data manually or automatically, based on the schedule, so that you can report on the latest data available in the HDInsight cluster. You can refresh data for an individual table or view a script separately for all the objects at once.

At the bottom right of the PowerPivot window, notice the icon to switch from Grid view to Diagram view, and vice versa. Click the second icon to switch to Diagram view (see Figure 15.13).

FIGURE 15.13
List of tables in a PowerPivot document—default, with no relationship.

NOTE

Transactional systems generally have relationships defined between their tables, to ensure data consistency with each small and frequent update. A data warehouse, however, either does not have this or defers it until reporting, to avoid overhead in maintaining these relationships during a bulk data load.

As you can see in Figure 15.13, the Hive tables we brought from the HDInsight cluster don't have a relationship yet defined. You can define the relationship, to do reporting across multiple tables or views.

To create a relationship, just select the appropriate column from one table and drag it to another appropriate column in another table.

Based on data, PowerPivot automatically identifies the relationship type (such as one-to-many). For example, you can see in Figure 15.14 that we have created these relationships:

▶ `Airline.AirlineId (one)` = `OnTimePerformance.AirlineId (many)`

▶ `Airport.AirpoitId (one)` = `OnTimePerformance.OriginAirportId (many)`

▶ `Cancellation.CancellationId (one)` = `OnTimePerformance.CancellationCode (many)`

▶ `Date.FlightDate (one)` = `OnTimePerformance.FlightDate (many)`

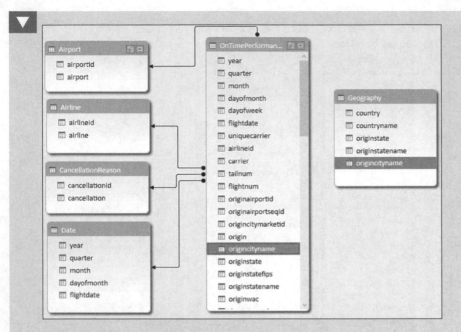

FIGURE 15.14
Establishing an appropriate relationship to create a data model.

NOTE

Role-Playing Dimension

You can even create a role-playing dimension that you can join to the same fact table multiple times, each time to a different column. This offers flexibility in examining the same data from different angles while using the same dimension. For example, in our case, the Airport dimension can be joined on `OriginAirportId` and `DestAirportId` with the OnTimePerformance fact table, to analyze it by both origin airport and destination airport. For the sake of simplicity and brevity, we have joined with the origin airport only.

If you try to create a relationship between the Geography dimension and the OnTimePerformance fact table on OriginalCityName, it will fail with the exception "duplicate values found." This failure occurs because more than one city has the same name (although in different states).

Hence, to make it unique, let's create a calculated column by concatenating the state with the city (see Figure 15.15), in both the Geography dimension and the OnTimePerformance fact table. You can name this column StateCity.

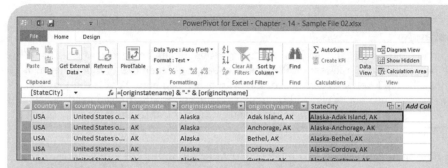

FIGURE 15.15
Creating a calculated column by using the formula = `[originstatename] & "-" &`
`[origincityname]`.

As you can see in Figure 15.16, you can establish a relationship between the Geography
dimension and OnTimePerformance fact table on the basis of the calculated column you created.
You can also see a four-level hierarchy in the Date dimension and a three-level hierarchy in the
Geography dimension.

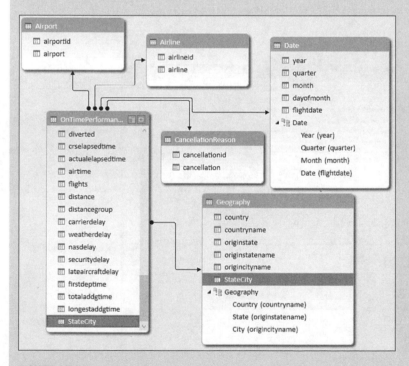

FIGURE 15.16
Establishing a many-to-many relationship and creating hierarchies.

NOTE

Dimension Hierarchy

A *hierarchy* is an arrangement of related attributes of a dimension in different levels, which aids in browsing the data. A hierarchy has a lowest level (called the *leaf level*), then one or more intermediate levels, and finally the top level. For example, for the Date dimension here, Year is the top level, Quarter and Month are intermediate levels, and Date is the leaf level. For the Geography dimension, County is the top level, State is the intermediate level, and City is the leaf level.

When analyzing data from PowerPivot data model, by default, summation is applied for all the numeric columns. You can also create your own calculations or measures with a custom formula. For example, we have created measures with the following formulas in the OnTimePerformance tab of the PowerPivot document (see Figure 15.17):

▶ TotalFlights:=SUM([flights])

▶ CancellationCount:=SUM([cancelled])

▶ AverageArrivalDelay:=AVERAGE([arrdelayminutes])

▶ AverageDepartureDelay:=AVERAGE([depdelayminutes])

▶ DivertedCount:=SUM([diverted])

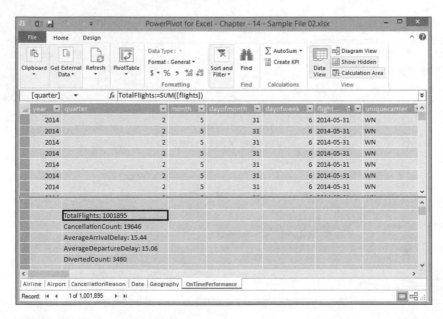

FIGURE 15.17
Creating custom calculations or measures.

By default, all the attributes and measures are visible to the end users in the client tool accessing it. Normally, you hide attributes or measures that are internal or that contain internal identification numbers, to avoid confusing end users.

For example, we have hidden all the attributes of the `OnTimePerformance` fact except the ones we created earlier as calculated measures; likewise we have hidden `AirlineId` from the Airline dimension, `AirportId` from the Airport dimension, and `CancellationId` from the CancellationReason dimension because end users do not normally use these attributes with identification during reporting.

To hide attributes, right-click the attributes and then click Hide from Client Tools.

NOTE

Hiding Attributes

Hiding an attribute is not the same as removing it from the model; a hidden attribute still exists as part of the model. By default, hidden attributes are not visible in client tools, although they can still be accessed using the Data Analysis Expressions (DAX) language.

DAX enables users to define custom calculations in PowerPivot tables (calculated columns) and in Excel PivotTables (measures). DAX includes some functions used in Excel formulas and additional functions that are designed to work with relational data and perform dynamic aggregation. See http://social.technet.microsoft.com/wiki/contents/articles/677.powerpivot-data-analysis-expressions-dax-language.aspx.

Reporting and Data Visualization with Excel

Two icons in the top-left corner of a PowerPivot document enable you to switch between Excel and PowerPivot. Click the Excel icon to switch to Excel or open the Excel document containing the PowerPivot model. Go to the Insert tab and then click PivotTable. In the Create PivotTable dialog box, select Use an External Data Source and then select airlinesdb (remember, this is the name you used for the embedded connection when you created a PowerPivot model) from the Connection in this Workbook section.

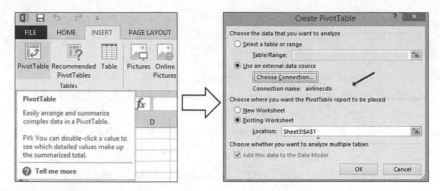

FIGURE 15.18
Accessing the PowerPivot model from Excel.

Now select the measures or calculations you want to analyze from the PivotTable Fields list, on the right side of the Excel document, by default. In Figure 15.19, we have selected all the custom measures we created in the PowerPivot model earlier in this section. To analyze this information by date, we have used the Date hierarchy (notice how the dates roll up into Month, the months roll up into Quarter, and quarters roll up into Year).

Row Labels	TotalFlights	CancellationCount	DivertedCount	AverageArrivalDelay	AverageDepartureDelay
⊟2014	1001895	19646	3460	15.44	15.06
⊟2	1001895	19646	3460	15.44	15.06
⊟5	499278	9513	1692	13.73	13.61
2014-05-01	16839	161	28	14.02	14.45
2014-05-02	16900	83	55	10.59	10.98
2014-05-03	13330	61	22	6.88	7.16
2014-05-04	16006	100	17	7.73	8.16
2014-05-05	16840	139	12	7.44	7.99
2014-05-06	16601	131	11	6.21	6.64
2014-05-07	16741	118	33	7.91	8.04
2014-05-08	16989	896	124	23.97	22.82
2014-05-09	17042	380	77	20.93	19.90
2014-05-10	13187	216	45	10.50	10.68
2014-05-11	15782	348	84	15.59	14.65
2014-05-12	16982	1131	212	24.82	22.44
2014-05-13	16701	1485	136	23.72	24.18
2014-05-14	16864	474	27	17.01	16.66
2014-05-15	17091	418	83	22.39	20.91
2014-05-16	17092	425	30	18.63	18.87
2014-05-17	13479	115	15	8.65	9.86
2014-05-18	16176	101	12	9.64	10.46
2014-05-19	17028	94	15	10.30	10.77
2014-05-20	16787	192	73	9.66	10.04
2014-05-21	16949	260	65	13.54	13.63
2014-05-22	17121	412	101	22.01	20.83
2014-05-23	17156	225	38	14.34	14.06
2014-05-24	13003	68	15	6.05	6.76
2014-05-25	13106	91	68	7.29	7.54
2014-05-26	16112	134	52	12.93	12.23
2014-05-27	16803	573	131	22.85	21.45
2014-05-28	16894	340	21	14.72	14.76
2014-05-29	17073	115	52	10.55	10.40
2014-05-30	17109	171	32	12.23	11.69
2014-05-31	13495	56	6	7.31	7.58
⊟6	502617	10133	1768	17.14	16.50
Grand Total	1001895	19646	3460	15.44	15.06

PivotTable Fields

ACTIVE   ALL

Choose fields to add to report:

⊿ Σ OnTimePerformance
  ☑ CancellationCount
  ☑ TotalFlights
  ☑ AverageArrivalDelay
  ☑ AverageDepartureDelay
  ☑ DivertedCount
⊿ ▦ Airline
  ☐ airline
⊿ ▦ Airport
  ☐ airport
⊿ ▦ CancellationReason
  ☐ cancellation
⊿ ▦ Date
  ▷ ☑ Date
  ▷ ▦ More Fields
⊿ ▦ Geography
  ▷ ☐ Geography
  ▷ ▦ More Fields

Drag fields between areas below:

▼ FILTERS

⫿ COLUMNS
  Σ Values ▼

⊞ ROWS
  Date ▼

Σ VALUES
  TotalFlights ▼
  CancellationCount ▼
  DivertedCount ▼
  AverageArrivalDelay ▼
  AverageDepartureDelay ▼

FIGURE 15.19
Analyzing data from PowerPivot in Excel.

When you have data in PowerPivot or Excel, you can use the full functionalities of Excel to explore and visualize your data in a table or with different charts. Next you see how you can add a Slicer (graphical filter) to slice your data as needed. Simply select the PivotTable, go to the Analyze tab, and click the Insert Slicer icon (this option is also available on the Insert tab). In the Insert Slicers dialog box, select any attributes of any available dimensions. For example, in our case, we chose Airline as the Slicer for this demo.

NOTE

Insert Timeline

If you have time-related data, you can even insert a timeline, which is a Slicer-based time control to analyze how your data changes over time (see Figure 15.20).

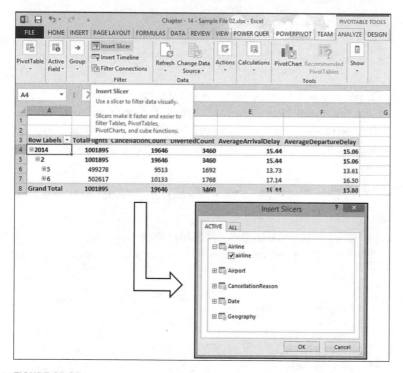

FIGURE 15.20
Adding a Slicer control.

Figure 15.21 shows how the interface should look after adding a Slicer to the Excel document for the airline we added.

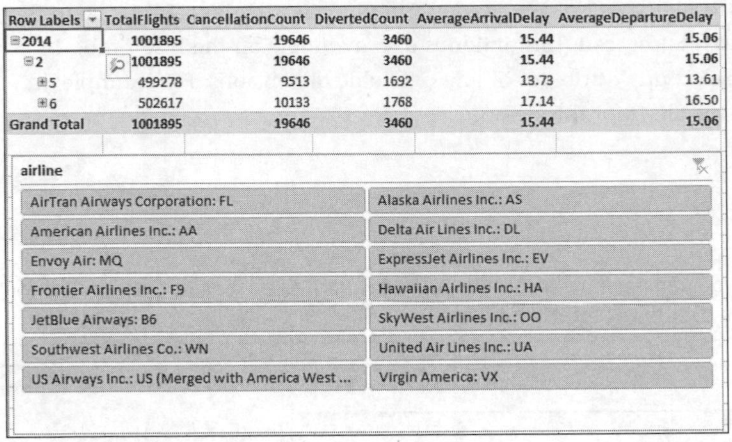

Row Labels ▾	TotalFlights	CancellationCount	DivertedCount	AverageArrivalDelay	AverageDepartureDelay
⊟2014	1001895	19646	3460	15.44	15.06
⊟2	1001895	19646	3460	15.44	15.06
⊞5	499278	9513	1692	13.73	13.61
⊞6	502617	10133	1768	17.14	16.50
Grand Total	1001895	19646	3460	15.44	15.06

airline	
AirTran Airways Corporation: FL	Alaska Airlines Inc.: AS
American Airlines Inc.: AA	Delta Air Lines Inc.: DL
Envoy Air: MQ	ExpressJet Airlines Inc.: EV
Frontier Airlines Inc.: F9	Hawaiian Airlines Inc.: HA
JetBlue Airways: B6	SkyWest Airlines Inc.: OO
Southwest Airlines Co.: WN	United Air Lines Inc.: UA
US Airways Inc.: US (Merged with America West ...	Virgin America: VX

FIGURE 15.21
Slicer in action.

As you can see in Figure 15.22, you can select one or more Slicer values to filter data in the PivotTable. We have selected just one Airline here (American Airlines Inc.), and you can see that all the measures have refreshed to show the values for just this airline. Click the icon on the right side of the Slicer dialog box to clear the Slicer or filter.

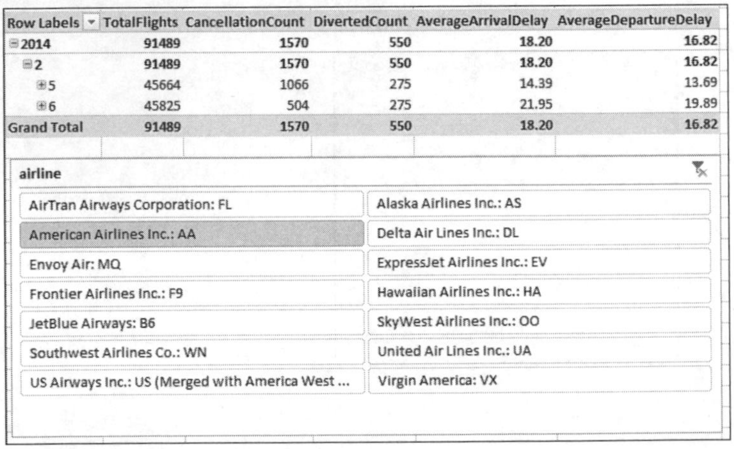

Row Labels ▾	TotalFlights	CancellationCount	DivertedCount	AverageArrivalDelay	AverageDepartureDelay
⊟2014	91489	1570	550	18.20	16.82
⊟2	91489	1570	550	18.20	16.82
⊞5	45664	1066	275	14.39	13.69
⊞6	45825	504	275	21.95	19.89
Grand Total	91489	1570	550	18.20	16.82

airline	
AirTran Airways Corporation: FL	Alaska Airlines Inc.: AS
American Airlines Inc.: AA	Delta Air Lines Inc.: DL
Envoy Air: MQ	ExpressJet Airlines Inc.: EV
Frontier Airlines Inc.: F9	Hawaiian Airlines Inc.: HA
JetBlue Airways: B6	SkyWest Airlines Inc.: OO
Southwest Airlines Co.: WN	United Air Lines Inc.: UA
US Airways Inc.: US (Merged with America West ...	Virgin America: VX

FIGURE 15.22
Data filtering based on Slicer selection.

Reporting and Data Visualization with Power View

Power View is an Excel add-in (supported in Excel 2013 and later) that supports intuitive, interactive, ad hoc data exploration, visualization, and presentation experience. It empowers end users to do ad hoc analysis and quickly create varieties of reports (in just few minutes, with just a few clicks) with different visualization options inside your own Excel.

In other words, it allows end users to spend less time formatting reports and more time visualizing the data to gain insights and digging into business questions or problems. Power View helps the users explore data in new ways, to uncover hidden insights and bring data to life with interactive visualization.

NOTE

Power View in SharePoint

Power View is also available as a feature in SharePoint Server 2010 and SharePoint Server 2013 Enterprise Edition, as part of the SQL Server 2012 Service Pack 1 Reporting Services add-in.

TRY IT YOURSELF ▼

Using Power View to Visualize Data

The Power View add-in might not be enabled already. If it isn't, you must follow the same procedure to enable it as you did for PowerPivot earlier in this hour.

Once Power View is enabled, click the Insert tab and then click the Power View icon (see Figure 15.23) in the same Excel document that contains the PowerPivot data model.

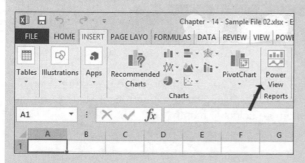

FIGURE 15.23
Launching Power View.

When you launch Power View, you will notice that the Power View tab appears in Excel now (see Figure 15.24). This tab has frequently used commands for the report designing and formatting stage. On the right side of the Power View report designer, you can see all the tables, along with their visible attributes and measures, from the PowerPivot model under the Power View Fields section. At the bottom of this, you can drag and drop attributes or measures to start analyzing. On the left side, you can see the report canvas to preview and format the data during report design.

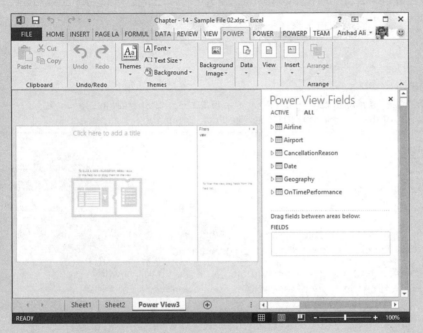

FIGURE 15.24
Power View Report Designer interface.

In Figure 15.25, we are analyzing the average Arrival Delay versus the average Departure Delay, by airline, in both tabular and bar-chart format. We have also added a month filter as `Tile` on the report header, to filter the report data based on the selected month.

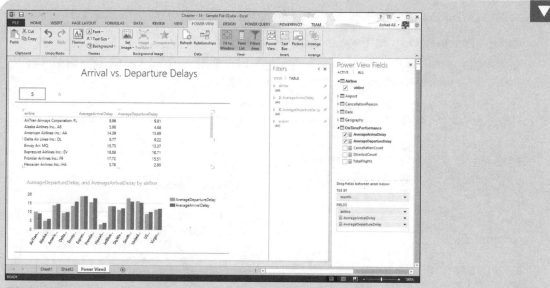

FIGURE 15.25
A sample Power View report based on data from the PowerPivot model (which, in turn, gets data from Hive tables) that shows Average Arrival versus Departure Delays.

Reporting and Data Visualization with Power Map

Power Map is another Excel add-in (supported in Excel 2013 and later) that extends the capability of Power View by enabling end users to visualize data in a three-dimensional (3D) map visualization format. It lets you plot geographical and temporal data visually, analyze it in 3D visualization format, and create an interactive, guided cinematic tour. This tour gives you a new way of seeing your data so that you can discover new insights. You can view your data in geographic space and see time-stamped data change over time (which you might not have seen in traditional 2D tables and charts). You also can share captured screenshots and guided interactive video tours with others.

NOTE

You can download Power Map from http://www.microsoft.com/en-us/download/details.aspx?id= 38395.

▼ TRY IT YOURSELF

Data Visualization in Power Map of Excel

After Power Map installs, you must enable it in Excel. You can follow the same procedure to enable it as you did for PowerPivot earlier in this hour.

After you enable it, click the Insert tab, click the Power Map icon, and then click the Launch Power Map icon (see Figure 15.26) in the same Excel document that contains the PowerPivot data model.

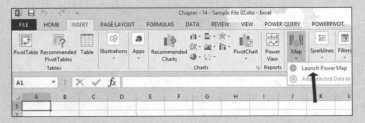

FIGURE 15.26
Launching Power Map.

Figure 15.27 shows the Power Map Report Designer. On the right side, specify columns from the data to associate it with the map so that it plots correctly; then click the Next button. For example, we mapped Country Name from data with the Country/Region field of the Map, and we mapped OriginStateName with the State/Province field of the map.

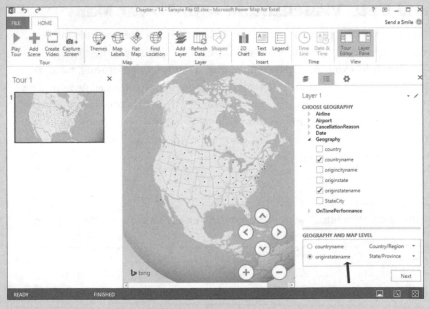

FIGURE 15.27
Power Map Report Designer Interface—Mapping geography data with Bing Map.

Next, select the Bar-chart icon and drag and drop the CancelledCount and DivertedCount measures from the OnTimePerformance fact table under the Height box (see Figure 15.28).

FIGURE 15.28
Creating a bar report plotted on the map—Flight Cancellation count versus Diverted count.

Figure 15.29 shows how your report should look. As you can see, Texas has the highest number of cancellations; if you hover over the bar, you will see the value associated with it.

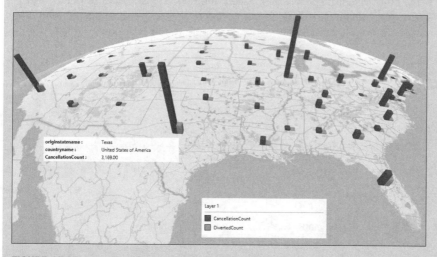

FIGURE 15.29
Bar chart report plotted on a 3D map—Flight Cancellation count versus Diverted count.

You can click the Add Scene icon on the ribbon to create another scene in the report. In Figure 15.30, we created another scene and added the AverageArrivalDelay and AverageDepartureDelay measures to analyze.

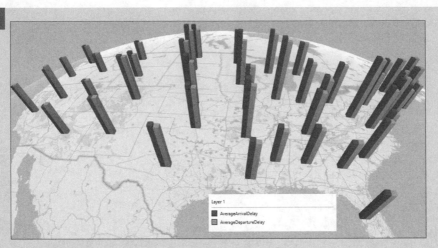

FIGURE 15.30
Bar chart report plotted on a 3D map—Average Arrival versus Departure Delay.

Now let's explore some other visualization options. Select the bubble-chart report this time, drag the airline attribute from the AIrlInes dimension to the Category box (to group by airline), and drag the TotalFlights measure from the OnTimePerformance fact table to the Size box.

FIGURE 15.31
Creating a pie chart report plotted on a 3D map—Total Flights Grouped by Airline.

Your report should look like Figure 15.32. You can hover over any pie and any chart to see its associated values. You can see here that the maximum number of flights from Georgia State comes from Delta Airlines.

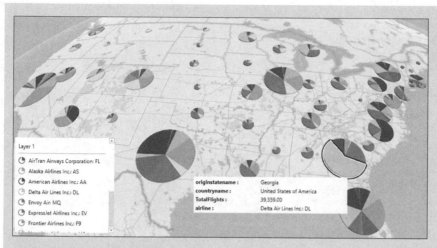

FIGURE 15.32
Pie chart report plotted on a 3D map—total flights, grouped by airline.

NOTE

The features of Power Map that we demonstrated are based on a recent Power Map Preview release. You can expect changes in the way it works as new versions are released. The final release of Power Map will include added features.

Accessing Hive Data from SQL Server

We discussed in detail using the Hive ODBC Driver to consume data from Hive in Excel and other related Excel add-ins for self-service BI by individuals or teams. The Hive ODBC Driver also lets you connect to your HDInsight cluster from Microsoft SQL Server and has related tools for corporate BI.

TRY IT YOURSELF ▼

Creating a Link Server in SQL Server

Using the following command, you can create a linked server in SQL Server to access Hive-based tables from an HDInsight cluster right within SQL Server or related tools such as SQL Server Analysis Services or SQL Server Reporting Services.

NOTE

When you create a linked server in SQL Server, it uses Microsoft OLE DB Provider for ODBC (MSDASQL). It wraps the ODBC Driver for Hive so that Hive appears as an OLE DB–based data source to linked server consumers.

```
EXEC master.dbo.sp_addlinkedserver
-- Name of your linked server
@server = N'HiveAccessFromSQL',
--Product name of the OLE DB data source to
--add as a linked server, it should be HIVE
@srvproduct=N'HIVE',
-- Unique Programmatic Identifier (PROGID) of the
-- OLE DB provider that corresponds to this data source
@provider=N'MSDASQL',
-- Name of the DSN - Based on bit-ness of SQL Server
-- you need to create 32-bit or 64-bit Hive ODBC DSN
@datasrc=N'HiveODBC64 to tyhdicluster',
-- Provider-specific connection string that identifies a unique data source
@provstr=N'Provider=MSDASQL;Persist Security Info=True;User
ID=tyhdiadmin;Password=<your password to connect to the cluster>;'
```

When a linked server is created, you can run distributed queries on the HDInsight cluster and retrieve the data back in SQL Server. As Figure 15.33 shows, you can verify the linked server in Object Explorer of SQL Server Management Studio (SSMS). You can expand it to see all the tables or views created in all the schemas in the connected HDInsight cluster or, more specifically, the Hive Server.

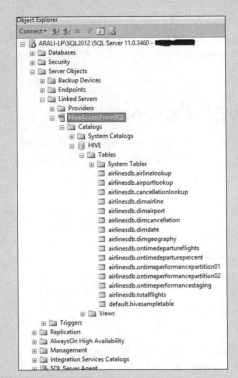

FIGURE 15.33
Linked server connected to the HDInsight cluster.

NOTE

Database Versus Schema

SQL Server and Hive define databases and schemas differently. In SQL Server, a database acts as a bigger logical container that has one or more schemas; those schemas contain tables or views. In Hive, however, a database and a schema are the same.

To overcome this difference, Hive ODBC Driver has added a synthetic database or catalog, called HIVE. All Hive schemas and databases are organized here (see Figure 15.33).

When you are connected to the HDInsight cluster via a linked server, you can run queries either in standard SQL (which the SQL Connector component of the Hive ODBC Driver transforms into an equivalent HiveQL query, as discussed in the section "Setting Up the Hive ODBC Driver" in Hour 14). Alternatively, you can directly write HiveQL using the OPENQUERY method to initiate pass-through query execution using a linked server.

In other words, OPENQUERY opens a connection to the Hive Server using a specified linked server and then executes a query as if it is executing from that server. OPENQUERY also enables you to join data that comes from Hive-based tables with the data available in SQL Server or data from other sources. You can then create a view of the joined data in SQL Server.

```
-- Using standard SQL with four part naming convention. This gets converted to
-- equivalent HiveQL and executed on the connected HDInsight cluster
SELECT * FROM [HiveAccessFromSQL].[HIVE].[airlinesdb].[ontimedeparturepercent]

-- Using OPENQUERY method to execute HiveQL queries on
-- the connected HDInsight cluster
SELECT * FROM OPENQUERY(HiveAccessFromSQL, 'SELECT * FROM airlinesdb.
ontimedeparturepercent')
```

CAUTION

While executing the previous scripts, you might encounter the following exception. This error arises because, by default, a column in a Hive table with the STRING data type tries to convert to VARCHAR (8000). This does not work, however, because, unlike the VARCHAR data type, the STRING data type has no maximum limit on size.

```
OLE DB provider "MSDASQL" for linked server "HiveAccessFromSQL" returned message
"Requested conversion is not supported.".
Msg 7341, Level 16, State 2, Line 4
Cannot get the current row value of column "[MSDASQL].airline" from OLE DB provider
"MSDASQL" for linked server "HiveAccessFromSQL".
```

To overcome the issue described in the previous Caution, you can change the Advanced options for the Hive ODBC DSN created, to make the maximum length of the STRING data type 8000 (you saw this in Figure 14.7 in the last hour). Be very careful with this change; it might cause precision lost and/or data truncation and you will end up getting incorrect data. After you have changed this option, you should be able to execute the earlier queries. See Figure 15.34 for the results.

	airline	ontimedeparturepercentage
1	American Airlines Inc.: AA	59.2072093605166
2	Alaska Airlines Inc.: AS	76.9984622201371
3	SkyWest Airlines Inc.: OO	64.914685167941
4	ExpressJet Airlines Inc.: EV	52.9091832599974
5	JetBlue Airways: B6	58.9430664022984
6	Frontier Airlines Inc.: F9	55.1225062179182
7	Southwest Airlines Co.: WN	38.5983657208745
8	Hawaiian Airlines Inc.: HA	81.8905721103157
9	Delta Air Lines Inc.: DL	62.6261651782804
10	United Air Lines Inc.: UA	47.1911176247798
11	US Airways Inc.: US (Merged with America West 9/...	66.1948444478669
12	Envoy Air: MQ	58.4561292616442
13	AirTran Airways Corporation: FL	53.933780688713
14	Virgin America: VX	64.8122197309417

FIGURE 15.34
Dataset returned from a Hive table in SQL Server.

To access the HDInsight cluster-wide configuration, the Hive ODBC driver includes a pseudo-table named `HIVE_SYSTEM` under the pseudo-schema named `HIVE_SYSTEM`. This table has two `STRING` data type columns: `ENVKEY` and `ENVVALUE`. You can run the following script to return Hive configuration entries in which the key contains the word `hive` (see Figure 15.35).

```
SELECT * FROM OPENQUERY(HiveAccessFromSQL, 'SELECT * FROM HIVE_SYSTEM.HIVE_SYSTEM
WHERE ENVKEY LIKE ''%hive%''');
```

	ENVKEY	ENVVALUE
332	hive.stats.reliable	false
333	hive.stats.retries.max	0
334	hive.stats.retries.wait	3000
335	hive.support.concurrency	false
336	hive.support.quoted.identifiers	column
337	hive.test.mode	false
338	hive.test.mode.prefix	test_
339	hive.test.mode.samplefreq	32
340	hive.tez.container.size	-1
341	hive.tez.input.format	org.apache.hadoop.hive.ql.io.HiveInputFormat
342	hive.tez.log.level	INFO
343	hive.tez.relocalize.am	true
344	hive.transform.escape.input	false
345	hive.txn.manager	org.apache.hadoop.hive.ql.lockmgr.DummyTxnManager
346	hive.txn.max.open.batch	1000
347	hive.txn.timeout	300
348	hive.txn.valid.txns	9223372036854775807:
349	hive.typecheck.on.insert	true
350	hive.udtf.auto.progress	false

FIGURE 15.35
Hive-related cluster-wide configuration.

Accessing Data from SQL Server Analysis Services

SQL Server Analysis Services (SSAS), a component of SQL Server, delivers online analytical processing (OLAP) and data mining functionalities for business intelligence applications. It supports OLAP by letting you design, create, and manage multidimensional or tabular structures that contain data aggregated from varieties of data sources, including HDInsight cluster.

SSAS has become a market leader, thanks to its performance, scalability, accessibility, reduced total cost of ownership, and relative ease of solution development. It offers a single unified BI platform, the Business Intelligence Semantic Model (BISM). BISM enables you to create either a multidimensional or a tabular data model so that you can utilize the expertise and power of both worlds. The model, which users create, is based on BISM and can integrate data from heterogeneous data sources, including an HDInsight cluster. Users can work intuitively with the data stored in the model, regardless of how the model was developed (whether it's multidimensional or tabular).

BISM is the one unified platform that powers all end-user experiences. It is accessed in an intuitive way using Reporting Services, Power View, PowerPivot, Excel, SharePoint, and more. A BISM model is conceptually divided into three layers: the Data Access layer, the Business Logic and Queries layer, and the Data Model layer (see Figure 15.36).

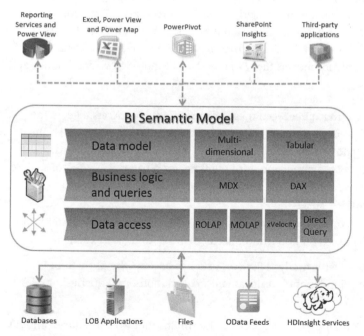

FIGURE 15.36
Business Intelligence Semantic Model (BISM).

Data Access Layer

The Data Access layer integrates data from heterogeneous data sources, including the HDInsight cluster. It uses two modes for data retrieval and management.

▶ **Cached data mode**—Cached data mode retrieves data from all the sources in the model during processing and stores it in a compressed data structure that is optimized for high-speed data access. MOLAP is the storage format used for the multidimensional model. It is optimized for OLAP and uses techniques such as prebuilt aggregates, bitmap indexes, and high degree of compression to deliver great performance and scale. XVelocity is an in-memory column store engine for tabular models that includes state-of-the-art data compression and scanning algorithms to deliver blazing fast performance with no need for indexes, precalculated aggregates, or tuning. The same XVelocity engine works behind PowerPivot data models as well. In fact, if you have already created a PowerPivot model, you can import it in a tabular model as a base.

▶ **Pass-through mode**—Pass-through mode pushes query processing and business logic down to the underlying data sources while querying. This exploits the capabilities of the source system and avoids the need to copy the data as part of the model processing. ROLAP is complementary to MOLAP, of the multidimensional model, whereas DirectQuery is complementary to xVelocity, of the tabular data model. Both attempt to push query evaluation, as much as possible, into the underlying data sources. ROLAP is optimized for large fact tables and relatively small dimension tables (star schema). DirectQuery is mostly neutral toward the back-end database structure. Note that, in SQL Server 2012, DirectQuery is supported only for models that are based on a single SQL Server relational data source.

The BISM developer must make a tradeoff between these two modes of data access, depending on application needs, local data storage requirements, and acceptable data latency. Given the latency involved while retrieving data from Hive-based tables, you should consider the cached approach instead of the pass-through approach most of the time, for a better query response time.

Business Logic and Queries Layer

BISM developers and client tools can choose between Multi-Dimensional Expression (MDX) and Data Analysis Expression (DAX) based on application needs, skill set, and user experience.

▶ **MDX**—MDX was introduced with Analysis Services and has become the de facto BI industry standard for multidimensional business logic, calculations, and queries for OLAP query access.

▶ **DAX**—DAX is an expression language based on Excel formulas that was introduced initially with PowerPivot and is built on tabular concepts (tables, columns, and relationships) for tabular models. DAX supports model development (such as when creating calculated columns, measures, and KPIs for tabular models and PowerPivot models), relationship navigation, context modification, and time intelligence. For example, we used DAX in the section "Accessing Hive Data from PowerPivot" to create measures and calculated columns.

Data Model Layer

BISM developers can choose between multidimensional or tabular model projects, based on the needs of their applications, their skill set, and the client tools that consume the model from a multidimensional or tabular model.

▶ **Multidimensional**—BISM supports traditional ways of creating a multidimensional model. It enables you to create a model with a cube and dimensions normally based on dimensional data model and star-snowflake schemas.

▶ **Tabular**—BISM also supports creating a tabular model based on the concept of tables and their relationships. It makes development much simpler because it is easier to understand.

NOTE

As of this writing, you can directly use the Hive ODBC Driver or DSN inside a tabular model but not in a multidimensional model. To create a multidimensional model based on data from Hive-based tables, you can create a linked server in SQL Server and then use the linked server in a multidimensional model to extract data from Hive tables.

You can learn more about SQL Server Analysis Services at http://msdn.microsoft.com/en-us/library/bb522607(v=sql.120).aspx.

NOTE

Klout Leverages SSAS to Hive and Gets Less Than 10 Seconds' Response Time on 1 Trillion Rows

Klout, a leading social network analytics company, leverages Hive ODBC Driver to bring relevant Hadoop data into SSAS by using HiveQL. SSAS then serves up the data for interactive and ad hoc analysis and reporting in Microsoft Excel and dashboards to provide insight into the Klout algorithms. In this way, Klout achieves an average query response time of less than 10 seconds on 1 trillion rows of data.

You can read about this success story in the white paper at http://msdn.microsoft.com/en-us/library/jj710329.aspx.

Accessing Data from SQL Server Reporting Services

SQL Server Reporting Services (SSRS) is another component of SQL Server that provides a full range of ready-to-use tools and services to help you author, deploy, and manage reports for your team and organization. SSRS is a server-based reporting platform that provides comprehensive reporting functionality to author and manage reports on data from a variety of data sources, including Hive-based data from an HDInsight cluster.

SSRS supports creating formatted, interactive, tabular, and graphical reports with rich sets of visualization options such as charts, maps, and sparklines. You can publish reports to the report server, where end users can view them in a web-based interface (browser) and export them to various formats. You can even publish your reports to the SharePoint farm, for better collaboration, instead publishing them to the default report server.

These are high-level options of creating SSRS reports on the data coming from Hive (HDInsight cluster):

▶ You can directly connect and consume data from Hive using the Hive ODBC Driver (see Figure 15.37).

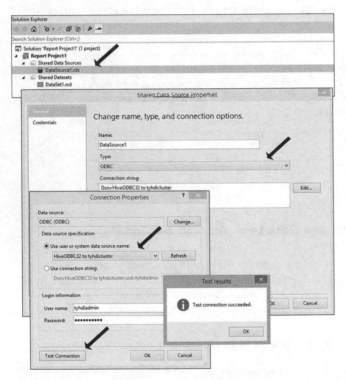

FIGURE 15.37
Using the Hive ODBC Driver or DSN in SSRS.

▶ You can consume data from a Hive table using the SQL Server linked server (you created this earlier in this section).

▶ You can consume data from a SSAS multidimensional or tabular model created on data from Hive tables or views.

Although it's possible to create reports by directly consuming data from Hive tables, this is not appropriate most of the time because of the latency involved in pulling data every time a report gets refreshed. Hence, you can create a SSAS multidimensional or tabular model based on data from Hive tables and then cache the aggregated data in the model during model processing so that users can access data for analysis in mere seconds.

NOTE

You can learn more about SQL Server Reporting Services at http://msdn.microsoft.com/en-us/library/ms159106.aspx.

Accessing HDInsight Data from Power Query

We discussed in detail using the Hive ODBC Driver to connect to the HDInsight cluster and retrieve the Hive-based data from Hive tables or views. These all require an operational HDInsight cluster because it needs to connect to the Hive Server for data exploration and extraction. You can provision an HDInsight cluster only when you want to refresh the data in Excel, PowerPivot, or Tabular model to minimize the cost, but you also can retrieve this data using Power Query without needing an operational HDInsight cluster.

As discussed in the past, by default, an HDInsight cluster stores and manages data in the Azure Storage Blob. Hence, you can directly query data from files available on the Azure Storage Blob without needing a running HDInsight cluster. Before we go into the details of using Power Query to retrieve this data for analysis, we need to briefly talk about Power Query itself.

Power Query is an Excel add-in (supported in both Excel 2010 and Excel 2013). It has an intuitive and interactive user interface that you can use to search, discover, acquire, combine, refine, transform, and enrich data from both a corporate intranet and the Internet (publically available data). You can think of Power Query as an extraction, transformation, and loading (ETL) or extraction, loading, and transformation (ELT) tool built into your familiar Excel to search or discover data from a wide variety of data sources.

NOTE

You can download the Power Query add-in from http://www.microsoft.com/en-us/download/details.aspx?id=39379.

When Power Query is installed, you must enable it in Excel. You follow the same procedure to enable it as you did for PowerPivot, earlier in this hour.

▼ TRY IT YOURSELF

Launching Power Query in Excel

After you have enabled Power Query, click the Power Query tab in the Excel document, click From Other Sources, and then click From Microsoft Azure HDInsight (see Figure 15.38).

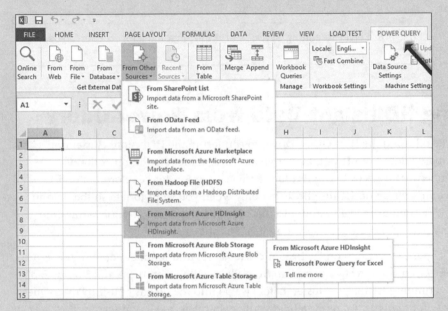

FIGURE 15.38
Launching Power Query in Excel to retrieve data from an HDInsight cluster.

You are prompted to enter the name of the Azure Storage account, followed by an access or account key to connect to it. After you specify this information, click Save to get connected to the specified Azure Storage account.

TIP
_____

To get an access or account key for your Azure Storage account, go to the Azure Management Portal, click the Storage icon on the left, and then select the storage account that was connected to your HDInsight cluster. Then click the Manage Access Key icon at the bottom to get both a primary and a secondary access key. You can use either of these. We recommend that you share the secondary key with other people so that you can rotate your secondary key while maintaining the primary key for your own.

_____

If the provided details are correct, you are connected to the Azure Storage account and a Navigator pane opens (see Figure 15.39). This gives you available containers on the connected Azure Storage account.

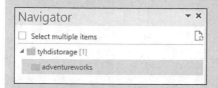

FIGURE 15.39
Navigator page once connected to the Azure Storage Blob.

Clicking any of the containers (you should click the default container for your HDInsight cluster) launches the Query Editor (see Figure 15.40). The Query Editor is a powerful component of Power Query that can transform, merge, and enrich your data. It also contains a list of steps applied, in case you want to revert to a previous step.

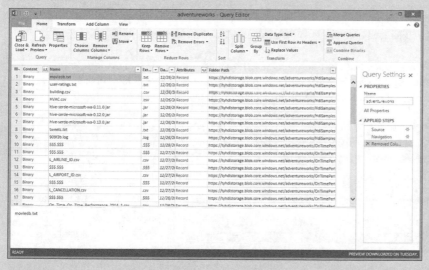

FIGURE 15.40
The Query Editor in Power Query.

In the Query Editor, you can apply a filter on the Folder Path column to contain only files and folders available at `/hive/warehouse` (the default folder for the Hive tables—see Figure 15.41).

Each file is considered binary data, so you can click the Binary link in Figure 15.41 to retrieve the data for the selected file. Data retrieved from the Azure Storage Blob is shown in the Query Editor, where you can apply a required transformation and merge it with other data sets, which is helpful if you have data in multiple files.

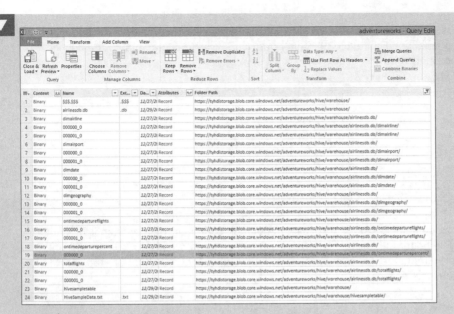

FIGURE 15.41
The Query Editor, filtered for files and folders available under `/hive/warehouse`.

When you are done with data transformation, close the Query Editor and load the data into an Excel document (see Figure 15.42). Now that you have data in an Excel document, you have full Excel capabilities to use for data exploration and visualization.

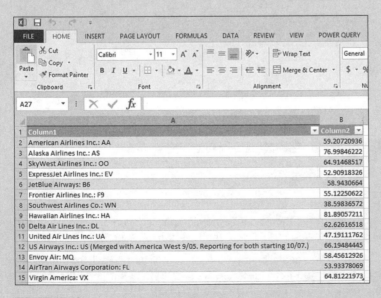

FIGURE 15.42
Data loaded back to Excel from the Query Editor.

Notice in Figure 15.42 that there is no header for the data, by default; this is because you are querying data directly from the underlying files, bypassing Hive Server or metadata. Hive tables and columns are stored as part of the Hive metadata, not as part of the underlying data files.

Summary

In this hour, you explored different options of consuming data from an HDInsight cluster or Hive tables from different Microsoft BI and reporting tools. You learned how to leverage Power BI tools (Excel, Power Query, PowerPivot, Power Query, and Power Map) to access Hive-based data for self-service BI.

You looked at how Hive-based data is consumed from SQL Server, SQL Server Analysis Service, and SQL Server Reporting Services for Corporate BI.

You also examined how you can use Power Query to consume data from the Azure Storage Blob (aggregated data stored on the Azure Storage Blob), even when an HDInsight cluster is not operational.

In the next hour, you focus on SQL Server Integration Services (SSIS) for building data integration packages to transfer data between an HDInsight cluster and a relational database management system (RDBMS) such as SQL Server.

Q&A

Q. What is Microsoft Power BI? What tools can be leveraged for self-service BI?

A. Microsoft Power BI is a cloud-based self-service BI solution for the enterprise. It empowers end users (people with all level of skills, including data analysts, power users, business users, data stewards, and folks from the IT department) and provides tools to take care of end-to-end business intelligence scenarios for self-service BI. Power BI is a broad umbrella that encompasses four Excel add-ins (Power Query, PowerPivot, Power View, and Power Map).

Q. How can you access Hive-based data from an HDInsight cluster for Corporate BI in SQL Server, SQL Server Analysis Services, and SQL Server Reporting Services?

A. SQL Server supports creating a SQL Server linked server to access Hive-based tables from the HDInsight cluster right within SQL Server or related tools, such as SQL Server Analysis Services or SQL Server Reporting Services. After a linked server is created, you can run distributed queries on the HDInsight cluster and retrieve the data back in SQL Server or related tools.

Q. Is there any way to consume data from an HDInsight cluster without an operational HDInsight cluster?

A. Yes. By default, HDInsight cluster stores and manages data in the Azure Storage Blob, so you can directly query data from files available on the Azure Storage Blob without having to run the HDInsight cluster using Power Query for analysis.

Exercise

Create a new tabular model by importing the PowerPivot model you created in the section "Accessing Hive Data from PowerPivot." Deploy this model to a tabular mode instance of SQL Server Analysis Services, process it, and explore and visualize the data using Excel. After a successful import, the tabular model should look like Figure 15.43.

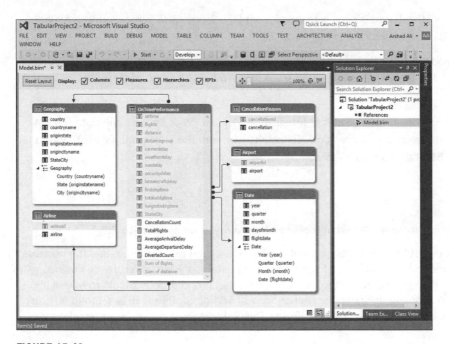

FIGURE 15.43
Tabular model based on data from Hive tables.

Integrating HDInsight with SQL Server Integration Services

What You'll Learn in This Hour:

▶ The Need for Data Movement
▶ Introduction to SSIS
▶ Analyzing On-time Flight Departure with SSIS
▶ Provisioning HDInsight Cluster

SQL Server Integration Services (SSIS) is a powerful platform for building enterprise-level data integration solutions. SSIS builds packages for *extracting* data from a variety of data sources, performing *transformations* on data, and *loading* the data to various destinations (ETL).

This hour discusses using SSIS to build data integration packages to transfer data between an HDInsight cluster and a relational database management system (RDBMS) such as SQL Server.

The Need for Data Movement

In a hybrid environment with an HDInsight cluster and SQL Server working as complementary technologies, the need for data integration becomes even more critical. An HDInsight cluster can store massive volumes of unstructured data and employ Map Reduce to provide analysis results in hours. SQL Server, on the other hand, works well with terabytes of structured data (a comparatively smaller volume), delivering query results in seconds.

Being able to transfer data to HDInsight for archival and long-term retention without losing the capability to perform analysis on data (although at a slightly slower speed) makes sense for historical data. At the same time, transferring the results of a MapReduce analysis from HDInsight Cluster into SQL Server works well for performing further reporting and analysis, as well as data integration and consumption by other systems.

The following sections explore the role of SSIS when creating ETL packages to transfer data between Hadoop and other sources and destinations (including SQL Server).

Introduction to SSIS

SSIS ETL workflow packages are created using graphical SSIS designer, which is a part of SQL Server Data Tools (SSDT). For more information on creating packages using designer, refer to http://msdn.microsoft.com/en-us/library/ms137973.aspx msdn link. An SSIS package consists of these main elements:

▶ Variables, for making decisions, storing configuration values, or handling intermediate processing results

▶ Tasks, for performing actions (a send mail task to send email notifications, a file system task to perform operations on files and directories, an execute process task to run an executable, and so on)

▶ Control Flow, containing tasks connected by precedence constraints

▶ Data Flow, containing data source and destination components and connection information

NOTE

Refer to the MSDN article at http://msdn.microsoft.com/en-us/library/ms141134.aspx for more details on SSIS package components.

NOTE

SSIS Holds the ETL World Speed Record for Loading 1TB in 30 Minutes

SSIS holds the extract, transform, and load (ETL) world speed record for loading 1TB in 30 minutes. See the Technet article at http://technet.microsoft.com/en-us/library/dd537533(SQL.100).aspx (dated March 2009) for details on how this was accomplished with SSIS following various best practices.

Analyzing On-time Flight Departure with SSIS

This scenario seeks to determine the on-time flight departure percentage for airlines using an SSIS workflow. It accomplishes the following tasks:

▶ Provisions HDInsight cluster on demand

▶ Invokes Hive queries for processing and summarizing user data stored in blob storage

▶ Loads the processing results to a SQL Server table

▶ Decommissions the HDInsight cluster to save cost

▶ Logs error messages (if any) upon failure

The Hive queries process the on-time flight departure data stored in blob storage to get the on-time flight departure percentage by airline. The results are transferred to a SQL Server/SQL Azure table.

Figure 16.1 represents the corresponding SSIS workflow.

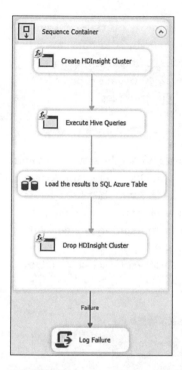

FIGURE 16.1
SSIS workflow to determine the on-time flight departure percentage.

Scenario Prerequisites

This scenario uses the on-time performance of airline flights data from the Research and Innovative Technology Administration, Bureau of Transportation Statistics (RITA). The data is available for download and analysis at http://www.transtats.bts.gov/ DL_SelectFields.asp?Table_ID=236&DB_Short_Name=On-Time.

You can download lookup data related to airline ID and descriptions here:

http://www.transtats.bts.gov/Download_Lookup.asp?Lookup=L_AIRLINE_ID

Download the prezipped on-time performance file for January 2014 and upload the unzipped CSV file to the blob store at /OnTimePerformance/Data/. Also download the lookup data related to airline ID and descriptions. Upload the lookup data file to blob storage at `/OnTimePerformance/Lookup/Airline/` location.

The Hive tables used in the scenario rely on `com.bizo.hive.serde.csv.CSVSerde` serde for interpreting CSV files. The Serde is defined in `csv-serde-1.1.2.jar`, which you can download at http://ogrodnek.github.io/csv-serde/.

Download the JAR file from the link. Upload the JAR file to blob storage at `/SSISWorkflow`. Also, copy the `HiveScripts.sql` file from the code samples accompanying this hour to `/SSISWorkflow` in blob storage. Create a folder named `C:\SSISScripts` on the machine, intended for running SSIS packages, and copy the `ProvisionHDInsightCluster.ps1`, `DropHDInsightCluster.ps1`, and `SubmitHiveJob.ps1` PowerShell script files.

Package Variables

Configuration elements such as the Azure subscription ID, the cluster name, the storage account name, and cluster credentials are used across different tasks. Using an SSIS variable for these common configuration elements makes sense. Figure 16.2 shows the SSIS variables used across tasks. The configuration elements can be easily configured from one place using variables, so you can easily connect to a different cluster or Azure subscription by configuring different values for corresponding variables. To view and edit the package variables, go to the Variables menu from the SSIS menu or right-click an empty space on the designer surface, and select Variables from the context menu.

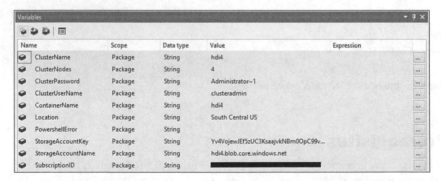

Name	Scope	Data type	Value	Expression
ClusterName	Package	String	hdi4	
ClusterNodes	Package	String	4	
ClusterPassword	Package	String	Administrator~1	
ClusterUserName	Package	String	clusteradmin	
ContainerName	Package	String	hdi4	
Location	Package	String	South Central US	
PowershellError	Package	String		
StorageAccountKey	Package	String	Yv4VojewJEf5zUC3KsaajvkNBm0OpC99v...	
StorageAccountName	Package	String	hdi4.blob.core.windows.net	
SubscriptionID	Package	String		

FIGURE 16.2
SSIS variables.

Setting Up Azure PowerShell for Automation

Before you can use Windows Azure PowerShell and SSIS for automating HDInsight cluster deployment, you must configure connectivity between the machine running SSIS and Windows

Azure. Simply download and import the PublishSettings file from Microsoft Azure. The publish file includes a management certificate with security credentials. This is required to set up certificate authentication between the machine running the SSIS package and Microsoft Azure.

To download and import publish settings, follow these steps:

1. Run Windows PowerShell as administrator.

2. Run the `Get-AzurePublishSettingsFile` command. This opens a web browser to the Microsoft Azure Management Portal sign-in page.

3. Sign in to the Microsoft Azure Management Portal to continue downloading the publish settings file.

4. Run the `Import-AzurePublishSettingsFile <publish setting file location>` command to import the publish settings.

Provisioning HDInsight Cluster

SSIS can invoke a Windows PowerShell script using the Execute Process task. PowerShell conveniently provisions and decommissions an HDInsight cluster on demand. `New-AzureHDInsightCluster` provisions a new HDInsight cluster:

```
New-AzureHDInsightCluster -Name $clusterName -Location $location
-DefaultStorageAccountName $storageAccountName -DefaultStorageAccountKey
$storageAccountKey -DefaultStorageContainerName $containerName  -ClusterSizeInNodes
$clusterNodes -Credential $clustercreds
```

Refer to the PowerShell script `CreateHiveTable.ps1` in the accompanying code samples for a full listing of a PowerShell script for creating a new HDInsight cluster.

NOTE

SSIS Tasks for Hadoop

The combination of PowerShell and the Execute Process task provides a convenient way to automate HDInsight cluster management tasks using SSIS. However, the growing popularity and adaption of HDInsight could result in native SSIS tasks for HDInsight cluster management, from either the codeplex community or Microsoft itself.

You can configure the Execute Process task to pass required parameters such as cluster name, location, and storage account name to the PowerShell script using variables declared earlier, along with the expressions in Figure 16.3.

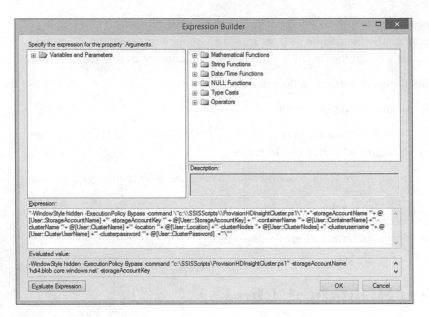

FIGURE 16.3
Execute Process task expression.

Similarly, you can use the `Remove-AzureHDInsightCluster` cmdlet to decommission an HDInsight cluster:

```
Remove-AzureHDInsightCluster -Name $clusterName
```

Refer to the PowerShell script `ProvisionHDInsightCluster.ps1` in the accompanying code samples for a full listing of a PowerShell script for creating a new HDInsight cluster.

Executing Hive Query

SSIS paired with PowerShell can execute Hive jobs using the `New-AzureHDInsightHiveJobDefinition` cmdlet. Refer to the `SubmitHiveJob.ps1` script in the accompanying code samples for a full listing of the PowerShell script for submitting a Hive job. The PowerShell script submits a `HiveScripts.sql` query for execution. The `HiveScripts.sql` in the accompanying code samples performs the following task:

▶ Creates `OnTimePerformance` and `AirlineLookup` external tables to consume CSV files at `/OnTimePerformance/Data` and `/OnTimePerformance/Lookup/Airline/`, respectively.

▶ Creates an `OnTimeDepartureData` table containing the airline ID and on-time departure percentage results from the Hive query.

Loading Query Results to a SQL Azure Table

SSIS data flow can move the query results from the Hive table `OnTimeDepartureData` to a SQL Azure table. You can connect an ODBC data source to Hive using the Hive ODBC driver, which you can download from http://www.microsoft.com/en-us/download/details.aspx?id=40886.

TIP

Installing both the 32-bit and 64-bit versions of the driver is recommended. At design time, Visual Studio relies on the 32-bit version of the driver because it's a 32-bit process, whereas the runtime utilizes the 64-bit version.

To configure the Hive ODBC data source, drag and drop the ODBC source component from the SSIS toolbox and create a new ODBC connection manager using the following connection string (see Figure 16.4):

```
DRIVER={Microsoft Hive ODBC Driver};Host=<cluster name>.azurehdinsight.net;Port=443;
Schema=default;RowsFetchedPerBlock=10000;HiveServerType=2;AuthMech=6;
DefaultStringColumnLength=4000
```

FIGURE 16.4
Configuring the Hive ODBC data source.

Provide the cluster username and password (you can set up expressions to configure these parameters to use values from the SSIS variables declared earlier) and click the Test Connection button to verify connectivity. Create a destination table in the SQL Server/Azure database to store the processing results, using the following command:

```
CREATE TABLE [dbo].[OnTimeDepartureData](
[Airline] [varchar](256) NOT NULL PRIMARY KEY,
[OnTimeDeptPercent] [float] NULL)
```

Add an Oleb Destination component and configure it to connect to the `OnTimeDepartureData` SQL Server/Azure database.

Executing the Package

You execute the SSIS package from within SQL Server Data Tools either by selecting Debug, Start Debugging from the menu or by pressing F5. The Execution Results tab shows the execution progress and any warnings or errors. When the package successfully executes, query the `OnTimeDepartureData` table. As Figure 16.5 shows, Hawaiian Airlines seems to have the highest percentage of on-time departures.

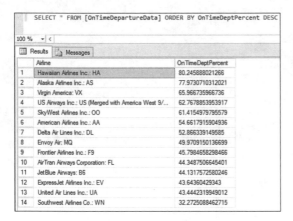

FIGURE 16.5
Airline on-time departure percentages.

NOTE

Other Ways to Build Data Integration Workflows

With unprecedented growth in the Hadoop ecosystem, multiple technologies have emerged in recent years for automating Hadoop jobs. One option, Oozie, is a workflow scheduler and coordination engine for managing Hadoop jobs. (Hour 20, "Performing Statistical Computing with R," covers Oozie workflows.) Oozie works well in scenarios that involve automation of jobs from inside an HDInsight cluster; in contrast, SSIS works outside HDInsight and can even spin up an HDInsight cluster on demand.

Summary

This hour introduced you to SQL Server Integration Services. Conventional relational database management systems, such as SQL Server and HDInsight, are complementary platforms. SSIS builds data integration workflows for transferring data between the two platforms and for automating management tasks, such as provisioning an HDInsight cluster on demand using Windows Azure PowerShell.

Q&A

Q. Is it possible to load data to HDInsight cluster using SSIS?

A. SSIS paired with PowerShell is a convenient way to transfer files to Windows Azure blob storage. You use the `Set-AzureStorageBlobContent` cmdlet for that purpose. Refer to http://azure.microsoft.com/en-us/documentation/articles/hdinsight-upload-data/#powershell for more details. The airline lookup and on-time performance CSV files that were loaded manually as a part of the scenario prerequisite also could have been loaded automatically using SSIS and PowerShell.

Q. Can SSIS packages execute on a defined schedule?

A. You can configure SSIS packages to run on a scheduled basis using either SQL Agent or Windows Task Scheduler (and dtexec). Refer to http://msdn.microsoft.com/en-us/library/ms141701.aspx for information on scheduling SSIS packages using SQL Agent. See http://msdn.microsoft.com/en-us/library/hh231187.aspx for information on running SSIS packages from the command line using the dtexec tool.

Quiz

1. How can SSIS be used to provision HDInsight cluster on demand?

2. Can data integration workflows for Hadoop be built in other ways?

Answers

1. PowerShell is a convenient way to provision and decommission an HDInsight cluster on demand. You use the `New-AzureHDInsightCluster` cmdlet to provision a new HDInsight cluster. Using the Execute Process task, you can invoke a PowerShell script to provision a new HDInsight cluster from within SSIS.

2. Yes, other workflow technologies are available for Hadoop. The most popular is Oozie, a workflow scheduler and coordination engine for managing Hadoop jobs from within an HDInsight cluster. Even a Pig job can be thought of as a high-level data integration workflow.

Using Pig for Data Processing

What You'll Learn in This Hour:

▶ Introduction to Pig Latin
▶ Using Pig to Count Cancelled Flights
▶ Using HCatalog in a Pig Latin Script
▶ Submitting Pig Jobs with PowerShell

Programming MapReduce jobs for data processing can be challenging and requires knowledge of Java program development. Pig provides a workflow-style procedural language, Pig Latin, that makes it easier to specify transformation operations on data. Pig Latin script is translated into a series of MapReduce jobs or a Tez DAG that performs the actual transformation and aggregation operations. Data analysts and researchers then can stay focused on data instead of worrying about the nuances of Java program development.

This hour provides an introduction to Pig for processing Big Data sets and details the steps involved in submitting Pig jobs to an HDInsight cluster.

Introduction to Pig Latin

Pig Latin is the Pig scripting language. Unlike SQL, which is a declarative language, Pig Latin is procedural. Pig Latin enables users to write data transformation operations as workflow-style steps. Pig Programs generally involve following three steps:

1. Load the data set of interest.

2. Run a series of data transformation operations.

3. Dump the processed data to screen or store it in a file. This executes a MapReduce program to produce the processed data.

Pig Initially Developed at Yahoo!

Pig was developed at Yahoo! in 2006 to enable researchers to query Big Data sets without worrying about the low-level details of writing MapReduce jobs. The goal was to develop an intermediate language between declarative SQL and low-level procedural MapReduce. In 2007, Apache adopted Pig, and it later became a Hadoop subproject.

Pig programs can run in two modes:

- ▶ Local mode, suitable for experimenting with Pig on small datasets.

- ▶ MapReduce mode, the default mode, which requires access to a Hadoop cluster. This mode is suitable for large datasets. Pig statements get translated to MapReduce jobs.

You can run Pig commands in batch mode by saving commands in a script file with a `.pig` extension or in interactive mode using Grunt, an interactive shell.

Using Pig to Count Cancelled Flights

This example uses on-time performance of airline flights data from the Research and Innovative Technology Administration, Bureau of Transportation Statistics (RITA) to determine the number of flights cancelled, grouped by flight cancellation reason. The data is available for download and analysis at http://www.transtats.bts.gov/DL_SelectFields. asp?Table_ID=236&DB_Short_Name=On-Time.

You can download lookup data related to cancellation codes and descriptions at http://www. transtats.bts.gov/Download_Lookup.asp?Lookup=L_CANCELLATION.

Uploading Data to an HDInsight Cluster for Processing

You can use a blob storage browser tool such as CloudXplorer to connect to the blob storage container being used as HDInsight cluster's file system and then upload the CSV file (see Figure 17.1).

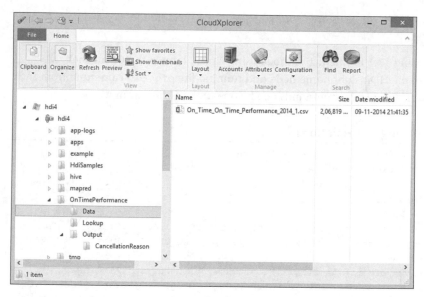

FIGURE 17.1
Uploading on-time performance flight data to blob storage.

Download the prezipped on-time performance file for January 2014 and upload the unzipped CSV file to the blob store at /OnTimePerformance/Data/On_Time_On_Time_ Performance_2014_1.csv. Also download lookup data related to cancellation codes and descriptions. Upload the lookup data file to the blob store at /OnTimePerformance/Lookup/L_ CANCELLATION.csv location.

Defining Pig Relations

A Pig relation is a collection of tuples. A relation is analogous to a table in a relational database. Pig Latin statements work with relations.

The Pig Latin LOAD statements in Listing 17.1 create two relations: OnTimePerformance and CancellationCodes, representing the on-time performance data and flight cancellation code descriptions, respectively. The USING clause in the LOAD statement specifies a function for loading data. In this case, CSVExcelStorage function is used to load a CSV file, specifying a comma as the field delimiter; multilines are not allowed inside fields, and system default options are used for line breaks and for skipping the header row. CSVExcelStorage uses the CSV conventions of Excel 2007.

To use the CSVExcelStorage function, you must register piggybank.jar. The schema for the relation is specified using the LOAD statement's AS clause. Because a data type has not been explicitly provided for fields, all fields are assumed to be of the type chararray, which is a string data type in Pig.

To run the code in Listing 17.1 in interactive mode using Grunt, launch the Grunt shell by remotely logging in to the HDInsight name node and running the pig.cmd command from the %PIG_HOME%\bin path. Submit the commands one by one at the Grunt prompt.

LISTING 17.1   Defining Pig Relations

```
-- Register piggybank.jar to use CSVExcelStorage
register %PIG_HOME%\lib\piggybank.jar;

-- Load OnTimePerformance data
OnTimePerformance = LOAD
'/OnTimePerformance/Data/On_Time_On_Time_Performance_2014_1.csv' USING
org.apache.pig.piggybank.storage.CSVExcelStorage(',', 'NO_MULTILINE', 'NOCHANGE',
'SKIP_INPUT_HEADER') AS
(Year,Quarter,Month,DayofMonth,DayOfWeek,FlightDate,UniqueCarrier,AirlineID,Carrier
,TailNum,FlightNum,OriginAirportID,OriginAirportSeqID,OriginCityMarketID,Origin,Ori
ginCityName,OriginState,OriginStateFips,OriginStateName,OriginWac,DestAirportID,Des
tAirportSeqID,DestCityMarketID,Dest,DestCityName,DestState,DestStateFips,DestStateN
ame,DestWac,CRSDepTime,DepTime,DepDelay,DepDelayMinutes,DepDel15,DepartureDelayGrou
ps,DepTimeBlk,TaxiOut,WheelsOff,WheelsOn,TaxiIn,CRSArrTime,ArrTime,ArrDelay,ArrDela
yMinutes,ArrDel15,ArrivalDelayGroups,ArrTimeBlk,Cancelled,CancellationCode,Diverted
,CRSElapsedTime,ActualElapsedTime,AirTime,Flights,Distance,DistanceGroup,CarrierDel
ay,WeatherDelay,NASDelay,SecurityDelay,LateAircraftDelay,FirstDepTime,TotalAddGTime
,LongestAddGTime,DivAirportLandings,DivReachedDest,DivActualElapsedTime,DivArrDelay
,DivDistance,Div1Airport,Div1AirportID,Div1AirportSeqID,Div1WheelsOn,Div1TotalGTime
,Div1LongestGTime,Div1WheelsOff,Div1TailNum,Div2Airport,Div2AirportID,Div2AirportSe
qID,Div2WheelsOn,Div2TotalGTime,Div2LongestGTime,Div2WheelsOff,Div2TailNum,Div3Airp
ort,Div3AirportID,Div3AirportSeqID,Div3WheelsOn,Div3TotalGTime,Div3LongestGTime,Div
3WheelsOff,Div3TailNum,Div4Airport,Div4AirportID,Div4AirportSeqID,Div4WheelsOn,Div4
TotalGTime,Div4LongestGTime,Div4WheelsOff,Div4TailNum,Div5Airport,Div5AirportID,Div
5AirportSeqID,Div5WheelsOn,Div5TotalGTime,Div5LongestGTime,Div5WheelsOff,Div5TailNu
m);
-- Load Cancellation Codes and Description
CancellationCodes = LOAD '/OnTimePerformance/Lookup/L_CANCELLATION.csv' USING
org.apache.pig.piggybank.storage.CSVExcelStorage(',', 'NO_MULTILINE', 'NOCHANGE',
'SKIP_INPUT_HEADER') AS (Code,Description);
```

Filtering Pig Relations

Records in the data pipeline are filtered using the FILTER statement. For example, the following pig statement filters the OnTimePerformance relation for cancelled flights and creates a new relation named CancelledFlight that contains only records with the Cancelled field value equal to 1 (cancelled flight records).

```
-- Get cancelled flights
CancelledFlights = FILTER OnTimePerformance BY (int)Cancelled == 1;
```

Grouping Records by Cancellation Code

A relation can be grouped by its fields using the GROUP operator. For example, the following Pig Latin statement groups cancelled flights by cancellation code:

```
-- Group by Cancellation Code
GroupedByFlightCancellationCode = GROUP CancelledFlights BY (CancellationCode);
```

GroupedByFlightCancellationCode relation contains tuples with two fields:

- ▶ The first field, group, contains the cancellation code.
- ▶ The second field is a collection of tuples of cancelled flights that correspond to a cancellation code (group key). This field takes the name of the original relation on which the grouping was applied.

Summarizing Cancelled Flights by Reason

The next step in the analysis involves summarizing the grouped data and generating as output the number of flights cancelled, by cancellation code. To accomplish this, the Foreach operator comes in handy. Foreach applies an expression to each record in the data pipeline and generates new records. For example, in the following statement, Foreach iterates through the GroupedByFlightCancellationCode relation and generates a new relation, named CancelledFlightCountByCode, that contains the fields CancellationReason (which is the group's key field) and Count (which contains the count of records in each group).

```
-- Count flight in each group
CancelledFlightCountByCode = FOREACH GroupedByFlightCancellationCode GENERATE group
as CancellationCode, COUNT(CancelledFlights) as Count;
```

Retrieving the Cancellation Description by Joining Relations

To generate the final output (the count of flights, by cancellation reason), you must retrieve the cancellation reason description that corresponds to the cancellation code from the CancellationCodes relation. This requires a join between the CancellationCodes and CancelledFlightCountByCode relations. You can use a Join operator to combine relations based on common fields.

```
-- Join Cancellation Codes with Cancelled flight data set
CancelledFlightCountWithReason = JOIN CancelledFlightCountByCode BY
CancellationCode, CancellationCodes By Code;
```

Saving Results to the File System

Before you can save the `CancelledFlightCountWithReason` relation to the file system, it must be subselected to select only the cancellation code description and count fields. The `Foreach` command achieves this:

```
ResultSet = FOREACH CancelledFlightCountWithReason GENERATE
CancellationCodes::Description as CancellationCode, CancelledFlightCountByCode::
Count as CancelledFlightCount;
```

Finally, you can use the `Store` statement to write this relation to the file system:

```
STORE ResultSet INTO '/OnTimePerformance/Output/CancellationReason';
```

To examine the CloudExplorer output file, navigate to the `/OnTimePerformance/Output` folder (see Figure 17.2).

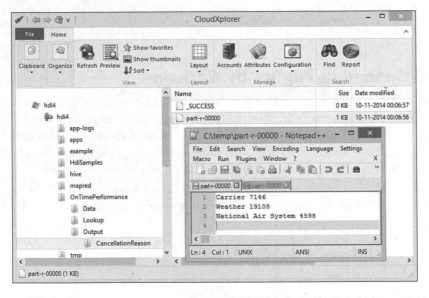

FIGURE 17.2
Examining final output.

Using HCatalog in a Pig Latin Script

Having filenames and schema hardcoded in Pig script files is a maintenance nightmare. Any change to input file location or schema causes breaking changes in all the dependent scripts. Fortunately, HCatalog works with Pig queries to abstract file paths and schema

definitions. For example, the following CREATE EXTERNAL TABLE statement creates an
OnTimePerformance HCatalog external table:

```
CREATE EXTERNAL TABLE OnTimePerformance (Year STRING,Quarter STRING,Month
STRING,DayofMonth STRING,DayOfWeek STRING,FlightDate STRING,UniqueCarrier
STRING,AirlineID STRING,Carrier STRING,TailNum STRING,FlightNum
STRING,OriginAirportID STRING,OriginAirportSeqID STRING,OriginCityMarketID
STRING,Origin STRING,OriginCityName STRING,OriginState STRING,OriginStateFips
STRING,OriginStateName STRING,OriginWac STRING,DestAirportID
STRING,DestAirportSeqID STRING,DestCityMarketID STRING,Dest STRING,DestCityName
STRING,DestState STRING,DestStateFips STRING,DestStateName STRING,DestWac
STRING,CRSDepTime STRING,DepTime STRING,DepDelay STRING,DepDelayMinutes
STRING,DepDel15 STRING,DepartureDelayGroups STRING,DepTimeBlk STRING,TaxiOut
STRING,WheelsOff STRING,WheelsOn STRING,TaxiIn STRING,CRSArrTime STRING,ArrTime
STRING,ArrDelay STRING,ArrDelayMinutes STRING,ArrDel15 STRING,ArrivalDelayGroups
STRING,ArrTimeBlk STRING,Cancelled STRING,CancellationCode STRING,Diverted
STRING,CRSElapsedTime STRING,ActualElapsedTime STRING,AirTime STRING,Flights
STRING,Distance STRING,DistanceGroup STRING,CarrierDelay STRING,WeatherDelay
STRING,NASDelay STRING,SecurityDelay STRING,LateAircraftDelay STRING,FirstDepTime
STRING,TotalAddGTime STRING,LongestAddGTime STRING,DivAirportLandings
STRING,DivReachedDest STRING,DivActualElapsedTime STRING,DivArrDelay
STRING,DivDistance STRING,Div1Airport STRING,Div1AirportID STRING,Div1AirportSeqID
STRING,Div1WheelsOn STRING,Div1TotalGTime STRING,Div1LongestGTime
STRING,Div1WheelsOff STRING,Div1TailNum STRING,Div2Airport STRING,Div2AirportID
STRING,Div2AirportSeqID STRING,Div2WheelsOn STRING,Div2TotalGTime
STRING,Div2LongestGTime STRING,Div2WheelsOff STRING,Div2TailNum STRING,Div3Airport
STRING,Div3AirportID STRING,Div3AirportSeqID STRING,Div3WheelsOn
STRING,Div3TotalGTime STRING,Div3LongestGTime STRING,Div3WheelsOff
STRING,Div3TailNum STRING,Div4Airport STRING,Div4AirportID STRING,Div4AirportSeqID
STRING,Div4WheelsOn STRING,Div4TotalGTime STRING,Div4LongestGTime
STRING,Div4WheelsOff STRING,Div4TailNum STRING,Div5Airport STRING,Div5AirportID
STRING,Div5AirportSeqID STRING,Div5WheelsOn STRING,Div5TotalGTime
STRING,Div5LongestGTime STRING,Div5WheelsOff STRING,Div5TailNum STRING) ROW FORMAT
SERDE 'com.bizo.hive.serde.csv.CSVSerde' STORED AS TEXTFILE LOCATION
'/OnTimePerformance/Data' tblproperties ("skip.header.line.count"="1");
```

The CREATE EXTERNAL TABLE statement uses the com.bizo.hive.serde.csv.CSVSerde
Serde to interpret CSV files. The serde is defined in csv-serde-1.1.2.jar, which you can
download from http://ogrodnek.github.io/csv-serde/. All the fields have been defined as strings.
The string data type maps to the chararray data type in Pig. Save the schema definition
script to a file with the extension .hcatalog and execute it in HCatalog using the following
command from the Hadoop command line:

```
%HCATALOG_HOME%\bin\hcat.py -f C:\Scripts\CreateTableScript.hcatalog
```

Before you can execute the script, copy csv-serde-1.1.2.jar into the Hive and Pig libraries at
%HIVE_HOME%\lib\csv-serde-1.1.2.jar and %PIG_HOME%\lib\csv-serde-1.1.2.jar.

Finally, launch Grunt with the useHCatalog switch for using HCatalog with Pig. Listing 17.2 shows how to use HCatalog with Pig. The HCatloader function reads data from HCatalog-managed tables.

LISTING 17.2   **Using HCatalog with Pig Queries**

```
-- Launching grunt with useHCatalog switch
pig -useHCatalog

-- Registering csv serde
register C:\apps\dist\pig-0.12.1.2.1.6.0-2103\lib\csv-serde-1.1.2.jar;

-- Creating OnTimePerformance relation from HCatalog schema definition
OnTimePerformance = LOAD 'OnTimePerformance' USING org.apache.hcatalog.pig.
HCatLoader();
```

Specifying Parallelism in Pig Latin

When executing pig queries in MapReduce mode, the PARALLEL keyword comes in handy for specifying the number of reducers. The PARALLEL clause works in conjunction with the group, join, distinct, and order operators. For example, you can set the number of reducers to 20 when grouping flights by cancellation code in the flight cancellation scenario using the following statement:

```
GroupedByFlightCancellationCode = GROUP CancelledFlights BY (CancellationCode)
PARALLEL 20;
```

Another way to set the number of reducers is to use the command set defaultllel. This sets the number of reducers at the script level. When the number of reducers is not explicitly specified, one reducer is used for every 1GB of input data, with an upper bound of 999 reducers.

NOTE

The PARALLEL Clause Does Not Affect the Number of Map Tasks

The PARALLEL clause does not affect the number of map tasks. Map parallelism is dependent on the size of the input, with one map for each HDFS block.

Submitting Pig Jobs with PowerShell

Pig jobs can also be submitted using PowerShell or .NET SDK. You create a new Pig job using the New-AzureHDInsightPigJobDefinition cmdlet and submit it to the HDInsight cluster for execution using the Start-HDInsightJob cmdlet.

Adding Azure Subscription

Before you create a new Pig job definition, you must make an Azure account available to Windows PowerShell. You add an Azure account to Windows PowerShell in two ways:

- ▶ With the `Add-AzureAccount` cmdlet
- ▶ With the `Import-AzurePublishSettingsFile` cmdlet

The `Add-AzureAccount` cmdlet uses Azure Active Directory authentication. The `Import-AzurePublishSettingsFile` cmdlet uses a management certificate to connect to Azure. Using the `Add-AzureAccount` cmdlet is the easier method, and it prompts for Azure account credentials.

TIP

When an access token is authenticated, it remains valid for 12 hours. Credentials must be reentered after the token expires.

Creating a Pig Job Definition

A Pig job definition requires specifying either a query string (using the `-Query` switch) or a script file (using the `-File` switch), along with indicating a status folder location for storing error log and standard output file (see Listing 17.3).

LISTING 17.3   Creating a Pig Job Definition

```
$statusFolder = "/OnTimePerformance/Output"
$QueryString = "CancellationCodes = LOAD
'/OnTimePerformance/Lookup/L_CANCELLATION.csv' USING
org.apache.pig.piggybank.storage.CSVExcelStorage(',', 'NO_MULTILINE', 'NOCHANGE',
'SKIP_INPUT_HEADER') AS (Code,Description);" +
"DUMP CancellationCodes;"
$pigJobDefinition = New-AzureHDInsightPigJobDefinition -Query $QueryString -
StatusFolder $statusFolder
```

Submitting a Pig Job for Execution

You create a Pig job with the `New-AzureHDInsightPigJobDefinition` cmdlet and then submit it for execution using the `Start-AzureHDInsightJob` cmdlet, specifying the cluster name and job definition object reference as arguments (see Listing 17.4).

LISTING 17.4 Submitting a Pig Job for Execution

```
$clusterName = "<<HDInsight Cluster Name>>"
$pigJob = Start-AzureHDInsightJob -Cluster $clusterName -JobDefinition
$pigJobDefinition
```

If you want to wait for job execution completion or failure and monitor the job progress, you can use the `Wait-AzureHDInsightJob` cmdlet. For example, the following command waits for a job to complete and times out after 3600 seconds:

```
Wait-AzureHDInsightJob -Job $pigJob -WaitTimeoutInSeconds 3600
```

Upon execution completion, the job `State`, `JobId`, and other information display (see Figure 17.3).

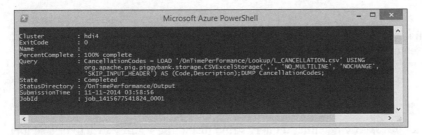

FIGURE 17.3
Pig job execution completion.

Getting the Job Output

The cmdlet `Get-AzureHDInsightJobOutput` retrieves the log output for a job by specifying the cluster name and `JobId` as parameters. With the cmdlet, you can retrieve various types of job logs, including standard output, standard error, task logs, and a summary of task logs. For example, the following command retrieves the standard output (`DUMP` command output) for the executed Pig job:

```
Get-AzureHDInsightJobOutput -Cluster $clusterName -JobId $pigJob.JobId -
StandardOutput
```

Figure 17.4 shows the job's standard output retrieved using the `Get-AzureHDInsightJobOutput` cmdlet.

FIGURE 17.4
Pig job output.

If any errors occur during processing, the job might not return any information upon completion. To troubleshoot in such scenarios and retrieve the error message, include the following code snippet at the end of the job definition:

```
Get-AzureHDInsightJobOutput -Cluster $clusterName -JobId $pigJob.JobId -
StandardError
```

Summary

This hour explored the use of Pig Latin for querying Big Data sets and examined the suitability of Pig Latin for scenarios involving data pipelines. The hour concluded by illustrating the steps involved in submitting a Pig job for execution to an HDInsight cluster.

Q&A

Q. Why was the programming language named Pig?

A. The exact origins of the name are unknown. The closest guess is that, like pigs— omnivorous animals that eat anything—Pig deals with any type of data: relational, nested, semi-structured, or unstructured. In line with the naming convention, the command shell is named Grunt and the shared JAR repository is named Piggybank.

Q. Pig and Hive seem almost equivalent. Both abstract the low-level details of programming the MapReduce job from the user. Is Pig really needed?

A. Many programmers prefer a procedural approach to querying data over a declarative approach, so programmers find Pig more comfortable to work with than Hive. Pig also is very suitable for scenarios that involve data pipelines in which many operations and transformations are to be applied to incoming data in stages. Achieving the same effect in Hive involves creating temporary tables for each stage, which is not a very elegant solution. Finally, researchers find Pig the best fit for their job. Although Hive works well in data warehousing scenarios, with data already cleansed and transformed, researchers sometimes need to deal with dirty data that requires some transformation and standardization. Pig works better than Hive in such scenarios.

Quiz

1. How are hardcoded path and schema definitions removed from Pig scripts?

2. How are parallel map tasks configured in Pig?

Answers

1. HCatalog is used with Pig queries to abstract file paths and schema definitions. Table schema are defined and managed using Hcatalog, and you can use the `HCatloader` function to read data from an HCatalog-managed table.

2. Map parallelism is dependent on the size of the input, with one map for each HDFS block. You can use the `PARALLEL` clause to specify a number of `reduce` tasks, but this does not affect the number of `map` tasks.

Using Sqoop for Data Movement Between RDBMS and HDInsight

What You'll Learn in This Hour:

▶ What Is Sqoop?

▶ Using Sqoop Import and Export Commands

▶ Using Sqoop with PowerShell

Sqoop facilitates data migration between relational databases and Hadoop. This hour introduces you to the SQL Server Sqoop connector for Hadoop and its use for data migration between Hadoop and SQL Server/SQL Azure databases.

What Is Sqoop?

Apache Sqoop is a data migration tool that facilitates the transfer of data between relational databases and Hadoop. Sqoop typically is used with HDInsight to import data from SQL Server (a relational database management system) to Hadoop, perform analysis with MapReduce, and export the analysis results to SQL Server for further analysis or visualizations with the Microsoft BI stack.

Sqoop uses Java Database Connectivity (JDBC) connectors to import and export data to relational databases. Sqoop connectors are available for most popular relational databases, including SQL Server, Oracle, and MySQL. Sqoop also provides faster bulk transfer connectors that use database-specific interfaces for faster transfers for certain relational databases. This is referred to as *direct mode transfer*. Direct mode transfer option is not yet available for SQL Server connector.

Importing Data to HDInsight Clusters

The following required Sqoop components are preinstalled on HDInsight clusters:

▶ Microsoft SQL Server JDBC driver

▶ SQL Server Sqoop Connector for Hadoop (part of Apache Sqoop 1.4 and not required to be installed separately)

You can use this Sqoop import command to import data directly from SQL Server/Azure SQL databases, without performing additional software installation:

```
%SQOOP_HOME%\bin\sqoop.cmd import --connect
"jdbc:sqlserver://SQL_Server;database=Database_Name;Username=Sql_User@ SQL_Server;
Password=Password;" --table Source_Table --m No_Of_Map_Tasks --target-dir
Destination_Directory
```

For example, the following command connects to the SQL Azure database named AdventureWorks, retrieves data for the DimCustomer table, and dumps it to the /AW/ DimCustomer location:

```
%SQOOP_HOME%\bin\sqoop.cmd import --connect
"jdbc:sqlserver://YourSQLAzureServer.database.windows.net;database=AdventureWorks;
Username=Sql_User@YourSQLAzureServer;Password=SQLAzurePassword;" --table
DimCustomer
--m 1 --target-dir /AW/DimCustomer
```

NOTE

Sqoop Network Connectivity

When using Sqoop, network connectivity is required between the HDInsight cluster and the target SQL Server instance, but corporate firewalls often restrict this for on-premises database servers. Hence, Sqoop is generally suited for data transfer to the SQL Azure database or to the SQL Server instance hosted on virtual machines running in Azure.

The imported data is dumped into a comma-delimited text file, which is the default import format. You can use the argument --fields-terminated-by to specify a different delimiter.

Note that the Sqoop import command launches a MapReduce job to connect to SQL Azure database and read the table data. The -m1 parameter specifies the number of parallel map tasks Sqoop should use to speed up the read operation. A value of 1 implies Sqoop should use a single map task to read data. In the case of multiple map tasks, the imported data is written to multiple files because each map task writes data imported by it in a separate data file.

CAUTION

Degree of Parallelism

Do not attempt to set the degree of parallelism to an unreasonable value. Setting a value beyond the MapReduce cluster capacity can cause the tasks to run serially and increase the import time. An unreasonably high number of concurrent connections also increases the load on the database server and impacts its performance.

By default, Sqoop uses the primary key column as the splitting column in a table to split the workload. If required, you can use the argument `split-by` to specify an alternative column. This is useful when the primary key is not uniformly distributed and could result in non-uniform load distribution between parallel tasks.

Sqoop also enables you to import a subset of table data. For example, you can use the `--columns` argument to specify a comma-delimited list of columns to include in importing from the table. You can limit the number of rows imported by using the `--where` argument and specifying a filter criteria. For even more control on the import, you can use the `--query` option to specify a SQL statement in place of `--table`, `--columns`, and `--where` arguments. For example, the following Sqoop command imports the first name, last name, and cars owned from the DimCustomer table by specifying a SQL query to get the results:

```
sqoop import --query 'SELECT FirstName,LastName,NumberCarsOwned FROM DimCustomer
WHERE $CONDITIONS' --split-by CustomerKey --target-dir /AW/DimCustomer
```

The SQL query includes a `$CONDITIONS` token that Sqoop replaces with the `split by` column name expression to split the workload.

Importing to Hive

Sqoop can also create Hive tables for imported data. Using the `--hive-import` argument with the Sqoop import command generates a Hive `CREATE TABLE` statement to create a table based on the schema definition in the relational data source. This prompts the `LOAD DATA INPATH` statement to load in the data to Hive. After the import, Sqoop invokes Hive to execute both these statements. You specify the Hive table name using the `--hive-table` option. If you don't specify a table name, Sqoop uses the source table name. Sqoop also provides an option to import data to a particular Hive partition using the `--hive-partition-key` and `--hive-partition-value` arguments.

NOTE

Row and Column Delimiters

The presence of row or column delimiter characters in the imported data troubles Hive's input parser. Be sure to specify unambiguous row or column delimiters using the `--fields-terminated-by` and `--lines-terminated-by` arguments. Another alternative is to use the `--hive-drop-import-delims` argument to remove delimiters from data.

Exporting Data from HDFS

Sqoop can also export data from HDFS to a database table. It can generate both insert and update statements to append data to an existing table or perform updates. In addition,

Sqoop can invoke stored procedures for each exported record. Export mode involves using the `--export-dir` and `--table` or `--call` arguments. The `--export-dir` argument specifies the HDFS directory containing the source data; the `--table` and `--call` arguments specify the destination table and stored procedure to be invoked, respectively. The insert and update operations are performed row by row, and no direct mode support for SQL Server is available yet.

As with import, you can use `--columns` to specify a comma-delimited list of columns for export. Columns not present in the export column list should either be nullable or have a default constraint defined. You can also use the argument `-m` to control the degree of parallelism (the number of parallel write operations).

By default, Sqoop export appends data to an existing table. To update existing records, you must specify an update key via the `--update-key` argument. If no records need to be updated in the destination table corresponding to an update key, the records are ignored. You can alter this behavior and instead perform a merge operation by using the `--update-mode` argument and specifying the `allowinsert` option. With this option, if a record exists in the destination table, it is updated; otherwise, a new row is inserted. Multiple rows also might get updated with a single input record if the update key does not uniquely identify destination records.

Understanding the Export Process

Sqoop splits the export process into multiple transactions. Multiple parallel write operations spawn separate database connections, each with separate transactions. Transactions are committed every 10,000 records. Multiple Map tasks run in parallel to export data, with each map task having its own transaction committed at periodic intervals, so a failed export command can result in partial export of data. You can avoid this scenario by transferring data initially to a staging table and then moving the data to the destination table in a single transaction. The argument `--staging-table` specifies the staging table during export.

Using Sqoop Import and Export Commands

This section illustrates the steps involved in using Sqoop import and export commands by first importing a data set from SQL Server (a relational database management system [RDBMS]) to Hadoop, performing analysis on imported data with MapReduce, and then exporting the results back to SQL Server, which can be used for further analysis or visualizations with the Microsoft BI stack. In practical scenarios, you will rarely need to import data to Hadoop from SQL Server. Instead, Sqoop is more often used to export the results of any analytics done on a Big Data set on Hadoop, to an RDBMS such as SQL Server.

Importing Data from SQL Server to Sqoop

The following steps describe the process of importing `DimCustomer` table data from Adventure Works to Hive, filtering it for married customers who own a house and have a yearly income of more than $100,000, and exporting the filtered results back to SQL Server. From a data volume perspective, `DimCustomer` is a small table. Exporting such a small data set to Hadoop might not make much sense in actual practice.

1. Launch the Hadoop command line.

2. Invoke the following command to import the DimCustomer table to Hive:

```
%SQOOP_HOME%\bin\sqoop.cmd import --connect
"jdbc:sqlserver://SQL_Server;database=Database_Name;Username=Sql_User@ SQL_
Server;
Password=Password;" --table Source_Table --m No_Of_Map_Tasks --hive-import
--hive-
drop-import-delims
```

3. Monitor the import MapReduce job for completion, when imported data then is loaded to the Hive table. Hive then prints an "import complete" message on the console (see Figure 18.1).

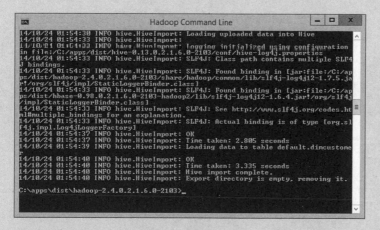

FIGURE 18.1
Importing data to Hive.

4. Execute the following `alter table` statement to add a new column titled `IsFiltered` to the `DimCustomer` table. Sqoop will later update this column to `1` for married customers who own a house and have a yearly income more than $100,000.

```
ALTER TABLE [DimCustomer] ADD [IsFiltered] BIT
```

5. Launch the Hive console from the Hadoop command line.

6. Hive uses an SOH, or Start of Heading (generated by pressing Ctrl+A), character as the default column delimiter, whereas Sqoop uses a comma as the default column delimiter. Use the following command to create the `FilteredCustomer` Hive table, using a comma as the column delimiter and specifying two columns: `CustomerKey`, for married customers who own a house and have a yearly income more than $100,000, and the `IsFiltered` flag, set to `1`.

```
CREATE TABLE FilteredCustomer ROW FORMAT DELIMITED FIELDS TERMINATED BY ',' AS
SELECT CustomerKey, 1 AS IsFiltered FROM DimCustomer WHERE MaritalStatus='M' AND
HouseOwnerFlag=1 AND YearlyIncome>100000
```

NOTE

Hive Query Results Cannot Be Directly Exported via Sqoop

You cannot directly export Hive query results via Sqoop. The best way to export Hive query results is to dump the result set into a Hive table and export the table contents instead.

7. Monitor the MapReduce job for completion, when the new Hive table `FilteredCustomer` will be created at `/hive/warehouse/filteredcustomer` (see Figure 18.2).

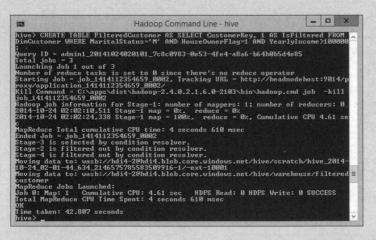

FIGURE 18.2
Creating the `FilteredCustomer` table in Hive.

8. Examine the file contents of the `/hive/warehouse/filteredcustomer` folder using the following command to examine the imported data:

```
hadoop fs -cat /hive/warehouse/filteredcustomer/000000_0
```

9. Finally, use the following command at the Hadoop command line to export the `FilteredCustomer` table to the SQL Server database. The export process updates the `IsFiltered` column in the SQL Server database using `CustomerKey` as the update key. When the export operation completes, the number of records exported is printed to console (see Figure 18.3).

```
%SQOOP_HOME%\bin\sqoop.cmd export --connect "jdbc:sqlserver://
SQL_Server;database=Database_Name;Username=Sql_User@ SQL_
Server;Password=Password;" --table SQL_Server_Table --m No_Of_Map_
Tasks --export-dir Source_Directory --update-key CustomerKey --columns
"CustomerKey,IsFiltered"
```

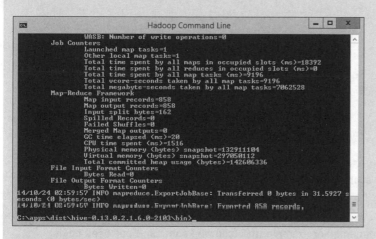

FIGURE 18.3
Exporting data to SQL Server.

Using Sqoop with PowerShell

The Sqoop export and import commands can also be conveniently invoked from PowerShell, without needing to remotely log in to the HDInsight Name node, using the New-AzureHDInsightSqoopJobDefinition cmdlet. As the following code snippet illustrates, the Command argument of the cmdlet specifies the Sqoop export/import command discussed earlier:

```
$clusterName="<HDInsight Cluster Name>"
# Creating a Sqoop job definition using New-AzureHDInsightSqoopJobDefinition cmdlet
$jobDef = New-AzureHDInsightSqoopJobDefinition -Command "export --connect ""export
--connect ""jdbc:sqlserver://SQL_Server;database=Database_Name;Username=Sql_User@
SQL_Server;Password=Password;"" --table SQL_Server_Table --m No_Of_Map_Tasks --
export-dir Source_Directory --update-key CustomerKey --columns
""CustomerKey,IsFiltered"""
# Invoking the job
```

```
$job = Start-AzureHDInsightJob -Cluster $clusterName -JobDefinition $jobDef #-Debug
-Verbose
# Waiting for job completion
Wait-AzureHDInsightJob -WaitTimeoutInSeconds 3600 -Job $job
```

The `Start-AzureHDInsightJob` cmdlet invokes the Sqoop job. The `Wait-AzureHDInsightJob` cmdlet tracks the progress and waits for job completion.

The `Get-AzureHDInsightJobOutput` cmdlet can troubleshoot job failures by retrieving errors logged to standard error stream, as the following code snippet illustrates:

```
Get-AzureHDInsightJobOutput -Cluster $clusterName -JobId $job.JobId -StandardError
```

Summary

This hour explored how to use Sqoop for migrating data between the HDInsight cluster and the SQL Server database, and concluded with a typical use case for Sqoop.

Q&A

Q. **While importing data with Sqoop, I cannot determine an unambiguous delimiter for text files. What are my options in such a scenario?**

A. When a chosen delimiter might occur in imported data, use qualifiers to avoid ambiguity. You can accomplish this by using the `--escaped-by` and `--enclosed-by` arguments of the Sqoop import command. For example, the following command encloses fields in an imported file in double quotes: `sqoop import --fields-terminated-by , --escaped-by \\ --enclosed-by '\"'`.

Q. **How can a Hive table using a default Hive column delimiter be exported to SQL Server using Sqoop?**

A. The argument `--input-fields-terminated-by` specifies the input column delimiter during Sqoop export. For a Hive table using the default Hive column delimiter, you should specify a value of `\0001` as the input delimiter instead of a comma.

Quiz

1. Does the presence of row or column delimiters in the imported data impact the Sqoop import to Hive?

2. What criteria does Sqoop use to split the workload during a parallel import?

Answers

1. The presence of row or column delimiter characters in the imported data can trouble Hive's input parser. Specify unambiguous row or column delimiters using the `--fields-terminated-by` and `--lines-terminated-by` arguments. Another alternative is to use the `--hive-drop-import-delims` argument to remove delimiters from data.

2. Sqoop uses the primary key column by default to split the workload. If required, you can use the argument `--split-by` to specify an alternative column. This is useful when the primary key is not uniformly distributed and could result in non-uniform load distribution between parallel tasks.

Using Oozie Workflows and Job Orchestration with HDInsight

What You'll Learn in This Hour:

▶ Introduction to Oozie

▶ Determining On-time Flight Departure Percentage with Oozie

▶ Submitting an Oozie Workflow with HDInsight .NET SDK

▶ Coordinating Workflows with Oozie

▶ Oozie Compared to SSIS

Data processing solutions require multiple jobs to be chained together to accomplish a processing task in the form of a conditional workflow.

Hour 16, "Integrating HDInsight with SQL Server Integration Services," discussed using SQL Server Integration Services (SSIS) to develop such workflows. This hour introduces Oozie, a workflow development component within the Hadoop ecosystem.

Introduction to Oozie

Oozie is a workflow scheduler and coordination engine for managing Hadoop jobs. The Oozie framework comes preinstalled with an HDInsight cluster. Oozie workflows are executed from a machine with the Oozie client tools installed. On an HDInsight cluster, Oozie frameworks can also be executed using either PowerShell or the Oozie client in the HDInsight .NET SDK. Oozie consists of these main parts:

▶ Workflow engine that supports workflow jobs of different types (MapReduce, Pig, Hive, Sqoop, and so on)

▶ Coordinator engine, responsible for running workflows based on time and data triggers

▶ Bundle engine, enabling users to manage the bundle or set of coordinator jobs

NOTE

Oozie was initially designed at Yahoo! to fulfill the need for a server-based workflow scheduling system for managing Hadoop jobs. It is still used extensively at Yahoo! for workflow orchestration and management. It was released to the open source community in early 2010.

Oozie Workflow

An Oozie *workflow* is a collection of actions. An Oozie *action* is a task that involves some processing or computation. Oozie actions include a MapReduce program execution, a Pig or Hive query execution, an Oozie subworkflow, and email notifications. You can also create custom actions.

NOTE

The Oozie Engine Leverages an HDInsight Cluster to Execute Actions

Oozie is a server-based workflow engine and only *triggers* workflow actions—the MapReduce framework is responsible for executing those actions. A workflow action simply invokes a job in a Hadoop subsystem (Hive, Pig, or plain old MapReduce). Oozie waits for an action completion notification before invoking the next action in the flow. This enables Oozie to leverage HDInsight cluster capabilities for load balancing workloads and handling failures.

A workflow arranges actions along with control nodes in a Directed Acyclic Graph (see Figure 19.1). This implies that the next action in the workflow cannot execute until the current action finishes execution. Nodes such as decision, fork, and join in Figure 19.1 control the execution path and hence are referred to as *control nodes*.

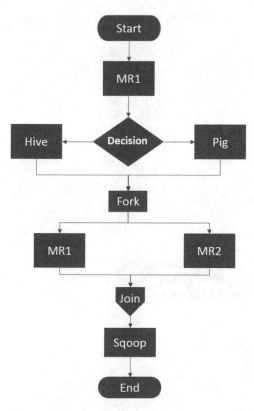

FIGURE 19.1
An Oozie workflow.

Determining On-time Flight Departure Percentage with Oozie

This scenario seeks to determine the on-time flight departure percentage for airlines using an Oozie workflow. Although the problem is easily solved with a single Hive query, the aim here is to illustrate Oozie workflow features. Four hive jobs are thus created to accomplish the following tasks:

▶ Create the required table structures

▶ Determine the total number of flights, by airline

▶ Determine the total number of on-time departure flights, by airline

▶ Join the result set of total flights and on-time departure flights, and determine the on-time departure percentage for each airline

Figure 19.2 shows these scripts organized as a workflow. Scripts to determine total flights and on-time departure flights execute in parallel.

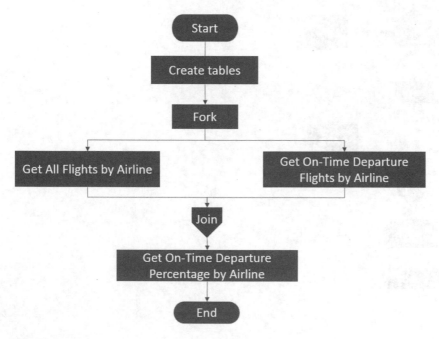

FIGURE 19.2
Workflow to determine on-time flight departure percentage.

The scenario uses on-time performance of airline flight data from the Research and Innovative Technology Administration, Bureau of Transportation Statistics (RITA). The data is available for download and analysis at http://www.transtats.bts.gov/DL_SelectFields.asp?Table_ID=236&DB_Short_Name=On-Time.

You can download lookup data related to airline ID and descriptions at http://www.transtats.bts.gov/Download_Lookup.asp?Lookup=L_AIRLINE_ID.

Scenario Prerequisites

Download prezipped on-time performance file for January 2014 and upload the unzipped CSV file to the blob store at /OnTimePerformance/Data/On_Time_On_Time_Performance_2014_1.csv. Also download lookup data related to airline IDs and descriptions.

Upload the lookup data files to the blob store at `/OnTimePerformance/Lookup/Airline/L_CANCELLATION.csv`.

Upload the HiveQL files `CreateTables.sql`, `HiveScriptDepPercent.sql`, `HiveScriptFinalOutput.sql`, and `HiveScriptTotalFlights.sql` from the code samples accompanying this hour to `/OozieWorkflow` on the blob store.

The Hive tables used in the scenario rely on `com.bizo.hive.serde.csv.CSVSerde` Serde to interpret CSV files. The Serde is defined in `csv-serde-1.1.2.jar`, which you can download from http://ogrodnek.github.io/csv-serde/. Download the JAR file from the link. Upload the JAR file to the blob storage at `/OozieWorkflow`. At this point, the contents of `/OozieWorkflow` should be similar to Figure 19.3.

FIGURE 19.3
Oozie workflow contents.

Creating an Oozie Workflow

Oozie workflows are defined in the Hadoop Process Definition Language (hPDL). Listing 19.1 shows an example of a basic Oozie workflow that executes a Hive action. The workflow action is named `CreateTables-Node` and defines two parameters—`OnTimePerformance_Data` and `Airline_Lookup`—passed to the `CreateTables.sql` script. The workflow has three control nodes. When the action successfully completes, execution control is passed to the `end` control node; upon failure, control goes to the `kill` control node.

LISTING 19.1   Defining an Oozie Workflow

```
<workflow-app xmlns="uri:oozie:workflow:0.2" name="hive-wf">
    <start to="CreateTables-Node"/>
    <action name="CreateTables-Node">
        <hive xmlns="uri:oozie:hive-action:0.2">
            <job-tracker>${jobTracker}</job-tracker>
            <name-node>${nameNode}</name-node>
            <configuration>
                <property>
                    <name>mapred.job.queue.name</name>
                    <value>${queueName}</value>
                </property>
                <property>
                    <name>oozie.hive.defaults</name>
                    <value>hive-default.xml</value>
                </property>
            </configuration>
            <script>CreateTables.sql</script>
            <param>OnTimePerformance_Data=${OnTimePerformance_Data}</param>
            <param>Airline_Lookup=${Airline_Lookup}</param>
        </hive>
        <ok to="end"/>
        <error to="fail"/>
    </action>
    <kill name="fail">
        <message>Workflow failed, error message[${wf:errorMessage(wf:lastErrorNo
de())}]
        </message>
    </kill>
    <end name="end"/>
</workflow-app>
```

You can define additional control operations in hPDL, such as `fork` and `join`, in the following manner:

```
<fork name="Fork-Node">
    <path start="HiveAllFlights-Node" />
    <path start="HiveOnTimeDep-Node" />
</fork>
<join name="Joining-Node" to="HiveDepPercent-Node"/>
```

The two actions `HiveAllFlights-Node` and `HiveOnTimeDep-Node` defined in the `fork` element are executed in parallel. The `join` control node waits for the operation to complete and passes on the control to the `HiveDepPercent-Node` control node.

You can easily extend the source code in Listing 19.1 and add both `fork` and `join` nodes and Hive actions to get the workflow that was defined in Figure 19.2. Refer to the `workflow.xml` file in the accompanying code sample for a full listing of the workflow source code.

Upload the `workflow.xml` file to `/OozieWorkflow` in blob storage.

Executing the Workflow

Before you submit the workflow for execution, you must create a `job.properties` file in the local file system (say, in the folder `c:\ooziescripts`) that contains the configuration elements and parameters required to execute the job (see Listing 19.2).

LISTING 19.2   Defining Job Properties

```
nameNode=wasb://hdi4@hdi4.blob.core.windows.net
jobTracker=jobtrackerhost:9010
queueName=default
oozie.use.system.libpath=true
oozie.wf.application.path=/OozieWorkflow/Workflow.xml
OnTimePerformance_Data=/OnTimePerformance/Data
Airline_Lookup=/OnTimePerformance/Lookup/Airline
```

You then execute the following command from the name node's `oozie_home\oozie-win-distro\bin` location to start the workflow execution:

```
oozie job -oozie http://namenodehost:11000/oozie/ -config c:\OozieScripts\job.
properties -run
```

Monitoring Job Status

The Oozie framework returns the workflow job ID after the workflow starts. You can use the job ID to track the workflow status. From the name node, navigate to http://namenodehost:11000/oozie/v0/job/*job-id?*show=log (replacing *job-id* with the actual job ID) to view the job log.

You can also use the command `oozie job -info job-id` to track workflow execution, as shown in Figure 19.4. The figure lists all four control nodes and four action nodes, along with the execution status for the workflow defined in Figure 19.2.

NOTE

Note that the MapReduce job ID is provided along with the four Hive actions. If an action fails, you can use the corresponding MapReduce job ID for further diagnostics.

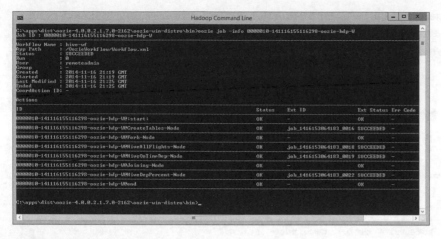

FIGURE 19.4
Monitoring Oozie workflow.

Querying the Results

The last Hive action in the workflow dumps the processed results into the
OnTimeDeparturePercent table. The following code queries the table to get the airlines
listed by their departure percentage (see Figure 19.5).

```
SELECT * FROM OnTimeDeparturePercent ORDER BY OnTimeDeparturePercentage DESC
```

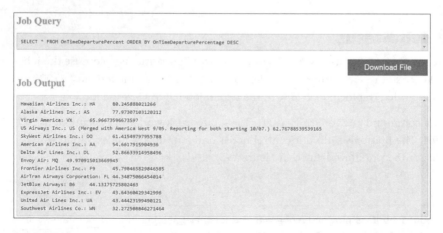

FIGURE 19.5
Querying the results.

According to the query results, Hawaiian Airlines seems to have the highest percentage of on-time departures for January 2014.

Submitting an Oozie Workflow with HDInsight .NET SDK

Azure PowerShell currently does not provide cmdlets for defining Oozie jobs. As a workaround, you can use the `Invoke-RestMethod` cmdlet to invoke Oozie web services. Oozie workflows can also be initiated from .NET applications using the HDInsight .NET SDK. The `OozieHttpClient` class defined in Microsoft .NET API for the Hadoop WebClient NuGet package can initiate an Oozie workflow on an HDInsight cluster. Listing 19.3 provides sample code to do the following:

▶ Create an Oozie job definition

▶ Pass the required parameters

▶ Submit the job and obtain a job ID for tracking

LISTING 19.3   Defining an Oozie Workflow

```
string azureStoreContainer = "storage_container";
string azureStore = "azure_store";
string hdInsightCluster = "cluster_name";
string hdInsightUser = "hd Insight User";
string hdInsightPassword = "password";
string workflowDir = "/OozieWorkflow/Workflow.xml";
string inputPath = "/OozieWorkflow/Input/";
string outputPath = "/OozieWorkflow/Output/";

var nameNodeHost = "wasb://" + azureStoreContainer + "@" + azureStore +
".blob.core.windows.net";
var OnTimePerformance_Data = "/OnTimePerformance/Data";
var Airline_Lookup = "/OnTimePerformance/Lookup/Airline";
var clusterAddress = "https://" + hdInsightCluster + ".azurehdinsight.net";
var clusterUri = new Uri(clusterAddress);

// Create oozie job
var client = new OozieHttpClient(clusterUri, hdInsightUser, hdInsightPassword);
var prop = new OozieJobProperties(hdInsightUser, nameNodeHost,
"jobtrackerhost:9010", workflowDir, inputPath, outputPath);
var parameters = prop.ToDictionary();

// Pass parameters
parameters.Add("oozie.use.system.libpath", "true");
parameters.Add("OnTimePerformance_Data", OnTimePerformance_Data);
parameters.Add("Airline_Lookup", Airline_Lookup);
```

```
// Submit job
var newJob = await client.SubmitJob(parameters);
var content = await newJob.Content.ReadAsStringAsync();
var serializer = new JsonSerializer();
dynamic json = serializer.Deserialize(new JsonTextReader(new
StringReader(content)));

// Job ID for progress tracking
string id = json.id;
await client.StartJob(id);
```

Coordinating Workflows with Oozie

In the real world, you often must trigger workflows either on a schedule or conditionally based on the availability of data or occurrence of an event. The Oozie Coordinator system comes in handy in such scenarios, providing features such as workflow scheduling and conditional execution.

A coordinator app consists of an XML job definition file (`coordinator.xml`) and a coordinator job properties file (`coordinator.properties`) containing the location of `coordinator.xml` and properties to be passed to the coordinator job.

Listing 19.4 defines a coordinator job that runs at the specified frequency (in minutes) between the specified start and the end time interval. It triggers a workflow definition (`workflow.xml`) at `/OozieWorkflow/`.

LISTING 19.4   Defining an Oozie Time-Based Coordinator Job

```
<coordinator-app name="coordinator_app1" frequency="${coordFrequency}"
start="${coordStartTime}" end="${coordEndTime}" timezone="${coordTimezone}"
xmlns="uri:oozie:coordinator:0.1">
    <action>
        <workflow>
            <app-path>/OozieWorkflow/</app-path>
        </workflow>
    </action>
</coordinator-app>
```

Listing 19.5 provides a sample definition of coordinator job properties, specifying values for properties related to the job schedule and location of the coordinator job definition (`coordinator.xml`) via the `oozie.coord.application.path` property.

LISTING 19.5 Defining the Properties of an Oozie Time-Based Coordinator Job

```
nameNode=wasb://hdi4@hdi4.blob.core.windows.net
jobTracker=jobtrackerhost:9010
queueName=default
oozie.use.system.libpath=true
oozie.coord.application.path=/OozieWorkflow/
coordFrequency=60
coordStartTime=2012-08-31T20\:20Z
coordEndTime=2013-08-31T20\:20Z
coordTimezone=GMT+0530
```

You submit Oozie coordinator jobs using the following command, providing the `coordinator.properties` file location using the `config` argument:

```
oozie job -oozie http://namenodehost:11000/oozie/ -config c:\OozieScripts\
coordinator.properties -run
```

Apart from the time-based coordination approach discussed so far, Oozie supports many other job-triggering mechanisms.

NOTE

For more details on the job-triggering mechanisms Oozie supports, refer to the Oozie specifications link from Apache at http://oozie.apache.org/docs/4.0.0/CoordinatorFunctionalSpec.html.

Oozie Compared to SSIS

Data processing workflows can be implemented in a range of ways using various toolsets. With HDInsight clusters, Oozie and SSIS are the preferred options. Hadoop users who have experience with other Hadoop distributions will naturally prefer to use Oozie with HDInsight. Integrating Oozie workflows with custom applications also works well because Oozie workflows can also be triggered using PowerShell and HDInsight .NET SDK. This does require some level of expertise with the .NET framework, however.

SSIS, on the other hand, is more suited for users who are familiar with SQL Server and who have experience developing SSIS workflows. SSIS also is the preferred choice when developers want to leverage the powerful data-handling capabilities of SSIS or when they are developing solutions targeting SQL Server. Furthermore, Visual Studio provides a rich set of visual development tools for SSIS, allowing rich visualization of nodes and connections in the workflow—it simplifies the process of developing SSIS workflows. SSIS can also be easily tied up with PowerShell and used to spin up an HDInsight cluster on demand to process data stored in Azure blob storage; that is not possible to achieve with Oozie.

Summary

This hour explored the use of Oozie to schedule and manage data processing workflows in an HDInsight cluster. Oozie workflows can be conveniently triggered from a .NET application using HDInsight .NET SDK. The Oozie workflow coordinator triggers workflows either on a schedule or conditionally, based on availability of data or occurrence of an event.

Q&A

Q. What is a control dependency directed acyclic graph of workflow actions?

A. Control dependency in a directed acyclic graph (DAG) of workflow actions implies that execution control cannot pass to the next action node in the workflow until the current action finishes execution. Simply put, the current action must finish before the next action in the flow can be executed. Oozie workflows also are strict DAGs and, hence, don't support cycles.

Q. Does Oozie workflow have a file system action?

A. Yes, Oozie has a built-in file system action (FS action) that supports the manipulation of HDFS files and directories. FS actions support commands such as `move`, `delete`, and `mkdir`.

Quiz

1. What are the main components of Oozie?

2. How can you monitor an Oozie job during execution?

Answers

1. Oozie consists of a workflow engine that supports workflow jobs of different types, a coordinator engine that is responsible for running workflows based on time and data triggers, and a bundle engine that enables users to manage a bundle or set of coordinator jobs.

2. You can track the workflow status using the Oozie workflow job ID, which Oozie returns after the workflow starts. You can view the job log by navigating to http://namenodehost:11000/oozie/v0/job/job-id?show=log (replace job-id with the actual job ID) on the `name` node. You also can use the command `oozie job -info job-id` to track workflow execution.

Performing Statistical Computing with R

What You'll Learn in This Hour:

▶ Introduction to R

▶ Integrating R with Hadoop

▶ Enabling R on HDInsight

R is a popular language among data scientists for analytics and statistical computing. However, R was not designed to work with Big Data because it typically works by pulling data persisted elsewhere into memory. Recent advancements have now made it possible to leverage R for Big Data analytics.

This hour introduces the R language and explores the approaches for enabling R on Hadoop.

Introduction to R

R is a popular open source scripting and interpreting language for statistical computing. R is a de facto language that data scientists use in statistical research, and it comes with standard packages to support statistical analysis. An R package is nothing but a collection of R functions. Analytic capabilities can be extended further by installing additional packages. R also has excellent graphic capabilities that are well suited to visualizing data. In addition, R provides options for loading and analyzing external data in different formats.

NOTE

R Is an Implementation of S

R is an implementation the of S programming language, which was originally developed by John Chambers at Bell Labs. R was developed at the University of Auckland by Ross Ihaka and Robert Gentleman. The name R comes from the first names of its authors.

Installing R on Windows

Before digging in to the steps in enabling R on Hadoop for Big Data analytics, it is useful to become familiar with the R programming environment by installing R on the Windows platform and trying some elementary scenarios.

You can download the R base package from the Comprehensive R Archive Network (CRAN) at http://cran.r-project.org/. CRAN is the go-to repository for R resources and documentation. R works on a number of standard platforms, including Windows, Mac, and UNIX.

To install R on a windows machine, navigate to the CRAN URL and select Download R for Windows. Download and install the R base distribution; then launch the installation wizard and install R with the default installation options. After installation, you will see a shortcut to launch the R console on your desktop.

Loading External Data

Knowledge of R data types is essential before you can start loading data in R for analysis. Understanding R data types is vital to selecting the most appropriate data type for loading and storing data.

The vector is the most basic object in R. A *vector* is a sequence of objects that belong to same data type. The function `c()` define vectors. The symbol `<-` is commonly used as the assignment operator in R. For example, the expression `x<-c(1,2,3,4)` defines a vector of numeric values and assigns it a variable x. Similarly, the statement `c(TRUE,FALSE,FALSE)` defines another vector of logical values.

R also supports the creation of a two-dimensional object called a *matrix*. A matrix can be created in several different ways. As one example, the expression `m<-matrix(nrow=2,ncol=3)` defines a matrix with two rows and three columns. The expression `m[1,1]<-2` assigns a value of 2 to the first element of the matrix (the element at the intersection of the first row and the first column).

Vectors contain objects belonging to the same data type, but R also supports a special type of vector, called a *list*, that can contain objects of different classes. For example, `x<-list(TRUE,1, "a")` defines a list with its first element of the logical data type, its second element of the numeric data type, and its final element of the character data type.

Data analysis generally is performed on structured data in tabular form, so R also supports the creation of data frames for storing tabular data. For example, the following R code snippet creates a simple data frame for storing flight data (flight number, origin city, and destination city):

```
flightNumber<-c(1,2,3)
originCity<-c("New York","Chicago","Los Angeles")
destinationCity<-c("Chicago","Los Angeles","New York")
flightData<-data.frame(flightNumber,originCity,destinationCity)
```

Figure 20.1 illustrates the creation of the flight data frame in the R console using this code snippet. The `print` function prints the flight data frame to the console.

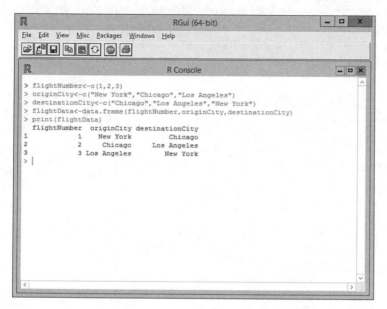

FIGURE 20.1
Creating a flight data frame in R.

You can conveniently create data frames from CSV files using the `read.csv()` function. For example, the following code snippet reads the on-time performance of airline flights data into an R data frame named `onTimePerfData`:

```
onTimePerfData<-read.csv("C:\\Data\\On_Time_On_Time_Performance_2014_1.csv",
header=TRUE)
```

NOTE

The Research and Innovative Technology Administration, Bureau of Transportation Statistics (RITA) tracks the on-time performance of airline flights. This information is available for download and analysis at http://www.transtats.bts.gov/DL_SelectFields.asp?Table_ID=236&DB_Short_Name=On-Time. The previous code snippet uses the prezipped data file for January 2014.

The parameter `Header=TRUE` in the `read.csv` function specifies that the first line of the CSV file contains the header information.

Performing Rudimentary Data Analysis

After the data is loaded into memory from the CSV file, it is available for analysis. To get acquainted with the dataset, the `str` function comes in handy. This function displays the structure of the dataset. For example, the `str(onTimePerfData)` command displays such information as the number of observations (or rows), variables (or columns), and data types, along with sample values for each column (see Figure 20.2).

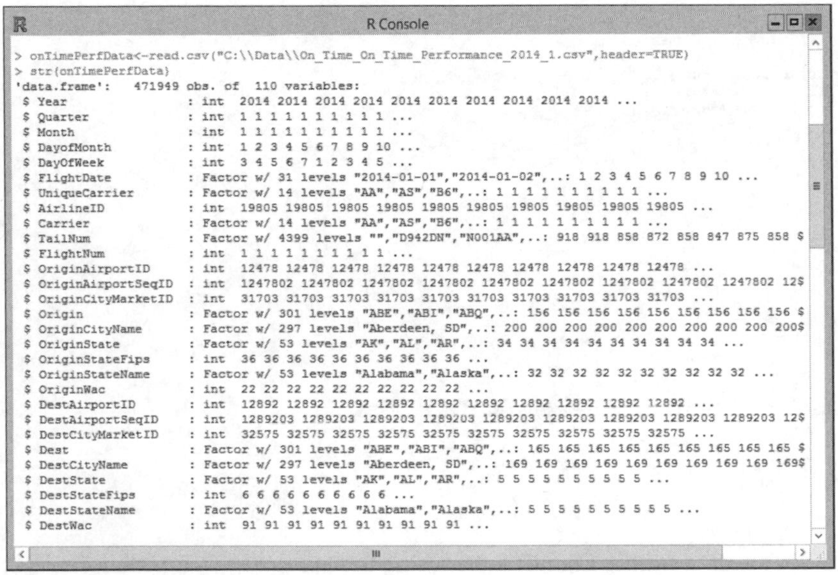

FIGURE 20.2
Using the `str` function to view the structure of the data frame.

R also has good graphics capabilities. ggplot2 is a popular visualization package in the R community. Its quick plot (`qplot`) function is a good starting point for first-time R users and provides most of the graphics capabilities, with a simpler syntax. The following code snippet installs the ggplot2 package and plots a bar chart showing the number of flights by carrier, stacked by cancellation code (see Figure 20.3):

```
install.packages("ggplot2")
library(ggplot2)
qplot(x=onTimePerfData$UniqueCarrier,
data=onTimePerfData,fill=factor(onTimePerfData$Cancelled),xlab="Carrier",
ylab="Flight Count")+labs(fill = "Flt Cancelled(1=Yes)")
```

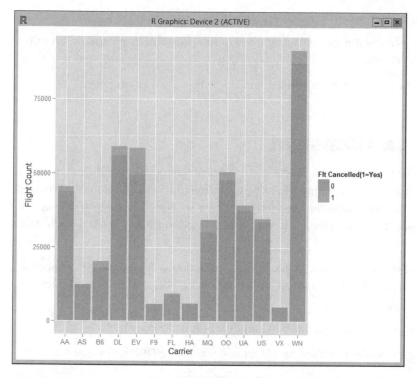

FIGURE 20.3
Using graphics in R.

Integrating R with Hadoop

Because R fetches data into memory, data analysis capabilities are limited by the amount of memory available. Furthermore, the central idea of Hadoop has been to move computing to data, not data to computing. Loading data persisted elsewhere into memory doesn't fit well with this core principle. This makes R unsuitable for Big Data analytics. With these limitations, why is there so much interest in enabling R on Hadoop? Why is R not being replaced by any other component from the Hadoop ecosystem for Big Data analytics?

The simple answer to the question is the overwhelming popularity of R among data scientists and statistical researchers. These groups of users are comfortable with R and will not easily switch to a different platform. More than 5,000 R packages are available on CRAN, contributed by a strong R user community. Furthermore, R is unmatched when it comes to performing statistical computations and data visualization.

Enabling R on Hadoop also provides the following benefits:

▶ Overcoming the memory limitation enables users to run statistical computations on full data sets instead of sample data.

▶ Distributed statistical computations can be run from within the R environment.

Enabling R on HDInsight

You can make R work with Big Data in a couple ways. A naive approach is to integrate R with Hadoop MapReduce via Hadoop streaming. Hadoop streaming, introduced in Hour 9, "Working with Microsoft Azure HDInsight Emulator," enables developers to create MapReduce programs in programming languages other than Java. However, writing MapReduce in R is not a trivial task for data scientists.

RHadoop aims to make the process easier by providing a collection of R packages with application programming interfaces (APIs) for Hadoop integration. It includes the following R packages, among others:

▶ The rmr package provides APIs for Hadoop MapReduce functionality in R.

▶ The rhdfs package provides functions for file management on HDFS/Azure blob storage.

▶ The rhbase package provides functions for interaction with HBase.

The rmr package enables R users to elegantly work with MapReduce programming from within the familiar R console. The `mapreduce()` function defined in the rmr package is the fundamental function for writing simplified MapReduce programs in R using RHadoop.

The function expects input data set and also mapper and reducer function definitions to be passed in as arguments. Later sections cover RHadoop in more detail.

Installing R on HDInsight

The custom Script Action feature introduced in Hour 11, "Customizing HDInsight Cluster with Script Action," enables you to customize an HDInsight cluster and install R. Microsoft provides a sample R installation script at https://hdiconfigactions.blob.core.windows.net/rconfigactionv02/r-installer-v02.ps1. To install R on Hadoop, provision a new HDInsight cluster with the Custom Create option from the Windows Azure management portal. On the Script Actions screen, provide the URL of the R installation script (see Figure 20.4).

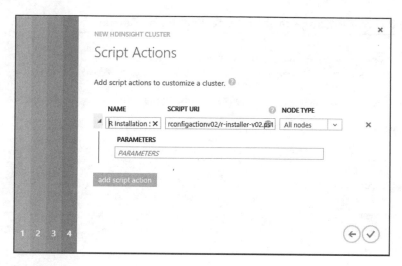

FIGURE 20.4
Installing R on an HDInsight cluster.

The script installs R version 3.1.1, the rmr2_3.1.2 package, and the rhdfs_1.0.8 package on all nodes of the cluster.

Using R with HDInsight

As discussed earlier, the `mapreduce()` function defined in the rmr package is the fundamental function for writing simplified MapReduce programs in R using RHadoop. The following code snippet describes the signature of the MapReduce function:

```
mapreduce (input, inputformat, output, outputformat, map, reduce)
```

The function expects input data set and also mapper and reducer function definitions to be passed in as arguments. Specifying the output location and output format parameters to the `mapreduce` function is optional. When these parameters are not specified, the output dataset is stored in a temporary location on the default file system; you can obtain a reference to this location using the following syntax:

```
output <- mapreduce (input, inputformat, output, outputformat, map, reduce)
```

The output data set is read from the output location using the `from.dfs` function. The function reads the output variable into memory from the file system and prints the result to the R console. Listing 20.1 shows this in action. The `mapreduce` function provides a reference to the output data set stored in a temporary location on the default file system.

LISTING 20.1 Using the rmr Package to Determine Flights, by Carrier

```
library(rmr2)
output=mapreduce(input="/OnTimePerformance/Data/OTP_Without_Header.csv",
        input.format=make.input.format(format='csv', mode='text', streaming.format
= NULL,
sep=',',col.names = c('Year','FlightDate','UniqueCarrier','TailNum','Origin','Dest'
,'CRSDepTi
me','DepTime','DepDelay','DepDelayMinutes','DepDel15','ArrDelay','ArrDelayMinutes',
'ArrDel15'
),stringsAsFactors=F),
        map=function(k,fields){
        keyval(fields$UniqueCarrier,1)
        },
        reduce=function(carrier,vv){
        keyval(carrier,length(vv))
        }
        )
from.dfs(output)
```

To understand the steps involved in using rmr2, consider the following scenario that determines the number of flights, by unique carrier, from a data file of flight information. Figure 20.5 illustrates the structure of the flight data file.

TIP

Although the figure shows the CSV file with a header, CSV files do not actually support headers. You must remove the header from the CSV file before executing the rmr2 workload.

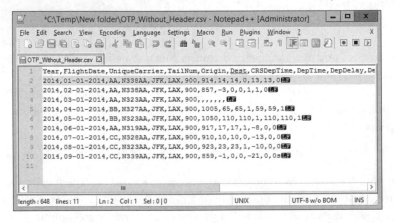

FIGURE 20.5
Flight data file.

Listing 20.1 provides the source code for using the `mapreduce` function defined in the rmr2 package to calculate the flight count, by `UniqueCarrier`. These parameters are passed to the function:

▶ The first parameter to the function specifies the location of the input file in blob storage.

▶ The second parameter specifies the format of the input file, indicating that it's a CSV file, using a comma as the field separator. Column names are also specified.

▶ The third parameter specifies the map function. This function uses the `keyval` function to create key-value pairs (with a unique carrier as the key and `1` as the value) that are passed on to the `reduce` function.

▶ The fourth parameter specifies the `reduce` function. This function counts the number of elements in the `value` vector (length of the `value` vector), grouped by unique carrier. It is returned as the final output and stored in a temporary location on the default file system.

▶ The `output` variable stores a reference to the temporary default file system location that contains the final output. The `from.dfs` function reads the output variable into memory from the file system and prints the result to the R console.

To execute the code in the Listing 20.1 on an HDInsight cluster, use a remote desktop connection to remotely log in to the name node of the cluster and launch the R console using the R console launcher icon on the desktop (see Figure 20.6).

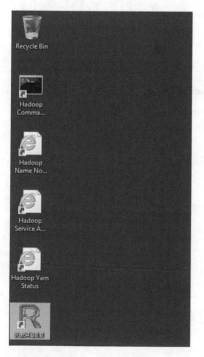

FIGURE 20.6
Launching the R console from the name node.

Paste the code in Listing 20.1 into the R console (see Figure 20.7). This triggers a Hadoop streaming MapReduce job from within the R console.

FIGURE 20.7
Using the rmr2 package with HDInsight.

When the job completes, you can print the final output to the R console by using the `from.dfs` function (see Figure 20.8).

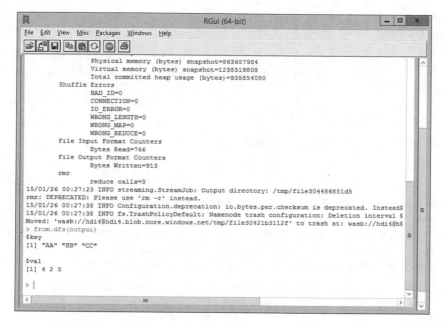

FIGURE 20.8
Displaying MapReduce output in the R console.

Summary

This hour explored integration of the R programming language, used for statistical computing, with Hadoop. You can set up R on an HDInsight cluster using the Script Action feature. RHadoop provides packages to integrate R with Hadoop. The rmr2 package simplifies the process of writing MapReduce programs using R.

Q&A

Q. Is it possible to program a map-only job using rmr?

A. Yes, specifying the `reduce` function argument in the `mapreduce` function is optional. Leaving out the `reduce` argument makes the job map only.

Q. How can I get help on issues related to R and RHadoop?

A. Subscribing to R mailing lists is the best way to discuss related issues and get help. You can find more details on the R mailing lists at http://www.r-project.org/mail.html link. For RHadoop, the Hadoop Google group https://groups.google.com/forum/#!forum/rhadoop is a public forum for discussions and questions. Apart from these resources, you can post related questions on Stack Overflow. HDInsight-specific issues and questions can also be posted on the MSDN forum for HDInsight at https://social.msdn.microsoft.com/forums/azure/en-US/home?forum=hdinsight.

Quiz

1. Why does R need to be integrated with Hadoop?

2. How can R be installed on an HDInsight cluster?

Answers

1. R is not capable of working with Big Data sets because it requires data to be loaded into memory for analysis. However, R is very popular in the data science community, which makes it indispensable in performing statistical computing and research. Integrating R with Hadoop overcomes the limitation of having data in memory and enables R users to work with Big Data sets instead of being forced to work with merely sample data, as in the past.

2. The custom Script Action feature, introduced in Hour 11, enables you to customize an HDInsight cluster and install R. Microsoft has a sample R installation script at https://hdiconfigactions.blob.core.windows.net/rconfigactionv02/r-installer-v02.ps1.

Performing Big Data Analytics with Spark

What You'll Learn in This Hour:

▶ Introduction to Spark
▶ Spark Programming Model
▶ Blending SQL Querying with Functional Programs

Spark is a top-level Apache project and has quickly become one of the most talked-about Big Data projects. Spark's in-memory computation model provides performance of up to 100 times faster than Hadoop MapReduce in scenarios involving interactive querying and iterative processing. In these scenarios, MapReduce spends a major chunk of time writing intermediate results and working sets to the file system. Spark, on the other hand, keeps the working sets in memory, thus saving a significant amount of time on disk I/O.

This hour provides an introduction to Spark, briefly explores the Spark programming model, and takes a look at Spark integration with SQL.

Introduction to Spark

Spark is a new Big Data computing engine that runs faster than MapReduce in scenarios that involve interactive querying and iterative processing. Spark relies on in-memory storage and computing, which works extremely well in iterative scenarios. Spark's in-memory computation engine can run programs up to 100 times faster than Hadoop MapReduce.

Spark eases Big Data development by providing a rich set of APIs with support for multiple languages, including Java, Scala, and Python. Spark also supports interactive querying via the Spark shell. Spark supports many storage systems as well, including HDFS, HBASE, and the Azure blob store.

Spark can run in different runtime environments, including YARN and Mesos, and also has a standalone mode. In addition, it provides more than 80 high-level operators, to ease parallel programming.

NOTE

Spark Started As a Research Project at U.C. Berkeley

Spark started as a research project in the AMPLab at U.C. Berkeley in 2009. It was open sourced in 2010 and later donated to Apache in 2013. In February 2014, Spark became an Apache Top Level Project.

Developers can either program against the Spark core engine or use high-level program tools to develop parallel applications. Spark offers the following higher-level programming tools that run on top of the Spark execution engine (see Figure 21.1):

▶ Spark SQL, for SQL querying capabilities

▶ Spark Streaming, for real-time stream-processing capabilities

▶ MLlib, a machine learning library

▶ GraphX, for graph analytics

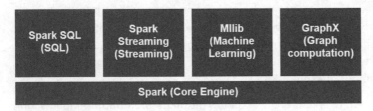

FIGURE 21.1
Higher-level programming tools Spark offers.

NOTE

Spark Holds the World Speed Record of Sorting 100TB of Data

According to benchmark numbers released by Databricks (the company founded by the creators of Spark), Spark performed a distributed sort of 100TB of data in 23 minutes, three times faster than the previous record, set by MapReduce, and using 10 times less computing power.

Installing Spark on HDInsight

The custom Script Action feature introduced in Hour 11, "Customizing the HDInsight Cluster with Script Action," enables you to customize the HDInsight cluster and install Spark.

To install Spark on Hadoop, provision a new HDInsight cluster with the Custom Create option from the Microsoft Azure Management portal. On the Script Actions screen, provide the URL of the Spark installation script (see Figure 21.2).

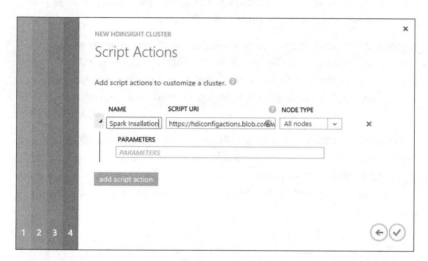

FIGURE 21.2
Installing Spark on an HDInsight cluster.

The script installs Spark version 1.0.2 on all nodes of the cluster.

Spark Programming Model

MapReduce has proven to be a highly successful programming model for performing data analysis on distributed Big Data sets. With the increased adoption and popularity of MapReduce, the expectation from the MapReduce framework has grown. However, the MapReduce framework has not been able to satisfy analysts in the following problem domains:

- ▶ Interactive querying and ad hoc data analysis

- ▶ Problems involving multiple iterations over a data set, such as graph processing and machine learning

- ▶ Real-time stream-processing scenarios

These problem scenarios have a similar processing pattern that involves multiple map reduce jobs running in succession, with each step accessing intermediate processing results from the previous step. The MapReduce framework writes out the intermediate results to the file system, which the next computation step then consumes. Data sharing between iterations over the disk involves considerable time spent writing intermediate results and working sets to the distributed file system and then reading those back in for processing by the next step.

Spark offers a new programming model that makes use of memory instead of the disk for data sharing between iterations. Reducing disk I/O enables Spark to achieve processing speeds up to 100 times faster than those of conventional MapReduce.

However, using memory for data sharing introduces new challenges for making the programming model fault tolerant. One solution for achieving fault tolerance is to replicate the memory contents to another node over the network. This solution is likely to cause performance problems, even over the fastest networks, because replication over a network is a time-consuming process.

Spark instead makes use of resilient distributed datasets (RDDs) for fault tolerance. RDDs are distributed objects that can be cached in memory across cluster nodes. Instead of replicating data, fault tolerance is achieved by keeping track of various high-level parallel operators applied on RDDs. If a node fails, the RDD is recomputed on a different node by applying the sequence of operations to a subset of data.

NOTE

More than 80 parallel operators can be applied to RDDs. Common ones include `map`, `reduce`, `groupBy`, `filter`, `joins`, `count`, `distinct`, `max`, and `min`.

When working with MapReduce, programmers primarily focus on breaking the problem into a set of Map and Reduce functions. With Spark, however, the approach is different. The Spark application consists of a driver program, in which the user either creates a new RDD by reading data from a file residing on a distributed file system or works with existing RDDs by applying various transformation operations.

Users can also choose to cache RDDs in memory and reuse them across operations, thus saving on disk I/O. Two types of RDD operations are transformations and actions, defined as follows:

▶ **Transformation operation**—Creates a new RDD from an existing one. In Spark, transformations are lazily evaluated when an action requires a computation to be performed. For example, applying a filter operation to a data set to filter records by a filter criterion does not cause any computation or data processing to be performed. The filter operation is not performed until an action operation, such as `count`, which requires a result to be computed, is applied to the data set. Lazy evaluation enables the Spark engine to optimize the steps in data processing workflow and reduces the memory footprint because expressions are evaluated and data is read only when needed.

▶ **Action operation**—Causes a computation to be performed.

Log Mining with the Spark Shell

To better understand the Spark programming model, consider a scenario that involves interactively loading log data (sample log data provided with the HDInsight cluster) into memory and querying error messages that match certain criteria. Figure 21.3 shows the contents of the sample log data provided with an HDInsight cluster, located at /example/data/sample.log in the blob store.

TIP

The file is a few kilobytes in size, but a similar kind of analysis can easily extend to bigger data files.

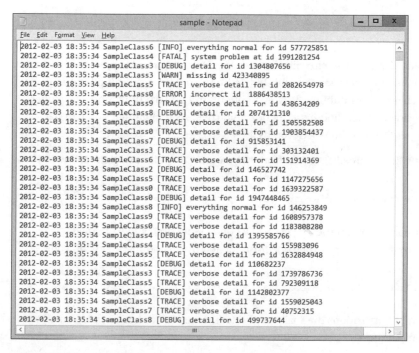

FIGURE 21.3
Sample log data provided with an HDInsight cluster.

To begin interactive analysis, launch the Spark shell by navigating to the `%SPARK_HOME%\bin` directory on the name node and issue the command `spark-shell.cmd`. This launches the Spark shell for Scala. (To use the Spark shell for Python, use the command `pyspark.cmd`.) Figure 21.4 shows the Spark shell for Scala.

FIGURE 21.4
Spark shell for Scala.

Spark's Scala interpreter requires some familiarity with the Scala programming language. *Scala* is an object-oriented language incorporating full-blown functional programming language features such as type inference, immutability, lazy evaluation, and pattern matching. Developers can use it to write concise, cleaner, and better-performing code. As a beginner, you can get started by using Scala as "Java without semicolons."

Start by creating a new RDD named `logFile` from the `sample.log` file using the following Scala code snippet:

```
val logFile = sc.textFile("/example/data/sample.log")
```

Next, apply filter transformation on the `logFile` RDD and create a new RDD named `errorsEntries` that contains an error message from the log file, using the following code snippet:

```
val errorsEntries= logFile.filter(_.contains("[ERROR]"))
```

Recall that transformation operations are lazily evaluated; so far, Spark has not performed any data processing or computation.

Because the `errorEntries` RDD will be queried multiple times, you can ask Spark to persist the RDD after evaluation using the following code snippet:

```
errorsEntries.persist()
```

Next, use the `count()` action operator to count the number of error log entries:

```
errorsEntries.count()
```

This causes the Spark engine to evaluate all transformation operations applied so far and compute the result of the `count` operation. Because you persisted the `errorsEntries` RDD, further actions and transformation operators applied on the RDD will not require reevaluation of the RDD from the flat file.

Perform the following actions one by one on the persisted RDD to count the number of error log entries related to `SampleClass1` and `SampleClass4` in the log:

```
errorsEntries.filter(_.contains("SampleClass1")).count()
errorsEntries.filter(_.contains("SampleClass4")).count()
```

Blending SQL Querying with Functional Programs

As discussed earlier, Spark also provides SQL querying capabilities using Spark SQL on top of the Spark engine. SQL querying using Spark occurs through Spark SQL. Spark SQL enables relational queries to be embedded in functional programs. This way, programmers can easily access the best of both worlds from the same programming environment.

NOTE

Shark Was the First Project That Allowed SQL Querying on Spark

Shark was the first project that supported running SQL queries on Spark. However, Shark worked by converting MapReduce operators generated by the Hive optimizer to Spark operators. Because the Hive optimizer was designed to work with MapReduce, this approach did not work. Spark SQL deviated from this approach and relies on an RDD-aware query optimizer, for better performance.

Following are the main components of Spark SQL:

- ▶ **Catalyst Optimizer**—Optimizes a logical query plan to achieve better query performance

- ▶ **Spark SQL Core engine**—Executes optimized logical query plans as operations on RDDs

- ▶ **Spark SQL**—Includes a Hive support layer for interaction with Hive

Spark SQL operates on SchemaRDD, which is nothing but schema information attached to an RDD. The schema information is essential for RDDs to efficiently be used in SQL as declarative queries.

Hive Compared to Spark SQL

Hive already provides SQL querying capabilities on Big Data, but it is not well suited for inter-active querying and ad hoc analysis. This can be attributed to the fact that the Hive execution engine relies on MapReduce on top of the distributed file system.

On the other hand, Spark SQL converts SQL queries to Spark operators and thus uses Spark run-ning on a distributed file system as the execution engine. This makes Spark SQL better suited for interactive querying and ad hoc analysis scenarios involving multiple iterations over the same set of data.

Still, Spark can also work with existing Hive tables. This makes switching from Hive to Spark SQL easy—you simply use a different client to query the same data.

Using SQL Blended with Functional Code to Analyze Crime Data

To appreciate the benefits of using Spark SQL and Spark's capability to blend SQL queries with functional programs, consider the following scenario involving the analysis of robbery-related crimes by location in Chicago. The end goal of the scenario is to list robbery locations sorted by number of incidents, in descending order.

The scenario uses the "Crimes—One year prior to present" dataset, available at https://data.cityofchicago.org/Public-Safety/Crimes-One-year-prior-to-present/x2n5-8w5q. The dataset reflects reported incidents of crime (with the exception of murders, for which data exists for each victim) that have occurred in the city of Chicago over the past year.

To download the data, click the Export button and select the CSV option from the Download As menu (see Figure 21.5).

The CSV file has the following schema:

```
CASE#,DATE  OF OCCURRENCE,BLOCK, IUCR, PRIMARY DESCRIPTION, SECONDARY DESCRIPTION,
LOCATION DESCRIPTION,ARREST,DOMESTIC,BEAT,WARD,FBI CD,X COORDINATE,Y COORDINATE,
LATITUDE,LONGITUDE,LOCATION
```

The columns PRIMARY DESCRIPTION (representing the primary crime type, such as ROBBERY) and LOCATION DESCRIPTION are of interest in this scenario.

TIP

Before you upload the CSV file to the blob store, remove the file header. This is easier than trying to skip it programmatically during processing.

After you trim the header, upload the CSV file at `/CrimeData/Crimes_-_One_year_prior_to_present.csv` in the default blob store that the HDInsight cluster uses.

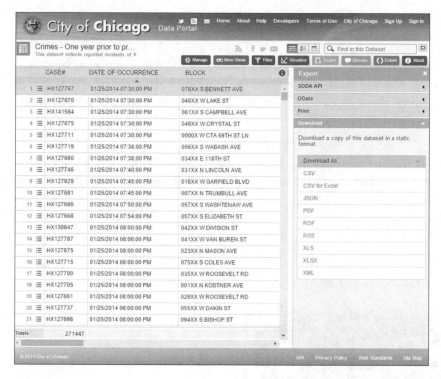

FIGURE 21.5
Downloading city of Chicago crime data.

Launch the Spark shell and start by creating a `SQLContext`. `SQLContext` provides functionality for working with SchemaRDDs, turning it into a table and using SQL queries against it.

```
val sqlContext = new org.apache.spark.sql.SQLContext(sc)
```

Import `SQLContext` to get access to all the public SQL functions and implicit conversions using the following statement:

```
import sqlContext._
```

Create a `case` class to define the schema of crime and location columns:

```
case class Crime(PRIMARY_DESCRIPTION: String, LOCATION_DESCRIPTION: String)
```

Next, create a new RDD from the CSV file that you uploaded to the blob store earlier and split it using a comma character to separate the columns. Extract columns 4 (primary description) and 6 (location) to create a SchemaRDD.

```
val crimes = sc.textFile("/CrimeData/Crimes_-_One_year_prior_to_present.csv").
map(line => line.split(",")).map(p => Crime(p(4),p(6)))
```

Register the SchemaRDD as a table. This makes it available for SQL querying.

```
crimes.registerAsTable("crimes")
```

Next, use `SqlContext` to invoke a SQL query against the registered table to extract robbery locations sorted by number of incidents, in descending order.

```
val robberiesByLocation = sqlContext.sql("SELECT LOCATION_DESCRIPTION,COUNT(*) AS
RobberyCount FROM crimes WHERE PRIMARY_DESCRIPTION='ROBBERY' GROUP BY
LOCATION_DESCRIPTION ORDER BY RobberyCount DESC")
```

The SQL query returns a collection of row objects as a result. From the result set, you can access individual columns (location and count of robberies) and print them to the console using the following code snippet:

```
robberiesByLocation.map(rob => "Location: " + rob(0)+" RobberyCount:
"+rob(1)).collect().foreach(println)
```

Figure 21.6 shows the results of the analysis. Most robberies seem to be happening on sidewalks and streets; the fewest appear to be happening at airports and police facility.

FIGURE 21.6
Analyzing robbery-related crimes by location in the city of Chicago.

This scenario illustrates the integration of Spark SQL with functional programming languages. Spark SQL makes it easy to mix and match SQL queries with functional code, enabling users to work with the best of both worlds without having to switch platforms.

Summary

This hour explored the in-memory computing capabilities of Spark. Having intermediate working sets in memory can make a big difference in processing times. The hour also explored the Spark programming model. Spark makes use of resilient distributed datasets (RDDs) for fault tolerance. Instead of replicating data, fault tolerance is achieved by keeping track of various high-level parallel operators applied on RDDs. The hour concluded with a discussion on the SQL querying capabilities of Spark and examined how to blend SQL with functional programs.

Q&A

Q. Can Spark work without Apache Hadoop?

A. Yes. Spark can be run outside the Hadoop ecosystem. Spark works well in standalone mode, where it requires a shared file system for storage.

Q. How does Spark process datasets that don't fit in memory?

A. Optimal performance is achieved when a distributed dataset fits in memory on each node. When a dataset does not fit in memory, Spark uses external operators to process the data on disk.

Quiz

1. What are some scenarios in which Spark outperforms Hadoop MapReduce?

2. What is an RDD?

Answers

1. Spark outperforms MapReduce in scenarios that involve interactive querying and ad hoc data analysis, as well as problems involving multiple iterations over a data set (for example, graph processing and machine learning and real-time stream processing scenarios).

2. Resilient distributed datasets (RDDs) are distributed objects that can be cached in memory across cluster nodes. Instead of replicating data, Spark achieves fault tolerance by keeping track of various high-level parallel operators applied on RDDs. When a node fails, the RDD is recomputed on a different node by applying a sequence of operations to a subset of data. More than 80 parallel operators can be applied to RDDs. Common ones include `map`, `reduce`, `groupBy`, `filter`, `joins`, `count`, `distinct`, `max`, and `min`.

HOUR 22
Microsoft Azure Machine Learning

What You'll Learn in This Hour:

▶ History of Traditional Machine Learning
▶ Introduction to Azure ML
▶ Azure ML Workspace
▶ Processes to Build Azure ML Solutions for Predictive Analytics
▶ Getting Started with Azure ML
▶ Creating Predictive Models with Azure ML
▶ Publishing Azure ML Models as Web Services

In the past few hours, you learned about Big Data, methods of storing it, and methods of doing data processing for historical analysis. Not only do organizations today need to do historical analysis to learn about what happened in the past but they also are more focused on doing *predictive analytics* to learn about future unknowns by analyzing trends and patterns in data collected from the past.

Predictive analytics has been in use for several years, but it was limited to only few large organizations that had data scientists or statisticians, along with the huge investment of time needed for implementation.

With the advent of emerging technologies such as Microsoft Azure Machine Learning, also known as Azure ML or MAML, the game has changed. Azure ML is extremely simple to use and easy to implement—analysts with varying backgrounds (even non-data scientists) can leverage it for predictive analytics.

As a user, you need to understand your data and how to set up and frame your problem. In this hour, you learn how to leverage Azure ML to quickly and easily build a predictive model.

History of Traditional Machine Learning

Traditionally, organizations performed diagnostic or descriptive analysis, based on what is known, to understand what happened in the past and what caused it to happen. They gained insight into historical data with reporting, KPIs, scorecards, and so on. For example, this type of analysis can use clustering or classification techniques for customer segmentation so that organizations can better understand customers and offer them products based on their needs.

Now organizations are looking for opportunities to do predictive Analytics to beat the competition, increase their market share, increase revenue by retaining and gaining more customers, and more. Predictive analytics focuses on learning the unknown to understand what can happen in the future based on identified patterns and trends using statistical and machine learning techniques on the data collected.

For example, predictive analytics can use time series, neural networks, and regression algorithms to predict future outcomes. Predictive analytics answers such questions as these:

▶ Which stocks should be targeted as part of portfolio management?

▶ Did some stocks show haphazard behavior? Which factors are impacting stock gains the most?

▶ How are users of e-commerce platforms, online games, and web applications behaving, and why?

▶ How do I optimize routing of my fleet of vehicles based on weather and traffic patterns?

▶ How do I better predict future outcomes based on identified patterns and trends?

▶ How can I anticipate customer churn? Which customers are likely to go, so that I can take proactive measures to retain them?

▶ What recommendation can be made for products or services to the customers based on customer behaviors?

NOTE

Machine Learning

"Machine learning, a branch of artificial intelligence, concerns the construction and study of systems that can learn from data. For example, a machine learning system could be trained on email messages to learn to automatically distinguish between spam and non-spam messages. After learning, it can then be used to classify new email messages into spam and non-spam folders."
—Wikipedia

With the help of machine learning, you can create data models from datasets by training the data. The model represents the dataset and generalizes to make predictions for the new data.

GO TO ▶ Refer to **Hour 1, "Introduction of Big Data, NoSQL, Hadoop, and Business Value Proposition,"** to review how datasets can reduce waiting times in the emergency room, predict disease outbreaks, and help with fraud detection and crime prevention, among many other scenarios.

Predictive analytics with machine learning is not a new concept. However, the traditional approach of machine learning had some problems:

▶ Machine learning was usually deployed in an on-premises infrastructure and was self-managed by a sophisticated engineering team.

▶ It had a steep learning curve for a rather complex processes using mathematical, statistical computing that requires trained, expert data scientists. The financial cost of having data scientists onboard and, at the same time, cleansing the data for correct and accurate inferences was often too costly (in both time and money) for companies to exploit their data, even though they realized that data analysis was an effective means of improving their services and optimizing their strategies.

▶ Building machine learning systems took a long time. It required data scientists to build the training sets and guide the machine learning system through its first step. The process was complex and expensive. In some cases, by the time a company started to realize the value of the model, the model might not be relevant to the current circumstances.

Introduction to Azure ML

Microsoft Azure ML is a new cloud-based machine learning platform offered as a fully managed cloud service. It enables data scientists and developers to efficiently embed predictive analytics into their applications. It also helps organizations use massive amounts of data in prediction and assists companies in forecasting and changing future outcomes. At the same time, it brings all the benefits of the cloud platform to the machine learning process.

NOTE

Simplicity and Ease with Azure ML

"You take data from your enterprises and make several hypotheses and experiment with them. When you find a hypothesis that you can believe in, that seems to work and it seems to validate, you want to put that into production so you can keep monitoring that particular hypothesis with new data all the time and track your predictions of what is going to happen versus what's actually happening and adjust your position. And that process is now so much easier now with Azure ML."
—Joseph Sirosh, Corporate Vice President, Machine Learning, Microsoft

http://www.citeworld.com/article/2366161/big-data-analytics/microsoft-azure-ml-overview.html

Azure ML offers a data science experience to make inferences from your massive amount of data and is not limited to data scientists only: Reduced complexity and broader participation through more user-friendly tooling makes it directly accessible to domain experts or business analysts. For example, its predefined templates, workflows, and intuitive user interface (UI) were built to help analysts or data scientists dig deeper and forecast future outcomes with predictive analytics much quicker than with traditional methods.

Although you still need to understand and formulate your queries appropriately, web- and workflow-based visual tools help you build questions easily from anywhere. You can publish machine learning APIs on top of the Azure ML platform so that others can easily hook them up from any enterprise application or even any mobile application for building intelligence by taking in new data and producing recommendations.

Benefits of Azure ML

Azure ML is extremely simple to use and easier to implement, so analysts with various backgrounds (even non-data scientists) can leverage it. As a user, you just need to know your data and know how to set up and frame your problem; then you can leverage Azure ML to build the predictive model.

Unlike traditional methods, in which an IT team with sophisticated programming experience handled deployment, you can handle Azure ML deployment yourself. Consider some of the benefits of using Azure ML:

▶ You don't need to install software or tackle hardware provisioning; its fully managed cloud service makes machine learning simple and powerful.

▶ Its web-based visual composition and modules support end-to-end data science workflow (which can be accessed from a variety of web browsers) in a drag, drop, and connect design approach.

▶ Azure ML uses best-in-class machine learning algorithms—the same that have run Xbox and Bing for years.

▶ It offers support for R. More than 400 R packages have already been ported, so you can start using it immediately. You can even use your own R packages with the model you are creating in Azure ML.

▶ You can quickly deploy Azure ML models as Azure web services, for both request response (for a smaller dataset) and batch scoring (for a larger dataset), with a few clicks and in just a few minutes.

▶ Azure ML offers a collaborative data science experience so that you can work with anyone, anywhere, via the Azure ML workspace.

The best part of Azure ML is that it is a tried and tested product based on more than 20 years of machine learning experience. Its powerful algorithms are being used in several Microsoft products, including Xbox, Kinect, Microsoft Malware Protection Center, Cortana, Skype Translator, and Bing. Microsoft released a data mining component or algorithms for predictive analytics with SQL Server 2005 (available in later versions as well).

Some early adopters of Azure ML are large retail customers that are being helped by MAX451 (http://blogs.technet.com/b/machinelearning/archive/2014/07/14/how-azure-ml-partners-are-innovating-for-their-customers.aspx), a Microsoft partner. The goal is to predict which products a customer is most likely to purchase next, based on e-commerce and brick-and-mortar store data, so that the companies can stock their stores even before demand rises.

Another Microsoft partner, OSISoft, is working with Carnegie Mellon University (http://www.microsoft.com/casestudies/Power-BI-for-Office-365/Carnegie-Mellon-University/University-Improves-Operational-Efficiency-Cuts-Energy-Consumption-by-30-Percent-with-BI-Solution/710000003921) on performing real-time fault detection and diagnosing energy output variations across university campus buildings. This will help predict and then plan for mitigation activities to reduce or optimize overall energy usage and cost, in a real-time scenario.

Azure ML Workspace

Azure ML introduces the notion of modeling with the Azure ML workspace, which you can think of as a container for data and an experiment for your projects and team. A data scientist can be part of more than one workspace and can easily switch between workspaces to contribute to them at the same time. More than one data scientist can access a specific workspace so that they all can collaboratively work on the data and experiment.

As the owner of an Azure ML workspace, you can invite others to contribute to the workspace. The workspace thus allows the group to work on the common project by gathering data, modules, and experiments for common use. These are some of the elements you typically find in an Azure ML workspace:

▶ **Datasets**—You identify datasets to be used in experiments that you create in the workspace. You can create a dataset by loading data from varieties of sources, such as your local system, Azure SQL database, Azure Blob, web or FTP sites, and online data. You can also create a dataset as an output from an experiment, to be used in other experiments. Azure ML includes several sample datasets to quickly learn the functionalities of Azure ML and see how to leverage it.

▶ **Modules**—A module is a component or algorithm that you use in your experiments. For example, you can use one module to bring data into the workspace and use another module with an algorithm to apply that. Azure ML includes varieties of modules, ranging from modules with data ingress functions to modules with training, scoring, and validation processes. Often a module has a set of parameters or properties that can configure the module's internal algorithms or behaviors.

▶ **Experiments**—An experiment is an Azure ML model that contains analytical modules that are connected for predictive analytics. While developing your experiment, you can run your experiment to analyze its outcome, save a copy of it (if needed), and then run it again. When you are satisfied with your experiment (you have trained an effective model), you can publish it as web service so that others can access your model. Experiments contain datasets and modules and exhibit these characteristics:

▶ An experiment contains either at least one dataset or module, or a combination of both.

▶ Datasets bring data for processing into the experiments and, hence, can be connected to modules only.

▶ Modules inside an experiment can get data from a dataset via input ports and can pass data to another module in the experiment via output ports.

▶ Some modules come with a set of parameters, so all the required parameters must be set for the module for it to function as expected.

▶ For a given module, all the input ports must be connected to the data flow to receive data to work on it.

▶ **Workspace configuration**—Details include the name of the workspace and users of the workspaces.

Azure ML Studio

Azure ML Studio is browser-based collaborative visual integrated development environment for machine learning solutions. It can be used from any device, from anywhere in the world, to build, test, and deploy predictive analytics solutions that operate on your own data. It has an easy-to-use, intuitive drag, drop, and connect interface for setting up your experiment. Azure ML Studio contains modules for each step of the data science workflow, including reading data from various sources (both on-premises and in the cloud), cleansing and transforming data, creating a training and test set, applying machine learning algorithms, and evaluating the resulting model. With these built-in modules, data scientists can avoid programming for a large number of common tasks and instead can focus on the data, their experiment design, and data analysis.

NOTE

Azure ML Studio contains best-in-breed built-in machine learning algorithms that you can use quickly; it also contains more than 400 open-source R packages that you can use securely in Azure ML; you can embed your own custom packages as well.

Hour 11, "Customizing HDInsight Cluster with Script Action," and Hour 20, "Performing Statistical Computing with R," covered installing R software while provisioning HDInsight and then using it. Here, however, we are referring to Azure ML as a predictive analytics platform that also includes several R algorithms or packages.

When you are finished with your model development, you can quickly (in minutes) and easily (with a few mouse clicks) deploy it in production as a web service for others; you don't have to spend several days doing this, as with the traditional approach of machine learning. When you deploy your model, Azure ML creates two web services, one for a request response to process and score individual requests, and one for batch data processing.

Processes to Build Azure ML Solutions

Creating an Azure ML solution is an iterative process that includes these iterative phases (see Figure 22.1):

▶ **Define/refine the business problem and objective**—You must first understand the business problem and define what you want to achieve. What's your end objective?

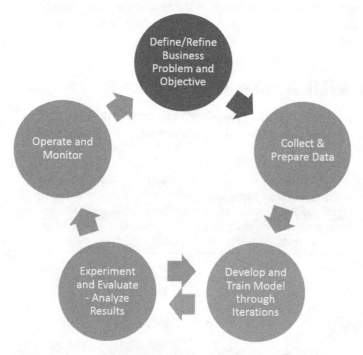

FIGURE 22.1
Azure ML solution development processes.

▶ **Collect and prepare data**—You must understand the domain and the data you need to solve the business problem. Then you can collect and start understanding the data, deal with vagaries and biases in data acquisition (missing data, outliers due to errors in the data collection process, more sophisticated biases from the data collection procedure, and so on).

▶ **Develop and train the model through iterations**—Frame the business problem in terms of an Azure ML problem—classification, regression, ranking, clustering, forecasting, outlier detection, and so on—to find trends and patterns in the data that lead to solutions. When you are developing and training Azure ML models, you don't need to be an expert in any programming language; you just need to visually connect datasets and modules to construct your predictive analysis model.

▶ **Experiment and evaluate, and analyze results**—Train, test, and evaluate the model to control bias or variance and ensure that the metrics are reported with the right confidence intervals (cross-validation helps here). Be vigilant against target leaks (which typically lead to unbelievably good test metrics). Note that this step is also iterative—you change inputs or machine learning algorithms to get different scores and for better evaluation.

▶ **Operationalize the Azure ML model and monitor the model's performance**—When you are sure that your developed Azure ML model solves the business problem, you can deploy the model to solve the business problem in the real world. Keep monitoring for its effectiveness in the real world.

Getting Started with Azure ML

As you can see in Figure 22.2, you first must obtain a Microsoft Azure subscription. If you have one already, you can use it, or you can choose to use a trial subscription for learning purposes.

NOTE
___
As of this writing, Microsoft offers a one-month free subscription with a $200 credit to spend on Azure services for signing up. (See http://azure.microsoft.com/en-us/pricing/free-trial/.) When you have access to the Microsoft Azure subscription, you can go to the Azure Management Portal (https://manage.windowsazure.com/) and create an Azure ML workspace.
___

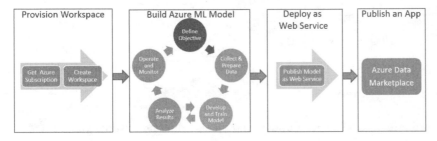

FIGURE 22.2
Azure ML development workflow.

You can create an Azure ML workspace by clicking the icon on the bottom left. You are prompted with a nice-looking user interface where you can select the Azure service you want to provision. For an Azure ML workspace, select Data Services, Machine Learning, Quick Create, and then specify the details to create an Azure ML workspace (see Figure 22.3).

FIGURE 22.3
Creating an Azure ML workspace in the Azure Management Portal.

After you have created the Azure ML workspace, you can click it to view its detail (see Figure 22.4). On this dashboard, you can manage access to the Azure ML workspace, manage web services, change the workspace owner, and so on. From here, you can log in to the Azure ML Studio (see Figure 22.4).

TIP

Alternatively, you can use https://studio.azureml.net/ to directly sign in to Azure ML Studio.

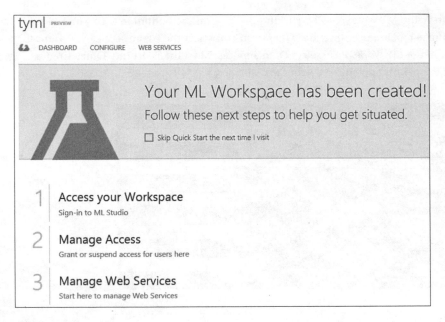

FIGURE 22.4
Viewing the details of the created Azure ML workspace.

When you are signed in to Azure ML Studio, you will see an interface similar to the Azure Management Portal, but with different options to work with Azure ML (see Figure 22.5). On the left side, you can see tabs, such as Experiments, to show all the experiments you have in workspace, along with sample experiments. The Web Services tab shows the deployed web services from the experiments. The Datasets tab displays the datasets you have created in the workspace. You can go to the Settings tab to change the name and description for the workspace, regenerate authorization tokens, change user access to the workspace, and so on.

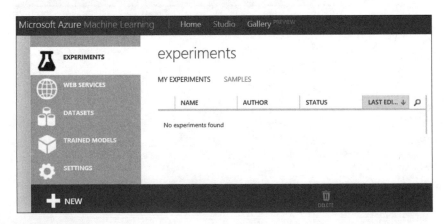

FIGURE 22.5
Azure ML Studio.

If you click the icon at the bottom left, you are prompted with a nice-looking user interface, where you can create a new dataset or a new experiment (see Figure 22.6). When you are creating an experiment, you have a choice to create a blank experiment and then start adding datasets or modules to it, or create an experiment based on samples available for learning purposes.

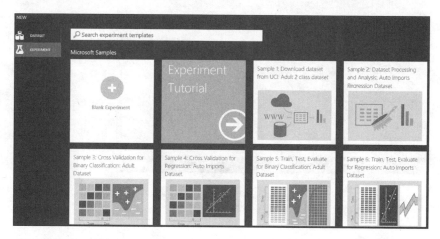

FIGURE 22.6
Creating a new experiment in Azure ML Studio.

When you create a blank experiment, your screen should look like Figure 22.7. On the left side, you can see different modules categorically grouped to use in your experiment. In the middle is a canvas to create your Azure ML data science workflow using different datasets and modules. On the right side are the properties of the workspace or the selected module in the canvas. At the bottom, you have options to zoom out or zoom in for better visibility of the data science workflow in the canvas, along with options to save the workspace or a copy of it.

For testing, you click the Run icon at the bottom to execute the Azure ML experiment. You also have options to publish an experiment by first creating a scoring experiment and then creating web services by publishing it.

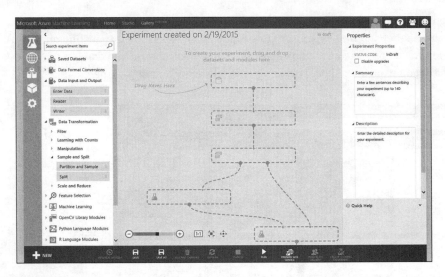

FIGURE 22.7
Azure ML Studio canvas to create an experiment and its workflow.

Retrieving Data into Azure ML Modules

You learned earlier that you can bring in the data from various sources either by creating a dataset from the local file system or by using a Reader module to bring in online data. Just drag a Reader module, available under the Data Input and Output group (or you can even search for a module in the search box at the top), to the canvas and set the properties appropriately (see Figure 22.8).

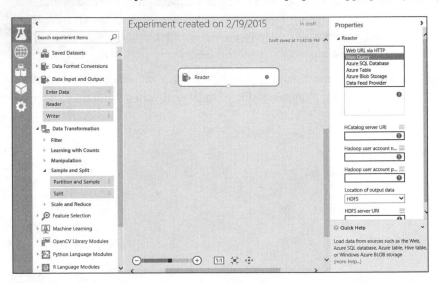

FIGURE 22.8
Reading data from a variety of sources using the Reader module.

When you have data, you can use it in further modules for preprocessing, such as cleansing data, removing duplicates, or joining two datasets, before you use it with Azure ML modules.

Now you can bring in online data using the Reader module, but before, you must give your experiment a meaningful name (in this case, we named it My First Experiment). Select the Reader module to bring in adults' income census data; to do that, specify Web URL via HTTP as the data source property and select http://archive.ics.uci.edu/ml/machine-learning-databases/adult/adult.data as the URL property. The format of this data is CSV with no header.

Click the output port (the tiny dot at the bottom) of the Reader module, and you will see disabled options to download or visualize the dataset (see Figure 22.9). This is because, even though you have pointed to the correct URL, you have not yet retrieved the data.

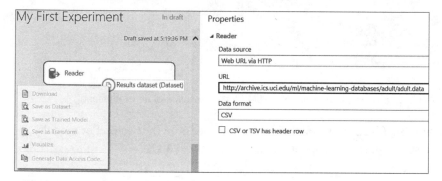

FIGURE 22.9
Creating a first experiment.

To retrieve the online data, you must run your experiment. After successful execution, if you click the output port of the Reader module again, you will see enabled options (see Figure 22.10).

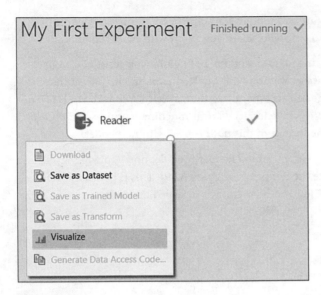

FIGURE 22.10
Visualizing the dataset (no data visualization takes place before the execution of an experiment).

Click Visualize (refer to Figure 22.10) to see the data that comes from that dataset or module, with some basic statistical information about the data (see Figure 22.11).

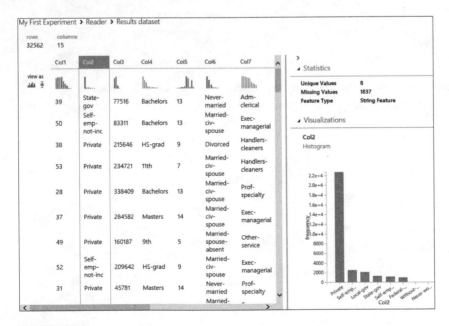

FIGURE 22.11
Saved data visualization.

Using the Descriptive Statistics Module

Now you can use the Descriptive Statistics module to find detailed statistical information of the dataset. Search for it in the search box, drag the Descriptive Statistics module onto the canvas, connect the output port from the Reader module to the input port of the Descriptive Statistics module, and run your experiment. Then click Visualize (see Figure 22.12).

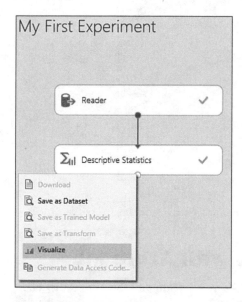

FIGURE 22.12
Visualizing data after experiment execution.

The Descriptive Statistics module profiles the data and creates a set of standard statistical measures that describe each column in the input table. The module does not return the original dataset, but instead generates a row for each column, beginning with the column name (in this case, you don't have a column name in the datasets, so you see Col1, Col2, and so on), followed by relevant statistics for that specific column, based on its data type (see Figure 22.13).

My First Experiment > Descriptive Statistics > Results dataset

rows 15   columns 23

view as

Feature	Count	Unique Value Count	Missing Value Count	Min	Max	Mean	Mean Deviation	1st Quartile	Median	3rd Quartile	Mode
Col1	32561	73	1	17	90	38.581647	11.189182	28	37	48	36
Col2	30725	9	1837								
Col3	32561	21648	1	12285	1484705	189778.366512	77608.21854	117827	178356	237051	{12301
Col4	32561	17	1								
Col5	32561	16	1	1	16	10.080679	1.903048	9	10	12	9
Col6	32561	8	1								
Col7	30718	15	1844								
Col8	32561	7	1								
Col9	32561	6	1								
Col10	32561	3	1								
Col11	32561	119	1	0	99999	1077.648844	1977.373437	0	0	0	0
Col12	32561	92	1	0	4356	87.30383	166.462055	0	0	0	0
Col13	32561	94	1	1	99	40.437456	7.583228	40	40	45	40
Col14	31978	42	584								
Col15	32561	3	1								

FIGURE 22.13
Data statistics collected using the Descriptive Statistics module.

Creating Predictive Models with Azure ML

Azure ML has numerous prebuilt models that both the Azure ML team and the community offer to help you quickly learn and get started with Azure ML. This section demonstrates one model from the Model Gallery that predicts income level (predicts whether an individual's income is greater than or less than $50,000), based on adult census data collected. Azure ML includes several datasets; one is the Adult Census Income Binary Classification dataset.

This is the same dataset you retrieved earlier using the Reader module, but this saved dataset has added a column header, for better clarity (see Figure 22.14).

workclass	fnlwgt	education	education-num	marital-status	occupation	relationship	race	sex	capital-gain	capital-loss	hours-per-week	native-country	income
39 State-gov	77516	Bachelors	13	Never-married	Adm-clerical	Not-in-family	White	Male	2174	0	40	United-States	<=50K
50 Self-emp-not-inc	83311	Bachelors	13	Married-civ-spouse	Exec-managerial	Husband	White	Male	0	0	13	United-States	<=50K
38 Private	215646	HS-grad	9	Divorced	Handlers-cleaners	Not-in-family	White	Male	0	0	40	United-States	<=50K
53 Private	234721	11th	7	Married-civ-spouse	Handlers-cleaners	Husband	Black	Male	0	0	40	United-States	<=50K
28 Private	338409	Bachelors	13	Married-civ-spouse	Prof-specialty	Wife	Black	Female	0	0	40	Cuba	<=50K
37 Private	284582	Masters	14	Married-civ-spouse	Exec-managerial	Wife	White	Female	0	0	40	United-States	<=50K
49 Private	160187	9th	5	Married-spouse-absent	Other-service	Not-in-family	Black	Female	0	0	16	Jamaica	<=50K
52 Self-emp-not-inc	209642	HS-grad	9	Married-civ-spouse	Exec-managerial	Husband	White	Male	0	0	45	United-States	>50K
31 Private	45781	Masters	14	Never-married	Prof-specialty	Not-in-family	White	Female	14084	0	50	United-States	>50K
42 Private	159449	Bachelors	13	Married-civ-spouse	Exec-managerial	Husband	White	Male	5178	0	40	United-States	>50K
37 Private	280464	Some-college	10	Married-civ-spouse	Exec-managerial	Husband	Black	Male	0	0	80	United-States	>50K
30 State-gov	141297	Bachelors	13	Married-civ-spouse	Prof-specialty	Husband	Asian-Pac-Islander	Male	0	0	40	India	>50K
23 Private	122272	Bachelors	13	Never-married	Adm-clerical	Own-child	White	Female	0	0	30	United-States	<=50K
32 Private	205019	Assoc-acdm	12	Never-married	Sales	Not-in-family	Black	Male	0	0	50	United-States	<=50K
40 Private	121772	Assoc-voc	11	Married-civ-spouse	Craft-repair	Husband	Asian-Pac-Islander	Male	0	0	40	?	>50K
34 Private	245487	7th-8th	4	Married-civ-spouse	Transport-moving	Husband	Amer-Indian-Eskimo	Male	0	0	45	Mexico	<=50K
25 Self-emp-not-inc	176756	HS-grad	9	Never-married	Farming-fishing	Own-child	White	Male	0	0	35	United-States	<=50K
32 Private	186824	HS-grad	9	Never-married	Machine-op-inspct	Unmarried	White	Male	0	0	40	United-States	<=50K
38 Private	28887	11th	7	Married-civ-spouse	Sales	Husband	White	Male	0	0	50	United-States	<=50K

FIGURE 22.14
Adult income census dataset.

The predictive model for predicting income level should look like Figure 22.15. We have divided the model in Figure 22.15 into different parts, to better explain each part of it. Part A in the model indicates adult income census dataset.

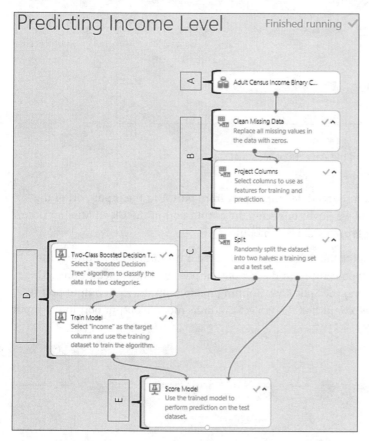

FIGURE 22.15
Predictive model to predict income level, based on trained data.

Part B in the model indicates preprocessing of the dataset; it contains the Clean Missing Data module to handle missing values and replaces it with some other values (in this case, we are replacing it with 0). It also contains the Project Columns module for choosing a subset of columns to use in downstream operations by excluding or including columns from the input dataset. In this case, as Figure 22.16 shows, we are excluding the workclass, occupation, and native-country column names because they contain a high number of missing values and would not contribute to an accurate prediction.

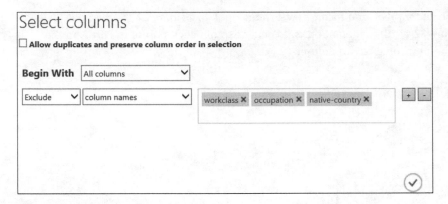

FIGURE 22.16
Column selector from the properties of the Project Columns module.

Next, we have connected the dataset module output port from part A to the input port of the Clean Missing Data module, and we have connected the output port of the Clean Missing Data module to the input port of the Project Columns module.

Part C of the model randomly splits the dataset into two parts: a training set for training the machine learning algorithm (60 percent) from the left output port, and a test set for predicting the income level (40 percent) using the Split Rows Splitting mode from the right output port (see Figure 22.17). Note that we have connected the Project Columns module output port to the input port of the Split module.

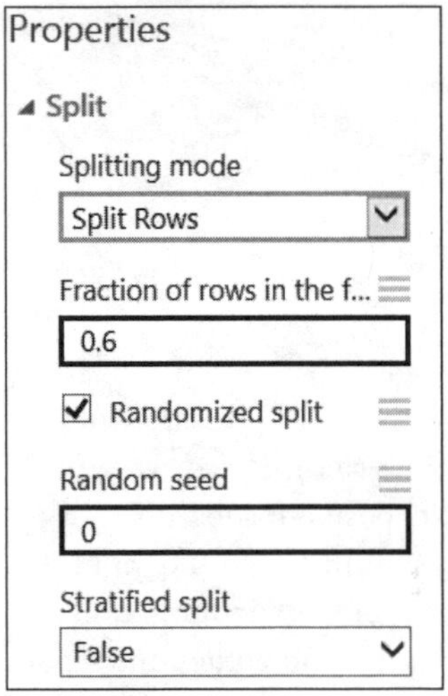

FIGURE 22.17
Split module properties.

NOTE

Training Sets Versus Test Sets

While developing, you normally split the data into training and testing sets. When you train an Azure ML model, you perform an initial analysis with a set of data to identify patterns, trends, and predictions and have them stored. You can then use this stored information to test the patterns in another set of new, incoming data.

Azure ML has several built-in machine learning algorithms to choose from. Part D of the model uses the Two-Class Boosted Decision Tree module, which is based on boosted decision trees to predict a target that has two possible values. The model also uses the Train Model module and specifies the income column from the dataset as the prediction target. The Train Model module takes a dataset that contains historical data from which to learn patterns.

Next, we have connected the output port of the Two-Class Boosted Decision Tree module to the left-side input port of the Train Model module, and connected the left output port of the Split module to the right input port of the Train Model module.

When the model has been trained, you can pass the model to the Score Model module to do predictions on tests or new datasets, as shown as Part E in Figure 22.15. We also have connected the output port of the Train Model module to the left input port of the Score Model, and connected the right output port of the Split module to the right input port of the Score Model module.

Now run the experiment. When it finishes running successfully, we click the output port of the Score Model module and then click Visualize. This brings up the scored dataset in Figure 22.18. Because we are using a classification model (Two-Class Boosted Decision Tree) to create the scores, the Score Model outputs a predicted value for the class (Scored Labels) and the probability of the predicted value (Scored Probabilities)—see Figure 22.18.

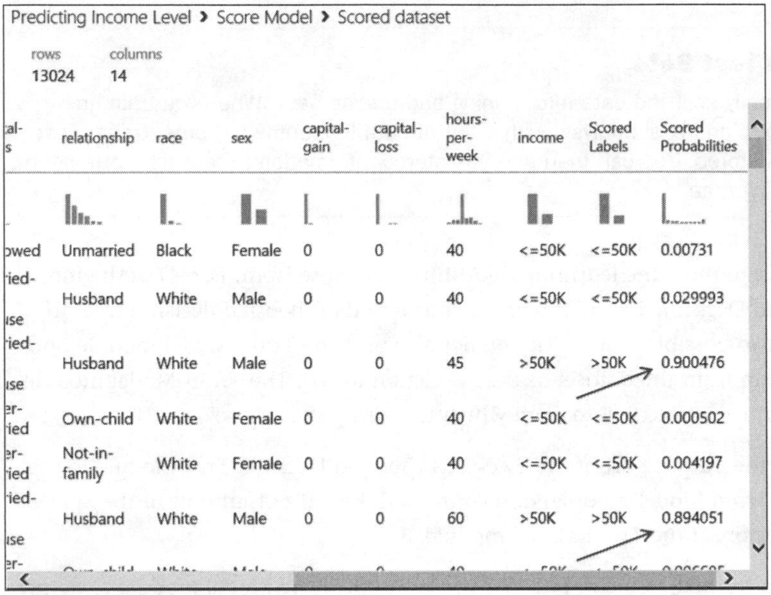

Predicting Income Level › Score Model › Scored dataset

rows 13024 columns 14

...al-s	relationship	race	sex	capital-gain	capital-loss	hours-per-week	income	Scored Labels	Scored Probabilities
...owed	Unmarried	Black	Female	0	0	40	<=50K	<=50K	0.00731
...ried-...se	Husband	White	Male	0	0	40	<=50K	<=50K	0.029993
...ried-...se	Husband	White	Male	0	0	45	>50K	>50K	0.900476
...er-...ied	Own-child	White	Female	0	0	40	<=50K	<=50K	0.000502
...er-...ied	Not-in-family	White	Female	0	0	40	<=50K	<=50K	0.004197
...ried-...se	Husband	White	Male	0	0	60	>50K	>50K	0.894051

FIGURE 22.18
Prediction with Scored Probabilities.

This experiment has not yet used the Evaluate Model module (you saw this in Figure 22.17). However, you can use that model to generate a set of metrics for evaluating the model's accuracy (performance) after you have generated a set of scores using the Score Model module.

When we used the Evaluate Model module, we got the result in Figure 22.19; notice that it was fairly accurate (higher numbers of true positives and true negatives, indicating correct predictions) in predicting the income level for individuals.

Figure 22.20 shows the definition and formulas for different metrics reported as part of the model evaluation process in Figure 22.19. The Receiver Operating Characteristic (ROC) plot and the Area Under Curve (AUC) plot are useful for comparing and selecting the best machine learning model for a given dataset.

TIP

A model with an AUC score near 1, and where the ROC curve comes close to the upper-left corner, has very good performance. A model with a score near 0.5 has a curve near the diagonal, and its performance is hardly better than a random predictor (http://blogs.msdn.com/b/andreasderuiter/archive/2015/02/10/performance-measures-in-azure-ml-accuracy-precision-recall-and-f1-score.aspx).

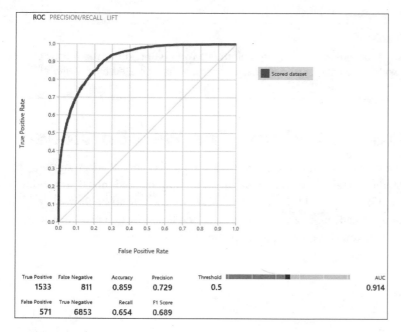

FIGURE 22.19
Model evaluation result.

True Positive (TP) - a positive instance that is correctly classified as positive
False Positive (FP) - a negative instance that is incorrectly classified as positive
True Negative (TN) - a negative instance that is correctly classified as negative
False Negative (FN) - a positive instance that is incorrectly classified as negative

$$\text{Accuracy} = \frac{TP + TN}{P+N} \qquad\qquad \text{Precision} = \frac{TP}{TP+FP}$$

$$\text{Recall} = \frac{TP}{TP+FN} = \frac{TP}{P} \qquad\qquad F_\beta = \frac{(1+\beta^2) \cdot precision \cdot recall}{\beta^2 \cdot precision + recall}$$

FIGURE 22.20
Definition and formula for evaluation results.

So far, you have seen just a simple example of Azure ML usage, but the possibilities are limitless. Azure ML includes dozens of other sample models, on different machine learning algorithms, available from both the Azure ML team and the community. For example, a restaurant recommender sample model would predict similar items that users might like, based on past habits and item characteristics. Similarly, a credit risk prediction sample model would predict credit risk based on the information given on a credit application.

NOTE

Sample Models Are Locked

By default, sample models are locked and you cannot edit them. You first need to save a copy of the sample model in your workspace—then you can use it as regular user-created model with all sort of functionalities.

Publishing Azure ML Models as Web Services

When you have a trained model ready for deployment as a web service, click the icon at the bottom of the Azure ML Studio to create a scoring experiment for your trained model. This adds web service input and output modules and takes out the dataset we used from the flow when published as a web service API (see Figure 22.21). It maintains the link, so when any change in the working experiment occurs, you can go back and update the scoring experiment.

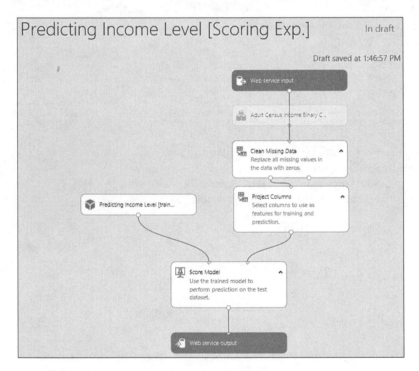

FIGURE 22.21
Scoring experiment for the learning model we created.

Next, you must run your scoring experiment. Upon successful execution, click the icon to publish your experiment as a web service API. You can visit the Web Services tab to view your web services API details (see Figure 22.22). As you can see, Azure ML creates two web services, one for a request response to process and score individual requests, and one for batch data processing and scoring.

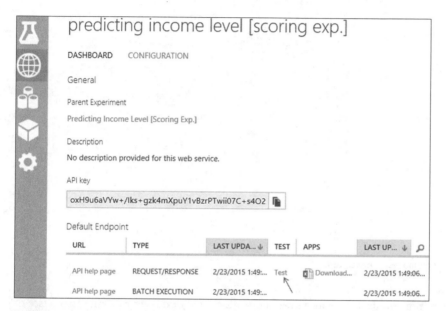

FIGURE 22.22
Published web service API.

Click the Test link for the request response web service API to quickly validate and test it (see Figure 22.23). You can enter data and quickly see scored labels and probabilities for the provided record. As you can see in Figure 22.22, it also provides a ready-to-use Excel client into which you can plug your own data to easily test your web service API.

FIGURE 22.23
Testing a request/response web service API.

We tested it for two individuals. One had a lower education level and fewer working hours, so income was predicted to be lower than $50,000. Another individual had a higher education level and more working hours, so income was predicted to be more than $50,000. The probabilities score was 90 percent (see Figure 22.24).

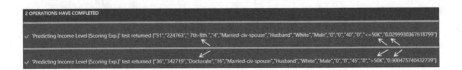

FIGURE 22.24
Test result of a web service API testing for two individuals.

After you have published your trained model as a web service, you can publish it to the Azure Marketplace for the general public (either free or as a paid service).

Summary

In this hour, you learned about Microsoft Azure Machine Learning (MAML, or Azure ML) and saw how it is a game changer for doing predictive analytics. You looked at processes to build Azure ML solutions, and you explored Azure ML components such as the Azure ML workspace and Azure ML Studio to get started with it quickly. You saw you can create and test your Azure ML experiment in Azure ML Studio and publish it as web service for wider access and use.

The next hour talks about Apache Storm and demonstrates how to use it to perform real-time stream analytics.

Q&A

Q. How does Azure ML differ from earlier machine learning approaches for predictive analytics?

A. Predictive analytics have been in use for several years now, but they have been limited to only a few large organizations that maintained data scientists or statisticians and had the huge investment of time and money needed for implementations. With the advent of emerging technologies such as Azure ML, the game has changed. Azure ML is extremely simple to use and easier to implement, so analysts with various backgrounds (even non-data scientists) can leverage it. As a user, you just need to know your data, know how to set up and frame your problem, and then leverage Azure ML to build the predictive model easily and quickly. Unlike with traditional methods, in which an ITM with sophisticated programming experience handled the deployment, you can deploy Azure ML yourself in a few minutes, with just a few clicks.

Q. How can you deploy your Azure ML models for wider use?

A. After you have trained your Azure ML model or experiment, you can deploy it as a scalable and fault-tolerant web service. The web services created are REST APIs that provide an interface for communication between external applications (such as web applications or mobile applications) and your predictive analytics models.

Q. When should you use a request/response web service, and when should you use a batch execution web service?

A. The request/response web service is a low-latency, high-scale web service that provides an interface to stateless models that are created and published from the experimentation environment. It accepts a single row of input parameters and generates a single row as output, although the output row can contain multiple columns.

The batch execution web service is used to asynchronously score a batch of input data records (high volume). The input for batch execution is similar to the data input used in the request/response web service. The main difference is that batch execution reads a block of records from a variety of sources, such as the Blob service and Table service in Azure, the

Azure SQL Database, HDInsight (hive query), and HTTP sources. The output for the batch execution contains the results of the scoring in a file in Azure Storage Blob, and data from the storage endpoint is returned in the response.

Exercise

Throughout this book, we have used publically available on-time performance of airline flights data from the Research and Innovative Technology Administration (RITA), Bureau of Transportation Statistics (BTS). This data is available as part of the Saved Datasets, along with weather forecasting data. A sample model predicts whether the arrival of a scheduled passenger flight will be delayed by more than 15 minutes. To create an experiment based on this sample, click the icon in the Azure ML Studio, search for the flight (see Figure 22.25), and then click Binary Classification: Flight Delay Prediction to create a copy of this sample.

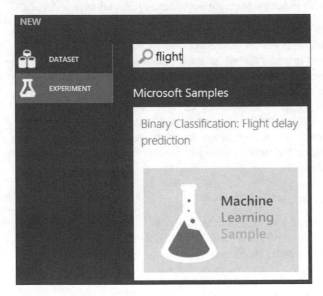

FIGURE 22.25
Search for the Flight Delay Prediction model.

Your model should look like Figure 22.26.

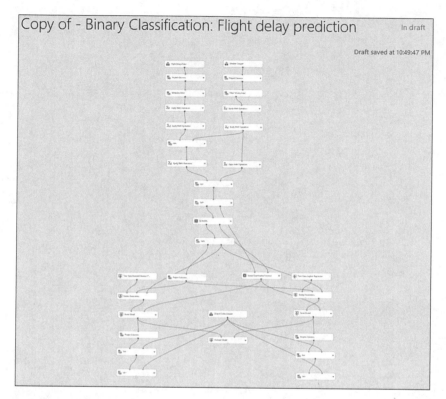

FIGURE 22.26
Flight Delay Prediction model.

You can go through each of module in the model to understand its functionalities and the values it delivers.

NOTE

You can find documentation of the model and a description of how it works at http://gallery.azureml.net/Details/837e2095ce784f1ba5ac623a60232027.

Performing Stream Analytics with Storm

What You'll Learn in This Hour:

▶ Introduction to Storm

▶ Using SCP.NET to Develop Storm Solutions

▶ Analyzing Speed Limit Violation Incidents with Storm

Hadoop MapReduce is well suited to batch processing; however, not all Big Data analytic problems fit in the batch processing model. For example, identifying trending topics on Twitter requires continuous processing of millions of incoming tweets. Similarly, providing music recommendations to users at Spotify requires continuously processing user activity for millions of subscribers. Apache Storm works well in such scenarios because it uses real-time continuous processing of data streams instead of processing data in batches.

This hour introduces Apache Storm and explores its use in performing real-time stream analytics.

Introduction to Storm

Storm is a distributed, fault-tolerant, real-time computation framework that supports continuous processing of data streams. Spouts feed data streams to a storm topology, and bolts apply transforms on streams. A network of spouts and bolts forms a Storm topology. Topologies in Storm are analogous to MapReduce jobs in Hadoop. Unlike a MapReduce job, which ends upon completion of processing, a topology keeps processing data streams continuously until execution is terminated.

NOTE

Storm Developed by Nathan Marz at BackType

Nathan Marz developed Storm at BackType, a social analytics company that Twitter later acquired in July 2011. BackType used Storm to process social media content such as tweets, comments, blogs, and Facebook content to derive meaningful insights for BackType customers.

Understanding the Storm Architecture

The Storm architecture is similar to the Hadoop MapReduce architecture, with some notable differences. A Storm cluster has two types of nodes:

▶ **Nimbus**—A master node runs a service called Nimbus, which is similar to the Hadoop JobTracker. Nimbus is responsible for assigning tasks to worker nodes and monitoring failures.

▶ **Supervisor**—Worker nodes run a service called Supervisor, which is similar to the Hadoop TaskTracker. Supervisor's role is to execute tasks assigned by Nimbus.

ZooKeeper handles coordination between Nimbus and Supervisors (see Figure 23.1).

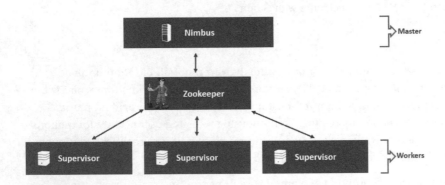

FIGURE 23.1
Storm cluster components.

Storm includes some important abstractions:

▶ **Stream**—A stream is an unbound sequence of Storm tuples. A Storm tuple is a named list of values.

▶ **Spout**—A spout feeds a data stream into the Storm system. A spout can read data from external sources (for example, event queuing systems such as the Azure Event hub or Apache Kafka, the de facto messaging system for Hadoop) and can also generate data (for example, generating random number data for testing).

▶ **Bolt**—A bolt processes one or more inputs and produces zero or more outputs. A bolt performs computations and transformations on input streams. A bolt can also write data to external destinations, such as a SQL Azure table or blob storage.

▶ **Topology**—A network of spouts and bolts forms a topology. Spouts feed a data stream to a topology. Bolts subscribe to one or more input streams and perform continuous computations on streaming data.

Figure 23.2 illustrates a Storm topology.

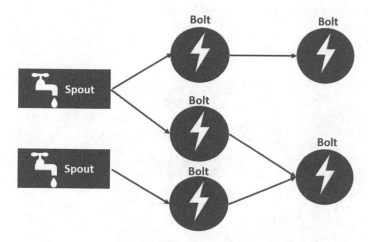

FIGURE 23.2
Storm topology.

Stream groupings control the way tuples are sent to bolts. The main types of groupings follow:

▶ **Shuffle grouping**—The tuple is sent to a randomly chosen bolt so that the load is equally distributed among bolts.

▶ **Fields grouping**—The tuple is sent to a bolt depending on the tuple fields. Tuples with the same value of chosen fields are directed to the same bolt. Field groupings are useful in counting scenarios and are discussed more with an example later in the "Analyzing Speed Limit Violation Incidents with Storm" section.

▶ **All grouping**—Copies of a tuple are sent to all bolts.

▶ **Global grouping**—All tuples from a spout are sent to a single bolt.

▶ **Direct grouping**—The stream source decides which tuple is directed to which bolt.

TRY IT YOURSELF ▼

Provisioning HDInsight Storm Cluster

Complete the following steps to provision the HDInsight Storm cluster:

1. Log in to the Microsoft Azure Management portal and select HDInsight from the left pane.

2. Select the option +NEW from the bottom-left corner of the portal.

3. Select Storm from the list of options (see Figure 23.3). In the appropriate spaces, enter a cluster name, the number of worker nodes required, and the password for admin account, and select an existing storage account.

4. Click the Create HDInsight cluster button to provision the cluster.

FIGURE 23.3
Provisioning the HDInsight Storm cluster.

Using SCP.NET to Develop Storm Solutions

The Stream Computing Platform (SCP) provides necessary .NET libraries for developing Storm solutions that target the HDInsight Storm cluster. SCP eases the process of creating Storm applications, with abstractions such as spouts, bolts, and topologies, using the .NET Framework.

HDInsight tools for Visual Studio install Storm project templates required for developing HDInsight Storm solutions using SCP.NET. HDInsight tools work with the following:

▶ Visual Studio 2012 with Update 4

▶ Visual Studio 2013 with Update 4

▶ Visual Studio 2013 Community Edition

▶ Visual Studio 2015 CTP6

Azure SDK 2.5.1 or higher is also required. Azure SDK and HDInsight tools for Visual Studio can be installed using the Microsoft Web Platform installer (see Figure 23.4).

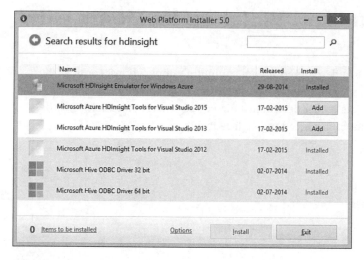

FIGURE 23.4
Installing HDInsight tools for Visual Studio.

After HDInsight tools for Visual Studio are installed, the Storm Application template becomes available in the list of installed HDInsight project templates (see Figure 23.5).

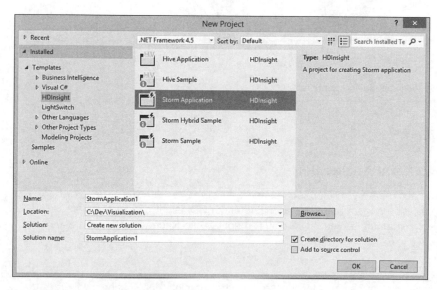

FIGURE 23.5
Storm Application project template.

Analyzing Speed Limit Violation Incidents with Storm

To appreciate the use of SCP.NET in developing stream computing applications, consider the following scenario for analyzing speed limit violation incidents at 10 different locations in New York City. Assume that license plate reader devices installed at 10 different locations provide tuples with the following information for incoming vehicle traffic:

▶ Event time stamp

▶ Location

▶ Vehicle registration number

▶ Speed

The scenario involves filtering the incoming stream to extract tuples with a speed of more than 60 mph and counting the number of extracted tuples by location (see Figure 23.6).

FIGURE 23.6
Storm topology for analyzing speed limit violations.

▼ TRY IT YOURSELF

Creating a New Storm Application

Launch Visual Studio and create a new project named `LicensePlateReaderApplication` using the Storm Application project template, available under HDInsight project templates. This creates a new project containing a predefined bolt and spout (see Figure 23.7).

NOTE

Refer to the accompanying code samples for this hour for the complete code listing.

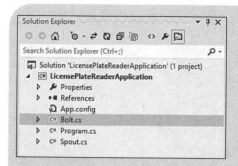

FIGURE 23.7
New project with a predefined spout and bolt.

Complete the following steps to create a license plate reader spout:

1. Use the following code snippet to create a new enum for `Locations`. The enum defines 10 city locations where license plate reader devices have been installed.

```
public enum Locations
{
    TimesSquare = 0,
    LexingtonAvenue = 1,
    BrooklynBridge = 2,
    PennStation = 3,
    CentralPark = 4,
    ColumbusCircle = 5,
    GrandCentral = 6,
    FifthAvenue = 7,
    WallStreet = 8,
    MadisonSquare = 9
}
```

2. Use the following code snippet to create the `LPREvent` class, which represents a tuple from a license plate reader device that contains information such as the time stamp, device location, vehicle registration number, and speed:

```
[Serializable]
public class LPREvent
{
    public DateTime TimeStamp { get; set; }
    public Locations Location { get; set; }
    public string VehicleRegNo { get; set; }
    public int Speed { get; set; }
    static Random = new Random();

    public static LPREvent CreateEvent()
```

```
    {
        return new LPREvent
        {
            TimeStamp = DateTime.Now,
            Location = (Locations)random.Next(10),
            VehicleRegNo = "xxxxx",
            Speed = random.Next(100)
        };
    }
}
```

The static function `CreateEvent` of the `LPREvent` class creates a new event object by populating random data for event location and speed to simulate an incoming vehicle.

3. Rename the existing spout to `LPRSpout` from the Solution Explorer. This also renames the class and all its references. Use the following code snippet to define the `LPRSpout` class:

```
public class LPRSpout : ISCPSpout
{
    private Context ctx;
    private Random r = new Random();

    public LPRSpout(Context ctx)
    {
        this.ctx = ctx;

        // Define output stream schema
        Dictionary<string, List<Type>> outputSchema = new Dictionary<string,
List<Type>>();
        outputSchema.Add("default", new List<Type>() { typeof(LPREvent) });
        this.ctx.DeclareComponentSchema(new ComponentStreamSchema(null,
outputSchema));
    }

    public static LPRSpout Get(Context ctx, Dictionary<string, Object> parms)
    {
        return new LPRSpout(ctx);
    }

    public void NextTuple(Dictionary<string, Object> parms)
    {
        // Emit a new LPR event to output stream
        ctx.Emit(new Values(LPREvent.CreateEvent()));
    }

    public void Ack(long seqId, Dictionary<string, Object> parms)
    {
```

```
                throw new NotImplementedException();
        }

        public void Fail(long seqId, Dictionary<string, Object> parms)
        {
                throw new NotImplementedException();
        }
}
```

The code snippet defines the spout's output stream schema. The `NextTuple` function emits a new tuple, with random values for speed and location, to the output stream by calling the `LPREvent` class's `CreateEvent` function. In a real-world scenario, the `NextTuple` function would read data from external sources (such as the Azure Service Bus or Event Hub Queue) and emit the data to the stream.

Next, complete the following steps to create a filter bolt to extract violations:

1. Rename the `Blot.cs` file from Solution Explorer to `FilterBolt.cs` and use the following code snippet to define the `FilterBolt` class. The code snippet defines input and output stream schemas. The `Execute` method filters out tuples with no violations from the input stream and emits only tuples that violate speed limit to the output stream.

```
public class FilterBolt : ISCPBolt
{
    private Context ctx;

    public FilterBolt(Context ctx)
    {
        this.ctx = ctx;

        // Define input stream schema
        Dictionary<string, List<Type>> inputSchema = new Dictionary<string,
List<Type>>();
        inputSchema.Add("default", new List<Type>() { typeof(LPREvent) });
        this.ctx.DeclareComponentSchema(new ComponentStreamSchema(inputSchema,
null));

        // Define output stream schem
        Dictionary<string, List<Type>> outputSchema = new Dictionary<string,
List<Type>>();
        outputSchema.Add("default", new List<Type>() { typeof(LPREvent) });
        this.ctx.DeclareComponentSchema(new ComponentStreamSchema(inputSchema,
outputSchema));
    }

    public static FilterBolt Get(Context ctx, Dictionary<string, Object>
parms)
    {
```

```
        return new FilterBolt(ctx);
    }

    public void Execute(SCPTuple tuple)
    {
        LPREvent = (LPREvent)tuple.GetValue(0);

        // Emit only tuple violating speed limit to output stream
        if (lprEvent.Speed > 60)
        {
            this.ctx.Emit(new Values(lprEvent));
        }
    }
}
```

To count the tuples that violate the speed limit, you must add a counter bolt to the topology. Complete the following steps to add a new bolt to the solution:

2. Right-click the Solution Explorer and select the New item option.

3. Select Storm Bolt as the template for the new item and name it `CounterBolt`.

4. Use the following code snippet to define the `CounterBolt` class:

NOTE

The bolt defines the schema only for the input stream. Because the bolt is a terminal node in the topology, output schema definition is not required. The `Execute` method of the counter bolt updates a SQL Azure table with a count of violations, by location.

```
public class CounterBolt : ISCPBolt
{
    private Context ctx;

    public CounterBolt(Context ctx)
    {
        this.ctx = ctx;

        // Define input stream schema
        Dictionary<string, List<Type>> inputSchema = new Dictionary<string,
List<Type>>();
        inputSchema.Add("default", new List<Type>() { typeof(LPREvent) });
        this.ctx.DeclareComponentSchema(new ComponentStreamSchema(inputSchema,
null));
    }

    public static CounterBolt Get(Context ctx, Dictionary<string, Object> parms)
    {
```

```
        return new CounterBolt(ctx);
    }

    public void Execute(SCPTuple tuple)
    {
        LPREvent = (LPREvent)tuple.GetValue(0);
        string location = lprEvent.Location.ToString();

        // Update SQL Azure table with violation counts by location
        DBHelper.UpdateCounters(location);
    }
}
```

Creating the Storm Topology

The `ITopologyBuilder` interface defines the Storm topology. Use the following code snippet to define the topology you saw illustrated in Figure 23.6. The code snippet adds an `lpr` spout to the topology, which emits the tuples.

The speed filter bolt consumes vehicle tuples to extract tuples that violate the speed limit. Because it does not matter which tuples are processed by which bolt instance, the shuffle grouping distributes the load equally among bolt instances.

Finally, the counter bolt consumes filtered tuples and acts as the terminal node in the topology. The counter bolt pushes violation counts by location into a SQL Azure table. `FieldsGrouping` routes incoming tuples so that tuples with the same locations are directed to the same bolt instance. This ensures that two or more bolt instances don't try to update the same row in the SQL Azure table at the same time.

```
public ITopologyBuilder GetTopologyBuilder()
{
    // Create LicensePlateReaderApplication storm topology
    TopologyBuilder = new TopologyBuilder("LicensePlateReaderApplication");

    // Add 'vehicles' lpr spout to the topology
    // The spout emits vehicle tuples
    topologyBuilder.SetSpout(
        "vehicles",
        LPRSpout.Get,
        new Dictionary<string, List<string>>()
        {
            {Constants.DEFAULT_STREAM_ID, new List<string>(){"vehicle"}}
        },
        1);

    // Add speed filter bolt to the topology
```

```
// The bolt emits over-speeding vehicle tuples
// Shuffle grouping is used to route incoming vehicle tuple
//       to randomly chosen bolt
topologyBuilder.SetBolt(
    "speedfilter",
    FilterBolt.Get,
    new Dictionary<string, List<string>>()
    {
    {Constants.DEFAULT_STREAM_ID, new List<string>(){"overspeedingvehicle"}}
    },
    1).shuffleGrouping("vehicles");

// Add vehicle counter bolt to the topology
// The bolt pushes the counts to a SQL Azure table
// FieldsGrouping is used to route incoming tuples, to ensure that
//       tuples with same location fields are directed to same bolt instance
topologyBuilder.SetBolt(
    "counter",
    CounterBolt.Get,
    new Dictionary<string, List<string>>()
    {
        {Constants.DEFAULT_STREAM_ID, new List<string>(){"location", "count"}}
    }
    , 1).fieldsGrouping("speedfilter", new List<int>() { 0 });

// Add topology configuration
topologyBuilder.SetTopologyConfig(new Dictionary<string, string>()
{
    {"topology.kryo.register","[\"[B\"]"}
});

    return topologyBuilder;
}
```

Creating the SQL Azure Table to Store Violation Counts

Use the following code snippet to create a SQL Azure table to hold speed limit violation counts
by location:

```
CREATE TABLE [dbo].[SpeedLimitViolationCount](
    [Location] [varchar](20) NOT NULL PRIMARY KEY,
    [VehicleCount] [int] NULL)
```

The following code snippet creates the stored procedure invoked by the counter bolt to update
speed limit violation counts by location. The stored procedure checks for the existence of a location in the table. If the location does not exist in the table, it creates a new record; otherwise, it
updates the violation counts for the existing record.

```
CREATE PROC [dbo].[usp_IncrementCount]
@LOCATION VARCHAR(20)
AS
IF EXISTS(SELECT 1 FROM SpeedLimitViolationCount WHERE Location=@LOCATION)
BEGIN
    UPDATE SpeedLimitViolationCount SET VehicleCount=VehicleCount+1 WHERE
Location=@LOCATION
END
ELSE
BEGIN
    INSERT INTO SpeedLimitViolationCount (Location,VehicleCount) VALUES(@
LOCATION,1)
END
GO
```

Submitting the Topology to the HDInsight Storm Cluster

To submit the Storm topology for execution, right-click the project and select Submit to Storm on HDInsight (see Figure 23.8).

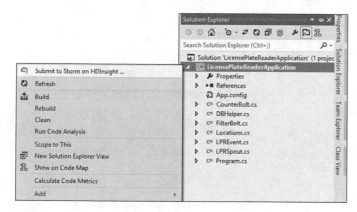

FIGURE 23.8
Submitting a topology to Storm.

At this point, you might be prompted to sign in to your Azure subscription associated with the Storm cluster. After signing in, select your Storm cluster from the drop-down list (see Figure 23.9).

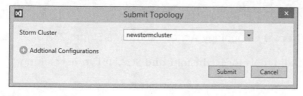

FIGURE 23.9
Selecting a Storm cluster.

To monitor the topology post submission, select the LicensePlateReader topology from the list of Storm topologies (see Figure 23.10). This brings up more information about the topology, options to perform additional actions (for example, pausing or terminating a topology, or rebalancing the topology to adjust parallelism after changing the number of nodes in Storm cluster), topology statistics, and information on spouts and bolts.

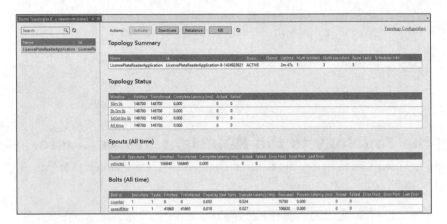

FIGURE 23.10
Selecting the Storm topology for monitoring.

Query the SpeedLimitViolationCount table repeatedly to see violation counts updated for each of the 10 locations (see Figure 23.11).

	Location	VehicleCount
1	BrooklynBridge	170
2	CentralPark	169
3	ColumbusCircle	170
4	FifthAvenue	185
5	GrandCentral	181
6	LexingtonAvenue	191
7	MadisonSquare	178
8	PennStation	202
9	TimesSquare	172
10	WallStreet	166

FIGURE 23.11
Querying the SpeedLimitViolationCount SQL Azure table.

To stop the topology, select the Kill option from the Topology Actions shown in Figure 23.10.

This scenario illustrates the use of Visual Studio tools for HDInsight and SCP.NET in developing stream computing applications.

Summary

This hour explored the stream analytics capabilities of Storm on HDInsight. A Storm topology is a network of spouts and bolts. Spouts feed data streams to a storm topology, and bolts apply transforms on streams. The SCP.NET SDK provides libraries for developing stream analytics applications using the .NET Framework. Visual Studio tools for HDInsight provide Storm project templates to aid in the development of Storm applications using Visual Studio and the .NET Framework.

Q&A

Q. Can I browse the Storm Dashboard through a web browser instead of Visual Studio?

A. Yes. You can access the Storm Dashboard through https://<clustername>.azurehdinsight. net/. An option to launch the Storm Dashboard for an existing cluster is also available from the Windows Azure Management portal.

Q. What are some of the advantages of using Storm?

A. The primary benefits are speed, fault tolerance, and guaranteed processing. Storm is capable of processing more than a million tuples per second, per node, and can automatically reassign tasks on node failure to other nodes. Furthermore, all this is done with a guarantee that the messages will be processed at least once.

Quiz

1. What are the different types of nodes on a Storm cluster?

2. List some of the important abstractions in Storm.

Answers

1. A Storm cluster has two types of nodes, a master node running a service called Nimbus and worker nodes running a service called Supervisor. Nimbus is similar to the Hadoop JobTracker; it is responsible for assigning tasks to worker nodes and monitoring failures. Supervisor is similar to the Hadoop TaskTracker and executes tasks that Nimbus assigns.

2. Spots, bolts, and topologies are the primary Storm abstractions. Spouts feed data streams to a Storm topology, and bolts apply transforms on streams. A network of spouts and bolts forms a storm topology.

Introduction to Apache HBase on HDInsight

What You'll Learn in This Hour:

▶ Introduction to Apache HBase
▶ HBase Architecture
▶ HDInsight Cluster Creation with HBase

In the past few hours, you looked in detail at how you can leverage HDInsight or the Hadoop cluster for storage and processing of Big Data. You explored how to write MapReduce jobs for batch mode data processing. You also looked at Hive and Pig, and you saw how they ease development and significantly reduce total development time. All these technologies work fine for processing Big Data in batch mode, which are often good for online analytics processing (OLAP) and which are supposed to take time. But what if you want a low-latency database that allows online transactional processing (OLTP) of Big Data (record-level processing) and also gives you random, near-real-time read/write access (record level) to your Big Data stored in Hadoop? This is where you can leverage Apache HBase.

Apache HBase is a low-latency, column-oriented NoSQL database that allows online transactional processing of Big Data stored in Hadoop. In this hour, you look at Apache HBase, when to use it, and how you can leverage it with HDInsight service. You also examine how HBase differs from Hive and how you can use Apache Phoenix as a SQL layer to manage and query data in HBase tables more efficiently and quickly.

Introduction to Apache HBase

Apache HBase is a distributed, versioned, column-oriented NoSQL database management system that runs on top of the Hadoop Distributed File System (HDFS). An HBase system consists of a set of tables. Each table contains rows and columns, much like a traditional relational table. Each table must have an element defined as a primary key, and all access attempts to HBase tables must use this primary key.

An HBase column represents an attribute of an object. HBase enables many columns to be grouped into column families so that the elements of a column family are all stored together. This differs from a relational table, in which all the columns of a complete given row are stored together.

HBase mandates that you predefine the table schema and specify the column families. However, it also enables you to add columns to column families at any time, making the schema flexible and adaptable to changing application requirements. It is well suited when you need random, near-real-time read/write access to sparse data sets, which are common in many Big Data use cases.

Row-Store Storage Versus Column-Store Storage

Unlike row-store storage, in which data from all the columns of a row are stored together, a column-oriented database stores data from a single column together. You might be wondering how a different physical layout representation of the same data (storing same data in columnar format instead of traditional row-wise format) can improve flexibility and performance. In a column-oriented database, flexibility comes from the fact that adding a column is easy, inexpensive, and applied row by row. Each row can thus have different set of columns, making the table sparse. In addition, storing data from single columns results in high redundancy and a greater degree of compression, improving overall performance.

Column-oriented or column-store databases, such as Apache HBase, are ideal for searching sites, blogs, and content management systems, as well as for counter analytics (when row access or a scan of a partial dataset is needed); they are not ideal for vertical aggregation, such as summations and averages (when scanning the complete dataset is needed). You can still use HBase scanning in these cases, but for better performance, you should use a MapReduce job when you want to process a large dataset completely, as in the case of vertical aggregation.

Recently, some RDBMS systems, such as SQL Server 2012 and onward, have begun to support storing data in a column-oriented structure. However, some NoSQL databases (such as Apache HBase) not only have support for column-oriented storage, but also can have a different scheme for each row (unlike RDBMS, in which the schema is fixed).

HBase can scale horizontally to thousands of commodity servers and petabytes of indexed storage in the form of tables. An HBase table can be referenced as the input and output for

MapReduce jobs or can be accessed either programmatically through Java, REST, Avro, and Thrift APIs or interactively using the HBase client shell.

While loading data into a table, HBase automatically shards or partitions data across multiple nodes or regions that scale linearly and automatically with new nodes. HBase leverages HDFS for storing HBase files, and HDFS ensures high availability and fault tolerance because replication is built in with HDFS.

When to Use HBase

Even though HBase provides create, read, update, and delete (CRUD) capabilities needed for OLTP systems, it might not be a good fit for all OLTP scenarios (HBase is not optimized for traditional transactional applications). You can use HBase in these situations:

▶ You need key-based access to data while storing or retrieving.

▶ You want database-style access (most users are accustomed to working with the tables, columns, and rows of a table) to the large-scale data sitting in Hadoop with CRUD capabilities for quickly reading from or writing to specific subsets of data.

▶ You have billions of rows with millions of columns of sparse data. If the data is too small, it might end up in one or two nodes, leaving the rest of the nodes of cluster idle. This defeats the whole purpose of distributed processing.

▶ The rows of a single table differ significantly in the number of columns. Basically, you have a schemaless or flexible design to handle sparse data or null data in most of the columns and want to support ongoing changes to the schema.

▶ You have single random selects and range scans by key. It would not perform well for relational analytics such as GROUP BY, JOIN, and WHERE column LIKE, and so on.

NOTE

HBase is not a replacement for traditional RDBMS systems. They both have different use cases and scenarios in which they can be used.

HBase can be good if you have a large volume of data to be stored by key in rows that don't conform well to a fixed schema and if you have data to be searched by key or a range of keys for retrieval and for querying. HBase is not suitable if you have a smaller dataset or you need complete SQL capability with the sophisticated Query Optimizer.

In summary, HBase is good choice for large, sparse datasets that are loosely coupled or denormalized (because joins are not supported in HBase) with a lot of concurrent clients for random, low-latency read-write access.

NOTE

Big Enterprises Leverage HBase

Several dozen big enterprises are already leveraging the power of HBase. For example, Facebook chooses to implement its messaging platform using HBase. Twitter leverages HBase for several applications, including people search, and as a time-series database for the operations team to handle cluster-wide monitoring and performance data. Many more companies are using HBase in their production systems, including Adobe, eBay, Yahoo!, Meetup, Netflix, and Stumbleupon. You can read success stories of some of the companies leveraging HBase at http://wiki.apache.org/hadoop/Hbase/PoweredBy.

HBase Architecture

As you can see in Figure 24.1, HBase Master handles Data Definition Language (DDL) operations, manages the region assignment to the HBase Region Servers of the HBase cluster, and ensures load balancing of regions across HBase Region Servers. You will also find three ZooKeeper instances running in the cluster (in some implementations, you will find more ZooKeeper instances, usually in odd numbers such as 3, 5, or 7, although three instances generally works fine), to maintain online configuration and distributed coordination such as master election. Without ZooKeeper instances, HBase does not exist.

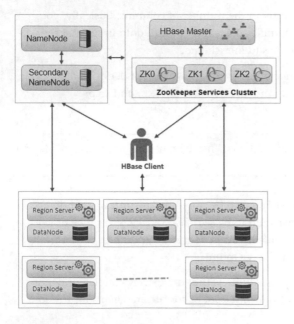

FIGURE 24.1
HBase physical deployment architecture.

In a typical HBase cluster, many HBase Region Servers typically are co-located with data nodes of HDFS (or they exist on worker nodes). They serve the requests (write, read, scan) from the HBase clients and send heartbeat signals to the HBase Master and ZooKeeper services cluster. The HBase Master and ZooKeeper are not involved in the data transfer path.

NOTE

Default Storage for HDInsight with the HBase Cluster

HBase clusters in HDInsight are also configured to store data directly in the Azure Storage Blob (as with the HDInsight cluster, discussed in Hour 6, "Getting Started with HDInsight, Provisioning Your HDInsight Service Cluster, and Automating HDInsight Cluster Provisioning"). This provides low latency and increased elasticity in performance/cost choices.

Customers thus can build their interactive websites or solutions that work with large datasets and that store data from millions of endpoints directly in the Azure Storage Blob, to be analyzed with HDInsight or the HBase cluster. As discussed earlier, you need HDInsight or an HBase cluster only as long as you need processing capabilities or power. When not in use, you can safely delete your HDInsight or HBase cluster to save on overall usage cost, because data is stored separately in the Azure Storage Blob.

While loading data into the HBase table, rows are automatically partitioned into regions. A *region* is a basic unit of scalability, a unit that accumulates a contiguous, sorted range of rows stored together for scaling. The association of a region with an HBase Region Server (for example, which region is stored on which HBase Region Server) is stored in a system table called hbase:meta, available in ZooKeeper.

NOTE

Failover Handling

HBase Region Server failure is handled automatically. The HBase Master reassigns regions from the failed HBase Region Server to available HBase Region Servers. Failure of the HBase Master itself, on the other hand, is addressed by keeping multiple instances of the HBase Master in the cluster.

Creating HBase Tables

An HBase client reaches out to the HBase Master for a table creation request. The HBase Master stores the table schema information, creates regions based on key-splits provided (if no key-split is provided, a single default region is created), and assigns regions to the HBase Region Servers. As you can see in the previous note, the assignment of regions to the HBase Region Server is updated in the system table hbase:meta, available with the ZooKeeper cluster.

Writing Data to HBase Tables

The HBase client reaches out to ZooKeeper for the location of the hbase:meta system table. After obtaining the location, the HBase client scans the hbase:meta system table to find the HBase Region Server that will handle the provided key. The HBase client directly reaches out to the identified HBase Region Server to insert, update, or delete the provided key/value pair. The HBase Region Server processes the incoming request and dispatches it to the region (where the specific key should belong—remember, the table is sorted on row key) to process the key where the operation is written to the Write Ahead Log (WAL); then key-values are added to the memory store (MemStore). Key-values stored in the MemStore are sorted on key and written to disk (in StoreFiles or HFiles) occasionally or when there is a memory pressure. In case of region failure, recovery is done based on the WAL.

NOTE

As the option for larger VM sizes are available, you should consider using VMs with more memory for HBase workloads or memory intensive processing.

With each memory flush to the disk, a new file is created. Note that two or more files might contain the same key because of the update or delete operations on that specific key. Therefore, while reading, HBase Region Server must scan all the files, although it employs some optimizations to filter out files based on the start row-key and end row-key of the file (remember that data inside a file is sorted on key), or by using the Bloom Filter on each file.

GO TO ▶ Refer to **Hour 5, "MapReduce—Advanced Concepts and YARN,"** for more about the Bloom Filter and how it works.

As you can see in Figure 24.2, the HBase client includes a client-side buffer to reduce frequent remote procedure calls (RPC) while writing. The write operation is logged into WAL, and data is written to the MemStore.

Subsequently, under pressure, the MemStore is flushed to disk, creating the StoreFile (one StoreFile per column family). The size of the MemStore is configured at the HBase Region Server level (percentage of the heap occupied by the MemStores), per table (size in megabytes of a single MemStore per column family in the region).

TIP

You can disable WAL to increase the write speed, but it might result in potential data loss, in case of HBase Region Server failure.

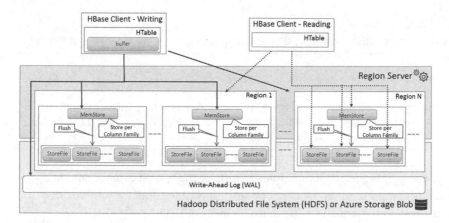

FIGURE 24.2
Reading and writing to an HBase table.

Reading Data from HBase Tables

The HBase client reaches out to ZooKeeper for the location of the hbase:meta system table. After obtaining the location, the HBase client scans the hbase:meta system table to find the HBase Region Server that should handle the provided row key. Then the HBase client directly reaches out to the identified HBase Region Server to get the specified key-value pair.

The HBase Region Server processes the incoming request and dispatches it to the region where the specific key is stored to process the key by scanning both the MemStore and the StoreFiles to find the specified row key.

Looking back at Figure 24.2, while reading, the data from the MemStore and the StoreFiles is combined (across all the regions and HBase Region Severs notified by ZooKeeper by looking into the hbase:meta system table). By default, the data with the latest time stamp or version is returned to HBase client.

Data Distribution and Storage

Data in HBase is stored in tables, which contain rows. A row is referenced by a unique key (stored as an array of bytes), which can be either a string, a long, or your own serialized data structure. Data inside a row is stored in columns, which are grouped in column families. You can identify a column data (also stored as an array of bytes) by row key × column family × column × time stamp.

TIP

The time stamp is optional. If you don't specify a time stamp, you get the latest version of the data.

NOTE

Rows keys are sorted lexicographically because row keys are stored as binary values; therefore, comparison is done at the binary level, from left to right. For example, 1, 2, 3, 4, 10, 11, 15, 20 values are sorted and stored as 1, 10, 11, 15, 2, 20, 3, 4.

A column family is a way of organizing or grouping your logically related column data to enable features such as compression, in-memory option, and version. Data for columns from a given column family is stored together in a file called StoreFile or HFile.

When you create an HBase table, you need to specify column families for that table. Typically, you have static column families or only rarely need to add new column families. Columns in a column family, however, are completely dynamic. In other words, for a set of rows, you can have a completely different set of columns in a given column family of the table. This gives flexibility in storing the data only when it is needed or available for given rows, thus minimizing storage space needed and requiring minimal time to scan the data while reading, for better overall performance.

Often you have a static small number of column families and a dynamic large number of columns (created at runtime) inside each available column family. For example, as you can see in Figure 24.3, for row 1, the row key is `david22`. The name column family has three column values, whereas the contactinfo column family has just one column value.

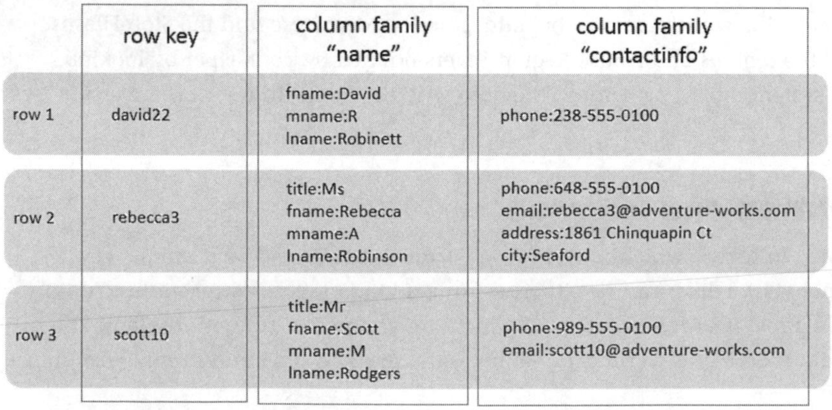

	row key	column family "name"	column family "contactinfo"
row 1	david22	fname:David mname:R lname:Robinett	phone:238-555-0100
row 2	rebecca3	title:Ms fname:Rebecca mname:A lname:Robinson	phone:648-555-0100 email:rebecca3@adventure-works.com address:1861 Chinquapin Ct city:Seaford
row 3	scott10	title:Mr fname:Scott mname:M lname:Rodgers	phone:989-555-0100 email:scott10@adventure-works.com

FIGURE 24.3
Example of rows and column families structure.

Likewise, for row 2, the row key is `rebecca3`; the name column family has four column values, and the contactinfo column family also has four column values. Similarly, for row 3, the row key is `scott10`; the name column family has four column values, and the contactinfo column family has two column values.

Typically, column families in a table are static or change very little. The columns inside a column family, however, are dynamic (with no fixed or predefined schema) and require only storage space for provided values (no storage space is needed for NULL). This results in an efficient solution for storing and managing a very large sparse dataset.

NOTE

Different Nomenclature

Different references or artifacts might use different nomenclature, but they essentially talk about the same thing. For example, one article might use *row* to represent a row in a table, *column family* to represent a group of logically related columns placed together, and *column* to refer to each specific column inside a column family. Another reference might use **column** to refer to a column family of the table and might use *cell* or *column qualifier* To refer to a column inside a column family:

ROW -> COLUMN FAMILY -> COLUMN
ROW -> COLUMN -> CELL or COLUMN QUALIFIER

As you can see in Figure 24.4, table data is sorted on row key values (for simplicity in illustration, we have used A, B, C, and so on for the values of row keys, although you can use any unique values for row keys) and is vertically partitioned into regions (a range of rows stored together) for scaling. Furthermore, a region is dynamically split into two or more regions if it becomes too big. Likewise, two or more small regions can be merged, to ensure that the size of the region remains similar.

NOTE

Region Size and Load Balancing

Regions have a configurable maximum size. When a region reaches its maximum size, it is split into two smaller regions (obviously, splitting is expensive), which can be assigned to the same region server or different ones. Regions are distributed evenly across HBase Region Servers of the cluster for load balancing.

Table 1

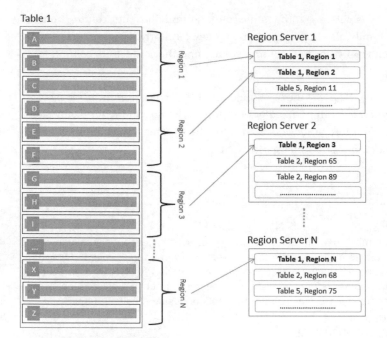

FIGURE 24.4
Data distribution across region servers.

To summarize, a table contains regions (defined by a start row key and an end row key). Each region contains a contiguous, sorted range of rows. Each row contains column families, and each column family contains cells or columns. Each cell or column can be identified with (row key, column family, column, time stamp) -> value or table[row key: column family : column : time stamp] = value.

Compaction of Data

An update to an existing row is considered a delete of the existing row and insertion of a new row with the new value. A delete, on the other hand, is not actually a physical deletion—it just logically marks a row as deleted. Over time, this results in duplicate keys (because of the update operation) and deleted keys (because of the delete operations) scattered around multiple files.

To handle this scenario, HBase has a process called *compaction* that removes duplicate keys and deleted keys by merging the contents of two or more files and removing the old files (see Figure 24.5).

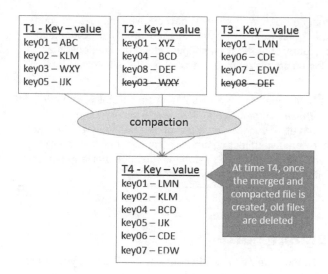

FIGURE 24.5
HBase compaction process.

Two types of compaction take place. Minor compaction combines the last few flushes (usually selects a few small, adjacent StoreFiles and rewrites them as a single StoreFile) and does not drop (filter out) deleted or duplicate or expired versions. Major compaction rewrites all StoreFiles by dropping deleted data and duplicate data whose values exceed the TTL (Time To Live) or the number of versions configured.

Creating HDInsight Cluster with HBase

As you learned in Hour 6, you have two main options for creating an HDInsight cluster with HBase. You can use Azure Management Portal to do it manually with an intuitive user interface, or you can use PowerShell scripting to automate the process.

Creating HDInsight with an HBase cluster differs little from creating a standard HDInsight cluster (which Hour 6 covered).

GO TO ▶ Because this hour highlights only the differences in creating HDInsight with HBase cluster, refer to **Hour 6** to review the step-by-step guide on how to create the HDInsight cluster.

NOTE

Integration of HDInsight and HBase Cluster with an Azure Virtual Network

Azure offers to create a virtual network to provision and manage virtual private networks (VPNs) in Azure so that you can directly access different Azure services or Azure virtual machines in a secure manner if they all belong to the same virtual network. With a virtual network, you can extend your Azure network to an on-premises network. In other words, you can seamlessly connect your cloud infrastructure or services to an on-premises datacenter (that is, connect cloud applications in a hybrid environment with applications running on-premises) by using point-to-site, site-to-site, or ExpressRoute connection.

You can integrate your HDInsight with an HBase cluster with a virtual network so that your other applications (part of the same virtual network) can communicate directly and securely with the HBase cluster. This provides improved performance because data movement does not go over multiple gateways or load balancers, but rather works via direct communication between web applications and HDInsight with the HBase cluster using HBase Java RPC APIs. The communication or data movement also happens over a secure communication path between them.

Using the Azure Management Portal

As you can see in Figure 24.6, on the first page of the New HDInsight Cluster Wizard, you must specify the name for your cluster (it should be unique on the `azurehdinsight.net` domain). Next, specify the cluster type as HBase for creating HDInsight with HBase cluster. Also specify the HDInsight version: As of this writing, the default (and only) version is 3.1, which is based on Hortonworks Data Platform (HDP) 2.1 and includes Hadoop 2.4 and the HBase 0.98 distribution from Hortonworks.

NOTE

For details on the latest HDInsight releases based on different Hadoop versions and the components each HDInsight release contains, go to http://azure.microsoft.com/en-us/documentation/articles/hdinsight-component-versioning/.

As you have learned, HBase runs on top of HDInsight (or Hadoop); so the first screen (shown in Figure 24.6) is the place where you need to specify whether you want to create only an HDInsight (or Hadoop) cluster or an HDInsight with HBase cluster. From the next screen of the wizard on, all options remain the same whether you are creating only HDInsight cluster or an HDInsight with HBase cluster as discussed in Hour 6.

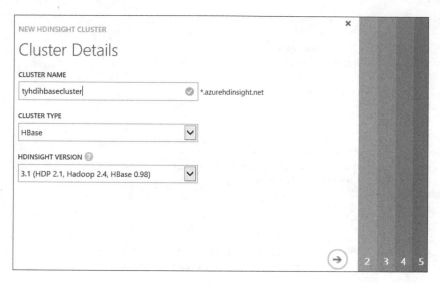

FIGURE 24.6
HDInsight with HBase Provision Wizard, page 1.

Using PowerShell Scripting

You can use the PowerShell script in Listing 24.1 to provision HDInsight with an HBase cluster. First, though, you must ensure that you have some prerequisites in place to use Azure PowerShell.

GO TO ▶ Refer to **Hour 6** for more details about the prerequisites for using Azure PowerShell.

In Listing 24.1, lines 2–11, you must specify parameters (name of the cluster, number of worker/data nodes in the cluster, data center location, and so on) required for creating HDInsight with an HBase cluster. Lines 14–27 check whether the specified storage account already exists and then either use that account or create a new one with the specified name (to be used as the default storage account for the HDInsight with HBase cluster).

Lines 29–45 check whether the storage account container already exists and then either use that account or create a new one with the specified name (to be used as the default storage account container for the HDInsight with HBase cluster).

LISTING 24.1 Provisioning HDInsight with HBase Cluster Using PowerShell Scripting

```
1: # Declare all the variables and specify their values
2: $location = "Central US"
3:
4: $defaultStorageAccount = "tyhdihbasestorage"
```

```
 5: $defaultStorageContainer = "adventureworks"
 6:
 7: $clusterAdminUserName = "tyhdihbaseadmin"
 8: $clusterAdminPassword = "Passw@rd01"
 9:
10: $clusterName = "tyhdihbasecluster"
11: $clusterSizeInNodes = 2
12:
13:
14: # Check if storage account already exists then use it
15: # or else create a new storage account with the specified name
16: $storageAccount = Get-AzureStorageAccount -StorageAccountName
    $defaultStorageAccount `
17:    -ErrorAction SilentlyContinue
18: if ($storageAccount -eq $null)
19: {
20:    Write-Host "Creating new storage account $defaultStorageAccount."
21:    $storageAccount = New-AzureStorageAccount –StorageAccountName
       $defaultStorageAccount `
22:        -Location $location
23: }
24: else
25: {
26:    Write-Host "Using existing storage account $defaultStorageAccount."
27: }
28:
29: # Check if specified storage container already exists then use it
30: # or else create a new storage container with the specified
31: # name in the specified storage account
32: $storageContext = New-AzureStorageContext –StorageAccountName
    $defaultStorageAccount `
33:    -StorageAccountKey (Get-AzureStorageKey $defaultStorageAccount).Primary
34: $storageContainer = Get-AzureStorageContainer -Name $defaultStorageContainer `
35:    -Context $storageContext -ErrorAction SilentlyContinue
36: if ($storageContainer -eq $null)
37: {
38:    Write-Host "Creating new storage container $defaultStorageContainer."
39:    $storageContainer = New-AzureStorageContainer -Name $defaultStorageContainer `
40:        -Context $storageContext
41: }
42: else
43: {
44:    Write-Host "Using existing storage container $defaultStorageContainer."
45: }
46:
47: # if cluster admin user name and password are specified use it
```

```
48: # or else prompt for entering user name and password for cluster administrator
49: if ($clusterAdminUserName -eq "" -or $clusterAdminPassword -eq "")
50: {
51:     Write-Host "Enter administrator credential to use when provisioning the
        cluster."
52:     $credential = Get-Credential
53:     Write-Host "Administrator credential captured successfully, please use these '
54:         credentials to login to the cluster when the script is complete."
55: }
56: else
57: {
58:     $clusterAdminPasswordSecureString = ConvertTo-SecureString
        $clusterAdminPassword `
59:         -AsPlainText -Force
60:     $credential = new-object -typename System.Management.Automation.PSCredential
        -argumentlist `
61:         $clusterAdminUserName, $clusterAdminPasswordSecureString
62: }
63:
64:
65: Write-Host "Creating HDInsight with HBase cluster : $clusterName in $location."
66:
67: New-AzureHDInsightCluster -Name $clusterName -Location $location `
68:     -ClusterType HBase `
69:     -Version 3.1 `
70:     -DefaultStorageAccountName ($defaultStorageAccount +
        ".blob.core.windows.net") `
71:     -DefaultStorageAccountKey (Get-AzureStorageKey $defaultStorageAccount).
        Primary `
72:     -DefaultStorageContainerName $defaultStorageContainer `
73:     -Credential $credential `
74:     -ClusterSizeInNodes $clusterSizeInNodes
75:
76: Write-Host "HDInsight with HBase cluster : $clusterName in $location created
        successfully."
```

Lines 47–62 are tricky. These lines first check whether you have specified any values for the cluster administrator (user and password). If so, they either use it or prompt the user to enter it during script execution. Be careful when you use variables to pass on values for the cluster administrator: These are stored as plain text in the script file.

Lines 67–74 create a new HDInsight with HBase cluster based on the configuration parameters specified. Notice that in Line 68 we have specified the ClusterType parameter value as HBase. This ensures that Microsoft Azure creates an HDInsight cluster with HBase already installed and configured on it. Figure 24.7 shows the result of the complete script (Listing 24.1).

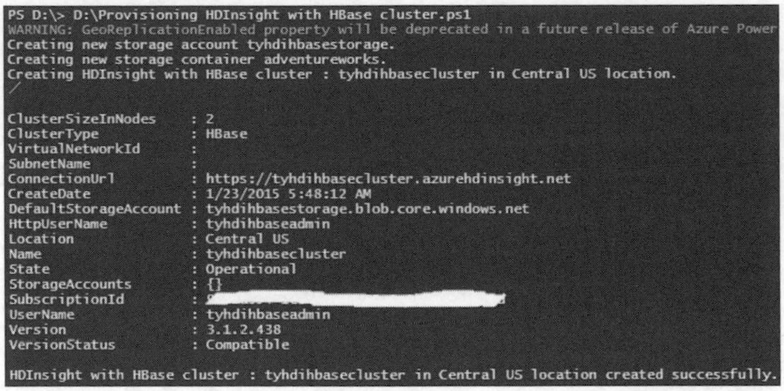

```
PS D:\> D:\Provisioning HDInsight with HBase cluster.ps1
WARNING: GeoReplicationEnabled property will be deprecated in a future release of Azure Power
Creating new storage account tyhdihbasestorage.
Creating new storage container adventureworks.
Creating HDInsight with HBase cluster : tyhdihbasecluster in Central US location.


ClusterSizeInNodes     : 2
ClusterType            : HBase
VirtualNetworkId       :
SubnetName             :
ConnectionUrl          : https://tyhdihbasecluster.azurehdinsight.net
CreateDate             : 1/23/2015 5:48:12 AM
DefaultStorageAccount  : tyhdihbasestorage.blob.core.windows.net
HttpUserName           : tyhdihbaseadmin
Location               : Central US
Name                   : tyhdihbasecluster
State                  : Operational
StorageAccounts        : {}
SubscriptionId         :
UserName               : tyhdihbaseadmin
Version                : 3.1.2.438
VersionStatus          : Compatible

HDInsight with HBase cluster : tyhdihbasecluster in Central US location created successfully.
```

FIGURE 24.7
Execution result of HDInsight with HBase cluster creation with PowerShell.

NOTE

Limitation on Azure Subscription

Some Azure subscriptions have a limit set. If you are trying to create a bigger cluster, you might encounter this issue: "New-AzureHDInsightCluster: Unable to complete the cluster create operation. Operation failed with code '400'. Cluster left behind state: 'Error'. Message: 'InsufficientResourcesCores'." If so, you need to either create a smaller cluster within the set limit or reach out to the Microsoft team to increase or remove the limit on your Azure subscription.

NOTE

HDInsight Emulator and HBase

As of this writing, the HDInsight emulator does not contain HBase; therefore, you can create an HDInsight with HBase cluster in Azure with the Azure subscription you have, or you can choose to use a trial Azure subscription for learning purposes. Microsoft gives you a one-month free subscription with $200 credit to spend on Azure services if you sign up. See http://azure.microsoft.com/en-us/pricing/free-trial/.

Verifying the Created HDInsight with HBase Cluster

When you have an up-and-running cluster, see Hour 6 to enable remote desktop connectivity to the head node of the cluster for remote logging. After enabling remote desktop connectivity, you can remotely log in to the head node of the cluster. Check out the Hadoop-related shortcut icons (including HBase) on the desktop of the machine (see Figure 24.8).

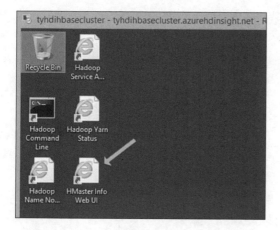

FIGURE 24.8
Shortcut icons on the desktop of the head node when connected via remote desktop connectivity.

Click the HMaster Info Web UI icon on the desktop to launch the HBase cluster dashboard. You can see the current ZooKeeper Quorum Master and other ZooKeeper backup nodes or servers (see Figure 24.9). You can also find all the HBase Region Servers in the cluster, along with the resources they have been allocated.

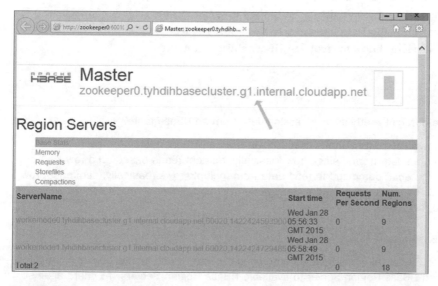

FIGURE 24.9
HBase cluster dashboard.

You can click different tabs in the HBase cluster dashboard to manage and monitor HBase Cluster and its different nodes (see Figure 24.10).

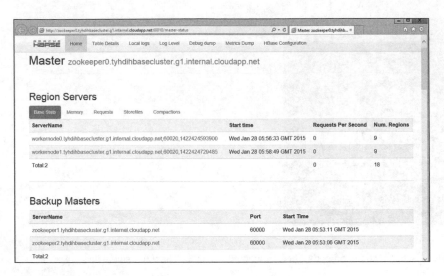

FIGURE 24.10
HBase cluster region and backup servers.

Summary

Apache HBase is a distributed, column-oriented NoSQL database management system that provides random, near-real-time read/write access to the large, sparse data sets (flexible schema) that are common in many Big Data use cases. In this hour, you learned about Apache HBase, including when to use it and how to create an HBase cluster on Azure.

Q&A

Q. **What are the different methods of accessing data from an HBase table?**

A. You can use two different methods to read data from an HBase table. You can use the `get` command to read data from a single row (basically, random reads based on a row key) or you can use the `scan` command to read data from multiple rows (basically, sequential row key scanning). The `scan` command usually works fast and defines both the start row key and the stop row key.

Q. **How does HBase handle failure?**

A. HBase Region Server failure is handled automatically. The HBase Master reassigns regions from the failed HBase Region Server to available HBase Region Servers. To guard against HBase Master failure, multiple instances of HBase Master are kept in the cluster. In the case of region failure, recovery is done based on the Write-Ahead Log (WAL). Also HBase leverages HDFS for storage of HBase files and HDFS ensures high availability and fault tolerance as replication is built in with HDFS.

Index

32-bit Hive ODBC drivers
  comparing, 372
  configuring, 373-377
64-bit Hive ODBC drivers
  comparing, 372
  configuring, 373-377

A

access control lists (ACLs), 154
accessing
  HDInsight data from Power
    Query, 417-421
  Hive data
    from Excel, 379-384
    from PowerPivot, 385-406
    from SQL Server Analysis
      Services (SSAS),
      413-415
    from SQL Server Reporting
      Services (SSRS),
      415-417
    from SQL Servers,
      406-417
  PowerPivot from Excel, 399
accounts, creating storage, 192
actions (Oozie), 456
Active Directory, 49
add method, 150
Add-AzureAccount cmdlet, 441
**Add-AzureHDInsightScriptAction
  PowerShell cmdlet, 281**
add-ins, 386

adding
  Slicer controls, 401
**airline departures, analyzing,
  360-361**
algorithms
  built-in machine learning,
    509-512
  compression-decompression,
    151
  regression, 492
ALTER DATABASE command, 328
ALTER INDEX command, 364
ALTER TABLE command, 337
Amazon Dynamo, 20
**Amazon Elastic MapReduce
  (EMR), 51-52**
Ambari, 50-51
analysis
  airline departures, 360-361
  canceled airline flights,
    362-363
  datasets, 358-360
  diagnostic (descriptive), 10,
    492
  flight delays, 256-261
  PowerPivot
    data models, 398
    in Excel, 399
  predictive, 11, 492
  prescriptive, 11
  speed limit violations,
    524-532
**Analytics Platform System
  (APS), 58**
Apache Ambari, 50-51

Apache Cassandra, 22

Apache Flume. *See* Flume

Apache Hadoop. *See* Hadoop

Apache HBase. *See* HBase

Apache HCatalog. *See* HCatalog

Apache Hive. *See* Hive

Apache Mahout. *See* Mahout

Apache Nutch, 65

Apache Oozie. *See* Oozie

Apache Pig. *See* Pig

Apache Spark. *See* Spark

Apache Sqoop. *See* Sqoop

Apache Storm. *See* Storm

Apache Tez. *See* Tez

application life-cycle
management, 160. *See also*
YARN

Application Manager, 163

Application Master, 166

    communication with, 169

    failures, 171-172

    uber-tasking optimization, 170

applications

    Apache Storm, creating,
    524-529

    Hive, creating, 310

    Tez, 317

APS (Analytics Platform System),
58

architecture

    Hadoop, 33

    Hadoop 2.0, 43-44

    HBase, 538-539

    HDFS (Hadoop Distributed File
    System), 33-35

        block placement and
        replication, 74-77

        deleting files, 86-87

        file split, 73-74

    handling failure, 83-85

    name nodes, 67-72

    reading from, 82-83

    writing to, 77-82

HDInsight

    clusters, 223-225

    storage, 240-241

    MapReduce, 35-36, 116-119

    Storm, 520-522

ASV (Azure Storage Vault), 241

atomicity, consistency, isolation,
and durability (ACID), 344

attributes, hiding, 399

authentication, 376

automatic failover, 99-100,
173-175

automating HDInsight, 199-212

availability (HA), 95-101

    automatic failover, 99-100

    failover detection, 99-100

    QJM (Quorum Journal
    Manager), 97-98

    shared storage using NFS,
    95-97

    in YARN, 173-175

Avro, 263-270

    Hadoop streaming, 273

AZCopy, 237

Azure. *See* Microsoft Azure

Azure Flat Network Storage, 242

Azure Management Portal,
280-281, 499

Azure ML (Microsoft Azure
Machine Learning), 48, 56-57,
491

    benefits of, 494-495

    built-in machine learning
    algorithms, 509-512

    data, reading, 492-502

Descriptive Statistics module,
505

history of machine learning,
491-493

overview of, 493-495

predictive models, 506-512

processes to build solutions,
497-498

web services, publishing as,
512-514

workflow, 498-505

workspaces, 495-497

Azure ML Studio, 496-497

Azure PowerShell, 237-239

    automation setup, 426-427

Azure storage, 47

Azure Storage Blob. *See* WASB

Azure Storage Explorer, 235-237

Azure Storage Vault (ASV), 241

Azure virtual networks, 545-546

Azure VNet, 49

B

bad records, handling, 157

base classes, extending, 130

Big Data

    business value proposition,
    26

    characteristics of, 12-13

        variability, 14

        variety, 13

        velocity, 14

        volume, 13

    data sources. See data
    sources

    Hadoop versus, 14-15

importance of managing,
15-16

phases of analytics

data acquisition, 46-47

data analysis, 47-48

data management, 49

data storage, 47

data visualization, 48-49

development and
monitoring, 49

usage scenarios, 27-29

BISM (Business Intelligence
Semantic Model), 413

bitmap indexes, 364

blacklisting

clusters, 155

per-MapReduce job, 155

blob storage. See also WASB
(Windows Azure Storage—Blob)

benefits, 234-235

data locality, 242-243

default file system,
configuring, 241-242

for HBase clusters, 539

HDFS versus, 234-235,
240-241

HDInsight

benefits, 223

Microsoft Azure, 233

AZCopy, 237

Azure PowerShell, 237-239

Azure Storage Explorer,
235-237

Hadoop command line,
239

HDInsight storage
architecture, 240-241

performance, 242-243

blocks (HDFS)

checksums, 83

management, 101

placement and replication,
74-77

rack awareness, 88-89

size of, 73-74

storage, 101

Bloom Filter objects, 149-150

bolts, 520

built-in counters, 159

built-in functions (Hive), 344-346

built-in machine learning
algorithms, 509-512

Bureau of Transportation
Statistics (BTS), 324

business intelligence (BI), 371

Business Intelligence Semantic
Model (BISM), 413

business value proposition of Big
Data and NoSQL, 26

C

C#

Avro, writing using, 263-268

MapReduce, programming,
270-273

caches

data modes, 414

DistributedCache
(MapReduce), 145-146

canceled airline flights, analyzing,
362-363

canceled flights scenario (Pig),
434-438

Pig relations

defining, 435-436

filtering, 436-437

grouping, 437

joining, 437

saving to file system, 438

summarizing, 437

uploading data, 434-435

Capacity Scheduler (MapReduce),
153-154

Cassandra, 22

Checkpoint process, 70-72

checkpoints, 221

checksums for data blocks, 83

cleanup function, 125, 130

client redirection on failover, 100

clients

communication with after
failures, 169

.NET, installing, 311

cloud services

Azure ML, 56-57

Hadoop clusters on, 55-56

HDInsight. See HDInsight

Microsoft Big Data solutions,
59-60

Power BI, 378-379

Cloudera, 50

Manager, 50

Support, 50

CloudXplorer, 324

Cluster Dashboards (Apache Hive),
299-301

clusters

blacklisting, 155

Hadoop, customizing, 190

HDFS clusters. See HDFS
clusters

HDInsight. See also HDInsight

accessing hive-based data
from, 379-384

architecture, 223-225

connecting from Visual
Studio, 303

deployment, 182-186

managing, 212-214

provisioning, 203-206

Tez, 318

codecs, 151

column families (HBase), 536, 541-544

column-store databases, 21-22, 536

columns

in Hive tables, 338

CombineFileInputFormat class, 123

Combiners (MapReduce), 114, 132-134

command line

Hadoop for Azure Storage Blob, 239

HDFS (Hadoop Distributed File System), 90-94

MapReduce, 139

command-line interfaces (CLIs), 139

Hive, 290-295

comma-separated value (CSV) files, 256, 324

COMMENT clause, 340

commodity hardware, HDFS and, 66

communication

with Application Master, 169

counters for, 158

compact indexes, 363

compaction of HBase tables, 544-545

components

Hadoop folders, 291

of YARN, 162-166

compression (MapReduce), 150-151

configure() function, 129

configuring

32-bit Hive ODBC drivers, 377-378

64-bit Hive ODBC drivers, 373-377

Azure ML (Microsoft Azure Machine Learning), 495-496

default file system, 241-242

HDInsight, verifying, 196-198

Hive ODBC data source, 429-430

Microsoft Azure storage emulator, 251-253

Microsoft Hive ODBC Drivers, 372-378

remote desktop connections, 193-195

connections

to existing connections, 392

HDInsight, 389

Microsoft Azure, 200

remote desktop, configuring, 193-195

contains method, 150

Context object (MapReduce), 139-140

Control Flow (SSIS), 424

coordinating Oozie workflows, 464-465

copyFromLocal parameter, 91

copyToLocal parameter, 91

cost-based optimization (CBO) engines, 319

costs

effectiveness of Hadoop, 32

of Microsoft Azure, 180

CouchDB, 23-24

counters (MapReduce), 158-159

CRAN (Comprehensive R Archive Network), 468

CREATE DATABASE command, 328

Create New Data Source Wizard, 374, 378

CREATE TABLE AS SELECT (CTAS) command, 341

CREATE TABLE command, 338

CREATE TABLE LIKE command, 341

CREATE VIEW command, 342

credit scoring and analysis, 27

crime data analysis scenario (Spark SQL), 486-489

cross-selling recommendations, 27

customer churn analysis, 27

customizing

counters, 159

HDInsight, 190

HDInsight clusters

consuming Script Actions, 280-282

identifying need for, 277-278

running Giraph job, 282-284

script development, 278-280

testing Script Action, 285

partitioning, 129

Cutting, Doug, 31, 263

D

daemons, 69

single nodes running on, 119

data

Big Data. *See* Big Data

semi-structured data, 12

structured data, 11

unstructured data, 11-12

Data Access layer, 414

data acquisition phase, tools needed, 46-47

data analysis

queries, 348-354

in R, 470

tools needed, 47-48

Data Analysis Expression (DAX), 414

data blocks, InputSplits versus, 122

data centers (Azure), 189

Data Definition Language (DDL), 297

data distribution in HBase tables, 541-544

data explosion, 12

Data Flow (SSIS), 424

data frames (R), 468

data integration. See also SSIS (SQL Server Integration Services)

importance of, 423

Oozie versus SSIS, 465

data locality

blob storage, 242-243

of HDFS, 66

Mapper class (MapReduce), 132

MapReduce, 115

data management phase, tools needed, 49

data manipulation language, 344

Data Model layer, 415

data nodes, 183

block placement and replication, 74-77

explained, 33-34

handling failure, 83-85

HDFS architecture, 67-69

heartbeat signals from, 97

Task Tracker co-location, 118-119

writing to HDFS, 77-82

Data Source Names (DSNs), 372, 375

data sources

Hive ODBC data source, configuring, 429-430

types of, 9-10

data sources, configuring ODBC, 372

data storage

tools needed, 47

data types in R, 468-469

data visualization phase

PowerPivot, 390-399

tools needed, 48-49

data wrapper classes, 127

databases

column-store databases, 21-22

document-oriented databases, 22-24

graph databases, 24

key-value store databases, 20-21

schemas, comparing, 328-331, 411

datasets

analysis, 358-360

Azure ML (Microsoft Azure Machine Learning), 495

DAX (Data Analysis Expression), 414

decompression, 151

default file system

configuring, 241-242

uploading data to, 239

defining

Oozie workflows, 459-461

Pig relations, 435-436

deleting files in HDFS, 86-87

deployment

Azure ML, 494

HDInsight clusters, 182-186

Microsoft Big Data solutions

cloud services, 59-60

on-premises, 58

descriptive (diagnostic) analysis, 10

Descriptive Statistics module, 505

detection, failover, 99-100

development

Azure ML processes, 497-498

Hive, 288

and monitoring phase, tools needed, 49

dfs.blocksize configuration property, 73-74

DFSAdmin, 94

diagnostic (descriptive) analysis, 10, 492

dialog boxes, ODBC Data Source Administrator (64-Bit), 373

dimensional modeling (DM), 391

dimensions, hierarchies, 398

direct mode transfer, 445

directed acyclic graph (DAG), 316

directories

in HDFS, 67

snapshots, 106

disease outbreak predictions, 29

DistributedCache (MapReduce), 145-146

document-oriented databases, 22-24

downloading publish settings, 426-427

Driver class (MapReduce), 134-138

DROP DATABASE command, 329

dynamic partition inserts, 355-358

E

ecosystems for Hadoop

Flume, 39-40

HBase, 39

HCatalog, 37

Hive, 36-37

Mahout, 39

MSBI (Microsoft Business Intelligence), 42

Oozie, 40

Pegasus, 41

Pig, 37-38

RHadoop, 41

Sqoop, 38

edit log file, 70

EMR (Amazon Elastic MapReduce), 51-52

emulators (HDInsight), 245-246

HBase and, 550

installation, verifying, 248-249

installing, 246-248

MapReduce job, 249-250

Microsoft Azure storage emulator, 251-253

Script Action, testing, 285

enabling R language

on Hadoop, 471-472

on HDInsight, 472-476

Enterprise Agreement (EA) model, 180

equi-joins, 347

ETL (extraction, transformation, and loading), 417

workflow packages, creating, 424

Excel, 48

Hive, accessing data from, 379-384

Power Query, launching, 417-421

reporting, 399-402

visualization, 399-402

executing

Apache Hive (HDInsight), 288-301

Hive queries, 288, 313-314, 428

HiveQL queries, 294

Oozie workflows, 461

Pig jobs, 441-442

PowerShell scripts, 200

SSIS packages, 430-431

Tez, 318, 365-368

exercises

Hadoop command line, 239

HDFS commands, 92-93

HDInsight name node services, 225-227

importing data from SQL Server to Sqoop, 448-451

installing HDInsight emulator, 246-248

running MapReduce job, 250

experiments

Azure ML (Microsoft Azure Machine Learning), 495-496

creating, 501

exporting Sqoop

data with PowerShell, 451-452

exercise, 448-451

export process, 448

from HDFS with, 447-448

extending base classes, 130

external data, loading in R, 468-469

external tables, programming, 335-338

extraction, transformation, and loading (ETL), 417

F

failover

automatic (YARN), 173-175

detection, 99-100

client redirection on, 100

with HBase, 539

with ZooKeeper, 228-230

failure, handling in HDFS, 83-85

Fair Scheduler, 152-153

Fast SQLPrepare, 376

fault tolerance

of Hadoop, 32

of HDFS, 66

MapReduce, 115

Spark, 482-483

federation, HDFS (Hadoop Distributed File System), 44-45, 101-103

fields grouping, 521

file system namespace of HDFS, 67

FileInputFormat class, 123

files

Avro, 263

comma-separated value (CSV), 256, 324

Optimized Row Columnar (ORC), 320

split in HDFS, 73-74

storage (Microsoft Azure), 234

filtering Pig relations, 436-437

first in, first out (FIFO) method, 152, 154

flexibility of Hadoop, 32

flight delays, analyzing, 256-261

flight departure analysis scenario (Oozie), 457-463

defining workflows, 459-461

executing workflows, 461

monitoring workflows, 461

prerequisites, 458-459

querying results, 462-463

flight departure analysis scenario (SSIS), 424-427

package variables, 426

prerequisites, 425-426

Windows Azure PowerShell automation, 426-427

Flume, 39-40, 46

folders, Hadoop components, 291

fraud detection and prevention, 27

FROM clause, 347

From Data Connection Wizard, 379

FS Shell, 90-94

fsimage files, 69-70, 221-222

Checkpoint process, 70-72

functions (MapReduce), 113

G

get parameter, 91

Get-AzureHDInsightJobOutput cmdlet, 442, 452

getPartition() function, 129

GFS (Google File System), 65

ggplot2, 470

Giraph

running jobs, 282-284

Script Action, installing with, 278-280

Google BigTable, 536

Google File System (GFS), 65

graphics in R, 470

graphs

databases, 24

mining, 41

grouping

Pig relations, 437

Storm, 521

Grunt, running code in, 436

H

HA (High Availability), 95-101

automatic failover, 99-100

failover detection, 99-100

QJM (Quorum Journal Manager), 97-98

Resource Manager, 173-175

shared storage using NFS, 95-97

Hadoop

architecture, 33

Avro, 263-270

Big Data versus, 14-15

characteristics of, 32

clusters, customizing, 190

command line, for Azure Storage Blob, 239

components folders, 291

compression-decompression, 150

ecosystems

Flume, 39-40

HBase, 39

HCatalog, 37

Hive, 36-37

Mahout, 39

MSBI (Microsoft Business Intelligence), 42

Oozie, 40

Pegasus, 41

Pig, 37-38

RHadoop, 41

Sqoop, 38

enabling R on, 471-472

explained, 31-32

licensing, 50

rack awareness, 88-89

serialization frameworks, 262-270

streaming, 146-148, 270-275

vendors

Amazon Elastic MapReduce (EMR), 51-52

Cloudera, 50

Hortonworks, 50-51

MapR Technologies, 51

Microsoft Big Data solutions, 52-57

Hadoop 1.0

Checkpoint-related configuration files, 71

limitations, 42-43

Hadoop 2.0

architecture, 43-44

Checkpoint-related configuration files, 71

hdfs dfs command, 94

HDFS new features, 44-46

Hadoop Distributed File System.
See HDFS

hadoop fs command parameters,
91-92

Hadoop MapReduce. *See*
MapReduce

handling

bad records, 157

features (MapReduce),
154-158

HBase, 22, 39, 47, 535-537

architecture, 538-539

HDInsight cluster creation,
545-551

Azure management portal,
546-547

Azure virtual networks,
545-546

PowerShell, 547-550

verifying, 550-551

success stories, 538

tables

compaction, 544-545

creating, 539

data distribution and
storage, 541-544

reading from, 541

writing to, 540-541

when to use, 537-538

HBase Master, 538-539

HBase Region Servers, 538-539

HCatalog, 37, 49, 368-369

in Pig Latin scripts, 438-440

HDFS (Hadoop Distributed File
System)

architecture, 33-35

block placement and
replication, 74-77

deleting files, 86-87

file split, 73-74

handling failure, 83-85

name nodes, 67-72

reading from, 82-83

writing to, 77-82

blob storage versus, 234-235,
240-241

command line, 90-94

data processing tools, 94

default file system,
configuring, 241-242

design goals, 66-67

exporting data with Sqoop,
447-448

Federation, 101-103

HA (High Availability), 95-101

automatic failover, 99-100

failover detection, 99-100

QJM (Quorum Journal
Manager), 97-98

shared storage using NFS,
95-97

Hadoop 1.0 versus Hadoop
2.0, 43

Hadoop 2.0 features, 44-46

HBase and, 535-537

HDInsight support, 224

new features in, 95-107

origin of, 65

rack awareness, 88-89

snapshot, 103-107

WebHDFS, 89-90

HDFS (Hadoop Distributed File
System) clusters

components, 219

name nodes, 220

secondary name nodes,
221-222

standby name nodes, 222

rack awareness, 88-89

hdfs dfs command, 94

HDInsight, 52, 58

Apache Hive, executing,
288-301

Apache Tez in, 287

benefits, 59

blob storage

for HBase clusters, 539

HDFS versus, 234-235

cluster customization

consuming Script Actions,
280-282

identifying need for,
277-278

running Giraph job,
282-284

script development,
278-280

testing Script Action, 285

cluster provisioning, 427-431

configuring Hive ODBC
data source, 429-430

executing Hive queries,
428

executing SSIS package,
430-431

clusters

accessing hive-based data
from, 379-384

architecture, 223-225

connecting from Visual
Studio, 303

creation with HBase,
545-551

deployment, 182-186

provisioning, 203-206

viewing Hive jobs, 306-308

configuring, verifying, 196-198

connections, 389

customizing, 190

data integration with SQL
Server, importance of, 423

default file system,
  configuring, 241-242

emulator, 245-246

  configuring Microsoft
    Azure storage emulator,
    251-253

  HBase and, 550

  Hive on, 294-295

  installing, 246-248

  running flight performance
    data on, 326-327

  running MapReduce job,
    249-250, 255-256

  testing Script Action, 285

  verifying installation,
    248-249

enabling R on, 472-476

high availability, 228-230

Hive, programming, 323-331

importing data with Sqoop,
  445-447

managing, 212-214

Microsoft Hive ODBC Drivers,
  371-378

name node services, 225-227

.NET SDKs, programmatically
  using, 311-316

overview of, 181-186

Power Query, accessing,
  417-421

PowerShell

  automating provisioning,
    199-212

  verifying setup, 207-212

provisioning, 186-198

R installation, 472-473

remote desktop connections,
  enabling, 193-195

services, provisioning, 186

Spark installation, 480-481

storage architecture, 240-241

Storm, provisioning clusters,
  521

tools for Visual Studio,
  302-311

topologies, submitting, 531

uploading data to, 434-435

HDInsight .NET SDK

  Script Action usage, 282

  submitting Oozie workflows,
    463-464

HDInsight Provision Wizard, 189

HDInsightUtilities module, 278

**HDP (Hortonworks Data Platform)
  on Windows, 52**

  on virtual machines, 60

head nodes, 183-184, 224

heartbeat signals, 97, 154

hiding attributes, 399

hierarchical files in HDFS, 67

hierarchies

  creating, 397

  dimensions, 398

high availability

  HDFS (Hadoop Distributed File
    System), 44

  HDInsight, 228-230

  of name nodes, 222

**history of machine learning,
  491-493**

Hive, 36-37, 47, 94

  Apache, 287

    executing HDInsight,
      288-301

    metastores, 289

    overview of, 287-288

  applications, creating, 310

  built-in functions, 344-346

  Cluster Dashboards, 299-301

data, SQL Server Reporting
  Services (SSRS), 415-417

development, 288

Excel, accessing data from,
  379-384

HDInsight

  emulators, 294-295

  programming, 323-331

importing data with Sqoop,
  447

indexing in, 363-365

jobs, viewing, 306-308

joins, 148

Microsoft Hive ODBC Drivers,
  371-378

PowerPivot, accessing,
  385-406

PowerShell scripting, 295-299

queries

  configuring Hive ODBC
    data source, 429-430

  executing, 288, 313-314,
    428

  writing, 309

RDBMS (Relational Database
  Management System),
  327-328

Serializer and Deserializer
  (SerDe), 340-343

Spark SQL versus, 486

SQL Server Analysis Services
  (SSAS), accessing, 413-415

SQL Servers, accessing,
  406-417

tables

  creating, 293, 309-321

  data load processes for,
    343-346

  programming, 331-340

  queries, 346-363

Hive Job Browser window, 307

HiveQL

Pig Latin versus, 38

queries, executing, 294

horizontal scalability, 101

of Hadoop, 44-45

of HDFS, 66

Hortonworks, 50-51

Hortonworks Data Platform (HDP) on Windows, 52

on virtual machines, 60

I

IaaS (Infrastructure as a Service), 179

IDEs (integrated development environments), Azure ML Studio, 496-497

IF EXISTS clause, 337

IF NOT EXISTS clause, 337

IF NOT EXISTS keyword, 328

Import Wizard, 388

Import-AzurePublishSettingsFile cmdlet, 441

importing

data from ODBC, 389

to HDInsight clusters with Sqoop, 445-447

to Hive with Sqoop, 447

publish settings, 426-427

Sqoop

data with PowerShell, 451-452

exercise, 448-451

tables, 389

indexes

in Hive, 363-365

InputFormat class (MapReduce), 121

InputSplit interface, 121

installing

Giraph with Script Action, 278-280

HDInsight, 196, 246-248

running MapReduce job, 249-250

verifying installation, 248-249

.NET clients, 311

R language

on HDInsight, 472-473

on Windows, 468

Spark on HDInsight, 480-481

integration of data. See data integration; SSIS (SQL Server Integration Services)

interfaces

command-line interfaces (CLIs), 139, 290-295

InputSplit, 121

RecordReader, 122

Tool (MapReduce), 139

WritableComparable<T>, 127

internal tables, programming, 331-335

J

Java, reading using Avro, 264-270

Java Virtual Machines (JVMs), 116, 124, 147

MapReduce, 151-152

Job History Server, 165, 225

job.properties file, creating, 461

jobs

completion of, 315

execution flow in YARN, 167-169

Hive, viewing, 306-308

MapReduce

execution flow, 119-140

programming, 255

request/response flow, 117-118

Pig, creating definitions, 441

scheduling, 152

JobTrackers, 35, 225

failure, 154

MapReduce, 115-116

joins

equi-joins, 347

MapReduce, 148-149

map-side, 148

Pig relations, 437

reduce-side, 149

Journal nodes, 97

K

Karmasphere Analyst, 52

key-value store databases, 20-21

blob storage, 239

Kimball, Ralph, 391

Klout, 415

L

layers

Data Access, 414

Data Model, 415

HDFS (Hadoop Distributed File System), 101

licensing Hadoop, 50

life science research, 28

linking SQL Server, 406-412

listings

defining job properties, 461

defining Oozie time-based coordinator job, 464

defining Oozie workflows, 460, 463

defining Pig relations, 436

defining properties of Oozie time-based coordinator job, 465

Giraph

installation script, 279

job submission, 284

HCatalog usage with Pig queries, 440

HDFS command-line interface example, 92

Pig

job definition creation, 441

job execution submission, 442

provisioning HDInsight with HBase cluster using PowerShell scripting, 547

rmr package usage, 474

lists (R), 468

load balancing, HBase regions, 543

load processes, Hive tables, 343-346

loading

data into PowerPivot, 391-397

external data in R, 468-469

local mode (Pig Latin), 434

LOCATION clause, 339

log mining with Spark, 483-485

ls parameter, 92

lsr parameter, 92

M

machine learning. See also Azure ML

built-in machine learning algorithms, 509-512

Descriptive Statistics module, 505

history of, 491-493

overview of, 493-495

predictive models, 506-512

processes to build solutions, 497-498

web services, publishing as, 512-514

workflow, 498-505

workspaces, 495

Mahout, 39, 48

management

Big Data, importance of, 15-16

blocks (HDFS), 101

HDInsight, 212-214

Management Portal (Azure), provisioning HDInsight, 186-198

many-to-many relationships, 397

map function, 125

Map function (MapReduce), 113

Mapper class (MapReduce), 124-128

Mapper function, 256

MapR Technologies, 51

MapReduce, 94

Application Master, 225

architecture, 35-36, 116-119

bad records, handling, 157

Bloom Filter objects, 149-150

C#, programming, 270-273

Capacity Scheduler, 153-154

Combiners, 132-134

compression, 150-151

Context object, 139-140

counters, 158-159

DistributedCache, 145-146

Driver class, 134-138

Fair Scheduler, 152-153

flight delays, analyzing, 256-261

Hadoop streaming, 146-148

handling features, 154-158

Hello World, 255-256

InputFormat class, 121

Java Virtual Machines (JVMs), 151-152

jobs

execution flow, 119-140

programming, 255

request/response flow, 117-118

running, 249-250, 472-476

scheduling, 152

JobTracker failure, 154

joins, 148-149

Mapper class, 124-128

mode (Pig Latin), 434

multiple input and output formats, 124

number of Mappers, 127-128

optimizing, 150-154

OutputFormat class, 123

overview of, 113-116

partitioning, 128-130

Reducer class, 130-132

Spark versus, 479, 481-483

speculative execution, 156-157

task failures, 155-156

TaskTrackers
  data node co-location,
    118-119
  failure, 154-155
Tez. See Tez
Tool interface, 139
YARN
  comparing, 45-46
  components of, 162-166
  failures in, 171-173
  Node Manager, 166-167
  overview of, 160-169
  uber-tasking optimization,
    170-171
map-side joins, **148**
matrix (R), **468**
maxbytes property, **170**
maxmaps property, **170**
maxreduces property, **170**
MDX (Multi-Dimensional
  Expression), **414**
membershipTest method, **150**
metadata
  layers (HCatalog), 368-369
  storage in name nodes,
    221-222
metastores (Apache Hive), **289**
methods, HDInsightUtilities
  module, **278**
Microsoft Analytics Platform
  System (APS), **58**
Microsoft Azure. See also
  HDInsight
  adding accounts to
    PowerShell, 441
  blob storage
    AZCopy, 237
    Azure PowerShell, 237-239
    Azure Storage Explorer,
      235-237

data locality, 242-243
  Hadoop command line,
    239
  for HBase clusters, 539
  HDFS versus, 234-235
  HDInsight storage
    architecture, 240-241
  performance, 242-243
Management Portal
  HDInsight cluster creation
    with HBase, 546-547
  provisioning HDInsight,
    186-198
overview of, 179-181
publish settings, downloading
  and importing, 426-427
storage emulator, configuring,
  251-253
storage services, 181,
  233-234
table storage, 20-21
virtual machines, 60
Microsoft Azure Machine Learning.
  See Azure ML
Microsoft Big Data solutions,
  52-57
  cloud services, 59-60
  on-premises, 58
Microsoft Business Intelligence
  (MSBI), 42, 54, 371
Microsoft Hive ODBC Drivers,
  371-378
  32-bit/64-bit IDBC drivers,
    comparing, 372
Microsoft OLE DB Provider for
  ODBC (MSDASQL), 409
Microsoft Power BI, overview of,
  378-379
Microsoft SQL Server Parallel
  Data Warehouse (PDW), 58
mkdir parameter, 91

models
  dimensional modeling (DM),
    391
  Enterprise Agreement (EA),
    180
  pay as you go (PAYG), 180
  predictive, machine learning,
    506-512
modules
  Azure ML (Microsoft Azure
    Machine Learning), 495
  Descriptive Statistics, 505
MongoDB, 23
monitoring
  HDInsight, 212-214
  Oozie workflows, 461
moving map-outputs, 129
MSBI (Microsoft Business
  Intelligence), 42, 54, 371
MSDASQL (Microsoft OLE DB
  Provider for ODBC), 409
Multi-Dimensional Expression
  (MDX), 414
multiple input and output formats
  (MapReduce), 124
multitenancy, 161, 166
  YARN, 45

N

name nodes, 220
  block placement and
    replication, 74-77
  explained, 33-34
  handling failure, 83-85
  HDFS architecture, 67-72
  HDInsight services, 225-227
  high availability, 222
  metadata storage, 221-222
  writing to HDFS, 77-82

namespaces, 101

naming Data Source Names (DSNs), 375

NAS (Network Attached Storage), 96

NDFS (Nutch Distributed File System), 65

.NET SDKs, 311-316

Network Attached Storage. See NAS

network connectivity (Sqoop), 446

Network File System. See NFS

New HDInsight Cluster Wizard, 187

New-AzureHDInsightCluster cmdlet, 427

New-AzureHDInsightHiveJob Definition cmdlet, 428

New-AzureHDInsightPigJob Definition cmdlet, 440

New-AzureHDInsightSqoopJob Definition cmdlet, 451

NFS (Network File System), shared storage using, 95-97

Nimbus, 520

Node Manager, 225
    failures, 172

Node Manager (YARN), 166-167

nodes
    clusters (Tez), 318
    head nodes, 224
    name nodes, 220
        HDInsight services, 225-227
        high availability, 222
        metadata storage, 221-222
    secondary name nodes, 221-222
    standby name nodes, 222

NoSQL
    benefits, 24-25
    business value proposition, 26
    limitations, 25
    RDBMS versus, 17-18
    types of technologies, 19
        column-store databases, 21-22
        document-oriented databases, 22-24
        graph databases, 24
        key-value store databases, 20-21
    usage scenarios, 27-29

number of Mappers, 127-128

Nutch Distributed File System (NDFS), 65

O

objects
    Bloom Filter, 149-150
    Context (MapReduce), 139-140

ODBC Data Source Administrator (64-Bit) dialog box, 373

OLTP (OnLine Transaction Processing), 19. See also HBase

OnLine Transaction Processing. See OLTP

on-premises deployment, 58

on-time flight departure analysis scenario (Oozie), 457-463
    defining workflows, 459-461
    executing workflows, 461
    monitoring workflows, 461
    prerequisites, 458-459
    querying results, 462-463

on-time flight departure analysis scenario (SSIS), 424-427
    package variables, 426
    prerequisites, 425-426
    Windows Azure PowerShell automation, 426-427

Oozie, 40, 49, 431, 455-456
    flight departure analysis scenario, 457-463
        defining workflows, 459-461
        executing workflows, 461
        monitoring workflows, 461
        prerequisites, 458-459
        querying results, 462-463
    SSIS versus, 465
    workflows, 456
        coordinating, 464-465
        submitting with HDInsight .NET SDK, 463-464

Optimized Row Columnar (ORC) files, 320

optimizing
    compression, 150-151
    MapReduce, 150-154
    uber-tasking optimization (YARN), 170-171

output of Pig jobs, 442-443

OutputFormat class (MapReduce), 123

P

PaaS (Platform as a Service), 179

parallelism
    MapReduce, 115
    in Pig Latin scripts, 440
    in Sqoop, 446

PARTITIONED BY clause, 340

partitioning

  dynamic partition inserts, 355-358

  MapReduce, 128-130

  switching/swapping, 354

  tables, 350-354

pass-through modes, 414

pay as you go (PAYG) model, 180

PDW (Microsoft SQL Server Parallel Data Warehouse), 58

Pegasus, 41, 48

performance, 161

  blob storage, 242-243

  MapReduce, 150-154

  Tez, 319

per-MapReduce job blacklisting, 155

Pig, 37-38, 47, 94

  canceled flights scenario, 434-438

    defining relations, 435-436

    filtering relations, 436-437

    grouping relations, 437

    joining relations, 437

    saving relations to file system, 438

    summarizing relations, 437

    uploading data, 434-435

  HCatalog, 438-440

  joins, 148

  Pig Latin scripting language, 433-434

  submitting jobs with PowerShell, 440-443

    adding Azure accounts, 441

    creating job definitions, 441

    execution of jobs, 441-442

    getting job output, 442-443

Pig Latin scripting language, 37-38, 433-434

  HCatalog usage, 438-440

  HiveQL versus, 38

plyrmr package, 41

PolyBase, 58

Power BI, 48, 378-379

Power Map, 54

  reporting, 405-406

  visualization, 405-406

Power Query, 54

  Excel, launching, 417-421

  HDInsight, accessing, 417-421

Power View, 54

  reporting, 403-404

  visualization, 403-404

PowerPivot, 48, 54

  data visualization phase, 390-399

  enabling, 386-390

  Hive, accessing, 385-406

  reporting, 390-399

PowerShell, 237-239

  Apache Hive, scripting, 295-299

  automation setup, 426-427

  HDInsight

    automating provisioning, 199-212

    cluster creation with HBase, 547-550

    verifying setup, 207-212

  HDInsight cluster provisioning, 427-431

    configuring Hive ODBC data source, 429-430

    executing Hive queries, 428

    executing SSIS package, 430-431

  Script Action usage, 281

  Sqoop and, 451-452

  submitting Pig jobs, 440-443

    adding Azure accounts, 441

    creating job definitions, 441

    execution of jobs, 441-442

    getting job output, 442-443

predictive analysis, 11, 492. *See also* Azure ML

predictive models (Azure ML), 506-512

prescriptive analysis, 11

pricing plans of Microsoft Azure, 180

private distributed cache files, 146

programming

  HDInsight .NET SDKs, 311-316

  Hive

    in HDInsight, 323-331

    tables, 331-340

  MapReduce

    in C#, 270-273

    Hello World, 255-256

    jobs, 255

    models for Spark, 481-483

    Serializer and Deserializer (SerDe), 340-343

properties

  Hive job, viewing, 308

  viewing, 304-306

provisioning HDInsight, 186-198, 427-431

  automating PowerShell, 199-212

  clusters, 203-206

  Hive

    ODBC data source, configuring, 429-430

    queries, executing, 428

  SSIS package, executing, 430-431

  Storm clusters, 521

public distributed cache files, 146

publish settings, downloading and importing, 426-427

publishing Azure ML as web services, 512-514

put parameter, 91

Q

QJM (Quorum Journal Manager), storage using, 97-98

queries

  data analysis, 348-354

  Hive

    executing, 288, 313-314

    tables, 346-363

    writing, 309

  HiveQL, executing, 294

  specifying, 393

Query Wizard, 382

queue storage (Microsoft Azure), 234

Quorum Journal Manager. See QJM

quorum-based storage, 228

R

R language, 41, 467

  data analysis, 470

  data types, 468-469

  enabling

    on Hadoop, 471-472

    on HDInsight, 472-476

  installing

    on HDInsight, 472-473

    on Windows, 468

rack awareness, 88-89

RDBMS (Relational Database Management System), 288

  Hive, comparing, 327-328

  indexes in, 365

  NoSQL versus, 17-18

RDDs (resilient distributed datasets), 482-483

reading

  data, Azure ML, 492-502

  from HBase tables, 541

  from HDFS, 82-83

RecordReader interface, 122

records, handling bad, 157

reduce function, 130

Reduce function (MapReduce), 114

Reducer class (MapReduce), 130-132

reduce-side joins, 149

refreshing PowerPivot models, 394

regions (HBase), 539

  load balancing, 543

regression algorithms, 492

Relational Database Management System. See RDBMS

relations (Pig)

  defining, 435-436

  filtering, 436-437

  grouping, 437

  joining, 437

  saving to file system, 438

  summarizing, 437

relationships, many-to-many, 397

remote desktop connections, enabling HDInsight, 193-195

Remove-AzureHDInsightCluster cmdlet, 428

replication

  deleting files and, 86-87

  HDFS blocks, 74-77

reporting

  Excel, 399-402

  Power Map, 405-406

  Power View, 403-404

  PowerPivot, 390-399

requests, job request/response flow (MapReduce), 117-118

Research and Innovative Technology Administration (RITA), 323

resilient distributed datasets (RDDs), 482-483

resource management, 160. See also YARN

Resource Manager, 163, 225

  failures, 172

  HA (High Availability), 173-175

responses, job request/response flow (MapReduce), 117-118

reuse of JVMs in YARN, 152

RHadoop, 41, 48-49

rhbase package, 41, 472

rhdfs package, 41, 472

rm parameter, 92

rmr package, 41, 472-476

rmr parameter, 92

ROW FORMAT DELIMITED FIELDS TERMINATED BY clause, 338

row-store databases, column-store databases versus, 536

rows, HBase data distribution and storage, 541-544

run function, 125, 130

running

    Giraph jobs, 282-284

    MapReduce jobs, 249-250

S

S language, 467

safe mode (HDFS), 83-85

saving Pig relations to file systems, 438

Scala, 484

scalability, 161

    of Hadoop, 32, 44-45

    of HDFS, 66

    MapReduce, 115

    of YARN, 45

Scheduler (Resource Manager), 163

scheduling

    Capacity Scheduler, 153-154

    Fair Scheduler, 152-153

    jobs, 152

schema-first systems, 17

schema-later systems, 18

schemas

    databases, comparing, 328-331, 411

    on read approach, 288

SCP (Stream Computing Platform), 522-523

Script Action

    with Azure Management Portal, 280-281

    with HDInsight .NET SDK, 282

    running Giraph job, 282-284

    script development, 278-280

    testing, 285

    version requirements, 278

    with Windows PowerShell, 281

scripting PowerShell (Apache Hive), 295-299

secondary name nodes, 221-222

    Checkpoint process, 72

    explained, 34, 69

    standby name nodes versus, 222

secure gateway nodes, 183

segregation of duties, 161

    MapReduce and YARN, 45

SELECT command, 342

semi-structured data, 12

semi-structured scalar data, serialization, 262

serialization frameworks (Hadoop), 262-270

Serializer and Deserializer (SerDe), 340-343

Server Explorer, 304

servers, linking SQL Server, 406-412

service-level agreements (SLAs), 153

services

    HDInsight. See also HDInsight

        name node, 225-227

        overview of, 181-186

    Microsoft Azure, 180

    Storage, 181

setup function, 125, 130

    HDInsight configuration, verifying, 196-198

shared storage using NFS (Network File System), 95-97

SharePoint, 48

    Power View in, 405

Shark, 485

SHOW DATABASES command, 328

show tables command, 291

shuffle grouping, 521

shuffling map-outputs, 129

signals, heartbeat, 97, 154

single node clusters, 36

Sirosh, Joseph, 56, 493

Slicer controls, adding, 401

snapshots, 45

    HDFS (Hadoop Distributed File System), 103-107

social network analysis, 27

sources of data. See data sources

Spark, 479-480

    HDInsight, installing on, 480-481

    log mining, 483-485

    MapReduce versus, 479, 481-483

    programming model, 481-483

Spark SQL, 485

    crime data analysis scenario, 486-489

    Hive versus, 486

speculative execution (MapReduce), 156-157

speed limit violations, analyzing, 524-532

spouts, 520

SQL (Structured Query Language), 183. See also NoSQL; SQL Servers

    crime data analysis scenario, 486-489

Hive versus, 486

Spark SQL, 485

SQL Azure tables, creating, 530-531

SQL Servers

Analysis Services (SSAS), 48, 54, 413-415

data integration with HDInsight, importance of, 423

Hive, accessing, 406-417

importing data

to HDInsight clusters, 445-447

to Sqoop, 448-451

Integration Services. *See* SSIS (SQL Server Integration Services)

linking, 406-412

Management Studio (SSMS), 302, 410

parallel data warehouse, 47

RDBMS, 47

Reporting Services (SSRS), 49, 54, 415-417

StreamInsight, 46, 48

Sqoop, 38, 46, 94, 445

exporting data

exercise, 448-451

export process, 448

from HDFS, 447-448

with PowerShell, 451-452

importing data

exercise, 448-451

to HDInsight clusters, 445-447

to Hive, 447

with PowerShell, 451-452

network connectivity, 446

SSAS (SQL Server Analysis Services), 48, 413-415

SSIS (SQL Server Integration Services), 47, 54, 423

ETL workflow packages, creating, 424

flight departure analysis scenario, 424-427

package variables, 426

prerequisites, 425-426

Windows Azure PowerShell automation, 426-427

HDInsight clusters, provisioning, 427-431

Oozie versus, 465

SSMS (SQL Server Management Studio), 410

SSRS (SQL Server Reporting Services), 415-417

standard input stream (STDIN), 146

standard output stream (STDOUT), 146

standby name nodes, 222

secondary name nodes versus, 222

Start-AzureHDInsightJob cmdlet, 441, 452

statistics

Descriptive Statistics module, 505

storage

accounts, creating, 192

blocks (HDFS), 101

emulator (Microsoft Azure), configuring, 251-253

NAS (Network Attached Storage), 96

QJM (Quorum Journal Manager), 97-98

services, 181, 233-234. *See also* specific types of storage (e.g. blob storage, table storage)

shared using NFS, 95-97

STORED AS clause, 338

Storm, 519-522

applications, creating, 524-529

architecture, 520-522

HDInsight, provisioning clusters, 521

SCP (Stream Computing Platform), 522-523

speed limit violations, analyzing, 524-532

SQL Azure tables, creating, 530-531

topologies

creating, 529-530

submitting, 531

stream analytics, 519. *See also* **Storm**

SCP (Stream Computing Platform), 522-523

speed limit violations, analyzing, 524-532

Stream Computing Platform (SCP), 522-523

streaming

access in HDFS, 67

Hadoop, 146-148, 270-275

structured data, 11

submitting topologies (HDInsight), 531

subscriptions, Microsoft Azure, 180, 201

summarizing Pig relations, 437

Supervisor, 520

swapping partitioning, 354

switching partitioning, 354

System Center Operations
  Manager, 49

T

Table Import Wizard, 389, 391

tables

columns (in Hive), 338

CREATE TABLE command, 338

external tables, programming,
  335-338

HBase

  compaction, 544-545

  creating, 539

  data distribution and
    storage, 541-544

  reading from, 541

  writing to, 540-541

Hive

  creating, 293, 309-321

  data load processes for,
    343-346

  programming, 331-340

  queries, 346-363

importing, 389

internal tables, programming,
  331-335

partitioning, 350-354

properties, viewing, 304-306

SQL Azure tables, creating,
  530-531

storage (Microsoft Azure),
  20-21, 234

temporary, 342

views, creating, 342-343

tabular data, serialization, 262

targeted campaigning, 27

task failures

MapReduce, 155-156

YARN, 171

Task Tracker, 225

data node co-location,
  118-119

tasks (SSIS), 424

TaskTrackers, 35

failure, 154-155

MapReduce, 115-116

TCP/IP, 82

Team Foundation Server, 49

temporary tables, 342

testing

requests/responses, 513

Script Action, 285

TextInputFormat class, 122

Tez

executing, 365-368

execution engines, 320

overview of, 287, 316-320

throughput of HDFS, 67

Timeline Server, 165

Tool interface (MapReduce), 139

tools

CloudXplorer, 324

ETL (extraction,
  transformation, and loading),
  417

for Visual Studio (HDInsight),
  302-311

topologies, Apache Storm, 520

creating, 529-530

submitting, 531

Trash folder (HDFS), 86-87

TRUNCATE TABLE command, 331

Try It Yourself. See exercises

types

of indexes, 363

of storage, 181

U

uber-tasking optimization (YARN),
  170-171

uniform resource identifier (URI),
  91

unstructured data, 11-12

uploading

  to default file system, 239

  to HDInsight clusters,
    434-435

URI (uniform resource identifier),
  91

usage scenarios for Big Data,
  27-29

user-defined aggregating functions
  (UDAFs), 345

user-defined functions (UDFs),
  345

user-defined table-generating
  functions (UDTFs), 345

V

variability characteristics of Big
  Data, 14

variables (SSIS), 424

  flight departure analysis
    scenario, 426

variety characteristics of Big Data,
  13

vectors (R), 468

velocity characteristics of Big
Data, 14

vendors for Hadoop

Amazon Elastic MapReduce
(EMR), 51-52

Cloudera, 50

Hortonworks, 50-51

MapR Technologies, 51

Microsoft Big Data solutions,
52-57

verifying

HDInsight

cluster creation, 550-551

configuration, 196-198

connections, 389

emulator installation,
248-249

PowerShell setup, 207-212

relationships (Azure/
PowerShell), 202

versioning in HBase, 536

viewing

Azure ML, 499

Hive jobs, 306-308

properties, 304-306

views, creating tables, 342-343

virtual machines in Microsoft
Azure, 60

Virtual Network (VNET), 189

virtual networks in Azure,
545-546

Visual Studio, 49

HDInsight tools for, 302-311

visualization

Azure ML, 505

Excel, 399-402

Power Map, 405-406

Power View, 403-404

PowerPivot, 390-399

volume characteristics of Big
Data, 13

W

Wait-AzureHDInsightJob cmdlet,
442

WASB (Windows Azure Storage—
Blob), 183-184, 240-241, 300

weather forecasting, 28

web services, publishing as (Azure
ML), 512-514

WebHDFS, 89-90

WHERE clause, 347

Windows

Hadoop on, 52-57

installing R, 468

windows, Hive Job Browser, 307

Windows Azure Storage—Blob
(WASB), 240-241

Windows PowerShell, 237-239

automation setup, 426-427

HDInsight cluster creation with
HBase, 547-550

HDInsight cluster provisioning,
427-431

configuring Hive ODBC
data source, 429-430

executing Hive queries,
428

executing SSIS package,
430-431

Script Action usage, 281

Sqoop and, 451-452

submitting Pig jobs, 440-443

adding Azure accounts,
441

creating job definitions,
441

execution of jobs, 441-442

getting job output,
442-443

WITH clause, 347

wizards

Create New Data Source
Wizard, 374, 378

From Data Connection Wizard,
379

HDInsight Provision Wizard,
189

Import Wizard, 388

New HDInsight Cluster Wizard,
187

Query Wizard, 382

Table Import Wizard, 389,
391

word counts, 126, 131, 135

worker nodes, 183

workflows

Azure ML, 498-505

coordinating, 464-465

flight departure analysis
scenario, 457-463

defining workflows,
459-461

executing workflows, 461

monitoring workflows, 461

prerequisites, 458-459

querying results,
462-463

Oozie, 456

submitting with HDInsight
.NET SDK, 463-464

workspaces (Azure ML),
495-497

WritableComparableT interface,
127

write once, read many, 66

writing

to HBase tables, 540-541

to HDFS, 77-82

Hive queries, 309

Y

YARN

automatic failover, 173-175

components of, 162-166

failures in, 171-173

job execution flow in, 167-169

MapReduce versus, 45-46

Node Manager, 166-167

overview of, 160-169

reuse of JVMs in, 152

uber-tasking optimization,
170-171

Z

**ZKFC (ZooKeeper Failover
Controller), 99, 228-230**

ZooKeeper

HBase and, 538-539

nodes, 183

quorums, configuring, 99

 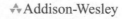